Selected Works of Michael Wallerstein

Michael Wallerstein was a leader in developing a rigorous comparative political economy of inequality, redistribution, and wage determination. His early death from cancer left both a hole in the profession and a legacy that will provide the foundation for research on these topics. This volume collects his most important contributions organized by topic, with each topic preceded by an editorial introduction that provides overview and context.

David Austen-Smith is the Earl Dean Howard Distinguished Professor of Political Economy at the Kellogg School of Management, Northwestern University. He is coauthor (with Jeffrey S. Banks) of two books on positive political theory and serves on the editorial boards of several journals in political science and economics.

Jeffry A. Frieden is professor of government at Harvard University. He specializes in the politics of international monetary and financial relations and is the author of three books, including, most recently, *Global Capitalism: Its Fall and Rise in the Twentieth Century* (2006), as well as the editor or coeditor of more than a dozen other books on related topics.

Miriam A. Golden is professor of political science at the University of California at Los Angeles. The author of two books, including *Heroic Defeats: The Politics of Job Loss* (Cambridge University Press, 1996), she has also published in journals such as the *American Political Science Review*, the *American Journal of Political Science*, the *British Journal of Political Science*, and *Comparative Political Studies*.

Karl Ove Moene is professor of economics at the University of Oslo and scientific advisor at the Center of Applied Research, Oslo, since 1987. He is the coauthor or coeditor of seven books, including *Trade Union Behaviour and Pay Bargaining and Economic Performance* (1993), coauthored with Robert Flanagan and Michael Wallerstein.

Adam Przeworski is Carroll and Milton Petrie Professor in the Department of Politics, New York University. A member of the American Academy of Arts and Sciences since 1991, he is the recipient of the 2001 Woodrow Wilson Prize and the author of thirteen books, including *States and Markets* (2003), *Democracy and the Rule of Law* (2003), and *Democracy and Development* (2000), published by Cambridge University Press.

Cambridge Studies in Comparative Politics

General Editor
Margaret Levi   *University of Washington, Seattle*

Assistant General Editor
Stephen Hanson   *University of Washington, Seattle*

Associate Editors
Robert H. Bates   *Harvard University*
Peter Lange   *Duke University*
Robert H. Bates   *Harvard University*
Helen Milner   *Princeton University*
Frances Rosenbluth   *Yale University*
Susan Stokes   *Yale University*
Sidney Tarrow   *Cornell University*
Kathleen Thelen   *Northwestern University*
Erik Wibbels   *University of Washington, Seattle*

Other Books in the Series

Lisa Baldez, *Why Women Protest: Women's Movements in Chile*
Stefano Bartolini, *The Political Mobilization of the European Left,*
    1860–1980: The Class Cleavage
Mark R. Beissinger, *Nationalist Mobilization and the Collapse of the Soviet*
    State
Nancy Bermeo, ed., *Unemployment in the New Europe*
Carles Boix, *Democracy and Redistribution*
Carles Boix, *Political Parties, Growth, and Equality: Conservative and Social*
    Democratic Economic Strategies in the World Economy
Catherine Boone, *Merchant Capital and the Roots of State Power in Senegal,*
    1930–1985
Catherine Boone, *Political Topographies of the African State: Territorial*
    Authority and Institutional Change

Continued on page 467

Selected Works of Michael Wallerstein

THE POLITICAL ECONOMY OF INEQUALITY, UNIONS, AND SOCIAL DEMOCRACY

Edited by

DAVID AUSTEN-SMITH
Northwestern University

JEFFRY A. FRIEDEN
Harvard University

MIRIAM A. GOLDEN
University of California, Los Angeles

KARL OVE MOENE
University of Oslo

ADAM PRZEWORSKI
New York University

 CAMBRIDGE
UNIVERSITY PRESS

CAMBRIDGE UNIVERSITY PRESS
Cambridge, New York, Melbourne, Madrid, Cape Town, Singapore, São Paulo, Delhi

Cambridge University Press
32 Avenue of the Americas, New York, NY 10013-2473, USA

www.cambridge.org
Information on this title: www.cambridge.org/9780521714853

First published 2008

Printed in the United States of America

A catalog record for this publication is available from the British Library.

Library of Congress Cataloging in Publication Data
Wallerstein, Michael, 1951–2006
Selected works of Michael Wallerstein : the political economy of inequality, unions, and
social democracy / edited by David Austen-Smith . . . [et al.].
    p. cm. – (Cambridge studies in comparative politics)
Includes bibliographical references and index.
ISBN 978-0-521-88688-8 (hardback) – ISBN 978-0-521-71485-3 (pbk.)
1. Economics. 2. Equality. 3. Labor unions. 4. Socialism. I. Austen-Smith, David.
II. Title. III. Series.
HB171.W216 2008
335.0092–dc22   2007029945

ISBN   978-0-521-88688-8 hardback
ISBN   978-0-521-71485-3 paperback

Contents

Preface and Acknowledgments

Michael Wallerstein's untimely death in January 2006 spurred us to compile this volume of Wallerstein's writings. The support that we received in this endeavor propelled the volume forward in record time. We thank Lewis Bateman, Scott Parris, and Kimberly Twist at Cambridge University Press, as well as the editor of this series, Margaret Levi, all of whom did much to make this project a reality. We also thank the anonymous reviewers of the manuscript for their speedy and helpful comments on the volume.

Finally, we are grateful for the support we have received from the entire Wallerstein family: Michael's parents, Bob and Judy; his sisters, Nina and Amy; his wife, Liz; and his children, Jonah and Hannah. This volume is dedicated to Michael's memory, but we hope that it will also offer some degree of comfort to the living.

1

General Introduction

Jeffry Frieden and Adam Przeworski

Michael Wallerstein's tragic death at the age of fifty-four deprived the world of one of its leading political economists. For twenty-five years Wallerstein had been in the forefront of rigorous analysis of the political economy of contemporary industrial societies. His research on relations between labor and capital, on labor organization, and on inequality and redistribution framed and advanced the study of central problems in modern politics and economics. This volume brings together Wallerstein's principal contributions, in the hope that their joint impact will demonstrate the scale of Wallerstein's achievement and advance the values that guided his life work.

Michael Wallerstein and Modern Political Economy

The modern study of political economy is quite recent. Forty years ago the term was barely used, and it was rare for scholars in the mainstream of the social sciences to study the interaction of political and economic forces. There were, to be sure, some scholars in the Marxist tradition, and others in the newer tradition of public choice theory, who analyzed aspects of the relationship between the economic and political systems. But there was no generally accepted field of political economy, and there was virtually no interaction between the two disciplines best suited to study it, political science and economics.

Today political economy is one of the most dynamic fields of investigation in both economics and political science, with a plethora of conferences and journals and handbooks of its own, displaying some of the biggest names

1

in the social sciences.[1] Three interrelated strands constitute contemporary political economy, all of them thriving. One is the impact of political factors on economic, and economic-policy outcomes. This includes investigations of electorally motivated business cycles, of the effects of partisan differences on policy, of the implications of different institutional settings for aspects of economic performance, and the like. A second strand of modern political economy is the impact of economic factors on politics. This includes the effect of economic interest groups on trade policy, and of such macroeconomic variables as unemployment and inflation on presidential voting. The third sort of political economy is methodological, and involves the use of economic models for the study of political interactions. Working together, these strands suggest political-economic equilibria, in which individuals and groups strive in the political arena for policies whose consequences they anticipate, while as economic agents they pursue their private objectives within the constraints of these policies. Together, these complementary and interrelated approaches have made substantial contributions to our understanding of how societies work.

Michael Wallerstein carried out path-breaking work in all three modes of political economy. He was one of the first political scientists to make extensive use of serious graduate training in modern economics. Wallerstein came to this blend of political science and economics by an unusual route. While a graduate student in political science at the University of Chicago in 1974, he enrolled in Adam Przeworski's course on the Marxist theory of the state. As the course went on, both Wallerstein and Przeworski concluded that this theory was based on an inadequate, often erroneous, understanding of the capitalist economy. Unlike those who reacted by engaging in increasingly arcane doctrinal debates, Wallerstein chose to traverse what was probably the deepest ideological divide of the time in search of the truth. He crossed the University of Chicago quadrangle to the Department of Economics, a stronghold of conservative market-oriented economic thinking dominated by the likes of Milton Friedman, George Stigler, Gary Becker, and Robert Lucas. These scholars were and remain giants of modern economics, but at the time the thought that a left-wing political scientist might have something to learn from them was practically heretical.

From Chicago's economists, Wallerstein obtained systematic training in economics, and became fascinated with the tools of economic analysis. Yet

---

[1] Such as the *Oxford Handbook of Political Economy* ed. Barry Weingast and Donald Wittman (Oxford: Oxford University Press, 2006).

he never abandoned his political commitment. Nor did he compromise his commitment to combining politics and economics, with a thorough command of both political science and economics. He brought theoretical and empirical rigor to the analysis of central issues in political economy, and did so with close attention to the implications for political action. Wallerstein was a pioneer in all dimensions of political economy: in bringing the most rigorous practices of both disciplines together, in exploring the interaction of politics and economics, and in applying economic methods to politics. He was also a pioneer in addressing questions typically associated with the Marxist left with tools usually associated with mainstream neoclassical economics.

Labor, Capital, and Politics

The early study of political economy was developed and applied to a series of questions about the interrelationship of politics and economics that had long exercised political scientists and economists. One strand of the developing approach focused on the role of special interests in affecting government policy, such as industrial lobbies for trade protection. Another strand emphasized the use of macroeconomic policy for electoral purposes, as in the political business cycles that were alleged to characterize many electoral democracies. Both strands were productive and engaging.

Michael Wallerstein's interests were broader. He was concerned to understand problems that have been central to modern capitalist societies since the rise of modern capitalism itself. Most generally, he wanted to know the conditions under which societies could achieve both material well-being and an equitable distribution of income. This led him to look at how labor, capital, and the government interacted, and the circumstances under which these interactions could result in improved conditions for labor while sustaining overall economic growth and prosperity. Four interrelated topics attracted Wallerstein's interest, in all of which he made important scholarly contributions. The topics are presented in detail in the introductions to the relevant parts of this volume; what follows is a summary treatment of the main outlines of the issue areas.

Relations between Labor and Capital

Wallerstein was particularly interested in a central problem in classical political economy, which had faded from view as both economics and political

3

science evolved away from their classical roots. This was how property-less workers could coexist with propertied capitalists when the immediate incentives of the working class all pointed toward the desirability of expropriating capital. With the rise of modern electoral democracies, in which the laboring classes were well represented, it was particularly hard to understand why class relations were as peaceful as they had turned out to be in the latter part of the twentieth century. Wallerstein rejected the simplistic notion that the working class simply did not know, or did not act upon, its own interests.

Wallerstein and his coauthor Adam Przeworski showed that workers can rationally forgo the benefits from expropriating capital, in the anticipation of greater gains in the form of a stream of future income that results from labor-capital cooperation. They extended this argument to show that it was similarly rational for a labor-based government to restrain its taxation to permit capitalists to retain a substantial share of their income.

In this and related work, Wallerstein demonstrated the great value and flexibility of rigorous political economy models of sociopolitical behavior. He also helped clarify important topics in both political science and economics. The role of labor-capital conflict in politics continues to be central in both analyses of contemporary politics, and in politics itself. So, too, does the set of policies best suited to improving the position of labor continue to be a subject of great concern to scholars, policy makers, and activists.

The Organization of Labor

Wallerstein's interest in how labor could organize itself both to bargain with capital and to further its interests in the political arena led him to investigate precisely how workers develop the collective institutions that they do. The extent and form of labor organization vary enormously from country to country, as well as having changed over time.

Here, too, Wallerstein brought to bear rigorous analytical tools. He developed theoretically grounded arguments and evidence to show why workers might be better organized in some countries than in others, and how their patterns of organization could affect the kinds of bargains labor unions would strike with employers.

As he worked on this set of topics, Wallerstein came to recognize the paucity of reliable data. He worked to rectify this, and, together with Miriam Golden and Peter Lange, put together a major new database on the organization of labor in advanced industrial societies. On the basis of these new statistical resources, he went on to try to understand the diversity of historical and contemporary experiences of national labor movements. Wallerstein rejected, for example, the simplistic notion so popular in the 1990s that labor's organizational strength had waned for good, showing – as would soon become clear – that in many industrial nations it continued to be powerful.

Labor and Redistributive Politics

One could hardly be interested in the role of labor in modern capitalist societies without being concerned with the impact of labor's political action on the distribution of income. Indeed, much of Wallerstein's early interest in the organization of labor unions was related to his belief that this could contribute to a more equitable distribution of income, not only between labor and capital but among different groups of workers. Wallerstein showed with his characteristic care and rigor that this was indeed the case, that the ways in which wage bargaining was carried out could have a powerful impact on wage dispersion, and in particular on the fortunes of poorer and less skilled workers.

From this finding, there were natural extensions to the role of labor in affecting the distribution of income and opportunities in society as a whole. With Karl Ove Moene and David Austen-Smith, Wallerstein examined the ways in which workers and the poor could attain a more equal society.

Labor and Social Democracy

In the European political arena, one of the principal means by which the working class has affected its position in society is by way of its organization into socialist and social democratic parties. These parties have become so much a fixture of the European political landscape that scholars have sometimes taken their origins, the sources of their strength, and their impact on policy for granted – just as their purported decline in the 1990s was widely (if prematurely) predicted.

Wallerstein's research on organized social democracy, again with Karl Ove Moene, demonstrated the foundations of the social democratic model and its implications for politics and policies in the industrialized nations. It also showed that the model continues to have contemporary relevance, as people around the world look for a way to combine markets and politics to create societies that are both prosperous and equitable.

Jeffry Frieden and Adam Przeworski

A Seminal Contribution

Michael Wallerstein made fundamental contributions to the development of modern political economy. His research brought political and economic factors together into an integrated picture of how modern societies operate. It did so with analytical rigor and empirical care, and pointed the way forward for generations of scholars to come. Wallerstein's research both reflected and enhanced his lifelong commitment to bettering the lot of the world's working people. His scholarly, political, and personal legacy is an enduring one that will long affect the analysis of modern societies.

Biographical Note

Michael Wallerstein was born in Topeka, Kansas, in 1951, and he was raised there and, later, in Marin County, California. He received his B.A. from Stanford University, and his Ph.D. from the University of Chicago in 1985. Wallerstein joined the Department of Political Science at the University of California, Los Angeles, in 1984, and taught there for ten years. His long-standing interest in Scandinavian social democracy led him to spend the 1989–1990 academic year in Norway, at the University of Oslo's Department of Economics and the Institute for Social Research.

In 1994, Wallerstein moved to Northwestern University's Political Science Department. He served as chair of the department from 1997 to 2000. In 2004, Wallerstein moved to the Yale University Department of Political Science, and soon after he was appointed the Charlotte Marion Saden Professor of Political Science. Always active in the political science profession, Wallerstein was a leading figure in both the Political Economy and the Comparative Politics Sections of the American Political Science Association, serving on both sections' executive councils, and as president of the Comparative Politics Section. He also served as a member of the Executive Council of the American Political Science Association. Wallerstein was a fellow of the American Academy of Arts and Sciences.

Michael Wallerstein died of brain cancer on January 7, 2006, shortly before his fifty-fifth birthday.

PART I

Class Conflict, the State, and Economic Limits to Democracy

2

Introduction

Adam Przeworski

The three articles included in this part reflect the intellectual preoccupations of the time when they were written. But they approached classical questions with new instruments of analysis and generated new answers.

The first puzzle they address concerns the strategies of labor movements under democratic conditions. What motivated this puzzle was the belief, held in the nineteenth century by thinkers across the entire political spectrum, from Thomas Macaulay to Karl Marx, that if workers were to gain political rights in the form of suffrage, they would use this right to confiscate property. Alternatively, if they were to win the right to freely associate, they would destroy productive property by making confiscatory wage demands. The conflict between capital and labor, Marx maintained, was irreconcilable. Even if the economy grew, "profit and wages remain as before in inverse proportions" (Marx 1952a: 37). In turn, Marx (1934, 1952b) and most of his followers expected that, faced with the threat of confiscation by the working class, the bourgeoisie would inevitably turn for protection to arms, and thus subvert democracy. Capitalism and democracy, therefore, could not coexist. Capitalist democracy could be "only the political form of revolution of bourgeois society and not its conservative form of life" (Marx 1934: 18), "only a spasmodic, exceptional state of things...impossible as the normal form of society" (Marx 1971: 198).

Yet they did coexist, uneasily in some countries at times, but quite peacefully and smoothly in several countries of Europe. When workers became organized into unions and parties, they were willing to moderate their wage demands and to obey the verdicts of the polls. And when they reached office in capitalist societies, workers' parties defended democracy, even when this defense entailed economic sacrifices and electoral defeats.

The explanations of this behavior that prevailed at the time among leftist critics of social democracy claimed either that workers were ideologically dominated by the bourgeoisie, who controlled the means of mass communication, or that they were repeatedly betrayed by their co-opted leaders. In these explanations, workers were thus either dupes or suckers, neither of which seemed plausible. Hence, the question Przeworski and Wallerstein posed was whether this strategy of the working-class movements could be understood in terms of their interests, that is, whether it was economically rational.

To examine this question, we studied a simple model of bilateral monopoly, in which one encompassing, centralized union chooses the labor share and identical competitive firms decide how much to invest.[1] In the Stackelberg equilibrium of this model, in which the union chooses labor's share of value added anticipating the investment decisions of firms, the union exercises a large degree of wage restraint. The reason is obvious: if a higher labor share causes firms to invest less, workers are trading off current for future consumption.[2] We concluded, therefore, that unless workers can expropriate capital and run firms on their own, the moderate strategy on the part of the union was rational. In turn, facing moderate demands, the bourgeoisie not only invests but can also live with democracy. As a result, a "democratic class compromise" naturally emerges, at least as long as everyone is sufficiently patient and the investment is sufficiently productive.[3]

The model of a centralized, encompassing union was sufficient to make a theoretical point about the rationality of wage restraint, but it did not generate comparative statics that would account for cross-national differences. To do so, we wrote several models allowing for different structures of unions. One parameter was the number of union federations; another was whether union agreements applied to nonmembers. The control variable of the unions was the wage rate (although we also studied Leontieff-like models in which bargaining includes employment), and we allowed wage rates to affect prices. What we found was that, as in the influential article by Calmfors and Driffill (1988), purely competitive labor markets and perfectly centralized unions dominated fragmented labor markets in employment and

---

[1] For a general review of bilateral monopoly models, see Wallerstein (1990a).
[2] The model assumed that workers consume all of their income, so that investment is financed entirely out of profits. This assumption was subsequently shown by Bertola (1993) to hold generally in a linear economy with concave utility functions.
[3] Subsequently, Przeworski (2005) and Benhabib and Przeworski (2005) have shown that such a compromise is also more likely in wealthier societies.

inflation. But we did not get far along this path, because we could not identify the effect of different externalities that particular federations imposed on one another, and in several aspects the results were indeterminate.[4]

The second puzzle concerned the pro-capital bias of democratic governments. These were the heady times of the Miliband-Poulantzas debate. Miliband (1970) amassed an impressive amount of evidence showing that capitalist state institutions tend to be staffed and directed by members of economic elites, claiming that this is why these institutions favor capital over labor. But neither he nor many others who followed him could solve the puzzle offered by socialist governments: why would they, too, favor capital? The answer given by Poulantzas (1973), as well as Lindblom (1977) and several others, was that this dependence of the state on capital was inevitable because capitalists controlled investment and the state, like everyone else, depended on investment decisions.

Our contribution to this debate was to rewrite the class-conflict model assuming that the state could tax the earnings of capital and transfer the revenue to workers. The government was now the Stackelberg leader, and it chose the tax rate that maximized the present value of workers' consumption. The result, as might have been expected, was that the state would choose exactly the same workers' consumption share as would a centralized union. Because the government had to anticipate investment decisions of firms, it had to stop well short of significant redistribution. The dependence of workers and of governments that represented them was thus "structural": the effect of the property structure of a capitalist society.

We were intrigued, however, by the following. This result holds if the instrument of the government is a tax on incomes; but, on paper at least, governments could free themselves from the structural dependence on capital if they would rely exclusively on taxes on consumption or their administrative equivalents, such as investment subsidies. Pure consumption taxes – economists tell us – are investment neutral. This result holds in a closed economy, but we suspected that it might not apply when capital can move across borders. As the third paper reproduced in this part shows, however, investment neutrality of consumption taxes is maintained in an open economy as long as the exiting capital is taxed at the same rate as domestic consumption.

The puzzle, then, became why labor governments would not shift from income to consumption taxes. We thought (Przeworski and Wallerstein

---

[4] Some of these results are echoed in Wallerstein (1990b).

11

1982b) that one reason neoliberal governments, which had just arrived in office in the United Kingdom and the United States, were liberalizing capital flows as well as eliminating investment subsidies and other programs that made taxes more neutral was precisely to expose wage earners to the constraint of investment. But even if the left-wing governments in Europe are more prone to rely on policy instruments to control investment, we did not anticipate that they would also give up controls over capital flows, while passively embracing the language of "trade-offs" between equality and efficiency, redistribution and growth, and the like. This puzzle we never solved.

A central conclusion of these analyses was that private ownership of productive resources limits the range of outcomes that can ensue from the democratic process. The state, regardless of who occupies its heights, by whom elected, and with what intentions, is constrained in any capitalist economy by the fact that crucial economic decisions, those affecting employment and investment, are a private prerogative.

Hence, the exclusive focus on the political process can be misleading. Institutions do matter, as do partisan differences. But how much? Unless this question is posed each time, we end up with an ideological view of the political process, a glorification of popular impotence. Indeed, the ideology of democratic capitalism is contradictory: people are simultaneously told that when they vote they choose and that some choices will result in their impoverishment because of the effect they have on the behavior of those who control the most important productive resources. Clearly, this ideology portrays the fact that property has this constraining power as impersonal and natural, just a fact of life. But the tension remains: if masses of people are disaffected from the political process, it is because what can be decided by voting is limited by the private ownership of capital. As Bobbio (1989) put it, "the question is not who votes but on what."

Since I continue to believe that this conclusion stands – more, that it is unduly ignored – let me argue for it in terms more general than the particular models reprinted here. First, however, disclaimers and caveats are necessary. I certainly do not want to argue in favor of Marxism *tout court*, and particularly not in favor of the version in which there are ready-made collective actors, classes, which are always in conflict, and of which one gains control over the state institutions and uses them to promote its interests. I believe this version explains little: classes are not ready-made actors, and economic interests constrain the state even when their bearers are not collectively organized. And – here comes the caveat – the thesis of

Introduction

structural dependence is only vaguely "Marxist": it is Marxist when it asserts that actions of governments are constrained by the interests of "capital," but the specific mechanism that it identifies to arrive at this conclusion is not one highlighted by Marx and his followers.[5] Conversely, this thesis can be derived outside the Marxist framework. What I want to offer, therefore, is just a trivial reminder that politics is constrained by the economy.

Capitalism is a system in which most productive resources are owned privately. Yet under capitalism property is institutionally distinct from political authority: this separation is necessary for markets to exist. As a result, there are two mechanisms by which resources can be allocated to uses and distributed among households: the market and the state. Individuals are simultaneously market agents and citizens. The market is a mechanism in which resources are allocated by their owners. The state is also a system that allocates resources, including those it does not own, with rights distributed differently from the market.

The market is a decentralized mechanism: households and firms decide how to allocate the resources they own. The state is a centralized mechanism: it coerces economic agents to do what they would have chosen not to do voluntarily. Depending on the political structure, the decisions of the state can be made by one individual, the "dictator," or can result from a process involving all citizens. Once reached, state policies are binding.

Given the coexistence of these two mechanisms, one concept of political-economic equilibrium is the following. Political actors reveal their preferences for policies by a variety of mechanisms ranging from voting to bribes to rioting; the state maximizes its objectives by adopting a policy, such as the tax rate; and then economic agents maximize their utility, subject to the constraint of the policy, by deciding how much to save and how much labor to supply. The result is an allocation of resources to uses and a distribution of incomes to households.

Structural dependence can be shown already at this level of abstraction:

1. Even if state policies are binding, economic agents enjoy some discretion in their decisions. Private agents may be legally prohibited from engaging in some actions at all, say producing PCBs; they may

---

[5] I owe this observation to Jon Elster. Here and there in Marx's writings, there are references to structural dependence, for example, at the beginning of *The Class Struggle in France, 1848 to 1850*, where he points out the dependence of the state on the Banque de France. But there is nothing for which some textual support could not be found somewhere in what Marx wrote, and he never argued structural dependence systematically.

be forced to allocate a part of their income to collective consumption; or they may be contingently subsidized for some decisions, say for investing. The degree to which policy constrains private actors varies from situation to situation. Yet short of the command equilibrium, households and firms have some latitude in allocating the disposable resources.

2. If private agents make decisions to maximize utility and if whatever generates utility is affected by state policy, then so will be the decisions of these agents. Examples abound: an income tax makes saving less attractive, insurance makes individuals more likely to take risks, etc. The degree of sensitivity of individual decisions to the policies depends on the specific policy instruments. Hence, policy instruments are characterized by specific elasticities of supply of productive inputs. Policies are *neutral* when they do not affect the supply of factors.

3. If the realization of the objectives of the state depends, for whatever reasons, on the outcome of decentralized decisions, then the state must anticipate the effect of policies on these decisions when choosing the optimal policy. The state is constrained in choosing policies by the effect of these policies on private decisions. In particular, if redistribution of incomes downward results in lowering total output, the optimal policy of an egalitarian state stops well short of equality. Since the state faces a trade-off between equality and efficiency, it chooses an internal solution.

4. One consequence of this dependence is that some allocations of resources and some distributions of welfare are inaccessible to the state even if they are technologically feasible given the endowments of the economy. Specifically, the state cannot redistribute incomes and generate an efficient allocation of resources at the same time.

As an illustration, let me present one non-Marxist version of this theory: the median voter model. Since this model is well known, I summarize it informally. Each individual is characterized by an endowment of labor or capital, and all individuals can be ranked from poorest to richest. Individuals vote on the tax rate to be imposed on incomes generated by supplying these endowments to production. The funds generated by this tax are either equally distributed to all individuals or spent to produce public goods equally valued by all individuals. Once the tax rate is voted on, individuals maximize utility by deciding in a decentralized way how much of their endowments to supply. The median voter theorem asserts that, when

Introduction

some additional technical conditions hold, there exists a unique majority rule equilibrium, this equilibrium is the choice of the voter with the median preference, and the voter with the median preference is the one with median income. Given this model, it can be shown that if decisions concerning the individual supply of endowments were completely insensitive to the tax rate (or if the state could order each individual how much to supply), then, under the typical conditions when the distribution of incomes is rightward skewed, the majority rule equilibrium would result in complete equality of post-fisc (tax and transfer) incomes. But if decentralized decisions are sensitive to the tax rate, that is, if positive tax rates generate deadweight losses, voters will anticipate this effect and the majority rule equilibrium will stop short of equality. Since perfect equality can be achieved only at the cost of reducing total output, citizens anticipate this constraint when they vote.

The median voter theorem attributes labor supply decisions to individuals and treats them as elastic. Yet we know that the labor supply of full-age males is highly inelastic, mainly because few individual agents can choose the number of hours they work in a continuous manner. In fact, labor withdraws its services collectively, by striking. Hence, even when the threat of strikes constrains government policy choice, the dependence of labor is not structural but political. The constraining power of capital stems from the fact that no collective organization or collective action is required for this constraint to bite: it is sufficient that each firm independently pursues its self-interest. Thus, while the state may be *politically* dependent on labor or innumerable other organized groups, it is *structurally* dependent only on capital.

Another model that analyzes the effect of taxes on investment has been offered by Barro (1990). In this model revenues generated by an income tax are used by the government to produce inputs complementary to private production, rather than being distributed to households or spent on public consumption goods. The state maximizes the rate of growth of the economy or, equivalently under a Cobb-Douglas production function, the present value of the utility of future consumption. As tax rates increase, firms respond first by increasing and then by lowering investment, and in equilibrium the rate of private savings is suboptimal in the sense that a higher level of consumption could be reached either in the command optimum or if a neutral tax were used. To put it in the language of structural dependence, the tax rate that maximizes consumption is higher than the tax rate that the state finds optimal when firms respond to it in a decentralized way.

15

One can cite alternative formulations, but the general logic is the same. Whenever private agents respond in a decentralized way to state policies, the policy choice and the actual allocation of resources and distribution of incomes are constrained by private decisions. The constraining power of agents with different endowments depends on the magnitude of these endowments and the elasticity with which they are supplied. Because the state is dependent on private decisions for the realization of its objectives, it is constrained in its policy choice and limited in the range of outcomes that it can generate.

Suppose that economic constraints are so overwhelming that any government, regardless of its base of support, ideology, electoral promises, or institutional framework, will end up following the same policy. Parties competing for office have different objectives, perhaps because they represent interests of different groups. As they seek to maximize the realization of these interests, they learn that they must anticipate the reactions of some specific actors: domestic and foreign creditors, private investors, or international aid donors. In the extreme case, whatever interests parties represent, they discover the same policy as the best way to satisfy them. The people have no choice: if they are well informed, voters may as well throw dice instead of voting; if they are not perfectly informed, they will vote only to find that they have been betrayed.

To the extent to which governments are structurally dependent on private agents, therefore, the scope of political decisions is limited. While to make the point I reverted to some caricatures, structural dependence need not imply that partisan and institutional differences are irrelevant. After all, not all democratic capitalist systems are the same. But a science of politics that ignores economic constraints on popular sovereignty misses what all democracies have in common, namely, that they exist in societies where the future of all depends on decisions of some, those who control productive resources. Popular sovereignty is constrained by private ownership of collective resources. The research question that continues to be open is to what extent democracy can be effective only within the limits imposed by markets and to what extent these limits can themselves be manipulated.

References

Aumann, Robert J., and Mordecai Kurz. 1977. "Power and Taxes." *Econometrica 45*: 1137–1161.

Barro, Robert J. 1990. "Government Spending in a Simple Model of Endogenous Growth." *Journal of Political Economy 98*: 103–125.

Introduction

Benhabib, Jess, and Adam Przeworski. 2005. "The Political Economy of Redistribution under Democracy." *Economic Theory*.

Bertola, Giuseppe 1993. "Factor Shares and Savings in Endogenous Growth." *American Economic Review 83*: 1184–1198.

Bobbio, Norberto. 1989. *Democracy and Dictatorship*. Minneapolis: University of Minnnesota Press.

Calmfors, Lars, and John Driffill. 1988. "Centralization of Wage Bargaining and Macroeconomic Performance." *Economic Policy 6*: 14–61.

Lindblom, Charles. 1977. *Politics and Markets*. New York: Basic Books.

Marx, Karl. 1934 [1852]. *The Eighteenth Brumaire of Louis Bonaparte*. Moscow: Progress Publishers.

Marx, Karl. 1952a. [1867] *Wage Labour and Capital*. Moscow: Progress Publishers.

Marx, Karl. 1952b [1851]. *The Class Struggle in France, 1848 to 1850*. Moscow: Progress Publishers.

Marx, Karl. 1971. *Writings on the Paris Commune*. Edited by Hal Draper. New York: International Publishers.

Miliband, Ralph. 1970. *The State in a Capitalist Society*. New York: Basic Books.

Poulantzas, Nicos. 1973. *Political Power and Social Classes*. London: New Left Books.

Przeworski, Adam. 2005. "Democracy as an Equilibrium." *Public Choice 123*:253–273.

Przeworski, Adam, and Michael Wallerstein. 1982a. "The Structure of Class Conflict in Democratic Capitalist Societies." *American Political Science Review 76*: 215–238.

Przeworski, Adam, and Michael Wallerstein. 1982b. "Democratic Capitalism at the Crossroads." *Democracy 2*: 52–68.

Przeworski, Adam, and Michael Wallerstein. 1988. "Structural Dependence of the State on Capital." *American Political Science Review 82*: 11–29.

Wallerstein, Michael. 1990a. "Class Conflict as a Dynamic Game." In Roger Friedland and Alexander F. Robertson (eds.), *Beyond the Marketplace: Rethinking Economy and Society*. Hawthorne, NY: Aldine de Gruyter.

Wallerstein, Michael. 1990b. "Centralized Bargaining and Wage Restraint." *American Journal of Political Science 34*: 982–1004.

Wallerstein, Michael, and Adam Przeworski. 1995. "Capital Taxation with Open Borders." *Review of International Political Economy 2* (3): 425–445.

3

The Structure of Class Conflict in
Democratic Capitalist Societies

Adam Przeworski and Michael Wallerstein

The combination of private ownership of the instruments of production
with representative political institutions based on widespread suffrage constitutes a compromise between workers, who consent to the private appropriation of profit by owners of capital, and capitalists, who accept the democratic institutions through which workers can make effective claims for an
improvement of their material conditions.

This form of societal organization was considered to be inherently unsta-
ble by Marx, who believed that capitalist democracy is "only the political
form of revolution of bourgeois society and not its conservative form of life,"
(1934, p. 18) "only a spasmodic, exceptional state of things... impossible
as the normal form of society." (1972, p. 198)[1] Once introduced, Marx
thought, political democracy would either be extended to the "social realm"
by workers nationalizing the means of production or subverted by capitalists using the ownership of capital to restore their political power. Yet in
many countries, capitalist democracy has persisted over long periods of
time.

Marx's predictions may have been false for at least two distinct reasons.
His followers have tended to accept a model of conflict in which interests of
classes are irreconcilably opposed to each other, a model that implies that
workers should always be hostile to capitalism and capitalists. If this model
is correct and if capitalism nevertheless survives in its democratic form, it
must be the result of the activities of some institutions, typically thought
to be the state, which provide physical repression, ideological domination,

---

[1] See Przeworski (1980).

This work has been supported by a grant from the National Science Foundation, No. SOC
78–04595.

cooptation of workers' leaders, or whatever else is necessary to perpetuate capitalism in the face of the permanent threat posed by workers.

But Marx may have erred in analyzing the nature of this conflict. Interests of workers and capitalists may not be irreconcilable under all circumstances, and workers may see the choice between capitalism and socialism differently depending upon the specific political and economic conditions under which they live. Their option may be the one defined by John Mitchell, President of the United Mine Workers, at the turn of the century: "Trade unionism is not irrevocably committed to the maintenance of the wage system, nor is it irrevocably committed to its abolition. It demands the constant improvement of the condition of the workingmen, if possible, by the maintenance of the present wage system, if not possible, by its ultimate abolition." (Quoted by Sombart 1976, p. 19.) And if workers opt for capitalism under some conditions, then the activities of the state acquire a different significance: the state institutionalizes, coordinates, and enforces compromises reached by a class coalition that encompasses both workers and capitalists.

Our purpose is to examine the structure of class conflict over material interests between workers and capitalists in democratic capitalist societies and to analyze the consequences of this structure for the theory of the state. We assume throughout that both workers and capitalists would adopt those courses of action which are most likely to benefit them. Generically, four such outcomes are conceivable: (1) a democratic capitalist compromise, (2) capitalist democracy without a compromise (tug-of-war), (3) dictatorial capitalism, and (4) socialism. First we examine the outcomes of conflicts under capitalist democracy; that is, the choice between compromise and its absence when the means of production are privately owned and democratic political institutions are preserved. Then we compare the best outcome workers can obtain under capitalist democracy with their welfare associated with the strategy of transition to socialism. Finally, we comment on the implication of the compromise for the theory of the state.

Capitalism and the Working Class

In a capitalist society profit is a necessary condition of continued production, consumption, and employment. Although in any society some part of the product must be withheld from current consumption if production is to continue and consumption is to increase, the distinguishing characteristic of capitalism is that most investment occurs out of profits, that part of the product which is withheld from the immediate producers. It is upon profits

19

that the renewal and enlargement of the capital stock depends. Hence, under capitalism private profit is a necessary condition for the improvement of the material conditions of any group in society. As Chancellor Schmidt put it, "The profits of enterprises today are the investments of tomorrow, and the investments of tomorrow are the employment of the day after" (*Le Monde*, July 16, 1976) and in place of employment he might as well have said production or consumption.

This dependence of accumulation upon profit can be formally described in a number of ways, among which we choose the simplest. We assume that net investment $\Delta K(t)$, where $K(t)$ is the capital stock, is equal to the rate of saving out of profits, s, multiplied by net profits, $P(t)$.[2]

$$\Delta K(t) = sP(t), s \leq 1 \tag{1}$$

In addition, we assume that the productivity of capital is constant and is measured by the output/capital ratio $1/c$.[3]

$$1/c = Y(t)/K(t) = \Delta Y(t)/\Delta K(t) \tag{2}$$

Net output $Y(t)$ is divided into net profits, $P(t)$, and wages, $W(t)$.[4]

$$Y(t) = P(t) + W(t) \tag{3}$$

---

[2] We make, here, the strong assumption that the entire wage bill is consumed. It is not crucial to our argument, however, If we acknowledge that workers do save and, following Pasinetti (1962), rewrite equation (1) in the test as $\Delta K(t) = s_p P(t) + s_p P(t) + Q(t)$, where s_p is the rate of saving out of profits, $P(t)$, and s_w is the rate of saving out of wages, $W(t)$, and workers' interest income, $Q(t)$, we get a more complicated model with similar results. If workers receive the same rate of return as capitalists, the results are identical. If, however, capitalists gain a fee for investing workers' savings, the results concerning workers' strategic behavior remain the same while capitalists become somewhat more disposed to compromise.

That being said, the strong assumption that workers' net savings are negligible is not an unreasonable simplification for a society like the United States where gross personal saving minus investment in housing and minus investment by unincorporated business averaged 1.1 percent of disposable income between 1949 and 1970 (Wallerstein 1979). In contrast, the rate of corporate saving in the United States in roughly the same period was estimated to range from 40 to 60 percent of profits (Odling-Smee 1973).

[3] The capital-to-output ratio constitutes a cumulative effect of past decisions by capitalists and it changes rather slowly, although it may exhibit long-term trends (Helmstädter 1973). The values of this parameter are fairly well known (Helmstädter 1973; Clough 1968; Kuznets 1966; Maddison 1964). In our subsequent analysis we assume that $c = 4$, as this value seems to be a reasonable estimate of the net incremental capital-to-output ratio in the advanced capitalist economies.

[4] That part of the national income accruing to wage earners, which we have designated $W(t)$, is actually a composite of different types of income. To disaggregate somewhat, we could write: $W = wL + \bar{w}(N - L)$, or, alternatively, $W = (\bar{w} - \bar{w})L + wN$, where N is the size of

Solving the three equations yields the time path of output.

$$Y(t+1) = (1+s/c)P(t) + W(t) \qquad (4)$$

Note that the quantity s/c represents the increase of output per unit of profit when capitalists invest at the rate s in an economy characterized by the capital/output ratio c.

$$s/c = \Delta Y(t)/P(t). \qquad (5)$$

Since the rate of investment can be at most equal to one, the productivity of capital, $1/c$, can be thought of as the upper bound on the increase of output due to each unit of profit.

Note finally that the rate of growth of such an economy depends upon the rate of profit and the rate of saving out of profit:

$$\Delta Y(t)/Y(t) = sP(t)/cY(t) = sP(t)/K(t) = sp(t), \qquad (6)$$

where $p(t) = P(t)/K(t)$ is the rate of profit. Hence the greater the rate of profit and the rate of investment out of profits, the greater the rate of growth. The rate of saving, s, characterizes the crucial aspect of the behavior of capitalists, since given the share of profit in the national income, their decisions to invest and thus to save determine the rate of growth of the economy.

Although profit is a necessary condition of economic growth, it is not a sufficient condition for the improvement of the material welfare of any particular group. First, capitalists may treat profits in ways that do not increase productivity: albeit under constraints, profits may be hoarded, consumed, exported, or just invested unproductively. Second, even if capitalists are frugal and efficient, no particular group can be in any way assured that it will be the beneficiary of the investment. Capitalists may themselves retain the entire additional output or they may share the gain exclusively with any of

the adult population that does not own capital, L is the number employed, w is the average wage rate, and W is the average transfer. Thus, w is either the average transfer to the unemployed or a "reservation wage" (McDonald and Solow 1981), or a basic maintenance payment accruing to all N independently of the employment status or a "citizen's wage" (Bowles and Gintis 1980) such as social security benefits, private pensions, and unemployment compensation. To proceed in this direction one must, first, modify our assumptions about production to include labor as a productive input; second, specify the preferences of workers over combinations of w, $\bar{w}$, and L, and third, stipulate who pays the citizen's wage. These modifications would be necessary to analyze class conflict over employment, rather than over investment and the distribution of income. This, however, is a project for the future.

a number of potential political allies. Their market relation with workers ends as the cycle of production is completed and wages are paid, and there is nothing in the structure of the capitalist economic system that would guarantee that workers would benefit because a part of the product (the profit) is currently withheld from them.

Faced with this system, organized workers have the following options:

1. To claim the entire capital stock ("means of production") from capitalists and to reorganize the system of production so that the decision to withhold from current consumption would be made by all individuals qua citizens. The investment fund would be deducted directly from the gross product, profit having been abolished as a juridical and as an economic category. This strategy would constitute a step toward socialism.
2. To claim the entire product or even a part of the capital stock without reorganizing the process of withholding from current consumption. This is a militant economicist strategy.
3. To claim less than the entire product, thus leaving a part in the hands of capitalists as profit, in exchange for some assurance that future material conditions would improve as a consequence. This strategy opens room for a class compromise with capitalists.

Class Compromise

The structural conditions of the capitalist organization of production delimit the form of any possible class compromise. Since the appropriation of profit by capitalists is a necessary but not a sufficient condition for an improvement of the material welfare of workers under capitalism, a class compromise is possible only on the condition that workers are reasonably certain that future wages will increase as a consequence of current profits. Any compromise must have the following structure: workers consent to the perpetuation of profits as an institution in exchange for the prospect of improving their material welfare within some future period. In terms of such a compromise, capitalists retain the capacity to withhold a part of the product because the profit they appropriate is expected by workers to be saved, invested, and utilized to increase output, with part of the increase distributed as gains to workers.

This general logic need not be always stated explicitly as the form of a particular compromise between labor and capital. Indeed, during the early period of the development of the working-class movement this compromise was limited to the right of workers to associate, to bargain collectively, and to strike. Eventually formal corporatist arrangements and explicit norms appeared, pegging wage increases to exceed increases in the cost of living, or to equal the growth of productivity, or to depend upon competitiveness in the international system. The norm tying increases of wages to the growth of productivity became the foundation of the compromise established during the expansionist period between 1950 and 1970. Nevertheless, whatever the explicit norm cementing a particular social compact, the underlying logic of compromise must relate future wages to current profits. The only conceivable reason for workers to consent voluntarily not to claim the capital stock is to treat current profits as a form of workers delegated investment.

Hence, any class compromise must have the form

$$\Delta \hat{W}(t) = F(P(t - i)), \quad i = 0, 1, \ldots, k, \ldots, \tag{7}$$

where $\Delta \hat{W}(t)$ represents the increase of wages between any successive periods t and $(t + 1)$ associated with a particular compromise, $P(t - i)$ gives the history of profits, and F is the rule that relates past profits to current wage increases. For the sake of simplicity, let this rule be

$$\Delta \hat{W}(t) = rP(t), r > 0. \tag{8}$$

A compromise is in force, therefore, when workers consent to any value of r which constitutes less than a claim to the capital stock and capitalists consent to institutions that would make it reasonably certain that wages would increase as a function of profits according to some rule such as (8). Workers consent to a capitalist organization of production when they choose and follow in practice any strategies that make possible the perpetuation of capitalist relations. Capitalists in turn accept a compromise when they consent to institutions that would permit workers to process their claims with some success: basically unions, parties, and a relatively autonomous state. This class compromise is precisely that which Marx found to be unreasonable: workers stop short of seeking social emancipation, capitalists of attempting political restoration. Workers consent to capitalism; capitalists consent to democracy.

Since workers make their consent conditional upon obtaining wage increases equal to the proportion r of current profits, this coefficient can be thought of as indicating the economic militancy of organized workers under particular historical conditions. A compromise is in force when workers are not so militant that their wage demands would make profits immediately negative, that is, when $r < (1 + s/c)$. This can be seen as follows: At any time t capitalists appropriate the amount of profit equal to $P(t)$ and during the period $(t,t + 1)$, they invest the fraction s of $P(t)$ at a rate of return equal to $1/c$. Therefore, at the time $(t + 1)$, with regard to which workers make claims at t, capitalists will have the amount $(1 + s/c)P(t)$. At time $(t + 1)$ they pay wage increases equal to $rP(t)$. Hence, an $r = (1 + s/c)$ is immediately confiscatory with regard to profits: it implies that workers appropriate the entire net product at $(t + 1)$. Any r larger than that means that workers claim capital stock.

Class compromise is expressed, therefore, in institutional arrangements that imply that some proportion r of current profits is to be transformed into wage increases, where $r < (1 + s/c)$. Class compromise is in force when workers and capitalists act in ways that presuppose the perpetuation of capitalist democracy as the form of organization of society.

Workers' Strategy

Organized workers would rationally opt for a compromise, consenting to profit as an institution, if this compromise would be preferable both to the outcomes associated with greater economic militancy under capitalism and to the result they would expect to attain by adopting a strategy of transition to socialism. Eventually we will introduce some of the complications that arise when workers consider the socialist alternative, but at this moment we will be concerned only with comparisons of the welfare that workers can attain by choosing different degrees of economic militancy under capitalism.

At any time, let it be $T = 0, 1, 2, \ldots$, workers decide how militant they should be economically, that is, what proportion of current profits they should immediately demand as wage increases. The effect of workers' decision made at time t is irrevocable in the sense that the part of the product not transformed into wages is irretrievably forsaken by workers and appropriated by capitalists who alone decide whether or not to invest it.

Workers choose their strategy on the basis of their expectations about the future. They decide by comparing the alternative futures they expect to occur as the result of their current course of action. These expectations are shaped by workers' analysis of the reaction of capitalists to their own course of action and of workers' perception of their power to enforce a compromise if one were to be concluded. Hence these expectations are conditional: they are molded by the conditions that hold when a decision is to be made.

Workers opt for a compromise if they think it to be the best course of action at a particular time. Note that workers may not receive the returns they expected when the decision was made, but they base their decision on what they expect to happen; they have, after all, no other grounds on which to base it.

Workers base present decisions on their expectations for the future, but they do not commit themselves to choose the same course of action again under different conditions. Hence no compromise is made once and for all. Neither the workers' consent to capitalism nor the capitalists' consent to democracy constitutes consensus, some kind of prior and immutable agreement about societal organization that would hold regardless of whether or not the interests of each class are being realized within it. A compromise holds if and only if it is continually in the best interest of workers and capitalists and only if it is repeatedly remade. A compromise is not a commitment for some indefinite or even limited future; it is an outcome of strategies chosen today which today appear optimal. If the compromise is to last the day after, it must be made again the day after, and it will be made only if it constitutes the best solution the day after.[5] Consent should not be seen as a state of mind or a prior commitment but as a characteristic of

---

[5] Hence although workers make strategic decisions repeatedly as conditions change, they make them independently at each occasion. This formulation of the problem implies that the game is modelled here as a static game played repeatedly but independently each time. This is not an iterative game as described by Taylor (1976), in which actors would make their current decisions anticipating subsequent decisions of their opponents and calculating the advantages to be derived by choosing strategies that are currently suboptimal. Neither is it a dynamic game, in which the solution is a function of time (Lancaster 1973, and Hoel 1975, 1978) in which actors would commit themselves at a particular time to follow definite strategies in the future. We do not see the problem as a dynamic game because we do not believe that any particular moment can be viewed as a privileged time at which to make a decision binding upon the future. In Lancaster's model the strategies to be chosen by workers and capitalists are the time paths of the wage share and the rate of saving out of profits, and these strategies are chosen once and for all for a finite horizon. What is unreasonable in our view is that in Lancaster's model the horizon is actually approached, and as a result at one moment workers and capitalists rush to consume as if there were no future. We prefer the assumption that every year is the first of the next h years with the view toward which workers and capitalists evaluate their strategies. We do believe, however, that the conflict we describe is in fact an iterative game in which the parameters are subject to trade-offs and are thus endogenous.

25

actions, of strategies, and of nothing beyond. Classes consent to a particular form of society when they choose strategies that entail the perpetuation of that form, because those strategies are in their best interests given the alternatives. Nothing else is involved.

How do workers decide upon their strategies? There are two considerations: the wages they expect in the future if the compromise holds and the risk that the compromise will not hold. Suppose first that actual wages follow the path stipulated by a compromise, that is, $W(t) = \hat{W}(t)$ for all $T \leq t \leq T + h$, where h is the horizon with which workers consider the future. If capitalists invest at the rate s in the economy characterized by the productivity of capital $1/c$, then the time path of compromise wages will depend upon the relation between r and s/c. Recall that

$$\Delta Y(t) = \Delta P(t) + \Delta W(t) = (s/c)P(t), \qquad \text{(from 3 and 5)}$$

and

$$\Delta W(t) = \Delta \hat{W}(t) = rP(t). \qquad \text{(from 8)}$$

It then follows that

$$\Delta P(t) = (s/c - r)P(t), \qquad (9)$$

or

$$P(t + 1) = (1 + s/c - r)P(t). \qquad (10)$$

There are three cases to consider[6] (see Figure 1):

If workers choose an r such that $r < s/c$, then wages will grow exponentially, following the exponential growth of profits. In this case we will say that workers are not militant or that they offer wage restraint.

If workers choose an r such that $s/c < r < (1 + s/c)$, then wages will grow rapidly at first and then stagnate at a fixed level as net profits decline to zero. Such a strategy we will call moderately militant.

If workers choose an r such that $r > (1 + s/c)$, then workers are highly militant. Wages will then experience a sharp increase as net profits immediately become negative. Since this strategy cannot lead to a compromise,

---

[6] Equation (10) is a first-order linear difference equation of the form $Y(t + 1) = aY(t)$, with the solution $Y(t) = a^t Y(0)$. For any $Y(0) > 0$, $Y(t)$ will be a monotonically increasing function of time if $a > 1$; it will monotonically decrease to zero if $0 < a < 1$; it will oscillate around zero if $a < 0$ (Goldberg 1973).

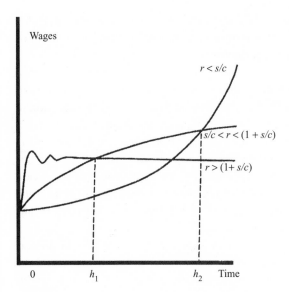

Figure 1

there is no reason to expect that subsequent wages would bear any relation to profits. If they did, wages would oscillate henceforth around a fixed level while profits would oscillate around zero.

One way to review these consequences of the workers' strategies is to observe that the non-militant workers would be best off after some time h_2, about a generation if time is measured in years; moderately militant workers would be best off during the period between some time h_1 and h_2; and highly militant workers would be best off during the initial period until h_1. The values of h_1 and h_2 depend upon the particular relation between r and s/c. The time span h_1 can be as short as a couple of years, whereas h_2 can be as long as thirty years.

In considering the effects of their actions workers cannot be certain, however, that the compromise would hold. Hence, their decision must depend upon the likelihood that capitalists will observe the terms of a compromise if one were to be concluded. Since the future becomes increasingly less predictable the further one looks into it, the wages workers would obtain at each moment in the future would weigh progressively less in the workers' decision, the further in the future they would occur. Hence, we assume that even if workers valued wage increases equally regardless of the magnitude

27

of current wages and were indifferent between certain consumption today and certain consumption in the future, they would nevertheless discount the future on the grounds of uncertainty.[7]

Since we assume below that capitalists also discount their future welfare on the grounds of uncertainty, we can treat similarly the determinants of risk facing each class. This risk is associated with the political and economic conditions at the time when a decision is made, specifically:

(1) The degree of bilateral monopoly. Unless workers are monopolistically organized, they cannot be certain that particular groups among them would not conclude their own agreements with their respective employers at the cost of other workers. Since capitalists cannot completely avoid competing with one another, each firm faces the danger that other firms would ride free on the costs of the compromise.[8]

(2) The institutionalization of labor-capital relations and the likelihood that a compromise would be enforced by the state. The question is whom the state would be capable and willing to coerce to prevent deviations from the compromise: capitalists, workers, or both? Partisan control over the state and the electoral prospects would constitute an important consideration in evaluating this risk.

(3) The ordinary risks inherent in investment owing to domestic and international economic fluctuations, domestic and international competition, technical change, and other economic factors.

Furthermore, the degree of risk born by capitalists when they invest depends in part upon the rigidity of their wage commitment. If wages are highly rigid, capitalists face the risk inherent in investment alone. If the wage bill can be reduced below the terms of the compromise when times are bad, much of the risk is borne by workers. To some degree, therefore,

---

[7] The assumption that anyone maximizes undiscounted values over infinite horizons is clearly unreasonable. As Ferejohn and Page put it, "The pie-in-the-sky quality of the overtaking rule no doubt disqualifies it as a practical decision rule" (1978, p. 271).

[8] To discuss this topic, as fundamental as it is, would be to open a can of worms. There are good reasons to believe that workers as well as capitalists are placed by a compromise into a prisoner's dilemma, in which each participant may find it preferable not to pay the costs of the compromise even if such a compromise is collectively optimal for the class. On the other hand, Roemer (1978) argues that workers have no choice but to opt for intra-class solidarity. Edel (1979) relies on a Taylor-like argument about the iterative nature of the prisoner's dilemma. Offe and Wiesenthal (1980) claim that workers can modify each other's preferences in the direction of solidarity by a process of "dialogue." We are skeptical about the validity of these arguments.

the uncertainty faced by capitalists is inversely related to the uncertainty confronting workers.

Let a, $a > 0$, be the rate at which workers discount the future on the grounds of uncertainty. The higher the a, the less certain it is at $t = 0$ that a compromise would hold in the future and the faster workers discount the future wages stipulated under a compromise. Given the level of wages associated with a particular compromise and the degree of workers' uncertainty, the workers' problem is to find a level of economic militancy that maximizes the current value of their discounted future wages, or

$$\max_r W^* = \sum_{t=0}^{t=b} (1 + a)^{-t} \hat{W}(t), \quad a > 0, \tag{11}$$

where the anticipated path of wages, $\hat{W}(t)$, is given by equations (8) and (10).[9]

Note that W^* depends upon workers' militancy, r, their horizon, b, their discount rate, a, the productivity of capital, $1/c$, and the saving behavior of capitalists, s. Thus $W^* = F(r; b,a,c; s)$. The productivity of capital, the horizon, and the rate of discount are fixed; they constitute the objective conditions of the moment. The behavior of capitalists with regard to saving is something workers must adjust to. Economic militancy is the strategic variable of workers, whose problem is to choose an r that maximizes W^* in the face of the investment strategy of capitalists, represented by s. Let $r^*(s)$ be the solution of equation (11); that is, the value of r which maximizes W^* given that capitalists invest at the rate s, when b, a, and c are given. Then $r^*(s)$ is the best reply strategy of workers (Harsanyi 1977, p. 102).

Workers must weigh the gains of immediate wage increases against the expected gains that would result in the future from less militant demands. Profits appropriated by capitalists who are investing at the rate s will increase output by s/c, or $\Delta Y(t)/P(t) = s/c$. Note also that the maximal return to output of a unit of profit, when all profits are invested, is given by the productivity of capital, $1/c$. We have, then, the following theorem: When the horizon is sufficiently long, workers' best reply will be a compromise level of r if their rate of discount, a, is less than the rate of return s/c. Otherwise they will be highly militant. Stated formally:

---

[9] Note that workers solve this problem repeatedly at each T, $T = 0,1,\ldots$, and we should have written W^*T as a sum going from $t = T$ to $t = T + b$. For convenience, we assume that we are examining one such decision, at $T = 0$.

Workers' Best-Reply Theorem

For all $h > H$, where H is some positive number,

$$r^*(s) > (1 + s/c) \quad \text{if } a > 1/c \text{ for any } s,$$
$$r^*(s) > (1 + s/c) \quad \text{if } a > s/c \text{ or } s < ac,$$
$$r^*(s) < (1 + s/c) \quad \text{if } a < s/c \text{ or } s > ac.$$

In the case of an infinite horizon, the workers best-reply strategy is given by a bang-bang function. When $a > s/c$, the workers' best reply is maximal militancy. When $a < s/c$, the workers' best reply approaches zero. (See Appendix for formal proof.)

What occurs when h is some finite number? Our numerical experiments indicate that for $c = 4$, H is approximately equal to 12; that is, for any $h > 12$, a maximally militant strategy will be best when $a > s/c$ and a compromise strategy will be best when $a < s/c$. (If $h < 12$, the best-reply strategy is to be maximally militant in all cases.) But, for any finite horizon, the workers' best-reply strategy does not suddenly jump from maximal militancy to zero. Rather, for $s > ac$, $r^*(s)$ is a continuous, monotonically decreasing, positive function. The higher the rate of saving above the product ac, the lower will be the workers' best-reply level of militancy.

One way to explain this theorem is that workers today would value equally the wages they anticipate receiving in each year of a compromise if for any two successive periods, the compromise wages would grow at such a rate that $W(t + 1) = (1 + a)W(t)$, or equivalently, $\Delta W(t) = aW(t)$. Now, we know that if a compromise were observed exactly, the wage path would follow the rule $\Delta W(t) = rP(t)$ for all t. Hence, the present value to workers who discount the future at the rate a of the wages they would obtain in any period of a compromise characterized by the level of militancy r, would be exactly constant if and only if $rP(t) = aW(t)$. The present value of each period's wages would be growing if $rP(t) > aW(t)$; otherwise it would be declining.

Suppose that $rP(t) = aW(t)$ for all t. Taking differences of both sides and dividing by $P(t)$ yields $r\Delta P(t)/P(t) = a\Delta W(t)/P(t)$. But $\Delta P(t)/P(t) = (s/c - r)$ and $\Delta W(t)/P(t) = r$. Hence, the present value of future wages stipulated under a compromise would remain constant if $a = (s/c - r)$. If $a < (s/c - r)$ or $r < (s/c - a)$, they would be growing over time. If $a > (s/c - r)$ or $r > (s/c - a)$, they would be falling.

Now, if workers are to benefit at all from current profits, r must be positive. The question then is whether there exists, under the conditions

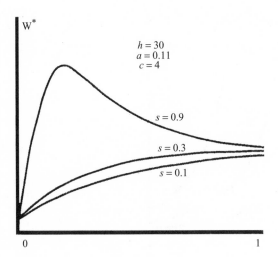

W*

h = 30
a = 0.11
c = 4

s = 0.9

s = 0.3

s = 0.1

0   1

Figure 2

given by s/c and a, a positive value of r such that the present value of future wages is growing. Such an r exists only if $(s/c - a) > 0$, or $s/c > a$. Under these conditions, workers will compromise for any $h > 12$. If the horizon is sufficiently long (where the sufficient length depends upon s/c and a), workers will opt for a strategy of wage restraint such that $r < (s/c - a)$, since the time path of growing discounted wages will eventually overtake any path of stagnant or declining discounted wages. If, on the other hand, $s/c < a$, then the present value of future wages will decline for any positive r and workers are best off highly militant, with immediate wage increases as large as possible.

The intuitive meaning of this theorem is apparent. Since s/c is the rate of increase of output per unit of profit, it constitutes the maximal rate at which wages could grow under a compromise. If the maximal conceivable growth of wages is lower than the rate at which workers discount their wage increases, then workers will be worse off if they consent to the appropriation of profits. But if output grows faster than workers discount the future; then workers will be better off choosing a strategy of compromise and waiting for future wage gains.

Figure 2 shows some illustrative functions $W^*(r, s)$ for $h = 30$. The lower segment portrays W^* when $a > s/c$ and the upper segment when $a < s/c$. When $a > s/c$, W^* is a monotonically increasing function of r, but when $a < s/c$, W^* has a maximum at a compromise level of militancy.

31

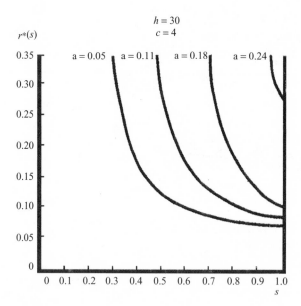

$r^*(s)$

$h = 30$
$c = 4$

a = 0.05   a = 0.11   a = 0.18   a = 0.24

Figure 3

Figure 3 presents the numerically derived function $r^*(s)$, that is, the level of militancy which maximizes W^* given workers' risk and the saving behavior of capitalists. As long as $a > 1/c$, this function will be larger than $(1 + s/c)$ for all s. If we assume $c = 4$, then at $a = 0.24$, the rate of saving must be as large as 0.96 for the workers' best reply to be a compromise value of r; at $a = 0.01$, a rate of saving equal to 0.04 will suffice.

These results do not yet constitute a prediction about workers' behavior, however, since the strategies that workers will choose depend upon the behavior of capitalists. Capitalists may be unwilling to increase their rate of saving to levels necessary for a compromise even when one is possible. In fact, capitalists can respond to each threat of workers with a threat of their own; if workers threaten to increase militancy, capitalists may threaten to lower their rate of saving. This, then, is what remains to be investigated.

Capitalists' Strategy

What would be the objective of capitalists in making compromises with workers? Clearly their chief preoccupation would be to maintain profits as the form in which a part of the product is withheld from current

32

The Structure of Class Conflict in Democratic Capitalist Societies

consumption. Yet the defense of the institution of private property is not sufficient: actual profits must be obtained. Furthermore, it seems unreasonable to assume that capitalists are nothing but "rational misers." Ultimately they are concerned not only about being able to reinvest profits but also being able to consume them. Capitalists are not simply workers' investing machines: they do have particularistic interests of their own. It seems reasonable, therefore, to assume that capitalists attempt to maximize their consumption, $C(t) = (1-s)P(t)$, over a period of h years. Moreover capitalists would discount future consumption in accordance with the uncertainty they face.

If the rate of discount for capitalists is b, then the problem faced by capitalists is to choose the value of the rate of saving, s, which maximizes the current value of their discounted future consumption given that workers choose the level of militancy, or

$$\max_s C^* = (1 - s) \sum_{t=0}^{t=h}(1 + b)^{-t}\hat{P}(t),\qquad(12)$$

where the anticipated path of compromise profits, $\hat{P}(t)$, is given by (10). The rate of saving, s, is the strategic variable of capitalists and $s^*(r)$ is their best reply strategy, that is, the value of s that maximizes C^* given a particular value of r, under conditions given by h, b, and c.

The best-reply strategy of capitalists is given by the following theorem. When their horizon is sufficiently long, capitalists' best reply will be to invest as long as the rate at which they discount the future is lower than their return on investment; otherwise they will disinvest. The capitalists' rate of return on investment is equal to the productivity of capital or the increase of output per unit of invested profits, $1/c$, minus the proportion of this unit of profit paid to workers, r. Hence, capitalists will find it best to invest at a positive rate if and only if $b < (1/c - r)$. Stated formally:

Capitalists' Best-Reply Theorem

For all $h > H$, where H is the same number as in the workers' best-reply theorem,

$$s^*(r) < 0 \text{ if } b > 1/c \text{ for any } r,$$
$$s^*(r) < 0 \text{ if } b > (1/c - r) \text{ or } r > (1/c - b),$$
$$s^*(r) > 0 \text{ if } b < (1/c - r) \text{ or } r < (1/c - b).$$

33

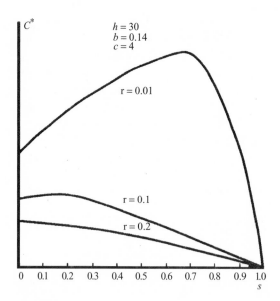

Figure 4

When the horizon is infinite, capitalists' best-reply strategy is a bang-bang function, equal to maximal investment or maximal disinvestment according to whether capitalists' discount rate, b is less than or greater than $(1/c - r)$. The proof is in the Appendix. For finite horizons, the capitalists' best-reply function must be derived numerically. For $b > 12$ (when $c = 4$), $s^*(r)$ is a continuous, monotonically decreasing function with $0 < s^*(r) < 1$ when $r < (1/c - b)$. The greater the restraint of workers' militancy below the quantity $(1/c - b)$, the higher the best-reply rate of saving by capitalists.

The intuitive meaning of the capitalists' best-reply theorem can be seen as follows. The quantity $(1/c - r)$ represents the maximal rate at which profits, and therefore consumption from profits, can grow given the level of militancy, r, stipulated under a particular compromise. If the maximum conceivable rate of growth of profits is less than the rate at which capitalists discount the future, capitalists are better off disinvesting. But if the maximal possible rate of growth of profits exceeds the capitalists' discount rate, a strategy of positive investment is optimal.

Figure 4 portrays some illustrative functions $C^*(s, r)$ for an $b = 30$, $c = 4$; Figure 5 shows the positive segment of the function $s^*(r)$ under the same conditions.

34

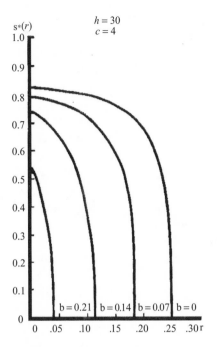

Figure 5

Conditions of Class Compromise: Basic Results

Thus far we have examined the best reply of each class to the behavior of the other class, that is, the solution to the maximizing problem facing each class when its opponent behaves in a fixed manner. The best-reply strategy is the optimal strategy if one's opponent is not acting strategically, but both classes do act strategically, and it is only reasonable to assume that each anticipates that the other will behave strategically. Each class must take into account not only the other's actions but also its reactions, not only the other's current strategy but also the likely response to its own choice of strategy. If, for example, workers' best-reply strategy to some positive rate of saving is to become highly militant, they cannot expect capitalists to continue saving if the workers' best-reply strategy is pursued. Workers must take into account that capitalists' best reply to high levels of militancy is to disinvest.

We define a pair of strategies (r, s) to be a solution to the game if neither class could do better with an alternative strategy given the anticipated response of its opponent. Hence, a solution is a pair (r, s) that, once chosen,

35

will be stable as long as conditions remain unchanged. Note that the intersection of the best reply functions $(r^*(s^*), s^*(r^*))$ constitutes a solution. Both classes are responding optimally to the current strategy of their opponent. This is the Nash (1954) equilibrium. In our model this solution occurs only when compromise breaks down.[10] The capitalists' best reply to high levels of militancy is to disinvest, and the workers' best reply to disinvestment is to be highly militant.

Suppose, however, that workers anticipate that capitalists will respond to any r with their best-reply strategy $s^*(r)$. Now the problem facing workers is to choose the level of militancy which maximizes the function $W^*(r; s^*(r))$, that is, one that maximizes workers' welfare given that capitalists will respond with $s^*(r)$ to any r workers might choose. Let this maximizing value of r be r^{**}. The pair $(r^{**}, s^*(r^{**}))$ is also a solution to the game. The level of militancy r^{**} is the optimal choice of workers given the anticipated response by capitalists and $s^*(r^{**})$ is by definition the capitalists' optimal response to the workers' strategy r^{**}. This is the Stackelberg (1952) solution with workers as the dominant player. Note that r^{**} is not necessarily in the workers' set of best-reply strategies, $r^*(s)$. The *function* $r^*(s)$ is defined as the maximum with respect to r of the function $W^*(r; s)$, each value of s constant, whereas the *number* r^{**} is defined to be the maximum with respect to r of the function $W^*(r; s^*(r))$, where $s = s^*(r)$ is a function of r.

Suppose now that it is the capitalists who anticipate that workers will adopt their best-reply strategy $r^*(s)$ to any rate of saving, s, capitalists choose. Capitalists would then seek to maximize $C^*(s, r^*(s))$. Let the maximizing value of s be s^{**}. The pair of strategies $(r^*(s^{**})_1 s^{**})$ is another solution of the game. Given their anticipations of the workers' response, the capitalists have chosen their best strategy, and the workers are responding optimally to the capitalists' choice. This is the Stackelberg solution with capitalists as the dominant player. Again, s^{**} need not be in the set of capitalists' best-reply strategies. The function $s^*(r)$ is the capitalists' best response to the workers' current level of militancy. The number s^{**} is the capitalists' optimal choice given that the workers will respond to any s with their best reply, $r^*(s)$.

The Nash equilibrium, which represents absence of compromise, is always possible. What remains to be investigated are the conditions for

---

[10] There is an exception. In the limiting case when $a = b = 0$, there is another Nash equilibrium at a point of compromise.

the existence of compromise, Stackelberg solutions. If the horizon is too short, $h < 12$, no compromise solutions exist. For any $h > 12$, however, the existence of compromise solutions depends entirely upon the relations between the discount rates a and b and the productivity of capital, $1/c$. In the subsequent discussion we assume $h > 12$. (In the numerical illustrations $h = 30$.) There are four cases to consider.

(i) $a > 1/c, b > 1/c$.

Both workers and capitalists face a large degree of uncertainty about whether any compromise would hold. The situation in France in 1936 provides a prototype: in France few workers were organized before 1936, there were almost no traditions of collective bargaining, several unions and parties competed for workers' support, and the very Matignon agreement was concluded under the pressure of spontaneous occupations of factories. Hence neither workers nor capitalists could expect that the agreement would last and, indeed, six weeks after it was concluded both parties began to undermine it: capitalists by dragging their feet in complying with the wage terms (specifically those concerning minimal wages and paid vacations), and by raising prices, and workers by striking and occupying factories again.

Under these circumstances workers find it best to be highly militant regardless of the saving rate chosen by capitalists, whereas capitalists find it optimal to disinvest regardless of workers' militancy, No compromise is possible. All three solutions collapse into one, the Nash equilibrium, at which $r^*(s) > 1 + s/c$ and $s^*(r) < 0$.

(ii) $a > 1/c, b < 1/c$.

Workers bear most of the risk, whereas capitalists are relatively certain they would obtain the profits specified by any compromise. This is the case when the degree of unionization is low or several unions compete with each other, capital-labor relations are weakly institutionalized, and workers have little influence over the state. The United States today would provide a prototypical case.

When $b < 1/c$, the best reply strategy of capitalists is to invest at a positive rate as long as workers are not highly militant: $s^*(r) > 0$ if $r < (1/c - b)$. The best reply strategy of workers, however, is to increase their militancy regardless of the rate of saving, since $a > 1/c$. One possibility is that workers would follow their best-reply strategy and capitalists would respond by disinvesting, a scenario that ends again without a compromise. But an alternative solution is also possible. Suppose first that for historical reasons

Adam Przeworski and Michael Wallerstein

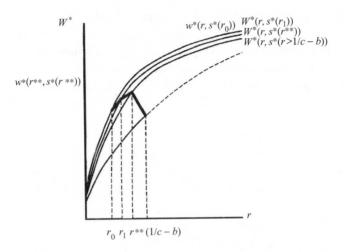

Figure 6

workers find themselves in a situation in which they have not been militant in the past and that they begin their current decision-making process by considering a non-militant value of r, say $r = r_0$. (Consult Figure 6 while following this argument.) If the workers choose r_0, then capitalists will choose $s_0 = s^*(r_0)$. Since the workers' best reply to any s is to increase their militancy, they will now consider moving to a new level $r = r_1$. Capitalists, in turn, will respond to the increase of militancy by lowering the rate of investment to $s_1 = s^*(r_1)$. The effect of the capitalists' adjustment will be to drop workers to a function $W^*(r, s_1)$, which is inferior to $W^*(r, s_0)$. If, however, r_1 is only slightly higher than r_0, capitalists will respond (see Figure 5) with a small reduction in their rate of investment, and workers will find that they are better off at the new point $(r_1, s^*(r_1))$ than they were before. Since workers' best reply to s_1 is again maximal militancy, workers will now consider raising their militancy further to $r = r^{**}$. Capitalists will lower their rate of saving to $s = s^*(r^{**})$, yet workers will still find they are better off at $(r^{**}, s^*(r^{**}))$ than at any lower value of r. Now as the workers consider increasing their militancy past the level $r = r^{**}$, they discover that the capitalists' best reply is to lower their rate of investment quite sharply, so that workers are worse off at an r slightly higher than r^{**} than they would be at r^{**}. Even though the workers' best response to any fixed rate of saving, including $s^*(r^{**})$, is maximal militancy, the capitalists' threat of disinvestment is effective in the region in which r is somewhat higher than

38

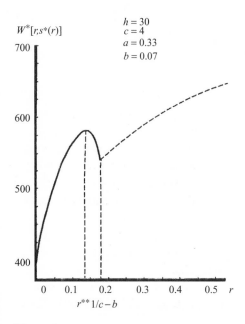

$W^*[r,s^*(r)]$

$h = 30$
$c = 4$
$a = 0.33$
$b = 0.07$

Figure 7

r^{**}. Indeed, the workers discover that if they keep increasing r gradually past r^{**}, they will be successively worse off as $W^*(r, s^*(r))$ keeps decreasing with higher levels of militancy. The threat of disinvestment will not be effective, however, in the entire range of $r > r^{**}$. As r reaches the value $r = 1/c - b$, capitalists will be disinvesting at the greatest possible rate, and their threat will be exhausted. If workers choose an $r > 1/c - b$, the compromise breaks down, workers seek to nationalize capital stock, and capitalists disinvest. Figure 7 presents a graph of the function $W^*(r, s^*(r))$, which is the array of choices facing workers when capitalists respond according to their best reply. There is a local maximum at r^{**} which constitutes a compromise solution and a local minimum at $1/c - b$.

Will the compromise $(r^{**}, s^*(r^{**}))$ constitute the solution? Unfortunately no answer can be given without additional assumptions. It will be the solution if workers do inherit a situation in which they have not been militant and if a sudden increase of militancy is unfeasible. This is not an unreasonable conjecture. Demands for large wage increases must be pressed through mass actions, strikes, demonstrations. A high level of militancy entails a high level of mobilization, and mobilization is a costly process that

39

requires resources and time. The compromise will also be the solution if workers have good reasons to fear the political consequences of a breakdown of compromise, a topic to which we return below.

(iii) $a < 1/c$, $b > 1/c$.

Workers are relatively certain to obtain the wages specified by any compromise while capitalists bear the brunt of uncertainty. This would be the case when workers are monopolistically organized, labor-capital relations are institutionalized, and workers are represented by parties that exert electoral influence. The Weimar Republic between 1924 and 1928, Italy between 1969 and 1976, and Great Britain at various times after 1951 would constitute good examples.

When $a < 1/c$, the workers' best-reply strategy is low or moderate militancy as long as the capitalists invest at a sufficient rate: $r^*(s) < (1 + s/c)$ if $s > ac$. The capitalists' best-reply strategy, however, is to disinvest regardless of the level of militancy. But capitalists must consider the workers' response. Figure 8 illustrates the function $C^*(s, r^*(s))$, the anticipated consequence of

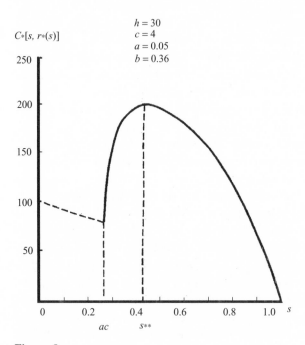

Figure 8

40

choosing each positive level of savings given that workers respond according to their best reply. The capitalists' choice is between $s^* < 0$, that is, disinvestment, which entails a breakdown of compromise (not shown) or the best compromise they can achieve, s^{**}. If the breakdown of compromise is sufficiently dangerous politically to capitalists, the solution $(r^*(s^{**}), s^{**}))$ will be chosen. Given s^{**}, workers reach a global maximum (under capitalism) at $r^*(s^{**})$, and this value represents a compromise strategy since $s^{**} > ac$. And for capitalists, the payoff from s^{**} is the most that can be gained from any compromise.

(iv) $a < 1/c, b < 1/c$.

Both capitalists and workers are quite certain they would obtain what would be expected under any compromise. There is a high degree of bilateral monopoly; capital-labor relations are highly institutionalized; the economy is well situated in the international system. Sweden after 1936 and before the mid-1970s would be a prototype. In Sweden, collective agreements began to be concluded at the turn of the century, and by 1905 a significant proportion of workers was covered by them. These agreements were made binding in a series of decisions by the Supreme Court which first enforced agreements among capitalists and then collective bargains in 1916. In 1920, Labor Courts were established and by 1926 parties could be sued in these courts for unfair bargaining practices. In 1938, a system of collective bargaining was centralized at the country-wide scale, a system that has continued with some modifications up to the present.

In this case, neither the adoption by workers of their best-reply strategy nor by capitalists of theirs would necessarily lead to conflict. Both solutions – $(r^{**}, s^*(r^{**}))$, where the compromise is enforced by the threat of disinvestment, and $(r(s^{**}), (s^{**}))$, where it is enforced by the threat of militancy – are feasible. Each class would prefer the other to depart from its best-reply strategy. Workers do better threatening capitalists with militancy to the solution $(r^*(s^{**}), s^{**})$, whereas capitalists are better off threatening workers to the solution $(r^{**}, s^*(r^{**}))$. The class which is forced to depart from its best-reply strategy ends up, in effect, paying the costs of the compromise. If both of the compromise solutions are superior for both players to the outcome that would result if they both obstinately pursued their best-reply strategies, workers and capitalists face a coordination problem (Schelling 1960). We will not pursue this topic further.

Table 1. *Illustrative Results* $b = 30$, $1/c = 0.25$, $1/(1 + a)(1 + b) = 0.7$[†]

		Workers Dominant				Capitalists Dominant				
a	b	r^{**}	s^{*}	W^{*}	C^{*}	r^{*}	s^{**}	W^{*}	C^{*}	Comments
0.43	0.00	.215	.655	483	541					$r > s/c$
0.35	0.05	.160	.615	557	548					$r > s/c$
0.33	0.08	.150	.585	578	529					$r < s/c$
$1/c$	0.15	.080	.540	701	548					$r < s/c$
0.23	0.16	.070	.505	726	534	.285	.960	1058	23	
0.16	0.23	.015	.225	787	505	.165	.765	1501	142	
0.15	$1/c$					.165	.715	1611	154	$r < s/c$
0.10	0.30					.140	.580	2325	185	$r < s/c$
0.09	0.32					.140	.540	2556	189	$r > s/c$
0.00	0.43					.140	.290	6809	204	$r > s/c$
0.43	0.43	no compromise solutions exist								$r > 1 + s/c$
0.00	0.00	.060	.810	19867	10023	.060	.810	19867	10023	$r < s/c$

†Except the last two rows for which $a = b$.

Conditions of Class Compromise: An Overview. At this point it is useful to disregard some of the details and summarize the results.

When both classes are highly uncertain about whether a compromise would hold, a compromise cannot be established. Workers become highly militant, regardless of the rate of saving, and capitalists seek to disinvest, regardless of militancy.

When workers are highly uncertain and capitalists relatively certain, a compromise may be established at a point at which workers are kept from increasing their militancy by capitalists' threat of disinvestment, whereas capitalists' optimal rate of investment is positive.

When the workers are relatively certain and the capitalists bear high risk, a compromise may be concluded at a point at which the capitalists are forced to save by the threat of militancy, whereas the workers' optimal level of militancy is not high.

When the workers and capitalists both face only moderate amounts of uncertainty, both a compromise concluded under the capitalists' threat of disinvestment and one reached under workers' threat of militancy are feasible. Either may be concluded.

For reference, some illustrative results are summarized in Table 1, for $b = 30$ and $c = 4$. Most entries in this table are obtained on the condition that class-specific discount rates are inversely related according to the equation $(1 + a)^{-1}(1 + b)^{-1} = 0.7$.

Supposing that compromises are concluded in the manner specified by our analysis, the question arises whether or not the outcomes reached will be efficient in the Pareto sense. (See Schelling 1978, for a general treatment of Pareto efficiency of n-person game equilbria.) The concept of the solution we have been using is essentially a non-cooperative one, since we have assumed that although workers and capitalists may choose their strategies in anticipation of the best reply of the opponent, they nevertheless choose these strategies independently rather than jointly. In fact, they need not negotiate at all: each class selects its optimal strategy and no negotiation need be involved. This is important since this concept of the solution means that the model does not presuppose the existence of any corporatist or consociational institutions that would involve direct negotiations. The model is general for all situations in which there is a fair degree of bilateral monopoly, even if all this means is that workers have only the right to associate and to strike, without any further relations with capitalists. But if the solutions obtained in this fashion are highly inefficient, that is, if workers and capitalists can simultaneously improve on these solutions by engaging in direct negotiations, then one would expect that corporatist arrangements must constitute an integral part of any compromise.

Numerical analysis indicates that the set of points that are Pareto superior to the equilibrium solutions is rather small; that is, that the room for improvement over the non-cooperative solutions is limited. Moreover, such an improvement is insignificant when compared with even a minute change in certainty. Workers are better off with a non-cooperative solution at $a = 0.30$ than with the best of the Pareto superior points to the non-cooperative solution at $a = 0.33$. They are better off with a non-cooperative solution at $a = 0.04$ than the best cooperative solution at $a = 0.05$. Hence, workers are better off struggling to increase their certainty that a compromise would hold rather than seeking to improve the terms of a less certain compromise. They are better off competing for political power than making deals with capitalists. Clearly the model does not preclude direct negotiations. Since, however, the non-cooperative solutions are not far from the Pareto efficient frontier, it would be wrong to expect that class compromise can occur only in the presence of institutional arrangements that involve direct negotiations.

Note, however, a major limitation of this model. We treat the political arrangements that determine the class differential risks and consequently rates of discount as the given conditions of the moment when decisions are made. These arrangements may change in time, but such change is exogenous to our model. All we say is that when conditions change, strategies will change as well, but our assumptions do not permit the players to trade off material gains for political power, that is, for a greater probability that class interests will be realized to a particular degree. (This is the definition of political power of Poulantzas 1973.) A more complicated model would treat the class differential rates of discount as endogeneous to the conflict and would allow such trades of material gains for greater certainty. Hence, to the extent to which corporatist arrangements can simultaneously increase the certainty of both classes, such arrangements will yield significantly superior outcomes.

More generally, note that although we assume that a particular compromise is reproduced over time if and only if the conditions a, b, and c under which it was originally arrived at remain the same, compromises break down in our model only for exogenous reasons. These reasons include a change of the political situation, characterized by a and b, and the change of the economic structure, characterized by $1/c$. Any change in the relation between class-specific discount rates and the productivity of capital will alter the structure of conflict and the solution associated with it. One instance of such change may be the exhaustion of the easy import substitution industrialization (O'Donnell 1973). Suppose that in a particular country workers enjoyed sufficient certainty, capitalists faced high risk, and a compromise was reached at the point where capitalists are threatened by militancy: $a < 1/c$, $b > 1/c$, $(r^*(s^{**}), s^{**})$. Suppose now that to continue the process of industrialization a large and lumpy investment must take place. This will mean that the capital-to-output ratio, c, will have to be increased temporarily, as capital stock is being amassed without the corresponding increase in output. It is then possible that $1/c$ will fall below the value of a and the compromise will break down. Faced with militant workers, capitalists may seek protection under an authoritarian regime.

Another source of exogenous change may originate from those workers or capitalists or both who are excluded from the compromise. Indeed, no compromise ever includes all workers and all capitalists, and at some stage those excluded from it may gather sufficient political strength to alter the terms of a compromise. This is what happened in several waves of rapid unionization of industrial workers, a good example being the United States in the 1930s.

Note that although the compromise solutions do not depend upon the initial conditions $W(0)$ and $P(0)$, there is one kind of compromise which threatens capitalists in the long run. For all finite horizons there exist values of a and b at which the compromise will be concluded with workers being moderately militant, that is, with $r > s/c$. In such cases profits decline exponentially to zero, and so does the rate of profit. Inspection of Table 1 shows that when $b = 30$ and $(1 + a)^{-1}(1 + b)^{-1} = 0.7$, workers may be moderately militant at the solution when $a > 0.33$ or $a < 0.09$. Thus, under such conditions the compromise leads to what has been described as "the profit squeeze" (Glyn and Sutcliffe 1972): a wage-induced secular fall of the rate of profit. The existence of a compromise does not preclude, therefore, the possibility that profits are falling.

Finally, reflecting upon the results we must re-examine the very concept of a compromise. At the outset, we have defined a compromise as a situation in which workers pursue strategies that entail positive profits, and capitalists consent to institutions that enable workers to pursue their claims with a reasonable chance of success. This definition was thus limited to the distributional aspect of class conflict. Yet as one would expect, we discovered in the course of analysis that any class compromise must also include a central feature of the process of production, namely the rate of investment out of profit. A compromise is thus a situation in which both workers and capitalists moderate their distributional claims, and capitalists choose a high rate of saving.

The rate of saving is an intrinsic feature of any compromise. An agreement concerning the rate of transformation of profits into wages would be too tenuous from the worker's point of view because it would leave open the question of whether capitalists would save and invest enough to make wage increases possible. The perennial complaint of the working-class movements is that capitalists are too lazy or too inefficient to be entrusted with the control over investment. Already in 1910 a French socialist noted the "timidity," the "uncertainty," the "lack of initiative" of capitalists. "We ask French employers," he continued, "to resemble the American employer class.... We want a busy, active, humming country, a veritable beehive always awake. In that way our own force will be increased" (Griffuelhes 1910, p. 331). And again, in 1975, Chiaramonte (1975, p. 31) complained in an official report to the Central Committee of the Italian Communist Party about a "disconcerting lack of ideas on the economic and industrial future of the country and on the productive prospects for their (capitalists') own industries. They continue to cling to productive, technical, and organizational policies adopted several dozen years ago...."

Investment cannot be left to the control of capitalists: this is an essential feature of any compromise. Having announced the austerity policy, having repeated that the P. C. I. is "not aiming at a worsening of the situation, . . . on an aggravation of the crisis," Chiaramonte continued immediately that "this does not mean that we in any way think it would be sufficient to limit the workers' pay claims and demands for greater control over working conditions to automatically obtain an increase in investment and productive reconversion" (1975, p. 34). What the P. C. I. demands in exchange for austerity is control over investment. Or, as the 1973 Conference of the Irish T. U. C. put it, "all workers must be guaranteed that their wage restraint will lead to productive and beneficial investment and not towards even further increases in the personal incomes of the privileged section of society. . . . " (Cited in Jacobsen 1980, p. 268).

Beyond Capitalist Democracy

What is the alternative to class compromise? We have referred to the breakdown of compromise without specifying what might occur in its stead. Indeed, our results concerning the conditions of class compromise are ultimately unsatisfying in that they are inconclusive. The decision to compromise depends, in the end, on a comparison of the best compromise that can be obtained with the consequences of no compromise. The question of the balance of political power becomes paramount; the outcome highly uncertain. We believe that any analysis based upon rational calculations of expected benefits is of limited value in moments of crisis. Conflicts are inherently laden with uncertainty, and this uncertainty is difficult to evaluate, not only for us but also for the protagonists of our story. Nevertheless we will seek to elucidate the choice that is involved in considering the transition to socialism as an alternative to either compromise or economic militancy under capitalism.

First let us clarify the outcomes that may occur in the absence of compromise. Generically, these are threefold.

(1) Workers have the political power to nationalize the means of production and to organize accumulation on a new basis. Profit is abolished as an economic and legal category and capitalism with it.

(2) Capitalists have the political power to impose a non-democratic solution. Recent experiences of Brazil, Chile, and Argentina demonstrate that profits grow under such regimes simultaneously with a dramatic fall in wages. Economic deprivation of workers as well as widespread physical repression are the hallmark of authoritarian regimes.

(3) Capitalists do not have the power to impose an authoritarian solution nor workers to impose socialism. In this case, the democratic capitalist system continues without compromise but rather with an uneasy stalemate, a prolonged "catastrophic" crisis described by Gramsci (1971, p. 210ff) with specific reference to the MacDonald government in Great Britain. This was perhaps the situation in several Western European countries after the defeats of general strikes fought on economic issues: Sweden in 1909, Norway in 1921, France in 1920, Great Britain in 1926. This may also be the situation in Great Britain today. These situations are characterized by high strike intensity and a fair amount of repression: they constitute a tug-of-war. Wages and profits oscillate sharply.

We will not investigate these alternatives any further but only specify the structure of choice involved in considering the socialist alternative. How would workers choose a strategy of transition to socialism? We will outline only a framework for such an analysis but will stop short of providing the analysis.

Note first that workers may embark upon the strategy of socializing the capital stock under two distinct conditions. The first has been described: compromise is impossible, workers make economic demands, provoke a political crisis, and in this crisis the only choice may come to be between socialism and authoritarian capitalism. This scenario, in which the transition to socialism originates from an economic crisis under capitalism, is the one typically envisaged by Marxists as the road to socialism. This is a scenario that leads to the *politique de pire*: in this view, the worse the economic situation under capitalism, the more likely socialism becomes. We are persuaded that this strategy of crisis mongering is unfeasible and irresponsible. As Varga warned in 1927, "If the working class creates conditions in which the profits of capitalists become impossible but at the same time the bourgeoisie is not defeated politically and the doctrine of the proletariat has not been established, the bourgeoisie, by means of implacable terror, crushes the working class in order to maintain the economic basis of the capitalist system and make possible the exploitation of labor" (Pirker 1965, pp. 133–4; translated by David Abraham).

Workers may, however, find socialism to be the attractive alternative under the same conditions under which they can conclude an attractive compromise under capitalism. If workers have political power that enables them to enforce compromises under capitalism, would they not use this power to transform the society into socialism? If socialism is preferable under the same conditions under which workers are able to conclude a compromise under capitalism, no compromise would ever be concluded by rational workers. Hence, the conditions of capitalist compromise must always include the superiority of such a compromise to the socialist alternative.

Let us speculate about the following scenario. Suppose that at some time $t = 0$ workers decide to nationalize the entire capital stock. At some later time $t = T$ the final nationalization bill is passed and the entire capital stock is socialized. During the remaining period, from $t = T$ to $t = b$, the institution of profit no longer exists and investment decisions are made by the entire society through some reasonable voting mechanism.

During the period $0 \leq t < T$, that is, until socialization is complete, the private ownership of capital remains intact. Faced with imminent nationalization, capitalists will disinvest as rapidly as possible. They cannot be prevented from disinvesting, and they cannot be taken by surprise: even Lange (1938), the foremost advocate of the "one stroke" nationalization strategy, admitted that some disinvestment would occur before capital stock is nationalized. Let $S^*(T)$ be the current value of discounted wages between $t = 0$ and $t = T$ when workers pursue a strategy of socialization and capitalists respond by disinvesting. It is likely that $S^*(T)$ will not be the most that workers could obtain between $t = 0$ and $t = T$. If $W^*(T)$ is the best they could do under capitalism, then the difference between these quantities is the cost of the transition strategy during this period.

At $t = T$ the capital stock becomes entirely nationalized and henceforth the economy operates in the following manner. The entire society now joins in the program of determining the optimal rate of saving out of total output, s_w, and the volume of investment is given by $\Delta K(t) = s_w Y(t)$.[11] Let q be the risk inherent in investment facing the socialist society. Then the problem to be solved would be:

$$\max_{s_w} S^* = (1 - s_w)Y(T) \sum_{r=T}^{r=b} (1 + q)^{-(t-T)}(1 + s_w/c)^{(t-T)}.$$

Let the rate of saving which solves this problem be s_w^*, and the resulting welfare of workers under socialism be $S^*(b - T)$.

---

[11] We hope that the reader will not mistake this model of socialism for a description of the Soviet Union or other Eastern European countries. In those countries investment decisions arise out of a game between central planners and managers, with a known effect of investing at a level higher than the preference of the population.

The total value of socialism to workers making a strategic choice at $t = 0$ would also depend, however, upon the risk that the socialist transition would be aborted or subverted under the pressure of the armed forces, foreign governments, foreign firms, or even by the workers themselves, if they object to the costs that have to be borne during the period $0 \leq t < T$. (See Kolm 1977 for some of these considerations.) Even if a nationalization law is passed by a parliament in accordance with all of the constitutional requirements, capitalists have numerous ways to fight back. If the probability that the socialist transition would be accomplished is $(1 - f)$ and the probability that the final outcome would be a capitalist dictatorship is f, then we can think of $kS^*(b - T)$, $k < 1$, as the expected value of the revolutionary attempt, where $kS^*(b - T) = (1 - f)S^*(b - T) + f$(material welfare under capitalist dictatorship). Note that k is likely to be closer to unity the greater the proportion of the capital stock is already publicly owned and the greater the electoral strength of the socialist parties.

The total value of pursuing a strategy of transition to socialism to workers at $t = 0$ can be thus thought of as: $S^* = S^*(T) + kS^*(b - T)$, where $S^*(T)$ and $S^*(b - T)$ are as given above. Note that this is again the current value of the socialist transition to workers at $t = 0$ when they decide whether or not to embark on this road. Hence, this value would be compared to the best workers can do under the particular conditions of democratic capitalism, $W^*(r, s)$, where (r, s) represents either a compromise or a tug-of-war.[12]

As we forewarned, we will not carry this discussion any further, mainly because we believe that this calculation involves too many imponderables to be taken seriously in practice. We wanted to clarify the nature of this

---

[12] Note some assumptions implicit in this formulation. First, we assume that workers living under capitalism evaluate socialism in the same terms as they do capitalism. Second, we assume that socialism is only as efficient as capitalism in allocating resources to uses; in our formalism, c remains the same after nationalization. Finally, we assume that workers compare their best possible, not their current, outcome under capitalism with socialism. The first of these assumptions would be rejected by those who maintain, with Heller (1975), that if socialism is to be preferable it is because it would satisfy needs other than those experienced by workers under capitalism. The second assumption would be rejected by the entire socialist tradition, which always maintained that socialism would be a more efficient, not only more just, system for satisfying material needs. Both of these assumptions should perhaps be rejected, but then the choice of socialism would be unproblematic. In turn, the last assumption is necessary to make the problem reasonable. Roemer (1982), for example, does not give workers a chance to improve their conditions under capitalism, whereas we did not give them a chance to opt for socialism in an earlier version of this paper.

decision, but we do not intend this to be a description of how the decisions to embark or not to embark upon the socialist path are in fact made.

Class Conflict and the State

Suppose for a moment, as did Marx, that the conflict over material interests is irreconcilable and that workers' pursuit of material interests leads them inevitably to the realization that these interests can be advanced if and only if the institution of profit is abolished altogether. Given this assumption, the reproduction of capitalist relations becomes problematic. Even if all the conditions for expanded reproduction of capital are fulfilled "of itself," "by the mere repetition of isolated acts of production" (Marx 1967, Vol. I, pp. 577–8), the survival of capitalist relation is no longer guaranteed when workers organize collectively to abolish them. One must then look beyond the system of production for the mechanisms by which capitalism is maintained. Hence a functionalist account of capitalist reproduction follows necessarily from this model of class conflict. For, if an irreconcilable conflict over the realization of material interests is characteristic of any capitalist society and if capitalism withstood this conflict during at least one hundred years, then some mechanisms external to class relations must be evoked to explain this durability. Whenever class conflict happens to generate a threat to the reproduction of capitalist relations, some mechanism, most often thought to be the state, must come to the rescue by repressing, organizing ideological domination, or coopting.

The gradual rejection of instrumentalist theories of the state (Miliband 1969) and their replacement by a model in which the state is viewed as relatively autonomous from class relations did not alter this functional logic. In the instrumentalist version, the state was acting predictably in defense of the interests of capitalists because it was directly populated by capitalists or like-capitalists. In the structuralist version, the state is seen as autonomous from particularistic interests of capitalists and as based on popular support: "the popular class state" (Poulantzas 1973). Yet somehow this state still manages to repress, to organize ideological domination, and to intervene where and when needed in ways designed to and having the effect of maintaining capitalism in the face of conflicts. Both the instrumentalist and autonomous theories of the state are functionalist theories, and although the instrumentalist theory is clearly at odds with the facts, it has at least the logical virtue of explaining why the state – concrete people functioning in concrete institutions – does all that is necessary to reproduce capitalist relations.

In fact, ultimately even the state as an institution disappears from this functionalist analysis. Since, by assumption, the state invariably responds to the functional requirements of capitalist reproduction and since its policies have, by assumption, the function of fulfilling these requirements, one can proceed from requirements to reproduction without bothering with the state at all. The very concept of the state is based on a reification. The state is ready-to-wear; it is tailored before class conflicts, as if in anticipation of those conflicts, appearing fully clothed whenever these conflicts threaten the reproduction of capitalist relations. The state is always given, already in its functional garb, before any conflicts occur, before any problems call for resolution.

Indeed, the perennial difficulty of any functionalist perspective is to account for the reasons why conflicts among specific groups under concrete historical circumstances would regularly result in the state performing its functions. It is quite true that once the manner in which a society responds to variations of historical conditions has been institutionalized, much of this response is automatic. To put it differently, each society organizes the mechanisms of its reproduction as a system. Yet it is equally apparent that the activity of institutions and the institutions themselves are the continual outcome of conflicts. Under concrete historical circumstances, particular groups enter into conflicts over particular issues, and the outcome of these conflicts is a particular organization and a specific set of policies of the state. What is not clear is why this policy would be predictably one that would have the function of reproducing capitalist relations. Clearly the answer to this question cannot be that the state reproduces capitalist relations because this "is" its function. This answer can be twofold: either the capitalist system is organized in such a manner that it is reproduced regardless of all conflicts, and then these conflicts, including class conflict, acquire the status of a superfluous ritual, as in Sahlins, or outcomes of conflicts do in fact determine the policies that the state pursues, in which case the burden of explanation is shifted to these conflicts and any concept of function becomes redundant.

These problems – an implausible account of reproduction, the inability to explain why the state pursues particular policies, and the reification of the state – are inherent in any functionalist perspective. Our claim, however, is that this perspective is made necessary by an incorrect model of class conflict in democratic capitalist societies. The very problem of reproduction appears as a functional one because the model of irreconcilable class conflict leads to the conclusion that capitalism could not have survived as a choice of the working class. Indeed, the working class appears in this model as a passive victim of repression, a perpetual dupe of ideological domination, or, at best, as repeatedly betrayed by its leadership.

If our model of class conflict is valid, then the need for this kind of a construction disappears. The policies pursued by the state in capitalist societies – the policies designed to invigorate and strengthen the capitalist system of social organization – are no longer viewed as functions of an autonomous state facing the threat of a revolutionary working class. These policies – and the state itself – now appear as an expression of a compromise: they are quite instrumental with regard to the interests of a class coalition that includes both capitalists and organized workers. When workers pursue strategies that lead to a compromise, the state does what appears necessary to reproduce capitalism because this is the choice of the workers as well as the capitalists. The organization of the state as an institution and the policies pursued by this institution constitute an expression of a specific class compromise.

Class compromise implies a particular organization of political relations, a particular relation between each class and the state, a particular set of institutions, and a particular set of policies. The state must enforce the compliance of both classes with the terms of each compromise and protect those segments of each class that enter into a compromise from non-cooperative behavior of their fellow class members. The state must induce individual capitalists to make the decisions required by the class compromise, shifting the terms of choice which they confront to produce the requisite aggregate effects as capitalists compete with each other. Finally, since the state of class compromise is a democratic state, it must see to it that the class coalition that forms the compromise can win popular support in elections, which implies that interests of those excluded from the particular coalition must also be taken into account. All of these indications lead, therefore, to the kind of state that was envisioned by Keynes when he claimed that "It is not the ownership of the instruments of production which it is important for the State to assume. If the State is able to determine the aggregate amount of resources devoted to augmenting the instruments and the basic rate of reward to those who own them, it will have accomplished all that is necessary" (1936, p. 378). Necessary, that is, to organize class compromise.

Appendix

In this Appendix we prove the best reply theorems of workers and capitalists for the case in which the horizon is infinite. To restate what is to be proven: when $b \to \infty$, the workers' best-reply strategy is given by the function $r^*(s)$, where

$r^*(s) > (1 + s/c)$ when $a > s/c$ or $s < ac$,
$r^*(s) \to 0$ when $a < s/c$ or $s > ac$.

and the capitalists' best-reply strategy is given by the function $s^*(r)$, where

$s^*(r) < 0$ when $b > (1/c - r)$ or $r > (1/c - b)$,
$s^*(r) \to 1$ when $b < (1/c - r)$ or $r < (1/c - b)$.

Since the math is less cumbersome, let us begin with the capitalists' best-reply function. From equation (10) in the text, we can write

$$P(t) = P(0)(g - r)^r, \text{ where, } g = (1 + s/c). \tag{A1}$$

Substituting this expression for $P(t)$ into equation (12), expanding the geometric series, and rearranging the terms yields:

$$C^* = -\frac{(1+b)(1-s)P(0)}{(s/c - (b+r))} + \frac{(1+b)(1-s)P(0)}{(s/c - (b+r))}\left[\frac{g-r}{1+b}\right]^{b+1} \tag{A2}$$

Consider first the case in which $b > (1/c - r)$. Since $s \leq 1$, it follows that $(1 + b) > (1 + s/c - r)$ or $(g-r)/(1 + b) < 1$. Therefore, as b approaches infinity, the second term vanishes. The derivative of the first term with respect to s is

$$\frac{\partial C^*}{\partial s} = \frac{(1/c - (b+r))(1+b)P(0)}{(s/c - (b+r))^2}.$$

Since $1/c - (b + r) < 0$ by hypothesis, this derivative is always negative, and capitalists will disinvest.

Suppose now that $b < (1/c - r)$, which is possible only if $1/c > b$. This presents capitalists with the following choice. If they choose an s such that $s/c < (b + r)$, then $(g - r)/(1 + b) < 1$, the second term vanishes, and C^* is bounded above for all b. If on the other hand, capitalists choose an s such that $s/c > (b + r)$, then $(g-r)/(1 + b) > 1$, from which it follows that the final term is positive and grows without bound as b increases. If b is sufficiently large, the latter choice will be superior. Now, as b approaches infinity, the function C^* is dominated by the second term of (A2). Taking its derivative with respect to s:

$$\frac{\partial C^*}{\partial s} = \left\{ \frac{\partial B}{\partial s} \left[\frac{g-r}{1+b} \right] + \frac{B(b+1)}{c(1+b)} \right\} \left[\frac{g-r}{1+b} \right]^b$$

where

$$B = \frac{(1+b)(1-s)P(0)}{[s/c - (b+r)]}.$$

Since $s/c > (b+r)$, $B > 0$ and the second term inside the brackets is positive. Since b is large, the second term dominates. Hence the derivative is positive for any s satisfying $s > c(b+r)$. Thus, when $b < (1/c - r)$, capitalists' best reply is to save at their maximal rate.

Note that throughout, current profits $P(0)$ are assumed to be positive. If profits, adjusted for cyclical fluctuations not included in our model, were not positive, capitalists would disinvest and compromise would break down.

The proof of the workers' best-reply theorem proceeds in the same way. From the definition of class compromise (equation 8), we can write

$$W(t) = W(0) + \sum_{t=0}^{i=t-1} \Delta(W)(i)$$

$$= W(0) + r \sum_{i=0}^{i=r-1} P(i). \tag{A3}$$

To get the expression for W^*, substitute (A1) into (A3), expand the geometric series, substitute the resulting expression for $W(t)$ into equation (11), expand the geometric series again, and collect and rearrange terms. The algebra is tedious but straightforward. The result is:

$$W^* = \frac{(1+a)}{a} \left[W(0) + \frac{rP(0)}{(r - (s/c - a))} \right]$$

$$- \frac{1}{a(1+a)^b} \left[W(0) + \frac{rP(0)}{(r - s/c)} \right] \tag{A4}$$

$$+ \frac{(1+a)rP(0)}{(r - s/c)(r - (s/c - a))} \left[\frac{g-r}{1+a} \right]^{b+1},$$

where $g = 1 + s/c$.

Let b approach infinity. Note first that since $a > 0$, the second term of W^* vanishes. Now consider the case in which $s/c < a$. It follows that $(g - r)/$

The Structure of Class Conflict in Democratic Capitalist Societies

$(1 + a) < 1$, which implies that the final term vanishes as well (since $g < (1 + a)$ and $r > 0$). Thus, W^* is dominated by the first term for b sufficiently large. The derivative of this term with respect to r is

$$\frac{\partial W^*}{\partial r} = \frac{(1 + a)P(0)(a - s/c)}{a(r - (s/c - a))^2}$$

Since, by hypothesis $(a - s/c) > 0$, this derivative is positive for any value of r. The best-reply strategy of workers is to be maximally militant.

Now let the rate of saving chosen by capitalists be such that $s/c > a$ (which is possible only if $1/c > a$). Workers face the following choice. If they choose an r such that $r > (s/c - a)$, then again $(g - r)/(1 + a) < 1$, the final term vanishes, and W^* is bounded above for all b. If workers, however, choose a less militant r such that $r < (s/c - a)$, the last term of W^* is positive and increasing without bound as b grows. Hence, for all b sufficiently large, the less militant choice is superior. Now as b approaches infinity, it is the last term of (A4) which dominates. Taking its derivative with respect to r:

$$\frac{\partial W^*}{\partial r} = \left\{ \frac{\partial A}{\partial r} \left[\frac{g - r}{1 + a} \right] - \frac{A(b + 1)}{(1 + a)} \right\} \left[\frac{g - r}{1 + a} \right]^b$$

where

$$A = \frac{(1 + a)r P(0)}{(r - s/c)[r - (s/c - a)]}.$$

Since $r < (s/c - a)$, $A > 0$ and the second term inside the brackets is negative. As b approaches infinity, this term dominates. Therefore, the derivative is negative for all values of r satisfying $r < (s/c\ a)$. When $a < s/c$, the workers' best reply is their minimal level of militancy. As the horizon becomes infinite, r^* approaches zero.

References

Bowles, Samuel, and Gintis, Herbert, 1980. The crisis of liberal democratic capitalism: the case of the United States. Presented at the annual meeting of the American Political Science Association, Washington, D.C.

Chiaramonte, Gerardo. 1975. Report to the Central Committee of the P.C.I. October 29–30. *Italian Communist*.

Clough, Shepard B. 1968. *European economic history*. New York: McGraw-Hill.

Edel, Matthew. 1979. A note on collective action, Marxism, and the prisoner's dilemma. *Journal of Economic Issues* 13:751–61.

Ferejohn, John, and Page, Talbot. 1978. On the foundations of intertemporal choice. *American Journal of Agricultural Economics* 78:269–75.

Glyn, Andrew, and Sutcliffe, Bob. 1972. *Capitalism in crisis*. New York: Pantheon Books.

Goldberg, Samuel. 1958. *Introduction to difference equations*. New York: John Wiley and Sons.

Gramsci, Antonio. 1971. *Prison notebooks*. New York: International Publishers.

Griffuelhes, Victor. 1910. L'Inferiorité des Capitalistes Francais. *Mouvement Socialiste* 226:329–32.

Harsanyi, John C. 1977. *Rational behavior and bargaining equilibrium in games and social situations*. Cambridge: Cambridge University Press.

Heller, Agnes. 1974. *The theory of need in Marx*. London: Allison and Busby.

Helmstädter, Ernst. 1973. The long-run movement of the capital-output ratio and of labor's share. In James Mirrlees and N. H. Stern (eds.). *Models of economic growth*. London: Macmillan.

Hoel, Michael. 1975. Aspects of distribution and growth in a capitalist economy. *Memorandum of the Institute of Economics*. Oslo, Norway: University of Oslo.

———(1978). Distribution and growth as a differential game between workers and capitalists. *International Economic Review* 19:335–50.

Jacobsen, John K. 1980. *Chasing progress*. Ph.D. dissertation. University of Chicago.

Keynes, John M. 1936. *The general theory of employment, interest, and money*. New York: Harcourt, Brace, Jovanovich.

Kolm, Serge-Christophe. 1977. *La Transition Socialiste: La Politique Economique de Gauche*. Paris: Editions du Cerf.

Kuznets, Simon. 1966. *Modern economic growth: rate, structure, and spread*. New Haven: Yale University Press.

Lancaster, Kelvin. 1973. The dynamic inefficiency of capitalism. *Journal of Political Economy* 81:1092–109.

Lange, Oskar. 1938. On the economic theory of socialism. In Benjamin Lippincott (ed.). *On the economic theory of socialism*. Minneapolis: University of Minnesota Press.

Maddison, Angus. 1964. *Economic growth in the west*. New York: W. W. Norton.

Marx, Karl. 1934. *The eighteenth brumaire of Louis Bonaparte*. Moscow: Progress Publishers.

———1967. *Capital*. New York: International Publishers.

———1972. *Writings on the Paris commune*. Edited by Hal Draper. New York: Monthly Review.

McDonald, Ian M., and Solow, Robert M. 1981. Wage bargaining and employment. *American Economic Review* 71:896–908.

Miliband, Ralph. 1969. *The state in capitalist society*. New York: Basic Books.

Nash, John. 1954. Equilibrium states in n-person games. *Proceedings of the National Academy of Sciences* 36:48–9.

Odling-Smee, J. C. 1973. Personal saving revisited – more statistics, fewer facts. *Oxford Bulletin of Economics and Statistics* 35:21–9.

O'Donnell, Guillermo A. 1973. *Modernization and bureaucratic-authoritarianism: studies in South American politics*. Berkeley: Institute of International Studies, University of California.

The Structure of Class Conflict in Democratic Capitalist Societies

Offe, Claus, and Wiesenthal, Helmut. 1980. Two logics of collective action: theoretical notes on social class and organizational form. *Political Power and Social Theory* 1:67–115.

Pasinetti, Luigi L. 1962. Rate of profit and income distribution in relation to the rate of economic growth. *Review of Economic Studies* 29:267–79.

Pirker, Theo, ed. 1965. *Komintern und Faschismus*. Stuttgart: Deutsche Verlags-Anstalt.

Poulantzas, Nicos. 1973. *Political power and social classes*. London: New Left Books.

Przeworski, Adam. 1980. Material bases of consent: politics and economics in a hegemonic system. *Political Power and Social Theory* 1:23–68.

Roemer, John E. 1979. Mass action is not individually rational: reply. *Journal of Economic Issues* 13:763–7.

Roemer, John E. 1982. *A practical theory of exploitation and class*. Cambridge: Harvard University Press.

Schelling, Thomas. 1960. *The strategy of conflict*. Cambridge: Harvard University Press.

Schelling, Thomas. 1978. *Micromotives and macrobehavior*. New York: W.W. Norton.

Sombart, Werner. 1976. *Why there is no socialism in the United States*. White Plains, N.Y.: International Arts and Sciences.

Stackelberg, H. von. 1952. *The theory of the market economy*. Translation and Introduction by A. T. Peacock. London: William Hodge.

Taylor, Michael. 1976. *Anarchy and cooperation*. London: John Wiley and Sons.

Wallerstein, Michael. 1979. *An estimate of savings out of wages in the United States, 1949–1970*. Unpublished. University of Chicago.

4

Structural Dependence of the State on Capital

Adam Przeworski and Michael Wallerstein

Capitalism is a system in which many scarce resources are owned privately, and decisions about allocating them are a private prerogative. Democracy is a system through which people as citizens may express preferences about allocating resources that they do not privately own. Hence the perennial question of political theory and of practical politics concerns the competence of these two systems with regard to each other. Is it possible for governments to control a capitalist economy? In particular, is it possible to steer the economy against the interests and preferences of those who control productive wealth?

The central and only distinctive claim of Marxist political theory is that under capitalism all governments must respect and protect the essential claims of those who own the productive wealth of society. Capitalists are endowed with public power, power which no formal institutions can overcome (Luxemburg 1970; Pashukanis 1951). People may have political rights, they may vote, and governments may pursue popular mandates. But the effective capacity of any government to attain whatever are its goals is circumscribed by the public power of capital. The nature of political forces that come into office does not alter these limits, it is claimed, for they are structural – a characteristic of the system, not of the occupants of governmental positions nor of the winners of elections.

During the past 20 years Marxists have developed several theories to explain why all governments in capitalist societies are bound to act in

For comments we are grateful to the members of the September Group, in particular Robert Brenner, to Sam Bowles, John Freeman, Max Haller, and Peter Lange. This work was supported by a grant from the National Science Foundation and by a German Marshall Fund Fellowship to Adam Przeworski.

the interests of capitalists. In one explanation, state managers internalize the goals of capitalists and use the state as an instrument on their behalf (Miliband 1969). Another explanation emphasizes the generic structural and functional limitations: under capitalism, the state cannot organize production (Offe 1975), mandate investment (Lindblom 1977), or command consumption, because these are prerogatives reserved to owners of private property. But the most daring, because the least contingent, theory claims that it does not matter who the state managers are, what they want, and whom they represent. Nor does it matter how the state is organized and what it is legally able or unable to do. Capitalists do not even have to organize and act collectively: it suffices that they blindly pursue narrow, private self-interest to sharply restrict the options of all governments. This is the theory of "structural dependence of the state on capital."

This theory begins with the hypothesis that the entire society depends on the allocation of resources chosen by owners of capital. Investment decisions have public and long-lasting consequences: they determine the future possibilities of production, employment, and consumption for all. Yet they are private decisions. Since every individual and group must consider its future, since future consumption possibilities depend on present investment, and since investment decisions are private, all social groups are constrained in the pursuit of their material interests by the effect of their actions on the willingness of owners of capital to invest, which in turn depends on the profitability of investment. In a capitalist society, the trade-off between present and future consumption for all passes through a trade-off between consumption of those who don't own capital and profits (Przeworski 1985, chap. 5).

Consider this dependence from the point of view of one group, wage earners. At any instant of time, wages and profits are indeed inversely related, as Marx argued in *Wage, Labour, and Capital* (1952a). In a world without a future, wage earners would be best-off consuming the entire product, indeed confiscating the capital stock. But wage earners care about their future as well as present income, and future wages depend on private investment. If firms respond to wage increases with less investment, wage earners may be best-off moderating their wage demands. Workers' future income depends upon the realization of capitalists' present interests.

While the theory is usually stated with regard to workers' wage demands, to the extent that material means are required to advance their welfare, structural dependence binds all groups: minorities struggling for economic equality, women wanting to transform the division of labor within the household, old people searching for material security, workers striving for safer working conditions, or the military seeking bombs. It is in this sense that capitalism is a class society: not in the sense that there are always two organized classes, but in the sense that the structure of property characteristic of capitalism makes everyone's material conditions dependent upon the private decisions of owners of wealth.

The theory of structural dependence continues with the inference that because the entire society depends on the owners of capital, so must the state. Whether particular governments have interests and goals of their own or they act on behalf of a coalition of groups or a class, the pursuit of any objectives that require material resources places governments in the situation of structural dependence. Politicians seeking reelection must anticipate the impact of their policies on the decisions of firms because these decisions affect employment, inflation, and personal income of voters: vote-seeking politicians are dependent on owners of capital because voters are. Even a government that was a perfect agent of wage earners could not and would not behave much differently from one that represents capitalists. If workers are best-off with a fair dose of wage restraint, a prolabor government will also avoid policies that dramatically alter the distribution of income and wealth. The range of actions that governments find best for the interests they represent is narrowly circumscribed, whatever these interests may be.

The reason the state is structurally dependent is that no government can simultaneously reduce profits and increase investment. Firms invest as a function of expected returns; policies that transfer income away from owners of capital reduce the rate of return and thus of investment. Governments face a trade-off between distribution and growth, between equality and efficiency. They can trade a more (or less) egalitarian distribution of income for less (or more) investment but they cannot alter the terms of this trade-off: this is the central thesis of the theory of structural dependence. Governments can and do choose between growth and income distribution; but because material welfare of any constituency depends upon economic growth as well as its share of income and because distribution can be achieved only at the cost of growth, all governments end up pursuing policies with limited redistributive effects.

At this moment the reader may remark that this is the neoliberal theory as well. It is. The Chicago school argues that all transfers of income cause deadweight losses. All support-maximizing governments, it is claimed, are tempered in their zeal for redistribution by the fact that owners of endowments will increasingly withdraw them from productive uses as taxes rise. (Bates and Lien 1985, Becker 1983, and Peltzman 1976 are presentations of formal models.) The difference between the two theories is that neoliberals are "pluralists"; that is, they are agnostic about the groups that have the power of inflicting the losses on the public by withdrawing their endowments. This difference should not obscure, however, the fact that both theories understand in the same way the relation between income distribution and investment.

The belief that under capitalism governments are structurally dependent on capital is widespread. Miliband (1969, 152) portrayed this dependence as follows: "Given the degree of economic power which rests in the 'business community' and the decisive importance of its actions (or its nonactions) for major aspects of economic policy, any government with serious pretensions to radical reform must either seek to appropriate that power or find its room for radical action rigidly circumscribed by the requirements of 'business confidence.'" Block (1977, 15) maintained that "in a capitalist economy the level of economic activity is largely determined by private investment decisions of capitalists. This means that capitalists, in their collective role as investors, have a veto over state policies in that their failure to invest at adequate levels can create major political problems for state managers." Lindblom (1977, 172, 175) observed that "because public functions in the market system rest in the hands of businessmen, it follows that jobs, prices, production, growth, the standard of living, and the economic security of everyone all rest in their hands.... In the eyes of government officials, therefore, businessmen do not appear simply as representatives of a special interest.... They appear as functionaries performing functions that government officials regard as indispensable." Offe (1975, 234) analyzed the predicament of the state vis-à-vis the private economy: "The political system can only make offers to external, autonomous bodies responsible for decisions: either these offers are not accepted, thus making the attempts at direction in vain, or the offers are so attractive in order to be accepted that the political direction for its part loses its autonomy because it has to internalize the aims of the system to be directed."

The theory of structural dependence can be evaluated in three ways. One method is to examine differences in policy choices and outcomes under different governments. Unfortunately, while there is much evidence that some policy outcomes covary with partisan orientations of governments, these findings cast little light on the existence of structural constraints that bind all governments. We cannot know whether the observed differences exhaust the realm of possibility. (The classical study was Hibbs 1977. See Cameron 1984, Castles 1982, Maravall 1979, and Shalev 1983 for literature reviews.) The second method is to examine the limiting cases: the experience of governments that came into office with programs of major transformations, in particular, programs of simultaneous nationalization of some industries and redistribution of income (Kolm 1977). All such governments either compromised their original program, including total reversals, like that committed by the French Socialists, or provoked profound economic crises and were overthrown by force, as was the government of the Unidad Popular in Chile. These experiences prompted Rueschemeyer and Evans (1985, 62) to observe that "even in countries where the state appears to be in the strongest position relative to private capital, . . . the state remains dependent on private capital, foreign and domestic, not only to promote accumulation but also to produce a surplus in which the state itself may share. The strict limits under which the state must operate in a dependent capitalist economy are grimly indicated by the severe problems confronted by social democratic regimes such as those of Salvador Allende in Chile and Michael Manley in Jamaica." Yet again, these experiences cannot speak to the issue of limits and possibilities: one can always cite some counterfactual actions that would have perhaps avoided the disasters. The issue concerns possibility and possibilities cannot be determined on the basis of limited historical experience. Hence, finally, the appropriate method to evaluate the hypothesis of structural dependence is to construct a formal model with which the internal logic of the theory can be explored and the robustness of its conclusions examined.

The Theory Reconstructed

Assumptions

To examine the validity of this theory, we need some assumptions. Suppose the society is composed only of wage earners and owners of capital. Wage earners consume all of their incomes and own no capital. There are firms, which receive the income from capital, invest some part of it, and distribute the rest to the shareholders. Let the net national income at time τ be $Y(\tau)$, let aggregate wages be $W(\tau)$, let investment be $I(\tau)$, and let profits net of investment be $P(\tau)$. Then $W(\tau) + I(\tau) + P(\tau) = Y(\tau)$. Let us implicitly define the share of wages in the national product, m, as $W(\tau) = Y(\tau)$. The volume of investment is $I(\tau) = s(1 - m)Y(\tau)$, where s is the rate of investment out of the total return to capital, $(1 - m)Y$. The volume of profits net of investment is then $P(\tau) = (1 - s)(1 - m)Y(\tau)$.

We make the simplest possible assumption about production: output is a linear function of capital. Expressed in terms of growth, $Y'(\tau) = \nu I(\tau) = \nu s(1 - m)Y(\tau)$, $\nu > 0$, where ν is the constant productivity of capital. The parameter ν represents the state of technology – the amount of additional output that can be produced when an additional unit is added to the capital stock. Thus, output grows at the rate of $\nu s(1 - m)$ per year. For example, if $\nu = .25$, $s = .50$ and $m = .80$, the economy is growing at an annual rate of 2.5 %.[1]

Firms make investment decisions. They are perfect agents of their homogeneous shareholders. Thus, firms maximize the utility that their shareholders derive from profits.[2] Shareholders derive their utility from present and discounted future consumption, where ϱ is the rate at which the future is discounted. For the sake of algebraic simplicity, we assume shareholders' utility in each period is given by a logarithmic utility function.[3] Let P^* represent the present value of shareholders' welfare: the value they attach today to a particular sequence of present and future consumption. Then P^* can be written

$$P^* = \int_0^\infty e^{-\varrho\tau} \ln[P(\tau)]d\tau, \varrho > 0. \tag{1}$$

Finally, wage earners derive their utility from consumption in the same manner.[4] Wage earners' welfare is given by

$$W^* = \int_0^\infty e^{-\varrho\tau} \ln[W(\tau)]d\tau.$$

[1] These figures are rough estimates for the postwar U.S. economy. Estimates of the productivity of capital can be found in Hill 1979. The others can be found in the National Income and Product Accounts published by the Department of Commerce. Of course, investment in physical capital is only one source of economic growth. We emphasize the role of investment in growth because that is the way the theory of structural dependence has been formulated.

[2] Alternatively and equivalently, firms maximize gross profits and distribute all income accruing to capital to shareholders, who then choose the rate of savings that maximizes their utility (see Hirshleifer 1970).

[3] We use the log function to simplify the presentation, but all of our results hold for the entire class of utility functions with a constant elasticity of marginal utility.

[4] Here we consider the rate of time preference ϱ to be risk-free and thus the same for all individuals who derive utility from consumption, whether they are workers or capitalists.

These assumptions are perhaps the simplest possible ones. Many can be complicated to introduce more descriptive realism without altering the qualitative conclusions. In the hope of remaining accessible to a wider audience, we assert the analytic results without proof in the text. Complete derivations are contained in the Appendix.

Structural Dependence without the State

Consider the economy without state intervention. The state is there: it enforces contracts, standardizes weights and measures, and the like, but it does not touch income or investment.

Firms choose a rate of investment to maximize P^* in Equation 1 given that the share of wages in income is m. The solution to this problem (for $m < 1$), as shown in the Appendix, is

$$s^*(m) = 1 - \frac{\varrho/v}{1 - m} = s^M, \tag{2}$$

where s^M stands for "market rate."[5] This is the investment rate firms will choose in the absence of taxes. Note that the rate of investment falls as the share of wages increases, $ds^*/dm < 0$.[6] Note also that the rate of investment is always less than 1, and it may be less than 0. Firms may find it optimal to disinvest. Indeed, as m approaches 1, s^M approaches negative infinity. Note, finally, that without taxes, shareholders are consuming the income share $(1 - s^*)(1 - m) = \varrho/v$, and firms are investing the share $I/Y = 1 - \varrho/v - m$ of national income. If $\varrho/v > 1$ or if the rate at which shareholders discount

---

We took a different approach in our earlier analysis of class conflict (Przeworski and Wallerstein 1982a), where rates of time preference reflected the differential risk faced by owners of firms and wage earners. Given the problem at hand, it seems better to consider time preferences risk-free and to model uncertainty explicitly. The effects of uncertainty are discussed in the final section.

[5] When workers' share m is greater than or equal to unity, profits are negative and firms will disinvest at the maximal rate.

[6] We treat investment in neoclassical fashion as the result of an intertemporal allocation of consumption by owners of capital. The Keynesian approach, in contrast, emphasizes the importance of investing to satisfy future demand. In a Keynesian model, the derivative ds^*/dm would be positive since wage increases put more money in the hands of people with a high propensity to consume. The problem of structural dependence cannot arise within a Keynesian framework where increasing wage earners' consumption accelerates investment and may even increase current profits. Indeed, one of the political appeals of Keynesian theory was the denial of any conflict of interests between wage earners and capitalists (see Skidelsky 1977 and Przeworski and Wallerstein 1982b).

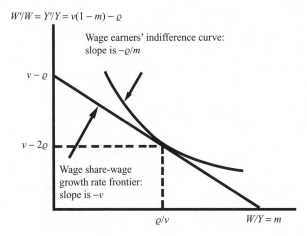

$W'/W = Y'/Y = v(1 - m) - \varrho$

Wage earners' indifference curve: slope is $-\varrho/m$

$v - \varrho$

$v - 2\varrho$

Wage share-wage growth rate frontier: slope is $-v$

ϱ/v $W/Y = m$

Figure 1 Wage Earners' Trade-off between Wage Share and Wage Growth.

the future exceeds the productivity of capital, firms will disinvest, whatever the wage share.

Because shareholders always maintain their current consumption at ϱ/v of income, any increase in the wage share must be exactly offset by a decline in the share of income going to investment: $d(I/Y)/d(W/Y) = -1$. Wage earners thus face a trade-off between the wage share and the rate of growth of national income (which determines the rate of growth of wages) as illustrated in Figure 1.

The straight line represents all possible combinations of the wage share and the rate-of-wage growth as income is transferred from wages to investment and vice versa. If wage earners were organized in a centralized union federation with sufficient power to set wages unilaterally, they would maximize W^* by choosing the point on the wage share-wage growth rate frontier that is tangent to their indifference curve where the wage share equals $m^{**} = \varrho/v.$[7] Regardless of the manner in which wages are determined, the

[7] In technical language, workers are behaving as Stackelberg leaders, firms as Stackelberg followers. This means that the unions anticipate the effect of their choice of wage share on firms' investment decisions, while firms respond optimally to whatever unions choose. We do not, in this paper, consider the alternative of firms leading and unions following, although we did previously in Przeworski and Wallerstein 1982a. The role of Stackelberg leaders poses a collective-action problem for firms. To act as Stackelberg leaders would demand that firms collectively invest more than is optimal for each individually.

We use the double asterisk to denote the optimal choice of the Stackelberg leader and the single asterisk to denote the best reply strategy or the optimal choice of the Stackelberg follower.

freedom of firms to determine the rate of investment suffices to maintain shareholders' current consumption share constant. In the absence of government intervention, wage earners can only increase wages at the expense of investment and, hence, of future wage increases. Wage earners are structurally dependent.

Structural Dependence of the State

Now let us consider a government that taxes and transfers income. The government imposes a tax either on income from capital or on wages and transfers the collected revenue to the other group. Taxes, T, are collected according to $T = t(1 - m)Y$, where t is the tax rate. If the tax rate t is positive, the tax is imposed on income from capital, and the revenue is transferred to wage earners. If the tax rate t is negative, the tax is imposed on wages, and the revenue is transferred to firms.[8]

Wage earners' share of national income is now $(W + T)/Y$, while the amount of net profits is

$$P = (1 - m)Y - I - T$$
$$= (1 - m)(m - s - t)Y.$$

The rate of investment firms choose now, given the tax rate and the share of wages in income, is

$$s^*(m, t) = (1 - t) - \frac{\varrho/v}{1 - m} = s^M - t.$$

With a tax on income from capital, tax payments come entirely out of investments. With a tax on wages, tax payments go entirely into investments. Shareholders continue to consume the same share of income as before, since $[1 - t - s^*(m,t)] = (1 - s^M)$. The share of income that is invested with taxes is $I/Y = 1 - m - \varrho/v - (1 - m)t$.

Thus the trade-off faced by the government between redistribution of income through taxation and investment is identical to the trade-off between wages and investment: $d(I/Y)/d(T/Y) = -1$. We can relabel the horizontal axis of Figure 1 to read $(W + T)/Y = m + t(1 - m)$, and use the same line to describe the possibilities facing the government as it raises or lowers the tax rate. The state is in the same situation as wage earners are.

---

[8] In this case, the rate at which wages are taxed is given by the equality $T = -t(1 - m)Y = t_w mY$, which implies that the tax rate imposed on wages is $t_w = -t(1 - m)/m$.

What will different governments do when confronted with this trade-off? Because shareholders' welfare declines as the tax rate increases, $dP^*/dt < 0$, a probusiness government would tax wage earners and transfer the income to firms: it would generate growth financed by workers. A purely procapitalist government, a government which sought to maximize P^*, would tax wages at the maximum feasible rate. A purely prolabor government, on the other hand, which sought to maximize W^* would have the same indifference curves as wage earners in Figure 1. Such a government would choose the tax rate such that $(W + T)/Y = m + t(1 - m) = \varrho/v$, or $t = (\varrho/v - m)/(1 - m)$.[9]

Thus procapital governments favor growth over wage earners' consumption while prolabor governments prefer greater consumption for wage earners at the cost of slower growth. No government, however, can reduce the share of income that owners of capital consume. Any additional income for wage earners, whether it consists of wage gains won at the bargaining table or of transfer payments won through elections, reduces total investment, dollar for dollar. As long as $\varrho/v < 1$, wage earners will moderate their claims on profits and so will governments representing wage earners.

Given this conclusion, it is not surprising that democracy appears so feeble when faced with the power of capital. "The institutional *form* of this state," write Offe and Runge (in Offe 1984, 121), "is determined through the rules of democratic and representative government, while the material *content* of state power is conditioned by the continuous requirements of the accumulation process." "The presumed sovereignty of the democratic citizenry," Bowles and Gintis (1986, 90) state succinctly, "fails in the presence of capital strike." The democratic process may bring governments with radically different bases of support into office but not governments with radically different programs.

Is the State Structurally Dependent on Capital? Statics

Taxes on Consumption out of Income from Capital

These conclusions are based, however, on an assumption that need not be true of capitalism in general. This assumption is that the only policy

[9] Wage earners who acquire complete control over tax policy through electoral victories achieve no more and no less than wage earners who gain complete control over private income distribution through collective bargaining: the outcome is the same in both cases. Note that the wage earners' optimal tax may be negative.

instrument governments can possibly use is a tax on income. This particular policy instrument leaves the state structurally dependent because utility-maximizing shareholders respond to tax increases with less investment. But governments can adopt policies that alter the trade-off between investment and income distribution. The inference that because society is dependent on capital, so must be the state is false.

In fact, all governments in developed capitalist countries tax, at different rates, the part of income from capital that is invested and the part that is consumed. Tax incentives for investment have been widely used, at least since the end of World War II. Depreciation allowances that differ from the rate at which plants and equipment actually wear out or become obsolete, investment credits, investment grants, special treatment of capital gains, and double taxation of profits distributed as dividends are only some of the most common deviations from a straight income tax. (For recent reviews of investment incentives in different countries, see Bracewell-Milnes 1980; Bracewell-Milnes and Huiskamp 1977; Commission of the European Community 1975; Hogan 1967; King and Fullerton 1984; Kopits 1981; Organization for Economic Cooperation and Development [OECD] 1979, 1983, 1984; Price, Waterhouse & Co. 1981.)

Let us distinguish the two taxes. The tax imposed on all income from capital (gross profits) is $T_i = t_i(I + P) = t_i(1 - m)Y$. We will refer to it as the "income tax." This is the tax we analyzed in the preceding section.

The tax imposed on shareholders' consumption is $T_c = t_c P = t_c(1 - s)$ $(1 - m)Y$. This is the "consumption tax."[10]

Suppose now that a government adopts a pure consumption tax, that is, $t_i = 0$ so that $t_c(1 - s)$ is the tax rate applied to the income from capital $(1 - m)Y$. The most important effect of using this instrument is that the rate of investment is not affected by this tax rate, whatever it is, as long as wages are constant (Auerbach 1983). Indeed, as shown in the Appendix, for any rate of taxation of consumption out of profits, firms continue to invest at the market rate given by Equation 2:

$$s^*(m) = 1 - \frac{\varrho/v}{1 - m} = s^M.^{11}$$

---

[10] The total tax rate imposed on income from capital is thus $t = t_i + t_c(1 - s) = (t_i + t_c) - t_c s = t_0 - t_1 s$, where $t_0 = t_i + t_c$ is the nominal tax rate and $t_1 = t_c$ is the rate of investment relief.

[11] This result may be nonintuitive: firms pay higher taxes and invest at the same rate as before. The reason is that this tax imposes the same cost on consumption now and in the future and thus does not change the optimal allocation of consumption over time.

We are thus already one step away from structural dependence: with this tax instrument a government can keep investment at its market-determined rate and distribute the remaining income of shareholders to wage earners. A pure prolabor government can set t_c close to 1, reduce shareholders' share of consumption almost to 0, yet keep the rate of investment unchanged at s^M.

This much is true when the wage share is fixed. But in some capitalist countries wage earners are highly organized in centralized union federations with the capacity to shape the private distribution of income. If a government uses a pure consumption tax, the union federation will maximize W^* by choosing the share of income given by $m^{**}(t_c) = (1 - t_c)\varrho/v$. The willingness of the unions to engage in the political exchange described by Pizzorno (1978), Hibbs (1978), and Korpi and Shalev (1980), in which lower wages are traded for increases in welfare programs is apparent: as the tax rate, and thus transfers of income, increase, the federation reduces its preferred private wage share.

Because consumption taxes do not affect the rate of investment and do reduce the share of wages that centralized unions will demand and because the rate of investment increases as the share of wages declines (Equation 2), increases in the tax on consumption out of profit can increase the rate of investment. The rate of investment resulting from a tax on consumption of income from capital when wages are set unilaterally by centralized unions will be

$$s^*[m^{**}(t_c)] = 1 - \frac{\varrho/v}{1 - (1 - t_c)\varrho/v},$$

which is a positive function of t_c, $ds^*/dt_c > 0$.[12] This, then, is the second step: in concertation with the union federation the government can increase investment.

Can it do both: reduce the income share consumed by shareholders and increase investment above market-determined levels? The answer is positive; but because an even stronger conclusion can be sustained, let us go directly there.

[12] This follows as long as the government chooses the tax rate t_c such that $(1 - t_c)\varrho/v < 1$. Otherwise firms will disinvest at the maximal rate no matter what the government does.

Adam Przeworski and Michael Wallerstein

Workers' Welfare under Socialism and Democratic Capitalism

The strong result is a vindication of the traditional social democratic strategy, formulated perhaps for the first time by Bernstein in 1898, elaborated by Henrik de Man in 1933, adopted by the Swedish Social Democrats in the 1930s, and codified in the German Social Democratic Programme of Bad Godesberg in 1959, namely, that a proworker state can control the capitalist economy in a manner that would bring the material welfare of wage earners to the same level they could reach under socialism.

Under capitalism, owners of capital stock control investment, while wage earners may at most control the distribution of private income. The strategic problem organized workers confront under capitalism is thus to choose the share of income, given that someone else determines investment. Under socialism, wage earners would control both the share of income going to investment and that going to consumption. Since capital stock would be collectively owned, there would no profit incomes; and the society as a whole, through some preference-revealing mechanism, would decide the distribution of income into investment and consumption.[13]

Wage earners' strategic problem under socialism would thus be to choose their share of income, knowing that whatever income they do not consume is invested. Technically, this is the same as setting $s = 1$ and choosing m to maximize W^*, which yields $m^*(1) = \varrho/v$. The rest of income goes to investment, or $I/Y = 1 - \varrho/v$. Associated with this allocation of resources is the level of wage earners' welfare under socialism $W^*(S)$. Given the technology and the time preferences, $W^*(S)$ represents the highest possible level of wage earners' welfare – the level they could attain if they controlled investment as well as income distribution.

Back to capitalism: consider the case with one big union and a government that chooses a pure consumption tax with the tax rate t_c close to 1. As t_c approaches 1,

$$(W + T)/Y = [m^{**} + t_c(1 - s^*)(1 - m^{**})] - \varrho/v$$

and

$$I/Y = s^*(1 - m^{**}) - 1 - \varrho/v,$$

[13] Obviously this notion of socialism should not be confused with Eastern European economies, where the decisions about allocation of resources are made by party bureaucrats.

70

which is the same as under socialism. As t_c approaches 1, wage earners' welfare under capitalism approaches the welfare they could obtain under socialism (Wallerstein and Przeworski, n.d.).

Would a government ever choose such a tax rate? To answer the question we need a language to characterize governments. Suppose the government's objective is to maximize G^*, which depends on the welfare of wage earners and shareholders according to $G^* = (W^*)^\gamma (P^*)^{1-\gamma}$, $0 < \gamma < 1$. Thus γ is the weight attached to the welfare of wage earners and $(1 - \gamma)$ is the weight given the welfare of shareholders. If γ approaches 1, labor's interests predominate; if γ approaches 0, the government exclusively favors capital.

The government's optimal tax on consumption out of income from capital is given implicitly by the equation

$$t_c = \frac{\gamma P^*}{\gamma P^* + (1 - \gamma)W^*}.\text{[14]} \tag{3}$$

Thus, as long as $0 < \gamma < 1$, the government will choose to tax consumption out of income from capital at a rate also between 0 and 1. In addition, the greater the weight given to wage earners' welfare, the higher will be t_c, or $dt_c/d\gamma > 0$. Finally, as γ approaches 1, t_c also approaches 1 and wage earners' welfare approaches that associated with socialism. Note that the share of national income that shareholders consume approaches 0, but shareholders' consumption in absolute terms may remain substantial. The conclusion is that when all wage earners are organized in one centralized union federation and the government is purely prolabor it will choose a tax on capitalist consumption the effect of which will be to bring wage earners' material welfare almost to the level they could obtain under socialism. Hence, at least when the union federation is willing to engage in a political exchange of private and public income, the state is not structurally dependent on capital.[15]

Caveats and Preliminary Conclusions

These conclusions are subject to a number of qualifications: (1) the results may depend on restrictive assumptions about workers' and shareholders'

---

[14] Both P^* and W^* contain t_c so, contrary to appearances, t_c is not isolated on the left-hand side of Equation 3.

[15] Whether a prolabor government in countries where unions are fragmented or weak could still bring wage earners' welfare arbitrarily close to the level they could attain under socialism with an appropriate set of taxes and transfers remains to be investigated.

preferences; (2) structural dependence may work through mechanisms other than investment; (3) the state may be dependent not on national but foreign investors; (4) interventionist governments may be inherently incapable of serving as perfect agents of any group's interests. Let us consider each in turn.

For the sake of mathematical tractability, we have worked with particularly simple specifications of the production and utility functions. Our conclusion does not depend on the assumption of a linear production function. Auerbach (1983) and Przeworski and Wallerstein (1985) present models of investment-neutral taxes on profits using the standard production function with diminishing returns to investment. Nor is our conclusion restricted to the case of logarithmic utility functions. The same results can be derived with any utility function with a constant elasticity of marginal utility.[16] We do not know, however, the generality of our results within the entire set of quasiconcave utility functions with which economists like to work.

Our results are sensitive to the assumption that firms care only about the present and future consumption of their shareholders. Owners of firms may not like encroachments on their prerogatives or the paying of taxes per se. Yet, the fact that owners of firms do not like something the government is doing, even if it touches them as profoundly as, say, a law increasing workers' rights at the workplace, is not sufficient to affect investment. Suppose firms maximize some more general utility function $V(P^*, x)$ where P^* is, as above, the welfare derived from present and future consumption and x is anything else that causes distress $(\partial V/\partial x < 0)$ as the Left comes to power. "Investment strikes" will occur only if $dx/ds > 0$. Note that control over the workplace will not do for x, because it is independent of investment. Dislike of paying taxes will cause firms to increase, not decrease, their rate of investment in the presence of taxes on shareholders' consumption. Thus, likely candidates for x are not obvious.

Our results are also sensitive to the assumption that workers care only about their consumption. If workers determine the supply of labor by balancing their marginal utility of leisure with their marginal utility of income, the replacement of private wages with transfer payments financed by a tax on consumption out of profits will reduce incentives to work as it increases incentives to invest.

---

[16] The family of utility functions with a constant elasticity of marginal utility is conventionally given by the formula $U(c) = [1/(1-b)]c^{1-b} + B, b > 0$, for $b \neq 1$ and $U(c) = \ln(c)$ for $b = 1$. The parameter b is the elasticity of marginal utility.

Structural Dependence of the State on Capital

The second objection is that our conclusion is valid at most with regard to a specific mechanism of structural dependence, namely, the dependence of future material welfare on investment. One might postulate other mechanisms that would render the state dependent on capital, for example, the need to finance state activities through borrowing (see Marx 1952b, written in 1850). The mechanism most often suggested by Marxist theoreticians is the following: governments depend on current levels of economic activity, therefore they depend on investment. This formulation is, however, incoherent: if governments are concerned with current levels of activity, current demand, or current employment, they can and would do many things other than worry about investment. In a Keynesian textbook they can reduce taxes on wages, increase public employment, or print money as well as reduce interest rates to stimulate investment. A concern with the short run would not lead to a preoccupation with investment. Investment matters mostly for the long run.

In general, however, it may be true that the state is structurally dependent through mechanisms other than the one analyzed here. A reasonable short-term model of dependence is yet to be developed, but our conclusion should not be taken to be more general than it is.

Third is the issue of international constraints. A clarification may be needed. In the analysis, export of capital was treated as equivalent to consumption from the point of view of the tax system: whatever is not invested in the particular economy is subject to the tax. Thus all that governments need to do, in order to use the tax system to induce domestic (as distinct from foreign) investment, is to ascertain the actual amount of domestic income and investment. And in spite of transfer pricing and other mechanisms by which firms can shift tax burdens from country to country, there seems to be a general agreement that by and large, governments do monitor international flows of income (Bracewell-Milnes 1980; Hartman 1985; OECD 1983). Governments that seek to attract new foreign investment are in a different and more constrained situation. High taxes on consumption out of profits that have no effect on the investment decisions of domestic firms (or of local subsidiaries of multinational firms) will deter new foreign investors. The most important and unresolved issue, however, concerns the range of choice that the government of any country has when domestic producers must trade in international markets in which competitiveness depends to a significant degree on relative labor costs.

Finally, we come to the problem of the limits of governmental competence. Government intervention in the economy creates a potential for vast inefficiencies in the allocation of investment and labor. Any system of investment incentives is vulnerable to inefficiencies due to differing effective rates on different assets (King and Fullerton 1984). Any system in which private consumption depends primarily on transfers rather than wages is vulnerable to inefficiencies due to misallocation of labor. The problem lies not only in the difficulty of designing neutral taxes or transfers but in their implementation. The very fact that the state acquires the capacity to intervene in the economy, that is, to affect material welfare of private actors, turns it into an attractive target of influence by these actors. What has thus developed as the eventual aftermath of the Keynesian revolution is a state that is strong in its capacity to intervene and that is highly vulnerable to private influence (Schmitter 1985; Skidelsky 1977). Diagnoses formulated within ideologically distant perspectives coincide in their anti-statist conclusions: Habermas's (1975) analysis of the crisis facing capitalism is identical to that of Stigler (1975). What may be thus wrong with our analysis is the assumption that interventionist governments can ever serve as perfect agents of the political forces that placed them in office. The economy is sick, the drugs are available, but the doctor may be a hack.

In sum, there may be limits to the ability of the state to redistribute consumption without discouraging private investment, because the economy depends on an inflow of capital from abroad (rather than the reinvestment of profit earned at home) or because private wages cannot be replaced by public income without undermining work incentives or because the government cannot be trusted with the discretion required by redistributive policies. But all of these reasons are less general than the claims of the theory of structural dependence.

Our analysis reveals a large range of economically feasible policies. Exclusive reliance on income taxes, that is, taxes that are independent of the rate of investment – whether these are imposed on capital or labor – allows owners of capital to choose the share of national income they want to consume and to ward off, by reducing the share of investment, all attempts both by unions and by governments to redistribute consumption. Under exclusive reliance on income taxes, the consumption of all groups other than shareholders, government included, is thus subjected to "market discipline." In contrast, if only consumption out of income from capital is taxed, governments can redistribute consumption without reducing investment. Acting in concert with unions willing and able to trade off wage demands for increased transfer payments, the government can increase investment and reduce capitalists' consumption share simultaneously.

Governments can choose different policies concerning distribution and growth and these policies can be effective. Specifically, governments can increase investment by reducing wage earners' consumption or by reducing the consumption of owners of capital. Since all social groups will seek to shift the costs of investment onto others, the outcome of the democratic process can matter greatly for the welfare of different groups under capitalism. The state is not structurally dependent.

These conclusions may seem banal, but they run against a substantial body of established theory. The Marxist theory presented in the first section is logically persuasive and historically plausible. Moreover, we demonstrated in the second section that as long as governments limit themselves, or are limited, to using a flat income tax, the state is structurally dependent on capital. And, importantly, Marxists are not the only theoreticians who come to the conclusion that the state is dependent: the language is different but this is the general thrust of theories of the state originating from the neoclassical economic theory, as exemplified by Peltzman (1976), Aumann and Kurz (1977), Busch and Mackay (1977), Becker (1983), Bates and Lien (1985), and innumerable others who conclude that all governments seeking support must anticipate the negative effect of taxes on private investment. Thus, there are good reasons to be theoretically surprised.

Is the State Structurally Dependent on Capital? Dynamics

Once they are in office, prolabor governments can use tax policies to bring the welfare of wage earners arbitrarily close to the level wage earners could attain if they controlled investment directly: this is the central conclusion we have reached thus far. This conclusion, however, holds only once the prolabor government is in office – more precisely, once the policy is in effect. The question that remains is what happens to investment and wage earners' welfare when firms anticipate that a prolabor party would or might win the next election and institute such tax policies.

Since the mathematical analysis is quite complicated, we present only the framework of analysis and the conclusions. Suppose that at time $\tau = 0$ a government characterized by γ_0 is in office and the tax rate is $t_c = t_0$. The government is highly procapitalist and this tax rate is close to 0. An election is to take place and firms expect that this election will be won by a prolabor government characterized by $\gamma_1 > \gamma_0$, which will eventually introduce, at time $\tau = 1$, a tax $t_c = t_1 > t_0$.[17] What rate of investment will be chosen during the period from $0 \leq \tau < 1$ if firms expect that tax rate to be higher at and after $\tau = 1$.

When firms do not anticipate a change in tax policy, they choose the rate of investment that maximizes $P^*(t_0)$ between $\tau = 0$ and infinity. If, however, they anticipate that the tax will increase at $\tau = 1$ and remain at the new level, they will choose a time path of investment $s(\tau)$ to maximize

$$\int_0^1 e^{-\varrho\tau} \ln[P(t_0, \tau)]d\tau + \int_1^\infty e^{-\varrho\tau} \ln[P(t_1, \tau)]d\tau.$$

The conclusion is the following: firms that anticipate a future increase in taxes will reduce investment in the period $0 \leq \tau < 1$ even if the tax is a pure consumption tax that will not lower investment in the period $\tau \geq 1$. The same holds for firms that are not certain about future tax policy but think taxes will rise with some positive probability. Thus, anticipations of certain or possible increases of taxes lead firms to lower their investment rate. Similarly, expectations of future tax decreases will cause current investment to increase. Pure consumption taxes are no longer investment-neutral when change is anticipated.

Thus "business confidence" – the expectation by firms concerning government policy – has direct consequences for the investment behavior of firms. Yet this conclusion should be distinguished from the view of Kalecki (1966; also Block 1977), who also saw in business confidence the constraint that any government under capitalism is forced to consider. In Kalecki's view, business confidence threatened investment even in a static case, when the government policy was already in place and no changes were anticipated. However, once a government has implemented a consumption tax, the investment rate is unaffected by the tax rate. It is the anticipation that a government would introduce or raise such a tax that erodes business confidence and lowers investment.[18]

---

[17] It makes no difference in the analysis if firms are certain taxes will increase at $\tau = 1$ or attribute some positive probability to a tax increase at $\tau = 1$. Uncertainty can be understood in this context as a situation in which firms attach subjective probability distributions to the outcomes of future elections or directly to future tax rates. Exactly the same analysis would apply if firms are uncertain about the future wage share or the future productivity of capital.

[18] Aubin and Goyeau (1986) have found that in France the prospect of an electoral victory of the Left (measured as the product of the support for the Left in the polls and the

Structural Dependence of the State on Capital

We suspect that many newly elected proworker governments abandoned or moderated their programs for wrong reasons, having mistaken the cost of anticipation of policies for the costs of policies themselves. The French Socialist party announced in the electoral campaign of 1981 that it would propose a law in favor of renters. Once elected, it prepared such a bill. In the meantime, the vacancy rate went up and so did rents. Having listened to a chorus of right-wing press, the government decided that the policy was too expensive and moderated the provisions of the law. Our analysis suggests that this may have been a mistake. The government never waited to discover the costs of the law. Instead, it panicked over the costs of anticipation which, by then, were sunk.

Ever since Winston Churchill sneered in 1924 that the Labour party was not fit to govern, parties of labor have been making desperate efforts to show their moderation and responsibility in administering the economy once in office. Yet once the decision to adopt a policy has been made and once the government has suffered the effects of anticipation, the government is best-off introducing the original program without any compromises. The time to compromise is not after the costs have already been paid.[19]

Since anticipated transitions to higher taxes are costly for wage earners' welfare, socialists are sometimes tempted to proceed "in one stroke" – to use the phrase of Oskar Lange, who thought that if a government has decided to go ahead with a socialist program at all, "it must go through resolutely . . . at a maximum speed" (1964, 125; also Kautsky 1925). This is not a new idea: Machiavelli advised, "When a prince takes a new state, he should calculate the sum of all the injuries he will have to do, and do them all at once, so as not to have to do new ones every day; simply by not repeating them, he will thus be able to reassure people, and win them over to his side with benefits" (1977, 28).

Our analysis suggests that socialist governments should never announce more than they intend to do and that they should do what they announced fully and quickly. Leon Blum was wrong to have waited to assume office after the Popular Front won the elections of 1936. Yet we do not know whether one stroke is better than many. Indeed, we cannot even determine whether or not workers' parties should seek to increase the tax on

proportion of the electoral term that has elapsed) contributes significantly to the explanation of investment in a model that includes measures of aggregate demand and the cost of capital.
[19] This does not mean, of course, that governments should stubbornly stick with all policies regardless of their effects. Some policies are simply bad policies.

shareholders' consumption. We know that once instituted, an increase in t_c will increase wage earners' welfare until or unless the socialist government is defeated and the policy reversed. But we also know that anticipation of this moment causes a fall in investment and is costly to wage earners' welfare in the period before the tax increase goes into effect. Thus, the question remains open whether the welfare of wage earners is improved. If workers are better-off when prolabor governments adhere to the status quo, then the state is structurally dependent in dynamic terms: some distributions of consumption are unattainable because the transition costs are too high.

Structural Dependence and Socialist Policies

The capitalist economy, in which owners of wealth and of the capacity to work make decentralized decisions about allocations of their endowments, regularly generates a number of effects that are experienced as profound deprivation by large segments of society. The market does not assure the material security of anyone who does not own wealth and is not able to earn a living. The market generates drastic inequalities, including inequality of opportunity. Finally, in cases where the private rate of return diverges from the social one, the market allocates resources to uses inefficiently. This has been the traditional socialist view of capitalism.

The perennial question has been what, if anything, can be done about it. Social Democrats in several countries developed a full-fledged program for steering the capitalist economy in the interest of people who depend on income from employment or cannot earn an income sufficient to survive. By controlling the capitalist economy, the state run by socialists could rationalize the economy as a whole and orient it toward the general welfare, the Swedish Social Democratic minister of finance discovered in the 1930s (Wigforss, as summarized by Lewin 1975, 286). Because capitalism became organized, it could be administered by socialists in the interest of the people, argued the eventual German Social Democratic minister of finance (Hilferding 1981). Ironically, it was Keynes who provided the policy instruments for controlling capitalist economies and perhaps the most eloquent statement of the social-democratic position: "It is not the ownership of the instruments of production which it is important for the state to assume. If the state is able to determine the aggregate amount of resources devoted to augmenting the instruments and the basic reward to those who own them, it will have accomplished all that is necessary" (1964, 378).

Even in its heyday, however, the social-democratic strategy was the subject of at least skepticism if not hostility from those who were persuaded that no government, not even one elected by "the people," could control investment and income distribution as long as the instruments of production were privately owned. The thesis that the state is structurally dependent on capital was used by critics of social democracy to argue that this strategy is unfeasible, since the ability of any government to determine the level of investment and the distribution of income is subject to a trade-off given by the self-interest of owners of the instruments of production.

Our contribution to this debate is as follows: Once in place, a tax on shareholders' consumption does not reduce investment. The state is not structurally dependent on capital in the sense that virtually any distribution of consumption between wage earners and shareholders is compatible with continual private investment. Yet anticipations of future threats to shareholders' consumption do reduce investment and impose costs on wage earners. Whether and when the future benefits to wage earners outweigh the costs incurred during the transition period remains an open question.

Appendix

Preliminaries

Given that the economy grows according to $Y'(\tau) = vs(1 - m)Y(\tau)$, the national income at any time is given by $Y(\tau) = Y(0)e^{vs(1-m)\tau}$. Wages, profits, investment, and taxes all constitute shares of this income as described in the text. All of our results are derived from the first-order conditions of a series of maximization problems. In all cases, it is easily verified that the second-order conditions for a maximum are satisfied.

Capitalists' Problem

Firms choose s to maximize

$$P^* = \int_0^\infty e^{-\varrho\tau} \ln[P(\tau)]d\tau = \frac{1}{\varrho}\left[\ln P(0) + \frac{vs(1 - m)}{\varrho}\right]. \tag{A-1}$$

Note that P^* is only well defined when $P(0) > 0$. To insure that this condition is met, we assume throughout that $m < 1$ or $\varrho/v < 1$.

Without taxes, $P(0) = (1 - s)(1 - m)Y(0)$. Firms thus choose the s that satisfies

$$\frac{\partial P^*(s, m)}{\partial s} = \frac{1}{\varrho}\left[\frac{v(1 - m)}{\varrho} - \frac{1}{1 - s}\right] = 0$$

which implies the choice

$$s^*(m) = 1 - \frac{\varrho/v}{(1 - m)} = s^M. \tag{A-2}$$

Capitalists are consuming the share $(1 - s^M)(1 - m) = \varrho/v$ and investing the share $s^M(1 - m) = (1 - m - \varrho/v)$.

With income and consumption taxes,

$$P(0) = [(1 - t_c)(1 - s) - t_i](1 - m)Y(0).$$

The first-order condition is now

$$\frac{\partial P^*}{\partial s} = \frac{1}{\varrho}\left[\frac{v(1 - m)}{\varrho} - \frac{1 - t_c}{(1 - t_c)(1 - s) - t_i}\right] = 0,$$

which yields

$$s^*(m, t_i, t_c) = 1 - \frac{\varrho/v}{(1 - m)} - \frac{t_i}{(1 - t_c)}. \tag{A-3}$$

In the case with only income taxes, $t_c = 0$ and Equation A-3 reduces to

$$s^*(m, t_i) = 1 - \frac{\varrho/v}{(1 - m)} - t_i = s^M - t_i. \tag{A-4}$$

Capitalists are consuming the share $(1 - s^* - t_i)(1 - m) = \varrho/v$ and investing the share $s^*(1 - m) = [(1 - m)(1 - t_i) - \varrho/v]$.

In the case with only consumption taxes, $t_i = 0$ and Equation A-3 reduces to

$$s^*(m, t_c) = 1 - \frac{\varrho/v}{(1 - m)} = s^M. \tag{A-5}$$

Now capitalists are consuming the share $(1 - t_c)(1 - s^*)(1 - m) = (1 - t_c)\varrho/v$ and investing the share $s^*(1 - m) = (1 - m - \varrho/v)$. As t_c goes to 1, capitalists' consumption share goes to 0.

Structural Dependence of the State on Capital

Workers' Problem

Unions choose m to maximize

$$W^* = \int_0^\infty e^{-\varrho\tau} \ln[W(\tau) + T(\tau)]d\tau$$

$$= \frac{1}{\varrho}\left[\ln[W(0) + T(0)] + \frac{vs(1-m)}{\varrho}\right]. \tag{A-6}$$

If there are no taxes and the unions treat s as exogenous, $W(0) = mY(0)$ and the solution to Equation A-6 (for $s > 0$) is given by

$$\frac{\partial W^*(m,s)}{\partial m} = (1/\varrho)[(1/m) - (vs/\varrho)] = 0,$$

which implies $m^*(s) = \varrho/vs$.

If firms invest according to their best reply $s^*(m)$ given by Equation A-2, $vs^*(1-m)/\varrho = [v(1-m)/\varrho - 1]$ in Equation A-6 and the solution to the workers' problem becomes

$$\frac{dW^*[m, s^*(m)]}{dm} = (1/\varrho)[(1/m) - (v/\varrho)] = 0$$

with $m^{**} = \varrho/v$.

With income and consumption taxes, $[W(0) + T(0)] = \{m + [t_i + t_c(1-s)](1-m)\}Y(0)$. If unions anticipate capitalists' response $s^*(m, t_i, t_c)$ as given by Equation A-3, the workers' solution is given by

$$\frac{dW^*}{dm} = \frac{1}{\varrho}\left[\frac{1-A}{m + (1-m)A + t_c\varrho/v} - \frac{1-A}{\varrho/v}\right] = 0 \tag{A-7}$$

where $A = t_i/(1 - t_c)$. Solving for m^{**},

$$m^{**}(t_i, t_c) = \frac{(1 - t_c)^2\varrho/v - t_i}{1 - t_c - t_i}. \tag{A-8}$$

Note that when $s = s^{**}(m, t_c, t_i)$, workers' share $(W + T)/Y = [m + (1-m)t_i/(1-t_c) + t_c\varrho/v]$. Therefore it follows immediately from Equation A-7 that when workers anticipate capitalists' best response s^* in choosing m, workers consume the share ϱ/v of national income.

In the case with only income taxes, $t_c = 0$ and Equation A-8 reduces to $m^{**}(t_i) = (\varrho/v - t_i)/(1 - t_i)$. In the case with only consumption taxes, $t_i = 0$ and Equation A-8 reduces to

$$m^{**}(t_c) = (1 - t_c)\varrho/v. \tag{A-9}$$

The Government's Problem

The government's objective function depends on the welfare of workers and capitalists according to the equation $G^* = (W^*)^\gamma (P^*)^{1-\gamma}$, $0 < \gamma < 1$. To find the government's optimal tax, we take the derivative

$$\frac{dG^*}{dt_i} = (W^*)^{\gamma-1}(P^*)^{-\gamma}\left[\gamma(P^*)\frac{dW^*}{dt_i} + (1 - \gamma)(W^*)\frac{dP^*}{dt_i}\right] = 0 \tag{A-10}$$

where t_i represents either t_i or t_c. Two cases were discussed in the text.

First we consider the income tax that would be chosen by a purely proworker government. Note that if $\gamma = 1$, then $G^* = W^*$. Thus, we substitute $s^*(m,t_i)$ (Equation A-4) into W^* (Equation A-6) and differentiate to obtain

$$\frac{dW^*}{dt_i} = \frac{(1 - m)}{\varrho}\left[\frac{1}{t_i(1 - m) + m} - \frac{v}{\varrho}\right] = 0,$$

which can be simplified to yield the solution $t_i = (\varrho/v - m)/(1 - m)$.

Now consider the case with a pure consumption tax, $t_i = 0$, and with unions choosing $m = m^{**}$. Substitute $m^{**}(t_c)$ (Equation A-9) and $s^*(m^{**},t_c)$ (Equation A-5) into W^* (Equation A-6) and take the derivative

$$dW^*/dt_c = 1/\varrho \tag{A-11}$$

Similarly, substitute $m^{**}(t_c)$ and $s^*(m,{}^{**}t_c)$ into P^* (Equation A-1) and differentiate

$$dP^*/dt_c = -t_c/\varrho(1 - t_c). \tag{A-12}$$

Combining Equations A-11 and A-12 with A-10 and rearranging terms yields $\gamma(1 - t_c)P^* - (1 - \gamma)t_c W^* = 0$, or

$$t_c = \frac{\gamma P^*}{\gamma P^* + (1 - \gamma)W^*}, \tag{A-13}$$

which implicitly defines the optimal t_c (since both P^* and W^* contain t_c). Thus, $0 < t_c < 1$ (since $0 < \gamma < 1$). It is readily checked that W^* does not explode as γ approaches 1. Therefore, as γ approaches 1, $(1 - \gamma)W^*$ approaches 0 and t_c approaches 1. Similarly, it is easily checked that P^* does not explode as γ approaches 0. Thus as γ goes to 0, γP^* goes to 0 and so does t_c. To find $dt_c/d\gamma$, differentiate Equation A-13 implicitly and rearrange terms to write

$$\frac{dt_c}{d\gamma} = \frac{(1 - t_c)p^* + t_c W^*}{\gamma P^* + (1 - \gamma)W^* + t_c/\varrho} > 0.$$

References

Aubin, Christian, and Daniel Goyeau. 1986. Political Influences on Private Economic Behavior: Corporate Investment in France 1972–84. Institut de Recherche et d'Analyse Politico-Economiques, Université de Poitiers. Typescript.

Auerbach, Alan J. 1983. Taxation, Corporate Financial Policy, and the Cost of Capital. *Journal of Economic Literature* 21:905–40.

Aumann, Robert J., and Mordecai Kurz. 1977. Power and Taxes. *Econometrica* 45:1137–61.

Bates, Robert H., and Da-Hsiang D. Lien. 1985. A Note on Taxation, Development, and Representative Government. *Politics and Society* 14:53–70.

Becker, Gary S. 1983. A Theory of Competition among Interest Groups for Political Influence. *Quarterly Journal of Economics* 48:371–400.

Block, Fred. 1977. The Ruling Class Does Not Rule: Notes on the Marxist Theory of the State. *Socialist Revolution* 33:6–27.

Bowles, Samuel, and Herbert Gintis. 1986. *Democracy and Capitalism*. New York: Basic Books.

Bracewell-Milnes, Barry. 1980. *The Economics of International Tax Avoidance*. Rotterdam: International Series of the Rotterdam Institute for Fiscal Studies.

Bracewell-Milnes, Barry, and Johan C. L. Huiskamp. 1977. *Investment Incentives: A Comparative Analysis of the Systems in the EEC, the US, and Sweden*. Deventer: Kluwer.

Busch, Winston C., and Robert J. Mackay. 1977. Private versus Public Sector Growth: A Collective Choice Approach. In *The Sources of Government Growth*, ed. Thomas E. Borcherding. Durham: Duke University Press.

Cameron, David R. 1984. Social Democracy, Corporatism, and Labor Quiescence: The Representation of Economic Interest in Advanced Capitalist Society. In *Order and Conflict in Contemporary Capitalism*, ed. John H. Goldthorpe. Oxford: Oxford University Press.

Castles, Francis G., ed. 1982. *The Impact of Parties*. London: Sage.

Commission of the European Community. 1975. *Tax Policy and Investment in the European Community*. Brussels: author.

Habermas, Jurgen. 1975. *Legitimation Crisis*. Boston: Beacon.

Hartman, David G. 1985. Tax Policy and Foreign Direct Investment. *Journal of Public Economics* 26:107–21.

Hibbs, Douglas A., Jr. 1977. Political Parties and Macroeconomic Policy. *American Political Science Review* 71:1467–87.

Hibbs, Douglas A., Jr. 1978. On the Political Economy of Long-Run Trends in Strike Activity. *British Journal of Political Science* 8:153–75.

Hilferding, Rudolf, 1981. *Finance Capital.* Boston: Routledge & Kegan Paul.

Hill, T. P. 1979. *Profits and Rates of Return.* Paris: Organization for Economic Cooperation & Development.

Hirshleifer, Jack. 1970. *Investment, Interest, and Capital.* Eaglewood Cliffs: Prentice-Hall.

Hogan, William T. 1967. *Depreciation Policies and Resultant Problems.* New York: Fordham.

Kalecki, Michal. 1966. *Studies in the Theory of Business Cycles, 1933–1939.* New York: A. M. Kelley.

Kautsky, Karl. 1925. *La révolution prolétarienne et son programme.* Brussels: L'Eglantine.

Keynes, John Maynard. 1964. *The General Theory of Employment, Interest, and Money.* New York: Harvest.

King, Mervyn A., and Don Fullerton. 1984. *The Taxation of Income from Capital: A Comparative Study of the United States, the United Kingdom, Sweden, and West Germany.* Chicago: University of Chicago Press.

Kolm, Serge-Christophe. 1977. *La Transition Socialiste.* Paris: Edition du Cerf.

Kopits, George G. 1981. Fiscal Incentives for Investment in Industrial Countries. *Bulletin of the International Bureau of Fiscal Documentation* 35:291–94.

Korpi, Walter, and Michael Shalev. 1980. Strikes, Power, and Politics in Western Nations, 1900–76. *Political Power and Social Theory* 1:301–34.

Lange, Oskar. 1964. On the Economic Theory of Socialism. In *On the Economic Theory of Socialism*, ed. Benjamin E. Lippincott. New York: McGraw Hill.

Lewin, Leif. 1975. The Debate on Economic Planning in Sweden. In *Sweden's Development from Poverty to Affluence, 1750–1970*, ed. Steven Koblik. Minneapolis: University of Minnesota Press.

Lindblom, Charles E. 1977. *Politics and Markets: The World's Political-Economic Systems.* New York: Basic Books.

Luxemburg, Rosa. 1970. *Reform or Revolution.* New York: Pathfinder.

Machiavelli, Niccolo. 1977. *The Prince*, ed. and trans. Robert M. Adams. New York: W. W. Norton.

Maravall, José M. 1979. The Limits of Reformism: Parliamentary Socialism and the Marxist Theory of the State. *British Journal of Sociology* 30:267–87.

Marx, Karl. 1952a. *Wage, Labour, and Capital.* Moscow: Progress.

Marx, Karl. 1952b. *The Class Struggle in France, 1848–1850.* Moscow: Progress.

Miliband, Ralph. 1969. *The State in Capitalist Society.* New York: Basic Books.

Offe, Claus. 1975. The Capitalist State and the Problem of Policy Formulation. In *Stress and Contradiction in Contemporary Capitalism*, ed. Leon Lindberg. Lexington: Lexington Books.

Offe, Claus. 1984. *Contradictions of the Welfare State*, Ed. John Keane. London: Hutchinson.

Organization for Economic Cooperation and Development. 1979. *The Taxation of Net Wealth, Capital Transfers, and Capital Gains.* Paris: author.

Organization for Economic Cooperation and Development. 1983. *International Investment and Multinational Enterprises.* Paris: author.

Organization for Economic Cooperation and Development. 1984. *Tax Expenditures: A Review of the Issues and Country Practices.* Paris: author.

Pashukanis, Eugene. 1951. General Theory of Law and Marxism. In *Soviet Legal Philosophy*, trans. Hugh W. Babb. Cambridge: Harvard University Press.

Peltzman, Sam. 1976. Toward a More General Theory of Regulation. *Journal of Law and Economics* 19:211–40.

Pizzorno, Alessandro. 1978. Political Exchange and Collective Identity in Industrial Conflict. In *The Resurgence of Class Conflict in Western Europe since 1968*, vol. 2, ed. Colin Crouch and Pizzorno. London: Macmillan.

Price, Waterhouse & Co. 1981. *Tax Policy Incentives to Capital Formation.* Prepared for the New York Stock Exchange study, U.S. Economic Performance in a Global Perspective. New York: New York Stock Exchange.

Przeworski, Adam. 1985. *Capitalism and Social Democracy.* Cambridge: Cambridge University Press.

Przeworski, Adam, and Michael Wallerstein. 1982a. The Structure of Class Conflict in Democratic Capitalist Societies. *American Political Science Review* 76:215–36.

Przeworski, Adam, and Michael Wallerstein. 1982b. Democratic Capitalism at the Crossroads. *Democracy* 2:52–68.

Przeworski, Adam, and Michael Wallerstein. 1985. A Comment on Katz. Mahler, and Franz. *American Political Science Review* 80:508–10.

Rueschemeyer, Dietrich, and Peter B. Evans. 1985. The State and Economic Transformation: Toward an Analysis of the Conditions Underlying Effective Intervention. In *Bringing the State Back In*, ed. Evans, Rueschemyer, and Theda Skocpol. Cambridge: Cambridge University Press.

Schmitter, Philippe C. 1985. Neo-Corporatism and the State. In *Political Economy of Corporatism*, ed. Wyn Grant. New York: St. Martin's.

Shalev, Michael. 1983. The Social Democratic Model and Beyond: Two Generations of Comparative Research on the Welfare State. In *Comparative Social Research.* Vol. 6, ed. Richard F. Tomasson. Greenwich, CT: JAI.

Skidelsky, Robert. 1977. The Political Meaning of the Keynesian Revolution. In *The End of the Kaynesian Era*, ed. author. New York: Holmes & Meier.

Stigler, George. 1975. *The Citizen and the State: Essays on Regulation.* Chicago: University of Chicago Press.

Wallerstein, Michael, and Adam Przeworski. 1988. Workers' Welfare and the Socialization of Capital. In *Rationality and Revolution*, ed. Michael Taylor. Cambridge: Cambridge University Press.

5

Capital Taxation with Open Borders

Michael Wallerstein and Adam Przeworski

1. Introduction

The central dilemma of social democratic thought today concerns the promise and the threat of freer markets. In the social democratic view, markets are mechanisms that simultaneously generate an efficient allocation of resources and an inegalitarian distribution of rewards. Of course, market outcomes are efficient only under restrictive conditions that rule out externalities, significant increasing returns to scale, monopoly power, and so forth. Nevertheless, the current consensus on the advantages of freer markets in ever-broader realms that encompasses most of the political spectrum from Right to Left belies the qualifications of economic theory. It is relatively easy for parties without egalitarian commitments to embrace policies of market liberalization. Social democrats are more conflicted. In order to reap the efficiency gains that markets make possible, must social democrats abandon their traditional commitment to mitigating the inequalities of wealth and income that markets engender?

This paper addresses this general question in the context of the taxation of income from capital and the liberalization of financial markets. The increased international integration of financial markets is commonly perceived as one of the most important changes in the world economy over the past twenty years. Exports and imports of capital have grown at twice the

An earlier version of this paper was presented at the 1990 Annual Meetings of the American Political Science Association. This version was prepared for publication in the *Review of International Political Economy*. We thank Jeff Frieden, Karl Ove Moene, Atle Seierstad, Geoffrey Garrett and Helen Milner for their help.

rate of trade in goods since 1980.[1] During the past decade, financial markets
have been liberalized in Japan, Italy, France, New Zealand, Norway, Sweden
and Denmark, i.e. in most of the advanced industrial societies that had significant regulatory controls over capital flows (OECD, 1989). Few political
restraints on the movement of capital remain among Western European
countries, whether or not they are inside the European Union (OECD,
1989).[2] If covered interest rate parity is used as the indicator of international
capital mobility, as Frankel (1989) suggests, financial market integration was
complete among advanced industrial societies by the end of the 1980s.[3]

Liberals (in the classical sense) have long urged the deregulation of capital markets, both for the sake of allocative efficiency and for the sake of the
constraints free capital markets place on government policy. In contrast,
social democrats had, in the past, frequently insisted that balanced growth,
full employment and macroeconomic stability required controls on capital
movements. But as planning and Keynesian policies of demand management have lost both intellectual and political support, the economic case
for capital controls has weakened.[4] Social democrats have long accepted
the principle that distributional objectives must be limited to those that
can be achieved without a large efficiency loss. Therefore, social democrats
have joined in the general move toward liberalization of financial markets,
in spite of their worries about the consequences.

It is clear that increased capital mobility sharpens the constraints on policy makers in the domain of monetary and exchange rate policy. But many
have advocated a much broader argument that increased capital mobility
has reduced the ability of governments to carry out redistributive policies
of all types. The argument seems particularly apt with regard to tax policy.[5]

---

[1] Figures are from the Bank for International Settlements, 60th Annual Report, cited by Jeff
Frieden (1990: 1).
[2] The only countries in Western Europe where 'the free play of market forces seem to remain
seriously hampered by institutional constraints,' according to the OECD (1989: 86), are
Iceland, Portugal and Greece. Portugal and Greece, along with Ireland and Spain, were
granted temporary exemptions from the EU requirement that all restrictions be removed
by 1990 (Tanzi and Bovenberg, 1990: 19).
[3] The covered interest rate is the rate of interest on bonds denominated in a common currency.
[4] See Epstein and Schor (1992) for a history of capital controls in the post-war period as well
as a Keynesian defense of capital controls as a vital instrument of macroeconomic policy.
See Quinn (1992) for a study of partisan differences in the adoption of financial restrictions.
[5] See, for example, Bird and McLure (1989), Lee and McKenzie (1989), McKenzie and Lee
(1991), Steinmo (1990, 1993) and Tanzi and Bovenberg (1990). The argument by Bates and
Lien (1985) that the taxation of factor owners is inversely related to factor mobility is more
abstract but similar.

As capital has become increasingly mobile across international borders, both corporate tax rates and the marginal personal tax rates facing high income investors have fallen. Between 1975 and 1989, Britain reduced the top marginal income tax rate from 83 to 40 per cent and lowered the corporate income tax from 52 to 35 per cent while broadening its base. During the Reagan administration in the United States, the marginal rate paid by the highest income bracket was reduced from 70 to 28 per cent (since raised to 31 per cent), while the tax on corporate profits was lowered from 46 to 34 per cent (again with a broadening of the corporate tax base). In Sweden, social democratic governments in the 1980s lowered the top marginal rates paid by individuals (from 82 to 50 per cent) and corporations (from 56 to 30 per cent) while increasing regressive consumption taxes (Steinmo, 1990, 1993).

Similar reductions in the top marginal income tax rate and in the corporate tax rate have occurred in almost every OECD country in the past decade (OECD, 1989). Between 1975 and 1989, the average corporate tax rate (including local taxes but excluding property taxes) among nineteen OECD countries fell from 49 per cent to 42 per cent (OECD, 1989: 182).[6] In the same time period, the average marginal rate paid to the central government by households in the top income bracket fell from 62 per cent to 46 per cent (OECD, 1989: 177). No country failed to reduce one of these two taxes and a large majority reduced both. Since most countries have broadened the tax base by removing special allowances and tax credits at the same time as tax rates were lowered, effective tax rates have fallen less than nominal tax rates. Yet, when changes in both the personal and corporate tax schedule are combined, the taxation of income from capital has significantly declined in most advanced industrial societies in the past decade (Steinmo, 1993).

The logic connecting pervasive reductions in taxes on income from capital with increased international mobility of capital is straightforward. In a world in which foreign investment is as easy as domestic investment, capital owners will shift their investments until post-tax rates of return are equal in all countries. Suppose that domestic capital owners can earn a fixed rate of return, r, by investing in foreign assets. If income invested abroad is not taxed while income earned from profits at home taxed at the rate of t, then investors must receive a pre-tax rate of return of at least $r/(1 - t)$ on their domestic investments. Any increase in the tax rate t raises the minimum

---

[6] The nineteen-country average excludes Iceland, Portugal, Greece, Turkey and Switzerland.

acceptable rate of return for domestic investments. While the profitability of already invested capital can be lowered, the post-tax profitability of new investments cannot. A unilateral increase in the tax on profits results in a permanent reduction in the country's stock of capital as investors increase the share of foreign assets in their portfolios. With open borders, the long-run burden of a tax on income from capital falls primarily on those groups in society who supply complementary factors of production, notably labor. The lower the cost of moving capital abroad, the argument goes, the less space there is for government policies that redistribute income from capital owners to others.[7]

Moreover, with internationally mobile capital, any country that increases the inflow of capital by unilaterally reducing its capital income tax rate imposes a negative externality on other countries. In calculating whether or not the increase in investment induced by a capital tax reduction is worth the loss of tax revenue, a country that neglects the loss imposed on other countries will set taxes below their optimal level (Giovannini, 1989). In addition, the ease with which many high-income workers can receive their compensation in the form of profit income rather than wages implies that lower taxes on income from capital create pressure to lower the top marginal tax rate on labor as well (Bird and McLure, 1989). Therefore, governments' declining ability to tax capital has an importance that is greater than the share of government revenues received from capital income taxes.

Two different remedies are frequently proposed for the problem of taxing internationally mobile capital. The first, favored by Giovannini (1989), is to change from a source-based system of taxation (where each country taxes capital income earned in its territory) to a residence-based system (where each country taxes the capital income of its residents, wherever the income is earned). Clearly, if countries taxed foreign investments at the same rate as domestic investments, the difficulty posed by capital mobility would vanish. In fact, most OECD countries, in principle, already have a residence-based system. In practice, however, the residence principle is compromised by various practices that treat foreign investment more favorably than domestic investment.[8] The greatest obstacles to effective source-based taxation, however, are the widespread banking secrecy and blocking laws that prevent countries from discovering the foreign earnings of their residents.

---

[7] Slemrod (1988) is a clear exposition of effects of a flat tax on capital income with international capital mobility.

[8] See Giovannini (1989) for details.

The critical weakness of effective source-based taxation is that it requires much greater coordination among countries in sharing records and prosecuting tax evasion than exists in the present or is likely to exist in the future. Giovannini is sanguine about the possibility of greater coordination among members of the European Union. Yet, unless the EU imposes controls on capital mobility with the rest of the world, cooperation within the EU will not be sufficient. Earnings that cannot be hidden inside the EU can easily be transferred outside.

The second remedy, favored by Tanzi and Bovenberg (1990) among others, is to harmonize tax systems within the EU through government agreement, thus removing differential tax rates yet avoiding the leveling downward to suboptimal levels of taxation that would result from unilateral actions. Again, the critical problem concerns tax harmonization with countries outside of the EU. While the joint determination of tax rates within the EU is easily imagined, collective tax setting with countries outside the EU seems even more Utopian than the collective pursuit of tax evaders. Thus neither remedy offers much hope of escaping the logic that predicts a downward leveling of taxes on income from capital (and high-paid labor as well) as a result of increased mobility of capital.

The model tracing the effects of international capital mobility on the ability of governments to tax income from capital rests on the simplifying assumption that capital income is taxed at a flat rate. Of course, the actual tax systems used by OECD countries are more complicated, even after the reforms of the 1980s. Almost half of OECD countries had some form of general investment allowance or investment tax credits in 1991 (OECD, 1991: 62). All OECD countries allow companies to deduct a depreciation allowance for investment in plant and equipment.

The simplification that capital income is taxed at a flat rate is not innocuous. It is critical in the sense that when one considers slightly more complicated tax systems that combine a flat tax on profits with a depreciation allowance for investment in plant and equipment, for example, the effects of corporate income taxation on investment change dramatically. In fact, the existence of neutral profit taxes, that is taxes on capital without effects on incentives to invest, has been discussed in the field of public finance in the context of a closed economy since the work of E. Cary Brown (1948).[9] The theory of capital taxation seems to suggest, contrary to the argument

[9] For more recent investigations of neutral capital taxes, see the Meade Committee (1978), Sinn (1987), Przeworski and Wallerstein (1988) and Howitt and Sinn (1989).

just summarized, that governments can tax internationally mobile capital without provoking a capital outflow provided they adopt the right type of tax. Moreover, cross-national evidence presented by Swank (1992, 1993) indicates that the relationship between financial openness and effective tax rates on capital income remains weak in advanced industrial societies, even after a decade of tax reform.

In this paper we argue for an intermediate position: international capital mobility does increase the constraints on taxation of income from capital, but to a much more limited extent than is commonly thought. In the second section of this paper, we review a standard result in the literature on taxes on income from capital that states that it is possible to tax uninvested profits without altering firms' investment plans. The argument has been made in the context of a closed economy by Abel and Blanchard (1983), Przeworski and Wallerstein (1988) and Howitt and Sinn (1989), among others. In this paper, we demonstrate that the argument remains valid in a model with free capital mobility as long as tax rates are constant over time. In the third section, we consider a case where the necessary conditions for taxing capital without distortionary effects cannot be satisfied, i.e., when future tax changes are anticipated. Only in this case does capital mobility increase the constraints on taxation of uninvested profits. Our results are summarized and qualified in the fourth and concluding section.

2. Neutral Capital Taxation with Free Movement of Capital

It is commonly thought that the taxation of income from capital necessarily distorts either investment or saving decisions. If the tax is residence-based, i.e., levied on all citizens regardless of the location of the investment, the return from saving is lowered. If the tax is source-based, i.e., levied on all capital income earned within the country regardless of the nationality of the investor, investment is shifted to low-tax countries. In this paper, we assume throughout that the government relies on source-based taxes because of the difficulty of collecting residence-based taxes in a world without capital controls. Moreover, as we will show, the claim that all source-based tax systems distort the location of investment is incorrect when tax rates are constant.

Suppose investors can choose either of two types of investments. The first type is investment in plant and equipment at home, denoted K, that produces a pre-tax income of $R(K)$ per period. Real capital is assumed to produce diminishing positive returns, or $R'(K) > 0$ and $R''(K) < 0$. In addition, we assume that real capital depreciates at the constant rate of δ. Letting $I_K(s)$ represent gross investment at home in period s, the domestic capital stock grows according to the equation

$$\dot{K}(s) = I_K(s) - \delta K(s).$$ (1)

We also impose the constraint that real gross investment cannot be negative, or $I_K(s) \geq 0$.

The second option investors have is to invest in foreign financial markets. Let the foreign monetary asset be denoted A and the global interest rate be r. The income investors receive in period s from their foreign investment is $r(s)A(s)$. Since monetary assets do not depreciate, we have

$$\dot{A}(s) = I_A(s)$$ (2)

where $I_A(s)$ represents investment abroad. Unlike investment in real assets, there is no reason to require $I_A(s)$ to be non-negative. Negative foreign investment is foreign borrowing. We do, however, require investors to remain solvent, which implies that $\lim_{s \to \infty} A(s) \geq 0$. This formulation with two types of investments is perhaps the simplest possible that contains all the necessary ingredients for studying capital taxation and capital formation when capital is easily moved across borders. Including additional types of investment, such as real investment abroad or monetary assets at home, adds nothing essential to the analysis.

Let the tax system be characterized by two parameters, the flat rate at which income from capital is taxed, t, and the present value of the depreciation allowance, z. Thus, the tax liability of recipients of income from capital can be written as

$$T(s) = t(s)[R(K(s)) - z(s)I_K(s)].$$ (3)

We assume that income from the foreign asset is not taxed at all (or, equivalently, that $r(s)$ represents the post-tax return on foreign assets). Consumption in each period, $C(s)$, equals income from both assets minus tax payments and new investment, both at home and abroad, or

$$C(s) = R(K(s)) + r(s)A(s) - I_K(s) - I_A(s) - T(s)$$
$$= [1 - t(s)]R(K(s)) - [1 - z(s)t(s)]I_K(s) + r(s)A(s) - I_A(s).$$ (4)

Assuming each investor has a per period utility function $U(C)$ with $U'(C) > 0$ and $U'' < 0$ and a subjective rate of time discount ρ, we can describe investors' behavior with the following problem.

Capital Taxation with Open Borders

Problem 1. Choose $I_K(S)$ and $I_A(S)$ to maximize

$$\int_0^\infty e^{-\rho s} U(C(s))\, ds \qquad (5)$$

with $C(S)$ given by equation (4), subject to equations (1) and (2) describing the growth of domestic and foreign capital and the constraints $I_K(s) \geq 0$ and $\lim_{s\to\infty} A(s) \geq 0$.

Instead of proceeding to solve Problem 1, consider an alternate formulation where the decisions of households and firms are separated. Assume all household investment is in the international financial market, or

$$C(s) = r(s)A(s) - I_A(s). \qquad (6)$$

The behavior of households is then given by

Problem 2. Choose $I_A(S)$ to maximize

$$\int_0^\infty e^{-\rho s} U(C(s))\, ds \qquad (7)$$

with $C(s)$ given by equation (6), subject to equation (2) and the constraint that $\lim_{s\to\infty} A(s) \to 0$.

Firms invest in domestic plant and equipment to maximize the present value of after-tax profits minus the cost of capital. Per period after-tax profits, $\pi(s)$, are given by:

$$\pi = [1 - t(s)]R(K(s)) - [1 - z(s)t(s)]I_K(s). \qquad (8)$$

The cost of capital to firms is $r(s)$, the international interest rate. Thus firms' investment decision can be written as

Problem 3. Choose $I_K(s)$ to maximize

$$\int_0^\infty \Delta(s)\pi(s)\, ds \qquad (9)$$

with $\pi(s)$ given by equation (8), subject to equation (1) and the constraint $I_K(s) \geq 0$. The discount factor $\Delta(s)$ is given by

$$\Delta(s) \equiv \exp\left\{ -\int_0^\infty r(u)du \right\} \qquad (10)$$

If the international interest rate, $r(s)$, is constant over time, then $\Delta(s) = e^{-rs}$.

Problem 1 is equivalent to Problems 2 and 3 in the sense that they imply identical solutions for $I_A(s)$ and $I_K(s)$.[10] In equilibrium, households act as if they invested exclusively in untaxed foreign assets regardless of their actual investment choices. Taxes on capital appear only in the firms' decision. This is why a source-based tax on income from capital does not distort household's saving decision. To study the impact of taxes on investment, we only need to analyze the solution of Problem 3, rather than the more complicated decision of investors in Problem 1.

From Problem 3 we have the Hamiltonian

$$\mathcal{H} = \Delta(s)\big\{[1 - t(s)]R(K(s)) - [1 - z(s)t(s)]I_K(s) + \lambda(s)[I_K(s) - \delta K(s)]\big\}$$
(11)

where $\lambda(s)$ represents the 'current value shadow price' of capital or the value to the firm (at time s) of marginal increase in its capital stock. The optimality conditions for Problem 3 are[11]

$$\lambda(s) - (1 - z(s)t(s)) \leq 0, \quad [\lambda(s) - (1 - z(s)t(s))]I_K(s) = 0$$
(12)

$$\dot{\lambda}(s) = (r(s) + \delta)\lambda(s) - (1 - t(s))R'(K(s))$$
(13)

$$\lim_{s \to \infty} \Delta(s)\,\lambda(s)K(s) = 0$$
(14)

Equation (12) indicates that the value of new capital, $\lambda(s)$, cannot exceed the cost of investment $[1 - z(s)t(s)]$, or else the firm could increase profits by investing more. If the value of new capital is less than the cost of investment (if $\lambda(s) < ([1 - z(s)t(s)])$), firms will not invest ($I_k(s) = 0$). Equation (13) states that the proportional change in shadow price of capital ($\dot{\lambda}(s)/\lambda(s)$) (capital gains) plus the gross marginal rate of return $(1 - t(s))R'(K(s))/\lambda(s)$ minus depreciation δ equals the opportunity cost of capital $r(s)$. Equation (14) requires the present value of the firm's capital stock in the infinite future to be zero. This last condition rules out acquisitions of capital that never benefit shareholders.

Consider the case of an interior solution with $I_K(s) > 0$ for some interval. It follows from equation (12) that $\lambda(s) = [1 - z(s)t(s)]$ and t $\dot{\lambda}(s) = -[\dot{z}(s)t(s) +$

---

[10] See Abel and Blanchard (1983) for a proof.
[11] Since $\mathcal{H}$ is concave in K and $I_{k'}$ the optimality conditions (12)–(14) are both necessary and sufficient (Seierstad and Sydsæter, 1987: 235).

$z(s)\dot{t}(s)$]. Combining these two equalities with equation (13) and rearranging terms yields

$$\frac{1 - t(s)}{1 - z(s)t(s)} R'K^*(s) - \delta = r(s) + \frac{\dot{z}(s)t(s) + z(s)\dot{t}(s)}{1 - z(s)t(s)} \tag{15}$$

as the condition that implicitly defines the optimal level of capital $K^*(s)$. The optimal investment choice for firms, then, is to invest in such a way that maintains their capital stock at the optimal level if possible. Otherwise firms should let capital decline through depreciation. Thus the optimal investment path can be written as

$$I_K^*(s) = \max(K^*(s) - (1 - \delta)K(s), 0). \tag{16}$$

A tax system is neutral with respect to investment if it raises revenue without changing the quantity of investment that firms select. In the absence of taxes on capital, that is if $t(s) = 0$ for all s, equation (15) reduces to

$$R'(K^*(s)) - \delta = r(s). \tag{17}$$

In the absence of taxes, firms equate the marginal product of capital, net of depreciation, with the cost of capital in the international financial market.

Comparing equations (15) and (17), the necessary and sufficient conditions for a neutral tax on capital follow immediately:

$$\dot{t}(s) = 0 \tag{18}$$

and

$$(1 - z)t = 0. \tag{19}$$

The first condition states that the tax rate must remain constant over time. The second condition states that if the tax rate is not zero, the full cost of investment must be deductible. (The two conditions together imply either $\dot{z}(s) = 0$ or $t = 0$.)

Equations (18) and (19) state that as long as $z = 1$, any constant tax rate $t < 1$ will have no deadweight cost.[12] This is the real cash flow tax

---

[12] The implication that a tax on profits will not alter firms' investment decisions provided firms' investment costs are fully and immediately deductible needs to be qualified when the tax approaches 100 per cent. If the most efficient way to provide managers with the proper incentive to maximize the market value of the firm is to make them partial owners, then the tax rate cannot approach unity without reducing the quality of managerial labor.

originally proposed by E. Cary Brown in 1948. The standard theory of capital taxation implies that a Left government could raise substantial revenue for redistributive purposes from owners of capital without any effect on private-sector investment, provided investment is fully deductible and the tax rate is stable.[13]

One way of understanding this result is to note that with $z = 1$, the tax on capital is equivalent to partial, non-voting ownership by the government. If the tax is set at $t = 0.5$, the government has become a passive partner in the firm with 50 per cent of the equity. It ought not to matter to management whether its stock is owned by the government or by pension funds or by thousands of individual shareholders, provided management has the same incentive to maximize profits. Nor does it matter that investments can be shifted into tax-free investments abroad. With $z = 1$, the government implicitly stands ready to share t per cent of the cost of investment in domestic capital in exchange for t per cent of the revenues the investment will generate. Any investment that would have been profitable without taxes remains profitable after taxes when the full cost of investment can be deducted from taxable income.

Another way to understand the neutrality of a real cash flow tax is that the tax discriminates against old capital. Old capital is taxed at the rate of t, but new capital faces a marginal tax rate of zero. Hence the choice of new capital or the level of investment is unaffected. The value of firm's stock of capital is reduced by the tax to $(1 - t)K$, however, since if the firm sold its capital it would have to pay tK in taxes (Howitt and Sinn, 1989). A tax on the firm's real cash flow is, thus, equivalent to tax on shareholders' wealth.

With free capital mobility, domestic investment depends on the rate of return abroad. The difference between a closed economy model and an open economy model is in the determination of $r(s)$ in equation (17). In the closed economy model, the interest rate is determined by the condition

---

[13] The Meade Committee (1978) and Howitt and Sinn (1987) prefer a tax on dividends to the tax on the firm's real cash flow. A dividend tax differs from the real cash flow tax by taxing income received from borrowing and exempting interest payments. Howitt and Sinn (1989) demonstrate that a dividend tax remains neutral even when changes in the tax rate are anticipated. However, the dividend tax, unlike the real cash flow tax, distorts the firm's choice between debt and equity financing. A full analysis of the dividend tax, thus, requires a model that allows consideration of the cost of financial distortions. For that reason, we concentrate on the real cash flow tax in this paper.

that investment must equal savings within each country. With free capital mobility, domestic interest rates are tied to the rate of return offered by foreign assets. If the country's excess supply or demand for capital is small relative to the pool of capital in global financial markets, and if foreign goods and assets are good substitutes for domestic goods and assets, then interest rates are exogenous. Even when these conditions are not satisfied, capital mobility sharply limits the feasibility of using interest rates as instruments of government economic policy. In contrast, capital mobility does not limit the feasibility of taxing income from capital at a high constant rate provided investment costs are fully deductible.

3. Anticipated Tax Increases

The two conditions for tax neutrality with a positive profit tax, that $i(s) = 0$ and $z = 1$, have quite different political implications. The condition that investment costs be deductible is compatible with any redistribution of uninvested profits through taxation and welfare expenditures. The condition that the tax rate be viewed by investors as constant over time limits the government to maintaining the status quo. A changing tax rate is incompatible with neutrality. Moreover, the impact of changes in the tax rate depends critically on whether or not capital is free to move across borders.

In this section we study the consequence of an one-time increase in the tax on profits, such as a Left government might want to implement. If the increase is not anticipated and if $z = 1$, the tax hike has no effect other than to reduce the wealth of capital owners and increase the revenues of the government. However, unanticipated tax increases exist only in models. Important policy changes do not happen in a democracy without prior public debate both inside and outside of parliament. Therefore, the important policy question concerns the impact of an anticipated increase in the tax on profits when capital is freely mobile.

Suppose, without loss of generality, that the tax rate t is initially zero. Suppose, further, that firms anticipate that the government will implement a new tax schedule with $t > 0$ and $z = 1$ at time $s = T$. Let $s = 0$ be the period when the future tax increase is initially anticipated. In addition, for simplicity of exposition, assume that the global interest rate is not expected to change, or $r(s) = r$ for all s. The problem facing firms now becomes:

Problem 4. Choose $I_K(s)$ to maximize

$$\int_0^T e^{-rs} [R(K(s)) - I_K(s)) \, ds + (1 - t) \int_T^\infty e^{-rs} [R(K(s)) - I_K(s)] \, ds \tag{20}$$

subject to equation (1) and the constraint that $I_K(s) \geq 0$.

This problem is solved backwards, by starting with the solution for $s \geq T$. By Bellmans's optimality principle, the optimal path of investment for $s \geq T$ must be the same as the path that would be chosen at $s = T$. But this is just Problem 3 with $\dot{t}(s) = 0$, $z = 1$ and $\Delta(s) = e^{-rs}$. It is easily verified that the stationary solution $\dot{\lambda}(s) = 0$ and $\dot{K}(s) = 0$ satisfies the optimality conditions (12)–(14) for $s \geq T$ where λ is given by

$$\lambda = (1 - t) \tag{21}$$

and $K = K^*$ is given implicitly by

$$R'(K^*) - \delta = r. \tag{22}$$

If $K(T) \leq K^*$, the optimal path of domestic investment is given by

$$I_K^*(s) = \begin{cases} K^* - 1(1 - \delta)K(T) & \text{for } s = T, \\ \delta K^* & \text{for } s > T. \end{cases} \tag{23}$$

Since we will show that $K(T) < K^*$, this is the relevant case. Again note the neutrality result: investment is independent of the tax rate once the tax is implemented and not expected to change further. Note also that, if t is set equal to zero, equations (21)–(23) define the solution before a tax increase is anticipated. In particular, equations (21) and (23) imply that $\lambda(s) = 1$ and $K(s) = K^*$ for $s < 0$.

Now we must solve Problem 4 for the period between $s = 0$, when the tax increase is first anticipated, and $s = T$, when the tax increase goes into effect. Since $t = 0$ during this period, the necessary condition for a maximum (10) states that $(\lambda(s) - 1) \leq 0$ and $(\lambda(s) - 1)I_K(s) = 0$. In addition, we know from equation (21) that $\lambda(T) = (1 - t)$. According to Pontryagin's theorem, $\lambda(s)$ must be continuous at $s = T$ (Seierstad and Sydsæter, 1987: 85–7).[14] There

---

[14] Note that the Pontryagin Maximum Principle remains valid in cases like the present where the Hamiltonian is discontinuous at a finite or countable set of time points (Seierstad and Sydsæter, 1987: 87). The costate variable $\lambda(s)$ must be continuous even at points where the optimal control $I_k^*(s)$ is not.

exists, therefore, some period of time, say between $s = T'$ and $s = T$, with $0 \leq T' < T$, where the solution of Problem 4 is given by

$$\lambda(s) < 1 \tag{24}$$

$$I_k^*(s) = 0 \tag{25}$$

$$K(s) = -\delta K(s) \tag{26}$$

In addition, it is easily shown that $\dot{\lambda}(s) < 0$ and $\ddot{\lambda}(s) < 0$ for $s \in (T', T)$.[15] A picture of a typical path of $\lambda(s)$ and $K(s)$ with $T' = 0$ is presented in Figure 1.

When capital is mobile, an anticipated increase of the tax rate t will cause a period of disinvestment at home immediately preceding the implementation of the tax. Once the tax is in place, disinvestment ceases and the capital stock is immediately brought up to its pre-tax level.

This contrasts sharply with the predictions of the closed economy model as presented, for example, by Abel and Blanchard (1983). In a closed economy, Abel and Blanchard show that an anticipated increase in a tax on uninvested profits will result in an *increase* in investment in the period preceding the tax increase, provided $\sigma = U'(C)/CU''(C)$ is less than one. When σ is constant, σ is investors' intertemporal elasticity of substitution, or the elasticity of the ratio of future to present consumption with respect to the rate of return.[16] Since empirical estimates of σ are well below one (Hall, 1988), this is the relevant case.

According to Abel and Blanchard, an anticipated tax increase can raise investment in a closed economy because, with declining marginal utility, investors prefer to smooth their consumption over time if possible. In a world without capital mobility, the only way to smooth consumption in anticipation of a future tax increase is to invest more before the tax goes into effect so that consumption will not have to fall as much after the tax

---

[15] For $s \leq T'$ we have the condition

$$\dot{\lambda}(s) = (r + \delta)\,\lambda(s) - R'(K^*) = 0$$

with $\lambda(s) = 1$. For $s \in (T', T)$, we have $\lambda(s) < 1$ and $K(s) < K^*$ (or $R'(K(s)) > R'(K^*)$) which together imply that $\dot{\lambda}(s) < 0$. Taking the second derivative:

$$\ddot{\lambda}(s) = (r + \delta)\,\dot{\lambda}(s) - R''(K)\dot{K}(s) < 0$$

for $s \in (T', T)$ since $\dot{\lambda}(s) < 0$, $R''(K) < 0$ and $\dot{K}(s) < 0$.

[16] The term σ is also the inverse of the coefficient of relative risk aversion. Since there is nothing stochastic in the model, the interpretation of σ as the intertemporal elasticity of consumption is preferable.

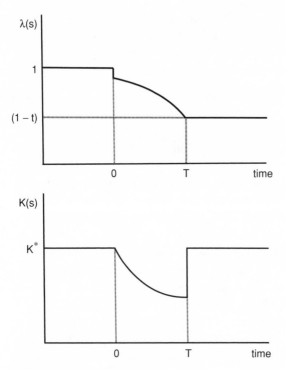

Figure 1

bites. If investors' intertemporal elasticity of substitution is less than one, this consumption-smoothing effect outweighs the incentive to consume before uninvested profits are taxed.

With international capital mobility, however, the consumption-smoothing motive becomes irrelevant. Households can smooth their consumption and escape the future tax at the same time by investing in tax-free assets abroad. Firms, for their part, reduce investment if the current tax deduction from investment does not compensate for the higher tax on earnings that will be imposed in the future. Even if $z = 1$ and the tax is neutral once it goes into effect, firms will postpone investment until after the tax is in place in order to obtain the benefit of the tax deduction.

4. Conclusion

A stable tax on income from capital has no effect on domestic investment whether or not capital is internationally mobile provided firms can deduct the full cost of domestic investment from taxable income. New capital cannot be taxed without a reduction in supply. Old capital, however, is in fixed supply and can be taxed without distortion. Since a tax on uninvested profits is a tax on old capital only, it has no adverse economic effects. The neutrality of a tax on profit with fully deductible investment is not preserved when the tax rate is expected to change, however. With international capital mobility, investment at home declines in the transitional period between when a tax increase is first anticipated and the tax increase is implemented.

If tax rates are stable, economic efficiency dictates that $z = 1$ but leaves t free to be set in accordance with the government's distributional goals. Table 1 presents estimates of the actual values of t and z that characterized systems of profit taxation in manufacturing in OECD countries in 1991. The tax rate, t, is the corporate tax rate applied by all levels of government. The value of t in OECD countries varies from a low of 10 per cent in Ireland to a high of 56 per cent in Germany with most countries clustered around 40 per cent.

All OECD countries rely on a depreciation schedule rather than allow an immediate deduction of the cost of investment. The parameter z in our model, however, can be redefined as the present value of the depreciation allowance. According to the OECD estimates, the actual value of z for investment in machinery is around 90 per cent in all but a few countries. The present value of the depreciation allowance for buildings is lower, with a median value of 70 per cent.

One commonly used measure of the inefficiency of the corporate tax system is the tax wedge, defined as the proportional difference between what firms' required return on investments would be in the absence of taxes and firms' required return with taxes. In the model of this paper, the tax wedge is given by the formula (from equation 15):

$$\left[1 - \frac{1 - t}{1 - zt} \right] = \frac{(1 - z)t}{1 - zt}. \tag{27}$$

If $z = 0$, the tax wedge is equal to the tax rate t. For $z = 1$, the tax wedge is zero.

The third and fifth columns of Table 1 present the tax wedge implied by the observed values of t and z. The median OECD country, with profit tax rate of 39 per cent and a depreciation allowance for machinery of 90 per cent in present value terms, has a tax wedge of 6 per cent for investment in machinery. If, for example, the required net return on the absence of taxes is 5 per cent and depreciation is 10 per cent, $r = 0.05$ and $\delta = 0.10$ in

Table 1. *Profit Taxation in Manufacturing in OECD Countries (1991)*

	t	z for Machinery	Implied tax Wedge for Machinery	z for Buildings	Implied Tax Wedge for Buildings
Australia	.39	.89	.06	.58	.21
Austria	.39	1.05	−.04	.89	.07
Belgium	.39	.94	.04	.80	.11
Canada	.36	.77	.12	.55	.20
Denmark	.38	.90	.06	.73	.14
Finland	.40	.90	.06	.75	.14
France	.34	.93	.04	.74	.12
Germany	.56	.92	.10	.80	.21
Greece	.40	.92	.05	.82	.11
Iceland	.45	.55	.27	.51	.28
Ireland	.10	.91	.01	.88	.01
Italy	.48	.85	.12	.63	.25
Japan	.50	.82	.16	.53	.32
Luxembourg	.39	.93	.04	.70	.16
Netherlands	.35	.88	.06	.65	.16
New Zealand	.33	.77	.10	.51	.19
Norway	.51	.90	.09	.75	.21
Portugal	.40	.90	.06	.74	.14
Spain	.35	.87	.07	.67	.15
Sweden	.30	.90	.04	.65	.13
Switzerland	.30	.90	.04	.73	.11
Turkey	.49	.88	.10	.73	.21
UK	.34	.89	.06	.70	.14
USA	.38	.91	.05	.63	.19
Median	.39	.90	.06	.70	.16

Data definitions and sources: The tax rate t is the combined corporate tax rate applied by all levels of government. The depreciation parameter z is the net present value of the depreciation allowance per unit of investment spending, assuming of a real interest rate of 3 per cent. Data are from OECD (1991: 69–71). The implied tax wedge is defined in the text.

Country notes: The corporate tax rates for Belgium, Canada, Finland, Japan, UK and the US do not include the special, lower tax rates for small businesses. The corporate tax rates for France and Germany are the tax rates that apply to retained earnings. The tax rate for the Netherlands is the rate for earnings above a threshold. Switzerland has a progressive tax on corporate profits. The figures in the table correspond to the OECD's estimate of the 'typical' tax rate in Switzerland. The figures for the US are based on an estimate of the average tax imposed by state and local governments.

equation (15), then tax system of the median OECD country raises the required gross return on investment in machinery from 15 per cent to (1.06)(0.15) or 15.9 per cent. Investments that yield a return greater than 15 per cent but less than 15.9 per cent would not be accepted because of tax considerations. For buildings, the median tax wedge of 16 per cent implies that firms would require a pre-tax gross return of (1.16) (0.15) or 17.4 per cent to invest.

The tax wedges calculated in Table 1 are the hypothetical tax wedges implied by the corporate tax rate and the depreciation allowance alone. Actual corporate tax systems include other tax instruments. Many OECD countries still have some form of general investment tax relief in addition to the depreciation allowance (OECD, 1991: 62). All OECD countries allow interest payments to be deducted from the tax base (OECD, 1991: 90). Thus, actual tax wedges are significantly less than those implied by calculations based upon the depreciation allowance alone. In the case of machinery at least, the aggregate tax wedge calculated by the OECD is very close to zero (OECD, 1991: 100).

In sum, prevailing systems of taxation of profits are close to neutral with regard to investment in machinery, and are only moderately harmful for investment in buildings. Given the possibility and, in the case of machinery, actuality of neutral taxes on profits, the argument that increased capital mobility forced all governments in the 1980s to reduce tax rates on profits can be rejected. A government worried about tax disincentives for domestic investment in a world with extensive capital mobility can easily increase z rather than reduce t.

The question remains, then, of what can explain the widespread reduction in the tax rate on income from profits that occurred in almost all OECD countries during the 1980s. In some countries, notably the United States and Great Britain, the reduction in taxes on income from capital can be explained in straightforward fashion as conservative governments rewarding their core constituents. In other countries, where the tax reductions were adopted by social democratic governments, employment concerns may have played a prominent role. As we have shown in this paper, international capital mobility increases the efficacy of changes in the profit tax as an instrument of macroeconomic policy. When capital is mobile across borders, the announcement of a future reduction of the tax on profits can induce an immediate increase in investment and employment that lasts until the tax goes into effect.

There is another aspect of the tax system that may explain a significant part of the general reduction of profit tax rates in the 1980s. In our model, we assumed a uniform tax rate and depreciation allowance for all types of plant and equipment. In fact, different assets are not treated equally. As the data presented in Table 1 reveal, all countries favor investment in machinery over investment in buildings. The most striking finding of the study of taxes on capital in the US, UK, Sweden and Germany by King and Fullerton (1984) was the variation of effective tax rates applied to different types of investment. Even if the tax system is roughly neutral with regard to the level of aggregate investment, profit taxes reduce the efficiency of investment when different assets are taxed at different rates. Proposals to eliminate tax loopholes and broaden the tax base obtained support from all sides of the ideological spectrum. As a matter of economics, the analysis of our paper indicates that there is no necessary connection between the efficiency of the system of profit taxes, which depends on both uniform treatment and full deducibility of investment costs, and the rate at which profits are taxed. As a matter of political feasibility, however, it may well have been necessary to compensate the losers of industry-specific tax exemptions with a general reduction in the tax rate.

Increased international integration of financial markets increases the social costs of the distortionary taxes on income from capital. What cannot be explained by the increased capital mobility is why most OECD countries responded by lowering the rate at which profits are taxed. Tax neutrality can be attained with either a zero tax on profits or 100 per cent deductibility of investment. Only the first alternative is incompatible with taxing the profits earned from the existing capital stock.

Similar conclusions may be warranted in regard to other taxes as well. Large differences in the value-added tax cannot survive the elimination of border controls. However, the value-added tax can, in principle, be replaced by an expenditure tax, levied like an income tax.[17] Taxes on labor may be constrained by free labor mobility, but the problem of movement to low-tax countries is mitigated by the fact that public services financed by taxes are generally only available to residents.

It is appealing to explain the general decline in support for redistributive policies in Western Europe and elsewhere in terms of the increased mobility of capital across national borders, which is often explained, in turn, by

---

[17] The base of an expenditure tax is income earned from all sources minus the change in total savings.

Capital Taxation with Open Borders

advances in computer and telecommunications technology. Technological determinism is a powerful argument. In addition, the simultaneous occurrence of financial market integration and the shift to more conservative policies lends the argument empirical plausibility. However, our analysis of taxes on income from capital with open capital markets indicates that a central link in the chain of reasoning is weak. That increased economic integration and capital mobility is forcing governments to modify prevailing systems of taxation is unassailable. The argument that increased international mobility of capital forces governments to reduce the amount of taxes collected from owners of capital is full of holes.

References

Abel, Andrew B., and Blanchard, Olivier J. (1983) 'An intertemporal model of saving and investment', *Econometrica* 51: 675–92.
Bates, Robert and Da-Hsiang D. Lien (1985) 'A note on taxation, development and representative government', *Politics and Society* 14: 53–70.
Bird, Richard M. and McClure, Jr, Charles E. (1989) 'The personal income tax in an interdependent world', paper presented at the International Seminar in Public Economics, Erasmus University, Rotterdam.
Brown, E. Cary (1948) 'Business-income taxation and investment incentives', in L. A. Meltzer and E. D. Domar *et al.* (eds) *Income, Employment and Public Policy: Essays in Honor of A. H. Hansen*, New York: W.W. Norton.
Epstein, Gerald A. and Schor, Juliet B. (1992) 'Structural determinants and economic effects of capital controls in the OECD', in Tariq Banuri and Juliet B. Schor (eds) *Financial Openness and National Autonomy*, Oxford: Clarendon Press.
Frankel, Jeffrey A. (1989) 'Quantifying international capital mobility in the 1980s', Cambridge, MA: NBER Working Paper No. 2856.
Frieden, J. (1990) 'International finance, national governments and economic interest groups', presented at the Conference on the Impact of the International Order on the National State, 5–7 September, Cambridge, England.
Giovannini, Alberto (1989) 'National tax systems versus the European capital market', *Economic Policy* 9: 346–86.
Hall, Robert E. (1988) 'Intertemporal substitution in consumption', *Journal of Political Economy* 96: 339–57.
Howitt, Peter and Sinn, Hans-Werner (1989) 'Gradual reforms of capital income taxation', *American Economic Review* 79: 106–24.
King, Mervyn A. and Fullerton, Don (1984) *The Taxation of Income from Capital: A Comparative Study of the United States, the United Kingdom, Sweden and West Germany*, Chicago: University of Chicago Press.
Lee, Dwight and McKenzie, Richard (1989) 'The international political economy of declining tax rates', *National Tax Journal* 62: 79–83.
McKenzie, Richard and Lee, Dwight (1991) *Quicksilver Capital: How the Rapid Movement of Wealth Has Changed the World*, New York: Free Press.

Meade Committee (1978) *The Structure and Reform of Direct Taxation: Report of a Committee Chaired by J. E. Meade*, London: Allen and Unwin.

OECD (Organization for Economic Cooperation and Development) (1989) *Economies in Transition*, Paris: OECD.

―――― (1991) *Taxing Profits in a Global Economy*, Paris: OECD.

Przeworski, Adam and Wallerstein, Michael (1988) 'The structural dependence of the state on capital', *American Political Science Review*, 82: 11–29.

Quinn, Dennis (1992) 'International capital flows: a twenty-one country study of financial liberalization 1950–1988', paper presented at the 1992 Annual Meetings of the American Political Science Association, Washington DC.

Seierstad, Atle and Sydsæter, Knut (1987) *Optimal Control Theory with Economic Applications*, Amsterdam: North-Holland.

Sinn, Hans-Werner (1987) *Capital Resource Taxation and Resource Allocation*, Amsterdam: North Holland.

Slemrod, Joel (1988) 'Effect of taxation with international capital mobility', in Henry J. Aaron, Harvey Galper and Joseph A. Pechman (eds) *Uneasy Compromise: Problems of a Hybrid Income-Consumption Tax*. Washington DC: Brookings Institution.

Steinmo, Sven (1990) 'The end of redistributive taxation? Tax reform in a globalizing world economy', paper presented at the 1990 Annual Meetings of the American Political Science Association, San Francisco, CA.

―――― (1993) *Taxation and Democracy: Swedish. British and American Approaches to Financing the Modern State*, New Haven, CT: Yale University Press.

Swank, Duane (1992) 'Politics and the structural dependence of the state in democratic capitalist nations', *American Political Science Review* 86: 38–54.

―――― (1993) 'Social democracy, equity and efficiency in an interdependent world', paper presented at the Annual Meetings of the American Political Science Association, 2–5 September, Washington DC.

Tanzi, Vito and Bovenberg, A. Lans (1990) 'Is there a need for harmoninzing capital income taxes within EC countries?' Working Paper 90/17, Washington DC: International Monetary Fund.

PART II

The Politics of Labor Organizations

6

Introduction

Miriam A. Golden

Empirical work on trade unions and organized labor in advanced nations underwent a resurgence beginning in the 1970s. The initial impetus was twofold: first, the strike wave that in the closing years of the 1960s swept across the European countries – most markedly France and Italy, but elsewhere as well (Crouch and Pizzorno 1978) – and second, the growing recognition in the years following the first oil shock in the winter of 1973 that wage militancy was a potentially important factor affecting inflation, unemployment, and ultimately economic growth (Bruno and Sachs 1985; Olson 1982). These two sets of events sparked new interest in problems of comparative trade unions, industrial relations, and wage militancy, problems that had lain largely outside the purview of political science in the preceding decades. Unions were now seen as political organizations, both in the sense that their internal organization exhibited political features and in the sense that their activities carried with them consequences of significance for the political realm.

This part includes four of Michael Wallerstein's most important contributions to the study of trade unions in advanced industrial economies. Although the papers display a range of analytic strategies, they are all concerned with understanding variations in union strength and organization, as well as the possible effects of these variations on wage outcomes. A central thread connecting all four essays concerns the centralization of collective bargaining, a core topic of Wallerstein's (1985) doctoral dissertation, to which he returned many times thereafter. Wallerstein's view was that groups of workers whose wages were set at the central level were better off than groups whose wages were set through a more fragmented, piecemeal bargaining process. Centralized bargaining helped workers who were most vulnerable in the market to pull up their wages, thereby effecting greater wage compression than otherwise would be the case. Because it led to more egalitarian wage outcomes, with the less well paid its main beneficiaries, centralized bargaining arrangements were, Wallerstein believed, normatively desirable.

Among the OECD countries, those with the most centralized collective bargaining processes – and therefore also highly egalitarian wage outcomes – were for most of the postwar era the Scandinavian social democracies. Wallerstein took a particular interest in these countries, becoming especially knowledgeable about them and spending a year in residence at the University of Oslo. However, although familiarity with the Scandinavian countries informed his work, he set this knowledge in cross-national context. He asked fundamentally comparative questions: how some union movements come to be highly organized, internally cohesive, and centralized in their wage-setting activities whereas others do not; whether these characteristics could endure in the face of the globalization and neoliberalism of the 1990s and after; and what are the systematic effects of these characteristics.

The intellectual context in which Wallerstein initially formulated these questions was dominated in political science by the concept of neocorporatism (Schmitter and Lehmbruch 1979) and subsequently the theme of varieties of capitalism (Hall and Soskice 2001). These two related literatures had in common the attempt to distinguish among types of political economies in the advanced nations, with the goal of assessing how these different types affected outcomes such as economic growth, unemployment, and inflation. The types themselves were distinguished using various criteria, among them the organization of the labor market and the system of industrial relations. The concept of neocorporatism, for instance, was meant to capture the centralized bargaining systems and integrated systems of elite policy making that led to the low strike levels, wage moderation, and wage compression observed in the Scandinavian nations. Wallerstein brought to this discussion the tools of economics and a deep commitment to the rigor of cross-national statistical analysis. He reformulated questions arising out of the neocorporatist literature in terms of variables instead of types of institutional arrangements or sets of countries. For instance, he asked how different degrees of bargaining centralization affected wage outcomes, how occupational change affected rates of union density, and how union density affected bargaining arrangements.

Initially, answering these questions systematically proved impossible, given the absence of precise and complete descriptive information about the

110

features of unions and bargaining structures across countries. Wallerstein was thus led to assemble data himself in his study of the political economy of trade unions in the advanced nations. The main dataset he worked on (first reported in Golden, Lange, and Wallerstein 1999; now available as Golden, Lange, and Wallerstein 2006) offered a range of systematic information, completing other important efforts of data assembly undertaken more or less simultaneously, such as Ebbinghaus and Visser (2000). A notable feature of the papers reprinted here is that they all take advantage of new datasets. Moreover, the three empirical papers included in this section are attentive not only to issues of data collection and dataset assembly, but also to those of concept definition and measurement, indicator construction, and other aspects of the empirical research process that require painstaking, and often hidden, effort.

In Chapter 7, "Union Organization in Advanced Industrial Democracies," Wallerstein takes on the challenge of explaining the very considerable variation in trade union density that we observe across the advanced nations, where unions organize less than 20 percent of the labor force in the United States but over 90 percent in Sweden. He proposes a novel explanation for this variation: the total size of the labor force in each country. Adopting the perspective of the union itself, as it decides how many resources to invest in organizing workers, Wallerstein contends that target density rates decline as the size of the labor force increases. The key to understanding why lies with his assumption that the cost to the union of convincing a worker to join is the same for each additional member regardless of whether the union has already organized only a few or many workers. It is as a result more expensive for the union to organize the same proportion of workers as the size of the pool increases. Unions in larger labor markets thus end up with a smaller proportion of the workforce as members, all else equal.

To evaluate this line of argument, Wallerstein first writes down a formal model and then tests it econometrically using data on union membership in 20 advanced industrial democracies in the 1970s. He finds the size of the labor force to be a consistent negative predictor of density: as the labor force size grows, a smaller proportion of the labor force joins trade union organizations. In large countries, such as the United States, a smaller fraction of the labor force is unionized than in small countries, such as Sweden, Belgium, or Norway.

Wallerstein's thesis proved controversial, eliciting a formal response by John Stephens and a rejoinder by Wallerstein in the *American Political Science Review* (Stephens and Wallerstein 1991). Stephens argues, contra

Wallerstein, that more concentrated industrial structures are associated with higher rates of union density, and that a reanalysis of Wallerstein's data using a proxy for industrial concentration produces results that do not allow us to untangle industrial concentration from country size. Stephens's view is that small countries exhibit greater industrial concentration, which in turn facilitates unionization. The main intuition underlying this argument is that there are economies of scale to organizing: membership drives in large establishments are proportionally less expensive than those that must be conducted across myriad small plants. Hence, where industrial concentration is greater, unions are able to organize higher proportions of workers for the same cost. Wallerstein's key response is that there is no evidence that the average plant size is larger in small countries, and that an absence of data on industrial concentration for nearly half of the countries in the sample weakens Stephens's analysis. Ultimately, then, the debate remains unresolved due to the unavailability of appropriate data.

The second of the four pieces included in this section is Wallerstein's Chapter 8, "Centralized Bargaining and Wage Restraint," a formal study of the mechanisms underlying the thesis that centralized bargaining both moderates overall wage levels and produces more egalitarian wage outcomes. The model builds on the distinction between complements and substitutes in production. Where workers are complements, both groups are necessary to produce the final output. An example is provided by the airline industry, which relies not only on pilots but also on workers in the food service industry and on air traffic controllers, each of which group is organized by a separate trade union. Examples of workers who are substitutes arise in settings where multiple unions organize similar workers; for instance, in Italy, where multiple competing confederations organize in each industry. Where workers compete as substitutes, their bargaining power is reduced unless they ally into a single bargaining unit because employers can use one group as strikebreakers against the other. Because of this, unions naturally seek to organize workers who are substitutes into a single bargaining unit; historically, the very process of unionization itself proceeds along these lines. Centralized bargaining occurs, in contrast, when complementary workers who are organized in different unions share a common bargaining arrangement, so that wages are set across otherwise distinct union organizations.

Wallerstein studies the effects of this type of bargaining arrangement on both real and relative wages. He examines how wage outcomes differ between centralized and decentralized wage setting, and shows how centralized wage setting, which organizes unions of complementary workers, leads to smaller wage differentials between groups of workers as well as a lower average rate of growth of real wages. The model builds on earlier studies of wage moderation under centralized bargaining (Calmfors and Driffill 1988). The innovation in Wallerstein's model consists in working out implications of the idea that centralized bargaining unites workers who are complements in productive activities; this carries with it specific implications for how centralized bargaining internalizes in union decision making what otherwise would be bargaining externalities.

The third essay in this section is a descriptive study of characteristics of union organization in twelve advanced industrial nations. Coauthored with Miriam Golden and Peter Lange, Chapter 9, "Postwar Trade-Union Organization and Industrial Relations in Twelve Countries," presents data collected by the three scholars on unions and industrial relations since 1980 along four dimensions: union density, coverage, concentration, and authority. On the final item, the authors present information on both unions and employers' organizations. They find that density has generally declined in the countries examined; that union coverage has likewise declined; and that the ability of traditional labor organizations to exercise representational monopoly has declined (interconfederal concentration) while national confederations have redundant consolidated their affiliates into fewer and larger organizations (intraconfederal concentration). The authority patterns within labor organizations have barely changed over the past few decades, however.

Wallerstein and his coauthors conclude that in only two countries (Britain and the United States) is there strong evidence of any very substantial weakening of organized labor along multiple dimensions. In other countries, unions appear to be undergoing decline on some dimensions, while on other dimensions their strength remains intact. The authors are reluctant to endorse the view that unions are not necessarily undergoing crisis, however. Rather, they argue that because union organizations continue to differ among nations, uniform patterns are difficult to discern.

This essay speaks to Wallerstein's characteristic caution and balance in empirical analysis, a studied reluctance to offer sweeping and therefore arguably inaccurate generalizations. Moreover, when Wallerstein makes strong statements about the world, these are couched in terms of relationships among variables at the subnational level rather than in terms of country-level characteristics. In this regard, he represented a new generation of scholarship in comparative politics, one inspired by the arguments advanced by Przeworski and Teune (1970), which argued for precisely such an approach.

In Chapter 10, "Unions in Decline? What Has Changed and Why", Wallerstein and his coauthor Bruce Western examine changes in union density, the coverage of union contracts, the centralization of wage setting, and union concentration in sixteen advanced industrial countries between 1950 and 1992. Using the dataset assembled by Golden, Lange, and Wallerstein (1999), Wallerstein and Western document that in the period since 1980, union density has declined in most of the countries included in the analysis, and wage bargaining has become more decentralized. At the same time, union organizations have become more concentrated, as national labor confederations have consolidated membership into smaller numbers of larger affiliates. Wallerstein and Western argue that existing theories appear to be inadequate to explain the recent declines in union organization. Instead, they suggest, some kind of break occurred in the 1980s; the world has changed fundamentally, so that the prior determinants of union organization no longer explain the changes we observe. Although they leave open the question of what this might be, this paper resonates with other work that identifies a period break in the political economy of the advanced nations after the oil shocks (Blanchard and Wolfers 2000).

If I were to summarize the intellectual contribution made by the four essays in this section, I would suggest it is threefold. First, these four essays all advance the proposition that the internal organization of trade unions is important for such economic outcomes as wage levels and relativities. In particular, the centralization of bargaining emerges as especially important. Second, the empirical essays in this section document that it is possible to measure characteristics of unions systematically across both time and countries, even for features that are less obviously quantifiable. Third, these essays demonstrate that once we do collect such data, it becomes more difficult to sustain sweeping generalizations about the politics of trade unions in the advanced nations.

References

Blanchard, Olivier, and Justin Wolfers. 2000. "The Role of Shocks and Institutions in the Rise of European Unemployment: The Aggregate Evidence." *Economic Journal 111* (462, March): 1–33.

Bruno, Michael, and Jeffrey Sachs. 1985. *The Economics of Worldwide Stagflation.* Cambridge: Harvard University Press.

Introduction

Calmfors, Lars, and John Driffill. 1988. "Bargaining Structure, Corporatism, and Macroeconomic Performance." *Economic Policy 3* (6, April): 13–61.

Crouch, Colin, and Alessandro Pizzorno, eds. 1978. *The Resurgence of Class Conflict in Western Europe since 1968.* 2 vols.; New York: Holmes & Meier.

Ebbinghaus, Bernhard, and Jelle Visser. 2000. *The Development of Trade Unions in Western Europe since 1945.* New York: Palgrave Macmillan.

Golden, Miriam A., Peter Lange, and Michael Wallerstein. 1999. *Dataset on Unions, Employers, Collective Bargaining and Industrial Relations for 16 OECD Countries.* Available at http://www.shelley.polsci.ucla.edu/data.

Golden, Miriam, Peter Lange, and Michael Wallerstein. 2006. *Union Centralization among Advanced Industrial Societies: An Empirical Study.* Available at http://www.shelley.polisci.ucla.edu/. Version dated June 16, 2006

Hall, Peter A., and David Soskice. 2001. *Varieties of Capitalism: The Institutional Foundations of Comparative Advantage.* New York: Oxford University Press.

Olson, Mancur. 1982. *The Rise and Decline of Nations: Economic Growth, Stagflation and Social Rigidities.* New Haven: Yale University Press.

Przeworski, Adam, and Henry Teune. 1970. *The Logic of Comparative Social Inquiry.* New York: Wiley.

Schmitter, Philippe C., and Gerhard Lehmbruch, eds. 1979. *Trends towards Corporatist Intermediation.* Beverly Hills: Sage Publications.

Stephens, John D., and Michael Wallerstein. 1991. "Industrial Concentration, Country Size, and Trade Union Membership," *American Political Science Review 85* (3, Sept.): 941–953.

Wallerstein, Michael. 1985. "Working Class Solidarity and Rational Behavior." Unpublished dissertation, Department of Political Science, University of Chicago.

7

Union Organization in Advanced Industrial Democracies

Michael Wallerstein

Few features of economic, social, or political life in industrialized democracies differ as much as the relative size of the trade union movement. The current density of union membership in the labor force ranges over almost the entire spectrum from above 90% in Sweden to under 20% in the United States (Goldfield 1987, 16). The level of unionization varies far more than such other characteristics of the labor force as the sectoral distribution of workers, the share of wages in GNP, rates of unemployment, or even the size of the public sector. Unionization rates vary more than such other forms of popular mobilization as electoral turnout or the share of the vote received by parties bearing communist, socialist, social democratic, or labor labels.

The economic effects of high levels of unionization are ambiguous. Unions that are large relative to the economy may simultaneously have more power in the labor market and more of an incentive to moderate their wage demands. A union that covers only a small fraction of an industry's work force, for example, can gain wage increases partly at the expense of employment among nonunion members, provided that union members have specialized skills not readily available elsewhere. In contrast, an industrial union covering the entire work force would be concerned with employment in all job categories. Bigger unions are not necessarily more militant unions (Cameron 1984; Olson 1982, chap. 4).

Part of this paper is drawn from a typescript coauthored with Adam Przeworski in 1984 entitled "Unionization as a Union Strategy." I am indebted to Jane Peterson and Robert Pahre for their assistance in gathering the data and to George Tsebelis, Miriam Golden, Jim DeNardo, Barbara Geddes, Jeff Frieden, Doug Rivers, Harold Wilensky, Gar Alperovitz, Richard Jankowski, Sandy Jacoby, Eric Rasmusen, and Michael Goldfield for their help and comments. Financial support was provided by the Institute for Industrial Relations, University of California, Los Angeles.

The political consequences of high levels of unionization are more straightforward. There is general agreement that, other things being equal, union movements representing a large share of voters are better able to influence policy. Union density is often used, either alone or in combination with measures of union centralization and unity, as an indicator of union power in cross-national comparisons of employment and welfare policy (Cameron 1984; Hicks 1988; Hicks and Swank 1984a, 1984b; Korpi 1983; Korpi and Shalev 1979, 1980; Stephens 1980). In addition, high levels of unionization are positively associated with the electoral support received by Socialist, Social Democratic, or Labor parties (Korpi 1983; Przeworski and Sprague 1986; Shalev and Korpi 1980; Stephens 1980).[1] Union density is an important – albeit not the only – determinant of union strength in the political arena as well as the market.

Table 1 presents union membership as a percentage of potential members (defined as all wage and salary earners plus the unemployed) in advanced industrial societies in the late 1970s.[2] The distribution of unionization rates was surprisingly uniform between the extremes of Sweden and Israel on the one hand and the United States on the other. In particular, while the United

[1] The direction of causality is unclear. This question is discussed below.

[2] Collecting data on union density is fraught with difficulties (Bain and Price 1980, chap. 1). Membership figures are provided by the unions with the inevitable result that their reliability varies from country to country. Union members are defined as the people listed on the unions' membership rolls. This is generally close to but larger than the number of people who pay union dues: apprentices and unemployed and retired workers are often exempted from the payment of dues, and all unions allow members to be in arrears for a period of time before being struck from the list. In France, however, the proportion of workers on the membership rolls who pay dues is probably around 10% (Adam 1983). In Israel, where individuals who are not economically active may join the General Federation of Labor (Histadrut) to gain access to the Histadrut's health care system, union membership exceeds the number of wage and salary earners by 50%. Unions may have an incentive to inflate their membership figures to impress employers or the government or to increase their representation in the national union confederation. On the other hand, unions also have an incentive to deflate their membership figures in order to reduce the dues owed the confederation. Goldfield (1987, 9) suggests that some of the reported decline in union density in the United States in the 1970s may be due to an increase in underreporting following large increases in the per capita taxes assessed by the AFL-CIO. Membership figures often include retired workers who maintain their membership and thus overstate the proportion of the work force that is unionized. At the same time, membership figures are often understated in that members of unions not affiliated with the major union confederations are excluded. In sum, in spite of the measurement error, there appears to be no clear bias in union membership figures. An additional difficulty in comparing union density figures stems from differences in the definition of the denominator. For this reason I collected figures for union membership, not union density, and divided by the number of wage and salary earners plus the unemployed for all countries except Israel.

Table 1. *Union Membership as a Percentage of Potential Union Members in Advanced Industrial Democracies (late 1970s)*

Country (Year)	Union Density
Sweden (1979)	82.4[a]
Israel (1979)	80.0[b]
Iceland (1975)	74.3
Finland (1980)	73.3
Belgium (1977)	71.9
Denmark (1980)	69.8
Ireland (1978)	68.1
Austria (1977)	65.6
New Zealand (1979)	59.4
Norway (1979)	58.9
Australia (1979)	51.4
Italy (1978)	50.6
United Kingdom (1976)	48.0
Germany (1979)	39.6
Netherlands (1979)	37.7
Switzerland (1979)	35.4
Canada (1980)	31.2
Japan (1979)	31.0
France (1979)	28.2
United States (1978)	24.5

Note: Potential union members are defined to be all wage and salary earners plus the unemployed. Data sources are listed in Appendix B. Union density in Luxembourg in 1978 was over 60% (Coldrick and Jones 1979). How much over is impossible to say as membership data for two of the three large labor organizations outside the main confederations are unavailable.

[a] Bain and Price (1980, 143) report a significantly higher unionization rate for Sweden – 92.9 – in 1977. Bain and Price note that their figure for Sweden includes retired union members which they estimate to comprise between 3% and 8% of the total (139).

[b] Dividing membership in the Histadrut by total wage and salary earners plus the unemployed results in a unionization rate of around 150%. Coldrick and Jones (1979, 1179) estimate that 85% of wage earners are members of the Histadrut while the estimate of the U.S. Department of Labor (1980, 145) is between 75% and 80%. The figure of 80% seems a suitable compromise.

States was at the low end of the spectrum, it was hardly in a class of its own. The unionization rates in France, Japan, and Canada were only slightly higher.

Cross-national differences in union density have increased since the mid-1950s, with unionization steadily declining in countries at the low end of the spectrum, such as the United States and Japan, while continually growing in countries at the high end, such as Sweden and Denmark (Bain and Price 1980; Troy and Sheflin 1985). Yet the relative positions of countries for which time series data exist have not changed much in the past three decades. In the postwar period the variation of union density among Western democracies far surpasses the variation over time within countries for which data are available.[3]

While there has been little work that attempts to explain cross-national differences in union density, there is a large and interesting empirical literature on the dynamics of union growth.[4] In fact Samuel Gompers was an early theorist. In 1904 he presented his view as follows: "From the formation of the first bona fide trade union movement in modern times, it has grown with each era of industrial activity and receded to some degree with each industrial depression, but with each recurring period of depression it has receded to a lesser degree than its immediate predecessors" (cited in Lorwin 1933, 233). This business cycle hypothesis was taken up by Commons and his associates at the University of Wisconsin (1918) and seemingly confirmed in empirical studies by Barnett (1916) and Weyworth (1917). During periods of high demand for goods and tight labor markets, the reasoning went, rising prices eroded real wages, prompting workers to join unions in defense of their real income while the greater effectiveness of strikes lowered the resistance of employers.

In the 1920s, however, the business cycle hypothesis suffered major damage by the failure of unions to grow. When unions began to rebound in the depths of the Great Depression, the procyclical hypothesis appeared decisively refuted. Dunlop (1949, 191) inaugurated a new phase of the discussion with an argument that union growth occurred either in periods of war when demand was particularly high and labor was in particularly short supply or in periods of "fundamental unrest," when the organization of unions

---

[3] This was not true prior to the Second World War. In Germany the unionization rate quadrupled from 1918 to 1920, then fell by one-half from 1922 to 1925. British union density tripled between 1910 and 1920 and fell by 50% in the subsequent decade 1920–30 (Bain and Price 1980). Of the eight countries studied by Bain and Price – Australia, Denmark, Canada, Germany, Sweden, the United Kingdom, and the United States – the United States and Canada had the lowest and second lowest union densities throughout the interwar period. Union density in Sweden, however, did not surpass German or British levels until the mid-1920s.

[4] This discussion of the literature on union growth is drawn from a survey by Przeworski (1984).

"represented a basic dissatisfaction with the performance of the economic system and the society in general." In the early 1950s Bernstein (1954) called for a "pluralist" conception of union growth allowing for different causes of union growth in different historical periods. In fact, Bernstein gave greatest emphasis to the impact of legislation. Shister (1953), similarly doubtful about the explanatory power of the business cycle hypothesis, argued that union leadership was decisive.

Ashenfelter and Pencavel (1969) initiated the third and final phase of the discussion by successfully fitting a relatively simple equation to union membership in the United States between 1904 and 1960. An econometric literature soon developed with scholars estimating time series models of union membership data from the turn of the century to the recent past in a half dozen countries (Bain and Elsheikh 1976; Hines 1964, 1969; Sharpe 1971; Swindinsky 1974). The thrust of the econometric results can be summarized in three findings: (1) the rehabilitation of the business cycle hypothesis – business cycle variables, primarily price inflation and secondarily unemployment and wage inflation, explain most of the variance of annual changes in union membership in all countries; (2) the saturation effect – as union density increases, union growth slows down; (3) the relative unimportance of political variables – political variables, by and large, did not have a discernable effect on union growth. For example, Bain and Elsheikh (1976) fit a business cycle model of union growth in four countries: the United Kingdom, United States, Australia, and Sweden. Only in Australia prior to 1913 and in the United States from 1937–47 did the fit of the model improve with the addition of a political dummy variable. Other political variables had no impact.

The new business cycle models have not escaped criticism. Moore and Pearce (1978); Sheflin, Troy, and Koeller (1983); and Fiorito (1982) have shown that the models lack stability: when estimated for the postwar period alone, many of the coefficients on the key cyclical variables lose significance and even change sign. Moreover, the connection between the statistical models of union growth and economic theory is vague. Unions tend to be portrayed as defending whatever happens to be the income of their current members rather than maximizing some objective function under the constraint of the response of employers or the government. Most importantly for my subject, the large national differences in union density remain a mystery when union growth is primarily explained by cyclical movements in prices and unemployment.

The prevalent explanations of the variance of unionization rates, whether in time series or cross-sectional studies, generally focus on circumstances that either increase the propensity of unorganized workers to join unions or reduce the cost of unionization for employers (Hirsch and Addison 1986, chap. 3). In contrast, I concentrate on the unions' decision to allocate resources to the recruitment of new members. From the traditional perspective, union growth occurs when workers organize unions. But it is equally true that union growth occurs when unions organize workers. In my analysis unions are the central actors.

That the level of unionization is the subject of strategic decisions made by union is still a novel perspective among scholars of comparative politics.[5] Craft unions – unions that restrict entry – are not very popular among those who are not members, scholars included. The restrictive practices of the American Federation of Labor are attributed to the "nativism" or the "racism" of U.S. workers. In Great Britain the "labor aristocracy" is charged not only with betraying their fellow class comrades but with sharing the spoils of imperialist exploitation. On the other hand, unions that are committed to organizing "every man who earns his livelihood either by his brain or his muscle" (in the words of Big Bill Haywood at the founding convention of the Industrial Workers of the World, quoted in Weinstein 1975, 9) are regarded as examples of selfless, if impractical, dedication to the ideals of class solidarity. In contrast to both views, unions are regarded here as organizations seeking to do the best for their members under different circumstances, whether at a particular time they aggressively mount organizing drives or let membership decline through attrition and retirement.

In the next section bargaining theory is used to model the impact of union density on the outcome of collective bargaining. The model is expanded in the third section to derive the level of unionization that maximizes the benefits received by union members. The central conclusion of the analysis – that the optimal union density is a negative function of the size of the potential union membership – is tested in the fourth section in a cross-sectional analysis of union density in advanced industrial societies where unions have been free to organize since World War II. In the concluding section the argument is generalized to encompass political objectives on

---

[5] This is no longer the case in the field of industrial relations. Block (1980), Freeman and Medoff (1984), and Goldfield (1987) all argue that a decrease in organizing effort by unions is part of the explanation of the postwar decline in union density in the United States.

the part of unions as well as organizations other than trade unions. Proofs of the propositions in the text have been collected in Appendix A.

A Model of Collective Bargaining and Union Density

Without a capacity to disrupt the supply of labor to employers, unions would be powerless participants in collective bargaining. As Wilkinson and Burkitt have written, "The ultimate sanction of union power is the ability to undertake strike action and so impose losses upon the employers of an industry" (1973, 113). The cost that unions can impose depends on the solidarity not only of their members but of all who could take their place. Unions seek to recruit new members because the presence of nonunion workers who can perform the same tasks as union members limits the gains unions can obtain at the bargaining table.

The impact of union density on the outcome of collective bargaining can be illustrated by introducing the level of unionization in a model of collective bargaining. Both unions and firms are assumed to be perfect agents of their (risk-neutral) constituents: firms maximize profits and unions maximize the expected income of union members. Let w be workers' income if they work and receive the union wage, and r their income if they are laid off or if negotiations break down and a strike ensues.[6] In addition, let the probability of remaining employed at a union job in the absence of a strike be denoted $\theta(L)$, where L represents the firms' demand for labor. Workers' expected income can be written, then, as

$$u = \begin{array}{l} \theta(L)w + [1 - \theta(L)]r \quad \text{if there is no strike} \\ r \text{ if strike occurs.} \end{array} \qquad (1)$$

The assumption in equation 1 that workers are risk-neutral – or maximize their expected income rather than their expected utility – simplifies the analysis without altering the conclusions regarding the optimal union size.[7]

[6] The assumption that workers receive the same income when on strike as when laid off is adopted purely for simplicity of exposition. Allowing the two to differ does not change my analytic conclusions significantly. Workers' reservation wage r is assumed to be strictly positive.

[7] Similarly, the assumption that workers care only about their expected income rather than a variety of pecuniary and nonpecuniary benefits such as seniority rights, grievance procedures, and working conditions is an inconsequential simplification. In the present context, all union demands that raise labor costs are equivalent.

Unless there is a strike, firms' profits, π, are defined to be the difference between their revenues, $R(L)$, and the wage bill wL. As is conventional, the marginal revenue product of labor is assumed to be positive and diminishing as employment increases with other inputs held constant, that is, $\partial R/\partial L > 0$ and $\partial^2 R/\partial L^2 < 0$. In the event of a strike, however, let firms' profits be denoted S. (The determinants of S will be elaborated shortly.) Thus, profits can be written as

$$\pi = \begin{array}{l} R(L) - wL \text{ if there is no strike} \\ S \text{ if a strike occurs.} \end{array} \qquad (2)$$

The cost of a strike to firms $[R(L) - wL - S]$ depends on the level of production that firms can maintain without the striking workers. In previous work it has generally been assumed that profits go to zero when a strike occurs (McDonald and Solow 1981). Yet the extent that a firm will have to reduce production depends, among other things, on the proportion of the firms' plants or workers that are organized and the availability and willingness of other workers to take the place of those on strike. Note that strike effectiveness depends on the proportion of the work force that refuses to work rather than the absolute number of strikers. Let M be the number of union members in the local bargaining unit, let $\Sigma M = m$ be the total membership of the union, let n be the total number of available workers with the requisite skills including both those in the union and those outside the union, and let $\mu = m/n$ be the proportion unionized or the union density. Then the profits received by firms during strikes can be written:

$$S = S(\mu, x) \quad \text{with} \quad \partial S/\partial \mu < 0 \quad \text{and} \quad \partial^2 S/\partial \mu^2 > 0. \qquad (3)$$

That $\partial S/\partial \mu < 0$ indicates that profits during a strike are a declining function of the proportion of the available workers who will refuse to work. It is assumed that $\partial^2 S/\partial \mu^2 > 0$ since, at least at high levels of unionization, further increases in union density must have a diminishing marginal impact on the union's power to reduce production (Block 1980). The variable x is a vector representing all of the factors besides the level of unionization that affect the profits or losses firms would sustain during a strike: the level of the firm's inventories or the demand for the firm's output, the support offered by an employers' association, the likely reaction of the government, legislation covering industrial conflict, etc.

Multiple solutions have been proposed to the bargaining problem. In one frequently studied case, however, where the number of union members in the bargaining unit exceeds or equals the demand for labor and all union

123

Michael Wallerstein

members are equally likely to be laid off, most bargaining solutions coincide. If $\theta(L) = L/M$ with $L \leq M$, the Nash, the Kalai-Smorodinsky, the Maschler-Perles, the proportional, and the Rubinstein solutions all yield identical results.[8] Moreover, this assumption of equal probability of layoffs is less outlandish than it appears. Lazear (1983) demonstrated that if workers are laid off strictly by seniority, unions that maximize workers' lifetime earnings will act as if to maximize $(L/M)w + [1 - (L/M)]r$ every period.

An intuitive derivation of the general bargaining solution when $\theta = L/M$ and $L \leq M$ proceeds by dividing the bargaining problem into two steps.[9] First, union members and the firm maximize the total income both sides would receive with a contract, $\pi + Mu = [R(L) - wL] + [wL + r(M - L)] = [R(L) - rL + rM]$, by agreeing to the level of employment given by the condition $\partial R/\partial L = r$. In an efficient bargain with risk-neutral workers, the level of employment is determined by the requirement that the marginal revenue product of labor equal labor's opportunity cost (Menil 1971).[10] Second, the aggregate gains to union members from an agreement, $(w - r)L$, is set equal to some share, say $\alpha(0 < \alpha < 1)$, of the gains received by both parties $(R - wL - S) + (w - r)L = (R - S - rL)$, which yields

$$w = \alpha[(R/L) - (S/L)] + (1 - \alpha)r \tag{4}$$

as the expression for union wages. Thus the wages of union members depend on the bargaining parameter, α; workers' productivity, (R/L); and the income of the firm and of workers should the two sides fail to agree, S and r. If union members could be replaced quickly with other workers

[8] Nash (1950) proved that the point on the feasibility set that maximizes the weighted geometric average of the bargaining gains is the unique solution that satisfies the axioms of Pareto optimality, the independence of affine transformations of the payoffs, and the independence of irrelevant alternatives (or, more appropriately, the irrelevance of unchosen alternatives). Other cooperative bargaining solutions drop one or more of Nash's axioms (except for Pareto optimality) and add other axioms until a different unique solution is defined. A nonaxiomatic approach to bargaining is developed by Rubinstein (1982), who reformulates the bargaining problem as a sequential game where offers and counteroffers are made until an agreement is reached. See Kalai 1985 for a recent review of cooperative bargaining theory and Sutton 1986 for an introduction to noncooperative bargaining theory. Note that the solutions differ in the case in which $L > M$ or in which the demand for labor in the plant exceeds the union local's membership (Wallerstein 1987).
[9] See Wallerstein 1987 for a more rigorous derivation of the Nash and proportional solutions for this model with $\theta(L) = \min(1, L/M)$.
[10] This is not true if unions maximize the expected utility of risk-adverse workers (McDonald and Solow 1981). However Clark (1984) finds evidence that labor contracts in the United States do satisfy this condition.

124

at the reservation wage, the firm's profit during a strike would be $S = R - rL$ and equation 4 would reduce to $w = r$. In noncooperative bargaining theory, the parameter α is determined by the relative impatience of the two sides. The more workers discount the future relative to firms, the lower is α.[11] In cooperative bargaining theory α is either set equal to one-half by an axiom of symmetry or left undetermined.

The impact of S on the bargaining outcome can be seen clearly by writing the expressions for the expected income of workers and their employers upon the conclusion of a labor agreement. Substituting equation 4 into equations 1 and 2, one obtains

$$Mu = \alpha[R(L) - S(\mu, x) - rL] + rM$$
$$\pi = (1 - \alpha)[R(L) - rL] + \alpha S(\mu, x). \tag{5}$$

As union density increases, a strike becomes more threatening (S falls) and union members obtain more of the joint surplus.[12]

The bargaining model is illustrated in Figure 1. The line with slope of -1 represents the set of feasible bargains. The solutions are the points of intersection of the bargaining frontier and the rays from the disagreement points with slopes of $(1 - \alpha)/\alpha$. As union density rises from μ^0 to μ^1, the disagreement point falls from $S(\mu^0)$ to $S(\mu^1)$, thereby raising the aggregate expected income of union members from Mu^0 to Mu^1 and reducing the profit of unionized firms from π^0 to π^1.

The Optimal Rate of Unionization from the Union's Perspective

If the story told in Figure 1 were complete, unions would always want to increase the level of unionization. But recruitment of new members is not free. Organizers must be paid. At times strikes must be called. According to estimates by Voos, the organizing cost of adding one additional union member in the United States ranged from $580 to $1,570 (1980 dollars) in the period 1964–77 (1984a, 44). Thus, if marginal costs were constant, unions would have had to spend an additional $100–300 million (1980

---

[11] In the noncooperative model, α approaches $\xi/(\varrho + \xi)$ as the time between making an offer and receiving a counteroffer goes to zero where ξ is the discount rate of the firm and ϱ is the discount rate of the union (Sutton 1986).

[12] Freeman and Medoff (1981, 567) estimate that an increase of 10 percentage points in union density at the industry level raises union wages by approximately 1.5% in U.S. manufacturing. They found no impact of union density at the industry level on nonunion wages.

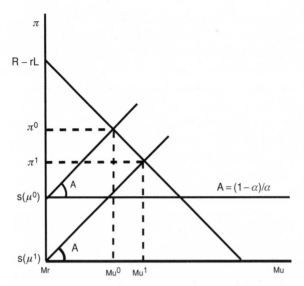

Figure 1 The Impact of Changes in Strike Effectiveness on the Bargaining Solution

dollars) per year between 1964 and 1977 to maintain union density at 1964 levels. This would have meant an increase of 50%–150% over what unions actually spent.[13] Labor legislation and the manner in which the legislation is enforced probably make union organizing particularly expensive in the United States (Freeman and Medoff 1984, chap. 15; Goldfield 1987, chap. 9; Rogers 1985). Unfortunately, comparative figures on organizing costs are unavailable. But unions in all countries that seek to recruit new members must devote resources to organizing.

Organizing costs depend on many factors: occupation (blue-collar workers are generally more highly organized than white-collar workers), plant size (large plants are more highly organized than small plants), and the threat of unemployment, as well as the political support or hostility toward union growth. In addition, organizing costs depend on the number of workers being organized.

[13] This calculation is based on the rough figure that union membership would have had to increase by 2.4 million – 185,000 per year – between 1964 and 1977 to maintain union density at its 1964 level (Goldfield 1987, 10). Voos (1984b, 56) presents organizing expenditures from 1953 to 1974 by 20 unions who collectively represent about half of the union members in the United States. I doubled Voos's figures and converted from 1967 to 1980 dollars according to the CPI to arrive at a ballpark estimate that total organizing expenditures were about $200 million in 1980 dollars per year.

126

To put these considerations in mathematical form, let the aggregate expenditures of the union on recruitment be written

$$C = C(z, y), \text{ with } \partial C/\partial z > 0 \quad \text{and} \quad \partial^2 C/\partial z^2 \geq 0, \tag{6}$$

where $z \equiv dm/dt \geq 0$ is the number of new members who are successfully recruited and y is a vector of all other factors – such as plant size, the business cycle, labor legislation, or employer resistance – that affect the total and marginal costs of recruitment.[14] The first inequality $-\partial C/\partial z > 0$ – states that costs increase as the number of workers being organized increases (Voos 1983). Otherwise, unions could achieve a larger membership by reducing their organizing efforts. The second inequality – $\partial^2 C/\partial z^2 \geq 0$ – states that marginal costs of organizing do not fall. This last assumption is necessary, at least in the neighborhood of the solution, for the existence of an optimum. If marginal costs are decreasing, unions can always do better by either expanding or contracting the scale of their organizing effort. Note that constant or increasing marginal costs does not mean that the cost per new member $C(z, y)/z$ is necessarily rising. If there are fixed costs in organizing, increasing marginal costs for all $z \geq 0$ imply a very plausible cost curve with average costs that initially fall and eventually rise as the scale of organizing increases.

Union members' expected income rises as union density grows. But union members must each pay organizing costs of $C(z,y)/m$ in union dues. From equation 5 the expected income of union members before union dues is $u = (\alpha/M)(R - S - rL) + r$. Therefore, the net income of union members in each time period is $u - (C/m) = (\alpha/M)(R - S - rL) + r - (C/m)$, which can be rewritten as $P - QS - (C/m)$, where $P \equiv [(\alpha/M)(R - rL) + r]$ and $Q \equiv \alpha/M$. Thus, a union that faithfully maximizes the present value of its members' net income with a discount rate of ϱ would choose the level of organizing activity $z(t)$ that maximizes the integral[15]:

$$\int_0^\infty e^{-\varrho t} \left[-QS[\mu(t), x] - \frac{C[z(t), y]}{m(t)} \right] dt, \tag{7}$$

where $\mu(t) \equiv m(t)/n$ and $z(t) \equiv dm/dt$.

---

[14] In previous work I allowed costs to depend also on the level of unionization in accordance with the saturation effect found in time series models of union growth. Since the saturation effect added nothing essential to the mathematical analysis, I removed it to avoid unnecessary complexity. See Wallerstein 1988b for details.

[15] The infinite time horizon is not critical. Letting the time horizon be finite and other modifications are discussed below.

The necessary conditions for an optimum are shown in the Appendix A to define a path of $\mu(t)$ that converges to a stationary level of unionization, denoted μ^* (provided $\mu(0) < \mu^*$ and $0 < \mu(t) < 1$ along the optimal path). This target union density depends on the union's rate of discount (ϱ), factors affecting the effectiveness of strikes (x), factors affecting the costs of organizing (y), and the size of the potential membership (n). The results can be summarized in the following four propositions. (All proofs are presented in Appendix A.)

Proposition 1. *As the union's discount rate ϱ increases, the target union density μ^* declines, or $\partial\mu^*/\partial\varrho < 0$.*

This is an intuitive result. Organizing drives are like an investment. The costs of recruiting new members are borne in the present while the benefits come in future negotiating rounds. The less union members care about the future, the higher the discount rate and the less unions invest in increasing the size of the union. This fits the common observation that high rates of turnover are associated with low rates of unionization.[16] For the same reason, unions with older members would devote fewer resources to organizing than unions with a young membership.

Proposition 2. *Any change that increases marginal strike effectiveness increases the target union density, or $\partial\mu^*/\partial x > 0$ if and only if $\partial^2 S/\partial\mu\partial x < 0$.*

Anything that increases the likely cost of a strike to the firm such as high levels of demand for the firms' output will increase the optimal unionization rate.[17] Defensive actions by employers' associations like the establishment of strike insurance funds may also propel unions to devote more resources to organizing by increasing the necessity of attaining high levels of density in order to strike effectively.

Proposition 3. *A change that increases total and marginal costs of recruiting new members in equal proportions will reduce the target union density, or $\partial\mu^*/\partial y < 0$ if $C(z, y) = yc(z)$ with $y > 0$.*

Proposition 3 is the counterpart of proposition 2. Changes that increase the cost of recruiting additional members, such as right-to-work legislation,

[16] It is also true that the costs of organizing in industries with high turnover are greater.
[17] If x is the price of the firm's output, $S(\mu,x) = xs(\mu)$, where $s(\mu)$ is the output that could be produced during a strike. Then $\partial^2 S/\partial\mu\partial x = \partial S/\partial\mu < 0$.

lower the target unionization rate.[18] Both propositions 2 and 3 can be readily understood with the analogy of unionizing drives as an investment. If the rate of return rises, the optimal level of investment will increase. If the cost of investing rises, the optimal level of investment falls. The focus here on the unions' preferred level of unionization is not in conflict with the usual attention given to political support for unions, the resistance of employers, and the sentiment of nonunion workers. The level of economic activity and the political environment affect the costs and benefits of organizing, in part, by influencing the willingness of nonunion members to join and employers to resist.

Proposition 4. *The target level of unionization declines as the size of the labor force increases, or $\partial \mu^* / \partial n < 0$.*

The union's optimal size may either rise or fall as the number of potential members increases. The effect of an increased number of potential members on the union's optimal density, however, is unambiguously negative. The benefits from an expansion of the union membership depend on the proportion of the relevant work force being organized. The costs, in contrast, depend in part on the absolute number of workers to be organized. Unions in large labor markets must pay a higher price than unions in small labor markets to achieve the same union density. Since the price is higher, unions in large labor markets purchase less. Even though there are more members to share the costs of organizing as the membership grows, unions maximize the net gains from organizing by organizing a smaller share of potential members when the number of potential members is large.

Many of the assumptions of the model can be easily relaxed or altered. Expected income maximization can be changed to expected utility maximization. The infinite time horizon can be replaced by a two-period model where the costs of organizing are paid in period 1 while the benefits of higher levels of unionization are received in period 2. The saturation effect noted in the time series literature can be incorporated by writing organizing costs as $C = C(z, y, \mu)$ with $\partial C / \partial \mu \geq 0$, $\partial^2 C / \partial \mu^2 \geq 0$, and $\partial^2 C / \partial z \partial \mu \geq 0$. Finally, greater realism can be added by including changes in union membership over time that are independent of organizing efforts according to the formula: $dm/dt = z(t) - \delta m(t)$, where $\delta m(t)$ represents the net effect of membership losses from retirements, quits, and layoffs and membership

---

[18] Ellwood and Fine (1987) find large decreases in union organizing at the state level after the passage of right-to-work laws.

gains from increases in employment in union shops. Most of these modifications entail increases in algebraic complexity; none alter the results.

Empirical Results

The analytical results are consistent with most of the standard explanations of variation in union density. The level of demand, the political support, plant size, occupational structure, and so on can all be understood as altering either strike effectiveness or the costs of organizing or both. What the model adds is a new potential explanation of differences in union density: the size of the labor pool. The size of the relevant work force from the point of view of a single union is the number of workers who are actual or potential substitutes in production. However, holding industry or occupation constant, the size of the relevant work force from the point of view of individual unions is likely to be related to the size of the work force of the country as a whole. Moreover, the size of the aggregate labor force is something that differs dramatically among advanced industrialized countries. The number of wage and salary and unemployed workers in the United States is 24 times the number in Sweden and over 1,000 times the number in Iceland. Perhaps the sheer number of potential union members explains an important part of cross-national variation in union density.

Dependent Variable and Sample

The dependent variable is total union membership in the late 1970s divided by the number of wage and salary earners plus the unemployed. The sample consists of the 20 advanced industrial societies that have been democracies since the end of the Second World War (with the exception of Luxembourg – for lack of adequate data). A theory premised on the choices of unions is applicable only where unions are independent of the government and can organize without fear of repression. In addition, instantaneous jumps to the optimal stationary level of union density are generally not optimal. Therefore, the unions' optimal level of density at any point in time depends on current levels of unionization as well as their target level of unionization. However, in countries where unions have been free to organize over a long period of time, the target level of union density might provide a good approximation for the actual levels attained. The countries included in the sample and their union density are listed in Table 1.

Independent Variables

Size of the Labor Force. The measure of size used is the natural log of the number of wage and salary earners plus the unemployed. Using the log of the potential membership implies that the percentage increase, rather than the absolute increase, matters for union density.[19]

Left Governments. Both common sense and the analytical results indicate that cross-national differences in the legal and political environment might have a significant impact on unionization rates. Government support that affects the cost of organizing new workers or the ability of unions to strike alters the unions' optimal level of unionization. Leftist governments are potentially important for union density for two reasons. First, leftist parties are particularly sympathetic to union views on labor legislation. Thus leftist party participation is as good a proxy as any available for the extent to which laws protect union organizing. Second, the implementation of labor law and political support more generally can be just as important as the laws themselves for union organizing. Therefore, I included an index of cumulative leftist party participation in government from 1919 to the year of the union density figure in the analysis.[20]

Yet just as leftist governments may enable or encourage unions to increase union membership, more encompassing unions may increase the votes received by leftist parties and the probability that leftist parties will govern. In many countries, union organizing was initially closely associated

[19] Using the raw size of the labor force would indicate that the addition of one million new workers would have the same impact whether it increased the labor force by 100% or only 5%.

[20] The index, developed by Wilensky (1981), gives each country from zero to three points for each year of leftist party participation in government depending on the Left's share of the parliamentary seats held by members of the governing coalition, the party of the prime minister, and whether the government has a majority in parliament. (There were no governments with leftist party participation in the presidential systems of the United States and the French Fifth Republic during the years of the index. Finland was treated as a purely parliamentary system.) Leftist parties include all Communist, Socialist, Social Democratic, and Labor Parties with the exception of the Socialist and Social Democratic Parties of Italy. Table 3 presents the country scores. An index of leftist party participation at the national level is a standard measure of the influence of leftist parties on public policy. Nevertheless, it is admittedly a rough measure that misses more subtle distinctions, such as the impact of leftist governments at the state or provincial level (possibly important in the Canadian case) or the difference between governments formed by center parties as opposed to conservative parties.

with and supportive of the political mobilization of workers by social democratic parties (Kassalow 1980; Przeworski and Sprague 1986; Shalev and Korpi 1980). Since leftist governments and union density are likely to be simultaneously determined, the method of two-stage standard least squares (SLS) was employed with a dummy variable for union centralization as the instrument.[21]

Trade Dependence. Another explanation of cross-national differences in union density, associated most prominently with the work of Cameron (1978) and Katzenstein (1985), emphasizes the impact of trade dependence. According to Katzenstein's argument, perceptions of vulnerability to the vicissitudes of international markets induce the leadership of both business and unions in trade-dependent economies to seek an institutional framework within which compromises can be achieved amicably and conflict avoided. Among other things, the institutional framework that Katzenstein associates with trade dependence entails high levels of union density (1985, 32–33, 91). Thus merchandise exports as a proportion of GDP was included in the analysis as a measure of trade dependence.

Proportion of the Work Force in Mining, Manufacturing, Utilities, and Construction ("Industry"). Countries differ in the mix of industries that make up the national economy. Since unionization rates vary by industry within the same country, it is possible that much of the cross-national variation in aggregate union density reflects cross-national variation in the distribution of workers among industries rather than differences in unionization rates, holding industry characteristics constant. Ingham (1974) and Cameron (1978), among others, have argued that differences in industrial structure explain much of the cross-national variation of the organization of the union movement, possibly including the level of unionization. It is doubtful that cross-national differences in average firm size are important: data collected by Wright (1985, 209) in Sweden and the United States on private sector employment by size of firm reveal virtually identical distributions for the two countries.

Nevertheless, important differences in industrial structure among countries may have an impact on the level of unionization. Cross-sectional

---

[21] After controlling for leftist governments and the size of the work force, union centralization is not significantly associated with union density. In contrast, the centralization of the union movement is frequently cited as contributing to the electoral success of social democratic parties (Korpi 1983; Stephens 1980).

studies of union density at the state or metropolitan level in the United States have found that unionization is significantly higher in areas with a large proportion of the work force in manufacturing, transportation, communications, and utilities and a small proportion in agriculture (Hirsch 1980). Therefore, the proportion of the national work force in the more heavily unionized sectors of mining, manufacturing, utilities, and construction was added as another independent variable.

Proportion of the Work Force in Blue-Collar Occupations. Blue-collar workers are generally more highly organized than white-collar workers. Like the proportion of workers in manufacturing, the proportion of workers in blue-collar occupations is significantly related to differences in unionization levels within the United States (Hirsch 1980; Hirsch and Addison 1986, chap. 3).[22] Accordingly the number of production workers, transport and equipment operators, and laborers as a proportion of the economically active population was also used in the statistical analysis, although the data on the distribution of the work force by occupation (collected by the International Labour Office from national censuses and labor force surveys) is not very reliable. No occupational data could be found for Belgium, Italy, or Iceland.

Results

Table 2 displays the results of the statistical analysis. Both ordinary least squares (OLS) and 2SLS estimates (with leftist government and union density as endogenous variables) are reported. The difference in the results obtained with the two methods is not large in this case. The size of the work force and the cumulative government of leftist parties are both strongly associated with cross-national differences in unionization. The coefficient on the log of potential membership (size) is consistently negative and significant at conventional levels of significance. A coefficient of -6.0 indicates that a doubling of the potential union membership would reduce union density by $\ln(2)(6.0) = (.69)(6.0) \approx 4.2$ percentage points. The coefficient on leftist party participation in government (left) is positive and also highly

---

[22] Goldfield (1987, chap. 7), in contrast, does not find a consistent relationship between occupational or industrial variables and the likelihood of union victory in National Labor Relations Board elections. Goldfield's result is exactly what one would expect if unions allocated their organizing efforts efficiently: all subgroups are roughly equally likely to support unionization at the margin.

Table 2. *Cross-Sectional Analysis of Union Density in Advanced Industrial Societies (late 1970s)*

	OLS (1)	2SLS (2)	OLS (3)	2SLS (4)	OLS (5)	2SLS (6)
Constant	98.6	90.4	77.7	70.3	83.4	75.5
	(7.04)	(4.97)	(2.73)	(2.18)	(2.27)	(1.61)
Size[a]	−6.52	−5.92	−5.98	−5.60	−6.35	−5.84
	(4.32)	(3.37)	(3.23)	(2.78)	(3.17)	(2.11)
Left[b]	.27	.36	.28	.33	.30	.34
	(3.73)	(2.62)	(3.68)	(2.66)	(3.82)	(2.05)
Trade[c]	−	−	.15	.16	−	−
			(0.59)	(0.62)		
Industry[d]	−	−	.34	.40	−	−
			(0.59)	(0.67)		
Blue-collar[e]	−	−	−	−	.33	.39
					(0.39)	(0.44)
R^2	.74	.72	.75	.75	.80	.79
Number of cases	20	20	20	20	17	17

Note: The dependent variable is union membership as a proportion of potential membership. Numbers in the parentheses are t-statistics (asymptotic t-statistics in the case of 2SLS). See Tables 1 and 3 and Appendix B for data and sources.

[a] Natural log of potential membership.
[b] Wilensky's (1981) index of left party participation in government cumulated from 1919 to the year listed in Table 1.
[c] Merchandise exports as a share of GDP.
[d] Employment in mining, manufacturing, utilities, and construction as a proportion of civilian employment.
[e] Production workers, transport and equipment operators, and laborers as a proportion of the economically active population.

significant. Its size indicates that one year of a social democratic majority government (three points in Wilensky's index) increases union density by approximately one percentage point. Together, size and leftist party partic-ipation explain about 70% of the variance.

In contrast, none of the other variables proved to be statistically signifi-cant in any combination. Adding either the proportion of the work force in industry or trade dependence to an equation with the proportion of blue-collar workers changed the sign of their coefficients from positive to nega-tive (not shown). After controlling for the size of the potential membership and the cumulative impact of leftist governments, neither trade dependence nor highly aggregated measures of industry and occupational characteristics contribute much to the explanation of cross-national variation in unionization levels.

The OLS and 2SLS estimates do well in accounting for the variation of union density by the size of the labor force and the cumulative participation of leftist parties in government. None of the predicted values (presented in Table 3) fall outside the permissible bounds of zero and one. Yet since the dependent variable is bounded on both ends, an unbounded linear relationship cannot be literally correct. In addition, the errors cannot be normally distributed. Both difficulties can be overcome with a logistic transformation of union density $\lambda = \ln[\mu/(1 - \mu)]$. Repeating the regressions of Table 2 with λ as the dependent variable (not shown) produced similar results with virtually identical t-statistics on all coefficients.

The insignificance of cross-national differences in the composition of economic activity in Table 2 may be an artifact of the high level of aggregation. More disaggregated comparisons can be done where data on union membership at the industry level is available. Bain and Price (1980, 38, 43–78, 89) have comparable union membership and labor force data for 15 sectors of the economy in the United States and Great Britain in 1974.[23] Unfortunately, the industry-level union membership data for the United States include Canadian members, who constitute 7%–8% of the total (100). One can calculate, however, what the British rate of unionization would be if Great Britain had the industrial mix of the United States. Let $\gamma^B(i)$ and $\mu^B(i)$ be the share of the work force and the union density in industry i in Britain, and let $\gamma^A(i)$ and $\mu^A(i)$ be the same for the United States. In 1974, the aggregate British unionization rate was $\Sigma\gamma^B\mu^B = 49.2$, while union density in the United States was $\Sigma\gamma^A\mu^A = 24.6$. Had Great Britain had the same distribution of workers among industries as the United States, British unionization in 1974 would have been $\Sigma\gamma^A\mu^B = 45.8$. Britain does have a greater share of workers in highly organized industries than the United States, but the different industrial mix accounts for less than 15% of the difference in aggregate union density. In the comparison of union density in the United States and Great Britain, at least, a more disaggregated

---

[23] The sectors of the economy are metal and machinery; clothing; food, drink, and tobacco; paper, printing, and publishing; leather and leather products; textiles; lumber and lumber products; chemicals, rubber, clay, glass, and stone; the residual manufacturing sector; transportation, utilities, and communication; construction; mining, quarrying, and oil; central government (excluding health care in Britain); state and local government, including education; and the residual (service sector).

Michael Wallerstein

Table 3. *Potential Union Membership, Cumulative Left Governments, Estimated, and Actual Union Density*

Country (Year)	Potential Membership (in Thousands)[a]	Index of Left Governments[b]	Estimated Density[c]	Actual Density
Sweden (1979)	3,931	111.84	81.1	82.4
Israel (1979)	997	73.17	75.5	80.0
Iceland (1975)	81	17.25	70.5	74.3
Finland (1980)	2,034	59.33	66.3	73.3
Belgium (1977)	3,343	43.25	57.7	71.9
Denmark (1980)	2,225	90.24	76.8	69.6
Ireland (1978)	886	0.00	50.2	68.1
Austria (1977)	2,469	48.67	61.4	65.6
New Zealand (1979)	1,050	60.00	70.5	59.4
Norway (1979)	1,657	83.08	76.0	58.9
Australia (1979)	5,436	33.75	51.4	51.4
Italy (1978)	15,819	0.00	33.1	50.6
United Kingdom (1976)	25,757	43.67	45.7	48.0
Germany (1979)	23,003	35.33	43.4	39.6
Netherlands (1979)	4,509	31.50	51.7	37.7
Switzerland (1979)	2,460	11.87	48.3	35.4
Canada (1980)	10,516	0.00	35.5	31.2
Japan (1979)	39.930	1.92	28.3	31.0
France (1979)	18,846	8.67	35.1	28.2
United States (1978)	92,899	0.00	22.6	24.5

Note: Data sources are listed in Appendix B.
[a] All wage and salary earners plus the unemployed.
[b] Wilensky's (1981) index of cumulative left governments from 1919 to the year in parentheses.
[c] Predicted values from equation 2 in Table 2.

comparison of the industrial strucure still does not explain much of the difference.

A large share of the cross-national variation of unionization rates can be explained with two variables: the cumulative impact of leftist governments and the size of the labor force. Differences between countries in terms of trade dependence or aggregate measures of the sectoral and occupational distribution of the work force appear much less important, although the data on the proportion of blue-collar workers are too weak to support any strong conclusions regarding the importance of the occupational structure.

These findings contrast sharply with the results of both time series analyses of union growth at the national level and cross-sectional analyses of

136

regional variation within the United States. The size of the labor force changes far too slowly to have a noticeable impact on annual changes of union density. In addition, the size of the local work force has no discernible impact on differences in union density among cities or states within the United States. The relevant labor market for most unions is national in scale, as evidenced by the predominance of unions organized at the national level. Even unions in industries that produce immobile goods, like construction, organize as national unions because of the mobility of workers. Instead, the significant variables in cross-sectional studies within the United States are the sectoral and occupational distribution of the work force, urbanization, and, in some but not all studies, the presence of right-to-work laws (Hirsch and Addison 1986, chap. 3).

The size of the work force does appear, however, to be a prominent explanation of cross-national differences in union density. In 1978 union membership as a proportion of wage and salary earners plus the unemployed in the United States was 24.5%, not very different from the predicted value in Table 3 of 22.6%. The average union density of the other 19 Western democracies was 55.6%. The estimated coefficients in Table 2 indicate that roughly 55%–60% of the gap between the United States and other advanced capitalist countries at the time can be attributed to the exceptional size of the U.S. labor force. The rest of the difference is accounted for by the absence – not unique to the United States – of any governments led by Socialist or Social Democratic parties.

Conclusion

I have introduced a new explanation of cross-national differences in union-ization rates: the size of the labor force. Size matters because union power in collective bargaining depends on the proportion of substitutable workers who will respect a strike, while the costs of recruitment depend in part on the absolute number to be recruited. Unions in smaller labor markets can achieve high levels of unionization more cheaply. A comparison of the costs and benefits of organizing new workers yields the conclusion that unions in larger labor markets will accept lower levels of unionization. Statistical analysis of cross-national differences in unionization rates among advanced industrial societies in the late 1970s indicates that the size of the labor force and the cumulative participation of leftist parties in government explain almost three-quarters of the variance.

The reasoning that relates the resources unions devote to recruitment to the size of the labor force is not limited to unions whose primary activity is collective bargaining. In some countries, seeking to influence public policies may be a more consequential activity than negotiating with employers. The political arena may be particularly important in countries like France, where unions lack a strong presence in the work place, as well as in countries like Sweden and Norway, where strong, centralized unions have frequently limited wage demands for the sake of aggregate economic performance.

The political influence of unions depends on many factors, including their ability to strike effectively and their capacity to affect electoral outcomes. In elections – as in strikes – the proportion of union supporters within the relevant population is what matters, not the absolute number of union supporters. While in theory the benefits of mobilizing additional voters might drop sharply once a prounion party gained a majority, in fact there is no advanced industrial democracy where a single party allied with the union movement consistently wins 50% or more of seats in parliament. Whether acting as an interest group or engaged in collective bargaining, the ability to provide benefits for members is likely to increase with the proportion who are union members, while costs depend partly on the number being recruited. The general argument remains applicable.

A negative relationship between the number of potential members and density of membership should also exist for organizations other than trade unions for whom the benefits depend on the proportion who have been recruited while costs depend on number being recruited. For example, the ability of cartels to raise prices depends on the market share controlled by cartel members. If the costs of monitoring compliance increase with the number of producers, cartel members maximize profits by attempting to incorporate a smaller proportion of potential members when the number of potential members is large.

Olson (1965) argued that very small groups may attain high levels of organization because each potential member receives a large share of the benefits of his or her contribution. But Olson's argument cannot explain the negative correlation of group size and the proportion organized among large groups, where individual incentives to contribute in the absence of selective incentives are negligible. In the case of unions and other organizations with structurally similar costs and benefits, the number of potential members may be an important determinant of membership density, not because of the impact of size on individuals' incentives to join but because of the effect of size on organizations' incentives to recruit.

Appendix A: Mathematical Proofs

The union's problem is to choose a nonnegative $z(t)$ to minimize

$$\int_0^\infty e^{-\varrho t}\left(QS[\mu(t), x] + \frac{C[z(t), y]}{m(t)}\right)dt \equiv \int_0^\infty \mathcal{J}[\mu(t), z(t), t]dt, \qquad \text{(A-1)}$$

where $\mu(t) \equiv m(t)/n$ and $z(t) \equiv dm/dt$. Consider the problem first without constraining $z(t)$ to be nonnegative. The optimal path of $z(t)$ is given by the Euler equation, $\partial \mathcal{J}/\partial_m = d[\partial \mathcal{J}/\partial z/]/dt$, or

$$(1/m)C_{zz}(dz/dt) = (1/m^2)C_z Z + (\varrho/m)(C_z - (1/m^2)C + (Q/n)S_\mu, \qquad \text{(A-2)}$$

where subscripts denote partial differentiation of S and C. In addition the Legendre condition, $\partial^2 \mathcal{J}/\partial z^2 = (e^{-\varrho t}/m)C_{zz} \geq 0$, must be satisfied along the optimal path (Tu 1984).

The optimal path of $\mu(t)$ defined by equation A-2 cannot be solved explicitly. However, the stationary value of μ implicit in equation A-2, denoted by μ^*, can be analyzed. Setting $dz/dt = z = 0$ in equation A-2, we have

$$H(\mu^*, \varrho, x, y, n) = (\varrho/m)C_z - (1/m^2)C + (Q/n)S_\mu = 0. \qquad \text{(A-3)}$$

If $C_{zz} > 0$, equation A-2 can be written as a system of first-order differential equations with $dm/dt = z(t)$ and dz/dt as given in equation A-2. Writing the linear approximation in the neighborhood of the stationary point we obtain

$$d\zeta/dt = A\zeta, \qquad \text{(A-4)}$$

where ζ is the vector (m, z) and A is a 2×2 matrix with $a_{11} = 0$, $a_{12} = 1$, $a_{21} = (m/C_{zz})(\partial H/\partial m)$, and $a_{22} = (m/C_{zz})(\partial H/\partial z)$. A necessary condition for the existence of a unique optimal path that approaches μ^* from any initial $\mu(0) \neq \mu^*$ is that the stationary solution $(m^*, 0)$ be a saddle point or that $|A| = -(m/C_{zz})(\partial H/\partial m) < 0$. Thus we have the additional condition that

$$\frac{\partial H}{\partial m} = -(\varrho/m^2)C_z + (2/m^3)C + (Q/n^2)S_{\mu\mu} > 0 \qquad \text{(A-5)}$$

at the stationary point.

If equation A-5 holds and $\mu(0) < \mu^*$, $z(t) \geq 0$ everywhere along the optimal path and the constraint that z be nonnegative is never binding.

Thus the solution to the constrained problem is identical to the solution to the unconstrained problem. If $\mu(0) > \mu^*$ the optimal solution to the unconstrained problem implies $z < 0$ as $\mu(t)$ approaches μ^*. In this case, the solution to the constrained problem is simply $z(t) = 0$ and $\mu(t) = \mu(0)$ as long as the parameters ϱ, x, y, and n remain constant. (This failure of $\mu(t)$ to converge to μ^* when $\mu(0) > \mu^*$ is a consequence of the simplifying assumption that $dm/dt = z(t)$. In the more general formulation with $dm/dt = z(t) - \delta m(t)$, where δ represents the net loss of membership that occurs when unions do not recruit new members, the optimal path of $\mu(t)$ may approach μ^* from any initial value when $\delta > 0$.)

Propositions 1–3 in the text are now readily proven. Differentiating H with respect to ϱ – treating μ^* as an implicit function of Q – yields

$$\frac{d\mu^*}{d\varrho} = -(\partial H/\partial m)^{-1}(1/mn)C_z < 0 \qquad \text{(A-6)}$$

since $C_z > 0$.[24] Differentiating H with respect to x yields

$$\frac{d\mu^*}{dx} = -(\partial H/\partial m)^{-1}(Q/n^2)S_{\mu x} > 0 \qquad \text{(A-7)}$$

if and only if $S_{\mu x} < 0$. Differentiating H with respect to y yields

$$\frac{d\mu^*}{dy} = -(\partial H/\partial m)^{-1}[(\varrho/mn)C_{zy} - (1/m^2 n)C_y], \qquad \text{(A-8)}$$

which may be positive or negative. If, however, $C(z, y) = yc(z)$ with $y > 0$, then $(\varrho/mn)C_{zy} - (1/m^2 n)C_y = (\varrho/mn)c'(z) - (1/m^2 n)c(z) = -(Q/yn^2)S_\mu$ by equation A-3. In this case

$$\frac{d\mu^*}{dy} = (\partial H/\partial m)^{-1}(Q/yn^2)S_\mu < 0, \qquad \text{(A-9)}$$

since $S_\mu < 0$.

To prove proposition 4, start with the impact of the size of the labor force on the stationary size of the union:

$$\frac{dm^*}{dn} = (\partial H/\partial m)^{-1}(Q/n^2)(\mu S_{\mu\mu} + S_\mu), \qquad \text{(A-10)}$$

[24] This equation assumes that $Q = \alpha/M$ is independent of ϱ, as in cooperative bargaining theory. In noncooperative bargaining theory, $d\alpha/d\varrho < 0$, in which case $\partial H/\partial \varrho = (1/m)C_z + (1/Mn)S_\mu(d\alpha/d\varrho)$. The term $\partial H/\partial \varrho$ is still positive, since S_μ and $d\alpha/d\varrho$ are both negative. Therefore, the sign of $d\mu^*/d\varrho$ is not altered.

which will be positive if $-(\mu S_{\mu\mu}/S_\mu) > 1$ and negative if $-(\mu S_{\mu\mu}/S_\mu) < 1$, where $-(\mu S_{\mu\mu}/S_\mu)$ is the elasticity of S_μ with respect to μ. However, the effect of n on the stationary union density does not depend on the elasticity of S_μ:

$$\frac{d\mu^*}{dn} = (1/n^2)[(dm^*/dn)n - m]$$
$$= (1/n^2)(\partial H/\partial m)^{-1}[(Q/n)S_\mu + (\varrho/m)C_z - (2/m^2)C]$$
$$= -(1/nm)^2(\partial H/\partial m)^{-1}C < 0, \tag{A-11}$$

since $(Q/n)S_\mu = -(\varrho/m)C_z + (1/m^2)C$ from equation A-3.

If $C_{zz} = 0$, then $C(z, y)$ must have the form $C(z, y) = C_0(y) + C_1(y)z$. Straight-forward calculation reveals that all of the above results continue to hold provided equation A-5 is satisfied.

Appendix B: Data Sources

Union membership. U.S. Department of Labor 1980 for all countries other than Iceland and Switzerland. Coldrick and Jones 1979 (p. 876) has membership figures for Iceland. See Troy and Sheflin 1985 (pp. 7–17) for Switzerland.

Potential membership (wage and salary earners plus the unemployed). Organization for Economic Cooperation and Development (OECD) 1984 for all countries but Israel, for which see Israel, Central Bureau of Statistics 1980 (p. 300).

Left government. Wilensky's index of leftist party participation in government is defined in Wilensky 1981. The composition of government coalitions from 1919 to 1980 is from Wallerstein 1988a. Mackie and Rose 1982 is the source for shares of seats in parliament.

Merchandise exports as a proportion of GDP in 1980. Export figures are from United Nations, Food and Agriculture Administration 1985. United Nations 1985 has GDP figures.

Employment in mining, manufacturing, utilities, and construction as a share of civilian employment in 1980. OECD 1984 (p. 34) for all but Israel, for which see Israel, Central Bureau of Statistics 1980 (pp. 316–317).

Production workers, transport and equipment operators, and laborers as a proportion of economically active population. International Labour Office (ILO) 1979–83. Census data, as opposed to labor force survey data, was used

141

whenever possible. Belgium and Iceland were excluded for lack of data. Italy was excluded because the figure reported by the ILO is implausibly low.

Union centralization. Dummy variable set equal to one for countries with highly centralized confederations according to Headey's (1970) classification. The Icelandic labor confederation was judged to be decentralized (U.S. Bureau of Labor Statistics 1956).

References

Adam, Gerard. 1983. *Le pouvoir syndical.* Paris: Dunod.

Ashenfelter, Orley, and John H. Pencavel. 1969. "American Trade Union Growth: 1900–1960." *Quarterly Journal of Economics* 83:434–48.

Bain, George S., and Farouk Elshelkh. 1976. *Union Growth and the Business Cycle.* Oxford: Basil Blackwell.

Bain, George S., and Robert Price. 1980. *Profiles of Union Growth: A Comparative Statistical Portrait of Eight Countries.* Oxford: Basil Blackwell.

Barnett, George E. 1916. "Growth of Labor Organization in the United States, 1897–1914." *Quarterly Journal of Economics* 30:780–95.

Bernstein, Irving. 1954. "The Growth of American Unions." *American Economic Review* 44:301–18.

Block, Richard N., 1980. "Union Organizing and the Allocation of Union Resources." *Industrial and Labor Relations Review* 34:101–13.

Cameron, David R. 1978. "The Expansion of the Public Economy: A Comparative Analysis." *American Political Science Review* 72:1243–61.

Cameron, David R. 1984. "Social Democracy, Corporatism, and Labor Quiescence: The Representation of Economic Interest in Advanced Capitalist Society." In *Order and Conflict in Contemporary Capitalism,* ed. John H. Goldthorpe. Oxford: Oxford University Press.

Clark, Kim B. 1984. "Unionization and Firm Performance: The Impact on Profits, Growth, and Productivity." *American Economic Review* 74:893–919.

Coldrick, Arthur P., and Philip Jones. 1979. *The International Directory of the Trade Union Movement.* New York: Facts on File.

Commons, John R., et al. 1918. *History of Labour in the United States.* New York: Macmillan.

Dunlop, John T. 1949. "The Development of Labor Organization: A Theoretical Framework." In *Insights into Labor Issues,* ed. Richard A. Lester and Joseph Shister. New York: Macmillan.

Ellwood, David T., and Glen Fine. 1987. "Effects of Right-to-work Laws on Union Organizing." *Journal of Political Economy* 95:250–73.

Fiorito, Jack. 1982. "American Trade Union Growth: An Alternative Model." *Industrial Relations* 21:123–27.

Freeman, Richard B., and James L. Medoff. 1981. "The Impact of the Percentage Organized on Union and Nonunion Wages." *Review of Economics and Statistics* 63:561–72.

Freeman, Richard B., and James L. Medoff. 1984. *What Do Unions Do?* New York: Basic Books.

Goldfield, Michael. 1987. *The Decline of Organized Labor in the United States.* Chicago: University of Chicago Press.

Headey, Bruce. 1970. "Trade Unions and National Wages Policies." *Journal of Politics* 32:407–39.

Hicks, Alexander. 1988. "Capitalism, Social Democratic Corporatism, and Economic Growth." *Journal of Politics* 50:677–704.

Hicks, Alexander, and Duane Swank, 1984a. "On the Political Economy of Welfare Expansion: A Comparative Analysis of Eighteen Advanced Capitalist Democracies, 1960–1971." *Comparative Political Studies* 17:81–119.

Hicks, Alexander, and Duane Swank. 1984b. "Governmental Redistribution in Rich Capitalist Democracies." *Policy Studies Journal* 13:265–86.

Hines, A. G. 1964. "Trade Unions and Wage Inflation in the United Kingdom 1893–1961." *Review of Economic Studies* 31:221–52.

Hines, A. G. 1969. "Wage Inflation in the United Kingdom 1948–1962: A Disaggregated Study." *Economic Journal* 79:66–89.

Hirsch, Barry T. 1980. "The Determinants of Unionization: An Analysis of Interarea Differences." *Industrial and Labor Relations Review* 33:147–61.

Hirsch, Barry T., and John T. Addison. 1986. *The Economic Analysis of Unions: New Approaches and Evidence.* London: Allen & Unwin.

Ingham, Geoffrey K. 1974. *Strikes and Industrial Conflict.* London: Macmillan.

International Labour Office. 1979–83. *Yearbook of Labour Statistics.* Geneva: ILO.

Israel. Central Bureau of Statistics. 1980. *Statistical Abstract of Israel 1980.* Jerusalem: Hamakor.

Kalai, Ehud. 1985. "Solutions to the Bargaining Problem." In *Social Goals and Social Organization: Essays in Memory of Elisha Pazner,* ed. Leonid Hurwicz, David Schmekller, and Hugo Sonnenschein. Cambridge: Cambridge University Press.

Kassalow, Everett M. 1980. "The Closed and Union Shop in Western Europe: An American Perspective." *Journal of Labor Research* 1:323–39.

Katzenstein, Peter. 1985. *Small States in World Markets: Industrial Policy in Europe.* Ithaca: Cornell University Press.

Korpi, Walter. 1983. *The Democratic Class Struggle.* London: Routledge & Kegan Paul.

Korpi, Walter, and Michael Shalev. 1979. "Strikes, Industrial Relations, and Class Conflict in Capitalist Societies." *British Journal of Sociology* 30:164–87.

Korpi, Walter, and Michael Shalev. 1980. "Strikes, Power, and Politics in Western Nations, 1900–1976." *Political Power and Social Theory* 1:301–34.

Lazear, Edward P. 1983. "A Microeconomic Theory of Labor Unions." In *New Approaches to Labor Unions,* ed. Joseph D. Reid. Greenwich, CT: JAI.

Lorwin, Lewis L. 1933. *The American Federation of Labor: History, Policies, and Prospects.* Washington, DC: Brookings.

Mackie, Thomas T., and Richard Rose. 1982. *The International Almanac of Electoral History.* 2d ed. New York: Free Press.

McDonald, Ian M., and Robert W. Solow. 1981. "Wage Bargaining and Employment." *American Economic Review* 71:896–908.

Menil, George de. 1971. *Bargaining: Monopoly Power versus Union Power*. Cambridge: MIT Press.

Moore, William J., and Douglas K. Pearce. 1976. "Union Growth: A Test of the Ashenfelter-Pencavel Model." *Industrial Relations* 15:244–47.

Nash, John F. 1950. "The Bargaining Problem." *Econometrica* 18:155–62.

Olson, Mancur. 1965. *The Logic of Collective Action*. Cambridge: Harvard University Press.

Olson, Mancur. 1982. *The Rise and Decline of Nations*. New Haven: Yale University Press.

Organization for Economic Cooperation and Development. 1984. *Labor Force Statistics 1962–1982*. Paris: OECD.

Przeworski, Adam. 1984. "Union Growth: A Review of the Literature." University of Chicago. Typescript.

Przeworski, Adam, and John Sprague. 1986. *Paper Stones: A History of Electoral Socialism*. Chicago: University of Chicago Press.

Rogers, Joel. 1985. "Divide and Conquer: The Legal Foundations of Postwar U.S. Labor Policy." Presented at the annual meeting of the American Political Science Association, New Orleans.

Rubinstein, Ariel. 1982. "Perfect Equilibrium in a Bargaining Model." *Econometrica* 50:97–109.

Shalev, Michael, and Walter Korpi. 1980. "Working Class Mobilization and American Exceptionalism." *Economic and Industrial Democracy* 1:31–61.

Sharpe, Ian G. 1971. "The Growth of Australian Trade Unions: 1907–1969." *Journal of Industrial Relations* 13:138–54.

Sheflin, Neil, Leo Troy, and C. T. Koeller. 1981. "Structural Stability in Models of American Trade Union Growth." *Quarterly Journal of Economics* 85:77–88.

Shister, Joseph. 1953. "The Logic of Union Growth." *Journal of Political Economy* 61:413–33.

Stephens, John D. 1980. *The Transition from Capitalism to Socialism*. Atlantic Highlands, NJ: Humanities.

Sutton, John. 1986. "Non-Cooperative Bargaining Theory: An Introduction." *Review of Economic Studies* 53:708–24.

Swindinsky, R. 1974. "Trade Union Growth in Canada, 1911–1970." *Relations Industrielles* 29:435–51.

Troy, Leo, and Neil Sheflin. 1985. *U.S. Union Sourcebook*. West Orange, NJ: Industrial Relations Data and Information Services.

Tu, Pierre N. V. 1984. *Introductory Optimization Dynamics*. Berlin: Springer-Verlag.

United Nations. 1985. *World Statistics in Brief*. New York: UN.

United Nations. Food and Agricultural Organization. 1985. *FAO Trade Yearbook, 1984*. Rome: FAO.

U.S. Bureau of Labor Statistics. 1956. *Labor in Iceland*. Washington, DC: Bureau of Labor Statistics.

Union Organization in Advanced Industrial Democracies

U.S. Department of Labor. 1980. *International Labor Profiles*. Detroit: Grand River Books.

Voos, Paula B. 1983. "Union Organizing: Costs and Benefits." *Industrial and Labor Relations Review* 36:57–91.

Voos, Paula B. 1984a. "Does It Pay To Organize? Estimating the Cost to Unions." *Monthly Labor Review* 107 (June): 43–44.

Voos, Paula B. 1984b. "Trends in Union Organizing Expenditures, 1953–1977." *Industrial and Labor Relations Review* 38:52–63.

Wallerstein, Michael. 1987. "Unemployment, Collective Bargaining, and the Demand for Protection." *American Journal of Political Science* 31:729–52.

Wallerstein, Michael. 1988a. "Parties in Government." University of California, Los Angeles. Typescript.

Wallerstein, Michael. 1988b. "Union Growth from the Unions' Perspective." Institute of Industrial Relations Working Paper no. 149. University of California, Los Angeles.

Weinstein, James. 1975. *Ambiguous Legacy: The Left in American Politics*. New York: New View-points.

Weyworth, William O. 1917. *The Organizability of Labor*. Baltimore: Johns Hopkins University Press.

Wilensky, Harold L. 1981. "Leftism, Catholicism, and Democratic Corporatism: The Role of Political Parties in Recent Welfare State Development." In *The Development of Welfare States in Europe and America*, ed. Peter Flora and Arnold J. Heidenheimer. New Brunswick, NJ: Transaction Books.

Wilkinson, R. K., and B. Burkitt, 1973. "Wage Determination and Trade Unions." *Scottish Journal of Political Economy* 20:107–22.

Wright, Erik O. 1985. *Classes*. London: Verso.

8

Centralized Bargaining and Wage Restraint

Michael Wallerstein

Introduction

During recent years extensive research has centered on corporatist patterns of interest representation and centralized systems of collective bargaining.[1] This research has associated corporatism and centralized bargaining with "labor quiescence," to use David Cameron's (1984) label for the combination of low strike rates and wage restraint. Labor quiescence, in turn, is claimed to contribute to successful economic performance: lower rates of inflation and unemployment, higher rates of investment, and a less pronounced slowdown of growth following the oil crises of the 1970s.

Union cooperation with government policies to curb the growth of wages has been a central theme in the research on corporatism in Western Europe. In one of the first contributions to a burgeoning literature, Gerhard Lehmbruch (1977) observed: "Incomes policies appear to constitute a core domain of liberal corporatism" (96). Similarly, Leo Panitch (1977) argued that in "virtually every" corporatist society, policies "designed to abate the

---

[1] The centralization of bargaining refers to the role of the peak associations of labor and capital in collective bargaining. In highly centralized bargaining systems, the peak associations typically negotiate a frame agreement on wages at the national level. In decentralized bargaining systems, each union negotiates independently at the industry or firm level. While there exist nearly as many definitions of corporatism as scholars working on the topic, the definition of corporatism when applied to Western European countries in the postwar period almost always includes centralized collective bargaining.

Work on this paper began as a joint research project with Adam Przeworski on pluralism, corporatism, and market competition. An early version was presented at the 1988 annual meeting of the American Political Science Association. I am grateful to Adam Przeworski, David Cameron, George Tsebelis, Michael Hoel, Steiner Holden, and Karl Ove Moene for their comments. Financial support was provided by National Science Foundation grant SES-87-12222 and the Institute of Industrial Relations, UCLA.

wage pressure of trade unions was the frontpiece of corporatist development" (74). Cross-national studies by Bruce Headey (1970) and Gary Marks (1986) have verified the existence of a close empirical relationship between union centralization and the successful implementation of voluntary incomes policies.

More recently, union centralization or corporatism has attracted the attention of economists seeking to account for the divergence in macroeconomic performance among advanced industrial societies since the mid-1970s. Michael Bruno and Jeffrey Sachs (1985) emphasize both the importance of "real wage moderation" for "achieving low inflation and low unemployment after a supply shock" (217) and the significance of corporatist institutions for moderating union wage demands. Studies by John McCallum (1986) and Charles Bean, Richard Layard, and Stephen Nickell (1986), among others, provide evidence associating corporatism or centralized bargaining with smaller increases in unemployment or superior trade-offs between unemployment and inflation.[2]

These empirical findings, however, remain highly controversial. The conventional wisdom in economics regarding the labor market is that competition and wage flexibility are good things. Yet centralized, encompassing trade unions are the unions that are least constrained by labor market competition. Moreover, the standardization of wages in different regions associated with centralized bargaining reduces the sensitivity of wage levels to local labor market conditions (Heitger 1987). In addition, centralized bargaining is often associated with a greater equality of wages in different occupations than many economists (and managers) think is efficient.[3] In Norway and Sweden in particular, the reduction of wage inequalities, or "wage solidarity," has been a prominent objective of the blue-collar confederations in centralized bargaining. Indeed, the compression of relative wages figures conspicuously in accounts of the increasing opposition to centralized

---

[2] Calmfors and Driffill (1988) argue that the relationship between union centralization and unemployment is U-shaped rather than monotonic with intermediate levels of centralization producing the worst outcomes. However, the hump-shaped pattern they observe is extremely sensitive to the outliers of Japan and Switzerland. Calmfors and Driffill point out that Switzerland, in particular, represents dubious evidence of the virtues of decentralized bargaining, as its low unemployment rate reflects the expulsion of immigrant labor. Another set of studies by Lange and Garrett (1985), Garrett and Lange (1986), and Hicks (1988) concludes that economic growth declined least in two sets of countries: those with both corporatist institutions and Left governments and those with neither.

[3] Freeman (1988) notes that Austria is an exception with high levels of both wage dispersion and union centralization.

147

Michael Wallerstein

bargaining by relatively well-paid workers in both countries (Ahlén 1988; Swenson 1989; Hernes unpublished paper, n.d.).

This paper presents a formal model in which the impact of centralized bargaining on both economic efficiency and wage equality can be derived. Given the small number of cases and the large number of factors that plausibly affect economic performance, the credibility of the empirical evidence on the benefits of centralized bargaining inevitably depends to an important degree on the strength of the theory explaining the results. While many have argued that centralized bargaining permits unions to achieve the Pareto optimal cooperative solution to some collective action problem (Schwerin 1980, 1982; Olson 1982; Lange 1984; Crouch 1985), the nature of the externality that causes centralized bargaining to differ from decentralized bargaining has generally not been well defined. Moreover, existing models in which all unions are assumed to benefit equally are ill suited for understanding the political conflicts over centralized bargaining within the union movement.

The next section briefly reviews recent theoretical studies of centralized bargaining and introduces the distinctive feature of the approach taken here: the interaction of different groups of workers who are complements in production. The third section presents a particular model of wage determination that allows for an explicit comparison of wages and growth under centralized and decentralized wage setting. The fourth section explores implications of the model for the effect of centralized wage setting on wage dispersion. The interaction of wage demands through wage leadership is contrasted with centralized wage setting in the fifth section. The sixth section concludes with a discussion of the puzzle posed by the instability of systems of centralized wage setting.

Complements and Substitutes in Production

Economists who have considered the interaction of multiple unions in collective bargaining have emphasized a number of different externalities. The most heretical from the perspective of economic theory, although the thought goes back at least to Keynes, is that workers care about relative wages in addition to real wage levels (Frank 1985; Blinder 1988). If all unions try to move up the wage hierarchy, none will change position (provided their relative bargaining strength has not changed). Wages will increase, however, and unemployment will increase. According to this explanation, centralized bargaining allows unions to restrain aggregate wage growth without altering relative wages. The difficulty with this approach is that centralized bargaining frequently changes relative wages as much as it restrains aggregate wage growth.

The externality emphasized by Jon Strand (1987) and Lars Calmfors and John Driffill (1988) comes from the impact of wages on consumer prices. In the model of Calmfors and Driffill, higher wages leading to higher prices in one industry can affect workers in other industries in two ways. The first effect is to lower real wages by increasing the cost of living. The second effect is to increase the demand for goods that are substitutes in consumption. Unions in substitute-producing industries gain from the higher demand for labor. The two effects push real wages in opposite directions. Unless one knows the elasticities of substitution between the goods produced by members of different unions and consumption patterns of union members, it is impossible to determine whether a confederation would demand higher or lower wages than its affiliates would acting independently.

Calmfors and Driffill argue that once bargaining is already moderately centralized, further centralization entails the amalgamation of workers who do not produce close substitutes. Therefore, moving from intermediate to high levels of centralization lowers wage demands. On the other hand, moving from highly decentralized to intermediate levels of centralization entails the unification of workers who do produce goods that are close substitutes, thereby increasing the unions' preferred wage level.

Other studies center the analysis on the financing of unemployment benefits: union members in one industry pay only a small share of the cost of supporting those who lose their jobs because of wage increases (Holden and Raaum 1989). However, the most important way in which workers in different unions interact is probably in the process of production. Many firms must bargain separately with more than one union, either because their work force is divided among craft unions, overlapping industrial unions or white- and blue-collar unions. A case study of labor relations in "a prototype for many large diversified conglomerates" in the United States describes bargaining with a dozen independent unions (Verma and Kochan 1985, 94). In large engineering firms in Britain, it is not unusual for the labor force to be represented by 15–20 separate unions (Bratt 1986). Where white-collar workers are unionized, they are generally organized in white-collar unions that act independently of the blue-collar work force. When professionals join unions, they rarely join the union that represents their secretaries.

In addition, firms depend on the labor of workers they do not directly employ. Airline companies depend on the labor of truck drivers and air controllers. A substantial part of the costs of production for many firms consists of payments for goods and services bought from other domestic producers. The manufacturing sector depends on the output of workers in utilities and transportation. The cost of new investment in plant and equipment depends on the price of capital goods and new construction. While capital goods may be imported, new factories must be built with local labor. The most important determinant of the cost of government services is the wage received by workers in the public sector. In general, labor costs are much less significant at the firm or industry level than at the national level. For example, labor costs average only 20% of revenues at the firm level in Great Britain (Calmfors and Driffill 1988, 52). Yet wages and salaries constitute 70% of value added at the national level.

Henrik Horn and Asher Wolinsky (1988) have recently shown that when employers negotiate with multiple unions, the centralization of bargaining can alter the unions' bargaining power.[4] Whether the unions acting jointly would obtain lower or higher wages depends on whether union members are substitutes or complements in production. The general argument is easily illustrated using Andrew Oswald's (1979) simple model of wage setting with two unions. In Oswald's framework, each union seeks to maximize a general objective function, U_i, that depends on the wage rate, w_i, and on something else that is in conflict with higher wages, x_i. The something else could be employment of union members or investment that promises to increase productivity and wages in the future. All that matters is that the union faces a trade-off between increases in w_i and increases in x_i.

In decentralized wage setting with two unions, the problem facing union A can be written as:

$$\max_{w_A} U_A(w_A, x_A) \quad \text{such that} \quad x_A = x_A(w_A, w_S) \tag{1}$$

where $\partial U_A/\partial w_A > 0$, $\partial U_A/\partial x_A > 0$ and $\partial x_A/\partial w_A < 0$. The optimal trade-off from the union's point of view is given by the condition that the welfare

---

[4] Part of Horn and Wolinsky's (1988) argument was anticipated in an unpublished paper by Hersoug (1985).

gained from a marginal increase in the wage rate is exactly balanced by the welfare lost from the impact of a wage increase on x_A, or:

$$\frac{\partial U_A}{\partial w_A} + \frac{\partial U_A}{\partial x_A}\frac{\partial x_A}{\partial w_A} = 0 \tag{2}$$

The second-order condition for a maximum implies that the LHS of equation (2) is a decreasing function of w_A.

A centralized confederation, in contrast, would set wages for both unions to maximize some objective function, V, that depends positively on the welfare of its two affiliates, U_A and U_B. Therefore, the centralized confederation chooses the pair of wages, w_A and w_B, to solve the problem:

$$\max_{w_A, w_S} V[U_A(w_A, x_A), U_B(w_B, x_B)]$$
$$\text{s.t.} \quad x_i = x_i(w_A, w_B), \quad i = A, B \tag{3}$$

where $\partial V/\partial U_A > 0$ and $\partial V/\partial U_B > 0$. In addition, $\partial x_i/\partial w_i < 0$ for both unions.

The wages that would be chosen by the union confederation are given by the first-order condition

$$\frac{\partial V}{\partial U_A}\left[\frac{\partial U_A}{\partial w_A} + \frac{\partial U_A}{\partial x_A}\frac{\partial x_A}{\partial w_A}\right] + \frac{\partial V}{\partial U_B}\left[\frac{\partial U_B}{\partial x_B}\frac{\partial x_B}{\partial w_A}\right] = 0 \tag{4}$$

for w_A and similarly for w_B. The first bracketed term represents the effect of a wage increase for union A on the welfare of union A, while the second bracketed term represents the effect of a wage increase for union A on the welfare of union B. The terms $(\partial V/\partial U_A)$ and $(\partial V/\partial U_B)$ represent the weights used by the central negotiators in aggregating preferences.

For a fixed w_B, the comparison of the wages demanded for union A under decentralized bargaining (equation 2) and centralized bargaining (equation 4) depends on whether $(\partial x_B/\partial w_A)$ is positive or negative. If $(\partial x_B/\partial w_A) > 0$, the members of the two unions are *substitutes* in production. Increases in wages paid to members of one union lead to increases in employment or wage growth for members of the other. In this case the second term in equation (4) is positive, implying that the term inside the first set of brackets is negative. From the second-order condition for a maximum, it follows that union A wages are *higher* with centralized wage setting.

On the other hand, if $(\partial x_B/\partial w_A) < 0$, the members of the two unions are *complements*. Increases in the wage paid to members of one result in lower wage growth or less employment for members of the other. Now the second term in equation (4) is negative, implying that the first term is positive. This implies, in turn, that union A's wages would be *lower* if they were set by the union confederation.

Both the case where separate unions represent substitutes and the case where separate unions represent complements can be observed. Examples of unions that represent substitutes occur where separate unions organize similar workers in the same workplace – as is common in Belgium, France, and Italy – or where unions are organized by enterprise – as in Japan. Cases of unions whose members are complements are provided by many of the examples given above: maintenance workers, flight attendants and pilots in the airlines; carpenters, plumbers, and electricians in construction; blue-collar, white-collar, and professional unions in manufacturing. In addition, workers in different industries are frequently complements, especially at high levels of aggregation.[5] Revenue per worker in manufacturing increases as labor costs in construction and transportation decline.

Horn and Wolinsky (1988) argue that workers who are substitutes have an incentive to organize in a single bargaining unit to maximize their ability to strike effectively. In fact, in Belgium and Italy (although not in France), the competing unions commonly form a joint bargaining committee to negotiate with management, while Japanese unions coordinate their wage demands in an annual spring offensive. In contrast, amalgamation decreases the strike threat of workers who are complements. If unions adopted the bargaining structure that maximized their bargaining power, each union would unite workers who are substitutes in production and remain separate from unions that represent workers who are complements in production.

The work of Horn and Wolinsky (1988) suggests that when and where unions are struggling to win recognition and to establish their bargaining power, they would concentrate on organizing workers who are substitutes. Only after unions have achieved substantial power over wages would unions representing complements in production have reason to accept the diminution of bargaining power that centralized bargaining entails.

---

[5] Thus, the move from company-level bargaining to industry-level bargaining might increase wage demands, while the replacement of industry-level bargaining with national-level bargaining would lower wage demands, resulting in the hump-shaped pattern claimed by Calmfors and Driffill (1988).

A Specific Model of Centralized and Decentralized Wage Setting

The impact of union centralization on wage demands cannot rigorously be deduced from the change in the optimal wage for one union holding other wages constant, however, since centralized bargaining alters the wages of all unions. The optimal wage demands of a centralized confederation must be compared with the equilibrium of decentralized bargaining where all unions simultaneously choose their best strategy. This section presents a particular model that is simple enough to illustrate the way in which centralization of unions might alter wage demands in equilibrium.

To focus attention on self-imposed wage restraint by unions that are complements in production, several strong assumptions are adopted. First, the assumption that unions have the power to set wages as they choose is retained. Thus, the model is really of wage setting rather than wage bargaining. Second, workers are assumed to be strong complements with no substitution possible among different types of workers or between capital and labor.

The Basic Model

Let there be two groups of workers, each represented by a potentially independent union, and one group of shareholders. Production requires capital and the labor of each group of workers in fixed proportions:

$$Y = \min(\nu K, \lambda_A L_A, \lambda_B L_B) \tag{5}$$

where Y is output, K is the stock of capital, L_A is the labor of members of union A, and L_B is the same for union B. The parameters ν, λ_A, and λ_B, represent the amounts of capital and both types of labor required in production. The production of one unit of output requires $(1/\nu)$ units of capital, $(1/\lambda_A)$ units of L_A, and so on. Profits are given by:

$$\pi = Y - w_A L_A - w_B L_B = (1 - m_A - m_B)Y \tag{6}$$

where $m_i \equiv (w_i L_i)/Y = w_i/\lambda_i$ is the share of income received by members of union $i = A, B$. Firms invest the share s of their income and distribute the rest to shareholders.

To emphasize the importance of employers' incentives to invest for economic growth, I assume that all investment is financed out of profits and that the rate of growth of output depends only on the growth of the capital

Michael Wallerstein

stock. In other words, growth is assumed to be unconstrained by either aggregate demand or the supply of labor. In particular, let technical progress be labor augmenting and equal to the rate of growth of the capital stock, or $\dot{v} = 0$ and $\dot{\lambda}_A/\lambda_A = \dot{\lambda}_B/\lambda_B = \dot{K}/K$ (where $\dot{x}$ denotes the change in x over time).[6] The growth of output is then determined by investment according to the equation:

$$\dot{Y}(t) = v\dot{K}(t) = vs(t)[1 - m_A(t) - m_B(t)]Y(t) \tag{7}$$

Firms are assumed to act as perfect agents of their owners: firms choose the rate of investment in each moment of time that maximizes shareholders' utility of present and future consumption, P^*, given by

$$P^* = \int_0^\infty e^{-\rho t} U\{[1 - s(t)]\pi(t)\}\, dt \tag{8}$$

where ρ is the (positive) rate at which shareholders discount the future.

Similarly, I assume that unions are also perfect agents of their constituents and that union members have the same preferences as shareholders. Therefore, each union chooses the time path of wages to maximize its members' utility from present and future wages, W_i^*, or

$$W_i^* = \int_0^\infty e^{-\rho t} U[w_i(t)]\, dt \tag{9}$$

What has been described is a dynamic game between shareholders and unions in the spirit of a model originally developed by Kelvin Lancaster (1973). Shareholders control the rate of investment over time, but unions control present and future wages. The welfare of both shareholders and workers depends on the share of income each consumes and the rate at which income grows. How fast income grows depends, in turn, on the share of income each actor is willing *not* to consume.[7]

[6] See Solow (1988) or Boskin (1988) for discussions of the dependence of the rate of technical progress on investment. The slightly less restrictive assumption that $\dot{\lambda}_i/\lambda_i = c_i(\dot{K}/K)$ for some positive constant c_i could easily be adopted at the cost of introducing two new parameters, c_A and c_B. However, the assumption that labor's productivity grows at the same rate as the capital stock is roughly consistent with the data presented by Layard and Nickell (1986).
[7] Pohjola (1984) analyzes a model with multiple unions that closely follows Lancaster's (1973) original specification in other respects. Some of the results that follow, particularly in equations (16)–(18), are similar to Pohjola's conclusions. See Wallerstein (1990) for a general review of models that analyze wage setting and investment as a dynamic game between unions and firms.

154

The model analyzed here differs from Lancaster's model (and Matti Pohjola's 1984 extension of the Lancaster model to the case with multiple unions) in three respects. The first is that the unions are modeled as dominant players vis-à-vis employers in the sense that each union anticipates the impact of its wage demands on subsequent investment decisions. In contrast, each firm is assumed to employ too small a proportion of the membership of each of the unions to consider the impact of its rate of investment upon union wage demands. Second, the time horizon is infinite, thus avoiding the unrealism of Lancaster's assumption that the unions and firms arrive at a period that both think will be the last.

Finally, instead of Lancaster's assumption that workers and shareholders are risk-neutral, here both are assumed to be risk-adverse with constant relative risk-aversion. The simplifying assumption that the coefficient of relative risk-aversion, $\gamma = -CU''(C)/U'(C)$, is constant has several advantages. The first is that it permits an explicit solution of the game to be derived with an infinite horizon. Second, the assumption that this particular measure of risk-aversion does not depend on consumption levels is supported by data on the household allocation of wealth among risky and risk-free assets (Friend and Blume 1975).[8] In keeping with empirical estimates, I assume that $\gamma \geq 1$.

Decentralized Wage Setting

To find a solution to the game with decentralized bargaining, start with the firms' decision. If, for some reason, the aggregate wage share ($m_A + m_B$) chosen by the unions does not vary over time, it is shown in the appendix that the best reply of shareholders is also invariant over time and equal to:

$$s^*(m_A, m_B) = \frac{1}{\gamma}\left(1 - \frac{\rho/\nu}{1 - m_A - m_B}\right) \qquad (10)$$

Note that the rate of investment, s^*, is an increasing function of the productivity of capital, ν, and a decreasing function of the discount rate, ρ, and the aggregate wage share, ($m_A + m_B$). Since $\gamma \geq 1$, s^* is always less than one (assuming the wage share $m_A + m_B$ is less than one). Shareholders would

---

[8] A constant coefficient of relative risk-aversion implies that the proportion of household wealth held in risky, as opposed to risk-free assets, should be roughly the same for all income levels. This is what Friend and Blume (1975) found. Utility functions with constant relative risk-aversion have the form $U(C) = a + b(1 - \gamma)^{-1}C^{1-\gamma}$ if $\gamma \neq 1$ and $U(C) = a + b \ln C$ if $\gamma = 1$ where $\gamma > 0$ and $b > 0$. Friend and Blume estimate γ to be close to two.

never want to invest all of their income. Shareholders would want to invest a negative amount or disinvest if their rate of return, $v(1 - m_A - m_B)$, fell below the rate at which they discount the future, ρ. Equation (10) indicates that a higher constant wage share reduces the investment share $I/Y = s(1 - m_A - m_B)$ in two ways. Both the profit share of income $(1 - m_A - m_B)$ and the optimal rate of investment out of profits s^* decline as the aggregate wage share increases.

Next consider the decision of union A. The most convenient way to write the union's choice is in terms of the wage share, $m_A(t) = w_A(t)/\lambda_A(t)$. If union A anticipates that firms will follow the rule given in equation (10) when choosing the rate of investment and if, for some reason, the wage share received by union B is constant over time, then it is shown in the appendix that the best reply of union A is also constant over time and equal to:

$$m_A^* = (1/\gamma)[(\rho/v) + (\gamma - 1)(1 - m_B)] \tag{11}$$

The optimal wage share, m_A^*, is an increasing function of discount rate, ρ, and a decreasing function of the productivity of capital, v. In addition, since $\gamma \geq 1$, union A's wage share is a nonincreasing function of the wage share received by members of union B: $(dm_A^*/dm_B) = -(\gamma - 1)/\gamma \leq 0$. Contrary to the envy effect discussed in the literature, here unions respond to an increase in the wage share of others by reducing their own wage share when $\gamma > 1$. The reason is that an increase in the wage share of one union threatens to lower investment and the future growth of income for all. Unions facing a decline in investment because of other unions' wage increases find it preferable to accept somewhat lower wages themselves to mitigate the slowdown of growth that would otherwise occur.

The problem facing union B is identical to the problem facing union A. Thus, if union A receives a constant wage share, the best reply of union B is also given by equation (11) with m_A instead of m_B on the RHS. Solving simultaneously for the best replies of unions A and B, one obtains the result that both unions demand the constant wage share of:

$$m_A^* = m_B^* = \frac{(\rho/v) + \gamma - 1}{2\gamma - 1} \tag{12}$$

Provided $2m^* < 1$ or, equivalently, $\rho < v/2$, equation (12) represents the Cournot-Nash solution among unions. Since all players find it optimal to choose time invariant strategies when the others choose time invariant strategies, the wage shares given in equation (12) and the rate of investment given in equation (10) represent a solution to the dynamic game. Moreover,

156

since the optimal strategies do not depend on the state variable Y, they constitute best replies to each other from any position in the game. Thus, the solution is subgame perfect.[9]

The last equation can be easily generalized to the case of $n \geq 1$ unions. The general Cournot-Nash solution among multiple unions is for each to demand the wage share of:

$$m^* = \frac{(\rho/v) + \gamma - 1}{1 + n(\gamma - 1)} \tag{13}$$

Each individual union demands less if the number of unions increases (when $\gamma > 1$), but the aggregate wage share, nm^*, increases. Thus, the rate of investment declines, and the economy grows more slowly as unions decline in size, provided their power to set wages is not also reduced.

There is, therefore, a monotonic relationship between the number of independent unions and the size of the aggregate wage bill in the equilibrium of decentralized bargaining in this model. In Mancur Olson's (1982) language, less encompassing unions internalize a smaller share of the costs of their wage increases. However, it is clear that such a monotonic relationship cannot continue to exist as the number of unions increases to the limit of one union per wage earner. No individual is essential for production. At some point an increase in the number of independent unions must reduce each union's bargaining power.

Centralized Wage Setting

With centralized bargaining, unions A and B allow their wages to be set by the national union confederation. Since in most countries, the affiliated unions determine the authority of the union confederation in wage setting, the preferences of the affiliated unions at least constrain the choices of the union central. Here, to keep the analysis as simple as possible, I assume that the union central chooses the time path of wages $W_A(t)$ and $W_B(t)$ to maximize a simple weighted average of the welfare of its affiliates:

$$V(W_A^*, W_B^*) = \alpha W_A^* + (1 - \alpha)W_B^* \tag{14}$$

The parameters α and $(1 - \alpha)$ are the political weights of unions A and B, respectively, in the union confederation, while the terms W_A^* and

---

[9] If $\rho \geq v/2$, the corresponding solution consists of maximal militancy and maximal disinvestment if maximal strategies exist. Other subgame perfect solutions are discussed below.

W_B^* represent the two unions' welfare as defined in equation (9). As in decentralized wage setting, the union central maximizes equation (14) subject to the constraint that investment is a decreasing function of aggregate wages.

Again writing the solution in terms of wage shares, it is shown in the appendix that if the union confederation anticipates that firms would invest according to their best reply strategy $s^*(m_A, m_B)$, it would set wages such that the wage shares received by unions A and B are constant over time and equal to:

$$m_A^* = \frac{M}{1+M}(1/\gamma)[(\rho/v)+\gamma-1], \quad \text{and}$$

$$m_B^* = \frac{1}{1+M}(1/\gamma)[(\rho/v)+\gamma-1], \quad \text{where} \tag{15}$$

$$M = \left[\frac{\alpha}{1-\alpha}(\lambda_A/\lambda_B)\right]^{1/\gamma}$$

Provided $\rho < v$, the union central demands a total wage share of $(1/\gamma)\,[(\rho/v)+\gamma-1]$ which it distributes to its affiliates according to the proportions $M/(1+M)$ and $1/(1+M)$.

The proportion received by union A, $M/(1+M)$ grows as its political weight in the union confederation, α, increases. If the political weight of union A approaches one (or, equivalently, if the political weight of union B approaches zero), union A receives close to the entire wage share: $M/(1+M) \to 1$ as $\alpha \to 1$. If α goes to zero, the entire wage share goes to union B: $M/(1+M) = 0$ if $\alpha = 0$. Of course, both extremes are incompatible with the voluntary participation of both unions in centralized wage setting. Note finally that if both unions are identical in the sense that $\alpha = 1/2$ and $\lambda_A = \lambda_B$, then $M = 1$, and each union receives half of the aggregate wage share.

The aggregate wage share received by members of the two unions together is lower with centralized wage setting than with decentralized wage setting. Let the total wage share $(m_A^* + m_B^*)$ be written (W/Y) with superscripts D and C representing decentralized wage setting and centralized wage setting respectively. Subtracting the aggregate wage share in decentralized wage setting (equation 12) from the aggregate wage share with centralized wage setting (equation 15), one obtains:

$$(W/Y)^C - (W/Y)^D = \frac{-1}{\gamma(2\gamma-1)}[(\rho/v)+\gamma-1] < 0 \tag{16}$$

since $\gamma \geq 1$. The union confederation demands less in aggregate, since it internalizes the negative impact of wage increases for union A on union B and vice versa.

Shareholders, in contrast, consume an equal or larger share when the union confederation sets wages. Letting (C/Y) denote the share of income consumed by shareholders, $(C/Y) = (1 - s^*)(1 - m_A^* - m_B^*$, we have:

$$(C/Y)^C - (C/Y)^D = \frac{(\gamma - 1)}{\gamma^2(2\gamma - 1)}[(\rho/\nu) + \gamma - 1] \geq 0 \qquad (17)$$

In addition, the share of aggregate income invested $(I/Y) = s^*(1 - m_A^* - m_B^*)$ is larger when wage setting is centralized:

$$(I/Y)^C - (I/Y)^D = \frac{1}{\gamma^2(2\gamma - 1)}[(\rho/\nu) + \gamma - 1] > 0 \qquad (18)$$

Since the rate of growth of income is a multiple of the investment share, $(\dot{Y}/Y) = \nu(I/Y)$, the economy grows more rapidly with centralized wage setting.

Shareholders clearly benefit from centralized wage setting. They are consuming at least as large a share of a faster growing pie. How union members rank centralized versus decentralized wage setting is less obvious. In aggregate, centralized unions accept lower present wages in exchange for more rapid growth and higher future wages. Whether this intertemporal trade-off enhances the welfare of the affiliated unions clearly depends on the share of the total wage share that each union receives.

However, a division of the aggregate wage share under centralized wage setting that improves the welfare of both unions in comparison to decentralized wage setting always exists. The optimal aggregate wage share from the union central's point of view maximizes the joint welfare of its two affiliates. Since the central's choice differs from the total wage share associated with decentralized wage setting, centralized wage setting must be superior by the Kaldor-Hicks criterion: the total wage share could be divided in such a way that both affiliates prefer centralized to decentralized wage setting. To give a concrete example, if workers' productivity is equal in the two unions, or $\lambda_A = \lambda_B$, and if $\gamma = 2$, which is roughly the value of γ estimated by Friend and Blume (1975), both unions prefer centralized wage setting as long as $.40 < \alpha < .60$.

159

Relative Wages

With decentralized wage setting, relative wages are determined by relative productivity. Since $m_A^* = m_B^*$ in the Cournot-Nash equilibrium and, by definition, $(w_A/w_B) = m_A\lambda_A)/(m_B\lambda_B)$, it follows that:

$$(w_A/w_B)^D = \lambda_A/\lambda_B \qquad (19)$$

The ratio of wages equals the ratio of labor productivity as measured by (λ_A/λ_B). The union central, in contrast, sets wages such that $(m_A^*/m_B^*) = M$ (equation 15). Using $w_i = m_i\lambda_i$ and the formula for M, one obtains:

$$(w_A/w_B)^C = \left[\frac{\alpha\lambda_A}{(1-\alpha)\lambda_B}\right]^{1/\gamma} \qquad (20)$$

Within the limits imposed by voluntary participation in centralized wage setting, relative wages can take any value depending on the political weights, α and $(1 - \alpha)$.

The case where the union confederation treats all members equally is of particular interest. Equality of treatment would be attractive if the leadership of the union confederation wishes to avoid showing favoritism to particular affiliates. If $\alpha = 1/2$, $(w_A/w_B)^C = (\lambda_A/\lambda_B)^{1/\gamma}$ under centralized wage setting, as opposed to (λ_A/λ_B) under decentralized wage setting. Note that, for any number x and $\gamma > 1$, $x^{1/\gamma} < x$ if $x > 1$ and $x^{1/\gamma} > x$ if $0 < x < 1$. Thus, when the two unions are given equal weights by the central confederation and $\gamma > 1$, we have either

$$(w_A/w_B)^D < (w_A/w_B)^C < 1 \quad \text{or} \quad (w_A/w_B)^D > (w_A/w_B)^C > 1 \qquad (21)$$

The ratio of wage rates is always closer to one with centralized wage setting. When the union confederation weighs both affiliates equally and when $\gamma > 1$, centralized wage setting reduces but does not eliminate wage differentials. In this sense the centralization of wage setting has a bias toward greater wage equality in this model.

Wage Setting with Wage Leadership

The polar cases of decentralized, simultaneous wage setting and centralized wage setting do not exhaust the possible patterns. There is an intermediate case where unions act autonomously, but one union acts as a wage leader. Here wage leadership means that one union sets its wages before

160

the other, anticipating how the other union will respond. Equivalently, wage leadership can mean that one union sets its wages as a multiple of the other. For example, in the 1970s the white-collar unions in Sweden began to demand "earnings development guarantees" in which increases in white-collar salaries would be set equal to the sum of the centrally negotiated blue-collar wage increase plus average wage drift (Swenson 1989, 149). It might seem that an informal linkage among union demands would have similar effects on aggregate wage demands as fully centralized wage setting. In fact, in this model, such a linkage results in equal or higher aggregate wage demands than when wage setting is either centralized or fully decentralized (holding the number of unions constant).

In the case where $\gamma = 1$, each union's wage demands are independent of the wages of the other (equation 11). Thus, whether one union anticipates the response of the other or not makes no difference. Yet the wages of other unions do influence wage demands in the case where $\gamma > 1$. Let union B be the wage leader, and choose W_B first. Union A then chooses w_A. Firms, as before, choose the rate of investment after unions set wages. Thus, the wage leader chooses $w_B(t) = m_B(t)\lambda_B(t)$ to maximize w_B^* anticipating the optimal responses of both union A and management. Union B's optimal wage share as wage leader is shown in the appendix to be constant over time and equal to:

$$m_B^* = (1/\gamma)[(\rho/v) + y - 1] \tag{22}$$

Union A then follows by demanding the wage share (obtained by substituting equation 22 into equation 11):

$$m_A^*(1/\gamma^2)[(\rho/v) + \gamma - 1] \tag{23}$$

Provided $\rho < v/(1 + \gamma)$, equations (22) and (23) represent the Stackelberg solution with union B as leader and union A as follower. Note the equivalence between being the first to fix wages and successfully demanding a fixed multiple of whatever the other union receives. If union B sets $m_B = \gamma m_A$ before the determination of union A's wages, the result is the same as choosing the wage share prescribed by equation (22).

The wage leader receives a larger share of income than the wage follower when $\gamma > 1$. In fact, the wage leader receives a larger income share than it would with simultaneous wage setting. The wage follower, in contrast, receives a smaller share in the Stackelberg solution than in the Cournot-Nash solution when $\gamma > 1$. Yet the wage follower does not reduce its wage share enough to keep the aggregate wage share from rising. The total wage share with a Stackelberg leader, denoted $(W/Y)^S$, exceeds the wage share resulting from decentralized wage setting, $(W/Y)^D$:

$$(W/Y)^S - (W/Y)^D = \frac{\gamma - 1}{\gamma^2(2\gamma - 1)}[(\rho/v) + \gamma - 1] > 0 \qquad (24)$$

when $\gamma > 1$. Similar calculations reveal that shareholders consume a smaller share and invest a smaller share in the Stackelberg equilibrium. With a smaller investment share, income grows at a slower rate.

The wage leader acts on the knowledge that the wages of the wage follower decline as the wages of the leader increase. This implies that investment is less responsive to the leader's wages than it would be if the wages received by others were fixed, as they are assumed to be by all actors in the Cournot-Nash equilibrium. Consequently, the wage leader chooses a higher wage. The wage follower responds by accepting a lower wage, but not low enough to prevent the profit share from also falling. Shareholders then react by reducing both their consumption and investment.

As wage leader, union B enjoys a higher level of welfare than in the Cournot-Nash equilibrium when $\gamma > 1$. Union B could have chosen the Cournot-Nash equilibrium if that had been optimal. That union B's wage share is larger in the Stackelberg equilibrium indicates that the additional income in the present more than compensates members of union B for the slower rate of wage growth.

Both the shareholders and wage followers are worse off, however. They receive smaller income shares in an economy that is growing at a slower rate. Thus, the wage follower and employers have reason to join a coalition to restrain wages of the wage leader, if possible. In Sweden the initial steps toward centralized bargaining in the 1930s were undertaken by a coalition of employers and unions in manufacturing. Their aim, according to Swenson's (1989) account, was to limit the wage increases obtained by unions in construction.

Conclusion

When workers, organized in separate unions, are complements in production, a wage increase obtained by any single union reduces shareholders' optimal level of investment. The consequence is a lower rate of growth of wages for all unions, not just the union that raised wages. Decentralized wage setters ignore this negative externality. Centralized wage setters who internalize the effect of wage increases on all union members (but not shareholders) demand less in aggregate. Decentralized wage setting is inefficient in the sense that the total wage share with centralized wage setting could be divided among the unions in such a way that members of all unions, as well as shareholders, are better off.[10]

Thus, the relationship among unions who are complements in production is similar, but not identical, to an iterated prisoner's dilemma game. Unlike an iterated game, the payoffs are not stable over time. Yet, as in the iterated prisoner's dilemma, joint wage setting potentially increases the welfare of both unions over what each finds optimal when taking the other's wage share as fixed.

It does not follow, however, that centralized bargaining is necessary for the achievement of wage restraint. The equilibrium of decentralized bargaining described in this paper is not the only subgame perfect equilibrium of the decentralized game. Any outcome that is superior to decentralized bargaining for all unions can also be a subgame perfect equilibrium supported by trigger strategies (Benhabib and Radner 1988; Holden and Raaum 1989).[11] In trigger strategy equilibra, all unions agree on some path of wages and sustain their agreement by threatening to revert to the Pareto inferior equilibrium forever if any union deviates.

Cooperation can exist in the absence of binding agreements, but it is more fragile. Equilibria supported by trigger strategies (or other strategies that punish defectors in subsequent rounds) rapidly become implausible as the number of actors increases. Moreover, informal coordination on a path of wages is made difficult by the inevitable conflicts over which wage path should be chosen. For example, should wage increases preserve traditional differentials or should all unions receive equal absolute wage gains? All of the problems that make cooperation difficult in centralized bargaining, where unions negotiate a binding agreement with each other as well as with employers, are all the more difficult to surmount when binding agreements among unions are absent. Descriptions of the interaction between blue-collar and white-collar confederations in Sweden and Norway in the 1970s and 1980s suggest ongoing battles over who will act as wage leader rather than informal cooperation (Swenson 1989; Elster 1989; Hernes Unpublished paper, n.d.).

---

[10] Centralized wage setting is not Pareto optimal, however, when one includes shareholders. A centralized agreement covering both wages and investment could make all parties better off.

[11] If the unions cannot detect a defection from the agreed upon strategy immediately, trigger strategy equilibria exist only if the discount rate is low enough.

163

Indeed, the real puzzle is not the instability of cooperation in the absence of centralized bargaining but the instability of centralized bargaining itself. In both Belgium and the Netherlands, centralized bargaining broke down to a significant extent during the 1960s and 1970s. In Sweden the breakup is more recent. White-collar unions in the engineering industry seceded from centralized bargaining in 1982. The metal workers bargained independently in 1983. In 1984 there was no central agreement as unions negotiated at the industry level. Although a national agreement was reached in 1985–86, industry-level bargaining returned in 1987–88. In the words of a recent observer: "The disintegration of the famous Swedish model of collective bargaining now seems beyond doubt" (Ahlén 1988, 1).

Centralized bargainers have learned to live with, and even welcome, limited defection at the local level. Locally negotiated wage increases above the wage levels specified in the national agreement, usually referred to as "wage drift," are an institutionalized part of industrial relations in countries with centralized bargaining. In fact, wage drift provides important benefits for both sides in collective bargaining. Firms that are experiencing a shortage of labor need to be able to attract workers by raising wages. In addition, wage drift gives workers an incentive to cooperate with management in raising productivity. Those workers who receive increases through drift clearly benefit. Finally, local union activists benefit, since local bargaining gives them something to do. Thus, wage drift is important for maintaining the union infrastructure at the plant level.

Wage drift does set a lower bound on wage restraint. In Norway, for example, wage drift rarely fell below 4% between 1963 and 1987, except when wage increases were restricted by legislation (Holden 1989; Høgsnes and Hanisch 1988). Nevertheless, most of the variance of annual wage growth in Norway is explained by variance in the central agreement, not by the relatively constant drift. While bargaining at the local level is an integral part of centralized bargaining systems in Scandinavia, the power of local officials is limited. Strikes are not permitted after the central agreement has been signed. Local union negotiators are restricted to threatening milder forms of industrial conflict, such as "working by the book" in attempting to increase wages above what has been negotiated centrally.

What centralized wage setting cannot survive is the defection of major unions, such as the metalworkers in Sweden. The position of the Swedish metalworkers illustrates the ambiguous impact of centralized wage setting on the welfare of workers whose wages are relatively high. On the one hand, Swedish metalworkers share the efficiency gains resulting from overall wage moderation. On the other hand, relatively well-paid metalworkers have been disadvantaged by the contraction of wage differentials sought by the blue-collar confederation.[12] In both Norway and Sweden, conflicts among unions over wage differentials have increased as union membership of highly paid white-collar and professional workers has grown and as wage differentials have shrunk.

In terms of the model of this paper, whether the potential benefits of centralization become actual benefits depends on the political weights used by the union confederation in choosing its wage demands. If α is too low, union A would prefer decentralized wage setting. If α is too high, it is union B that would defect. Yet this explanation is insufficient, since there always exists some α that makes members of both union A and union B better off. If α reflects the outcome of prior bargaining among the two unions over the wage demands of the union confederation, all models of bargaining presume that the outcome for both unions will not be worse than what they could obtain in decentralized bargaining. No equilibrium strategy for either union could entail demanding an α such that the other union would prefer to set wages separately. Of course, the limits on the weight given the interests of any particular unions may not be obvious to the central bargainers. In practice, union leaders may have to learn the constraints imposed by voluntary participation in centralized bargaining through trial and frequent error.

Yet, it is also possible that in this instance bargaining theory is not descriptively accurate. To extend an example used earlier, if members of unions A and B are equally productive, their wages under decentralized bargaining would be equal. In this case, if $\gamma = 2$, centralized wage setting increases the welfare of both unions for any α roughly between .40 and .60. In contrast, consider the case where the productivity of union A workers is twice the productivity of workers in union B. Now (with $\gamma = 2$) α must be greater than .56 for centralization to benefit union A. If the union confederation treats both unions equally, that is if $\alpha = .50$, the cost of reduced wage differentials exceeds the gains from aggregate wage

---

[12] The fact that Swedish employers in the metalworking industry encouraged metalworkers to break away from the central agreement seems to contradict the result that shareholders always gain from centralized wage setting. The most common explanation is that employers wanted to increase wage differentials to attract skilled workers (Lash 1985). The explanation provided by a representative of the national employers' association (SAF) is that, with increased conflict within the blue-collar confederation, centralization had already broken down in substance, albeit not yet in form (personal discussion).

moderation for members of union A. To get an agreement that is Pareto superior to decentralized wage setting, the confederation must favor the relatively advantaged union.

Yet such favoritism conflicts with the norm of equal concern as well as the norm of helping those who are relatively disadvantaged, both prominent norms among union members and union officials (Swenson 1989; Elster 1989). There may be times when union members find the prospect of poorer aggregate economic performance less repellent than assenting to a wage distribution that they regard as unfair.

Appendix

Investment

Firms choose the time path of investment, $s(t)$, to maximize

$$\int_0^\infty e^{-\rho t} U[C(t)]\, dt \quad \text{s.t.} \quad \dot{Y}(t) = vs(t)[1 - m_A - m_B]Y(t) \tag{A.1}$$

where $C(t) = [1 - s(t)](1 - m_A - m_B)Y(t)$ represents shareholders' consumption and $\dot{x} = dx/dt$ for any variable x. Note that workers' share is considered by firms to be exogenously fixed at $(m_A + m_B)$.

The Hamiltonian for this problem is

$$H = e^{-\rho t}\{U[C(t)] + \mu(t)vs(t)(1 - m_A - m_B)Y(t)\} \tag{A.2}$$

where $\mu(t)$ is the implicit value to shareholders at time t of a marginal increase in aggregate income. From the optimality conditions $\partial H/\partial s = 0$ and $\partial H/\partial Y - d(e^{-\rho t}\mu)/dt$, the following conditions for an optimal path can be obtained:

$$U'[C(t)] = v\mu(t) \tag{A.3}$$

and

$$\dot{\mu}(t) = [\rho - v(1 - m_A - m_B)]\mu(t) \tag{A.4}$$

The first condition (A.3) stipulates that the marginal cost of forgone consumption be equated with the marginal benefit of investment. The second condition (A.4) states that the rate of change of the value of output to shareholders is equal to the discount rate minus shareholders' rate of return. In addition, the optimal path of investment must satisfy the transversality condition that the present value of output obtained in the distant future goes to zero as the distant future stretches to infinity, or $e^{-\rho t}\mu(t)Y(t) \to 0$ as $t \to \infty$. Otherwise, shareholders would be placing a positive value on output that would never increase their consumption possibilities.

To solve for the optimal path of investment, find the time derivative of marginal utility: $dU'[C(t)]/dt = U''(C)\dot{C} = U''(C)(1 - m_A - m_B)$ $[(1 - s)\dot{Y} - \dot{s}Y)]$. From (A.3) this must equal $\nu\dot{\mu}$. Using (A.4) to write $\dot{\mu}$ and rearranging terms, one obtains:

$$U''(C)C\left[\frac{\dot{Y}}{Y} - \frac{\dot{s}}{(1-s)}\right] = \nu\mu[\rho - \nu(1 - m_A - m_B)] \tag{A.5}$$

Using the constraint in (A.1) to write $(\dot{Y}/Y)$, the first order condition $U'(C) = \nu\mu$ (equation A.3) and the symbol γ to represent the coefficient of proportional risk aversion, $\gamma = -CU''(C)/U'(C)$, the last equation can be rewritten as

$$\nu s(1 - m_A - m_B) - \frac{\dot{s}}{(1-s)} = (1/\gamma)[\nu(1 - m_A - m_B) - \rho] \tag{A.6}$$

Equation (A.6) cannot be solved explicitly in the general case where γ depends on $C(t)$ and thus on $s(t)$. For the family of utility functions where γ is constant, however, a solution for (A.6) can be found by setting $\dot{s} = 0$ and $s(t) = s^*$ where

$$s^* = \frac{1}{\gamma}\left(1 - \frac{\rho/\nu}{1 - m_A - m_B}\right) \tag{A.7}$$

Solving for the time path of $Y(t)$ and $\mu(t)$ when $s(t) = s^*$, one can verify that s^* satisfies the transversality condition as well. Therefore, s^* satisfies the necessary conditions for the optimal path. Since the Hamiltonian is concave, the necessary conditions are also sufficient.

Decentralized Wage Setting

A similar procedure is used to solve the maximization problem of the union. Union A chooses the wage share $m_A(t)$ to maximize

$$\int_0^e e^{-\rho t} U[w_A(t)]\, dt \quad \text{s.t.} \quad \dot{\lambda}_A(t) = \nu s^*[1 - m_A(t) - m_B]\lambda_A(t) \tag{A.8}$$

where $w_A(t) = m_A(t)\lambda_A(t)$, s^* is shareholders' optimal rate of investment given in equation (A.7), and the other unions' wage share m_B is assumed by union A to be constant. Note that in the derivation of s^*, it was assumed that m_A and m_B were constant, just as union A assumes that s^* and m_B do not vary over time. However, there is no inconsistency if constant wage shares turn out to be optimal for unions A and B when the other's wage share and the rate of investment are also constant.

The unions' Hamiltonian is

$$H = e^{-\rho t}\{U[m_A(t)\lambda_A(t)] + (\mu(t)/\gamma)[\nu(1 - m_A(t) - m_B) - \rho]\lambda_A(t)\} \quad \text{(A.9)}$$

where $\mu(t)$ now represents the value to members of union A of a marginal increase in aggregate income per union member. The optimality conditions can be written

$$U'[w_A(t)] = \nu\mu(t)/\gamma \quad \text{(A.10)}$$

and

$$\dot{\mu}(t) = (1/\gamma)[(\gamma + 1)\rho - \nu(1 - m_B)]\mu(t) \quad \text{(A.11)}$$

Differentiating (A.10), substituting (A.11) for $\dot{\mu}(t)$, using the equality $U'(w_A) = \nu\mu/\gamma$ and rearranging terms yields

$$(\dot{\lambda}_A/\lambda_A) + (\dot{m}_A/m_A) = (1/\gamma^2)[\nu(1 - m_B) - (1 + \gamma)\rho] \quad \text{(A.12)}$$

If γ is constant, (A.12) can be solved by setting $\dot{m}_A = 0$ to yield

$$m_A^* = (1/\gamma)[(\rho/\nu) + (\gamma - 1)(1 - m_B)] \quad \text{(A.13)}$$

Since the constant wage share $m_A(t) = m_A^*$ satisfies the transversality condition, m_A^* fulfills the necessary conditions for the optimal path. As before, the concavity of the Hamiltonian implies that the necessary conditions are sufficient.

Centralized Wage Setting

The union confederation chooses $m_A(t)$ and $m_B(t)$ to maximize

$$V(W_A^*, W_B^*) = \int_0^\infty e^{-\rho t}\{\alpha U[w_A(t)] + (1 - \alpha)U[w_B(t)]\}\, dt, \text{ s.t.}$$
$$\dot{\lambda}_i(t) = \nu s^*[1 - m_A(t) - m_B(t)]\lambda_i(t) \quad \text{(A.14)}$$

for $i = A, B$. As before, s^* is shareholders optimal response to $(m_A + m_B)$ as given in equation (A.7).

168

The Hamiltonian can be written as

$$H = e^{-\rho t}\{\alpha U(m_A \lambda_A) + (1 - \alpha)U(m_B \lambda_B)$$
$$+ (1/\gamma)[\nu(1 - m_A - m_B) - \rho](\mu_A \lambda_B + \mu_A \lambda_B)\} \tag{A.15}$$

There are now three optimality conditions:

$$\alpha \lambda_A U'(w_A) = (1 - \alpha)\lambda_B U'(w_B) = (\nu/\gamma)(\mu_A \lambda_A + \mu_B \lambda_B) \tag{A.16}$$

and

$$\dot{\mu}_A = (1/\gamma)[(1 + \gamma)\rho - \nu(1 - m_B)]\mu_A - \nu m_A(\lambda_A/\lambda_A)\mu_B] \tag{A.17}$$

and

$$\dot{\mu}_B = (1/\gamma)[(1 + \gamma)\rho - \nu(1 - m_A)]\mu_B - \nu m_B(\lambda_A/\lambda_B)\mu_A] \tag{A.18}$$

Following the familiar steps of differentiating the first and the third terms in (A.16) and substituting (A.17) and (A.18) for $\dot{\mu}_A$ and $\dot{\mu}_B$, one can obtain

$$(\dot{\lambda}_A/\lambda_A) + (\dot{m}_A/m_A) = (1/\gamma^2)[\nu - (1 + \gamma)\rho] \tag{A.19}$$

If γ is constant, $\dot{m}_A$ can be set to zero and (A.19) solved to yield

$$(m_A^* + m_B^*) = (1/\gamma)[(\rho/\nu) + \gamma - 1] \tag{A.20}$$

The aggregate wage share $(m_A^* + m_B^*)$ satisfies the transversality conditions for μ_A and μ_B.

Equation (A.20) defines the union confederation's optimal choice of the aggregate wage share $(m_A^* + m_B^*)$ when γ is constant. Equation (A.16) determines the division of the aggregate wage share among the two unions. Note, from footnote 8, that $U'(C) = bC^{-\gamma}$ where b is any positive constant for the family of utility functions with a constant coefficient of proportional risk-aversion. Therefore, $U'(w_A)/U'(w_B) = (w_A/w_B)^{-\gamma}$, which can be rewritten as $(m_A \lambda_A/m_B \lambda_B)^{-\gamma}$. From (A.16) we also know that $U'(w_A)/U'(w_B) = [(1 - \alpha)\lambda_B]/\alpha \lambda_A$. Solving for (m_A/m_B), we have

$$(m_A/m_B) = \left[\frac{\alpha}{(1 - \alpha)}(\lambda_A/\lambda_B)^{1-\gamma}\right]^{1/\gamma} \tag{A.21}$$

169

Michael Wallerstein

Stackelberg Leadership

The problem faced by the Stackelberg leader is similar to choosing the optimal wage share, holding other wages constant (equations A.8–A.13). Instead of (A.9), the Hamiltonian for the wage leader (union B) is

$$H = e^{-\rho t}\{U[m_B(t)\lambda_B(t)] + (\mu(t)/\gamma^2)[\nu(1 - m_B) - (1 + \gamma)\rho]\lambda_B(t)\}$$

(A.22)

where m_A^* from (A.13) has been substituted for m_A. The optimality conditions are

$$U'[w_B(t)] = \nu\mu/\gamma^2$$

(A.23)

and

$$\dot{\mu}(t) = (1/\gamma^2)[(1 + \gamma + \gamma^2)\rho - \nu]\mu$$

(A.24)

Differentiating (A.23), making substitutions and rearranging terms produces

$$(\dot{\lambda}_B/\lambda_B) + (\dot{m}_B/m_B) = (1/\gamma^3)[\nu - (1 + \gamma + \gamma^2)\rho]$$

(A.25)

When γ is constant, (A.25) can be solved by setting $\dot{m}_B = 0$ to obtain

$$m_B^* = (1/\gamma)[(\rho/\nu) + \gamma - 1]$$

(A.26)

Since $m_A(t) = m_B^*$ satisfies the transversality condition and the Hamiltonian is concave, m_B^* fulfills the necessary and sufficient conditions for a maximum.

References

Ahlén, Kristina. 1988. "Recent Trends in Swedish Collective Bargaining: Collapse of the Swedish Model." *Current Sweden* (Stockholm: Swedish Institute) 358:1–3.

Bean, Charles, Richard Layard, and Stephen Nickell. 1986. "The Rise in Unemployment: A Multi-Country Study." *Economica* 53:S1–S22.

Benhabib, Jess, and Roy Radner. 1988. "Joint Exploitation of a Productive Asset: A Game-Theoretic Approach." Photocopy, New York University and AT&T Bell Laboratories.

Blinder, Alan. 1988. "The Challenge of High Unemployment." *American Economic Review* 78:1–15.

Boskin, Michael J. 1988. "Tax Policy and Economic Growth: Lessons from the 1980s." *Journal of Economic Perspectives* 2(4): 71–97.

Bratt, C. 1986. *Labour Relations in 18 Countries*. Stockholm: SAF.

Bruno, Michael, and Jeffrey Sachs. 1985. *The Economics of Worldwide Stagflation*. Cambridge: Harvard University Press.

Centralized Bargaining and Wage Restraint

Calmfors, Lars, and John Driffill. 1988. "Bargaining Structure, Corporatism, and Macroeconomic Performance." *Economic Policy* 3:13–61.

Cameron, David R. 1984. "Social Democracy, Corporatism, and Labor Quiescence: The Representation of Economic Interest in Advanced Capitalist Society." In *Order and Conflict in Contemporary Capitalism*, ed. John H. Goldthorpe. Oxford: Oxford University Press.

Crouch, Colin. 1985. "The Conditions for Trade-Union Wage Restraint." In *The Politics of Inflation and Economic Stagnation*, ed. Leon N. Lindberg and Charles S. Maier. Washington, DC: Brookings Institution.

Elster, Jon. 1989. *The Cement of Society*. Cambridge: Cambridge University Press.

Frank, Robert S. 1985. *Choosing the Right Pond*. New York: Oxford University Press.

Freeman, Richard B. 1988. "Labour Market Institutions and Economic Performance." *Economic Policy* 3:64–80.

Friend, Irwin, and Marshall E. Blume. 1975. "The Demand for Risky Assets." *American Economic Review* 65:900–22.

Garrett, Geoffrey, and Peter Lange. 1986. "Economic Growth in Capitalist Democracies, 1974–1982." *World Politics* 38:517–45.

Headey, Bruce W. 1970. "Trade Unions and National Wages Policies." *Journal of Politics* 32:407–39.

Heitger, Bernhard. 1987. "Corporatism, Technological Gaps, and Growth in OECD Countries." *Weltwirtschaftliches Archiv* 123:463–73.

Hernes, Gudmund. Unpublished paper, n.d. "Karl Marx and the Dilemmas of Social Democracies: The Case of Norway and Sweden." In *Experimenting with Scale*, ed. Philippe Schmitter. Cambridge: Cambridge University Press.

Hersoug, Tor. 1985. *The Importance of Being Unimportant: On Trade Unions' Strategic Position*. Memorandum from the Department of Economics No. 12. Oslo: University of Oslo.

Hicks, Alexander. 1988. "Social Democratic Corporatism and Economic Growth." *Journal of Politics* 50:677–704.

Holden, Steiner. 1989. "Wage Drift and Bargaining: Evidence from Norway." *Economica*, 56(224):419–432.

Holden, Steiner, and Oddbjørn Raaum. 1989. *Wage Moderation and Union Structure*. Memorandum from the Department of Economics, No. 6. Oslo: University of Oslo.

Horn, Henrik, and Asher Wolinsky. 1988. "Worker Substitutability and Patterns of Unionization." *Economic Journal* 98:484–97.

Høgsnes, Geir, and Ted Hanisch. 1988. *Incomes Policy and Union Structure: The Norwegian Experience during the Seventies and Eighties*. Working Paper 88:8. Oslo: Institute for Social Research.

Lancaster, Kelvin. 1973. "The Dynamic Inefficiency of Capitalism." *Journal of Political Economy* 81:1092–109.

Lange, Peter. 1984. "Unions, Workers, and Wage Regulation: The Rational Bases of Consent." In *Order and Conflict in Contemporary Capitalism*, ed. John H. Goldthorpe. Oxford: Clarendon Press.

Michael Wallerstein

Lange, Peter, and Geoffrey Garrett. 1985. "The Politics of Growth." *Journal of Politics* 47:792–827.

Lash, Scott. 1985. "The End of Neo-Corporatism? The Breakdown of Centralized Bargaining in Sweden." *British Journal of Industrial Relations* 23:215–39.

Layard, Richard, and Stephen Nickell. 1988. "Unemployment in Britain." *Economica* 53:S121–169.

Lehmbruch, Gerhard. 1977. "Liberal Corporatism and Party Government." *Comparative Political Studies* 10:91–126.

Marks, Gary. 1986. "Neocorporatism and Incomes Policy in Western Europe and North Americs." *Comparative Politics* 18:253–77.

McCallum, John. 1986. "Unemployment in the OECD Countries in the 1980s." *Economic Journal* 96:942–60.

Olson, Mancur. 1982. *The Rise and Decline of Nations.* New Haven: Yale University Press.

Oswald, Andrew J. 1979. "Wage Determination in an Economy with Many Trade Unions." *Oxford Economic Papers*, 31:369–85.

Panitch, Leo. 1977. "The Development of Corporatism in Liberal Democracies." *Comparative Political Studies* 10:61–90.

Pohjola, Matti. 1984. "Union Rivalry and Economic Growth: A Differential Game Approach." *Scandinavian Journal of Economics* 86:365–70.

Schwerin, Donald S. 1980. "The Limits of Organization as a Response to Wage-Price Problems." In *Challenge to Governance: Studies in Overloaded Politics*, ed. Richard Rose. Beverly Hills: Sage.

——— 1982. "Incomes Policy in Norway: Second-Best Corporate Institutions." *Pollty* 14:464–80.

Solow, Robert. 1988. "Growth Theory and After." *American Economic Review* 78:307–17.

Strand, Jon. 1987. *Oligopoly with Monopoly Unions.* Working Paper No. 33. Stockholm: Trade Union Institute for Economic Research.

Swenson, Peter. 1989. *Fair Shares: Unions, Pay, and Politics in Sweden and West Germany.* Ithaca: Cornell University Press.

Verma, Anil, and Thomas Kochan. 1985. "The Growth and Nature of the Nonunion Sector within a Firm." In *Challenges and Choices Facing American Labor*, ed. Thomas Kochan. Cambridge: MIT Press.

Wallerstein, Michael. 1990. "Class Conflict as a Dynamic Game." In *Beyond the Marketplace: Rethinking Economy and Society*, ed. Roger Friedland and A. F. Robertson. New York: Aldine de Gruyter.

9

Postwar Trade-Union Organization and Industrial Relations in Twelve Countries

Miriam A. Golden, Michael Wallerstein,
and Peter Lange

Ten years ago, when the volume *Order and Conflict in Contemporary Capitalism* (Goldthorpe 1984) was published, conventional academic wisdom regarding the future of trade unions and corporatism in western Europe was optimistic. As numerous contributors to that earlier volume emphasized, systems of industrial relations involving encompassing unions, in which authority was concentrated in either a small number of large industrial unions or in national confederations, had performed remarkably well in the decade after the first oil price shock of 1973. Most contributors to the Goldthorpe volume shared the view articulated by Peter Lange (1984) that unions could be thought of as playing an *n*-person prisoner's dilemma in which decentralized action among organizations resulted in collectively suboptimal outcomes. Unions would accept greater wage restraint collectively, the argument went, but not willingly concede acting individually. The prisoner's dilemma analogy suggested that the more encompassing the union movement, the greater the concentration among unions, and the more centralized the authority of the peak associations, the more likely it

The data reported here were collected as part of a project funded by the National Science Foundation entitled "Union Centralization among Advanced Industrial Societies." Data collection and research assistance were provided by Allyson Benton, Bronwyn Dylla, David Ellison, Miongsei Kang, Preston Keat, Bernadette Kilroy, Danise Kimball, Amie Kreppel, Brian Lawson, Sydney Mintzer, Jonathan Moses, Stephen Newhouse, and Carolyn Wong at UCLA and Torben Iversen, Brian Loynd, Jessica Rouleau, and Lyle Scruggs at Duke University. The graphics were produced by Allyson Benton, Pia Kaiser, and Stephen Newhouse. Financial support came from the National Science Foundation, SES-9309391 and SES-9108485 to UCLA and SES-9110228 and SBR-9309414 to Duke University. Additional support came from UCLA's Institute of Industrial Relations and the Committee on Research of the Academic Senate, as well as from the Center for German and European Studies at the University of California at Berkeley.

was that the collectively optimal cooperative solution could be obtained. David Cameron (1984), among others, provided support for this view with evidence showing that corporatism was associated with wage restraint and low strike rates, as well as with lower inflation and less unemployment than in noncorporatist OECD countries.

The concern with how the organizational features of trade unionism affect economic performance and the optimism about the relative merits of corporatism were premised on an important if often inexplicit assumption: that unions themselves would remain effective agents for the promotion of the economic interests of workers. More specifically, it was typically assumed that in the advanced industrial economies, unions would continue to represent a source of wage pressure which, if not controlled through political-organizational means, could threaten macroeconomic performance. The powerful and centralized unions characteristic of corporatism were seen as one end of a continuum, while the other was characterized by countries in which a relatively small subset of workers was strongly unionized and likely to remain so while the remainder of the work force was exposed to market forces with relatively little institutional protection. Labor militancy, whether overtly on show or successfully controlled by astute union leaders, was expected to be a permanent feature in the former group countries, buttressed by the full-employment economy believed characteristic of advanced capitalism, while organized workers in the latter group would also retain market power.

Today, trade unions and corporatist bargaining arrangements appear much less durable than they did ten years ago. A series of stylized facts fuels this suspicion. There is a general perception that unions are suffering from declining membership and influence (Visser 1992). Instead of supporting centralized bargaining, employers aggressively promote the decentralization of wage setting to the level of the firm or even the individual employee (Katz 1993). Unions have become less unified and more fragmented as workers have grown increasingly heterogeneous in their interests and identities (Locke and Thelen 1995). Such changes are commonly believed to be occurring across the advanced countries, marking a presumed crisis of trade unionism and of corporatist bargaining institutions. As a result, today unions in OECD countries are viewed as either weak and decentralized, with little power to affect wages and conditions in the labor market, or as stronger but declining in power and whose ability to affect economic outcomes has been restricted primarily to the firm, industry, and/or regional levels. Almost no one argues that unions retain the strength and cohesion they often exhibited a few decades ago.

Two explanations for the decline in unions over the past decade dominate current thinking. The first emphasizes the impact of changes in technology in altering workplace relations and occupational structures in ways that are detrimental to the unity of union movements. Gudmund Hernes (1991) and Karl Moene and Michael Wallerstein (1993b), for example, argue that the proliferation of small and highly specialized groups of workers with extraordinary market power has resulted in greater fragmentation and decentralization of unions in the Nordic countries, where collective bargaining used to be especially encompassing and centralized. Wolfgang Streeck (1993) and Jonas Pontusson and Peter Swenson (1996) emphasize the decentralizing effect of the widespread adoption of new production technologies, technologies that place a premium on product differentiation and rapid responses to changes in consumer demand. Peter Lange, Michael Wallerstein, and Miriam Golden (1995) and Geoffrey Garrett and Christopher Way (1995) have pointed to the destabilizing impact of the growing weight of public sector workers in the union movement.

The second main explanation of union decline concerns the impact of increased economic integration, or what has come more generally to be termed "globalization." Melvin Reder and Lloyd Ulman (1993) argue that economic integration has eroded the ability of unions to raise wages above the level that would exist in the absence of unions. As long as unions' ability to "take wages out of competition" stops at national borders while product markets have expanded to include the entire European Union, the room for union-negotiated wage increases is sharply reduced. Such union weakness is only exacerbated by the growth in capital mobility and increasing potential for firms to "exit," or to threaten to "exit," if union demands threaten their competitiveness and profits. Likewise, Dani Rodrik (1996: 2) stresses that because globalization has led to an increased substitutability of unskilled labor, "globalization makes it difficult to sustain the post-war bargain under which workers would receive continued improvements in pay and benefits in return for labor peace and loyalty." In contrast to this view but also in a context of globalization, Wolfgang Streeck and Philippe Schmitter (1991) emphasize the declining room for discretionary macroeconomic policies on the part of national governments in an integrated Europe. Without the ability to manage demand, Schmitter and Streeck argue, governments have little need for union cooperation and unions have little incentive to organize collectively in order to be able to deliver wage restraint for policy conces-sions. Finally, Timothy McKeown (1999), echoing the perspective adopted by Rodrik, argues that increasing levels of international trade in the advanced industrial economies have weakened the market power of less skilled workers while potentially increasing that of their more skilled coun-terparts, a transformation that is bound to affect the largest industrial unions, whose membership largely comprises the less skilled.[1]

What is striking about both these lines of interpretation of union decline is that they imply a *widespread* and *permanent* weakening of unions. The decline of trade unions and corporatist bargaining institutions is viewed as a product of deep and irreversible transformations of the social struc-tures of the advanced industrial economies and of their positioning in the international economy. Globalization, for instance, has become the latest in a series of supposedly impersonal and uncontrollable forces sweeping the advanced countries (and indeed the less developed nations as well) whose effects can only be borne but not circumvented or even very greatly con-trolled. The requirements for successful economic competition in a new global economy are believed to be largely incompatible with strong and cohesive unions and with centralized collective bargaining.

If this is the case, then we should see exactly what many observers claim is occurring: a process of convergence underway among industrial rela-tions systems of the OECD countries toward the noncorporatist end of the continuum. Yet this view encounters a basic problem: some prominent industrial relations specialists argue that what is most striking in European industrial relations today is the divergence of national experiences and the absence of a general pattern of union decline (Hyman 1994; Traxler 1994, 1995).

Such divergent views about the simple facts of the situation mean that before we can begin to compare the relative explanatory power of different putative causes of union decline and fragmentation and their impact on the conditions that permitted corporatist practices, we need better data on how much has really changed in industrial relations in the past ten years. To date, almost all discussions have been largely anecdotal. The primary purpose of this chapter is to present more systematic information on the extent to which the organizational strength of unions and employers' associations may have actually changed in the past decade.

---

[1] The impact of trade with the Third World on the demand for unskilled and semiskilled labor in Europe and North America is subject to a vigorous debate. See Freeman 1995, Richardson 1995, and Wood 1995 for three views.

We summarize data concerning twelve countries: Austria, Britain, Canada, Denmark, Finland, France, Germany, Italy, Japan, Norway, Sweden, and the United States. This group includes the most and least corporatist countries in the OECD, as well as the countries with the largest populations.[2] We chart changes in these countries along four dimensions, each of which has often been considered a condition for union strength and corporatist bargaining. First, we summarize changes in union *density*, or the share of the work force belonging to unions. Second, we investigate the extent of union *coverage*, or the share of the work force covered by a union agreement. Third, we present data on changes in union *concentration*, both between union confederations and within union confederations. Fourth, we compare the *authority* held by different levels of union and employer organizations. Finally, we summarize our findings and discuss what can be inferred regarding the nature and sources of change in the institutions of industrial relations and the implications of such changes for future union strength and bargaining practices.

Union Density

Union density – the proportion of eligible employees who become union members – is usually taken as the first and perhaps most fundamental measure of union strength. This is easily justified. Only in very unusual circumstances is union density an unimportant indicator of the ability of organized labor to attract mass support and of its potential to mobilize workers for industrial action.[3] Trends in density are therefore usually considered significant indicators of the state of trade unionism more generally.

Reinforcing the dominant and relatively pessimistic interpretation of contemporary unionism, Jelle Visser, the OECD's foremost authority on union density (Visser 1989, 1990, 1991), describes recent trends by noting that "in fourteen of the eighteen countries [considered] unionization levels fell in the 1980s" (Visser 1992: 18). Visser's analysis shows that only in Sweden, Finland, Norway, and Canada did aggregate union density rates remain stable or increase between 1980 and 1989. While Visser is careful

---

[2] See Golden and Wallerstein 1996 and Wallerstein, Golden, and Lange 1997 for additional data not presented here.

[3] In countries such as Italy and France, where membership is not obligatory and rival union confederations exist, rates of strike participation and rates of participation in elections for union representatives may surpass membership rates by very large amounts, making the latter weaker proxies for union strength than elsewhere.

177

to note the continuing diversity of unionization rates and trends among countries, his interpretation of the recent period resonates with the more general sense of union crisis that is often encountered in the comparative literature.

While it is certainly true that in most OECD countries trade unions have not experienced recent growth, examining only the 1980s leads to conclusions that may be unwarranted. In Table 9.1, we present union density rates for our twelve countries since 1950 in five-year intervals. By extending the time span from one to four decades, a more nuanced and qualified interpretation of changes in membership levels emerges. Over the longer postwar period, union density in most of the countries studied has increased and then fallen back, but usually to a level still above that where it began in 1950.[4]

Comparing density rates in 1989 with those that obtained in 1950, we can group countries into two classes: those in which density has increased or remained stable, and those where it has fallen, which we define as a decline of more than 10 percent off the original 1950 value. Over the forty-year period, most of the countries we examine (seven of the twelve) exhibit either stable or increasing rates of union density.[5] Quite substantial increases have occurred in Denmark, Finland, Norway, and Sweden. Perhaps not surprisingly, as Bo Rothstein's work alerted us (1992), three of these are countries in which trade unions control unemployment funds.[6] Although officially employees who suffer job loss need not be union members to receive unemployment insurance, in these countries access to unemployment funds is facilitated by union membership. In only five of the twelve countries – Austria, France, Italy, Japan, and the United States – has density undergone a decline over the postwar era, taking the 1989 value against that from 1950.

As frequently observed in the literature, decline has indeed been more widespread if we examine trends only since 1980. Seven of our twelve countries experienced declines of greater than 10 percent between 1980 and 1989. Undoubtedly decline has multiple causes, including vast ongoing

---

[4] This generalization is not true of Finland or Sweden, where density rose throughout the period, nor is it true of Japan, where it has declined since 1950. The other nine countries experienced increases, and then more recent declines in union membership.

[5] We class Germany and the United Kingdom as cases of stability, since density declined less than 10 percent in both countries (from 34 to 31 percent in Germany and from 41 to 38 percent in the United Kingdom).

[6] A fourth country where unions control unemployment funds is Belgium, which also had high and stable union density throughout the 1980s.

Table 9.1. *Net Union Density at Five-Year Intervals (1950–1989) and Unadjusted Coverage (1990) for Twelve Countries (Percentages)*

	Net density									Unadjusted Coverage, 1990
	1950	1955	1960	1965	1970	1975	1980	1985	1989	
Austria	57.51	58.39	57.38	56.43	54.86	51.04	50.35	48.43	45.52	71
Canada	32.77	36.09	27.59	25.58	29.05	31.81	33.16	32.83	32.70	38
Denmark	53.30	54.68	60.10	61.32	60.16	68.19	76.34	78.50	74.39	74[c]
Finland	31.47	31.12	32.67	37.62	51.93	65.92	70.35	69.00	71.94	95
France	30.88	19.95	19.57	19.71	21.55	21.61	17.56	15.19	10.15	92[c]
Germany	34.17	34.72	35.01	33.52	32.95	34.61	34.33	32.08	30.77	76
Italy	40.27	33.10	23.05	23.36	33.37	43.57	44.13	36.23	33.53	83
Japan	36.47[a]	35.59	31.34	34.60	34.49	33.61	30.28	27.79	25.36	21[d]
Norway	44.26	46.42	57.66	57.31	55.56	51.47	55.74	54.10	53.84	75[e]
Sweden	66.66	68.62	70.08	64.92	66.18	72.85	78.01	81.26	82.89	83
United Kingdom	40.59	40.90	40.70	40.63	44.65	47.58	48.61	40.47	38.26[b]	47
United States	28.38	31.20	29.35	26.95	25.85	23.11	20.24	17.22	14.76	18

[a] Data from 1953.
[b] Data from 1988.
[c] Data from 1985.
[d] Data from 1989.
[e] Data from 1992.

occupational shifts from industry to tertiary employment, where unions typically have more difficulty enrolling members. Indeed, as we will note in greater detail, unionization has recently tended to increase only in those few countries – found especially in Scandinavia – where union movements have been unusually successful in recruiting white-collar workers. In addition, however, in countries where unions do not administer unemployment insurance, density rates have tended to track labor market conditions, albeit with a lag (see Western 1993 and 1997). By this reasoning, part of the decline that we observe in density rates in the 1980s is a function of sustained weak demand for labor, a view also supported by the analysis undertaken by Peter Lange and Lyle Scruggs (1996). If this is correct, density rates can be expected to recover, at least in part, when and if unemployment rates decline significantly in Europe.[7]

It is worth noting explicitly that the best-known cases of union decline, including the United States, are not representative of more general trends across the countries we study. The United States, like France and Japan, has exhibited a secular decline in membership rates over many decades, a decline clearly independent of fluctuations in the business cycle and short-term changes in labor market conditions. In the United States, as in France and Japan, density rates have dropped steadily over the past decades even when unemployment rates have improved. There is, moreover, evidence for the United States that density is responding at least as much to changes in national public policy as to labor market conditions (Goldfield 1987). But the evidence for our twelve countries shows that trends in unionization rates in the United States should not be taken as representative of trends elsewhere.

Overall, the data on union density suggest three conclusions. First, substantial differences in density trends characterize our twelve countries. There is no uniform pattern of decline even in the period since 1980, even if it is the most common trend since then. Second, even among union movements that have experienced declining density in the past decade, decline, when seen in a longer temporal perspective, often becomes more clearly short-term and hence somewhat less striking. Most countries in our sample have experienced increases and more recently declines in density. If the first did not herald a permanent strengthening of labor movements, neither may the second indicate their permanent weakening. Rather than

---

[7] For a review of the causes of persistent unemployment in Europe, see Alogoskoufis et al. (1995).

decrying purported union decline, perhaps we should be looking for the systematic cross-national causes of fluctuations in union membership. Third, density rates, far from converging across countries, remain vastly different and this difference has increased dramatically since 1950. In 1989, density ranged from 15 percent to 83 percent (in the United States and in Sweden, respectively), whereas density rates in 1950 ranged only from 28 percent to 66 percent (again, in the same two countries). Despite all the recent attention to common technological changes, occupational shifts, and globalization, labor movements in advanced countries are becoming more dissimilar in their abilities to attract members, not more alike.

Union Coverage

Coverage rates refer to the proportion of employees who are covered by collectively bargained contracts.[8] Because many employees who are not union members are nonetheless covered by collectively bargained agreements, the degree of union coverage is a more accurate measure of the extent to which unions affect wage levels in the economy than is the rate of union membership. Substantial declines in union coverage would indicate an erosion of the ability of trade unions to influence wage levels. Stable and high coverage, by contrast, suggests that unions continue to have an important role in wage setting despite whatever declines in membership may have occurred in recent years. Coverage rates have rarely been used as measures of union strength, however, because comparative data have been almost entirely unavailable. Now, Franz Traxler (1994, 1996) has compiled and made available data on collective bargaining coverage rates among selected OECD countries. In Table 9.1, we present figures on coverage for our twelve countries in 1990.

In the 17 countries Traxler examines (of which the twelve studied here are a subset), coverage was (with the exception of the Japanese case) always at least as extensive as unionization, and often a good deal more so (see Traxler 1994: 173, chart 5.1), as observation of the data reported in Table 9.1 corroborates. The latter phenomenon occurs in a variety of ways. In some cases, firms are legally required to pay a collectively bargained wage to all employees, regardless of their union status. In other cases, employers'

---

[8] Although we are really interested in collectively bargained wage contracts, the available data refer only to collectively bargained contracts generally. While some of these probably do not set wages, undoubtedly most do.

associations mandate that the firms affiliated with them pay collectively bargained wages to all employees. And in remaining cases, finally, govenments may extend the collective agreement to entire industries, for instance, by ministerial decree.

As a result of these various measures, which vary considerably country by country, coverage in 1990 was very high (greater than 70 percent) in eight of the twelve countries studied here. In the remaining four – Canada, Japan, the United Kingdom, and the United States – unionization rates are modest and extension mechanisms nonexistent. Only this specific combination of variables produces low coverage. All of the continental European countries that we study are, by contrast, characterized by high union density, extension mechanisms, or both.

We know few studies that have tracked coverage over time. In a recent paper, Simon Milner (1995) presents data that he compiled on union coverage in Britain between 1895 and 1990. Over the course of the twentieth century, Milner finds that coverage has increased from below 10 percent in 1900 to a peak of 73 percent in 1973. For the recent period, Milner finds significant change in the extent of coverage in Britain. Whereas coverage increased in the early 1970s, it declined slightly in the latter part of the decade and then slipped precipitously in the 1980s, falling to its latest estimate of only 47 percent in 1990. This is, indeed, a dramatic and major decline in the extent to which collectively bargained wages are paid to British employees.

Are British findings generalizable? Traxler (1994: 185), surveying existing data on seven of our countries (and four that we do not cover) for the decade from 1980 to 1990, argues that they are not. The decline in coverage in Britain is the most extreme instance of decline that he finds, and decline itself, he shows, has been limited to only a handful of the countries investigated. Coverage rates in the 1980s remained largely stable in Canada, Finland, and Germany, increased in France, and declined in the United States, Japan, and Great Britain. Moreover, the decline in Japan was relatively modest (from 28 to 23 percent). As a result, it seems unlikely that there has been a widespread or general collapse in the ability of unions to negotiate wages for large numbers of nonunion employees.

We can also investigate the relationship between coverage and density visually in order to obtain more information to assess whether union strength is generally declining. Figure 9.1 presents a scatterplot showing the relationship between the degree of unionization in a country in 1989 and its degree of bargaining coverage the next year. Traxler himself, working with a

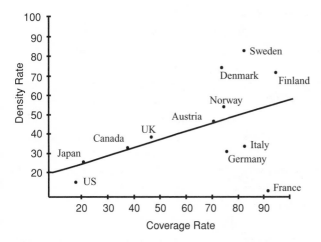

Figure 9.1 Net density versus unadjusted coverage in twelve countries (*c*. 1990).

larger sample of countries, found that "there is only a modest positive correlation ($r = 0.41$) between the two rates" (1994: 174). Nevertheless, as inspection of the scatterplot reveals, the relationship between density and coverage is quite clearly positive, especially if one removes the deviant French case. As density rises, so too does coverage. The line that we have fitted shows this quite well.

More careful review of the scatterplot reveals that the variance of coverage rates is much greater at low levels of union density than at high levels. Low levels of union membership (say, 40 percent or less) correspond to extremely variable levels of coverage, levels that range from under 20 percent (the U.S. case) to more than 90 percent (the French case, where unionization in 1989 was only 10 percent but coverage an astonishing 92 percent). Low unionization is thus entirely indeterminate in its relation to coverage. However, once union membership exceeds a certain threshold – about 40 percent – coverage rates are uniformly greater than 70 percent.[9]

Particularly striking is the uniformly high level of union coverage in Europe, especially on the continent, and despite the diversity of union density rates. Although more than half of European workers do not belong to unions, relatively few workers on the continent are not covered by a union-negotiated collective agreement, at least among the countries for

[9] There are only two countries (Germany and France) with density rates below this threshold where coverage exceeds 60 percent.

which we have data. Across Europe, four out of five workers receive wages that reflect the outcome of a process of collective bargaining. In North America and Japan, by contrast, the wages and salaries of most employees are determined in competitive labor markets.

How do these data reflect on the issues of union crisis, its generalizability, and its likely duration? While the absence of long-term longitudinal data does not allow us to examine trends for the entire postwar era, the high rates of coverage that obtain in continental Europe speak against the union crisis hypothesis. Even in 1990, all of the continental countries on which we present data boasted coverage rates above 70 percent. These figures indicate that unions continue to bargain over the wages of most wage and salary earners in continental Europe. This is not to say that unions today bargain as effectively on behalf of their workers as they did earlier, but it does mean that their institutional role in the bargaining process remains largely intact and that they often continue to be able to take a large portion of wages "out of competition."

Union Monopoly and Concentration

Many see signs of union decline in aspects of union organization other than membership and the coverage afforded by union contracts. Even if collective bargaining still covers 80 percent of the work force on the continent in western Europe, unions are seen as less unified and therefore less influential than they used to be. The dominant argument in the literature is that unions across the OECD countries have experienced a loss of internal cohesion. Richard Hyman (1994: 11) characterizes the prevalent view: "A further aspect of changing union effectiveness and representativeness concerns the balance between unity and division: the inter- and intra-union dynamics of solidarity and sectionalism. It is a familiar argument that European trade unions in harder political and economic times have displayed a loss of cohesion at best, or at worst have been riven by internecine conflicts."

In this section, we investigate changes in concentration, or the extent to which single organizations of workers organize potential constituents. Concentration indicates the ability of a small number of actors to dominate decision making. In principle, the smaller the number of actors, the easier it is to prevent free riding and therefore to obtain collectively optimal outcomes (Golden 1993).

We distinguish two dimensions of concentration. The first, *interconfederal* concentration, refers to the number of actors and their relative size at the confederal level. We measure interconfederal concentration by the number of peak-level union confederations and the distribution of union members among them. As a summary measure, we also provide figures on the proportion of total union members enrolled in any of the major confederations, where major is defined as any confederation with at least 5 percent of total union membership in at least one year between 1950 and 1989. The second dimension of concentration, *intraconfederal* concentration, refers to the number of actors and their relative size within each confederation. Our indicators of intraconfederal concentration are the number of affiliated national unions and the share of members belonging to the largest affiliate and the largest three affiliates. In many cases, measures of interconfederal and intraconfederal concentration have changed in opposite directions over the four decades on which we have data.

As regards interconfederal concentration, our countries divide into three groups, as illustrated by the data reported in Table 9.2. In six of the twelve countries, interconfederal concentration has clearly declined over the postwar period. This is true of Norway, Sweden, Denmark, Finland, France, and Italy. In the four Nordic countries, the confederations are divided along essentially occupational lines. In all four, the main blue-collar confederation has lost ground relative to confederations of white-collar and professional workers. To some extent, this reflects changes in the composition of the labor force. More importantly, the change reflects the sharp increase in union membership among white-collar and professional workers that has occurred in these countries. In France and Italy, the decline of interconfederal concentration is linked to the political decline of the Communist parties of those two countries. In both cases, the relative size of the Communist-allied union confederation has declined throughout the postwar period.

In the second group of countries, comprising Austria, Germany, and the United Kingdom, interconfederal concentration has not changed very much in the past forty years. In Austria, the main confederation's monopoly status is enshrined in law. No other confederation enjoys legal recognition. As in Austria, little change in interconfederal concentration has occurred in the United Kingdom, where the Trades Union Congress (TUC) remains the country's predominant peak association for labor. In Germany, the share of union members in the largest confederation has fallen since 1950, but the decline is small and was arrested part way through the period. No decline in the German confederation's organizational cohesiveness has been observed since 1970.

Table 9.2. *Interconfederal Concentration at Five-Year Intervals (1950–1989) for Twelve Countries (Percentages)*

	1950	1955	1960	1965	1970	1975	1980	1985	1989
Group 1									
Denmark									
LO	84.48	81.98	81.51	78.82	78.37	67.28	69.56	69.72	67.95
FTF	–	10.55	11.84	12.56	13.65	14.92	15.44	15.40	15.40
AC	–	–	–	–	–	3.13	3.88	3.69	4.84
Total	84.48	92.53	93.35	91.38	92.02	85.33	88.88	88.81	88.19
Finland									
SAK/FFC	70.38	66.42	48.83	39.71	68.71	65.80	62.68	59.14	58.55[a]
TVK/TOC	18.12	16.56	23.69	23.61	22.28	21.00	19.72	21.02	19.57
SAJ	–	–	11.43	16.89	–	–	–	–	–
Akava	–	–	–	–	4.48	9.30	9.85	11.99	13.28
STTK	–	–	–	–	2.89	6.20	7.00	7.30	7.75
Total	88.50	82.98	83.96	80.21	90.99	86.80	82.40	80.16	99.15
France									
CGT	75.50	61.83	54.40	49.14	47.70	44.00	37.02	31.19	n.a.
FO	9.07	13.71	15.43	16.30	17.39	16.49	19.71	24.75	n.a.
CFTC	8.68	13.04	16.28	2.40	2.25	2.32	3.11	4.15	n.a.
CFDT	–	–	–	16.16	17.22	19.01	19.77	20.35	n.a.
Total	93.24	88.57	86.11	88.13	87.94	86.45	84.97	86.67	n.a.
Italy									
CGIL	88.99	85.53	75.45	70.03	56.32	54.55	52.43	53.42	52.54
CISL	22.82	27.37	38.68	40.42	34.60	34.66	34.88	34.35	35.32
UIL	n.a.	n.a.	n.a.	n.a.	n.a.	n.a.	15.35	15.20	15.04
Total	111.81[b]	112.9[b]	114.13[b]	110.45[b]	90.92	89.21	102.67[b]	102.96[b]	102.89[b]
Norway									
LO	100.00	100.00	81.93	80.92	78.29	75.23	71.30	67.47	65.00
AF	–	–	–	–	–	8.16	9.80	12.01	16.76
YS	–	–	–	–	–	–	9.27	11.19	14.82
Total	100.00	100.00	81.93	80.92	78.29	83.39	90.36	90.66	96.58
Sweden									
LO	79.00	77.23	75.86	71.61	65.98	62.90	61.00	60.27	58.63
TCO	16.80	18.83	20.10	23.34	28.26	31.20	29.91	32.04	33.03
SACO/ SACO-SR	1.43	2.38	2.92	3.96	4.52	5.41	6.45	7.47	8.34
Total	97.22	98.43	98.87	98.91	98.75	99.51	97.36	99.78	100.00
Group 2									
Austria									
OeGB	100.00	100.00	100.00	100.00	100.00	100.00	100.00	100.00	100.00
Germany									
DGB	90.93	84.05	80.54	79.67	81.35	82.10	81.72	80.70	81.56
DBB[c]	2.00	7.12	8.21	8.52	8.74	8.10	8.51	8.32	8.23
DAG[d]	5.13	5.79	5.69	5.76	5.59	5.24	5.13	5.24	5.22
CGB	n.a.	n.a.	2.53	2.71[d]	2.36	2.50	2.99	3.21	3.16
Total	98.06	96.96	96.96	96.66	98.05	97.95	98.35	97.47	98.18
UK									
TUC	84.87	83.23	82.65	84.95	84.11	85.06	94.02	91.08	85.93[e]

	1950	1955	1960	1965	1970	1975	1980	1985	1989
Group 3									
Canada									
TLC/CLC	37.78	38.03	76.96	74.34	75.11	70.86	66.79	56.83	56.58^e
CCL	24.84	22.87	–	–	–	–	–	–	–
CTCC/	6.59	6.32	6.98	9.45	9.54	6.02	5.37	5.66	5.23
CNTU									
Total	69.21	67.21	76.96	74.34	75.11	70.86	66.79	56.83	61.81
Japan									
JCTU/Sohyo	47.88	49.21	48.88	41.88	36.90	36.32	36.79	35.15	31.95
Rengo	–	–	–	–	–	–	–	–	44.53
JTUC/Domei	–	9.93	12.06	16.35	17.75	18.00	17.48	17.40	–
Churitsuroten	–	–	–	9.69	12.06	10.88	10.98	12.54	–
Zenroren	–	–	–	–	–	–	–	–	–
Total	47.88	49.21	48.88	41.88	36.90	36.32	36.79	35.15	76.49
United States									
AFL/AFL-CIO	57.68	60.36	75.93	79.86	71.60	73.56	68.99	77.12	79.93
CIO	24.78	25.97	–	–	–	–	–	–	–
Total	82.46	86.33	75.93	79.86	71.60	73.56	68.99	77.13	79.93

Notes: n.a. = not available. – = not applicable.
^{a} Finnish data for 1989 are from 1988.
^{b} See data sources for a discussion of why Italian totals exceed 100%.
^{c} Data from 1951.
^{d} Data from 1964.
^{e} British data for 1989 are from 1988.

Finally, there is a third set of countries, comprising the United States, Canada, and Japan, in which interconfederal concentration has increased over the forty years thanks to mergers of rival confederations. In both the United States and Canada, mergers of rival confederations occurred early in the postwar period. Since then, interconfederal concentration has followed divergent paths in the two countries, with membership in unions outside the main confederation declining modestly in the United States but increasing in Canada. In Japan, the merger of rival confederations is quite recent.

There appears to be a relationship between union density and changes in interconfederal concentration. The country in which a merger of rival confederations has occurred in recent years – Japan – is one where union membership has fallen significantly as a share of the labor force.[10] In contrast,

[10] The Netherlands is another example of a country where rival confederations have merged and union membership had declined significantly. See Wallerstein, Golden, and Lange 1997, for additional information.

Table 9.3. *Intraconfederal Concentration (1950–1990) for Eleven Countries (Percentages)*

Country and Confederation	1950			1955		
	Number of Affiliates	% in Largest Affiliate	% in Largest 3 Affiliates	Number of Affiliates	% in Largest Affiliate	% in Largest 3 Affiliates
Austria						
OeGB	16	15.7	39.8	16	17.5	43.6
Canada						
TLC/CLC	80	8.1	20.0	88	9.1	22.6
CCL	27	19.9	47.2	27	16.6	42.6
Denmark						
LO	57	36.7	52.5	54	36.1	53.8
Finland						
SAK	38	16.7	34.6	39	15.1	35.5
TVK	31	29.2	57.1	23	31.3	67.7
Germany						
DGB	16	24.8	48.8	16	27.2	51.0
Italy						
CGIL	n.a.	22.1	45.9	n.a.	23.4	45.3
CISL	n.a.	21.9	46.5	n.a.	16.6	32.0
UIL	n.a.	n.a.	n.a.	n.a.	n.a.	n.a.
Japan						
JCTU/Sohyo	32	19.7	47.1	37	18.8	46.2
Rengo	–	–	–	–	–	–
JTUC/Domei	–	–	–	14	49.3	93.3
Norway						
LO	39	11.0	31.1	43	11.0	30.8
AF	n.a.	n.a.	n.a.	n.a.	n.a.	n.a.
YS	n.a.	n.a.	n.a.	n.a.	n.a.	n.a.
Sweden						
LO	44	17.2	32.7	44	17.6	34.6
TCO	43	22.0	40.9	42	24.5	43.5
United Kingdom						
TUC	186	15.9	35.2	183	15.3	35.2
United States						
AFL/AFL-CIO	108	12.8	27.0	137	12.4	29.5

Notes: n.a. not available; – not applicable.

	1960			1965			1970	
Number of affiliates	% in Largest Affiliate	% in Largest 3 Affiliates	Number of Affiliates	% in Largest Affiliate	% in Largest 3 affiliates	Number of Affiliates	% in Largest Affiliate	% in Largest 3 Affiliates
16	18.3	46.1	16	18.7	48.4	16	18.6	48.6
07	7.3	18.6	110	9.3	23.1	110	9.2	24.9
–	–	–	–	–	–	–	–	–
53	32.9	55.0	50	30.8	56.5	45	28.7	56.0
25	16.8	46.2	24	24.7	54.2	31	16.2	39.0
26	28.0	57.2	29	25.2	51.2	29	17.6	42.0
16	28.9	52.4	16	30.6	53.7	16	33.1	56.6
n.a.	22.7	40.9	n.a.	15.8	36.6	n.a.	15.3	38.8
n.a.	14.8	28.2	n.a.	12.1	29.3	n.a.	14.2	33.7
n.a.	n.a.	n.a.	n.a.	n.a.	n.a.	n.a.	n.a.	n.a.
57	15.8	40.0	63	18.7	39.0	63	20.9	40.3
–	–	–	–	–	–	–	–	–
23	44.2	82.0	22	31.6	52.6	26	26.6	47.7
41	12.7	32.0	40	13.6	33.4	35	15.1	36.6
n.a.	n.a.	n.a.	n.a.	n.a.	n.a.	n.a.	n.a.	n.a.
n.a.	n.a.	n.a.	n.a.	n.a.	n.a.	n.a.	n.a.	n.a.
44	19.2	36.9	38	21.2	41.9	29	22.0	46.3
37	27.2	46.4	32	30.2	48.7	23	28.9	49.0
83	15.3	35.9	172	16.3	36.7	150	16.3	36.9
36	7.9	19.9	130	8.3	19.7	123	6.8	17.8

189

Table 9.3 *(continued)*

Country and Confederation	1975			1980		
	Number of Affiliates	% in Largest Affiliate	% in Largest 3 Affiliates	Number of Affiliates	% in Largest Affiliate	% in Largest 3 Affiliates
Austria						
OeGB	16	18.9	48.7	15	20.4	48.7
Canada						
TLC/CLC	113	9.7	25.5	91	11.0	28.2
CCL	–	–	–	–	–	–
Denmark						
LO	40	27.3	55.1	33	25.0	56.7
Finland						
SAK	28	16.4	38.4	29	15.2	40.4
TVK	23	18.4	40.3	19	21.1	48.6
Germany						
DGB	16	34.7	57.8	17	33.8	56.7
Italy						
CGIL	24	13.7	37.8	22	13.0	35.3
CISL	41	14.4	33.3	38	13.1	31.0
UIL	n.a.			32	11.1	30.0
Japan						
JCTU/Sohyo	64	25.9	46.9	50	27.6	49.6
Rengo						
JTUC/Domei	28	22.2	46.4	31	21.3	44.5
Norway						
LO	35	16.4	40.0	33	19.2	48.4
AF	32	22.5	49.2	32	21.8	49.5
YS	n.a.	n.a.	n.a.	15	23.9	54.6
Sweden						
LO	25	23.7	50.7	25	24.2	54.9
TCO	24	27.7	49.8	21	28.3	54.6
United Kingdom						
TUC	111	17.9	38.1	109	17.1	35.1
United States						
AFL/AFL-CIO	112	7.4	18.7	105	7.6	21.2

| | 1985 | | | 1990 | |
Number of Affiliates	% in Largest Affiliate	% in Largest 3 Affiliates	Number of Affiliates	% in Largest Affiliate	% in Largest 3 Affiliates
15	20.8	49.3	15	20.5	49.1
96	14.0	34.1	90	16.0	35.9
–	–	–	–	–	–
31	22.6	54.7	30	22.7	54.6
28	17.0	41.1	24	18.8	42.8
15	18.4	51.2	15	22.3	50.9
17	33.1	56.8	16	34.4	58.6
19	9.9	27.6	18	8.7	24.5
17	10.2	25.4	21	7.2	20.0
29	9.2	26.8	29	8.2	24.0
50	29.0	51.6	–	–	–
			81	13.9	32.9
32	22.8	46.4	–	–	–
34	21.8	49.8	29	25.4	61.6
36	22.4	49.7	40	19.7	49.8
15	23.0	56.1	17	18.6	52.5
24	28.0	57.5	23	28.5	57.8
21	23.9	49.3	21	23.7	48.1
91	15.1	33.9	76	15.1	33.8
96	7.6	22.6	89	n.a.	n.a.

in the three countries in our sample where density has increased over time – Denmark, Finland, and Sweden – interconfederal concentration has fallen as the share of membership organized by the largest confederation has declined relative to the whole organized work force. Density has been increasing in these countries as new confederations have successfully enrolled previously unorganized groups of workers. Indeed, the emergence of new, occupationally specific union confederations has probably enhanced the ability of the union movement generally to organize such workers. They appear more likely to join an organization tailored to their needs than a general confederation of both blue- and white-collar employees.

In contrast to the diversity of trends we observe in interconfederal concentration, there is a widespread tendency toward increased intraconfederal concentration among the countries in our sample, as illustrated by the data presented in Table 9.3.[11] The number of unions affiliated with the main confederation has declined significantly since 1950 in Great Britain and the United States, as well as in the four Nordic countries of Norway, Denmark, Sweden, and Finland. The largest decline in the number of affiliates, measured as a percentage of the number of affiliates in 1950 or 1970, occurred in Great Britain. In 1950, the main British confederation had 186 affiliates, whereas four decades later, it had only 76. Another dramatic case is Denmark, which, like Britain, has historically housed a large number of craft unions. Three unions in the main confederation have recently reorganized into five bargaining units. In Germany and Austria, the number of affiliates remains unchanged while the concentration of members in the largest affiliates has increased slightly. Declines in the number of affiliates can also be observed in Italy, although we have data only since 1975. The only countries of our twelve whose major confederations have witnessed increases in the number of affiliated unions since 1950 are Canada (although here the number has been falling since about 1970) and Japan.

Our other measures of intraconfederal concentration – the share of membership held by the largest single and largest three affiliates – likewise show a general tendency to increase across almost all of our countries. Unions have rationalized their organizations by reducing their number of affiliates and concentrating more members in their largest affiliates in all countries except where the number of affiliates was already small at the beginning of the postwar period.

[11] We have been unable to obtain affiliate figures for France; hence Table 7.3 offers data on the other eleven countries only.

Overall, our data show a common tendency toward greater concentration within confederations but divergent trends with regard to concentration among union confederations. The latter seems systematically related to changes in union density. Where density has fallen, there has been a tendency for concentration to increase, as unions have responded to membership losses with mergers. Where density has risen, there has been a tendency for concentration to decline, as the growth of new members has occurred largely outside the traditionally dominant union organizations. Indeed, we suspect that the ability of organized labor to cope successfully with the occupational shifts away from employment in industry and toward the tertiary sector depends heavily on organizational specialization and hence proliferation.

This latter phenomenon suggests that unions may be caught in a dilemma. The share of the work force in the traditional core of the union movement – blue-collar workers in manufacturing, transportation, mining, and construction – is declining. Those union movements to have responded successfully in organizing the growing share of the work force in white-collar and professional occupations have experienced splits along occupational lines. This is what has occurred in the four Nordic countries. White-collar and professional workers there exhibit a preference to join their own distinctive confederations rather than those traditionally dominated by blue-collar workers. Conversely, those unions that have preserved their unity across occupational lines have generally suffered declines in union density.[12] The main German confederation has been unique in successfully preventing a significant decline in union density while nonetheless maintaining its dominant organizational position within the German union movement. Not surprisingly, Germany is also exceptional in its degree of stability in the manufacturing work force as a share of the total labor force; that is, occupational shifts have not been as important there as elsewhere.

Authority in Unions and Employers' Organizations

The authority of different levels of organization – national, industry, and local – in wage negotiations and industrial conflict is a central component of every measure of corporatism. Moreover, the changing roles of union confederations, national unions, and shop floor organizations in collective

---

[12] This is very similar to the electoral dilemma faced by socialist parties in western Europe described by Przeworski and Sprague (1986).

bargaining and industrial conflicts are central elements of the current debate over the degree to which traditional patterns of industrial relations have been shattered and wage-setting processes decentralized. In this section, we examine the authority of union confederations and national industrial unions, as well as the autonomy of shop floor bodies. We also investigate the authority of peak business associations and national affiliates over their member enterprises.

We distinguish statutory authority from participation in wage determination or the predominant level of wage setting. Statutory authority refers to what lower levels of union organization can or cannot do without the permission of the central confederation as specified in the confederation's constitution or, in a few cases, national law. Participation in wage setting refers to the activities of the confederation during wage negotiations. While the extent of confederal participation in wage setting can change with every bargaining round, statutory authority only changes when the organization's statutes are revised. In this chapter, we present data only on statutory authority, although elsewhere we also investigate the involvement of central confederations in wage setting (see Wallerstein and Golden, forthcoming; Wallerstein, Golden, and Lange, 1997; and Golden and Wallerstein 1996).

Our assessment of the authority of the central confederations and the industry-level union and employer organizations rests on the rules as specified in organizational statutes for a number of related reasons. First, it is simply easier to gather hard evidence of constitutional change than of informal changes of processes and relations among various levels. Fewer inevitably arbitrary judgment calls are required. Second, statutory authority may have a larger impact than is readily visible. If actors in a subordinate position restrict their activities to those that higher levels will not veto, the higher levels may effectively delimit the actions of lower levels even though an actual veto is never observed. However, the gulf between formal and actual authority can be particularly wide at the enterprise level. Where actual practice differs from formal authority at the enterprise level, we report what we believe to be customary practice. Third, many of the more informal changes that occur in authority relations are better captured by our data on confederal involvement in private sector collective bargaining, presented in Golden and Wallerstein (1996) and Wallerstein, Golden, and Lange (1997).

We examine the statutory authority of actors at three levels of union organizations: the peak confederal level, a major national union (typically the leading metalworking or engineering union), and the shop floor organization.[13] As regards national unions, it proved difficult to collect information on how national unions function generally, and we have therefore almost always used the country's national metalworking or engineering federation as emblematic of national trade unionism more generally. This is not because we necessarily believe that these unions are "average," but instead because they often play a pattern-setting role, thereby influencing wage growth throughout the labor force. For the same reason, the metalworkers' or engineers' union is typically the most frequently studied and about which, therefore, most information is publicly available.

Our index of union authority is meant to assess the extent to which each of the three levels wields authority in wage bargaining vis-à-vis the other two. Thus, we have been principally concerned with the extent to which each level maintains independent resources – its own strike fund, its own authority to sign collective agreements, independence in calling and settling disputes – and the degree to which each level controls the selection of officers or influences the wage bargaining of other levels. As a rule, a positive answer indicates a greater degree of authority or autonomy for the level in question, and a negative answer, the reverse.[14]

We have collected parallel data on employers' organizations. The hypothesis that employers have been systematically attacking centralized bargaining and attempting to push collective bargaining down to lower levels could be verified with evidence of devolution of authority within employers' organizations. For employers, we have distinguished only the peak-level confederation and the national (i.e., sectoral) employers' organizations, since it hardly makes sense to assess the authority of the firm in a free-market context. At the national level, we have considered the metalworking or engineering sector as representative, as we did for organized labor.

---

[13] In general, we report on shop floor union organization. However, in Austria and Germany, where works councils are both more important than shop floor union organization and where the former are effectively if informally dominated by the latter, we report on works councils instead.

   In some countries, regional unionism may also play an important role in collective bargaining (this is true, for instance, of Germany, where bargaining is almost all regional in scope), but it is generally so difficult to collect data on regional union organizations that we have omitted this level entirely. For the German case, we have merged the national and regional levels for coding purposes.

[14] A negative answer to the question of whether shop stewards cannot be dismissed or replaced from above indicates that they *can* so be, whereas a positive response indicates shop steward autonomy in this matter.

Table 9.4. *Statutory Authority in Major Union Confederations and Their Metalworking Affiliates (1950–1992) for Twelve Countries*

	Austria	Canada	Denmark	Finland 1950–71	Finland 1972–92	France
Peak-level confederation	Oegb	CLC	LO	SAK	SAK	All
Appoints leaders of lower levels	Yes	No	No	No	No	No
Signs own wage agreement	No	No	No	Yes	Yes	No
Has own strike fund	Yes	No	No	Yes	No	No
Veto power over wage agreements signed by affiliates	Yes	No	No	Yes	No	No
Participates in demand formulation and/or bargaining of lower levels	Yes	No	Yes	Yes	No	No
Veto power over strikes by affiliates	Yes	No	Yes	Yes	No	No
National metalworkers, auto workers, or engineers	Metall	CAW/USA	Metall	Metall	Metall	All
Appoints leaders of local or shop stewards	No	No	No	No	No	n.a
Signs wage agreement without countersignature from above	No	Yes	Yes	Yes	Yes	Yes
Can initiate strike action without approval from above	No	Yes	Yes	No	Yes	Yes
Has own strike funds	No	Yes	Yes	Yes	Yes	n.a.
Veto power over wage agreements signed by locals	No	Yes	No	Yes	Yes	n.a.
Participates in demand formulation and/or bargaining by lower levels	No	Yes	No	Yes	Yes	n.a.
Veto power over strikes by lower levels	Yes	Yes	Yes	Yes	Yes	n.a.
Shop stewards or work councillors in metalworking	Metall[a]	CAW/USA	Metall	[b]	[b]	[b]
Recognized by union and/or legal statute	Yes	Yes	Yes	Yes	Yes	Yes

Note: n.a. = not available.
[a] Information concerns shop stewards generally, but probably also extends to those in the metalworking industries.
[b] Information concerns works councillors.

Germany	Italy 1950–68	Italy 1969–92	Japan	Norway	Sweden	United Kingdom	United States
DGB	All	All	All	LO	LO	TUC	AFL-CIO
No	Yes	Yes	No	No	No	No	No
No	Yes	No	No	Yes	Yes	No	No
No	No	No	No	Yes	Yes	No	No
No	Yes	No	No	Yes	No	No	No
No	Yes	Yes	No	Yes	Yes	No	No
No		No	No	Yes	Yes	No	No
IG-Metall	All	All	IMF-JC	Felles.	Metall	AUEW/CSEU	UAW/USA
No	n.a.	No	No	No	No	No/Yes	Yes/No
Yes	No	Yes	No	Yes	Yes	No/Yes	Yes
Yes	n.a.	Yes	Yes	No	No	Yes/Yes	Yes
Yes	No	No	No	Yes	Yes	Yes/No	Yes
No	n.a.	No	No	No	Yes	No/Yes	Yes
No	n.a.	Yes	Yes	Yes	Yes	Yes/–	Yes
Yes	n.a.	No	No	Yes	Yes	Yes/No	Yes
IG-Metall[a]	[b]	All	[b]	[b]	[b]	Engineering	UAW/USA
Yes	No	Yes	Yes	Yes	Yes	Yes	Yes

Table 9.4 *(continued)*

	Austria	Canada	Denmark	Finland 1950–71	Finland 1972–92	France
Are elected rather than appointed from above	Yes	Yes	Yes	Yes	Yes	Yes
Cannot be dismissed or replaced from above	Yes	No	No	Yes	Yes	n.a.
Right to strike without approval from above	No	No	No	No	No	Yes
Automatically receive strike funds or control own	No	No	No	No	No	No
Right to negotiate local or enterprise wage agreements	Yes	No	Yes	Yes	Yes	Yes
Right to bargain without external officials present	Yes	No	Yes	No	No	Yes
Sign wage agreements without countersignature from above	Yes	No	Yes	Yes	Yes	Yes
Participate in wage bargaining delegation of higher levels	Yes	Yes	No	No	No	n.a.

Our results for unions and employers' associations are presented in Tables 9.4 and 9.5 respectively. Among union movements, the data show that most are characterized by shared governance; that is, there are relatively few unions in which a single level exercises uncontested authority. In particular, shop floor union bodies in all the countries considered except the United States and Canada enjoy some notable degree of autonomy in decision making, and thus some potential for independent action.[15]

[15] It is interesting that shop floor autonomy is lowest in the two countries where collective bargaining is traditionally considered among the most decentralized. This may be less paradoxical than it appears, however, if we consider that higher levels of union organization may require much more authority over enterprise union representatives than where bargaining is more often located at the level of the enterprise itself. Without such authority, superordinate levels would be in danger of allowing bargaining outcomes to occur that they could not control. Where, by contrast, bargaining occurs at higher or on multiple levels, shop floor union representatives can enjoy greater autonomy because their ability to affect outcomes is intrinsically less.

Germany	Italy		Japan	Norway	Sweden	United Kingdom	United States
	1950–68	1969–92					
es	No	Yes	Yes	Yes	Yes	Yes	Yes
es	No	No	Yes	Yes	Yes	No	No
No	n.a.	Yes	Yes	No	No	No	No
No	No	No	Yes	No	No	No	Yes
es	No	Yes	Yes	Yes	Yes	Yes	No
es	No	Yes	Yes	Yes	Yes	Yes	No
es	No	Yes	Yes	Yes	Yes	No	No
No	No	Yes	n.a.	No	No	No	Yes

With this qualification, we can still classify the twelve cases according to the authority of different levels. Peak-level union confederations in Austria, Norway, and Sweden, as well as in Finland until 1971 and Italy until 1968, are the only major confederations in our twelve countries to enjoy very significant statutory authority over lower levels. Not surprisingly, Austria, Norway, and Sweden (and to a lesser extent Finland) are considered classically corporatist cases. The other extreme is found in Japan and to a slightly lesser extent in Italy after 1969, where neither national nor confederal bodies exercise significant authority over shop floor union agents. Canada, Denmark, Finland after 1971, France, Germany, the United Kingdom, and the United States, finally, are all cases where national unions seem to exercise the greatest authority, authority that is, as we have noted, shared with shop floor bodies in all cases except the North American.

Among employers' organizations, the data reported in Table 9.5 show that the peak level exercised substantial authority over national affiliates in Denmark, Finland, Italy until 1962 (although the lack of complete

199

Table 9.5. *Statutory Authority in Central Employer Organizations and Their Metalworking Affiliates (1950–1990) for Ten Countries*

Employers' organizations	Austria	Denmark	Finland	France	Germany	Italy	Japan	Norway	Sweden	United Kingdom
Peak-level confederation	BWK	DA	STK	ONPF	BDA	Confindustria[a]	Nikkeiren	NAF/NHO	SAF[x]	CBI
Appoints officials of lower levels	No	No	No	No	No	n.a./No	No	No	No/No	No
Signs own wage agreement	No	No	Yes	No	No	n.a./No	No	Yes	Yes/No	No
Has own strike funds	No	Yes	Yes	No	No	n.a./No	No	Yes	Yes/Yes	No
Veto power over wage agreements signed by affiliates	No	Yes	No	No	No	Yes/No	No	Yes	Yes/Yes	No
Participates in demand formulation and/or bargaining of lower levels	Yes	Yes	Yes	No	Yes	n.a./Yes	Yes	Yes	Yes/Yes	No
Veto power over lockouts by affiliates	No	Yes	Yes	No	No	n.a./No	No	Yes	Yes/Yes	No
Metalworking or engineering industry federation	All	Unknown	FIMET	UMM	All	Federmeccanica[b]	None	TBL	VF	EEP[d]
Signs wage agreement without countersignature from above	Yes	n.a.	Yes	Yes	Yes	n.a.	–	Yes	Yes	Yes/No
Can initiate lockout without permission from above	Yes	n.a.	No	Yes	Yes	n.a.	–	No	No	Yes/n.a.
Has own strike funds	Some	n.a.	Yes	Yes	Yes	No	–	No	Yes	Yes/No
Veto power over wage agreements signed by members	No	n.a.	No	No	No	No	–	No	Yes	No/No
Participates in demand formulation and/or bargaining at lower levels	No	n.a.	No	No	Yes	Yes	–	Yes	Yes	No/No
Veto power over lockouts by members	Yes	n.a.	Yes	No	Yes	No	–	Yes	Yes	Yes/No

Notes: Data on Austria reflect industry-level employers' associations, not metalworking in particular. n.a. = not available. – = not applicable.
[a] 1950–1962/1963–1992.
[b] 1971+.

information must temper this assessment somewhat), Norway, and Sweden until 1990. Peak-level organizations in Austria, France, Germany, post-1963 Italy, Japan, and the United Kingdom held very little authority over affiliates. In Canada and the United States, finally, employers are not organized into peak-level associations, and these countries are thus absent from the table.

These data suggest two interesting conclusions. First, the extent of authority over lower levels enjoyed by the central organizations of labor and of business in any particular country can be quite different. For instance, the classically corporatist countries of Austria, Denmark, Germany, Norway, Sweden, and Finland exhibit high levels of statutory authority on either the employers' or the union side, but not necessarily both. This is somewhat surprising, given that one might have expected the two kinds of organizations to mirror each other organizationally in order to be equally effective in coordinating collective bargaining.

One reason they do not, we suspect, speaks to our second conclusion. There is simply much less of a relationship than might have been anticipated between the extent to which central organizations exercise statutory authority over lower levels and the extent to which they actively intervene in and control the practice of collective bargaining from year to year. Indeed, substantial discrepancies often obtain, as we detail elsewhere (Wallerstein, Golden, and Lange, 1997). In Austria, for instance, the central organization of labor exercises relatively significant authority over lower levels, but collective bargaining nonetheless occurs exclusively at the industry level. The Finnish central confederation, by contrast, exercises little statutory authority over its affiliates but nonetheless bargains regularly on their behalf. In France, likewise, the central confederations enjoy almost no statutory authority, but their role in collective bargaining has been very extensive thanks to numerous important agreements they have signed regulating benefits and working conditions.

It is surprising that statutory authority and the extent of central intervention in wage setting do not necessarily coincide. The economic effects of these two different ways of centralizing industrial relations may be more or less equivalent, although that remains an empirical question deserving further research. Nonetheless, it would not necessarily be accurate to infer that central organizations directly intervene in collective bargaining just because they exercise a high degree of statutory authority, just as it would be inaccurate to infer that they enjoy significant authority on paper just because they play important roles in the bargaining process. These two indicators do not necessarily go together, implying that collecting separate data on each may be required to assess the effects of centralization more generally on economic outcomes.

Our data on statutory authority thus show large variations among countries. However, there is almost no variation over time. In most countries, the authority relations that were established after World War II (if not earlier) endure even today. The major exceptions on the union side are Italy and Finland, which witnessed changes in union authority relations in the 1960s and 1970s. In Italy, these entailed a decentralization of confederal authority, and the concomitant empowerment of shop floor union organizations. In Finland, whereas the statutory changes also weakened the authority of the main confederation, the national industrial unions were the main beneficiaries rather than shop floor organizations. Moreover, the Finnish changes were part of the process of unifying rival confederations and establishing a centralized system of wage negotiations that would serve as a national framework for subsequent industry-level agreements. The only other exceptions to the general pattern of little change is the weakening of the authority of the British engineering federation of employers in the late 1980s and of the Swedish employers' confederation in 1982 and again in 1990, when the organization's peak bargaining unit was dismantled.

The general absence of change in patterns of internal authority in trade unions and employers' organizations in the postwar period is quite remarkable. If there is a crisis of unions, they are certainly not responding by undertaking significant statutory changes, or by adapting union statutes to the powerful external economic forces presumably at work. Authority relations also show little reflection of the changes in inter- and intraconfederal concentration discussed earlier. Employers, moreover, are generally not following the lead offered by British and Swedish organizations and devolving authority to lower levels, thereby rendering peak-level offices relatively ineffective and forcing unions to adjust accordingly.

Of course, as we have already suggested, these findings may tell us little about changes underway in collective bargaining. At least in some countries, notably Sweden and Britain, bargaining became significantly less centralized in the 1980s. While this is confirmed by the shifts in authority relations undertaken by employers over their affiliates, we suspect that in other countries, bargaining may devolve substantially even in the absence of statutory alterations.[16] Suffice it to say here, however, that diversity in formal authority remains as great as it has been historically and few changes are to be noted. This, in turn, means that in unions in which the formal authority of the center was considerable in the past, it remains so today.

Conclusion

In this chapter, we have examined changes in industrial relations along the dimensions of union membership; union coverage; concentration, both interconfederal and intraconfederal; and statutory authority, both for employers and for unions. Our main findings are summarized here.

Union membership as a share of the work force has declined in most countries in our sample since 1980, in some cases dramatically. Nevertheless, this trend must be qualified in two ways. First, in the countries where the unions provide unemployment insurance – Denmark, Sweden, and Finland – union density continued to increase in the 1980s. Second, the trend of declining membership disappears in some countries if one begins with a baseline of 1950 or 1970 rather than 1980. A long-term decline in union membership over most of the postwar period is true in only a minority of countries, albeit a minority that contains a majority of the work force of our sample.

In Great Britain, Japan, and the United States, the coverage of collective agreements appears to have declined as union membership has declined. In continental Europe, by contrast, coverage remains high and stable. In spite of the decline in union membership, almost all western European workers, outside of Britain, work for wages that were negotiated by a trade union.

Two trends are evident with regard to interconfederal concentration. Among the Nordic countries, which have some of the highest rates of union density in the world, interconfederal concentration has declined as the growth of unions has occurred largely outside the traditional, blue-collar, socialist confederations. Among some of the countries with the greatest decline in union membership, such as Japan, interconfederal concentration has increased as previously rival confederations have united. With regard

---

[16] In Italy, for instance, a dramatic decline in the level of central intervention in collective bargaining occurred just at the end of our data set (in 1992), when the country's wage indexation system was dismantled. This is not reflected, to the best of our knowledge, in changes in the extent of statutory authority on either the employers' or union side, however.

to intraconfederal concentration, there is a nearly universal trend to reducing the number of affiliates except in cases where this number was already quite low.

The lack of change in statutory authority in most countries is quite notable. By and large, the statutory authority established during the interwar years or immediately after World War II has remained unchanged, even, in some countries, in spite of big changes in the organizational structure of the confederations or the practice of wage negotiations. Moreover, the few changes that did occur in the postwar period in trade unions were concentrated in the 1960s and early 1970s. There has been little change in authority relations in response to the more recent demands for greater decentralization that has come from employers in some, albeit not all, countries, even among employers' associations themselves.

Overall, there is more diversity and fewer common trends occurring across the OECD nations than most scholars have assumed. Some features of union movements in some countries have remained largely unchanged, whereas others have changed but not in predictably similar ways. Thus, our data support the view that industrial relations institutions and trade unions have by and large proved quite resilient in the face of considerable domestic and international economic pressures in the past two decades. In only two of the twelve countries we investigate, Britain and the United States, is there broad and conclusive evidence of a dramatic decline in the influence of unions: secular declines in membership, a sharp falloff in coverage, and efforts to merge unions in order to respond to growing weakness. These are the only countries where organized labor exhibits decline along multiple indicators. And in these countries, we suspect that government policy and politics played at least as important a role as the market in promoting such catastrophic collapse.

Were the proponents of the union crisis hypothesis correct, we might expect to have seen substantial changes in authority relations within both labor movements and employers' organizations within the past decade. With the decentralization of bargaining purportedly underway, one would have expected that employers' organizations would have devolved authority to lower levels. We have found no evidence to support this claim, however, except in Britain and Sweden.

These findings do not appear consistent with arguments that changes in domestic sociooccupational structures or in international economic relationships are (already) creating a crisis in trade unions across the advanced industrial countries. Yet the conclusion that unions have proved more resilient than commonly believed may be premature. There are three possible lines of argument supporting such skepticism.

First, our categories may be too crude to pick up the relevant changes underway; that is, perhaps beneath the surface of seeming institutional resilience as measured by the cross-national indicators we have gathered, extensive de facto changes have been occurring in the interactions among levels of unions and employers' organizations over wage bargaining.

Second and related, we have not included direct measures of the centralization of wage setting in this chapter. The level of collective bargaining can change even when the statutory authority of the different organizations remains constant. Thus, perhaps the formal resilience of the institutional trappings of centralization hides substantial bargaining decentralization. Sweden is the most visible illustration of such a possibility. There, a clear decentralization of wage setting has occurred since 1983 with no change in the statutory authority of the union confederation (although changes have occurred in the statutory authority of the employers' confederation). Yet we know from other work that significant changes in the actual practice of wage setting is far from universal. Sweden and Britain, in this regard, represent exceptions rather than the rule (Golden and Wallerstein 1996; Wallerstein, Golden, and Lange 1997).

Finally, it is possible that the changes anticipated have yet to come. While we cannot exclude such a possibility, we nonetheless remain impressed by the relative absence of change in trade-union organization and industrial relations systems despite more than two decades of apparent pressures for such changes. This suggests that possibly the pressures working against trade unions and preexisting patterns of collective bargaining have been overstated.

Underlying each of these doubts about our preliminary conclusions is a more general criticism: that what is being measured does not indicate the extent of union strength, the ability of unions effectively to promote the interests of their members and workers more generally, or the current and future state of corporatist practices. In other words, skeptics would argue that beneath the surface of relative stability on some of the dimensions we examine and relative divergence on others, there is actually a convergence toward unions that are weaker, more divided, and more decentralized. Obviously, we cannot counter such skepticism with data, for we do not have it, nor do they. Nonetheless, some concluding observations can be offered.

First, the lack of a uniform pattern of union decline by virtually any available measure causes us to be skeptical of *all* general explanations for *why* unions are declining. General explanations seem to explain too much. Only in terms of recent membership trends is union decline widespread, and here the evidence points as much to mass unemployment as to domestic and international structural changes as the underlying cause (Western 1993, 1997).

Second, on all other dimensions that we examine, significant change is limited to a minority of countries. Only the United States and the United Kingdom have witnessed union decline along multiple dimensions. These two cases both point to the importance of government policy. The United States and the United Kingdom are the only countries in our sample where conservative governments actively encouraged employers to engage in a frontal attack on union power. The rapidity of union decline in these two countries is a stark reminder of the vulnerability of unions to political attack, but it says little about the vulnerability of unions to occupational change or international economic transformations.

This brings us to our final point. In the majority of the countries we have studied, unions have retained most of the *institutionally based* capacities for the defense of worker interests that they had prior to the 1980s. Indications of union weakness, such as declining union density since 1980, must be weighed against indications of continuing union strength, such as the high levels of union coverage in continental Europe. The continued authority of central confederations, where they enjoyed such authority earlier, is more evident in the data than a trend toward greater decentralization, except in Sweden and Britain. The current weakness of unions appears, in most countries, to be more a product of sustained unemployment (and occasional political assault) than an instance of institutional decay.

If there is little evidence of institutional change in most countries, that may be because existing institutions have important benefits for employers and governments as well as for unions. Interpretations stressing the apparent weakening of organized labor and trade unionism rest on the implicit assumption that existing institutional arrangements embody union successes, successes that had been gained at the expense of and in opposition to employers. Such a view underlies the widespread belief that employers would dismantle corporatist institutions as soon as possible – that is, once the economic tide turned against labor. But what if these very institutions – including those providing high coverage, relatively cohesive union organization, and relatively strong central authority – embody compromises between labor and capital, compromises from which both parties benefit? If this is so, then it is much less surprising that industrial relations systems have been weathering the economic turmoil of the post–oil-shock decades with such little substantial change.

Data Sources

Table 9.1: Net Union Density

Except for Japan, membership data refer to union members who are neither retired nor self-employed. Data for Japan formally refer to total union membership (i.e., they include retired and self-employed). However, there should be no difference between net and total Japanese union membership, since the retired and self-employed are not allowed to join unions there.

All data were drawn from Jelle Visser, "Trade Union Membership Database" (unpublished data base, Department of Sociology, University of Amsterdam, 1992), heretofore referred to as the 1992 Visser data base. We are grateful to Visser for having made the data available to us, and for allowing us to reprint it here.

The deflator used in constructing the figures is the dependent labor force, also drawn from the Visser data base. Visser's data, in turn, were largely drawn from the OECD.

Tables 9.2 and 9.3: Interconfederal and Intraconfederal Concentration

Data on membership in individual union confederations and their affiliates were collected from individual country sources. Most confederations do not make separate figures available on the number of retired members, and membership in individual confederations therefore includes pensioners (except for organizations that do not allow persons who retire to maintain their membership). For Table 9.2, the deflator used is thus total union membership (i.e., membership including retired and self-employed members), drawn from the 1992 Visser data base. (Note that the deflator is thus not identical to the membership data reported in Table 9.1.)

We have included in our analyses of interconfederal concentration only those confederations on which it proved possible to collect relatively complete and accurate annual data. As a result, the table omits specifically listing very tiny confederations (those with less than 5 percent of total union membership in at least one year) as well as membership in unions unaffiliated with any confederation. The difference between the proportion of union members in the major confederations that are listed by name and total union membership thus reflects membership in very minor confederations and unaffiliated unions.

Sources for figures on individual confederations and their affiliates are listed below by country.

Austria *ÖGB Tätigkeitsbericht* and the *Wirtschafts-und Sozialstatistisches Taschenbuch.*

Canada Confederal membership for the period 1960–1990 from David J. Arrowsmith, *Canada's Trade Unions: An Information Manual* (Kingston, Ontario: Industrial Relations Centre, Queen's University, 1992). For 1950–1955, data were drawn from Bureau of Labour Information, *Directory of Labour Organizations in Canada* (Canada: Minister of Supply and Services, various years), which was also the source for all data on affiliates.

Denmark *Statistisk årbog,* various years. Data on unaffiliated white-collar union are not included in the official statistics until 1975. In addition, the number of affiliates of the Danish LO does not include affiliates too small to be listed in the statistical yearbook (affiliates with less than 300 or 500 members, depending on the year).

Finland *Suomenon tilastollinen vuosikirja,* various years. In the schism that led to the formation of the rival SAJ from 1960–1969, some SAK affiliates left the SAK to join the SAJ while other affiliates split in two. The data in Table 9.3 refer to the SAK alone.

France Confederal membership from Jelle Visser, *European Trade Unions in Figures* (Deventer, Netherlands: Kluwer Law and Taxation Publishers, 1989).

Germany *Statistisches Jahrbuch,* and for 1950, from Walter Müller-Jentsch, *Basisdaten der industriellen Beziehungen* (Frankfurt am Main: Campus, 1989). The *Statistisches Jahrbuch,* as of 1956, notes explicitly that it does not include all professional organizations. As of 1991, figures include both East and West Germany, since the *Statistisches Jahrbuch* does not provide disaggregated figures. We have assumed that DHV figures are included in those for the CGB as of 1959. Data for the CGB for 1959–1985 are from Visser, *European Trade Unions in Figures,* for 1986–1987 from Müller-Jentsch, *Basisdaten der industriellen Beziehungen;* 1988–1992 from the

Statistisches Jahrbuch. Data for the DAG and DBB in 1950 from Visser, *European Trade Unions in Figures.* The data are actually from 1951 (there are no 1950 figures available). The CGB figure for 1965 is likewise from 1964. Data on the DHV for 1950–1952 from Visser, *European Trade Unions in Figures,* and for 1953–1958 from the *Statistisches Jahrbuch.* Data for the DGB and its affiliates for 1950 from Müller-Jentsch, *Basisdaten der industriellen Beziehungen.*

Italy Confederal figures for the CGIL, CISL, and UIL for 1950–1976 from Romagnoli, ed., *La sindacalizzazione tra ideologia e pratica: il caso italiano 1950/1970,* vol. 2 (Rome: Edizione Lavoro, 1990). Data on membership in the UIL is unavailable until 1977. Confederal figures for the period 1977–1990 from CESOS, *Le relazione sindacale in Italia* (Rome: Edizione Lavoro, various years). Membership in CISL affiliates for 1970 from Romagnoli 1990, tables 3.1–3.12. Membership in CISL affiliates and number of affiliates for 1975 and 1980 courtesy of CISL, Rome. Membership in CGIL affiliates for 1970 and 1975 from Romagnoli 1990, tables 3.1–3.12. Membership in CGIL affiliates and number of affiliates for 1980 from Dipartimento Organizzazione della Cgil Nazionale, *CGIL anni '80: l'evoluzione delle strutture organizzative* (Rome: Editrice Sindacale Italiana, 1981), pp. 386–387. Affiliate data for the UIL for 1980 from UIL, Servizio Organizzazione. Data on affiliates for all confederations for 1985 from CESOS, *Le relazione sindacali in Italia: rapporto 1985/86* (Rome: Edizione Lavoro, 1987).

Japan Data on affiliates in 1970 from *Japan Labor Bulletin* ("Directory of Major Trade Unions in Japan"), various years. All other membership figures, including affiliate data prior to 1970, are drawn from the *Year Book of Labour Statistics,* various years.

There is a break in the series for total union membership as of 1953, when figures first include members who are not likewise affiliated with a "unit" union. Prior to 1953, this type of "direct affiliation" was not included in the statistics.

Norway *Statistisk årsbok,* various years.

Sweden *Statistisk årsbok, för Sverige,* various years.

United Kingdom Membership in the TUC, number of affiliates, and membership in affiliates from the *Report of the Annual Trades Union Congress* (London: TUC, various years).

United States   Figures for the AFL, the CIO, and the AFL-CIO from 1950 through 1983 are from Leo Troy and Neil Sheflin, *U.S. Union Sourcebook: Membership, Finances, Structure, Directory* (West Orange, N.J.: Industrial Relations and Information Services, 1985). Data covering later years are from the *Directory of U.S. Labor Organizations*.

Tables 9.4 and 9.5: Statutory Authority in Unions and Employers' Organizations

The data presented in these tables were compiled from a series of country code books assembled by the authors. The information was gathered initially by research assistants, who consulted available secondary sources in both English and the country language, as well as through questionnaires sent to union and employer organizations. The actual coding was undertaken by the authors. Code books are available from the authors upon request.

Figure 1: Union Coverage and Density

Except for Italy, all data on unadjusted coverage rates are from Franz Traxler, "Collective Bargaining: Levels and Coverage," in OECD, *Employment Outlook*, July 1994 (Paris: OECD), 167–194, or Franz Traxler, "Collective Bargaining and Industrial Change: A Case of Disorganization? A Comparative Analysis of 18 OECD Countries," paper presented at the 1996 annual meeting of the American Political Science Association, San Francisco, August 29–September 1. In cases where Traxler provides different figures in 1996 from those published in 1994, we used the later figures.

To calculate the Italian unadjusted coverage rate, we took the size of the total work force and subtracted the self-employed, the unemployed, and managerial personnel, using government figures available in Pietro Ichino, *Il lavoro e il mercato. Per un diritto del lavoro maggiorenne* (Milan: Mondadori: 1996), 14. This resulted in a figure that represented the number of regularly and irregularly employed wage and salary workers. Given Italy's extension laws, we assumed that all regularly employed dependent wage and salary earners were covered by collective agreements. The coverage rate is thus the percentage of regularly and irregularly employed who are covered by agreements.

Traxler distinguishes what he calls the unadjusted and the adjusted coverage rates. The unadjusted coverage rate is the proportion of employees covered by a collective agreement in relation to the total number of employees in a country, regardless of whether they enjoy bargaining rights. The adjusted coverage rate takes as the deflator only those employees who legally enjoy the right to bargain. In most cases where there is a difference, it is because public employees (or certain groups of them) are legally prohibited from collective bargaining. We have chosen to work with the unadjusted coverage rate because it more nearly captures the extent to which collective agreements regulate the terms of employment throughout the economy. Laws prohibiting collective barganing are, like laws extending agreements to firms and employees even when they fail to subscribe to such agreements, endogenous to the concept of coverage.

The data on density are the same as those reported for 1989 in Table 9.1.

10

Unions in Decline? What Has Changed and Why

Michael Wallerstein and Bruce Western

Introduction

Unions are in big trouble, as everyone knows. Under attack by conservative politicians, battered by overseas competition, threatened by capital flight, bewildered by changes in the nature of work, and shackled by an outmoded egalitarian ideology, unions increasingly appear like large but aging dinosaurs struggling to adapt as the climate changes. The proportion of workers who belong to unions is in decline. Centralized systems of wage-setting are breaking apart. Incentive pay schemes and profit-sharing arrangements subvert negotiated wage scales. Wage inequality is growing while the median wage stagnates. Past achievements are under attack as European governments blame "labor market rigidities," i.e. the legal and contractual protections that current workers enjoy, for persistently high unemployment. Even the unions' traditional political allies, the social democratic and labor parties, are keeping their distance, having discovered that being too closely tied to the unions is a political liability.

As is usually the case, what everyone knows to be true is not completely wrong but not completely right either. In this paper, we aim to describe, as precisely as the data allow, what is and is not known about the changing terrain of industrial relations in advanced industrial societies in the postwar period. We survey the empirical research that seeks to explain cross-national and longitudinal variation in union organization and wage-setting procedures. We do not attempt to provide country-by-country descriptions.[1]

---

[1] Several edited collections provide complementary overviews of the literature. Golden & Pontusson (1992), Kitschelt et al (1999), and Iversen et al (1999) all contain a mixture of case studies and quantitative studies of unions and collective bargaining in advanced industrial

Instead, we emphasize the patterns of change and stability in key aspects of labor organizations and wage-setting institutions across the major member countries of the Organisation for Economic Co-operation and Development (OECD). Although there is great interest in changes that have occurred in the recent past, the lags in data collection are such that we are forced to end our study in 1992.

Unions are heterogeneous institutions. The extent to which union-negotiated agreements determine the pay received by union members and by nonmembers, the participation of unions in aspects of the employment relation other than pay, and the involvement of unions in labor training and policy making vary across countries, across time, and frequently across industries within countries. Moreover, the sources of union power are equally heterogeneous across time and place. Unions, to varying degrees in different countries and different time periods, have become able to influence the terms of employment by threatening work stoppages, by participating in governmental bodies with statutory authority, by obtaining political support in parliament, and by offering employers services that employers value.

Within a short essay, we cannot hope to cover the full range of differences among unions as organizations. Instead, we concentrate on the core activity of unions in all advanced industrial societies, which is to represent workers in negotiations with employers concerning pay. We begin with a discussion of the share of the work force that belongs to unions and the share of the work force whose wages are covered by collective agreements. We discuss the extent to which wage setting is centralized through collective bargaining practices or through political intervention. We discuss the trend in union concentration. Each of these sections describes the fundamental facts concerning both cross-national variation and change over time. In addition, we summarize the evidence concerning the causal mechanisms that best explain the differences and changes that the data reveal. The essay concludes with a brief discussion of the impact of changes in union organization and wage-setting institutions on equality and economic performance.

Union Density and Coverage

To analyze cross-national variation in union organization, we follow Bain & Price (1980:2), who define a union as "an organization of employees

---

societies. Ferner & Hyman (1998 [1992]) contains an excellent set of country-by-country descriptions of industrial relations in Western Europe.

which seeks to represent the job interests of its members to employers and in some circumstances to the state, but which is not dominated by either of them." This definition conveys the main idea of a voluntary organization of employees whose chief purpose is collective bargaining over wages and working conditions. Unions can then be distinguished from professional associations, such as the American Medical Association. Professional associations, though they do represent members' "job interests," generally include significant numbers of self-employed professionals in private practice. The Bain & Price definition excludes professional associations from union membership counts but includes organizations of credentialed wage earners such as teachers, nurses, or social workers.

The extent of union organization is typically measured by union density. Union density expresses the number of union members as a percentage of the number of people who could potentially be union members. This potential constituency usually includes all wage and salary earners and sometimes the unemployed. A distinction can be drawn between gross density statistics that count unemployed and retired members, and net density statistics that include employed union members only. Union members are defined as persons whom the unions count as members. In the case of employed workers, this is equivalent to persons who pay union dues.

Table 1 summarizes trends in gross union density through the postwar period for a group of 18 OECD countries (see also Visser 1991). The table shows three distinct patterns of variation. First, three groups of countries differ in their general level of unionization. Belgium, Denmark, Finland, and Sweden share very high unionization rates. By 1992, the total number of union members in these four countries nearly equaled or exceeded the total number of wage and salary earners. A large, heterogeneous group of countries unionized between a third and two thirds of their national labor markets. At the bottom of the scale, a group of six low-density countries organized less than a third of the work force in 1992.

Second, unionization in the industrialized democracies steadily diverged over the three decades from 1950. This divergence is reflected in the increasing standard deviation reported in Table 1. At the beginning of the postwar period, union density varied in a small band between about 30% and 60%. Unions – and industrial relations institutions more generally – showed much greater variation 30 years later, when the gap between the most and least organized countries had increased to 70 percentage points.

Third, the pattern of divergence in unionization that describes most of the postwar period was replaced by a convergent pattern of union decline

Table 1. *Union Density and Labor Market Institutions*[a]

	Density 1950	Density 1980	Density 1992	Level[b] 1965–1992	Left[c] 1965–1992	Ghent[d]	Coverage[e] 1990
High-density countries							
Belgium	36.9	76.6	80.5	0.50	0.23	Yes	90
Denmark	58.2	86.2	91.6	0.78	0.43	Yes	74
Finland	33.1	85.8	111.4	0.63	0.48	Yes	95
Sweden	62.1	89.5	111.3	0.85	0.73	Yes	83
Middle-density countries							
Australia	56.0	52.4	39.6	0.68	0.40	No	80
Austria	62.2	65.3	53.2	0.33	0.72	No	71
Canada	26.3	36.1	37.0	0.11	0.67	No	38
Germany	36.2	41.3	41.2	0.33	0.40	No	76
Ireland	38.6	63.4	53.5	0.54	0.15	No	
Italy	47.4	60.5	68.0	0.77	0.18	No	83
New Zealand	49.4	46.0	25.9	0.62	0.34	No	
Norway	53.8	65.3	67.7	0.91	0.56	No	75
UK	45.1	56.3	41.3	0.33	0.35	No	47
Low-density countries							
France	30.9	19.7	9.4	0.33	0.31	No	92
Japan	46.2	31.2	24.5	0.33	0.00	No	21
Netherlands	36.2	39.9	31.0	0.63	0.18	No	60
Switzerland	40.1	34.5	30.0	0.33	0.29	No	43
US	28.4	24.9	15.3	0.07	0.26	No	18
Mean	43.7	54.2	51.8	0.51	0.37		65.4
S.D.	11.4	21.5	30.7	0.25	0.20		24.7

[a] Union density taken from Visser's [1992 (unpublished), 1996] gross density series. Figures sometimes exceed 100 in 1992 because gross density here is defined on all wage and salary earners whereas union membership data include the retired and unemployed.

[b] Level is the 1965–1992 average level of collective bargaining, rescaled to vary from zero to one, measured by the scale of Golden et al (1999).

[c] Left is the 1965–1992 average of the proportion of cabinet seats held by left parties (see Western & Healy 1999).

[d] Ghent indicates countries with Ghent systems of unemployment insurance.

[e] Coverage refers to the share of workers covered by a collective bargaining agreement in 1990, taken from Traxler's (1994) unadjusted series.

during the 1980s. Although the average level of unionization dropped just three points between 1980 and 1992, some countries suffered spectacular declines. Falling unionization was especially severe in the English-speaking countries. Union density fell by 20 points in New Zealand, by 15 points in the United Kingdom, by 12 points in Australia, and by 10 points in Ireland

and the United States. Among non-English-speaking countries, Austria, France, and the Netherlands also suffered large declines in unionization. Out of all the industrialized democracies surveyed, only Finland and Sweden enjoyed strong union density growth through the 1980s.

Explanations of unionization should be able to account for these three patterns of union density variation. The dominant account of cross-sectional variation has emphasized the impact of labor market and state institutions (e.g. Visser & Ebbinghaus 1999, Western 1997, Rothstein 1989). The effects of leftist parties in government, collective bargaining centralization, and union-controlled unemployment insurance have received detailed empirical treatment. Labor and social democratic parties have been instrumental in expanding union rights and lowering the cost of unionization. In particular, leftist governments significantly facilitated public sector unionization in the 1950s and 1960s. In contrast, conservative parties have actively resisted unions through labor legislation and in industrial relations. Centralized collective bargaining is claimed to raise unionization by extending union agreements to nonunion workplaces, thereby defusing employer opposition to the expansion of union membership. Centralized union confederations also restrict interunion competition and coordinate organizing efforts among union affiliates. Finally, unions play a significant role in the distribution of unemployment benefits in the four high-density countries. The Ghent system, in which unemployment insurance is administered by the unions, enables union officials to protect union rates from competition from the unemployed through their discretion in the determination of the conditions under which unemployment becomes "involuntary" (Rothstein 1989). In addition, the Ghent system keeps workers in contact with their union during spells of joblessness.

Measures of leftist government, bargaining centralization, and the Ghent system are reported in Table 1. Bargaining level represents an index (described in more detail in the next section) of the extent to which wages are set at the level of the plant, the industry, or the economy as a whole. Leftist parties include socialist, social democratic, and labor parties, as well as the Liberal and New Democratic Parties in Canada and the Democratic party in the United States. Regressing 1992 union density on these two institutional variables and a dummy variable for the presence of a Ghent system yields the following estimates:

$$\text{Density} = 7.58 + 43.1 \text{ Level} + 31.9 \text{ Left} + 45.8 \text{ Ghent,}$$
$$(0.8) \quad (3.1) \quad\quad (2.0) \quad\quad (5.5)$$

where t statistics are in parentheses, and $R^2 = 0.85$. This simple cross-sectional regression shows a close association between union organization and labor market and state institutions. The estimates indicate that a difference of about 40 points in union density is explained by the difference between national and local-level collective bargaining. About a quarter of the 85-point difference in union density between Sweden and Japan is attributed to variation in the electoral success of social democratic and socialist parties. In addition, Ghent system countries enjoy, on average, close to a 50-point advantage in unionization.

Although institutional conditions can explain cross-sectional variation in unionization, time-series variables are needed to explain divergence in union growth and union decline in the 1980s. The leading longitudinal explanation claims that workers convert market power into collective action in response to fluctuating economic conditions. In this business cycle account, poor economic conditions weaken labor's market power and increase employer resistance to unions. A strong economy improves labor's hand by increasing the benefits of collective action and lowering employer opposition. Operationally, the business cycle theory has taken many different forms, but the impact of two variables stands out. Union membership is positively related to inflation but negatively associated with unemployment. Relatively strong inflation and unemployment effects were reported in a large econometric literature that covered union membership trends in Australia, Canada, Sweden, the United Kingdom, and the United States (Hines 1964, Ashenfelter & Pencavel 1969, Sharpe 1971, Swindinsky 1974; also see the reviews of Bain & Elsheikh 1976:26–57 and Hirsch & Addison 1986:52–56).

Despite reasonable empirical results, the business cycle approach takes a thin view of labor movements. The key agents – workers and employers – respond to exogenously shifting market conditions. This approach discounts active efforts by workers to construct shared interests through mobilization. The strategic role of unions is also bracketed from analysis. In contrast to the business cycle approach, other researchers have focused on the mobilizing efforts of militant workers and unions. The role of worker militancy as a source of union growth was developed and largely abandoned by economists but rehabilitated by political sociologists. Dunlop's (1949) work on the early development of US unions associated spurts in labor movement growth with periods of intense strike activity. According to this analysis, the strike waves of the 1890s and the 1930s were critical moments. Comparative researchers observed that unions grew rapidly in the wake of strike waves, not only in the United States of the 1930s, but also in Sweden in the 1910s, in Italy after 1969, and in France for most of the twentieth century (Korpi 1978:211–12, Regalia et al 1978, Tilly 1986:369). In this political theory, strike activity raises unionization by mobilizing workers around a collective project. In some cases, strikes are explicitly intended to obtain union recognition and rights to collective bargaining (Griffin et al 1990:179).

The organizing problem of the union has been studied by examining effects of labor-force size and growth (Wallerstein 1989, 1991). In this perspective, the benefits of unionization depend on the proportion of the work force organized, but the cost of organization to the union depends on the absolute number of new union members recruited. As a result, the optimal level of unionization for the union falls as the size of the labor force increases. Although this idea was originally examined in a cross-sectional sample of 20 industrialized democracies, strong results were also found in time-series analysis (Western 1997:119). Estimates indicate that the union organizing task is more difficult when the labor force is growing quickly (Western 1997:119).

Longitudinal and institutional explanations can be combined in models that treat time-series effects as conditional on time-invariant institutional conditions. In this approach, institutions not only raise or retard unionization but also affect the strategic calculations of unions and the impact of labor market competition. Western (1997) followed a hierarchical approach in which he estimated country-specific coefficients in a time-series model of annual change in density for the period 1950–1985. Longitudinal predictors in this model included inflation, unemployment, strike activity, the growth of the dependent labor force, and leftist-party participation in government. The country-specific, time-series coefficients were assumed to depend on a measure of centralized bargaining and a dummy variable for the Ghent system of unemployment insurance. Table 2 reports Western's results, describing how the level of bargaining and the Ghent system affect the impact of unemployment, strikes, and leftist government on density.

Data from only 18 countries in a highly parameterized model with error at both the micro and macro levels yield only modest statistical precision. Nevertheless, the point estimates indicate that the effects of labor market institutions on the relationship between union growth and the economic environment may be substantial. Consider first the impact of

Table 2. *Effects of Labor Market Institutions on Times-Series Coefficients**

Time-Series Coefficients	Intercept	Level	Ghent
Unemployment	−0.17	0.16	0.04
	(−0.21, −0.13)	(0.08, 0.24)	(−0.05, 0.12)
Strike volume	0.19	−0.12	−0.02
	(0.11, 0.27)	(−0.24, 0.00)	(−0.13, 0.09)
Leftist government	0.33	−0.28	−0.17
	(0.10, 0.56)	(−0.64, 0.16)	(−0.75, 0.39)

* The parentheses contain the 80% confidence intervals. The first row in the table gives the estimates obtained from the regression $b_{ui} = \gamma_{u0} + \gamma_{u1}$ level$_i$ + γ_{u2} Ghent$_i$ + error$_{ui}$, where b_{ui} is the estimated coefficient for unemployment in country i derived from the regression of the change in union density on a constant, inflation, unemployment, strike volume, labor force growth, and leftist government. A similar procedure was followed for the coefficient on strike volume and leftist government. See Western (1997:109–21) for additional details. The coefficients for *level* differ from Table 7.3 in Western (1997:116) due to a rescaling of *level* so that it varies between zero and one as in Table 1.

unemployment on union density. According to the estimates in Table 2, the impact of unemployment on the annual change in union density is strongly negative in a country, such as the United States, that has decentralized bargaining (level ≈ 0) and a government-run system of unemployment insurance (Ghent = 0). In contrast, in such countries as Sweden or Denmark, with centralized bargaining (level ≈ 0.8) and a union-run system of unemployment (Ghent = 1), the rate of unemployment has almost no impact on the growth of union density [−0.17 + (0.16)(0.8) + 0.04 ≈ 0]. The key intuition of business cycle explanations ties the fortunes of labor movements to the fortunes of the economy, with unions growing when labor markets are tight and declining when labor markets are slack. The estimates reported in Table 2 (as well as in Pedersen 1982 and Freeman 1989) suggest that unions can maintain their memberships and even grow during periods of high unemployment when bargaining is centralized and unions administer the system of unemployment insurance.

Table 2 shows important institutional effects on the impact of industrial conflict and the partisan composition of government as well. In decentralized countries without the Ghent system, union growth is substantially higher when the volume of strikes is high. In countries with centralized bargaining, the volume of strikes is much less important for union growth. When bargaining is centralized, strikes frequently represent protests against wage restraint imposed by centralized agreements negotiated by the top union leadership. Finally, the partisan composition of government can have a large impact on union growth in countries with decentralized bargaining, where employers have a strong incentive to resist unions. With centralized bargaining, employers have less reason to resist unions, since the wages of union members and nonmembers are the same (Freeman 1989) and election results have little impact on union growth or decline. In sum, the vulnerability of unions to periods of high unemployment or government by parties with ties to business depends on the set of labor market institutions that unions and employers have established to regulate and moderate their conflicts.

To study the decline of union density in the 1980s, Western (1997: ch. 9) used the hierarchical model of union growth to form forecasts for the period 1974–1989. Where union density decline was modest – as in Canada, Norway, or Sweden – trends in unionization in the 1970s and 1980s were predicted accurately. The performance of the model for the healthier labor movements suggested a continuity in the statistical regime of union growth from the 1960s to the post-oil shock period. However, using information from the 1950s and 1960s provided little leverage on the major falls in union density of the 1980s. Where declining unionization was dramatic (as in the Netherlands, France, the United Kingdom, or Ireland), the model fared poorly. The declines in unionization are much larger than we would predict given the historical pattern of union growth in the 1950s and 1960s.

The failure of standard models to predict the large declines of union organization that occurred in a significant number of countries in the 1980s suggests that a new causal process may be driving the disorganization of labor markets in the industrialized democracies. Two explanations have been studied in some detail. First, a number of researchers have related union decline to declining employment in manufacturing industries (Bell 1973:137–42, Troy 1990, Visser 1991). However, the changing occupational structure does not fare well as an explanation of union decline. First, the timing is wrong. The employment share of secondary industries in OECD countries fell at about the same rate in the 1970s as in the 1980s, but unions generally grew in the 1970s and declined only in the later decade. Second, industry-level membership figures reveal large declines of union density within manufacturing in countries with large declines of union density overall (Western 1997:154). A successful account of contemporary deunionization must explain falling union density within industries where unions have traditionally been strong.

The second approach to union density decline has emphasized changes in the political and institutional environment. Howell (1995) emphasizes the importance of the Thatcher governments' labor law reforms in explaining the sharp decline of union membership in the United Kingdom between 1980 and 1992. Western (1997: ch. 11) examined the year with the greatest acceleration of decline in union density since the mid-1970s. Western found that the acceleration of decline was more likely to occur when the left had suffered an electoral defeat and when bargaining was decentralized. Such studies are suggestive, but we are still some distance from having an empirical model that can adequately account for the cross-national and longitudinal variation in union density since the mid-1970s.

A decline in the proportion of workers who belong to unions is not the same thing as a decline in the proportion of workers covered by union contracts. The last column of Table 1 displays the share of the work force that was covered by union contracts in 1990. In such countries as the United States, Canada, Japan, and the United Kingdom, the coverage of union contracts is roughly equivalent to the share of the work force that belongs to unions. In English-speaking countries, apart from Australia, and in Japan, coverage has declined as density has fallen. In Australia and on the European continent, however, union contracts frequently cover far more workers than belong to unions. If countries are weighted by the size of their labor forces, the average density in Australia and continental Europe was 46.4 in 1990. The weighted average coverage rate for the same set of countries in the same year was 79.9. Outside of the United States, Japan, Canada, and the United Kingdom, four out of five workers are covered by a union contract, although less than half of the work force belongs to unions. Moreover, the share of workers covered by collective agreements remained roughly constant in continental Europe between 1980 and 1990 (Traxler 1994), even in countries where union density declined significantly.

The reasons for the difference between coverage and density are varied. In all countries, union and nonunion members who work side by side in the same plant receive the same wage. (Closed and union shops are rare in Europe. Thus, most plants have less than 100% union membership.) In Germany, the majority of workers are employed by members of an employers' confederation. In Austria, membership of employers in the relevant employers' confederation is mandated by law. In both Germany and Austria, the terms of wage agreements negotiated between a union and an industry-level employers' association are binding on all firms that belong to the employers' association, whether or not their workers belong to the

221

union.[2] In France, Belgium and, to a lesser extent, the Netherlands, union-negotiated contracts are regularly extended by government act to cover all workers in the industry.

Falling union density is a major problem for unions, even when coverage remains high. A high level of coverage says little about the unions' financial health or ability to mobilize supporters in a conflict with employers. Yet, the high levels of coverage in Europe, outside of the United Kingdom, indicate that collective bargaining has declined much less than union membership has. In spite of the significant decline in union membership in some countries, the large majority of workers in Western Europe continue to work under conditions governed by a collective bargaining agreement.

The Centralization of Wage Setting

Collective bargaining always entails a centralization of wage setting relative to a purely competitive labor market. At the very least, workers' pay and other aspects of employment are decided at the level of the plant or company when pay is covered by a collective agreement. However, pay may be decided at much higher levels. In most advanced industrial societies (albeit not in the United States, Canada, and the United Kingdom), a majority of workers are covered by multi-employer agreements negotiated at the level of the industry. In a few countries, multi-industry agreements covering the entire private sector have been the norm for substantial periods of time.

Why is the level of centralization important? The dominant understanding of the impact of the level of bargaining is as follows.[3] If wages are set at the plant or company level, unionization enables workers to obtain a share of the extra profit, or rents, that some firms enjoy by having lower costs than their competitors. If the product market is competitive, however, workers' possible wage gains are limited by the firm's inability to cover higher labor costs with higher prices. With purely local bargaining, collective bargaining changes the distribution of the firm-specific rents between workers on the

---

[2] The dependence of coverage on employers' membership in the employers' association gives unions an important stake in the organizational health of employers' associations. See Thelen (1999) for a discussion of the depth of union concern in Germany with the declining organizational strength of German employers.

[3] See Moene et al (1993) and Calmfors (1993) for surveys of the theoretical literature on the impact of centralized wage setting on economic performance. See Flanagan (1999) for a survey of the empirical literature.

one hand and management and shareholders on the other, but otherwise it has a limited impact on economic performance.

If unions set wages at the industry level, however, workers can raise wages throughout the industry. (The presence of foreign competition changes the argument, as discussed below.) If all firms in the industry face higher wage costs, the price of output is forced up. In effect, industry-level wage setters can exert monopoly power in the product market in a closed economy, with union members receiving monopoly profits in the form of higher wages. Employers may also benefit from industry-level bargaining, relative to local bargaining, since their ability to partially cover the higher wages with price increases lessens the negative impact of wage gains on profits. But now, there may be significant losses for groups who are not represented at the bargaining table. Wage increases that lead to price increases reduce the real income of workers in other industries. In addition, since higher prices imply lower sales and less employment, wage increases hurt workers who are priced out of a job and hurt taxpayers who pay for the unemployment benefits received by workers who have been laid off. In sum, industry-level wage setting stands accused of allowing the externalization of the costs of higher wages and of generating an inefficient allocation of resources.

If, however, unions and employers centralize wage setting so that wages throughout the economy are set simultaneously, the wage agreement will be neutral with regard to relative prices. Workers' ability to exert monopoly power disappears. In other words, national wage setters internalize many of the externalities of industry-level wage setting, and thus, the theory goes, they would choose outcomes as efficient as decentralized bargaining (Calmfors & Driffill 1988). Moreover, if the central wage agreement contains an industrial peace obligation, i.e. a prohibition on strikes once the central agreement is signed and ratified, workers in low-cost firms are unable to obtain a share of firm-specific rents, as they could with local bargaining. Thus, fully centralized bargaining with an industrial peace obligation may result in the best possible outcome for employers, short of having no unions at all. However, since the determination of the wage distribution becomes an explicitly political decision with highly centralized wage setting, centralization may unleash forces that employers cannot control.

Whether or not centralized bargaining has a desirable impact on profits, wages, and aggregate economic performance is a subject of continuing controversy that we return to in the conclusion. In this section, our primary

Table 3. *The Centralization of Wage Setting**

	1950–1959	1960–1972	1973–1981	1982–1992
Australia	0.67	0.67	0.67	0.70
Austria	0.47	0.33	0.33	0.33
Belgium	0.33	0.33	0.50	0.64
Canada	0.00	0.00	0.38	0.00
Denmark	1.00	1.00	0.92	0.52
Finland	0.73	0.74	0.63	0.58
France	0.33	0.36	0.33	0.33
Germany	0.33	0.33	0.33	0.33
Italy	0.67	0.67	0.67	0.88
Japan	0.00	0.24	0.33	0.33
Netherlands	1.00	0.81	0.79	0.48
Norway	0.87	0.95	0.96	0.82
Sweden	0.73	1.00	1.00	0.64
Switzerland	0.33	0.33	0.33	0.33
UK	0.00	0.40	0.50	0.00
US	0.00	0.14	0.00	0.00
Mean	0.47	0.52	0.54	0.43
S.D.	0.36	0.32	0.28	0.28
Confederal involvement				
Mean	0.30	0.35	0.32	0.26
S.D.	0.31	0.32	0.30	0.26
Government involvement				
Mean	0.30	0.33	0.39	0.31
S.D.	0.28	0.21	0.24	0.20

* The country data represent the scores on a four-category scale of the level or bargaining, described in the text. The confederal involvement and government involvement data represent the average scores on scales of confederal participation in wage setting and parliamentary participation in (private-sector) wage setting, respectively. All data have been scaled to vary between zero and one. The raw values for the three scales are taken from Golden et al (1999).

concern is to describe how centralization has changed during the postwar period. Table 3 presents data on the centralization of private-sector wage setting in 16 countries during 1950–1992. The main variable in the table is the country's score on a four-category scale of the level of wage setting. The four categories are (*a*) predominantly local or company-level wage bargaining, (*b*) predominantly industry-level wage bargaining, (*c*) national-level wage bargaining without an industrial peace obligation, and (*d*) national-level wage setting with an industrial peace obligation.

Wages can be centralized in two basic ways. The first is via direct negotiations between peak associations of unions and employers. The second is via government intervention. The scale of the level of wage setting combines both, but confederal involvement and government intervention can be examined separately. At the bottom of the table, we list the average scores on an 11-category scale of confederal involvement and a 15-category scale of government intervention.[4] The 16 countries have been coded on all three scales on an annual basis. The table reports the average scores during various time periods.

On average, the level of wage setting increased from the 1950s to the 1960s and increased again from the 1960s to the 1970s. After 1981, however, the average level of centralization has declined. Particularly sharp declines in centralization occurred in four of the 16 countries: Denmark, the Netherlands, Sweden, and the United Kingdom. However, not all countries moved in the same direction. In Belgium and in Italy, for example, the average level of wage setting was higher between 1982 and 1992 than at any earlier time in the postwar period. Overall, the estimated change in centralization from the 1970s to the 1980s is only -0.11 on the four-point scale – a marginally significant difference. Thus, without further analysis, the data provide some support for the arguments that wage setting has become increasingly decentralized since the early 1980s (Lash & Urry 1987, Katz 1993, Katz & Darbishire 1999), and those who emphasize, instead, the continuing diversity of national experiences (Hyman 1994, Traxler 1995, Wallerstein et al 1997, Wallerstein & Golden 1997).

There is an interesting distinction between centralization via confederal involvement and centralization via parliamentary act. Whereas the average level of confederal involvement in wage setting was highest in the "Golden Age" from 1960 through 1973, government involvement increased sharply in the period between the two oil shocks. The initial response of many governments to the first appearance of rising unemployment and rising inflation was to seek greater control over the rate of wage increases. After 1982, however, both confederal and government involvement in wage setting declined significantly.

---

[4] Descriptions of the categories can be found in Wallerstein (1999) or in Golden et al (1999). Two limitations of the data should be noted. The first is that the data cover changes in wage-setting institutions in the private sector only. Wage setting in the public sector is usually organized differently. The other limitation is that the data refer only to wage setting, which may be centralized while other aspects of the employment relation that are covered by collective agreements are decided at the level of the firm or plant.

Michael Wallerstein and Bruce Western

There are three approaches to explaining both the pattern of cross-national variation and change over time. The first approach might be labeled micro-Marxism. In the micro-Marxist approach, scholars have sought to explain the rise and decline of centralized bargaining institutions as the results of changes in technology and the organization of production. Ingham (1974) argued that centralized bargaining institutions arose in countries, such as Sweden, where industrialization was late and rapid. The consequence of rapid industrialization, according to Ingham, was a relative similarity of production methods and working conditions across factories and industries that made centralized bargaining feasible. Piore & Sabel (1984) and Pontusson (1991) emphasize the association of the establishment of centralized wage setting with the growth of "Fordist" methods of production, in which large numbers of workers are doing similar tasks.

The recent decline in centralized bargaining, according to the micro-Marxist approach, stems from the changes in technology and the organization of production that require greater flexibility and/or differentiation of work and terms of employment. Katz (1993), Streeck (1993), Pontusson & Swenson (1996), and Iversen (1996) argue that the rise of "diversified quality production" and "flexible specialization" necessitates greater differentiation of pay and a stronger connection between individual or team performance and rewards than centralized wage setting allows. A related explanation spotlights changes in the occupational structure. Hernes (1991) and Moene & Wallerstein (1993), for example, argue that the proliferation of small and highly specialized groups of workers with extraordinary market power had a destabilizing impact on the centralized bargaining systems in the Nordic countries.

The second broad approach to explaining the rise and decline of centralization focuses on the impact of international trade. Our discussion of the impact of centralization on collective bargaining outcomes rested on the assumption of a closed economy. In a small open economy, however, the prices of traded goods are independent of domestic wage costs. Thus, industry-level bargaining advantages workers in the sheltered sector relative to workers in the traded-goods sector. As a consequence, workers and employers in the traded-goods sector may form an alliance to centralize bargaining in order to restrain wage increases in sectors that do not face international competition. This, in brief, is Swenson's (1989, 1991) explanation of the establishment of centralized wage-setting institutions in Sweden and Denmark. Katzenstein's (1983, 1985) argument that

226

centralized wage-setting institutions arise in small open economies as an adaptation to the risks associated with international openness has a similar flavor. If the Nordic countries and the Low Countries adopted centralized bargaining institutions because of their high levels of trade dependence, it appears paradoxical that centralization is declining as economic openness increases. Wood (1994), Leamer (1993), Rodrik (1996), and McKeown (1999) offer a resolution of the paradox by arguing that increased international competition from rapidly industrializing developing countries, a new phenomenon, has reduced the demand for unskilled and semiskilled workers in advanced industrial societies while increasing the demand for their more skilled counterparts. To the extent that centralized wage setting prevents wages from falling at the bottom of the labor market, the argument goes, employers and governments increasingly seek decentralized alternatives. Although most observers argue that trade with the Third World has weakened unions relative to employers in recent years, Thelen (1999) makes the interesting argument that increasing international competition has weakened employers' associations most of all. As Thelen points out, centralized wage setting requires that both sides of the employment relationship are sufficiently organized to bargain collectively. If employers' associations collapse, so will centralized bargaining.

In yet another twist on the argument that globalization leads to decentralization, Lange et al (1995), Garrett & Way (1995), and Iversen (1996) point out that the unionized work force may be less dependent on trade today than in the early postwar period. Because productivity gains in the traded-goods sector outrun productivity gains in the sheltered sector, the share of workers who face international competition has declined even as the value of trade as a share of gross domestic product has increased. In particular, the share of union members who work in the public sector has grown in almost all countries. According to this line of argument, centralized institutions received widespread support among both unions and employers in the Nordic countries when the union movement was dominated by workers in the traded-goods sector. As sheltered-sector unions grew in size and influence in Northern Europe, the ability of employers in the traded-goods sector to restrain the wages of sheltered-sector workers through centralized bargaining declined. Whereas centralized wage setting functioned to restrain wages of sheltered-sector workers in the early postwar period, now employers seek to achieve the same goal of wage restraint through decentralization.

Michael Wallerstein and Bruce Western

Table 4. *Ordered Probit Analysis of the Level of Wage Setting*[a]

Independent Variable	Estimated Coefficient	t-statistic	Mean of Independent Variable
Lagged dependent variable	1.29	14.1	0.688
Industry[b]	0.599	3.08	0.792
Authority[c]	0.424	6.79	0.794
Concentration[d]	−4.70	3.00	0.088
1982–1992[e]	−0.524	3.04	0.256
Lagged unemployment[f]	7.28	2.71	0.039
Lagged inflation[g]	2.43	1.70	0.052
First cut	1.752		
Second cut	3.010		
Log-likelihood index[h]	0.53		

[a] Dependent variable is a three-category scale of the level of wage setting as described in the text, with assigned values of one, two, and three. There are 630 observations (15 countries, 1950–1992). The countries are the same as in Table 3.
[b] Industry is a dummy variable equal to one if industry-level bargaining predominates in the absence of centralization.
[c] Authority is an index of the statutory authority of the employers' confederation.
[d] Concentration is the Herfindahl index described in Table 5.
[e] 1982–1992 is a dummy variable equal to one for 1982–1992.
[f] Unemployment from the OECD. All other variables are from the Golden et al (1999) data set.
[g] Inflation data indicate the proportional change in the CPI from the Summers & Heston (1991) data set.
[h] Log-likelihood index is $1-(LL/LL_0)$, where LL is the log likelihood of the model and LL_0 is the log likelihood when the only independent variable is a constant.

A third approach views centralization as a response to macroeconomic difficulties. In this argument, countries centralize wage setting to restrain wage growth in pursuit of greater price stability or lower unemployment (Headey 1970, Flanagan et al 1983, Martin 1984, Streeck & Schmitter 1991). The argument is transparent when wage setting is centralized through the adoption of incomes policies. Even in the absence of incomes policies, unions and employers may adopt centralized negotiations in order to collectively reduce wage growth in the face of high unemployment.

The view of centralization as a solution to macroeconomic problems receives support from the ordered probit regression reported in Table 4. Since we lack systematic data on the shift from industry-level bargaining to plant-level bargaining in the United States and United Kingdom, the

228

dependent variable in Table 4 is a tripartite scale where the lowest level of centralization is either plant- or industry-level bargaining, the middle level represents national wage setting without an industrial peace obligation, and the highest level represents national wage setting with an industrial peace obligation. The independent variables are (a) the lagged dependent variable, (b) a dummy variable indicating whether industry-level or plant-level wage setting predominates when wage setting is not centralized at the national level, (c) an index of the statutory authority of the peak association for employers (described below), (d) the Herfindahl index of union concentration (described below), (e) a dummy variable for the period 1982–1992, (f) the rate of inflation from year $t-1$ to year t, and (g) the rate of unemployment in year $t-1$.

Countries are more likely to centralize wage setting when wage setting was centralized in the previous year. Countries in which industry-level bargaining predominates when not centralized are more likely to centralize wage setting than countries in which plant-level bargaining predominates. It is also not surprising that centralized wage setting is more likely to be adopted in countries in which the employer's peak association has substantial statutory authority over affiliated firms. The index of statutory authority is a threefold scale based on (a) whether the employers' confederation has veto power over wage contracts signed by members, (b) whether the employers' confederation can veto lockouts by members, and (c) whether the employers' confederation has its own conflict funds. It is interesting to note that the parallel index for the union confederation did not fit the data as well. The authority of the employers' confederation over its members appears to be more important for the success of centralized wage setting than the authority of the union confederation over its members. This could indicate that the employers are usually the driving force behind centralization, as Swenson (1991) argues, or that employers face a more severe collective action problem than unions do, as Thelen (1999) argues. The Herfindahl index is a measure of the extent to which the union movement is dominated by a small number of large unions, described below. The negative coefficient on union concentration may imply that centralization and concentration are substitutes. Countries with high levels of concentration, such as Germany and Switzerland, have less need for centralized procedures to coordinate wage setting.

The negative coefficient for the dummy variable for the period 1982–1992 implies a substantial decline in the likelihood of centralization after

1982. Before 1982, the probability of adopting centralized wage setting, with or without an industrial peace obligation, for a country at the mean of all of the other independent variables was estimated to be 0.48.[5] After 1982, the probability of adopting a centralized wage-setting procedure dropped to 0.28 (holding the other independent variables constant at their mean). The estimated impact of an increase in the unemployment rate of one percentage point, when all other variables are at their mean, is to increase the probability of centralization by three percentage points.

Thus, if unemployment increased from 4% to 5% before 1982, and all other independent variables are at their mean, the probability that a country will adopt a moderately or highly centralized system of wage setting is estimated to increase from 0.48 to 0.51. An increase in inflation is estimated to have about one third the impact of an increase in unemployment. In other words, a three-percentage-point increase in the rate of inflation is estimated to have the same impact as a one-percentage-point increase in the rate of unemployment. Supplementary regression (not shown) revealed that measures of trade openness (imports plus exports over gross domestic product), size (the number of wage and salary earners), and the partisan composition of government (leftist-party participation in government) do not have significant effects on the likelihood of centralized wage setting after controlling for the variables in Table 4.

In sum, macroeconomic difficulties, in particular rising unemployment and rising inflation, are important determinants of the adoption of central-ized systems of wage setting. Other explanations, however, are not nec-essarily wrong. There has been a significant decline in the reliance on systems of centralized wage setting to reduce unemployment since 1981. Whether that change is a consequence of changes in the organization of production, of increased international competition, or of a political shift to

---

[5] The likelihood that a country adopts a decentralized system of wage setting in year t is $\Pr(\beta'x + u < \mu_1) = \Pr(u < \mu_1 - \beta'x) = \Phi(\mu_1 - \beta'x)$, where β is the vector of coefficients, x is the vector of independent variables for country i in year t, μ_1 is the first cut point, and $\Phi(\cdot)$ is the cumulative density function for the standard normal distribution. Thus, if all independent variables other than the dummy for 1982–1992 take their mean values, $\bar{x}$, we have $\Phi(\mu_1 - \beta'\bar{x}) \approx \Phi(0.055) \approx 0.52$ before 1982 and $\Phi(\mu_1 - \beta'\bar{x}) \approx \Phi(0.579) \approx 0.72$ after 1982. To calculate the impact of a marginal change in a variable x_i, we use $\partial\Phi(\mu_1 - \beta'\bar{x})/\partial x = -\beta\phi(\mu_1 - \beta'x)$. For unemployment, assuming all other independent variables take their mean values, we have $\beta\phi(\mu_1 - \beta'\bar{x}) \approx -(7.28)(0.398)$ before 1982 and $-\beta\phi(\mu_1 - \beta'\bar{x}) \approx -(7.28)(0.337)$ after 1982. In either case, the marginal impact of an increase in unemployment of 0.01 is to reduce the likelihood of decentralized wage setting by 0.03. The marginal impact of a change in inflation is calculated in a similar fashion.

the right by social democratic as well as conservative parties is anybody's guess.

Union Concentration

Even in the absence of centralized bargaining, industry-level unions may coordinate their demands and employers' associations may coordinate their responses. Alternatively, a union, such as the German metal workers, may act as the wage leader and negotiate a contract that is then copied in the other industries. If the German metal workers and metal-working employers understand that their contract will be copied by all, the result may be similar to what would be achieved by fully centralized bargaining [though Wallerstein's (1990) model demonstrates that the result with a wage leader may be very different from fully centralized bargaining]. Thus, Golden (1993) argues that centralization may be less important than concentration, where concentration refers to the extent to which union members are concentrated in a few large unions, as opposed to being divided into a large number of smaller organizations. If the number of actors is small enough, coordination of wage setting is likely whether or not wages are explicitly set in a centralized manner.[6] More recently, increasing concentration among unions in the English-speaking countries may capture an alternative dynamic in which unions merge to expand membership in a context where new organization has stalled (Chaison 1996).

To see how concentration has changed over time, we use the Herfindahl concentration index, defined as $H = \sum_{i=1}^{n} S_i^2$, where S_i is the share of confederal membership in the ith largest affiliate and n is the total number of affiliates in the confederation. The Herfindahl index represents the probability that two confederation members who are selected at random would belong to the same affiliate. Since we have membership data only for the three largest affiliates and for the total number of affiliates, we approximated the Herfindahl index using the formula $H^* = S_1^2 + S_2^2 + S_3^2 + (n-3)S_4^2$, where $S_4 = (1 - S_1 - S_2 - S_3)/(n-3)$. Table 5 presents the approximate Herfindahl indices for the main blue-collar confederations of 15 countries during the postwar period. In countries with more than one blue-collar

[6] Concentration might be measured between confederations (the degree to which union members belong to a single confederation) or within confederations (the degree to which union members belong to the same unions within the confederation). Since concentration between confederations is uncorrelated with all other measures of concentration and centralization (Golden & Londregan 1998), we focus on concentration within confederations.

Table 5. *Herfindahl Index of Union Concentration**

	1950–1959	1960–1972	1973–1981	1982–1992
Australia	0.014	0.018	0.019	0.017
Austria	0.088	0.099	0.103	0.105
Belgium	0.101	0.098	0.104	0.095
Canada	0.041	0.024	0.030	0.047
Denmark	0.148	0.130	0.123	0.118
Finland	0.062	0.088	0.068	0.076
Germany	0.120	0.144	0.159	0.158
Italy	0.097	0.075	0.073	0.073
Japan	0.111	0.089	0.097	0.078
Netherlands	0.108	0.115	0.181	0.157
Norway	0.045	0.055	0.079	0.114
Sweden	0.056	0.081	0.114	0.136
Switzerland	0.156	0.169	0.177	0.180
UK	0.046	0.050	0.053	0.046
US	0.025	0.018	0.019	0.025
Mean	0.081	0.084	0.093	0.095
S.D.	0.044	0.045	0.052	0.050

* Entries represent the average Herfindahl index for within-confederal concentration during the time period at the head of the column. The approximation formula is described in the text. In countries with more than one major blue-collar confederation, the data refer to the average weighted by each confederation's membership. Data are from the Golden et al (1999) data set. The raw data are available at five-year intervals. Missing values were added by linear interpolation.

confederation, we used a weighted average of the Herfindahl indices for each confederation, weighting each confederation by its relative size in terms of membership.

Within confederations, there is a trend toward greater concentration over time, as Windmuller (1981) observed almost 20 years ago. The mean Herfindahl index has increased steadily since 1950, although the change over time is small relative to the cross-national differences. Norway, Sweden, and the Netherlands show the largest increase in the Herfindahl index. If we measured concentration by the number of affiliates of the blue-collar confederations, Britain and the United States would show the largest increases in concentration (Golden et al 1999). For example, the British Trades Union Congress had 186 affiliates in 1950 and only 76 affiliates in 1990. In fact, the only countries whose number of affiliates has not declined over the postwar period are those whose number of affiliates was already small in 1950.

Conclusion

From 1950 to the 1970s, the average levels of union density, union concentration, and the centralization of wage setting were all increasing among advanced industrial societies. In spite of the diversity of national experiences, the general pattern is one in which the labor market was becoming increasingly organized and regulated. Since the early 1980s, however, most indicators of union strength and centralized wage setting have declined on average. Average density has declined since 1980 to a limited extent if each country is weighted equally. If countries are weighted in proportion to the size of their labor force, however, the fall in density is large. The decline in centralization, if judged from the raw figures, is not large. Controlling for macroeconomic conditions and the partisan composition of government, however, the likelihood of centralized wage setting declined sharply in the 1980s. The main exception to the trend toward greater decentralization is the steady but small increase in union concentration. Increased concentration, however, may reflect pressures to merge operations in the face of declining membership.

Does it matter whether union membership is falling and wage setting is becoming less centralized? The effect on equality is large. The more decentralized the system of wage setting, the more unequal the distribution of wages and salaries (Freeman 1988; Blau & Kahn 1996; D Rueda, J Pontusson, unpublished manuscript; Wallerstein 1999). Wallerstein (1999), for example, finds that the index of the centralization of wage setting, the Herfindahl index of concentration and union density, explains most of the cross-national and longitudinal variance in wage inequality among advanced industrial societies since 1980. But whether high levels of union density and centralized wage-setting institutions are associated with high or low unemployment is no clearer today than when Bruno & Sachs published the first systematic study of the question in 1985 [see, for example, the recent exchange between Siebert (1997) and Nickell (1997) on the causes of unemployment in Europe]. Part of the difficulty is that wage-setting institutions are only part of the institutional environment that may be relevant for macroeconomic performance. Lange and Garrett argued that what matters is not the centralization of wage setting but the interaction between the centralization of wage setting and the partisan composition of government (Lange & Garrett 1985, Garrett & Lange 1986, Garrett 1998). Hall (1994), Hall & Franzese (1998), Iversen (1998), and Soskice & Iversen (2000) argue that what matters is the interaction of the

233

centralization of wage setting and the independence of the central bank. The number of countries is small enough that the number of interaction terms soon overwhelms the data. (Combining longitudinal and cross-national variation in pooled time-series analyses does not help as much as might be expected, since there is strong dependence over time in the unemployment rate.)

Table 4 points to a different difficulty. If systems of centralized wage setting are adopted, in part, as a response to macroeconomic difficulties, the system of wage setting is endogenous (as argued by Flanagan 1999). In order to estimate the impact of wage-setting institutions on macroeconomic performance, we need to simultaneously estimate the impact of macroeconomic performance on the choice of wage-setting institutions. Clearly, to jointly estimate the choice of wage-setting institutions and the impact of wage-setting institutions is a difficult task given the limited data available. But empirical studies of the impact of wage-setting institutions on macroeconomic performance that treat wage-setting institutions as exogenous, i.e. virtually all existing studies, are attempting to draw inferences from biased estimates. In spite of the large literature on economic performance and labor market institutions, we still know little about the magnitude of the tradeoff between equality and economic performance, or even whether a tradeoff exists.

Acknowledgments

We thank Ernesto Calvo and Jomy Joseph Alappattu for research assistance. Financial assistance was provided by the National Science Foundation (SBR-9809014) and the Russell Sage Foundation. We thank Kathleen Thelen for helpful comments.

References

Ashenfelter O, Pencavel JH. 1969. American trade union growth: 1900–1960. *Q. J. Econ.* 83:434–48

Bain GS, Elsheikh F. 1976. *Union Growth and the Business Cycle.* Oxford, UK: Blackwell

Bain GS, Price R. 1980. *Profiles of Union Growth: A Comparative Statistical Portrait of Eight Countries.* Oxford, UK: Blackwell

Bell D. 1973. *The Coming of Post-Industrial Society: A Venture in Social Forecasting.* New York: Basic Books

Blau FD, Kahn LM. 1996. International differences in male wage inequality: institutions versus market forces. *J. Polit. Econ.* 104:791–837

Unions in Decline? What Has Changed and Why

Bruno M, Sachs J. 1985. *The Economics of Worldwide Stagflation.* Cambridge, MA: Harvard Univ. Press

Calmfors L. 1993. Centralization of wage bargaining and macroeconomic performance: a survey. *OECD Econ. Stud.* 21:161–91

Calmfors L, Driffill J. 1988. Bargaining structure, corporatism and macroeconomic performance. *Econ. Policy* 3:13–61

Chaison GN. 1996. *Union Mergers in Hard Times.* Ithaca, NY: Cornell Univ. Press

Dunlop JT. 1949. The development of labor organizations: a theoretical framework. In *Insights into Labor Issues*, ed. R Lester, J Shister, pp. 163–93. New York: Macmillan

Ferner A, Hyman R, eds. 1998 (1992). *Industrial Relations in the New Europe.* Oxford, UK: Blackwell. 2nd ed.

Flanagan RJ. 1999. Macroeconomic performance and collective bargaining: an international perspective. *J. Econ. Lit.* 37:1150–75

Flanagan RJ, Soskice DW, Ulman L. 1983. *Unionism, Economic Stabilization and Incomes Policies: European Experience.* Washington, DC: Brookings Inst.

Freeman RB. 1988. Labour market institutions and economic performance. *Econ. Policy* 3:64–80

Freeman RB. 1989. *On the divergence in unionism in developed countries. NBER Work. Pap. No. 2817.* Cambridge, MA: Nat Bur. Econ. Res.

Garrett G. 1998. *Partisan Politics in the Global Economy.* Cambridge, UK: Cambridge Univ. Press

Garrett G, Lange P. 1986. Economic growth in capitalist democracies, 1974–1982. *World Polit.* 38:517–45

Garrett G, Way C. 1995. The sectoral composition of trade unions, corporatism and economic performance. In *Monetary and Fiscal Policy in an Integrated Europe*, ed. B Eichengreen, J Frieden, J von Hagen, pp. 38–61. Berlin: Springer

Golden M. 1993. The dynamics of trade unionism and national economic performance. *Am. Polit. Sci. Rev.* 87:439–54

Golden M, Lange P, Wallerstein M. 1999. *Dataset on Unions, Employers, Collective Bargaining and Industrial Relations for 16 OECD Countries.* http://www.shelley.polisci.ucla.edu/data

Golden M, Londregan J. 1998. *Globalization and industrial relations.* Presented at Annu. Meet. Am. Polit. Sci. Assoc., Boston, MA, Sept. 3–6

Golden M, Pontusson J, eds. 1992. *Bargaining for Change: Union Politics in North America and Europe.* Ithaca, NY: Cornell Univ. Press

Griffin LJ, McCammon HJ, Botsko C. 1990. The "unmaking" of a movement? The crisis of US trade unions in comparative perspective. In *Change in Societal Institutions*, ed. M Hallinan, D Klein, J Glass, pp. 109–94. New York: Plenum

Hall P. 1994. Central bank independence and coordinated wage-setting: their interaction in Germany and in Europe. *Ger. Polit. Soc.* 31:1–23

Hall P, Franzese R. 1998. Mixed signals: central bank independence, coordinated wage-bargaining and European monetary union. *Int. Org.* 52:505–35

Headey BW. 1970. Trade unions and national wages policies. *J. Polit.* 32:407–39

235

Hernes G. 1991. The dilemmas of social democracies: the case of Norway and Sweden. *Acta Social.* 34:239–60

Hines AG. 1964. Trade unions and wage inflation in the United Kingdom 1948–1962: a disaggregated study. *Econ. J.* 79:66–89

Hirsch BT, Addison JT. 1986. *The Economic Analysis of Unions: New Approaches and Evidence*. London: Allen & Unwin

Howell C. 1995. Trade unions and the state: a critique of British industrial relations. *Polit. Soc.* 23:149–83

Hyman R. 1994. Industrial relations in Western Europe: an era of ambiguity? *Ind. Relat.* 33:1–24

Ingham G. 1974. *Strikes and Industrial Conflict: Britain and Scandinavia.* London: Macmillan

Iversen T. 1996. Power, flexibility and the breakdown of centralized wage bargaining: the cases of Denmark and Sweden in comparative perspective. *Comp. Polit.* 28:399–436

Iversen T. 1998. Wage bargaining, hard money and economic performance: theory and evidence for organized market economies. *Br. J. Polit. Sci.* 28:31–61

Iversen T, Pontusson J, Soskice D, eds. 1999. *Unions, Employers and Central Banks: Wage Bargaining and Macroeconomic Policy in an Integrating Europe.* Cambridge, UK: Cambridge Univ. Press

Katz HC. 1993. The decentralization of collective bargaining: a literature review and comparative analysis. *Ind. Labor Relat. Rev.* 47(1):3–22

Katz HC, Darbishire O. 1999. *Converging Divergences: Worldwide Changes in Employment Systems*. Ithaca, NY: Cornell Univ. Press

Katzenstein P. 1983. The small European states in the international economy: economic dependence and corporatist politics. In *The Antinomies of Interdependence*, ed. JR Ruggie, pp. 91–130. New York: Columbia Univ. Press

Katzenstein P. 1985. *Small States in World Markets: Industrial Policy in Europe*. Ithaca, NY: Cornell Univ. Press

Kitschelt H, Lange P, Marks G, Stephens JD, eds. 1999. *Continuity and Change in Contemporary Capitalism*. Cambridge, UK: Cambridge Univ. Press

Korpi W. 1978. *The Working Class in Welfare Capitalism*. London: Routledge

Lange P, Garrett G. 1985. The politics of growth. *J. Polit.* 47:792–827

Lange P, Wallerstein M, Golden M. 1995. The end of corporatism? Wage setting in the Nordic and Germanic countries. In *Workers of Nations: Industrial Relations in a Global Economy*, ed. S Jacoby, pp. 76–100. Oxford, UK: Oxford Univ. Press

Lash S, Urry J. 1987. *The End of Organized Capitalism*. Oxford, UK: Polity

Leamer E. 1993. Wage effects of a US-Mexican free trade agreement. In *The Mexico-US Free Trade Agreement*, ed. PM Garber, pp. 57–125. Cambridge, MA: MIT Press

Martin A. 1984. Trade unions in Sweden: strategic responses to change and crisis. In *Unions and Economic Crisis: Britain, West Germany and Sweden*, P Gourevitch, A Martin, G Ross, S Bornstein, A Markovits, C Allen, pp. 190–359. London: Allen & Unwin

Unions in Decline? What Has Changed and Why

McKeown T. 1999. The global economy, post-Fordism and trade policy in advanced capitalist states. In *Continuity and Change in Contemporary Capitalism*, ed. H Kitschelt, P Lange, G Marks, JD Stephens, pp. 11–35. Cambridge, UK: Cambridge Univ. Press

Moene KO, Wallerstein M. 1993. What's wrong with social democracy? In *Market Socialism: The Current Debate*, ed. P Bardhan, J Roemer, pp. 219–35. Oxford, UK: Oxford Univ. Press

Moene KO, Wallerstein M, Hoel M. 1993. Bargaining structure and economic performance. In *Trade Union Behavior, Pay Bargaining and Economic Performance*, ed. RJ Flanagan, KO Moene, M Wallerstein, pp. 63–154. Oxford, UK: Oxford Univ. Press

Nickell S. 1997. Unemployment and labor market rigidities: Europe versus North America. *J. Econ. Persp.* 11(3):55–74

Pedersen PJ. 1982. Union growth in Denmark 1911–39. *Scand. J. Econ* 84:583–92

Piore M, Sabel C. 1984. *The Second Divide: Possibilities for Prosperity*. New York: Basic Books

Pontusson J. 1991. *Fordism and social democracy: towards a comparative analysis*. Presented at Annu. Meet. Am. Polit. Sci. Assoc., Washington, DC, Aug. 29–Sept. 1

Pontusson J, Swenson P. 1996. Labor markets, production strategies, and wage bargaining institutions: the Swedish employer offensive in comparative perspective. *Comp. Polit. Stud.* 29(2):223–50

Regalia I, Regini M, Reyneri E. 1978. Labour conflicts and industrial relations in Italy. In *The Resurgence of Class Conflict in Western Europe Since 1968*, ed. C Crouch, A Pizzorno, 1:101–58. London: Macmillan

Rodrik D. 1996. *Globalization and labor, or: If globalization is a bowl of cherries, why are there so many glum faces around the table?* Presented at CEPR Conf. Regional Integration, La Coru, Spain, April 26–27

Rothstein BO. 1989. Marxism, institutional analysis and working-class power. *Polit. Soc.* 18:317–46

Sharpe IG. 1971. The growth of Australian trade unions: 1907–1969. *J. Ind. Relat.* 13:144–62

Siebert H. 1997. Labor market rigidities: at the root of unemployment in Europe. *J. Econ. Persp.* 11(3):37–54

Soskice D, Iversen T. 2000. The non-neutrality of monetary policy with large price or wage setters. *Q. J. Econ.* 115: In press

Streeck W. 1993. The rise and decline of neocorporatism. In *Labor and an Integrated Europe*, ed. L Ulman, B Eichengreen, WT Dickens, pp. 80–101. Washington, DC: Brookings Inst.

Streeck W, Schmitter PC. 1991. From national corporatism to transnational pluralism: organized interests in the single European market. *Polit. Soc.* 19(2):133–64

Summers R, Heston A. 1991. The Penn World Table (Mark 5): an expanded set of international comparisons, 1950–1988. *Q. J. Econ.* 106:327–68

Swenson P. 1989. *Fair Shares: Unions, Pay and Politics in Sweden and West Germany*. Ithaca, NY: Cornell Univ. Press

Swenson P. 1991. Bringing capital back in, or social democracy reconsidered. *World Polit.* 43(4):513–44

Swindinsky R. 1974. Trade union growth in Canada, 1911–1970. *Relat. Ind.* 29:435–51

Thelen K. 1999. Why German employers cannot bring themselves to dismantle the German model. In *Unions, Employers and Central Banks: Wage Bargaining and Macroeconomic Policy in an Integrating Europe*, ed. T Iversen, J Pontusson, D Soskice, pp. 138–169. Cambridge, UK: Cambridge Univ. Press

Tilly C. 1986. *The Contentious French*. Cambridge, UK: Belknap

Traxler F. 1994. Collective bargaining: levels and coverage. *OECD Employment Outlook* July:167–94

Traxler F. 1995. Farewell to labor market associations? Organized versus disorganized decentralization as a map for industrial relations. In *Organized Industrial Relations in Europe: What Future?*, ed. C Crouch, F Traxler, pp. 3–19. Aldershot, UK: Avebury

Troy L. 1990. Is the U.S. unique in the decline of private sector unionism? *J. Labor Res.* 11:111–43

Visser J. 1991. Trends in trade union membership. *OECD Employment Outlook* July: 97–134

Visser J. 1996. Unionisation trends revisited. CESAR Res. Pap. 1996/2. Cent. Res. Eur. Soc. Ind. Relat., Amsterdam

Visser J, Ebbinghaus B. 1999. When institutions matter. *Eur. Sociol. Rev.*

Wallerstein M. 1989. Union organization in advanced industrial democracies. *Am. Polit. Sci. Rev.* 83:481–501

Wallerstein M. 1990. Centralized bargaining and wage restraint. *Am. J. Polit. Sci.* 34:982–1004

Wallerstein M. 1991. Industrial concentration, country size and union membership: response to Stephens. *Am. Polit. Sci. Rev.* 85:949–53

Wallerstein M. 1999. Wage-setting institutions and pay inequality in advanced industrial societies. *Am. J. Polit. Sci.* 43:649–80

Wallerstein M, Golden M. 1997. The fragmentation of the bargaining society: wage-setting in the Nordic countries, 1950–1992, *Comp. Polit. Stud.* 30(6):699–731

Wallerstein M, Golden M, Lange P. 1997. Unions, employers associations and wage-setting institutions in North and Central Europe, 1950–1992. *Ind. Labor Relat. Rev.* 50(3):379–401

Western B. 1997. *Between Class and Market: Postwar Unionization in the Capitalist Democracies*. Princeton, NJ: Princeton Univ. Press

Western B, Healy K. 1999. Explaining the OECD wage slowdown: recession or labor decline. *Eur. Sociol. Rev.* 15:233–49

Windmuller JP. 1981. Concentration trends in union structure: an international comparison. *Ind Labor Relat. Rev.* 35:43–57

Wood A. 1994. *North-South Trade, Employment and Inequality*. Oxford, UK: Clarendon

PART III

Inequality and Redistribution

11

<hr>

Introduction

David Austen-Smith

Although a great deal of Michael Wallerstein's work concerns the inequality of income, wages, and wealth, very few of his papers contain significant normative claims beyond those of economic efficiency. Of course, the fact that Wallerstein eschewed any substantive normative discussions in his work does not imply that he held no views on the fairness or otherwise of particular patterns of wage and income inequality; far from it. Rather it reflects his belief that, before any compelling normative case can be made regarding any given distributions of income or wealth, it is necessary to understand as deeply as possible exactly how such distributions come about. And while there are a great many reasons offered in the literature for levels and changes in income inequality, Wallerstein focused on exploring how political-economic institutions influence and support particular distributions of income.

In the early 1980s, the ratio of wages earned by those in the 50th percentile of the wage distribution to those in the 10th percentile was 1.96 in the US, 1.64 in France, and 1.31 in Sweden. By the late 1990s, the ratios were 2.1, 1.59, and 1.39, respectively.[1] Over the same period, evidence from a set of eighteen OECD countries (including the US, France, and Sweden) indicates, first, a strong negative correlation between pretax income inequality and government spending on "safety net" insurance against loss of income and, second, a negligible relationship between pretax income inequality and any purely redistributive government spending in favor of the poor.[2] Finally, controlling for differences in income and wealth, the extent of income redistribution and public good provision in

<hr>

[1] Data reported in Oskarsson (2005), Table 1.
[2] Moene and Wallerstein (2001b, reprinted in Chapter 13).

localities with racially heterogeneous populations is lower than in more racially homogeneous localities.[3] How might such facts be explained? What accounts for the different levels and changes in wage inequality across countries over time? Why is the extent of governments' redistributive "safety net" policies inversely related to the degree of income inequality? Why does racial heterogeneity at given income levels lead to lower levels of fiscal redistribution and public good supply? The three papers by Wallerstein reproduced in this volume document some of his efforts to shed light on, if not provide definitive answers to, these specific questions. Thus, the papers exemplify both Wallerstein's belief in the importance of undertaking serious positive analysis before committing to any particular normative prescription, and his focus on political-economic institutions as fundamental for understanding income distribution.

The idea that centralized wage bargaining might account for relatively egalitarian distributions of pay has been in the literature for a while. For example, Freeman (1980, 1996) and Card (1996) identify a positive relationship between the degree of unionization and pay equality in the US; Hibbs and Locking (1995) document a similar relationship for Sweden; and Blau and Kahn (1996) compare wage inequality and the institutions of wage bargaining across the US and several other countries. Wallerstein's principal contribution in his 1999 article, "Wage-Setting Institutions and Pay Inequality in Advanced Industrial Societies," the first selection reprinted in this section (Chapter 12), is the exploitation of a far richer cross-national and intertemporal institutional dataset to disentangle various distinct aspects of centralization in wage bargaining and so identify which particular aspects are important for aggregate pay inequality and which are marginal.[4] His main result is that it is the degree of centralization in wage bargaining that most matters for pay inequality, and not the particular form that such centralization takes. Thus, two otherwise identical economies that differ only in the way wage bargaining is centralized (e.g., through unionization in one case and through the state per se in the other), but which nevertheless exhibit the same degree of centralization, can be expected to have essentially the same distribution of wages. Moreover, Wallerstein provides extensive evidence in support of the robustness of this finding and shows that it is independent of whether a country is a "social market economy" (that is,

[3] Alesina, Baqir, and Easterly (1999).
[4] Much of the novel data here derives from collaborative projects with, among others, Miriam Golden and Peter Lange.

Germany, Austria, the Netherlands, Belgium, or the Scandinavian countries) or not. Although other variables (such as trade patterns, government employment and ideology, and so forth) certainly influence wage inequality, their effects vary among nations, and – unlike the degree of centralization – none are robust across alternative specifications of the empirical model.

The independence of Wallerstein's empirical finding from other characteristics of political-economic organization, particularly government ideology or the institutional form of centralization, is striking. For instance, there is clearly a positive correlation between wage inequality and the extent to which a country uses proportional representation in electing its legislature (see, e.g., Atkinson, Rainwater, and Smeeding 1995; Birchfield and Crepaz 1998; Austen-Smith 2000). Thus, Wallerstein's analysis raises both theoretical and empirical questions about exactly why these other characteristics might vary so much in their impact relative to that of centralization. Oskarsson (2005) pursues the issue empirically, not only confirming that the degree of centralization in wage bargaining is the critical explanation for wage inequality, but also going on to show that it systematically influences the channels through which other characteristics, such as the openness of the economy or the ideological leaning of the government, affect the distribution of pay. For instance, "trade with less developed countries... and government employment have inegalitarian effects on the wage distribution, whereas leftist governments and unionism compress wages. However, given centralized wage bargaining these effects gradually disappear or, in some cases, change direction" (2005: 359). Oskarsson's results thus provide an explanation for Wallerstein's inability to find any systematic and robust influence of explanatory variables beyond the degree of centralization and suggest an important set of questions for future research, questions that Wallerstein broadly anticipated in his discussion (see especially section 6 of his paper).

While the "Wage-Setting..." paper (Chapter 12) is wholly an empirical investigation into what determines wage inequality, the second article reprinted below, "Inequality, Social Insurance, and Redistribution" (Chapter 13) by Moene and Wallerstein, develops both a theoretical model and an empirical assessment thereof. Most, if not all, of the formal political economy literature on redistributive taxation assumes a proportional tax rate on income, with total revenues distributed more or less evenly as lump-sum transfers across the population. In the canonical model (Romer 1975; Meltzer and Richard 1981), those with incomes above the mean are net losers from such transfers, whereas those with incomes less than the mean benefit on balance, and the level of taxation is determined by the median voter under majority preference collective choice. The main prediction generated by this model and subsequent variants is that the degree of redistribution is increasing in the difference between mean and median income. The empirical literature, however, fairly uniformly rejects this hypothesis (e.g., Perotti 1996).

Moene and Wallerstein's contribution starts with the observation that not all redistributive taxation is motivated by purely egalitarian motives; rather, some redistributive taxation funds social insurance policies to protect individuals from a loss of income due to unemployment, sickness, and other untoward events. And, as remarked earlier, in this regard there is evidence of an inverse relationship between income inequality and the extent of government spending on social insurance policies. Moene and Wallerstein build an infinite-horizon model in which individuals in any given period work in either a high-wage or a low-wage sector, or are unemployed and dependent exclusively on benefits from redistributive taxation. For convenience, high-wage earners are assumed to have job security, and there is a fixed share of permanently unemployed persons. Low-wage earners, however, may move in and out of unemployment, depending on the realization of some underlying stochastic shocks. Specifically, in any period there is an exogenous, time-invariant probability that any particular low-wage earner will become unemployed, and similarly an exogenous time-invariant probability that a temporarily unemployed person will find a low-wage job. Under the assumption that the stochastic process is Markov, there is a steady state to the system in which the shares of the population filling each category are fixed, and it is the properties of the steady state that the authors analyze. Wages are taxed at the majority-preferred rate, and tax revenues are allocated in part to the unemployed (who pay nothing) and in part across the working population as a lump-sum, purely inequality-reducing benefit.

The first question addressed with the model concerns how the majority-preferred tax rate varies with the share of tax revenues allocated for insurance purposes (i.e., to the unemployed) relative to that allocated to income redistribution among workers. The result here is that the more unequal the wage distribution, the higher is the majority-preferred tax rate when revenues are used for redistribution among workers, and the lower is the tax rate when revenues are used for social insurance purposes. Thus the model yields the empirical findings connecting government insurance policies and inequality, and therefore, if social insurance is the primary goal of

redistributive taxation, the result also runs counter to the canonical association of greater redistributive spending with greater inequality. On the
other hand, when relatively little is spent on social insurance, Moene and
Wallerstein's results are consistent with the standard prediction.[5]

The next step is to endogenize both the tax rate and the spending mix
between insurance and pure redistribution. As is well understood, such
multidimensional collective choice processes typically have no well-defined
majority-preferred policy bundle; rather, for every proposed tax rate and
share of revenues devoted to, say, insurance spending, there is an alternative
proposal that is majority-preferred (Plott 1967). To finesse the problem,
Moene and Wallerstein assume collective decisions are made using issue-by-
issue voting (Shepsle 1979): first the majority-preferred level of taxation is
decided, and then, conditional on this decision remaining fixed, the shares of
revenues are determined. This procedure yields interesting results, central
among which is that, graphed as a function of the low wage with the high
wage fixed, total government spending on insurance and redistribution is
V-shaped: an increase in inequality, first, induces a lower share of revenues
devoted to social insurance, and second, induces a fall in aggregate welfare
spending (i.e., taxes) when initial inequality is low, but third, induces a rise
in aggregate welfare spending when initial inequality is high.

Moene and Wallerstein's findings are suggestive, and the preliminary
empirical evidence presented later in the article provides some, albeit
not conclusive, support. Perhaps more importantly, the theory itself is
incomplete: as the authors remark, the model is limited both by the particular model of collective choice used to identify the principal comparative-
static results, and by the absence of any private insurance market in the
economy. The robustness of their results to the inclusion of such a market
is an important and, at the time of writing, open question. The article is significant in large part because it demonstrates the substantive importance of

---

[5] In a complementary article, Moene and Wallerstein (2001a) develop a static model of redistribution with a continuum of incomes subject to stochastic shocks. In this model, all individuals are taxed at a common proportional rate, as in the article reprinted in Chapter 13, but
the redistributive policy is a little different. The policy provides a common benefit level to
those with minimal income, and, as income rises, the benefit an individual receives declines
at a rate of $1 - \alpha$ times posttax earnings: if $\alpha = 0$, all tax revenue is targeted to the poorest
people in society, and if $\alpha = 1$ the redistribution is universalistic. In this setting, their main
result is that the majority-preferred level of welfare spending is increasing in α. And the
intuition here is simply that α and the likelihood of being a benefit recipient are inversely
related. This result and supporting intuition are clearly consistent with the results of their
dynamic model reprinted here.

taking explicit account of exactly how redistributive revenues are targeted for a proper understanding of redistribution policy.

Wage inequality is not only affected by details of the wage-bargaining institutions or by the reallocation of pretax earnings from the rich or employed to the poor or unemployed. There are, for instance, education subsidies and labor market regulations designed to alter the incentives and opportunities for various sorts of worker to enter more lucrative employment than might otherwise be available to them. One important example of such policies is affirmative action, and this is the subject of the third (and wholly theoretical) article reprinted here, Austen-Smith and Wallerstein's "Redistribution and Affirmative Action" (Chapter 14), which focuses on the interaction between fiscal redistribution and affirmative action policy within an equilibrium political economy model.

The formal political economy literature on understanding how, as observed earlier, racial heterogeneity within a society leads to less redistribution, all else held constant, is relatively small but growing. Important contributions to this literature include articles by Roemer (1998), who looks at how racial (or religious) attitudes influence the level of fiscal redistribution in a spatial model of elections; Roemer and Lee (2004), who develop the approach further to account for how racial prejudice influences welfare policy more generally; and Alesina and Glaeser (2004), who argue, inter alia, that politicians have strategic incentives to utilize racism to influence redistributive policy choice. A common feature of these efforts is the presumption of some degree of prejudice, or mutual distrust, across racial divides. Although such characteristics are surely present in society, using racial preferences to account for why redistributive policy seems to depend on racial fractionalization is a little unsatisfactory. At the very least, it is useful to explore just how far one might get without such an assumption. In their paper, Austen-Smith and Wallerstein consider an environment in which individuals are distinguished by an educational level and an ascriptive characteristic, race. No individual or firm in the model is motivated by any sort of prejudice. Nevertheless, due to presumed historical discrimination, the racial minority is assumed to be relatively disadvantaged educationally as a group; thus the economic prospects of members of this group are less than those of a typical member of the racial majority. The reason for excluding prejudice is not that this is necessarily realistic, but that it permits identifying how (ex post) fiscal redistribution and (ex ante) affirmative action policies interact through the purely economic incentives facing people in the society: different mixes of policy induce different incentives to create employment opportunities and different wage schedules in the labor market, which in turn affect individuals' preferences over the policy mix itself.

More specifically, the economy is a labor market in which the distribution of job opportunities is endogenous and workers are randomly matched with firms; moreover, a worker's productivity, and thus her wage, at any given firm depends on her education and the realization of a match-specific random variable. Workers with low productivity are assigned to unskilled, low-wage jobs, whereas those with sufficiently high productivity are assigned to skilled jobs where wages are discretely higher and increasing in productivity. Fiscal policy in the model is then purely redistributive, with revenue from a proportional tax on high wages financing a uniform benefit to workers with low wages; and affirmative action is assumed to consist in a mandatory minimal share of minority workers per firm hired into high-wage jobs. Since providing skilled jobs is costly to the firm, the fiscal policy and the affirmative action constraint substantially affect the allocation of productive labor and the supply of high-wage jobs.

All individuals are assumed to be self-interested income maximizers who therefore evaluate policy alternatives solely in terms of their implications for expected net wages. In contrast to the electoral approach due to Roemer (1998) among others, policy choice is determined in the model through a legislative bargaining process among three factions: one each representing, respectively, the high- and the low-wage earners from the racial majority, and a third representing the interests of the minority workers. Among the results here are that the expected level of fiscal redistribution is lower when affirmative action is an available policy instrument than when it is not, and that the skilled majority workers and the racial minority gain, at the expense of the less skilled, from having affirmative action available as a policy instrument. Moreover, the overall reduction in wage inequality is lower when affirmative action is an available policy instrument than when it is not.

As with Wallerstein's work with Moene discussed above, Austen-Smith and Wallerstein's results have a good intuition but are predicated on a fairly special model, albeit one in which both economic and political decisions are explicitly modeled and integrated. For example, both Roemer, and Alesina and Glaeser are clearly correct in thinking that electoral politics is a key ingredient to any satisfactory account of how racial fractionalization affects policy choice in general and welfare policy in particular, and its absence from Austen-Smith and Wallerstein's analysis constitutes a gap that needs filling.

David Austen-Smith

In sum, the three contributions reprinted here illustrate well Wallerstein's conviction that understanding wage inequality is an important task and that the right approach to doing this is essentially one that integrates both the economics and the politics of redistribution. He was among the first to pursue this conviction with such tenacity and at such a high level of academic rigor.

References

Alesina, A., R. Baqir, and W. Easterly. 1999. "Public Goods and Ethnic Divisions." *Quarterly Journal of Economics 114* (4): 1243–1284.
Alesina, A. and E. Glaeser. 2004. *Fighting Poverty in the US and Europe: A World of Difference.* Oxford: Oxford University Press.
Atkinson, A. B., L. Rainwater, and T. Smeeding. 1995. "Income Distribution in European Countries." Working Paper 9535. Dept. of Applied Economics, University of Cambridge.
Austen-Smith, D. 2000. "Redistribution under Proportional Representation." *Journal of Political Economy 108* (4): 1235–1269.
Birchfield, V., and M. L. Crepaz. 1998. "The Impact of Constitutional Structures and Collective and Competitive Veto Points on Income Inequality in Industrialized Democracies." *European Journal of Political Research 34* (1): 175–200.
Blau, F., and M. Kahn. 1996. "International Differences in Male Wage Inequality: Institutions versus Market Forces." *Journal of Political Economy 108* (2): 791–837.
Card, D. 1996. "The Effect of Unions on the Structure of Wages: A Longitudinal Analysis." *Econometrica 64* (4): 957–979.
Freeman, R. 1980. "Unionization and the Dispersion of Wages." *Industrial and Labor Relations Review 34* (1): 3–24.
Freeman, R. 1996. "Labor Market Institutions and Earnings Inequality." *New England Economic Review* May/June: 157–168.
Hibbs, D., and H. Locking. 1995. "Wage Compression, Wage Drift and Wage Inflation in Sweden." *Labour Economics 77* (1): 1–32.
Meltzer, R., and S. Richard. 1981. "A Rational Theory of the Size of Government." *Journal of Political Economy 89* (3): 914–927.
Moene, K., and M. Wallerstein. 2001a. "Targeting and the Political Support for Welfare Policies." *Economics of Governance 2* (1): 3–24.
Moene, K., and M. Wallerstein. 2001b. "Inequality, Social Insurance and Redistribution." *American Political Science Review 95* (4): 859–874.
Oskarsson, S. 2005. "Divergent Trends and Different Causal Logics: The Importance of Bargaining Centralization when Explaining Earning Inequality across Advanced Democratic Societies." *Politics and Society 33* (3): 359–385.
Perotti, R. 1996. "Growth, Income Distribution, and Democracy: What the Data Say." *Journal of Economic Growth 1* (1): 149–187.
Plott, C. 1967. "A Notion of Equilibrium and Its Possibility under Majority Rule." *American Economic Review 57* (3): 787–806.

Introduction

Roemer, J. 1998. "Why the Poor Don't Expropriate the Rich." *Journal of Public Economics 70* (3): 399–424.

Roemer, J., and W. Lee. 2004. "Racialism and Redistribution in the United States: A Solution to the Problem of American Exceptionalism." Working Paper. Yale University.

Romer, T. 1975. "Individual Welfare, Majority Voting and the Properties of a Linear Income Tax." *Journal of Public Economics 14* (1): 163–185.

Shepsle, K. 1979. "Institutional Arrangements and Equilibrium in Multidimensional Voting Models." *American Journal of Political Science 23* (1): 27–59.

12

*Wage-Setting Institutions and Pay
Inequality in Advanced Industrial Societies*

1. Introduction

There are large differences in the distribution of wages and salaries across
advanced industrial societies and, in some countries, significant change over
time in the recent past. In the United States, a worker who somehow man-
aged to rise from the 10th decile of the wage distribution to the 90th decile
would have received a pretax wage gain of 440 percent in 1990. To accom-
plish the same feat in 1980 would have taken a wage gain of only 380
percent. Both figures are in sharp contrast to the 98 percent increase that
a Norwegian worker would obtain in going from the 10th to the 90th
decile in the wage distribution in 1990. While countries may differ even
more in the distribution of income from capital or transfer payments, the
preponderance of labor earnings in total income is such that differences
in the distribution of wages and salaries account for most of the cross-
national variation in measures of the distribution of income among the
nonelderly.[1]

---

[1] In the United States, the correlation between labor earnings and total income, defined to be
revenue from all sources before taxes but after transfers, is .938 (Díaz-Giménez, Quadrini,
and Rios-Rull 1997, 6).

This chapter draws upon data that were collected as part of a project funded by the National
Science Foundation entitled "Union Centralization Among Advanced Industrial Societies"
directed by Peter Lange, Miriam Golden, and Michael Wallerstein. Financial support came
from the National Science Foundation, SES-9309391 and SES-9108485 to UCLA and SES-
9110228 and SBR-9309414 to Duke University. I thank Jelle Visser and Duane Swank for
allowing me to use unpublished data they collected and Lyle Scruggs for his help in putting
the data set together. I thank Miriam Golden, Peter Lange, Karl Ove Moene, Matthew Rabin,
John Stephens, Margaret Levi, David Olson, Bruce Western, and Douglas Hibbs for useful
discussions and comments on earlier drafts.

In the United States, the growth of wage inequality since 1980 blunted the usual impact of economic growth on poverty alleviation. The prolonged economic expansion that began in 1982 had little effect on the proportion of the US population with incomes below the poverty line until the mid 1990s, in sharp contrast to the significant declines in poverty that occurred during earlier economic expansions in the postwar period (Blank 1997). While employment increased strongly, the gain in hours at work was more than offset by declining real wages for low-wage workers. With less income and more hours at work, the welfare of the poor unambiguously declined.[2]

Before 1980, when the distribution of income was relatively stable, wage inequality attracted relatively little scholarly attention. In response to the growth of wage inequality since 1980 in the United States, however, the study of the determinants of wage inequality has acquired greater urgency with a large and growing literature that is increasingly comparative in scope.[3] My purpose here is to document and discuss the importance of wage-setting institutions for the distribution of earnings and, hence, for the distribution of income. In particular, the data strongly indicate that the more wages are determined in a centralized fashion, whether through centralized collective bargaining or parliamentary action, the more equal the distribution of earnings. Conversely, the more wages are set in decentralized bargaining between unions and firms at the plant level or between individual workers and their employers, the more unequal the wage distribution. In fact, it is difficult to find other variables that matter once the institutional variation in wage-setting is controlled for.

The existence of an empirical relationship between wage-setting via collective bargaining and the compression of pay differentials has been noted in the literature on wage inequality. Freeman (1980) and Freeman and Medoff (1984) observed that unions in the United States reduce inequality both within unionized establishments and between unionized establishments. More recent studies by Card (1996), Freeman (1996), Dinardo, Fortin, and

---

[2] The political consequences of growing income inequality are less clear than the social consequences. Lipset (1960), among many others, argued that high levels of income inequality are associated with high demand for redistributive policies and political instability. Yet, in the recent past, growing income inequality in the US has been accompanied by reductions in welfare spending (Gramlich, Kasten, and Sammartino 1993; Moffitt, Ribar, and Wilhem 1998). See Moffitt, Ribar, and Wilhem (1998) and Moene and Wallerstein (1998) for studies of the impact of inequality on political support for welfare programs.

[3] Levy and Murnane (1992) is an early survey of the literature on the growth of earnings inequality in the US. The more recent survey by Gottschalk and Smeeding (1997) compares changes in earnings and household inequality in the US with other OECD countries.

Michael Wallerstein

Lemieux (1996), and Fortin and Lemieux (1997) converge in estimating that the decline in union density in the United States can account for about 20 percent of the rise in wage inequality during the 1980s. In a comparison of wage dispersion in the United States with wage dispersion in nine other countries using micro-data sets, Blau and Kahn (1996) conclude that the greater wage inequality in the United States exists in spite of supply and demand conditions that would have produced the opposite result if wage-setting were equally decentralized everywhere.

In comparing wage inequality across countries, the share of the work force covered by collective bargaining is less important than cross-national differences in bargaining institutions, in particular, cross-national differences in the centralization of wage-setting and the concentration of unions. Hibbs and Locking (1995) document the dramatic impact of the egalitarian wage policy pursued by the Swedish unions through centralized bargaining on the distribution of wages in Sweden, as well as the rise in inequality after bargaining was decentralized in the early 1980s. Erickson and Ichino (1994) demonstrate a large compression of wages in Italy due to the combination of the cost of living index, the *scala mobile*, and significant levels of inflation between 1975 and 1983. Freeman (1988) considers the relationship between centralized wage-setting and wage equality to be so close that he uses measures of wage dispersion as a proxy for the centralization of bargaining.

Here, the determinants of the inequality of pay are studied using a new data set that includes much better information regarding cross-national and temporal differences in wage-setting institutions for sixteen advanced industrial societies over the period 1950–1992. The central advantage of the new data set is the availability of time-series data on a variety of different aspects of wage-setting institutions, including the involvement of union and employer peak associations in wage-setting, government involvement in (private-sector) wage-setting, the level at which wages are set, and the concentration of membership both within and between union confederations, on a yearly or five-yearly basis for most of the postwar period.

With richer institutional data, the relationship between wage-setting institutions and wage inequality can be established with greater accuracy. With separate series on different aspects of wage-setting institutions for sixteen countries, we can investigate which institutional differences matter for wage equality and which do not. In addition, the impact of institutional differences in wage-setting can be compared with other possible determinants of wage inequality such as international openness, the partisan composition of government, the size of government, or the supply of highly educated labor. Finally, with time-series data on wage-setting institutions, we can investigate the extent to which institutional change can explain the cumulative changes in the wage distribution from 1980 to 1992 among the major developed countries.

In the literature, it is common to refer to systems of centralized wage-setting as "corporatist." In this case, the conflation of centralization and corporatism is misleading. As is demonstrated below, centralization by means of parliamentary intervention in wage-setting has the same impact on wage equality as centralization by means of collective bargaining between peak associations of unions and employers. While bargaining between peak associations is largely confined to the countries conventionally labeled as corporatist, government intervention in wage-setting is not. Thus, centralization of wage-setting is a more precise description of what matters for wage inequality.

The body of my paper is organized as follows. The measures of wage inequality, institutional variation and other independent variables are described in Section 2. The estimation procedure is outlined in Section 3. Section 4 presents the empirical results on the determinants of pay inequality. Section 5 discusses the extent to which the empirical model can account for the change in wage inequality over time in those countries with the greatest change in wage equality. The implications of the empirical findings for understanding how institutions shape the wage distribution are discussed in Section 6. Section 7 concludes. The data sources are described in the appendix.

2. Measures of the Dependent and Independent Variables

Neither the equality of pay nor the variety of institutional differences in wage-setting are simple concepts to measure. Thus, it is necessary to begin with a discussion of how the dependent and independent variables are defined.

2.1. Pay Inequality

The measure of pay inequality that is used as the dependent variable is derived from the ratio of the wage received by the worker at the 90th percentile, w_{90}, to the wage received by the worker at the 10th percentile, w_{10}, for both sexes reported in OECD (1996) from 1980 through

253

1992.[4] No single statistic can encompass all important aspects of the wage distribution. For the purpose of studying the impact of wage-setting institutions on wage compression, however, a statistic like the w_{90}/w_{10} ratio has two important advantages over alternative measures such as the Gini coefficient or the variance of the log of wages. The first is that measurement error is most serious in the upper and lower tails of the wage distribution.[5] The w_{90}/w_{10} ratio is, therefore, a more reliable statistic than measures that are sensitive to reported wages at the top and bottom of the wage scale.

The second advantage of the w_{90}/w_{10} ratio sterms from its insensitivity to wage differentials among observationally equivalent workers. With centralized wage-setting, workers in similar positions with similar credentials and seniority must be treated identically since information about individual employees is not available at levels of centralization higher than the firm. The standardization of wages for workers with identical credentials in identical job categories lowers the variance of the wage distribution, but does not affect the w_{90}/w_{10} ratio. Thus, if centralization has an effect on the w_{90}/w_{10} ratio, that effect is due to something other than the reduction of inequality that occurs solely because of informational constraints.

Figure 1 presents the w_{90}/w_{10} ratios for the sixteen countries included in the study in three different years: 1980, 1986, and 1992.[6] The correlation of the w_{90}/w_{10} ratio and the w_{50}/w_{10} ratio, where w_{50} is the median wage, is very high (around .93). The distribution of w_{90}/w_{10} ratios is positively skewed, with wage inequality in the US and Canada substantially higher than the other fourteen countries. Moreover, the w_{90}/w_{10} ratio cannot be less than one by definition, which is incompatible with the standard assumption that the error term has a normal distribution. Therefore, for

---

[4] To be precise, the data refer to gross (pretax) wages and salaries received by full-time workers. Nonwage benefits are not included.

[5] The wage data come from either labor market surveys or administrative data such as collected by the social security system, depending on the country. In either case, the data are generally "top-coded" where reported earnings above some threshold x are recorded as being equal to x. The problem at the bottom the wage distribution is the absence of reliable measures of earnings that are hidden from the tax authorities.

[6] The countries in Figure 1 are Norway (NOR), Sweden (SWE), Denmark (DNK), Belgium (BEL), Finland (FIN), Italy (ITA), (West) Germany (GER), Netherlands (NLD), Switzerland (CHE), Australia (AUSTRL), Japan (JPN), France (FRA), Great Britain (GBR), Austria (AUT), Canada (CAN), and the United States (USA). Data for the years 1980, 1986, and 1992 were used whenever possible. In cases with missing data, I used data from the closest available year. (See the appendix for details.) There is no data for Belgium or the Netherlands before 1985. There is no data for Switzerland before 1991. The data source is OECD (1996, Table 3.1, 61–62).

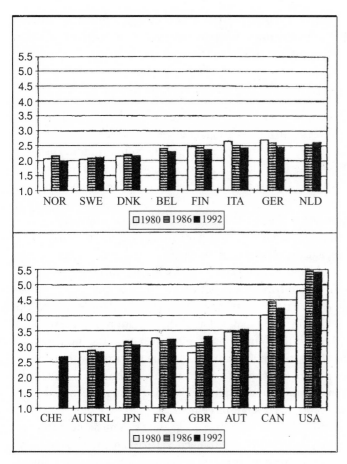

Figure 1 90/10 wage ratio.

the purposes of estimation, the w_{90}/w_{10} ratio was transformed according to the formula

$$y = \ln \left(\frac{w_{90} - w_{10}}{w_{10}} \right) \tag{1}$$

to obtain a measure of pay inequality that can take any value between negative infinity (indicating that the 90th percentile worker and the 10th percentile worker receive equal pay) and positive infinity.[7] A value of $y = 0$

---

[7] The results presented below are not sensitive to the logarithmic transformation. Similar results are obtained with w_{90}/w_{10} as the dependent variable.

Michael Wallerstein

indicates that $[(w_{90} - w_{10})/w_{10}] = 1$ or that the wage differential between the 90th and 10th percentile workers is 100 percent, roughly the level of wage dispersion found in Norway and Sweden.

2.2. Measures of Institutional Differences in Wage-Setting

The set of independent variables contains measures of confederal and government involvement in wage-setting, the level at which wages are predominantly set, the concentration of union membership within and between union confederations, union density, and union coverage. Additional details regarding the data and the list of data sources are contained in the appendix.

The Centralization of Wage-Setting As scholars of comparative industrial relations have frequently noted, there are large cross-national differences in the level at which wage agreements are negotiated and in the role of the peak associations of unions and employers in collective bargaining. First, there is the general distinction between systems of industrial relations in which wage contracts are largely negotiated at the plant level (the US, Canada, Great Britain, and Japan prior to the initiation of industry-wide coordination through the annual spring offensive) or at the industry level (all of the other countries in the sample). Among countries with industry-wide bargaining, there is a wide range with respect to the role played by the peak associations of unions and employers, ranging from none to peak-level negotiation of a centralized wage agreement.

Moreover, to focus on the collective bargaining system alone is too narrow. Wage-setting can also be centralized via parliamentary action. All governments have an impact on the distribution of pay via their role as employer of a significant share of the work force. Most governments also have some role in private-sector wage-setting. At one end of the spectrum, governments do no more than legislate a minimum wage or extend the terms of collective agreements to nonunion workers. At the other cod of the spectrum, governments directly determine private sector wages through arbitration or the imposition of mandatory wage controls.

Table 1a and 1b presents the scales devised by Golden, Lange, and Wallerstein to measure confederal and government involvement in private-sector wage bargaining.[8] Confederal involvement is measured for every

[8] For descriptions of the changes in wage-setting institutions during the postwar period revealed by the data, see Wallerstein, Golden, and Lange (1997), Wallerstein and Golden (1997), and Golden, Wallerstein, and Lange (1998)

Wage-Setting Institutions and Pay Inequality

Table 1a. *Index of Confederal Involvement in Wage-Setting*

1. Confederation(s) uninvolved in wage-setting in any of the subsequent ways.
2. Confederation(s) participates in talks or in formulation of demands for some affiliates.
3. Confederation(s) participates in talks or in formulation of demands for all affiliates.
4. Confederation(s) negotiates non-wage benefits.
5. Confederations(s) negotiates a part of the wage agreement, such as the cost-of-living adjustment.
6. Confederation(s) represents affiliates in mediation with centralized ratification.
7. Confederation(s) represents affiliates in arbitration.
8. Confederation(s) bargains for affiliates in industry-level negotiations.
9. Confederation(s) negotiates national wage agreement without peace obligation.
10. Confederation(s) negotiates national wage agreement with peace obligation.
11. Confederation(s) negotiates national wage agreement with limits on supplementary bargaining.

Table 1b. *Index of Government Involvement in Wage-Setting*

1. Government uninvolved in wage setting.
2. Government establishes minimum wage(s).
3. Government extends collective agreements.
4. Government provides economic forecasts to bargaining partners.
5. Government recommends wage guidelines or norms.
6. Government and unions negotiate wage guidelines.
7. Government imposes wage controls in selected industries.
8. Government imposes cost-of-living adjustment.
9. Formal tripartite agreement for national wage schedule without sanctions.
10. Formal tripartite agreement for national wage schedule with sanctions.
11. Government arbitrator imposes wage schedules without sanctions on unions.
12. Government arbitrator imposes national wage schedule with sanctions.
13. Government imposes national wage schedule with sanctions.
14. Formal tripartite agreement for national wage schedule with supplementary local bargaining prohibited.
15. Government imposes wage freeze and prohibits supplementary local bargaining.

Table 1c. *Index of the Level of Wage-Setting*

1. Local wage-setting.
2. Industry-level wage-setting.
3. Centralized wage-setting without sanctions.
4. Centralized wage-setting with sanctions.

bargaining round, usually every two years. Government involvement is measured annually. The rankings of categories reflect both the role of the central confederations (or government) and the degree to which central agreements constrain wage negotiations at lower levels.

Central agreements generally impose a floor on wages. In the absence of an industrial peace clause, industry and local-level negotiators are free to bargain and to strike for additional wage increases above the increase specified in the central agreement. With an industrial peace clause, bargaining at lower levels is permitted but strikes and lockouts are prohibited for the duration of the central agreement. Although other forms of industrial action, such as go-slow or work-to-rule actions, may be allowed and no clause in a contract can prevent wildcat strikes, the existence of an industrial peace clause significantly increases the ability of central wage-setters to control the aggregate wage increase in multi-level bargaining (Moene, Wallerstein, and Hoel 1993, chapter 12). Thus, agreements that contain peace clauses are considered to be more centralized than those that do not.

In the scale for government involvement, presented in Table 1b, wage-setting by Parliament is judged to be more centralized than wage-setting by a government-appointed arbitrator. An arbitrator's mandate is to craft an agreement that is acceptable to both unions and employers, thereby avoiding industrial conflict. For Parliament, in contrast, the government's macroeconomic goals may be the primary consideration. The scale distinguishes between a government-imposed wage contract, government participation in tripartite talks in which a wage contract is negotiated as part of a broader package, and government attempts to influence the wage agreement without formally participating in the wage negotiations.

In addition to using separate indices for confederal and government involvement, two other summary measures of centralization were constructed. The first combines the confederal and government involvement scores by rescaling both indices to have a common range of [0,1] and then using the maximum of the two. A second summary measure of centralization, summarized in Table 1c, is a four-category scale indicating the level at which wages are predominantly set for each country for each year. A score of three indicates centralized wage-setting with sanctions on lower-level bargaining whether by centralized collective bargaining or government action. A score of two indicates centralized wage-setting without sanctions on subsequent lower-level bargaining. A score of one indicates wage-setting at the level of the industry while a score of zero indicates the predominance of wage-setting at the level of the firm or the individual employee-employer pair. The country means of the index of the level of wage-setting over the time period 1950–1992 are displayed later in Table 5 in the appendix.

Union Concentration Centralization measures explicit coordination of wage-setting among workers in different firms or different industries. However, there can be a substantial degree of implicit coordination that may achieve much the same outcome in the absence of a centralized procedure. A particular union, the German metalworkers for example, may act as the wage leader. If the wage agreement signed in the leading industry is quickly adopted in other industries, and the wage negotiators in the leading industry understand that the terms of their agreement will rapidly spread throughout the economy, the outcome may be a wage schedule that is not very different from what would result from the direct negotiation of a centralized agreement covering the private sector as a whole.

An important determinant of the ability of unions and employers to coordinate wage settlements implicitly in the absence of a formal centralized agreement may be the extent to which the union side is dominated by a small number of actors or the degree of concentration of union membership (Golden 1993). In the data set, concentration is measured along two dimensions. The first is between confederations, or the extent to which union members belong to a single confederation rather than being divided among multiple confederations. The measure used is the Herfindahl index between confederations:

$$H_B = \sum_{j=1}^{N}(S_j)^2 \qquad (2)$$

In Equation 2, S_j is the share of total union members who belong to confederation j, and N is the total number of confederations. The Herfindahl index of concentration between confederations is the probability that two union members, picked at random, will belong to the same confederation.[9]

Another dimension of concentration is the extent to which the membership of a single union confederation is concentrated within a small number of affiliates. To measure concentration within each confederation, an approximate Herfindahl index was constructed using the membership of the

___

[9] Members of unions unaffiliated with a confederation are not included, due to the difficulty of obtaining reliable membership figures for independent unions in all sixteen countries.

three largest affiliates and the total number of affiliates. The approximate Herfindahl index of concentration within confederations is defined as:

$$H_w = \sum_{j=1}^{3}(s_j)^2 + \left[1 - \sum_{j}^{3} s_j\right]^2 \frac{1}{n-3} \tag{3}$$

where s_j is the share of the confederation's members who belong to the jth largest union, and n is the total number of affiliates in the confederation. H_w represents an approximation of the probability that two members of confederation i, picked at random, will belong to the same affiliate. The formula for H_w in Equation 3 implicitly assumes that the fourth through nth unions are the same size. Thus, Equation 3 is an underestimate of the true Herfindahl index, but the underestimate is not large in practice. The approximate Herfindahl was calculated for the main blue-collar confederation, where there is a dominant blue-collar confederation. In countries with multiple major blue-collar confederations, such as Italy or the Netherlands, the average Herfindahl index for each blue-collar confederation was used, weighted by the confederation's share of total union membership.[10] Unfortunately, membership by affiliate is unavailable in France, so the Herfindahl index of concentration within confederations is only available for fifteen countries. Both measures of concentration were calculated every five years from 1950 though 1990. (See Table 5 in the appendix for the country means of H_w from 1950–1990.)

Union Density and Coverage   Studies of the influence of unions in the US almost always use union density as the measure of union influence. Here, density is defined as union members who work as employees divided by the total number of wage and salary earners. Thus, the definition of union density excludes workers who are retired, unemployed, or self-employed from both the numerator and the denominator.

A different measure of the extent to which unions influence the aggregate wage distribution is coverage, defined to be the share of the work force covered by a collective agreement. In some countries, such as the US, Canada, Japan, and Great Britain, there is a close correspondence between union density and coverage. In other countries, coverage far exceeds density for a

---

[10] The Belgian figure for within-confederal concentration reflects only the Catholic confederation, as membership figures by affiliate are unavailable for the socialist confederation. Since the two confederations have close to the same (small) number of affiliates, the two are assumed to be equally concentrated.

variety of reasons. In France and Belgium, coverage is frequently extended by government decree. In Germany and Austria, a labor agreement signed by the employers' association is binding on all affiliated firms whether or not the firm's employees are union members, and most employees work for employers who belong to the employers' association. In fact, membership of firms in the relevant employers' association is mandated by law in Austria. Not only is union coverage much higher than union density in continental Europe, but coverage has remained stable since 1980 in continental Europe, even in countries where union density has declined.[11] While union density figures are available for the entire postwar period, union coverage figures are available only for 1980 and 1990. The data for union coverage in 1990 is presented in Table 5 in the appendix.

2.3. Other Independent Variables

Partisan Variables Given the extensive government involvement in private-sector wage-setting in many advanced industrial countries, the ideology or the constituency of the government might have an impact on wage equality. In particular, social democratic governments might push for greater wage equality than conservative governments. Left government is measured by the share of cabinet portfolios held by socialist, social democratic, or labor parties as a proportion of all cabinet portfolios. Alternatively, it is sometimes argued that the important political divide is not between the socialist camp and the rest, but between both left and center parties, on the one side, and conservative parties on the other. Therefore, the proportion of cabinet portfolios held by conservative parties was also included, following the classification of Castles and Mair (1984).

International Openness Wood (1994) argues that increasing international trade is responsible for much of the rise in the inequality of pay in the US and, to the extent that the wage-setting system allows wages at the bottom to fall, in other advanced industrial societies as well. Trade dependence, as measured by imports plus exports as a share of GDP, was included to test the direct impact of trade on pay inequality.[12]

[11] In 1990, the unweighted average of union density was 46.8 percent while the unweighted average of union coverage was 76 percent for the eleven countries of the sample in continental Europe.
[12] In fairness, it should be noted that what matters for the wage distribution, according to standard trade theory, is the impact of trade on relative prices in the domestic economy

Michael Wallerstein

The Size of the Public Sector Wage equality might be affected by the size of the public sector. Katz and Krueger (1991) show that public sector wages are more compressed than private sector wages in the US. If public sector wages are generally more compressed than private sector wages, then public sector employment as a share of total employment might be an important determinant of aggregate wage inequality. The size of the public sector in terms of government spending as a share of GDP may also be important. On the spending side, generous welfare policies may increase the bargaining power of low-wage workers by providing better options outside the labor market. On the revenue side, Hibbs and Locking (1996) suggest that high marginal tax rates reduce the cost of wage compression for high wage workers, since much of the extra income that high wage workers would receive with a less compressed wage scale would be taxed away.

Education Finally, one might expect to find more compressed wage scales in countries with a relatively large supply of highly educated labor.[13] Two measures of the supply of educated workers on the wage distribution are used. The first is the mean number of years of higher education among persons between the ages of 15 and 64. The second is the mean number of years of education at all levels for the same age bracket.

3. Statistical Procedures

The adjustments to the wage distribution that occurs from one year to the next are always small, whatever the wage-setting system. Workers' relative wages in year t are strongly dependent on their relative wages in year $t - 1$. The most compelling empirical specification of the evolution of the distribution of pay is the error-correction model. The underlying assumption is that there is an equilibrium wage distribution associated with a given set of wage-setting institutions and other determinants of relative pay, but that the adjustment to the equilibrium distribution is not instantaneous. The actual wage distribution is modeled as a weighted average of the equilibrium

which may not be accurately proxied by the ratio of imports plus exports to GDP. For a review of the debate over the importance of international trade in explaining the rise of pay inequality in the US, see Freeman (1995), Richardson (1995), and Wood (1995).

[13] At the same time, if additional years of schooling have a relatively small effect on future earnings, the number of persons who seek higher education may be reduced (Edin and Topel 1995). Thus, it is impossible to say a priori whether the correlation between a large supply of educated workers and wage equality should be positive or negative.

262

wage distribution, which changes as the wage-setting environment changes, and the wage distribution that existed in the previous period.

Formally, let $y_i^*(t)$ be the equilibrium wage dispersion for country i at time t. The equilibrium wage dispersion is the level of wage dispersion that, once obtained, would not change provided there was no change in the exogenous variables. Different wage-setting institutions and other exogenous factors are assumed to affect the equilibrium wage distribution in the standard linear fashion

$$y_i^*(t) = X_i(t)'\beta + v_i^*(t) \tag{4}$$

where $X_i(t)$ is a vector of independent variables associated with country i at time t and $v_i^*(t)$ is a random error term associated with the equilibrium wage distribution.

The actual wage dispersion at time t, denoted $y_i(t)$, is assumed to be equal to the wage dispersion at time $t - 1$ plus an adjustment that depends on the difference between the wage dispersion at time $t - 1$ and the equilibrium wage dispersion at time t, or

$$y_i(t) = y_i(t - 1) + (1 - \lambda)[y_i^*(t) - y_i(t - 1)] + v_i(t) \tag{5}$$

where λ is a parameter indicating the speed at which the distribution of wages adjust and $v_i(t)$ is a random error term. Combining Equations 4 and 5, we have

$$y_i(t) = \lambda y_i(t - 1) + (1 - \lambda)X_i(t)'\beta + u_i(t) \tag{6}$$

where $u_i(t) = [v_i(t) + (1 - \lambda)v_i^*(t)]$. I assume, initially, that $E[u_i(t)^2] = \sigma^2$ for all i and all t and that $E[u_i(t)u_j(s)] = 0$ if either $i \neq j$ or $t \neq s$.[14]

Rather than work with annual data, the statistical analysis is performed with the three cross-sectional panels of data displayed in Figure 1. There were several reasons for this choice. First, one of the institutional variables that turns out to be important is only available in five-year intervals. Second, the annual change in the wage distribution is small relative to the measurement error in the data on wage dispersion.[15] Cumulating the change in

---

[14] Both fixed period effects and fixed country effects are introduced later.

[15] Some sense of the extent of measurement error can be obtained by comparing w_{90}/w_{10} ratios derived from different surveys of the same country in the same year (OECD 1996, annex 3A: 100–103). The correlation of the annual change in wage inequality derived from different surveys of the same country is frequently close to zero. See Rueda and Pontusson (1998) for a study of wage inequality based on annual pooled time series data. The major difference between Rueda and Pontusson's results and the results in this paper are discussed below.

dependent and independent variables over approximately six years has the effect of increasing the variance of the independent variables relative to the noise in the data.

Let t_0 be the first year for which we have wage dispersion data for country i. This is usually 1980, but in some countries it is 1981 or even, in the case of Germany, 1983. Let t_1 be 1986, unless 1986 data are missing for country i, in which case $t_1 = 1987$. Finally, let t_2 be the last year for which we have wage dispersion data. This is 1992 for most countries, but 1991 for Norway and Italy and 1990 for Denmark. Then, for country i, repeated substitution using Equation 6 yields

$$y_i(t_1) = \lambda^{(t_1 - t_0)} y_1(t_0) + \sum_{k=0}^{t_1 - t_0 - 1} \lambda^k [(1 - \lambda) X_i(t_1 - k)' \beta + u_i(t_1 - k)] \qquad (7)$$

for $y_i(t_1)$ and a similar expression for $y_i(t_2)$. Since data for the independent variables are available for many years prior to t_0, $y_i(t_0)$ can be estimated without knowing $y_i(t_{-1})$ by making repeated use of Equation 6 to obtain

$$y_i(t_0) = \sum_{k=0}^{\infty} \lambda^k [(1 - \lambda) X_i(t_0 - k)' \beta + u_i(t_0 - k)] \qquad (8)$$

In practice, the Golden, Lange, Wallerstein data set only goes back to 1950. Therefore, in estimating Equation 8, it was assumed that $X_i(1980 - k) = 0$ for $k > 30$ for all independent variables except the constant. With regard to the variables pertaining to wage-setting institutions, this is equivalent to assuming that the distribution of wages was determined in decentralized markets in all sixteen countries prior to 1950. Such an assumption is clearly false, but to the extent that the assumption matters, it biases the coefficients toward zero given the high correlation between the centralization of bargaining in the postwar period and the centralization of bargaining before 1950.[16]

---

[16] An additional problem is that some of the data is not available on an annual basis. The Herfindahl indices between and within confederations are available every five years starting in 1950. Before cumulating, these data series were completed by linear interpolation between data points. The change in Herfindahl indices is small, so the use of interpolated data has little effect on the results. Coverage is available only in 1980 and 1990. Again, linear interpolation was used to fill in the data after 1980. To fill in the rest of the series, coverage was assumed to be constant in the three decades prior to 1980. While this is a strong assumption, the data do show that coverage was nearly constant in the decade following 1980. Nevertheless, coverage is measured with a great deal more error than the other independent variables used in this study.

In sum, for each country i the following system of equations was estimated:

$$\tilde{y}_i = \tilde{X}_i \beta (1 - \lambda) + \tilde{u}_i \tag{9}$$

where

$$\tilde{y}_i = \begin{pmatrix} y_i(t_0) \\ y_i(t_1) - \lambda^{(t_1 - t_0)} y_i(t_0) \\ y_i(t_2) - \lambda^{(t_2 - t_1)} y_i(t_1) \end{pmatrix}$$

$$\tilde{X}_i = \begin{pmatrix} \sum_{k=0}^{t_0 - 1950} \lambda^k X_i(t_0 - k) \\ \sum_{k=0}^{t_1 - t_0 - 1} \lambda^k X_i(t_1 - k) \\ \sum_{k=0}^{t_2 - t_1 - 1} \lambda^k X_i(t_2 - k) \end{pmatrix}$$

and

$$\tilde{u}_i = \begin{pmatrix} \sum_{k=0}^{\infty} \lambda^k u_i(t_0 - k) \\ \sum_{k=0}^{t_1 - t_0 - 1} \lambda^k u_i(t_1 - k) \\ \sum_{k=0}^{t_2 - t_1 - 1} \lambda^k u_i(t_2 - k) \end{pmatrix}$$

Stacking the set of equations for each country, the variance structure of the error term in Equation 7 can be written succinctly as[17]

$$E(\tilde{u}\tilde{u}') = I \otimes \Omega$$

where I is a 16×16 identity matrix and

$$\Omega = \frac{\sigma^2}{1 - \lambda^2} \begin{pmatrix} 1 & 0 & 0 \\ 0 & 1 - \lambda^{2(t_1 - t_0)} & 0 \\ 0 & 0 & 1 - \lambda^{2(t_2 - t_1)} \end{pmatrix}$$

Once λ is determined, the system of equations in 9 can be estimated by GLS. The parameter λ was estimated by maximum likelihood.[18]

---

[17] The symbol $\otimes$ indicates the Kronecker product.

[18] Assuming that the error term is normally distributed, the GLS estimate maximizes the likelihood function for a fixed λ. Thus, the procedure outlined here would be identical to finding the maximum likelihood estimators for Equation 7 if the estimate of λ was recalculated for every specification of the exogenous variables. See Greene (1993, chapter 13) for a discussion of the properties of the GLS estimator.

Table 2. *Centralization, Concentration, Coverage, and Pay Inequality*

	(1)	(2)	(3)	(4)	(5)	(6)	(7)
Constant	.918	1.06	1.17	1.33	1.42	1.57	1.48
	(9.96)	(11.8)	(17.5)	(10.7)	(14.2)	(10.4)	(4.12)
Confederal Inv.	−.0469						
	(3.80)						
Government Inv.	−.0165						
	(0.98)						
Maximum		−.0650					
		(6.24)					
Level of			−.0234	−.0165	−.0191	−.0182	−.0159
Wage-Setting			(10.3)	(5.34)	(6.93)	(7.03)	(3.91)
Concentration			.0171				
			(1.79)				
Conf. Concentration Within				−.116	−.134	−.164	−.040
				(3.01)	(3.55)	(4.00)	(0.34)
Conf. Density			−.0122				
			(0.75)				
Coverage				−.0215	−.0148	−.0196	−.0635
				(1.72)	(1.45)	(2.00)	(1.68)
Fixed effects							
Period	no	no	no	no	no	yes	yes
Country	no	no	no	no	no	no	yes
N	44	44	44	41	41	41	40
Buse R^2	.431	.481	.716	.818	.796	.844	.959

Notes: The dependent variable is ln $[(w_{90} - w_{10})/w_{10}]$. GLS estimation with $\lambda = .95$. The absolute value of the t-statistics are reported in the parentheses. "Constant" refers to the quasi-differenced constant given by setting $x_i(t) = 1$ in Equation 9. There are three period dummies and thirteen country dummies, with the country dummies quasi-differenced in the same way as the constant term. Equations 4–7 exclude France for lack of data on concentration within confederations. Equation 7 also excludes Switzerland for lack of time series data on the Swiss wage distribution. The F-statistics for period fixed effects in (6) and (7) are 3.54 (with [3,34] degrees of freedom) and 7.46 (with [3,20] degrees of freedom) respectively. The F-statistic for country fixed effects in (7) is 4.35 (with [13,20] degrees of freedom). The Buse R^2 is equal to $1 - (SS_{res}/SS_{const})$ where SS_{res} is the sum of squares of the residuals of the regression and SS_{const} is the sum of squares of the residual when "constant" is the only independent variable (Buse 1973).

4. Empirical Results

The impact of wage-setting institutions on the inequality of wages and salaries is presented in Table 2. The value of λ used in the regressions, $\lambda = .95$, is the value that maximizes the likelihood function with a weighted constant (as described in the notes at the bottom of the table), the level of wage-setting and the Herfindahl index of concentration within confederations as independent variables. The maximum likelihood value of λ

changes only slightly with the inclusion of different sets of independent variables.[19]

Consider, first, the first three equations of Table 2. When the index of confederal involvement and the index of government involvement are added to the regression equation separately, both coefficients are negative, indicating that greater centralization reduces wage inequality, but only the coefficient on confederal involvement is bounded away from zero with standard confidence intervals. Combining the two indices by taking the value of whichever is larger substantially increases the fit of the regression line. But the simple fourfold index of the level of wage-setting produces an even better fit, explaining more than 70 percent of the variance with a single variable. The level of wage-setting consistently outperforms the other measures of centralization whatever other independent variables are added, including the addition of dummy variables for both time periods and countries. When the level of wage-setting and one of the other measures of the centralization of wage-setting are combined in the same equation, only the level of wage-setting receives an estimated coefficient significantly different from zero.

Specification 4 adds the Herfindahl indices for concentration between and within confederations, along with density and coverage. The results indicate that the concentration of confederation members among a small number of affiliates is associated with greater pay equality. In contrast, the coefficient on the Herfindahl index between confederations is invariably estimated to have the wrong sign regardless of the other variables that are added to the regression equation. Equation 4 also indicates that union density has a substantially smaller impact on pay inequality than the coverage of union contracts. Equation 5 presents the regression equation with the institutional variables that work best: the level of wage-setting, concentration within confederations, and coverage.

To check the robustness of the results, Equation 5 was reestimated with fixed period and country effects in Equations 6 and 7. The point estimate of the coefficient on level of wage-setting is somewhat reduced with the addition of fixed country and period effects, but it still remains significant at the 1 percent significance level in all specifications. Concentration within confederations has very little variance over time within countries. Thus, the addition of country fixed effects removes almost all of the explanatory

---

[19] The robustness of the results with respect to different values of λ is investigated below.

Michael Wallerstein

power of the Herfindahl index. With the data we have, it is impossible to distinguish the impact of union concentration from unobserved country-specific effects. Finally, the estimate of the coefficient on coverage is sharply increased by the addition of fixed period effects.

If we accept the point estimates in Equation 6 of Table 2, the long-term impact of a permanent change in the system of wage-setting from a system of plant or individual-level bargaining (as in Britain, Canada, or the US), to a system of industry-level bargaining (as in Switzerland, Austria, or Germany), is to reduce the wage differential $(w_{90} - w_{10})/w_{10}$ by 30 percent, since $\exp(-.018/(1 - \lambda)) = \exp(-.36) \approx 0.70$. A decline of two steps in the four step scale, for example, a lasting move from highly centralized bargaining, as in Sweden before 1983, to a system of industry-level bargaining would raise the predicted wage differential by 50 percent $(\exp(-.72) \approx 0.5)$ in the long run.

The most concentrated union confederations in the data set are the German and Swiss confederations. The estimate of the long-term impact of the difference between the Herfindahl index for the German DGB (about .16 in 1990) and the Herfindahl index of the least concentrated confederation in the data set, the Australian ACTU (about .02 in 1990), on the $(w_{90} - w_{10})/w_{10}$ wage differential is $\exp(-(.14)(.16)/(1-\lambda)) \approx 0.63$, which is roughly the same magnitude as the estimated difference between local and industry-level bargaining. Finally, the impact of increasing the coverage of union contracts from the US level (18 percent in 1990) to the average level of coverage in continental Europe (74 percent in 1990), would reduce $(w_{90} - w_{10})/w_{10}$ in the US by roughly 20 percent in the long run since $\exp(-(.02)(.56)/(1 - \lambda)) \approx 0.80$.

The first two columns of Table 3 present estimates of the impact of the partisan composition of government, economic openness, and the size of the public sector on wage inequality controlling for the level of wage-setting concentration within confederations and coverage. The first column of Table 3 includes a time trend. The second column replaces the time trend with fixed period effects.[20] To save space, Equations 1 and 2 in Table 3 only report the results of adding the six additional independent variables at the same time. Adding subsets of the six additional independent variables does not change the general pattern of results, except for the interaction of government employment and government spending noted below.

[20] There are not enough degrees of freedom to add fixed country effects to the set of independent variables in Table 3.

268

Wage-Setting Institutions and Pay Inequality

Table 3. *Pay Inequality and Other Explanatory Variables*

	(1)	(2)	(3)	(4)
Constant	1.51	1.92	1.39	1.43
	(10.4)	(9.75)	(6.05)	(6.28)
Level of Wage-Setting	−.0179	−.0187	−.0192	−.0184
	(6.03)	(7.58)	(5.88)	(5.86)
Concentration	−.182	−.201	−.111	−.0184
	(3.75)	(4.83)	(1.90)	(2.33)
Coverage	−.0295	−.0267	−.0099	−.0124
	(2.43)	(2.61)	(0.72)	(0.92)
Left Government	.0021	.0090		
	(0.23)	(1.11)		
Right Government	−.0093	−.0117		
	(1.27)	(1.92)		
Trade Dependence	−.0134	−.0261		
	(1.32)	(2.61)		
Government Employment	−.0971	−.0845		
	(1.83)	(1.89)		
Government Spending	.0864	.0720		
	(1.93)	(1.92)		
Year	0			
	(0)			
Higher Education			.170	.169
			(1.33)	(1.34)
Total Education			−.0811	−.0300
			(1.96)	(0.59)
Period Dummies	no	yes	no	yes
N	41	41	26	26
Buse R^2	.839	.896	.858	.886

Notes: The dependent variable is ln $[(w_{90} - w_{10})/w_{10}]$. GLS estimation with $\lambda = .95$. The absolute value of the t-statistics are reported in the parentheses. Concentration refers to concentration within confederations. The constant term and the Buse R^2 are described in the notes to Table 2. The F-statistics for the period fixed effects in (2) and (4) are 5.31 (with [3,29] degrees of freedom) and 2.22 (with [2,18] degrees of freedom) respectively. France is excluded because of missing concentration data. The 1992 panel is excluded from (3) and (4) because of missing data for mean years of education.

The data decisively reject the hypothesis that the participation of social democratic, socialist, or labor parties in government reduces wage inequality or that the participation of conservative parties in government increases wage inequality. These results indicate that partisan composition of government does not have a *direct* effect on wage inequality. To the extent that left governments are more likely to encourage centralized bargaining

269

by the unions or to intervene directly in wage-setting, however, the partisan composition of government may have an important indirect effect.

In addition, the cross-national data fail to support the claim that the increase of wage inequality in the US since 1980 is a consequence of increased trade. The hypothesis that growing trade dependence, as measured by imports plus exports as a share of GDP, is associated with greater wage inequality is contradicted by the negative point estimate of the coefficient on trade dependence. Countries with high levels of trade dependence tend to have relatively egalitarian wage distributions, even after controlling for the fact that countries with high levels of trade dependence have relatively centralized systems of wage-setting. Nor is there evidence of any time trend in the inequality of pay in the cross-national data. Note that the absence of a positive time trend does not mean that wage inequality has remained constant over time on average. Rather, the zero time trend implies that the change in average inequality of pay is fully explained by the change in the means of the other independent variables.

The impact of increased public sector employment is to reduce wage inequality as expected but only at a given level of government spending as a share of GDP. If government spending is removed from the set of independent variables, the point estimate for the coefficient on public sector employment is close to zero. The hypothesis that government spending reduces wage inequality, in contrast, is rejected. At given level of public sector employment, greater government spending as a share of GDP is associated with higher, not lower, wage inequality. This pattern appears to correspond to Esping-Andersen's (1990) distinction between the social democratic emphasis on the public provision of services and the Christian Democratic emphasis on cash transfers in welfare policy, with the former associated with greater wage equality than the latter.

Evidence on the impact of the supply of educated workers on wage equality is presented in Equations 3 and 4 of Table 3. Missing data force the dropping of the last time period which reduces the sample size from 41 to 26. More years of higher education (college and above) in the labor force is associated with greater wage inequality, controlling for mean years of education at all levels. In contrast, more years of education below the college level is associated with lower wage inequality. This pattern of results is consistent with a simple economic model of the labor market in which an increase in the education of the less-educated workers raises wages at the bottom, while the reduction of relative wages for workers at the top of the pay scale induced by centralized wage-setting lowers students' incentives to pursue higher education. By this argument, a reduction in average years of higher education is a consequence of wage compression and should be removed from the set of independent variables. Equation 4 in Table 3 indicates that the estimate of the impact of average years of education at all levels is sensitive to the inclusion of fixed period effects.

In sum, while independent variables like government employment, government spending, and the number of years of schooling appear as significant determinants of wage inequality in some specifications, only the level of wage-setting is robust in the sense that the estimated coefficient is stable and both statistically and substantively significant no matter what else is included on the right hand side of the regression equation. If we exclude fixed country effects, the estimate of the impact of concentration within confederations is also robust. Finally, if we include fixed period effects, the coverage of collective agreements is almost always significant. Moreover, there is a sense in which the coverage of union contracts must be important if collective bargaining institutions are important. Highly centralized bargaining that covered a vanishingly small fraction of the work force could not have a large impact on the aggregate wage distribution.

Table 4 illustrates how the estimates of the coefficients on the level of wage-setting, concentration within confederations and coverage change with different values of λ, the parameter for the speed of convergence to the equilibrium wage distribution. At $\lambda = .95$, a transitory shock to the wage distribution loses half its impact in 13.5 years. Increasing the value of λ to $\lambda = .975$ doubles the half life of a transitory shock to 27 years while reducing λ to $\lambda = .9$ cuts the half life of a transitory shock by roughly 50 percent to 6.5 years. Reducing λ further to $\lambda = .8$ reduces the half life of a temporary shock to only three years. To compare the magnitudes of the estimated coefficients with different values of λ, the estimates are divided by $(1-\lambda)$, labeled "long-term coefficients" in Table 4. The long-term coefficient is equal to the eventual impact of a permanent one unit change in the independent variable on ln $[(w_{90} - w_{10})/w_{10}]$. The lower and upper bounds of the 95 percent confidence interval of the long-term coefficient are also reported. As Table 4 indicates, the main effect of increasing the assumed value of λ is to raise the estimate of the magnitude of the impact of the level of wage-setting and to reduce the precision of the estimates of the coefficients on concentration and coverage.

Finally, we test the argument of Rueda and Pontusson (1998) that the determinants of wage inequality differ in two sets of countries, the "social market economies" (SMEs) consisting of Austria, Germany, Finland,

Table 4. *Robustness of Results with Respect to* λ

	Coefficient	*t*-statistic	Long-term Coefficient	(Lower, Upper)
Level of Wage-Setting				
λ = .8	−.0522	6.52	−.261	(−.341, −.181)
λ = .9	−.0306	7.62	−.306	(−.386, −.226)
λ = .95	−.0182	7.03	−.364	(−.468, −.260)
λ = .975	−.0128	5.91	−.512	(−.688, −.336)
Concentration				
λ = .8	−.610	5.37	−3.05	(−4.19, −1.91)
λ = .9	−.313	5.51	−3.13	(−4.27, −1.99)
λ = .95	−.164	4.00	−3.28	(−4.92, −1.64)
λ = .975	−.101	2.83	−4.04	(−6.90, −1.18)
Coverage				
λ = .8	−.0775	2.51	−.388	(−.697, −.079)
λ = .9	−0342	2.27	−.342	(−.644, −.040)
λ = .95	−.0200	2.00	−.400	(−.800, 0)
λ = .975	−.0124	1.49	−.496	(−1.160, .170)

Notes: The dependent variable is ln $[(w_{90} - w_{10})/w_{10}]$. GLS estimation with λ as indicated in the first column. All regressions include the three variables listed in the table, a constant term as described in the notes to Table 2 and fixed period effects. Concentration refers to concentration within confederations. The absolute value of the *t*-statistics are reported in the third column. The long-term coefficient is equal to the coefficient listed in the second column divided by $(1 - \lambda)$. The fifth column presents the 95 percent confidence interval for the long-term coefficient.

Denmark, Sweden, Norway, the Netherlands, and Belgium and the rest. Dividing the sample in two and redoing the estimates with a constant level of wage-setting, concentration within confederations, and coverage as independent variables, the *F*-statistic that tests the null hypothesis that the SME and nonSME samples are drawn from the same population is 1.43 with (4,33) degrees of freedom without fixed period effects and 1.77 with (7,27) degrees of freedom with fixed period effects. Neither statistic is significant at the 5 percent significance level. Thus, the null hypothesis that the institutional determinants of wage inequality are the same in the social market economies and the nonsocial market economies is not rejected by the data.

5. Change over Time

There is much greater variation in both wage-setting institutions and wage inequality between countries than over time within a twelve-year period.

One implication is that the close relationship between institutions and pay inequality revealed in the statistical analysis is largely driven by the cross-sectional variation. Nevertheless, there is sufficient longitudinal variation for the impact of the level of wage-setting and the coverage of union contracts to be evident, even when cross-national differences are removed from the data using fixed country effects as shown in the last column of Table 2.

How well do the institutional variables highlighted in this study explain the changes that occurred in the wage distribution between 1980 and 1990 in the US and elsewhere? In the US, the 90/10 wage differential ($[w_{90} - w_{10}]/w_{10}$) increased by 15.7 percent between 1980 and 1992. The decline in coverage, from 26 percent in 1980 to 18 percent in 1990, can only explain an increase in the wage differential of about 1 percent. The fading effects of past periods of more centralized bargaining explains another 2 percent increase.[21] Together, the changes in wage-setting institutions only account for around 3/16 or 19 percent of the increased inequality in the US, an estimate that is very close to the conclusions of the single-country studies of the US discussed in the introduction.

The increase of wage inequality was even greater in Great Britain than in the US in the 1980s in percentage terms. Between 1980 and 1992, the British 90/10 wage differential rose from 1.79 to 2.31, an increase of 29 percent. Coverage declined sharply in the same period, from 70 percent to 47 percent, which can explain an increase of about 3 percent. More significant for the distribution of wages was the decentralization of wage-setting. From 1965 through 1979, wage-setting was frequently centralized in Britain through a series of income policies. According to the estimates in Table 2, the abandonment of income policies by the Conservative governments after 1980 and the decentralized bargaining that followed would be expected to increase the 90/10 wage differential in 1992 by around

---

[21] The counterfactuals of this section were computed by calculating counterfactual values of the relevant independent variables and comparing the difference in the predicted values using the point estimates of Equation 6 in Table 2. To determine the counterfactual scores for coverage in the US and Britain, the cumulative value of coverage was recalculated assuming that no change in coverage occurred after 1980. To determine the importance of the declining impact of past episodes of more centralized bargaining in the US and Great Britain, the cumulative score of bargaining level in 1980 was converted into a constant annual bargaining level score by multiplying by $(1-\lambda)$. The constructed annual bargaining level score was then assumed to be the actual annual bargaining level score from 1980 through 1992. Finally, to determine the impact of changes in bargaining level in Italy, Norway and Sweden between 1980 and 1992, the cumulative score for bargaining level was recalculated under the assumption that no change in bargaining level occurred after 1980.

10 percent. Together, decentralization and declining coverage account for close to half of the increase in wage inequality that occurred.

Sweden, like Britain, witnessed a significant decline in the centralization of wage-setting, albeit from a much more centralized starting point in 1980. The famous Swedish pattern of highly centralized wage agreements negotiated by union and employers' confederations came to an end in 1983. In subsequent years, the role of the peak associations and government in wage-setting fluctuated from bargaining round to bargaining round, but centralized wage-setting with an industrial peace obligation was never reestablished during the sample period. Wage inequality did increase in Sweden, but less than would be predicted on the basis of the decentralization of wage-setting that occurred. According to the point estimates in Table 2, the decline in bargaining level in Sweden raised the expected wage differential by approximately 17 percent. According to the OECD data, the actual increase in the 90/10 wage differential was around 6 percent.[22]

Not all change in wage-setting institutions was in the direction of greater decentralization between 1980 and 1992. In Italy, government involvement in wage-setting increased in 1984 with the legislative enactment of the cost-of-living index. In Norway, centralized wage negotiations between the union and employer's confederations were resumed in 1988 after a period of less centralized bargaining in the early and mid-1980s. In both countries, the decline in wage inequality that occurred between 1980 and 1992 was close to what would be predicted by the increased centralization of wage-setting.

6. Discussion

One can think of wage-setting institutions as varying along a continuum from bilateral negotiations between an individual employer and an individual employee to centralized negotiations covering the entire wage distribution conducted by elected representatives, whether the negotiators are office-holders in the union and employers' confederations or members of Parliament. The data strongly suggest that the more the wage schedule is

---

[22] The data on blue-collar wages in Swedish manufacturing industries reported in Hibbs and Locking (1995) show a much larger increase in wage inequality after 1983 than the OECD data. See Iversen (1996), Pontusson and Swenson (1996), and Wallerstein and Golden (1997) for contrasting accounts of the change in bargaining institutions in Sweden and other Nordic countries in the 1980s.

determined collectively, whether the coordination is achieved by the explicit centralization of wage-setting or through the implicit cooperation of a small number of actors, the more egalitarian the distribution of pay. Collective choice of wages leads to greater wage equality than decentralized wage-setting.

It might appear that a connection between collective pay-setting and greater wage equality must exist, almost by definition, since a wage agreement covering a work force of any size must specify a general rule rather than a list of individual pay levels. However, it is easy to write general rules for pay raises that do not compress relative wages. For example, a collective agreement or legislative act stating that all wages should increase by x percent per year would preserve existing differentials. The strength of the relationship between collective pay-setting and relatively egalitarian outcomes should be seen as an important fact begging for an explanation.

There may be multiple reasons for the strong association of collective wage-setting with relatively egalitarian wage distribution. In fact, three different types of explanation can be distinguished: "economic" explanations that are based on considerations of economic efficiency, "political" explanations that refer to the way wage-setting institutions affect the relative influence of different groups of workers, and "ideological" explanations that point to the impact of wage-setting institutions on the application of widespread norms.

The economic explanations start from the premise that the wage differentials that emerge from decentralized interactions among employers and employees in the labor market are inefficient in some way. Consider, for example, an economy with decentralized wage-setting institutions in which strong unions exist in some industries but not in others or in some plants but not in others in the same industry. Even equally strong unions will differ in terms of the tradeoff they face between wage increases and employment that stem from differences in the productive process and the elasticity of demand for output. Among employers of nonunion labor, some firms may have substantial monopsony power while other firms have none. In such an economy, wages for equivalent workers in the unionized sector would differ according to workers' share of the monopoly rents, which vary across both industries and individual firms, while wages in the nonunionized sector would differ according to the monopsony power of employers.

Both in markets where workers' wages are higher than the competitive wage, due to monopoly power, and lower than the competitive wage, due to monopsony power, employment is inefficiently low and the relative price of output too high. There is both a misallocation of labor and a misalignment of prices. In this scenario, centralized wage-setting, by imposing a rule like equal pay for equal work, generates a wage distribution that may be closer to the textbook model of a perfectly competitive labor market than does decentralized wage-setting in actual markets. Although some workers and some firms would be worse off, aggregate income may be higher if local rents are reduced through a process of centralized wage-setting (Moene and Wallerstein 1997).

Another example of a model in which the wage differentials associated with decentralized wage-setting are inefficiently large is provided by the winner-take-all reward structure described by Rosen (1981) and Frank and Cook (1995). Winner-take-all markets are markets in which workers' rewards depend, at least in part, on their performance relative to other workers. Thus, the best musicians earn much more money than musicians with only slightly less talent, since, with modern audio technology, we can all listen to the best. The huge rewards that are obtained by the best musicians induce many to enter the competition, although logic dictates that almost all who compete to be best will fail. There is a social gain from recording the best musician rather than the second best, but the gain is only the possibly small difference in quality between the two. The private gain to being best, in contrast, may be huge. Thus, there is too much entry into winner-take-all markets with decentralized wage-setting. If, by centralized agreement, the prize from winning in winner-take-all markets were reduced, there would be fewer entrants in winner-take-all contests which could increase the efficiency of the allocation of labor in the economy as a whole.

There are many other reasons why the reduction of wage differentials might lead to lower rather than higher efficiency. Moreover, even in circumstances where greater equality is more efficient, an explanation in terms of efficiency is insufficient in the sense that a change that increases total income but not everyone's income may be blocked by those who would lose. Nevertheless, the possibility that wage compression within some range yields efficiency gains in some dimensions that offset efficiency losses in others may be an important part of the explanation of why institutions matter so much for the distribution of pay.[23] If there were a large, self-evident,

---

[23] As suggested by a study of the impact on productivity growth of wage compression in Sweden by Hibbs and Locking (1995), the reduction of wage differentials probably has multiple effects on economic performance, some beneficial and some not, such that the net effect varies over time and place.

economic cost from imposing changes in relative pay through collective processes of wage-setting, workers in countries with compressed wage scales would be paying a high price to satisfy their desire for greater equality. If pay inequality has little net effect on productivity within a wide range, however, institutions promoting wage compression could persist even in the absence of widespread willingness to accept lower incomes for the sake of greater equality.

The political explanation of the association of centralized wage-setting with egalitarian wage distributions is simply that centralization alters the influence of different groups in the wage-setting process. Freeman and Medoff (1984) argue that the wage structure in a nonunion labor market is shaped by the preferences and outside options of mobile workers who employers are trying to attract or retain while the structure of wages under collective bargaining reflects the preferences of the median voter in elections for union leadership or contract ratification. In general, a mean-preserving reduction in wage inequality will raise the pay received by the median wage-earner (and all other workers with wages below the mean) given the positively skewed shape of the wage distribution.

Moreover, as Moene and Wallerstein (1997) show, employers as well as low-wage workers may benefit from a wage policy that raises the wages of low-wage workers and lowers the wages of high-wage workers even when wage compression is inefficient. Moene and Wallerstein examine a model with heterogeneous employers and heterogeneous workers in which wage differentials arise from competition among employers to obtain more skilled employees. It is demonstrated that the wage differentials associated with the decentralized equilibrium are both efficient, in the sense that social surplus is maximized, and unjust, in the sense that differences in pay exceed differences in workers' abilities or efforts. In this model, reducing the wage differential between high and low-skilled workers increases both profits and the wages of low-wage workers as long as the average wage is kept low enough to clear the labor market. The possibility that employers can benefit from wage compression is important in understanding the history of centralized bargaining in Northern Europe. As Swenson's (1989, 1991) research has documented, the centralized wage-setting procedures in Scandinavia were created with the active support of the employers' associations.

The ideological explanation starts from the premise, well documented in the experimental literature, that people care about fairness as well as about their own income (Thaler 1989; Rabin 1998). The fact that people care about fairness does not, by itself, separate decentralized from collective decision making. Even with completely decentralized wage-setting, firms that disregard workers' concern with fairness when designing their pay policies suffer the consequences in terms of the morale and productivity of their work force.

Although concerns with fairness exist whatever the institutional environment, the centralization of wage-setting may have a large impact by altering how the norm of fairness is applied. In decentralized bargaining, the norm of equal sharing results in a wage that depends on the worker's usefulness to the firm and his or her alternative opportunities. In centralized pay-setting, the same norm of equal sharing results in pay that depends on the importance of the work force as a whole and their outside opportunities as a group. The larger the fraction of workers who are considered as a group in the wage-setting process, the more egalitarian the potential impact of applications of equal sharing rules. The association of pay equality and collective or political processes of wage determination may be due to the way wage-setting institutions shape the application of norms of fairness as much as to the way wage-setting institutions affect the ability of different groups to pursue their self-interest.

7. Conclusion

The most important institutional factors in explaining the degree of wage inequality in advanced industrial societies are (a) whether wages are set locally, at the industry-level or at the level of the economy as a whole, (b) the extent to which wage-setting is dominated by a few large unions that are able to coordinate informally, and (c) the extent to which union contracts cover the labor force. The more wages and salaries are set in a centralized manner, the more egalitarian the distribution of wages and salaries.

This finding points to three lines of research, at least, that deserve further work. The first is to examine the economic costs and benefits of the reduction of wage differentials associated with centralized wage-setting. In particular, it is common to attribute a significant part of the high levels of unemployment in many European countries to the high wages received by relatively low-wage workers. However, some European countries with much more compressed wage scales than the US, such as the Netherlands and Norway, have unemployment rates as low as in the US. Thus, the nature of the connection between wage compression and macroeconomic performance is far from settled.

The second area for future research is to ascertain the generality of the egalitarian bias in centralized decision-making procedures. One would guess, for example, that public insurance programs are more egalitarian than private insurance or that even the earnings-related component of public pension systems is more egalitarian than private pensions. The third area for future research is to better understand the source of the egalitarian bias of collective decision making that is so strongly evident in the process of wage determination.

Appendix: Data Sources

All data used in this paper are available from the author in an Excel file upon request.

Wage Differentials: Data for all countries except the US is from OECD (1996, 61–62). The US data is from OECD (1993, 159–161) for 1980–1989 and from OECD (1996, 61–62) for 1990–1992. Data for the years 1980, 1986, and 1992 were used whenever possible. In cases with missing data, I used data from the closest available year. Thus, the earliest year of data is 1981 for Canada and 1983 for Germany. For Austria and Norway, the 1986 data actually refer to 1987. The last data point is 1991 for Norway and Italy and 1990 for Denmark.

Wage-setting institutions: Data on the level of wage-setting and concentration within and between confederations are from the Golden, Wallerstein, and Lange data set on unions, employers' associations, and collective bargaining procedures for sixteen countries from 1950–1992. Concentration data are available only at five-year intervals. A complete series was created by assuming no change between 1990 and 1992 and constant linear change in each five-year period. For a few countries, missing data at the beginning of the series were filled in by extending the first available value back to 1950. The Golden, Wallerstein, and Lange data set is available on the web at www.shelley.polisci.ucla.edu/data. Selected data on the level of wage-setting, concentration within confederations, and coverage are presented in Table 5.

Union density: Data are from Visser (1996) for 1970–1992 and from Visser (1992) for 1950–1969. To make the two series compatible, Visser's (1992) figures were adjusted to remove unemployment union

Table 5. *Selected Data on Centralization, Concentration, and Coverage*

	Average Level 1950–92	Cumulative Level 1992	Average Concentration 1950–90	Cumulative Concentration 1992	Coverage 1990
Australia	2.02	36.2	.017	0.31	.80
Austria	1.09	18.3	.099	1.82	.71
Belgium	1.33	26.5	.100	1.73	.90
Canada	0.21	4.2	.034	0.68	.38
Denmark	2.58	39.9	.130	2.20	.74
Finland	2.02	33.6	.075	1.34	.95
France	1.02	18.0			.92
Germany	1.00	17.8	.144	2.72	.76
Great Britain	0.67	10.7	.049	0.87	.47
Italy	2.16	41.0	.080	1.34	.83
Japan	0.67	15.5	.095	1.52	.21
Netherlands	2.30	34.5	.136	2.65	.60
Norway	2.70	47.9	.069	1.60	.75
Sweden	2.53	42.8	.093	2.02	.83
Switzerland	1.00	17.8	.169	3.12	.43
United States	0.14	2.2	.022	0.40	.18

Notes: "Level" is the level of wage-setting index. "Concentration" is the Herfindahl index of concentration within confederations (H_W). Columns 1 and 3 present the average value over the period for which data were collected. Columns 2 and 4 present the cumulative value in 1992, defined by the formula $X_i^*(1992) = \sum_{k=0}^{42}(.95)^k X_i(1992 - k)$ where $X_i(t)$ is the value of variable X for country i in year t. Data sources are described in the appendix. Data for concentration within confederations is missing for France.

members from the numerator and unemployed workers from the denominator.

Coverage: Data are unadjusted coverage figures from Traxler (1994). Data are only available for 1980 and 1990. To create a complete series, the 1990 value was extended forward through 1992, the 1980 value was extended backward to 1950, and the figures between 1980 and 1990 were filled in through linear extrapolation.

Partisan composition of government: Data are from Duane Swank's Eighteen Nation Pooled Time Series Data Set. See Swank (1992).

Trade dependence: Data are from the Summers and Heston data set, described in Summers and Heston (1991).

The size of the public sector: Data on government outlays (at all levels) as a share of GDP are from the OECD, *Economic Outlook*, various years. Government outlay data begins in 1960. Data on public employment as a share of the work force are updated data originally published in Cusack, Notermans, and Rein (1989).

Stock of human capital: Data on the mean number of years of tertiary education and the mean number of years of schooling at all levels are from the Nehru, Swanson, and Dubey data set described in Nehru, Swanson, and Dubey (1995).

References

Blank, Rebecca. 1997. *It Takes a Nation*. Princeton: Princeton University Press.

Blau, Francine D., and Lawrence M. Kahn. 1996. "International Differences in Male Wage Inequality: Institutions versus Market Forces." *Journal of Political Economy* 104:791–837.

Buse, A. 1973. "Goodness of Fit in Generalized Least Squares Estimation." *American Statistician* 27:106–108.

Card, David. 1996. "The Effect of Unions on the Structure of Wages: A Longitudinal Analysis." *Econometrica* 64:957–979.

Castles, Francis, and Peter Mair. 1984. "Left-Right Political Scales: Some 'Expert' Judgements." *European Journal of Political Research* 12:73–88.

Cusack, Thomas, T. Notermans, and M. Rein. 1989. "Political Economic Aspects of Public Employment." *European Journal of Political Research* 17:471–500.

Díaz-Giménez, Javier, Vincenzo Quadrini, and José-Víctor Ríos-Rull. 1997. "Dimensions of Inequality: Facts on the U.S. Distributions of Earnings, Income, and Wealth." *Federal Reserve Bank of Minneapolis Quarterly Review*. Spring: 3–21.

Dinardo, John, Nicole M. Fortin, and Thomas Lemieux. 1996. "Labor Market Institutions and the Distribution of Wages, 1973–1992: A Semiparametric Approach." *Econometrica* 65:1001–44.

Edin, Per-Anders, and Robert Topel. 1995. "Wage Policy and Restructuring: The Swedish Labor Market Since 1960." In *Reforming the Welfare State*, ed. Richard B. Freeman and Robert Topel. Chicago: University of Chicago Press.

Erickson, Christopher L., and Andrea C. Ichino. 1994. "Wage Differentials in Italy: Market Forces, Institutions, and Inflation." In *Differences and Changes in Wage Structures*, ed. Richard B. Freeman and Lawrence F. Katz. Chicago: University of Chicago Press.

Esping-Andersen, Gøsta. 1990. *The Three Worlds of Welfare Capitalism*. Princeton: Princeton University Press.

Fortin, Nicole M., and Thomas Lemieux. 1997. "Institutional Changes and Rising Wage Inequality: Is There a Linkage?" *Journal of Economic Perspectives* 11:75–96.

Frank, Robert H., and Philip J. Cook. 1995. *The Winner-Take-All Society*. New York: Penguin.

Freeman, Richard B. 1980. "Unionization and the Dispersion of Wages." *Industrial and Labor Relations Review* 34:3–24.

Michael Wallerstein

Freeman, Richard B. 1988. "Labour Market Institutions and Economic Performance." *Economic Policy* 3:64–80.

Freeman, Richard B. 1995. "Are Your Wages Set in Beijing?" *Journal of Economic Perspectives* 9:15–32.

Freeman, Richard B. 1996. "Labor Market Institutions and Earnings Inequality." *New England Economic Review* May/June: 157–168.

Freeman, Richard B., and James L. Medoff. 1984. *What Do Unions Do?* New York: Basic Books.

Golden, Miriam. 1993. "The Dynamics of Trade Unionism and National Economic Performance." *American Political Science Review* 87:439–454.

Golden, Miriam, Michael Wallerstein, and Peter Lange. 1998. "Trade Union Organization and Industrial Relations in the Postwar Era in 12 Countries." In *Continuity and Change in Contemporary Capitalism*, ed. Herbert Kitschelt, Peter Lange, Gary Marks, and John Stephens. Cambridge: Cambridge University Press.

Gottschalk, Peter, and Timothy Smeeding. 1997. "Cross-National Comparisons of Earnings and Income Inequality." *Journal of Economic Literature* 35:633–687.

Gramlich, Edward M., Richard Kasten, and Frank Sammartino. 1993. "Growing Inequality in the 1980s: The Role of Federal Taxes and Cash Transfers." In *Uneven Tides: Rising Inequality in America*, ed. Sheldon Danziger and Peter Gottschalk. Cambridge: Harvard University Press.

Greene, William H. 1993. *Econometric Analysis*. New York: Macmillan.

Hibbs, Douglas A. Jr., and Håkan Locking. 1995. "Solidarity Wage Policies and Industrial Productivity in Sweden." *Nordic Journal of Political Economy* 22:95–108.

Hibbs, Douglas A. Jr., and Håkan Locking. 1996. "Wage Compression, Wage Drift, and Wage Inflation in Sweden." *Labour Economics* 77:1–32.

Iversen, Torben. 1996. "Power, Flexibility, and the Breakdown of Centralized Wage Bargaining: The Cases of Denmark and Sweden in Comparative Perspective." *Comparative Politics* 28:399–436.

Katz, Lawrence, and Alan Krueger. 1991. "Changes in the Structure of Pay in the Public and Private Sectors." In *Research in Labor Economics*. Vol. 12, ed. Ronald Ehrenberg. Greenwich Conn.: JAI Press.

Levy, Frank, and Richard Murnane. 1992. "US Earnings Level and Earnings Inequality: A Review of Recent Trends and Proposed Explanations." *Journal of Economic Literature* 30:1333–1381.

Lipset, Seymour Martin. 1960. *Political Man: The Social Bases of Politics*. Garden City N.Y.: Doubleday and Company.

Moene, Karl Ove, and Michael Wallerstein. 1997. "Pay Inequality." *Journal of Labor Economics* 15:403–430.

Moene, Karl Ove, and Michael Wallerstein. 1998. "Inequality and Redistribution." Unpublished manuscript. University of Oslo and Northwestern University.

Moene, Karl Ove, Michael Wallerstein, and Michael Hoel. 1993. "Bargaining Structure and Economic Performance." In *Trade Union Behavior, Pay Bargaining and Economic Performance*, ed. Robert Flanagan, Karl Ove Moene, and Michael Wallerstein. Oxford: Oxford University Press.

Moffitt, Robert, David Ribar, and Mark Wilhelm. 1998. "The Decline of Welfare Benefits in the US: The Role of Wage Inequality." *Journal of Public Economics* 68:421–452.

Nehru, Vikram, Eric Swanson, and Ashutosh Dubey. 1995. "A New Database on Human Capital Stock in Developing and Industrial Countries: Sources, Methodology and Results." *Journal of Development Economics* 46:379–401.

Organization for Economic Cooperation and Development. 1993. *Employment Outlook*. July 1993. Paris: OECD.

Organization for Economic Cooperation and Development. 1996. *Employment Outlook*, July 1996. Paris: OECD.

Pontusson, Jonas, and Peter Swenson. 1996. "Labor Markets, Production Strategies, and Wage Bargaining Institutions: The Swedish Employer Offensive in Comparative Perspective." *Comparative Political Studies* 29:223–250.

Rabin, Matthew. 1998. "Psychology and Economics." *Journal of Economic Literature* 36:11–46.

Richardson, J. David. 1995. "Income Inequality and Trade: How to Think, What to Conclude." *Journal of Economic Perspectives* 9:33–56.

Rosen, Sherwin. 1981. "The Economics of Superstars." *American Economic Review* 71:845–858.

Rueda, David, and Jonas Pontusson. 1998. "Wage Inequality and Varieties of Capitalism." Unpublished manuscript. Cornell University.

Summers, Robert, and Alan Heston. 1991. "The Penn World Table (Mark 5): An Expanded Set of International Comparisons, 1950–1988." *Quarterly Journal of Economics* 106:327–368.

Swank, Duane. 1992. "Politics and the Structural Dependence of the State in Democratic Capitalist Nations." *American Political Science Review* 86:38–54.

Swenson, Peter. 1989. *Fair Shares: Unions. Pay and Politics in Sweden and West Germany*. Ithaca: Cornell University Press.

Swenson, Peter. 1991. "Bringing Capital Back In, or Social Democracy Reconsidered." *World Politics* 43:513–544.

Thaler, Richard H. 1989. "Anomalies: Interindustry Wage Differentials." *Journal of Economic Perspectives* 3:181–193.

Traxler, Franz. 1994. "Collective Bargaining: Levels and Coverage." *OECD Employment Outlook*, July: 167–94.

Visser, Jelle. 1989. *European Trade Unions in Figures*. Deventer, Netherlands: Kluwer Law and Taxation Publishers.

Visser, Jelle. 1992. *Trade Union Membership Database*. Unpublished manuscript. University of Amsterdam.

Visser, Jelle. 1996. "Unionisation Trends Revisited. Centre for Research of European Societies and Industrial Relations, Amsterdam." CESAR Research paper 1996/2.

Wallerstein, Michael, and Miriam Golden. 1997. "The Fragmentation of the Bargaining Society: Wage-Setting in the Nordic Countries, 1950–1992." *Comparative Political Studies* 30:699–731.

Wallerstein, Michael, Miriam Golden, and Peter Lange. 1997. "Unions, Employers Associations and Wage-Setting Institutions in North and Central Europe, 1950–1992." *Industrial and Labor Relations Review* 50:379–401.

Wood, Adrian. 1994. *North-South Trade, Employment and Inequality.* Oxford: Clarendon Press.

Wood, Adrian. 1995. "How Trade Hurt Unskilled Workers." *Journal of Economic Perspectives* 9:57–80.

13

Inequality, Social Insurance,
and Redistribution

Karl Ove Moene and Michael Wallerstein

How do changes in the inequality of income affect political support for welfare policy? Starting with the economic models of Romer (1975), Roberts (1977), and Meltzer and Richard (1981), the conventional view is that increased inequality in pretax earnings leads to greater political demand for redistributive policies. The logic is simple and compelling. If the majority of the electorate receives a below-average income and if an increase in inequality causes above-average incomes to rise and below-average incomes to fall, then it is reasonable to think that demands for public policies to reduce the gap between rich and poor will increase.

The argument of Romer (1975) and Meltzer and Richard (1981) is best illustrated by comparing two hypothetical lognormal income distributions with the same mean but different levels of inequality as shown in Figure 1. As the figure shows, the greater the variance of a distribution like the lognormal distribution that is skewed to the right, the greater the gap between median and mean income. In the models of Romer (1975), Roberts (1977), and Meltzer and Richard (1981), political competition drives the level of welfare spending toward the ideal point of the median income voter. The greater the gap between the pretax earnings of the median income voter and average (mean) income, the greater is the level of spending preferred by the median income voter and the higher is the equilibrium level of welfare spending. •

The authors thank three anonymous referees and the editor, Ada Finifter, for their suggestions. We also thank Jim Alt, David Austen-Smith, Steve Davis, Daniel Diermeier, Geoffrey Garrett, Douglas Hibbs, Torben Iversen, John Roemer, David Soskice, and Duane Swank for helpful comments. We thank the Cost of Inequality Project of the MacArthur Foundation and the Norwegian Research Council for financial support.

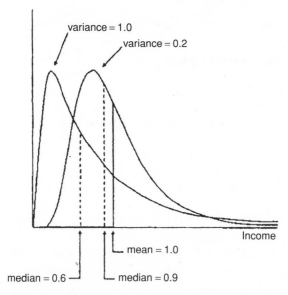

Figure 1 Two Hypothetical Lognormal Income Distributions with the Same Mean and Different Levels of Inequality.

The relationship between the inequality of pretax earnings and welfare expenditures is important because it shapes our understanding of the relationship between political and economic equality. According to the conventional view, a change in the economic environment that causes the income distribution to grow more unequal increases political support for redistributive policies. In other words, the public favors redistributive policies as the need for them increases. Although voters are assumed to care only about their own welfare, the result is a welfare policy that varies appropriately with the needs of the poor. In addition, if greater equality reduces the demand for redistributive policies and if those policies inhibit growth, then reduced income inequality promotes growth (Alesina and Rodrik 1994; Persson and Tabellini 1994).

In this article, we demonstrate that a more complete theory leads to different conclusions. Support for some kinds of welfare spending may increase as inequality rises, but support for other kinds is lower when inequality is higher. In particular, our framework implies that greater inequality in pretax earnings is associated with less, not more, spending on welfare policies targeted to people who have lost their market income because of layoffs,

286

accidents, or ill health. Both theory and the data on welfare expenditures in 18 advanced industrial countries suggest that one political consequence of greater income inequality is less support for policies that constitute a significant share of the welfare budget.

Our framework combines two different approaches to understanding the sources of political support for welfare policy. In the first view, as expressed in most economic models and the large literature in political science and sociology that emphasizes the political strength of the working class in cross-national studies of welfare spending, welfare policy is fundamentally about redistribution from rich to poor.[1] Self-interested voters support welfare policy up to the point at which their gain from income redistribution matches their share of the cost. In the second view, the essence of welfare policy is the public provision of insurance, and self-interested voters support welfare policy to obtain protection against risks that private insurance markets fail to cover.[2]

These two views appear to have very different political implications. Critics frequently view welfare programs as redistributive policies that distort incentives and reduce the efficiency of the economy. Supporters often argue, in contrast, that welfare policies provide insurance to all and enhance efficiency to the extent that the public sector protects against risks that are difficult or impossible to cover through private insurance markets. In fact, the policy implication of either view is not obvious. On the one hand, one might think that welfare policies are fundamentally redistributive but favor increased spending on the ground that the benefit of greater equality outweighs the efficiency loss. On the other hand, one might consider welfare policies as social insurance but think that the demand for insurance could be better satisfied by private firms.

Our purpose is to investigate the contrast between the redistributive and the insurance views in terms of how inequality affects political support for welfare spending. Consider an increase in income inequality that lowers the income of the median voter but leaves mean income unchanged. In the

---

[1] The early literature on the role of social democratic parties and organized labor in the expansion of welfare policies is surveyed by Shalev 1983. For more recent studies, see Esping-Andersen 1990; Hicks 1999; Hicks and Swank 1992; Huber, Ragin, and Stephens 1993; and Huber and Stephens 2001.

[2] For studies of social welfare as publicly provided insurance, see Barr 1992; Casamatta, Cremer, and Pestieau 2000; De Donder and Hindricks 2000; Sinn 1995; and Wright 1996.

redistributive model, the wider this gap, the more the median voter gains from welfare expenditures. In the insurance model, in contrast, the demand for insurance declines with income, holding risk constant, assuming that insurance is a normal good. If median-voter income decreases and the risks covered by social insurance do not change, then support for spending on social insurance will decline.

In our judgment, both approaches provide essential ingredients for an adequate understanding of the politics of welfare policy. Social insurance policies comprise a large part of the welfare budget. Even means-tested policies can be viewed as protection against the residual risk of income loss that social insurance policies do not cover. At the same time, public insurance is commonly provided and financed in a manner that is redistributive ex ante, in that voters with lower expected income receive insurance on more favorable terms than do voters with higher expected income. Thus, without specifying how the policy is designed, one cannot tell which aspect – redistribution or insurance – dominates in determining the effect of inequality on support for welfare spending.

Our article is related to two strands of the recent theoretical literature on the politics of welfare policy. The first consists of studies of how income or wealth inequality affects support for redistributive policies. This literature can be subdivided according to whether the emphasis is on the cost of redistributive policies (Moffitt, Ribar, and Wilhelm 1998; Rodriguez 1998; Saint-Paul 1998),[3] voters' empathy toward the poor or the unlucky (Kristov, Lindert, and McClelland 1992; Piketty 1995),[4] or voters' demand for insurance versus redistribution (Bénabou 2000; this article).[5] The second

---

[3] Moffitt, Ribar, and Wilhelm (1998) argue that a reduction in the earnings of low-wage workers increases the cost of welfare policies by lowering the incentive of welfare recipients to find work. Saint-Paul (1998) argues that if inequality increases due to a decline in the income of the poor, the mean income may fall relative to the median, which will increase the cost of redistribution to the median voter. Rodriguez (1998) maintains that higher inequality increases the ability of the rich to evade redistributive taxes by political lobbying.

[4] Kristov, Lindert, and McClelland (1992) argue that voters are more willing to support benefits for others like themselves. Thus, support for welfare declines as the gap between the poor and the middle grows. Piketty (1995) maintains that willingness to support redistributive policies depends on beliefs regarding the relative importance of luck and effort in determining earnings. In Piketty's model, a negative income shock can shift the equilibrium in such a way that support for redistributive policies may either increase or decrease, depending on the status quo ante.

[5] In Bénabou's (2000) model, inequality and spending on egalitarian policies that promote efficiency are simultaneously determined. Bénabou does not consider differences in the targeting of welfare benefits, which is the focus here.

strand of literature examines the effect of benefit targeting on political support for welfare expenditures (Casamatta, Cremer, and Pestieau 2000; De Donder and Hindricks 1998, 2000; Gelbach and Pritchett 1997; Moene and Wallerstein 2001b). We bring these two strands together to examine (1) how benefit targeting alters the effect of income inequality on support for welfare expenditures and (2) how the inequality of income affects the share of the welfare budget targeted to different groups. Our mathematical framework is similar to the model Wright (1996) uses to study the effect of economic growth on welfare expenditures. Most recently, Iversen and Soskice (2001) apply the same framework to study how different types of training affect welfare support.

In the following section we develop a model in which government spending is characterized by two parameters: a tax rate that determines the level of aggregate welfare spending and a distributive parameter that determines how welfare benefits are targeted. This framework encompasses both the redistributive and the insurance views of welfare policy, depending on the type of targeting. We then show how targeting can alter the influence of inequality on voters' choice of the level of benefits. When the beneficiaries are predominantly persons who are employed, we obtain the conclusion of the redistribution models: When a rise in inequality reduces the income of the median voter relative to the mean, support for welfare expenditures increases. When the beneficiaries are those without earnings, however, the response to greater inequality is predicted by the insurance model: A reduction in the median income, holding the mean constant, reduces support for welfare expenditures.

We also investigate the simultaneous choice of the level and targeting of benefits. When targeting is endogenous, benefits aimed at those without earnings decline as income distribution becomes more skewed. Thus, when increases in inequality reduce the income of the median relative to the mean, benefits targeted to those without earnings are reduced, both as a share of GDP and as a share of government spending. The situation regarding benefits targeted to the employed is more complicated. If income distribution is not too unequal, a majority of voters prefer all welfare payments to be targeted to the unemployed. If the distribution of income is sufficiently skewed, benefits aimed at the employed are an increasing function of the skewness, as in the pure redistribution model. We test these propositions with data on welfare spending and the inequality of wages and salaries in eighteen advanced industrial countries from 1980 to 1995.

Basic Assumptions

We present our theory in the context of a simple model of the economy that contains two essential ingredients: uncertainty regarding future income on the part of a significant fraction of the population and heterogeneity among voters in terms of both their income and the risks they face. We will assume that the population is divided into three groups. The share σ_0 is permanently outside the labor market and has no income other than transfer payments. The share σ_L is the group of wage earners who receive a wage of w_L when employed. The share σ_H is the high-income group and receives w_L, with $w_H > w_L$. We assume that the three groups exhaust the population, so that $\sigma_0 + \sigma_L + \sigma_H = 1$.

Wage earners may be employed or not. We assume that the probability of employed wage earners losing their source of income (whether due to lay off, injury, or illness) within period dt is αdt. The probability that workers who have lost employment will find a new job within dt is βdt. For simplicity, both α and β are assumed to be constant.[6] The Markov process described by the parameters α and β converges to a steady state distribution of wage earners in which the fraction $\beta/(\alpha + \beta)$ are working. Alternatively, $\beta/(\alpha + \beta)$ denotes the fraction of time that each wage earner expects to be employed in the long run. The high-income group faces a lower risk of losing earnings than do wage earners. For simplicity, we set the risk of job loss for high-income earners to zero.[7]

The population without earnings consists of the share who are permanently outside the labor market, σ_0, plus a share who are temporarily without employment, $[\alpha/(\alpha + \beta)]\sigma_L$; the workforce consists of high-income earners, σ_H, plus the share of low-income earners who are employed, $[\beta/(\alpha + \beta)]\sigma_L$. It simplifies the notation to introduce a symbol $e \equiv \sigma_H + [\beta/(\alpha + \beta)]\sigma_L$ for employed share of the population. We will assume that the majority of people are employed, or $e > 1/2$. In addition, we assume that the high-income groups constitute a minority, or $\sigma_H < 1/2$. It follows that the employed wage earners are the median income earners.

We represent fiscal policy with two parameters. The first is the flat tax rate on earnings, t, that determines aggregate government spending per

---

[6] In a more general model, the probability of obtaining employment, βdt, would be partly a matter of agents' efforts rather than a parameter. Making β endogenous is discussed briefly in a later section.
[7] We discuss the consequence of relaxing this assumption below.

capita, $T(t)$. We write the requirement that tax receipts equal expenditures as

$$T(t) = \tau(t)e\bar{w}, \tag{1}$$

where $\bar{w}$ is the average wage, $\bar{w} \equiv (1/e)[\sigma_H w_H + (\beta/(\alpha + \beta))\sigma_L w_L]$, and $\tau(t)$ represents tax revenues as a share of earnings. The function $\tau(t)$ implicitly incorporates the deadweight cost of taxation. We assume, therefore, that $\tau(t)$ is a strictly concave function (the deadweight cost of taxation rises at an increasing rate as the tax rate rises), with $\tau'(0) = 1$ (there is no deadweight cost when the tax rate is zero) and $\tau(0) = \tau(1) = 0$ (tax revenues are zero when the tax rate is zero or when taxes are confiscatory).[8]

The second policy parameter, γ, represents the share of welfare spending received by employed persons. The remaining share, $(1 - \gamma)$, is assumed to go to programs aimed at those without earnings. Thus, the posttax and transfer consumption of a person with a pretax income of w is

$$c_E(w) = (1 - t)w + \frac{\gamma T(t)}{e}, \tag{2}$$

where $\gamma T(t)/e$ is the welfare benefit received by each employed person. The consumption of those without earnings is

$$c_N = \frac{(1 - \gamma)T(t)}{1 - e}. \tag{3}$$

Implicit in equation 3 is an assumption that all persons without earnings receive the same benefit, regardless of their history of employment or earnings.[9] If $\gamma = 0$, then welfare policy is targeted at those without work. If $\gamma = 1$, then the benefits go exclusively to those with earnings. (We assume throughout that $0 \leq \gamma \leq 1$.) A universalistic policy that pays the same benefit to all, regardless of employment status, is implied by $\gamma = e$. Our assumptions regarding the distribution of pre- and posttax and transfer income are summarized in Figure 2.

---

[8] To model the costs of taxation explicitly, we could set $\tau(t) = tb(t)$, where $b(t)$ is the appropriately defined hours worked, derived from worker preferences over consumption and leisure. Alternatively, we could assume that hours worked are fixed and that $t - \tau(t)$ represents the costs of collecting taxes, with the cost assumed to be an increasing, convex function of t.

[9] Such an assumption is stronger than necessary. All the results go through in a more general model in which the benefits targeted to those without earnings partly depend on past wages or contributions as long as there is some minimum benefit that everyone without earnings receives.

	Permanently Out of Work	Temporarily Out of Work	Wage Earners	High-Income Earners
Population Share	σ_0	$[\alpha/(\alpha+\beta)]\sigma_L$	$[\beta/(\alpha+\beta)]\sigma_L$	σ_H
After-tax Earnings	0	0	$(1-t)w_L$	$(1-t)w_H$
Transfer Payment	$\dfrac{(1-\gamma)T(t)}{1-e}$	$\dfrac{(1-\gamma)T(t)}{1-e}$	$\dfrac{\gamma T(t)}{e}$	$\dfrac{\gamma T(t)}{e}$

(Between Temporarily Out of Work and Wage Earners: βdt above, αdt below)

σ_0	The share of the population permanently without work
σ_L	The share of the population who are wage earners
σ_H	The share of the population who are high-income earners
αdt	The probability that employed wage earners will lose their earnings within the period dt
βdt	The probability that wage earners without employment will obtain employment within dt
$(1-t)$	The share of earnings remaining after taxes are paid
w_L	The earnings of wage earners
w_H	The earnings of high-income earners
γ	The share of aggregate social insurance spending received by the employed
$T(t)$	Total social insurance expenditures as a function of the tax rate
e	The share of the population who are employed

Figure 2   The Distribution of Income.

We also assume that all individuals have identical preferences over consumption, described by a standard utility function, $u(c)$, with the following characteristics: (1) $u''(c) < 0$, (2) $u'(c) \to \infty$ as $c \to 0$, and (3) $\mu \equiv -cu''(c)/u'(c) > 1$. Assumption 1 states that individuals are risk averse. Assumption 2 means that individuals always want some insurance to cover a nonnegligible risk that they may have nothing. Assumption 3 implies that insurance is a normal good or that the demand for insurance increases as income rises. Empirical estimates of μ, usually called the coefficient of relative risk aversion, consistently conclude that $\mu \geq 1$ (Friend and Blume 1975). We assume $\mu > 1$ to simplify our discussion. How the description of the results would have to be modified to encompass the borderline case of $\mu = 1$ is easily seen from the mathematics.

Assuming that individuals live forever, the expected lifetime utility for a wage earner can be derived from the asset equations:

$$rV^E = u(c_E(w)) - \alpha(V^E - V^N), \tag{4}$$
$$rV^N = u(c_N) + \beta(V^E - V^N), \tag{5}$$

where V^E is the expected lifetime utility of a person currently employed, V^N is the expected lifetime utility of a person temporarily not employed, $u(c_i)$ is the instantaneous utility of consumption when employed ($i = E$) or when not employed ($i = N$), and r is the discount rate.[10] Equations 4 and 5 can be solved for the expected lifetime utilities of starting out in the two different states. We will concentrate on the expected lifetime utility of employed wage earners, which is conveniently written as

$$v \equiv rV^E = \left(\frac{\beta + r}{\alpha + \beta + r} \right) u(c_E(w_L)) + \left(\frac{\alpha}{\alpha + \beta + r} \right) u(c_N). \quad (6)$$

Equation 6 indicates that the expected lifetime utility of an employed wage earner consists of a weighted average of expected utility in the two states, with the current state of being employed weighted more heavily, the greater is the discount rate. Self-interested workers care about the benefits received by the unemployed because of the chance that they may be without employment sometime in the future. Of course, voters may care about those without earnings out of altruism as well as self-interest. In this case, the parameter r might be interpreted as reflecting concern for the poor as well as concern for the future. The lower is r, the greater the weight given to the welfare of those without earnings in wage earners' choice of how to cast their ballots.

Choosing the Level of Benefits with Exogenous Targeting

We first investigate the political choice of the level of benefits when targeting is fixed. The investigation of the choice of t for a fixed γ provides a general framework in which the contrasting predictions of the two models of welfare spending – as redistribution and as public insurance – can be compared and shown to depend on how benefits are targeted. In addition, the model of choosing t for a fixed γ may be applicable in circumstances in

[10] To understand equation 4, observe that lifetime expected utility (for individuals who live forever) can be written as the sum of current utility during period dt plus expected lifetime utility one period in the future, discounted by the discount factor e^{-rdt} : $V^E = u(c_E)dt + e^{-rdt}[(\alpha dt)V^N + (1 - \alpha dt)V^E]$. Future expected lifetime utility equals the expected lifetime utility of someone without employment with probability αdt. With probability $(1 - \alpha dt)$, lifetime utility remains unchanged. Rearranging terms, letting $dt \to 0$, and using the fact that $(1 - e^{-rdt})/dt \to r$ as $dt \to 0$ yields equation 4. The derivation of equation 5 is similar. The assumption that individuals live forever can be relaxed by replacing r with $r/(1 - e^{rH})$ in equations 4 and 5, where H is the voter's life expectancy. (We thank an anonymous referee for this observation.)

Karl Ove Moene and Michael Wallerstein

which changing the funding level is politically easier than altering a program's design.

With γ fixed, the level of taxation and benefits preferred by wage earners is given by the first-order condition

$$\frac{dv}{dt} = \left(\frac{\beta + r}{\alpha + \beta + r}\right) u'(c_E)[\gamma \tau'(t)\bar{w} - w_L]$$
$$+ \left(\frac{\alpha}{\alpha + \beta + r}\right) u'(c_N)\left[\frac{(1-\gamma)\tau'(t)e\bar{w}}{1-e}\right] = 0, \tag{7}$$

or, by rearranging,

$$\left(\frac{\beta + r}{\alpha}\right)\left[\frac{u'(c_E)}{u'(c_N)}\right] - \left(\frac{e}{1-e}\right)\left[\frac{(1-\gamma)\tau'(t)}{(w_L/\bar{w}) - \gamma\tau'(t)}\right] = 0 \tag{8}$$

The first term in equation 8 represents the marginal rate of substitution between consumption when employed and consumption when unemployed, and the second term represents the marginal rate at which income can be transferred via the welfare system from a workers' earnings when employed to income when not employed. The strict concavity of $u(c)$ and $\tau(t)$ guarantees that the second-order condition for a maximum is satisfied. In this model, all groups have single-peaked preferences. Therefore, we can identify the political equilibrium as the preferred tax rate of the median group of income recipients, or the value of t that solves equation 8.

From equation 8 it is apparent that a decrease in the discount rate r or an increase in voters' altruism induces voters to raise $u'(c_E)/u'(c_N)$ or to increase the redistribution of income from c_E to c_N. Conversely, a rise in the cost of taxation, as represented by a decrease in the marginal tax yield $\tau'(t)$, induces voters to lower $u'(c_E)/u'(c_N)$ or to reduce the redistribution of income from c_E to c_N.[11] It is sometimes argued that the more policy benefits are targeted to the majority with earnings, the higher is the level of political support.[12] Within our framework, this argument is partially correct. Differentiating equation 7 with respect to γ yields $dt^*/d\gamma > 0$, where t^* is the median group's preferred tax rate. Thus, the more benefits targeted to the employed, the higher is the benefit level the employed majority will support.

[11] The effect of deadweight costs on political support for redistributive policies is emphasized in Becker 1983, 1985.
[12] See, for example, the exchange between Skocpol (1991) and Greenstein (1991).

Inequality, Social Insurance, and Redistribution

An increase in the funding of benefits may not benefit the poor, however, if the benefits are targeted more broadly. The question of whether less targeting to the poor benefits the poor concerns the sign of

$$\frac{dc_N}{d\gamma} = \left(\frac{e}{1-e}\right)\bar{w}\left[(1-\gamma)\tau'(t^*)\frac{dt^*}{d\gamma} - \tau(t^*)\right],$$

which can be either positive or negative, depending on the concavity of the function $\tau(t)$. It is straightforward to show that $dc_N/d\gamma > 0$ when the deadweight cost of taxation is negligible (i.e., when $\tau(t) \approx t$), whereas $dc_N/d\gamma < 0$ when the deadweight cost of a marginal increase in taxation increases rapidly (i.e., when $|\tau''(t)|$ is sufficiently large).

Our topic, however, is how changes in income inequality affect support for welfare expenditures. Consider the effect of a mean-preserving spread in the wage distribution, that is, an increase in w_H and a reduction in w_L, such that the average wage remains constant. To investigate the importance of a change in w_L on wage earner support for welfare, holding $\bar{w}$ constant, define

$$\Psi(w_L, \gamma) \equiv u'(c_E)[\gamma\tau'(t)\bar{w} - w_L]$$

as the part of equation 7 that depends on w_L. The sign of dt^*/dw_L is the same as the sign of

$$\frac{\partial\Psi(w_L, \gamma)}{\partial w_L} = u'(c_E)(\mu\xi - 1), \tag{9}$$

where

$$\xi \equiv \frac{dc_E}{d(1-t)}\frac{(1-t)}{c_E} = \frac{(1 - t[w_L - \gamma\tau'(t)\bar{w}])}{(1-t)w_L + \gamma\tau(t)\bar{w}}$$

is the elasticity of consumption when working with respect to $1-t$.[13] Since $\mu > 1$ and $\xi \leq 1$, the sign of $\partial\Psi/\partial w_L$ in equation 9 is not clear.

There are two special cases in which the sign of $\partial\Psi/\partial w_L$ is immediate, however. The first is the case of $\gamma = 1$, in which the employed receive all the

[13] To derive equation 9, start with

$$\frac{\partial\Psi}{\partial w_L} = u''(c_E)(1-t)[\gamma\tau'\bar{w} - w_L] - u'(c_E)$$

and use the definition $\mu = -c_E u''(c_E)/u'(c_E)$ to write $u''(c_E) - \mu u'(c_E)/c_E$. Equation 10 follows immediately.

295

benefits. If $\gamma = 1$, we have $w_L - \gamma \tau' \bar{w} = 0$ from equation 7, which implies that $\xi = 0$. In this case, equation 9 reduces to

$$\frac{\partial \Psi(w_L, 1)}{\partial w_L} = -u'(c_E) < 0. \tag{10}$$

Thus, workers with lower wages prefer higher benefits $(dt^*/dw_L < 0)$ when benefits are targeted at the employed.

The second special case is $\gamma = 0$, in which benefits are targeted exclusively at those without earnings. Since $\gamma = 0$ implies that $\xi = 1$, equation 9 reduces to

$$\frac{\partial \Psi(w_L, 0)}{\partial w_L} = u'(c_E)(\mu - 1) > 0. \tag{11}$$

Thus, an increase in the earnings of the median income group, w_L, increases their preferred benefit level $(dt^*/dw_L > 0)$ when benefits are aimed at those without earnings.

The effect of increased inequality on political support for welfare spending is summarized in the following proposition.

Proposition 1. *A mean-preserving spread in the income distribution (i) reduces the median voter's preferred level of benefits when benefits are targeted to those without employment but (ii) increases the median voter's preferred level of benefits when benefits are targeted to the employed.*

Proof. According to equation 10, a decline in the median voter's wage reduces his or her demand for welfare benefits if $\gamma = 0$. According to equation 11, a fall in the median voter's wage increases his or her demand for welfare benefits if $\gamma = 1$. Since $\Psi(w_L, \gamma)$ is continuous in γ, the conclusions hold for γ near zero and near one as well.[14]

A mean-preserving spread of the pretax income distribution has two effects on the choice of benefits. On the one hand, an increase in inequality represents a decline in income for workers with income below the mean. The wage reduction increases employed workers' resistance to paying taxes to finance benefits for those not working. On the other hand, greater inequality lowers the ratio of the median voter's income to mean income, thereby lowering the tax that must be paid by low-wage workers to

---

[14] We conjecture that ξ is generally a monotonic declining function of γ, which would imply the existence of a unique $\bar{\gamma} \epsilon (0, 1)$ such that $dt^*/dw_L > 0$ for $\gamma < \bar{\gamma}$ and $dt^*/dw_L < 0$ for $\gamma > \bar{\gamma}$.

finance a given level of benefits. A reduction in the price of providing benefits increases the willingness of low-wage voters to support higher benefit levels. Thus, in addition to an income effect that leads the median voter to reduce his or her preferred level of expenditures, there is a substitution effect that works in the opposite direction.

Alternatively, the two effects can be described as a redistribution effect and an insurance effect. For any value of $\gamma < 1$, welfare policy both redistributes income and provides insurance. A rise in inequality increases the redistributive effect of the welfare system, to the benefit of workers with below-average income. At the same time, an increase in inequality, holding average income constant, implies a reduction in the income of workers whose incomes are below average. Voters whose wages decline prefer to reduce the amount of insurance they buy. Which effect dominates depends on the coefficient of relative risk aversion, μ, and on the targeting of welfare benefits, γ.

Consider first the effect of voters' risk aversion for a fixed value of γ. If $\mu = 1$, that is, if voters' risk aversion is at its lower bound, then the insurance benefit provided by the welfare system is less important, and greater inequality increases the median voter's preferred tax rate for all $\gamma > 0$. If μ is sufficiently large, that is, if voters are sufficiently risk averse, then the insurance aspect of welfare dominates, in which case greater inequality lowers the median voter's preferred tax rate.

Alternatively, for a fixed $\mu > 1$, whether the redistributive or the insurance effect dominates can be understood as a function of benefit targeting. When benefits are mostly paid to the employed (when γ is close to one), the redistributive aspect dominates, and the preferred benefit level of the median income earner increases as inequality grows. This is the case described by the standard redistribution model. When benefits are mostly paid to those without earnings (when γ is close to zero), however, the insurance aspect dominates, and the preferred benefit level of the median income earner declines as inequality increases.

Equation 11 implies that, in comparing different countries with similar average income and similar distribution of the risk of income loss, support for spending on benefits targeted to the unemployed rises as the skewness of the income distribution declines. Equation 11 does not imply that support for spending on benefits aimed at the unemployed is a positive function of income when comparing the preferences of voters located at different points in the income distribution. When the risk of job loss is correlated with income, such that low-income voters face a greater probability of income loss than high-income voters, the relationship between a voter's position in the income distribution and support for spending on policies targeted to the unemployed can go either way. In our simple model, high-income voters are assumed to face no risk of income loss, so they prefer less welfare spending than low-income voters for all values of γ and μ.

The model in this section can be generalized in a variety of ways without altering the conclusions. The simplifying assumption that there are only two types of workers, lower paid and higher paid, can be replaced by the assumption of any finite number of types, or even a continuum of types. The assumption that only wage earners are subject to the risk of income loss can be replaced by assuming a general distribution of this risk. As long as the risk for workers with lower income is the same as or greater than the risk for workers with higher income, all the results of this section remain unchanged. Also, one might consider a different environment in which wages each period are random draws from a known wage distribution. In this case, one can investigate the effect of an increase in uncertainty regarding future wages, holding expected wage and risk of job loss constant. The results are similar. If welfare benefits are targeted to the employed, then an increase in uncertainty regarding future wages raises the preferred level of benefits of the median voter. If welfare benefits are targeted to those without employment, an increase in uncertainty regarding future wages reduces the median voter's preferred level of benefits.[15]

The assumption that the probability of obtaining employment, βdt, is not affected by changes in taxes and benefits could be relaxed to allow β to be a function of the difference in welfare between those with and without earnings. The result would be to introduce an additional mechanism whereby increased inequality causes reduced welfare spending; as described by Moffitt, Ribar, and Wilhelm (1998), voters cut benefits to the poor as wages fall in order to restore work incentives. Another extension would allow self-insurance (or saving) to compete with public insurance against income loss. The possibility of saving would enable the share of the population with no need for social insurance to be made endogenous. Such an extension might introduce a third reason for the association of greater inequality with lower welfare spending insofar as greater inequality increases the relative share of the electorate who prefer self-insurance to public insurance.

[15] See Moene and Wallerstein 1998 for details on the mathematical analysis of the effect of an increase in uncertainty on support for welfare spending.

Choosing Both Benefit Levels and Targeting

The targeting of benefits is as much a political decision as the level of welfare spending. Thus, a general model of the politics of welfare must include the political choice of targeting. Consideration of a second dimension of political choice is made difficult, however, by the general absence of a majority rule equilibrium in two dimensions without additional assumptions about the political process. We begin by characterizing the optimal policy of the median income group, as in the previous section. We then describe two alternative models of the political process, both of which imply that the policy preferred by the median income group constitutes the political equilibrium in the context of our particular model.

We concentrate, as before, on employed wage earners who receive w_L and face the risk αdt of losing their source of earnings within period dt. Wage earners' ideal policy is the combination of t and γ that maximizes their expected lifetime utility (equation 6), subject to the constraint that $\gamma \geq 0$ or that total benefits paid to those without employment, $(1 - e)c_N$, cannot exceed total expenditures, $T(t)$. The constraint that $\gamma \leq 1$, or that $c_N \geq 0$, is never binding, given our assumption that $u'(c) \to \infty$ as $c \to 0$. The first-order conditions for the solution can be written as

$$\left(\frac{\beta + r}{\alpha} \right) \left[\frac{u'(c_E)}{u'(c_N)} \right] - \left(\frac{e}{1 - e} \right) \left[\frac{(1 - \gamma)\tau'(t)}{(w_L/\bar{w}) - \gamma\tau'(t)} \right] = 0, \tag{12}$$

$$\gamma \left\{ \left(\frac{\beta + r}{\alpha} \right) \left[\frac{u'(c_E)}{u'(c_N)} \right] - \left(\frac{e}{1 - e} \right) \right\} = 0. \tag{13}$$

The first-order condition with respect to t, equation 12, is identical to equation 8. We now must consider the first-order condition with respect to γ as well.

Equation 13 indicates that there are two cases to be considered. In the first, the constraint is not binding, or the optimal choice of γ, denoted γ^*, is greater than zero. In this case, the first-order conditions can be written as

$$\tau'(t)\bar{w} - w_L = 0, \tag{14}$$

$$\left(\frac{\beta + r}{\alpha} \right) \left[\frac{u'(c_E)}{u'(c_N)} \right] - \left(\frac{e}{1 - e} \right) = 0. \tag{15}$$

Equation 14 determines the optimal tax rate as the rate at which the marginal revenue gain from an increase in the tax rate, $\tau'(t)\bar{w}$, just equals the marginal cost to wage earners, w_L, in line with the pure redistribution model. The optimal tax is zero when $w_L = \bar{w}$, since $\tau'(0) = 1$, and it rise as $w_L/\bar{w}$ declines, since

$$\frac{dt^*}{dw_L} = \frac{1}{\tau''(t)\bar{w}} < 0. \tag{16}$$

With the optimal tax rate determined by equation 14, the optimal allocation of tax revenues between benefits targeted to those with and without earnings is given implicitly by equation 15. Equation 15 represents the standard condition that the marginal rate of substitution between consumption when employed and consumption when not employed must equal the cost of transferring income from a worker's earnings when employed to income when not employed. For a fixed welfare budget, the cost of transferring benefits from those without earnings to the employed is the relative size of the two groups, $e/(1 - e)$. Equation 15 indicates that a change in the distribution of income that causes a decline in w_L must be matched by a decline in the benefits received when not employed to keep the ratio $(\beta + r)u'(c_E)/\alpha u'(c_N)$ unchanged:

$$\frac{dc_N}{dw_L} = \frac{(1 - t)[e/(1 - e)](\beta + r)u''(c_E)}{(\beta + r)u''(c_E) + [e/(1 - e)]^2 \alpha u''(c_N)} > 0. \tag{17}$$

It follows from equations 16 and 17 that

$$\frac{d\gamma^*}{dw_L} = \frac{1}{\tau(t)\bar{w}}\left[(1 - \gamma)\frac{\tau'(t)}{\tau''(t)} - \left(\frac{1-e}{e}\right)\frac{dc_N}{dw_L}\right] < 0.$$

Employed workers who suffer a decline in earnings prefer a partial offset of the wage reduction through an increase in the benefits targeted to themselves.

The second case to consider is the binding constraint, or when $\gamma^* = 0$. In this case, the first-order condition with respect to t simplifies to

$$\left(\frac{\beta + r}{\alpha}\right)\left[\frac{u'(c_E)}{u'(c_N)}\right] - \left(\frac{e}{1 - e}\right)\left[\frac{\tau'(t)\bar{w}}{w_L}\right] = 0. \tag{18}$$

Wage earners would like to lower t and raise money with a lump-sum tax (i.e., set γ below zero), but lump-sum taxes are ruled out by the constraint. Therefore, wage earners prefer to transfer less money from c_E to c_N than they would if lump-sum taxes were possible. From proposition 1, we know that $dt^*/dw_L > 0$ when $\gamma = 0$.

In order to visualize the wage earner's optimal policy, it is helpful to rewrite the policy choice as a choice of aggregate expenditures, $T(t)$, and a

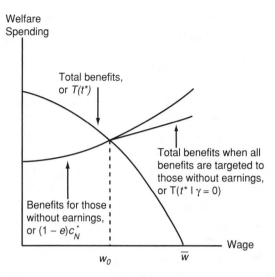

Figure 3 Preferred Policy of Employed Wage Earners.

choice of the total transfers that are disbursed to those without earnings, $(1 - e)c_N$. These choices are graphed in Figure 3. The curve $T(t^*)$ represents wage earners' unconstrained optimal aggregate welfare expenditures, which decline as w_L increases. The curve $(1 - e)c_N^*$ represents the unconstrained optimum with respect to the benefits targeted to those without earnings. This curve is an increasing function of w_L from equation 17. Since $T(t^*) = 0$ when $w_L = \bar{w}$, whereas $(1 - e)c_N^*$ is always positive and increasing in w_L, the two curves must cross at a wage level below $\bar{w}$, denoted w_0 in the figure. If $w_L < w_0$ wage earners' optimal choice of benefits targeted to themselves is given by the difference between $T(t^*)$ and $(1 - e)c_N^*$. For $w_L \geq w_0$, the constraint that $\gamma \geq 0$ or that $T(t) \geq (1 - e)c_N$ binds. The constrained optimum with $\gamma^* = 0$ or $T(t^*) = (1 - e)c_N$ is represented by the curve $T(t^* \mid \gamma = 0)$. That $T(t^* \mid \gamma = 0)$ is an increasing function of w_L is a restatement of part (i) of proposition 1.

The comparative static results implicit in Figure 3 are summarized as follows.

Proposition 2. *A mean-preserving increase in inequality that lowers the income of the median voter (i) reduces wage earners' preferred level of benefits targeted to those with no income, (ii) reduces wage earners' preferred level of aggregate spending when initial inequality is sufficiently small, but (iii) increases wage earners' preferred level of aggregate spending when initial inequality is sufficiently large.*

Proof. Part (i) states that c_N^* is an increasing function of w_L (equation 17 and proposition 1, part (i)). Part (iii) states that $T(t^*)$ is an increasing function of w_L for $w_L < w_0$ (equation 16), and part (ii) states that $T(t^* \mid \gamma = 0)$ is a decreasing function of w_L for $w_L > w_0$ (proposition 1, part (i)).[16]

When workers' income falls, their demand for redistribution increases, and their demand for insurance against loss of earnings declines. When the wage is sufficiently low, relative to the mean, the preferred level of aggregate spending provides more than enough to finance the preferred level of insurance, which leaves money in the budget to be distributed to employed workers and high-income earners. As the wage rises relative to the mean, however, wage earners' demand for insurance increases, and their demand for redistribution falls. Eventually, the wage rises above the threshold $w_L = w_0$, and wage earners prefer the entire welfare budget to be targeted to those without earnings. With $\gamma = 0$, wage earners face the conflict between redistributive and insurance motives for supporting welfare spending, described in the previous section. According to proposition 1, the insurance motive dominates when $\gamma = 0$, in the sense that the preferred benefit level rises with w_L.

In the previous section, when γ was assumed to be fixed, political choice was one-dimensional, and the political equilibrium could be identified with the optimal policy of the median income group. Proposition 2 implies that the same reasoning can be applied with regard to the simultaneous choice of t and γ when the median income is sufficiently close to the mean. If $w_L \geq w_0$ in Figure 3, a majority of voters prefer to target all benefits to those without earnings. (The γ that is optimal for wage earners who have lost their earnings and for those who never work is always less than or equal to the γ preferred by employed wage earners.) Given majority support for $\gamma = 0$, part (i) of proposition 1 applies. The ideal policy combination of employed wage earners is preferred by a majority to all feasible policy alternatives.

In the case in which w_L is sufficiently low, such that employed wage earners prefer a policy combination with some spending targeted to the employed ($w_L < w_0$), however, no policy has the property of being preferred by a majority to all feasible alternatives. To specify an outcome, one must add some additional assumptions about the political process. We

---

[16] Bénabou (2000) derives a similar V-shaped relationship between redistributive spending and inequality from a different set of assumptions regarding preferences, risk, and the fiscal system.

consider two approaches that can be used to select an equilibrium. The first assumes issue-by-issue voting, as in Shepsle (1979). If t and γ are decided in separate parliamentary votes, then the outcome is the policy combination preferred by employed wage earners, regardless of which policy vote is first, since employed wage earners are the median group in both policy dimensions.[17] The second approach assumes electoral competition between two parties or two coalitions of parties that have distinctive constituencies.[18] Suppose the leftist party seeks the support of wage earners and the poor, and the rightist party seeks the support of wage earners and voters with income above the median. If the party system prevents the formation of an alliance of the rich and poor against the middle, the wage earners' preferred policy is again a stable political equilibrium. Although other plausible approaches might yield other equilibria, we proceed to investigate the extent to which the pattern of government spending in advanced industrial societies fits the preferences of the median income group as described in proposition 2.

Inequality and Welfare Spending in 18 Countries, 1980–95

Definition of Variables

According to proposition 1, for the case of exogenous targeting, and proposition 2, for the case of endogenous targeting, an increase in the skewness of the income distribution reduces the share of GDP that the median income group prefers to spend on benefits for those who have lost their earnings. In the notation of the model, the preferred level of $(1 - e)c_N = (1 - \gamma)T(t)$ is a decreasing function of the skewness of the income distribution. In addition, the two propositions imply that an increase in skewness reduces the share of government spending that the median income group prefers to allot to benefits aimed at those without earnings.[19] In this section, we show that

[17] Let (t_0^*, γ_0^*) be the optimal policy of the poor, (t_1^*, γ_1^*) the optimal policy of workers temporarily without earnings, (t_2^*, γ_2^*) the optimal policy of employed wage earners, and (t_3^*, γ_3^*) the optimal policy of high-income earners. In the case with $w_L < w_0$, it is straightforward to show that $0 = \gamma_0^* \leq \gamma_1^* < \gamma_2^* < \gamma_0^* = 1$ and that $0 = t_3^* < t_2^* = t_1^* < t_0^* = t_{max}$, where t_{max} is the tax rate that maximizes $T(t)$.

[18] See Roemer 1998, 1999, and Austen-Smith 2000 for theoretical studies of political competition among constituency-based parties over redistributive policies.

[19] More precisely, the model implies that $(1 - e)c_N / T(t) = (1 - \gamma)$ is a declining function of the skewness of the income distribution as long as $\gamma > 0$. Given the existence of government expenditures for purposes other than insurance and redistribution, however, it is reasonable to expect that, if our model is correct, spending on insurance should increase as a share of total government spending as skewness falls, even when the $\gamma \geq 0$ constraint is binding.

both these implications of the model fit the data on welfare expenditures in advanced industrial societies during 1980–95.[20] Spending on social insurance against income loss is lower in countries where the income distribution is highly skewed, whether measured as a share of GDP or as a share of total government expenditures.

To measure *Spending on Insurance Against Income Loss*, we sum expenditures in seven categories: disability cash benefits, occupational injury and disease, sickness benefits, services for the disabled and elderly, survivors' benefits, active labor market programs, and unemployment insurance. Both government expenditures and mandated private expenditures are included. Government spending on health care does not fit in this category because in seventeen of the countries coverage is provided to all, regardless of income or employment status. The exception is the United States, which targets substantial programs to the elderly and the poor. To include health care spending would significantly overstate expenditures aimed at the unemployed in the seventeen countries, but to exclude it might understate benefits targeted to those without employment in the United States. Therefore, we added 100% of government spending on health care to the benefits received by those without earnings in the United States, but we only added 42% in the other countries. The latter figure is the government share of total health care expenditures in the United States in 1990 (OECD 1994).[21]

Our measure of insurance against the risk of income loss excludes old age cash benefits, family benefits, housing benefits, and benefits for other contingencies. Many family and housing programs cover those without employment, but many do not, and we have no way of estimating how the spending in these areas is divided among different types of households. Pensions are a large category of spending that is received by persons who are not employed. Although public pensions insure against investment risks inherent in private pensions, the loss of income upon retirement is an expected event in a way that the loss due to sickness or layoffs is not. Thus, we exclude government pension programs from our measure. Spending on insurance against income loss is still substantial even with pensions excluded. Among

[20] The countries in the Organization for Economic Cooperation and Development (OECD) data set are Australia, Austria, Belgium, Canada, Denmark, Finland, France, Germany, Italy, Japan, Netherlands, New Zealand, Norway, Portugal, Sweden, Switzerland, the United Kingdom, and the United States. These are the countries for which the OECD (1993, 1996) has published measures of wage and salary inequality.
[21] The statistical results are not changed significantly if government spending on health care is excluded from the insurance category.

the eighteen countries in our sample, it averaged 10% of GDP or 20% of total government spending from 1980–95.

According to most models, the aspect of income distribution that matters politically is the comparison of the median wage to the mean. The absence of data, however, compels us to use the ratio of earnings at different percentiles of the wage distribution as a proxy. If we approximate the empirical distribution of wages and salaries with the lognormal distribution, then the ratio of the median to the mean wage can be written as

$$\frac{\text{median wage}}{\text{mean wage}} = \exp(-\sigma^2/2),$$

where σ^2 is the variance of the log of wages and salaries.[22] This variance, in turn, can be derived from the ratio of wages at any two percentiles of the wage distribution, according to the formula

$$\sigma = k_{ij} \ln(w_i/w_j),$$

where w_i and w_j are the wages at the ith and jth percentiles, respectively, with $i > j$, and where k_{ij} is a positive constant that depends on i and j. It follows that the ratio of the median wage to the mean wage is a strictly decreasing function of the wage ratio w_i/w_j for any i and j with $i > j$.

In theory, any ratio w_i/w_j is an equally good proxy for the ratio of the median to the mean. Our proxy for the skewness of the income distribution, *Inequality* (90/10), is derived from the ratio of pretax earnings as between the 90th percentile and the 10th percentile of the distribution of wages and salaries. These data are available for eighteen industrialized countries from 1979–80 through 1995–96 (OECD 1996). Taking the log of $[w_{90}/w_{10}) - 1]$ improves the fit slightly. Therefore, we use

$$\text{inequality } (90/10) = \ln\left(\frac{w_{90} - w_{10}}{w_{10}}\right)$$

as our proxy for the skewness of the income distribution. All the statistical analyses were redone using the w_{50}/w_{10} and the w_{90}/w_{50} ratio in place of the w_{90}/w_{10} ratio to check that our findings are robust with respect to the choice of proxy.[23] Because wage inequality data are not available annually

[22] According to Aitchison and Brown (1957), the distribution of wages and salaries is closely approximated by the lognormal distribution apart from the upper and lower tails.
[23] See Moene and Wallerstein 2001a for the full set of regression equations using the w_{50}/w_{10} and the w_{90}/w_{50} wage ratios. In addition, our results do not depend in a significant way on whether one uses $\ln[(w_{90}/w_{10}) - 1]$ or $\ln(w_{90}/w_{10})$ or (w_{90}/w_{10}) as the proxy.

for the entire data set, we took the average of all data points for each country in the periods 1980–94, 1985–89, and 1990–94, which yielded (3)(18) = 54 possible data points. After removing cases with no inequality data for one or more of the five-year periods, we were left with 50 observations.[24]

Welfare spending today is highly correlated with welfare spending in the recent past. Budgets are adjusted up or down from the status quo. For the eighteen countries, if one regresses spending on social insurance against income loss as a share of GDP in 1985, 1990, and 1995 on spending as a share of GDP five years earlier, one obtains

$$(\text{Spending/GDP})_{it} = 1.60 + 0.913 \, (\text{Spending/GDP})_{it-5},$$

where the standard error of the coefficient in front of the lagged dependent variable is 0.05, and $R^2 = 85.5$. It is clear that the influence of past spending on current decisions cannot be ignored in empirical work.

In addition to a *Lagged Dependent Variable*, we control for the rate of unemployment (*Unemployment*), government by conservative parties (*Right Government*), the turnout for elections to the lower house of parliament (*Turnout*), and the proportion of the population over age 65 (*Percentage Elderly*). The rate of unemployment is potentially an important determinant of spending on unemployment insurance, active labor market policies, and even disability insurance (countries with high levels of joblessness may classify some of the unemployed as disabled) (Pampel and Williamson 1989). Because our measure of spending on insurance against income loss includes survivors' insurance and expenditures on health for those not in the labor market, the share of the population who are elderly also may affect spending levels. Whether one views the fraction of the population who are over age 65 or who are unemployed as measuring need or measuring political influence has a subtle implication for measument choice. As an indicator of need, the relevant control is the share of each group in the year at which expenditures are measured. As an indicator of political influence, the relevant control is an average of the size of each group in the preceding five years, since policy changes lag shifts in the electorate. We let the data decide this issue. The unemployment rate fits the data much better if measured in the same year

[24] The excluded cases were Belgium 1980–84, Portugal 1980–84, and Switzerland 1980–89. The method for calculating wage inequality in the United States was changed in the early 1990s. To construct a continuous time series starting in 1980 for the United States, we used the older series reported in OECD 1993 together with the extension of the older series reported in OECD 1996.

that we measure social insurance benefits. With regard to the proportion of elderly, using the average over the preceding five years fits slightly better, although the difference is small.

In the literature on partisanship and welfare spending, the early emphasis was on the division between socialist or social democratic parties and center/Right parties (Korpi 1983; Stephens 1979). Like many before us, we find that the most important division is between the Left/center and the Right (Castles 1982; Esping-Andersen 1990). Because the Left versus center/Right division was never significant in any of our regressions, we only report results based on the classification conservative versus Left/center. Our measure of conservative government is the share of cabinet seats held by conservative parties (Castles and Mair 1984; Huber and Inglehart 1995).

Turnout also may have an important effect on political support for spending to insure against the risk of income loss (Franzese 1998; Liphart 1997). We include the average turnout in elections in the lower house of parliament in the preceding five years. Summary statistics and data sources for all the variables are presented in the Appendix.

Among the earliest findings of the empirical literature is that welfare spending is higher as a share of GDP in countries with a higher level of GDP per capita (Wilensky 1975). Yet, like most other researchers whose data set is limited to countries with relatively high GDP per capita, we found that this factor had no explanatory power. Therefore, we did not include GDP per capita in the set of independent variables. In addition, we used no controls for union strength, such as density or centralized wage-setting, since these two are among the most important determinants of the inequality of earnings distribution (Freeman 1988; Hibbs and Locking 2000; Rueda and Pontusson 2000; Wallerstein 1999). It should be noted that government spending has little influence on the inequality of pretax wages and salaries after controlling for the effect of wage-setting institutions (Wallerstein 1999). Thus, the inequality of pretax wages and salaries can be considered exogenous with respect to spending on social insurance benefits.

Testing the Model

Regressions results with spending on social insurance against income loss as a share of GDP as the dependent variable are presented in Table 1.[25] The

---

[25] The panel-corrected standard errors are estimated assuming that $E(\epsilon \epsilon') = \Sigma \otimes I$ where Σ is a general 18×18 variance-covariance matrix for the error terms associated with the

Table 1. *Effect of Inequality on Government Spending for Insurance against Loss of Income as a Share of GDP in Eighteen Countries, 1980–95*

	1	2	3	4	5
Lagged dependent variable	.761* (.063)	.734* (.073)	.789* (.069)	.778* (.068)	.757* (.063)
Inequality (90/10)	−2.17* (0.33)	−1.93* (0.35)	−2.52* (0.55)	−1.83* (0.39)	
Unemployment	.118 (.073)	.122 (.072)	.117 (.082)	.060 (.071)	.119 (.077)
Turnout	−.053* (.012)	−.050* (.011)	−.043* (.015)	−.044* (.011)	−.053* (.014)
Rightist government	−.013* (.004)	−.013* (.005)		−.013* (.004)	−.013* (.005)
Percentage elderly		.108 (.108)			
Inequality (50/10)					−1.31* (0.53)
Inequality (90/50)					−1.53 (0.97)
adj. R^2	90.0	90.1	88.3	90.3	89.8
N	50	50	50	49	50

Note: The table shows OLS estimation. The dependent variable is insurance benefits for loss of income as a share of GDP. Parentheses contain panel-corrected standard errors. All regressions include a constant. Column 4 excludes Finland 1995.
*$p ≤ .05$.

first column is our basic specification. The estimated effect of the skewness of the wage distribution on spending as a share of GDP is strongly negative, as predicted by the model. Among advanced industrial societies, countries with a more skewed distribution spend less on insurance against income loss than countries with more a egalitarian distribution. The estimated effect of an increase in inequality (90/10) by one standard deviation (.378) reduces spending on insurance against income loss as a share of GDP by (2.17)(.378) ≈ 0.8 percentage points in five years. In the long run, such an increase reduces that spending by 0.8/(1 − .761) ≈ 3.3 percentage points.[26] This is a large effect. For example, consider the contrast between average spending on insurance against income loss in the Netherlands (15% of GDP), ranked highest in this category in the sample, and United States (8% of GDP). Given that the difference for the inequality (90/10) variable between the Netherlands and the United States averaged 1.44 –0.43 ≈ 1.0, the long-run difference in their spending as a share of GDP we can expect on that basis is (2.17)(1.0)/(1 − .761) ≈ 9 percentage points, compared to an actual difference of 7 percentage points.

The estimated effect of turnout on spending as a share of GDP is also negative. Higher turnout is associated with less spending on insurance against the risk of income loss, controlling for the skewness of income distribution. The simplest explanation is that the propensity to vote is positively correlated with age as well as income. Indeed, Franklin (1996, 220), in an analysis of survey data from 21 European countries and the United States, found that the effect of age exceeds that of income.[27] When turnout is low, the elderly may comprise a larger share of voters than when turnout is high. Because some of the insurance benefits going to those without earnings are

eighteen countries and I is the 3×3 identity matrix for the three time periods. See Beck and Katz 1995 or Greene [1993] 1997, 651–69 for a discussion of the estimation of panel-corrected standard errors.

[26] The coefficients reported in Table 1 represent the short-run effect of a unit change in the independent variables on the dependent variables, where the short run is within five years, since all variables are measured in five year intervals. The long-run effect of a unit change in the independent variables is given by the short-run effect divided by (1 − .761), where .761 is the estimated coefficient on the lagged dependent variable. The long run refers to the total cumulative effect of a permanent change in one of the independent variables as time goes to infinity.

[27] Franklin (1996, 220) divided his sample into five age and income categories. The difference in turnout between the top and bottom age quintiles was approximately 30 percentage points (from 58.8% to 88.9%); the difference in turnout between the top and bottom income quintiles was roughly 15 percentage points.

309

disproportionately received by the older voters (obvious examples are dis- ability and survivors' insurance), the negative estimated effect of turnout on spending may reflect the fact that smaller electorates contain a relatively larger proportion of elderly than do larger electorates.

As an additional control for the age distribution of the electorate, we added the proportion of the population who are elderly to the set of inde- pendent variables in the second column of Table 1. Note that cross-national differences in turnout far exceed cross-national differences in the share of the population over age 65, as shown in Table A-1. Thus, it is not surprising that the standard error of the estimated effect of the percentage elderly is much larger than the standard error of the estimated effect of turnout. The point estimates indicate that both a high share of elderly in the population and a low turnout are associated with higher benefits.

There are two ways in which income distribution can affect spending for insurance against income loss. The first is to induce all parties to shift their platform in the direction of the policy preferred by the median income group. This is implicit in the first column of Table 1. The second mech- anism is to alter the likelihood of an electoral victory of the parties that are most committed to social insurance policies, that is, the parties of the Left and center. In this case, government by rightist parties is an endoge- nous variable that reflects the distribution of income. If income distribution affects policy by affecting the likelihood of a conservative electoral victory, then inclusion of rightist government as a control variable will underesti- mate the influence of income on social insurance benefits as a share of GDP. The third column of Table 1 shows that the estimated effect of inequality (90/10) does increase in absolute value when government by the Right is removed as a control, but the difference is not large.[28]

The last two columns of Table 1 present several checks on the robust- ness of our results. Tests of the influence of individual data points revealed that the case of Finland in 1995, an outlier with an unemployment rate of 17.4%, has a large influence on the estimates. Its extraordinarily high rate significantly increases the range over which unemployment varies in the data and allows more precise estimates of the coefficients. As the fourth

---

[28] Standard economic theory suggests that unemployment also may be endogenous, in the sense of being affected by both the distribution of wages and the generosity of unemploy- ment benefits. Yet, the correlation of unemployment and our measure of wage inequality is close to zero. Moreover, the removal of the unemployment rate from the set of controls had little effect on the estimated coefficients of the variables that remained.

Inequality, Social Insurance, and Redistribution

Table 2. *Effect of Inequality on Government Spending for Insurance against Loss of Income as a Share of Government Expenditures in Eighteen Countries, 1980–95*

	1	2
Lagged dependent variable	.845* (.105)	.851* (.089)
Inequality (90/10)	−1.33* (0.27)	−1.74* (0.28)
Turnout	−.060* (.013)	−.064* (.013)
Rightist government	−.008 (.009)	−.008 (.010)
Unemployment	−.042 (0.78)	
Percentage elderly	.131 (.101)	
adj. R^2	84.9	85.3
N	46	46

Note: The table shows OLS estimation. The dependent variable is insurance benefits as a share of government expenditures. Parentheses contain panel-corrected standard errors. All regressions include a constant. New Zealand and Portugal 1995 are deleted because of missing data. *$p \le .05$.

column of Table 1 shows, removing the case of Finland 1995 greatly reduces the estimated effect of unemployment and slightly reduces the estimated effect of inequality (90/10).

In column 5, we replace the w_{90}/w_{10} ratio with w_{50}/w_{10} and w_{90}/w_{50} to test the argument of Kristov, Lindert, and McClelland (1992) that support for social insurance depends on the social affinity felt by the median group toward the poor. Kristov and his colleagues argue that such affinity is a negative function of the distance between the middle and the poor, as measured by the w_{50}/w_{10} ratio, and a positive function of the distance between the middle and the rich, as measured by the w_{90}/w_{50} ratio. Thus, the estimated coefficient for inequality (50/10) should be negative, and the estimated coefficient for inequality (90/50) should be positive. According to our model, in contrast, both measures are equivalent proxies of income skewness. Column 5 indicates that the estimated coefficients for both are virtually the same, negative number.

Our model implies that countries with a highly skewed distribution of wages and salaries spend less on insurance against income loss as a share of either government expenditures or GDP. This is tested in Table 2. The dependent variable is social insurance spending as a share of government spending, defined as total outlays by all levels of government minus gross capital formation and other capital expenditures. Because the signs of the estimated coefficients for both unemployment and the share of elderly in

311

column 1 are contrary to our prior beliefs, we removed both controls in column 2.[29] Both specifications in Table 2 show a strong, negative relationship between spending on insurance against income loss as a share of government spending and the skewness of the wage distribution. Together, columns 1 and 2 imply that a long-lasting increase in inequality (90/10) by one standard deviation reduces social insurance spending as a share of government outlays by between $(1.33)(.378)/(1 - .851) \approx 3.4$ and $(1.74)(.378)/(1 - .851) \approx 4.4$ percentage points in the long run.

Our model generates weaker predictions regarding the relationship between the skewness of income distribution and total spending on benefits for both the employed and people without earnings. The V-shaped relationship between skewness and $T(t)$ described in proposition 2 and illustrated in Figure 3 is compatible with any empirical relationship between our measure of inequality and $T(t)$ except for an upside-down V. A further obstacle to testing the predictions of our model regarding $T(t)$ is the difficulty in measuring government spending on benefits for the employed. Defined narrowly to be transfer payments received by the median group of wage earners, these benefits as a share of GDP are close to zero in all advanced industrial societies; this is consistent with our model if the income distribution in those societies is sufficiently egalitarian that a majority prefers transfer payments be targeted to those without earnings.[30] An alternative approach is to equate $T(t)$ with total social expenditures as defined by the OECD (1999), which includes insurance benefits to those without earnings (about 40% of the total), pensions (about 30% of the total) and other transfer payments and in-kind benefits that do not depend on employment status.[31]

Column 1 of Table 3 reveals a strong, negative relationship between income inequality and social expenditures as a share of GDP, as Rodríguez (1998) has shown. If one looks for a V-shaped relationship between social expenditures and income inequality, it can be found. Searching the data for a critical level of inequality that generates the strongest V-shaped relationship yields the division described in columns 2 and 3. In those two cases the sample is divided according to whether $w_{90}/w_{10} < 3.15$ (the distribution of

---

[29] Since spending on pensions reduces the share of government spending on insurance against income loss, we expected the coefficient on the percentage elderly to be negative.

[30] Family benefits, the only transfer payments likely to be received by a voter with median income, average 1.4% of GDP among advanced industrial societies (OECD 1999).

[31] Social expenditures include government spending on health and housing but not on education.

Table 3. *Effect of Inequality on Social Expenditures as a Share of GDP in Eighteen Countries, 1980–95*

	1 (Entire Sample)	2 ($w_{90}/w_{10} < 3.15$)	3 ($w_{90}/w_{10} \geq 3.15$)
Lagged dependent variable	.749* (.065)	.715* (.078)	.730* (.089)
Inequality (90/10)	−2.87* (0.79)	−5.88* (2.59)	4.06 (2.99)
Turnout	−.069* (.022)	−.117* (.035)	.034 (.036)
Rightist government	−.019* (.007)	−.013 (.010)	−.028* (.008)
Unemployment	.259* (.089)	.288* (.098)	.765* (.207)
Percentage elderly	.320 (.221)	.112 (.249)	.964* (.340)
adj. R^2	92.2	91.8	95.9
N	50	34	16
$F(7, 36)$			1.55

Note: The table shows OLS estimation. The dependent variable is total social expenditures as a share of GDP. Parentheses contain panel-corrected standard errors in column 1, OLS standard errors in columns 2 and 3. All regressions include a constant. The F-statistic tests the null hypothesis that the coefficient vectors in the last two columns are identical. *$p \leq .05$.

income is at least as equal as in Japan) or $w_{90}/w_{10} \geq 3.15$ (the distribution of income is at least as unequal as in France). The point estimates in columns 2 and 3 indicate a V-shaped relationship between spending and inequality, but the F-statistic fails to reject the null hypothesis that the coefficients in the two subsamples are identical.

To summarize the empirical evidence, there is strong support for the model's predictions regarding insurance against income loss. In advanced industrial societies, the more positively skewed the distribution of pretax earnings, the lower is government spending on insurance against income loss, whether measured as a share of GDP or total government spending. There is also a strong negative relationship between aggregate social expenditures as a share of GDP and income inequality. In other words, there is little empirical support for a purely redistributive model of welfare expenditures. The empirical relationship between inequality and political support for welfare programs, we suggest, cannot be adequately understood without considering welfare policies as publicly provided insurance.

Conclusion

We have developed the implications of the view that welfare policies are publicly financed insurance that pays out benefits relative to contributions in a redistributive manner. At the extreme ends of the income scale, the insurance aspect is dwarfed by the redistributive aspect. The poor in our model receive benefits and do not contribute at all, and the rich have no need for publicly financed insurance. But the middle group of voters in our model benefit from both aspects of welfare policies. When the redistributive and insurance benefits are considered simultaneously, the effect of increasing inequality on political support for welfare policies depends critically on the way in which benefits are targeted. Increased income inequality that is associated with an increased gap between median and mean income increases political support for redistributive benefits received by the employed but reduces support for publicly provided insurance against income loss. When the targeting of benefits is endogenous, the model continues to imply that support for spending on insurance against the risk of income loss declines as the gap between the median and the mean increases. Regression results indicate that greater inequality is associated with lower spending on programs to insure against income loss among eighteen advanced industrial countries from 1980 to 1995, as a share of both GDP and total government spending.

Our approach does not yield a clear prediction regarding how support for insurance against the risk of income loss varies across individuals with different incomes. In our model, the demand for welfare spending comes from those who never work and low-wage workers who may lose their employment. High-wage workers, who, by assumption, face no risk of income loss, oppose spending on social insurance to the extent that they vote in a self-interested manner. In reality, however, the risk of income loss rises gradually as one moves up the income scale. Whether self-interested workers earning a higher income would support more or less spending on insurance against the risk of job loss than workers earning lower income depends on their relative risk as well as their relative wage.[32] Our conclusion that a more unequal distribution of income leads to less support for social insurance is conditional upon holding constant the distribution of the risk of income loss.

Theoretically, the largest gap in our approach is the absence of a private alternative to publicly provided insurance. We have concentrated on the loss of income, a risk that cannot be insured privately. The politics of the demand for insurance when there is a private alternative involves different considerations. The policies that constitute the welfare state are heterogeneous in their bases of political support. One model will not encompass them all.

---

[32] Iversen and Soskice (2001) find that support for welfare expenditure declines as survey respondents' income increases, controlling for the specificity of skills.

Empirically, there is strong support in our sample for the proposition that countries with more skewed income distributions spend less on insurance against income loss. A simple cross-sectional comparison of wage inequality and spending on social insurance yields a clear negative relationship. That relationship holds up surprisingly well using panel data with a lagged dependent variable; that variable alone explains 85% of the variance. The results can be destroyed, however, by removing all the cross-sectional variation with a full set of country dummy variables, as Devroye (2000) shows. The variation in wage inequality within countries is too small over the fifteen years we studied to provide a reasonable test of the model's implications. To test the relationship using a fixed-effects model, we need measures of wage inequality and spending on benefits targeted to those without employment over a longer period. We also need more empirical work on the categories of welfare expenditures that do not consist of insurance against income loss. The political contests over pensions or government spending on health care may differ significantly from the political contest over programs that insure against the loss of income. Finding the level of disaggregation that best explains the dynamics of political support for welfare policies should be high on the agenda of future work.

Appendix

Descriptive statistics for all the variables used in the data analysis are presented in Table A-1. Insurance against income loss refers to spending on welfare program targeted to those without earnings, excluding pensions, as described in the text. Data are for 1985, 1990, and 1995 in the case of social insurance benefits, government spending and unemployment. All the other variables represent the average value for the periods 1980–84, 1985–89, and 1990–94. See note 20 for the countries in the sample. The source for spending on social insurance, health care, and pensions is OECD (1999). Wage inequality (i/j) is $\ln[(w_i - w_j)w_j]$, as described in the text. The data on wage inequality are from OECD (1996) and, in the case of the United States, OECD (1993). The share of government spending, the share of elderly in the population, and unemployment figures are from OECD (1997). Conservative government is based on Swank (1992), updated using recent issues of *Keesing's Record of World Events*. The classification of parties in terms of Right versus center and Left is based on Castles and Mair (1984), updated with Huber and Inglehart (1995). Turnout refers to elections for the lower house of parliament or for president in the United States. The source for

315

Karl Ove Moene and Michael Wallerstein

Table A-1. *Summary Statistics*

Variable	Mean	S.D.	Minimum	Maximum
Insurance for income loss/GDP	9.8	3.4	3.6	15.7
Insurance for income loss/govt. spending	21.8	4.4	13.6	30.0
Social expenditures/GDP	23.0	6.2	11.3	33.4
Inequality (90/10)	.604	.378	−.020	1.50
Inequality (90/50)	−.333	.264	−.755	.336
Inequality (50/10)	−.463	.393	−1.17	.365
Unemployment	7.2	3.1	1.6	17.2
Rightist government	41.5	36.7	0	100
Turnout	78.5	13.2	40.0	95.6
Percentage elderly	13.5	2.1	9.5	17.7

turnout is Blais and Dobryzynska (1998). The data set is available from the authors upon request.

References

Aitchison, John, and J. A. C. Brown. 1957. *The Lognormal Distribution.* Cambridge: Cambridge University Press.

Alesini, Alberto, and Dani Rodrik. 1994. "Distributive Politics and Economic Growth." *Quarterly Journal of Economics* 109 (May): 465–90.

Austen-Smith, David. 2000. "Redistributing Income under Proportional Representation." *Journal of Political Economic* 108 (December): 1235–69.

Barr, Nicholas. 1992. "Economic Theory and the Welfare State: A Survey and Interpretation." *Journal of Economic Literature* 30 (June): 741–803.

Beck, Neal, and Jonathan Katz. 1995. "What to Do (and Not to Do) with Time-Series Cross-Sectional Data in Comparative Politics." *American Political Science Review* 89 (September): 634–47.

Becker, Gary S. 1983. "A Theory of Competition among Pressure Groups for Political Influence." *Quarterly Journal of Economics* 98 (August): 371–400.

Becker, Gary S. 1985. "Public Policies, Pressure Groups, and Dead Weight Costs." *Journal of Public Economics* 28 (December): 329–47.

Bénabou, Roland. 2000. "Unequal Societies: Income Distribution and the Social Contract." *American Economic Review* 90 (March): 96–129.

Blais, André, and Agnieszka Dobrzynska. 1998. "Turnout in Electoral Democracies." *European Journal of Political Research* 33 (March): 239–61.

Casamatta, Georges, Helmuth Cremer, and Pierre Pestieau. 2000. "Political Sustainability and the Design of Social Insurance." *Journal of Public Economics* 75 (March): 341–64.

Castles, Francis G. 1982. "The Impact of Parties on Public Expenditure." In *The Impact of Parties: Politics and Policies in Democratic Capitalist States*, ed. Francis Castles. London: Sage. Pp. 21–96.

Castles, Francis, and Peter Mair. 1984. "Left-Right Political Scales: Some 'Expert' Judgements." *European Journal of Political Research* 12 (January): 73–88.

De Donder, Philippe, and Jean Hindriks. 1998. "The Political Economy of Targeting." *Public Choice* 95 (January): 177–200.

De Donder, Philippe, and Jean Hindriks. 2000. "The Politics of Redistributive Social Insurance." Department of Economics. University of London. Typescript.

Devroye, Dan. 2000. "Voting for Inequality." Department of Government. Harvard University. Unpublished paper.

Esping-Andersen, Gösta. 1990. *The Three Worlds of Welfare Capitalism.* Princeton, NJ: Princeton University Press.

Franklin, Mark N. 1996. "Electoral Competition." In *Comparing Democracies: Elections and Voting in Global Perspective*, ed. Lawrence LeDuc, Richard Niemi, and Pippa Norris. Thousand Oaks, CA: Sage. Pp. 216–35.

Franzese, Robert J. 1998. "Political Participation, Income Distribution and Public Transfers in Developed Democracies." Department of Political Science. University of Michigan, Ann Arbor. Typescript.

Freeman, Richard B. 1988. "Labour Market Institutions and Economic Performance." *Economic Policy* 6 (April): 64–80.

Friend, Irwin, and Marshall E. Blume. 1975. "The Demand for Risky Assets." *American Economic Review* 65 (December): 900–22.

Gelbach, Jonah B., and Lant H. Pritchett. 1997. "Indicator Targeting in a Political Equilibrium: Leakier Can Be Better." Washington, DC: World Bank Policy Research Working Paper 1523.

Greene, William H. [1993] 1997. *Econometric Analysis.* Upper Saddle River, NJ: Prentice Hall.

Greenstein, Robert. 1991. "Universal and Targeted Approaches to Relieving Poverty: An Alternative View." In *The Urban Underclass*, ed. Christopher Jencks and Paul Peterson. Washington, DC: Brookings Institution. Pp. 437–59.

Hibbs, Douglas A., and Håkan Locking. 2000. "Wage Dispersion and Productive Efficiency: Evidence for Sweden." *Journal of Labor Economics* 18 (October): 755–82.

Hicks, Alexander. 1999. *Social Democracy and Welfare Capitalism: A Century of Income Security Politics.* Ithaca, NY: Cornell University Press.

Hicks, Alexander, and Swank, Duane. 1992. "Politics, Institutions and Social Welfare Spending in the Industrialized Democracies, 1960–1982." *American Political Science Review* 86 (September): 658–74.

Huber, Evelyne, Charles Ragin, and John D. Stephens. 1993. "Social Democracy, Christian Democracy, Constitutional Structure and the Welfare State." *American Journal of Sociology* 99 (November): 711–49.

Huber, Evelyne, and John D. Stephens. 2001. *Development and Crisis in Advanced Welfare States.* Chicago: University of Chicago Press.

Huber, John, and Ronald Inglehart. 1995. "Expert Interpretations of Party Space and Party Locations in 42 Societies." *Party Politics* 1 (1): 73–111.

Iversen, Torben, and David Soskice. 2001. "An Asset Theory of Social Policy Preferences." *American Political Science Review* 95 (December): 875–93.

Karl Ove Moene and Michael Wallerstein

Korpi, Walter. 1983. *The Democratic Class Struggle.* London: Routledge and Kegan Paul.
Kristov, Lorenzo, Peter Lindert, and Robert McClelland. 1992. "Pressure Groups and Redistribution." *Journal of Public Economics* 48 (July): 135–63.
Lijphart, Arend. 1997. "Unequal Participation: Democracy's Unresolved Dilemma." *American Political Science Review* 91 (March): 1–14.
Meltzer, Allan H., and Scott F. Richard. 1981. "A Rational Theory of the Size of Government." *Journal of Political Economy* 89 (October): 914–27.
Moene, Karl Ove, and Michael Wallerstein. 1998. "Rising Inequality and Declining Support for Redistribution." Department of Political Science. Northwestern University. Typescript.
Moene, Karl Ove, and Michael Wallerstein. 2001a. "Inequality, Social Insurance, and Redistribution: Additional Statistical Tables." Department of Political Science. Northwestern University. Typescript.
Moene, Karl Ove, and Michael Wallerstein. 2001b. "Targeting and Political Support for Welfare Spending." *Economics of Governance* 2 (1): 3–24.
Moffitt, Robert, David Ribar, and Mark Wilhelm. 1998. "The Decline of Welfare Benefits in the U.S.: The Role of Wage Inequality." *Journal of Public Economics* 68 (June): 421–52.
Organization for Economic Cooperation and Development. 1993. *Employment Outlook,* July 1993. Paris: OECD.
Organization for Economic Cooperation and Development. 1994. *New Orientations for Social Policy.* Paris: OECD.
Organization for Economic Cooperation and Development. 1996. *Employment Outlook,* July 1996. Paris: OECD.
Organization for Economic Cooperation and Development. 1997. *Statistical Compendium 1997/2* [CD-ROM]. Paris: OECD.
Organization for Economic Cooperation and Development. 1999. *Social Expenditure Database, 1980–1996* [CD-ROM]. Paris: OECD.
Pampel, Fred C., and John B. Williamson. 1989. "Welfare Spending in Advanced Industrial Democracies 1950–1980." *American Journal of Sociology* 93 (May): 1424–56.
Persson, Torsten, and Guido Tabellini. 1994. "Is Inequality Harmful for Growth?" *American Economic Review* 84 (June): 600–21.
Piketty, Thomas. 1995. "Social Mobility and Redistributive Politics." *Quarterly Journal of Economics* 110 (August): 551–84.
Roberts, Kevis W.S. 1977. "Voting over Income Tax Schedules." *Journal of Public Economics* 8 (December): 329–40.
Rodríguez, Caballero, and Francisco Rafael. 1998. "Essays on the Political Economy of Inequality, Redistribution and Growth." Department of Economics. Harvard University. Ph.D. diss.
Roemer, John E. 1998. "Why the Poor Do Not Expropriate the Rich in Democracies: A New Argument." *Journal of Public Economics* 70 (December): 399–424.
Roemer, John E. 1999. "The Democratic Political Economy of Progressive Income Taxation." *Econometrica* 67 (January): 1–20.

Romer, Thomas. 1975. "Individual Welfare, Majority Voting, and the Properties of a Lienar Income Tax." *Journal of Public Economics* 14 (May): 163–85.
Rueda, David, and Jonas Pontusson. 2000. "Wage Inequality and Varieties of Capitalism." *World Politics* 52 (April): 350–83.
Saint-Paul, Gilles. 1998. "The Dynamics of Exclusion and Fiscal Conservatism." Department of Economics. Universitat Pompeu Fabra and CEPR. Typescript.
Shalev, Michael. 1983. "The Social Democratic Model and Beyond: Two Generations of Comparative Research on the Welfare State." *Comparative Social Research* 6: 316–51.
Shepsle, Kenneth A. 1979. "Institutional Arrangements and Equilibrium in Multidimensional Voting Models." *American Journal of Political Science* 23 (February): 27–59.
Sinn, Hans-Werner. 1995. "A Theory of the Welfare State." *Scandinavian Journal of Economics* 97: 495–526.
Skocpol, Theda. 1991. "Targeting within Universalism: Politically Viable Policies to Combat Poverty in the United States." In *The Urban Underclass*, ed. Christopher Jencks and Paul Peterson. Washington, DC: Brookings Institution. Pp. 411–36.
Stephens, John D. 1979. *The Transition from Capitalism to Socialism*. Atlantic Highlands, NJ: Humanities Press.
Swank, Duane. 1992. "Politics and the Structural Dependence of the State in Democratic Capitalist Nations." *American Political Science Review* 86 (March): 38–54.
Wallerstein, Michael. 1999. "Wage-Setting Institutions and Pay Inequality in Advanced Industrial Societies." *American Journal of Political Science* 43 (July): 649–80.
Wilensky, Harold L. 1975. *The Welfare State and Equality*. Berkeley: University of California Press.
Wright, Randall. 1996. "Taxes, Redistribution, and Growth." *Journal of Public Economics* 62 (November): 327–38.

14

Redistribution and Affirmative Action

David Austen-Smith and Michael Wallerstein

1. Introduction

Many scholars have observed that the politics of redistribution in the US is intertwined with the politics of race. Writing in the 1950s, Lipset and Bendix (1959) argued that the "social and economic cleavage" created by discrimination against blacks and Hispanics "diminishes the chances for the development of solidarity along class lines" (1959: 106). Myrdal (1960), Quadagno (1994) and, most recently, Gilens (1999) claim that racial animosity in the US is the single most important reason for the limited growth of welfare expenditures in the US relative to the nations of Western Europe. According to Quadagno (1994), political support for Johnson's War on Poverty was undermined by the racial conflicts that erupted over job training and housing programs. Alesina et al. (1999) find that localities in the US with high levels of racial fragmentation redistribute less and provide fewer public goods than localities that are racially homogeneous. Alesina and Glaeser (2004) conclude that racial conflict is one of the most important reasons for the low level of redistribution in the US compared to Europe.

The dominant approach in studies of race and redistributive politics in the US is to focus on the manner in which race affects voters' preferences regarding redistributive policies. Kinder and Sanders (1996) and Alesina and La Ferrara (2000) find that the sharpest contrast in preferences for redistributive policies in the US today is not between rich and poor or between men and women, but between whites and blacks. Moreover, the racial gap in public opinion towards redistributive policies is not eliminated when personal income or personal experience with unemployment are included as control variables (Kinder and Sanders, 1996). Gilens (1999)

320

and Luttmer (2001) find evidence that American voters are more willing to support redistributive policies if the perceived beneficiaries are of the same race.

In contrast, the more formal approach to the political economy of redistribution has largely ignored the role of race or divisions rooted in individuals' ascriptive characteristics. Assuming individuals differ only in the single dimension of wealth or income, the focus has been on how changes in income distribution or in the political franchise influence majority preferences over redistributive fiscal policy; Romer (1975) and Meltzer and Richard (1981) are the seminal contributions.[1] Likewise, most formal models of affirmative action (e.g. Lundberg, 1991; Foster and Vohra, 1992; Coate and Loury, 1993; Chung, 2000) have focused on the implications of affirmative action policies for labor market outcomes rather than on the political choice of affirmative action when alternative redistributive policies are also on the agenda.

In this paper, we study the effect of social cleavages on the politics and economics of redistribution due to the introduction of an additional dimension of potential redistribution; that is, affirmative action. Motivated in principle by perceptions of past and current injustice, affirmative action is a political decision designed to influence pre-wage labor market allocations; and fiscal redistribution is a political decision designed to influence post-wage allocations of income. It is reasonable, therefore, that individuals' induced preferences over the two sorts of policy should be related: affirmative action (differentially) affects the ex ante opportunities for both black and white workers to secure more lucrative employment which, in turn, affects their views regarding the appropriate level of ex post fiscal redistribution. Furthermore, the relative supply of more or less lucrative employment opportunities is itself likely to be influenced by both affirmative action and fiscal policy.

To explore the sorts of tradeoff above, we build a general equilibrium political economy model in which individuals differ in their exogenously given stock of human capital and some ascriptive characteristic. In our application, we suppose the ascriptive characteristic is race with blacks being the minority group; the racial gap in earnings is captured by the minority having

[1] The most salient exceptions to one-dimensional models of redistribution are models of competition between special interests: see, for example, Grossman and Helpman (2001) and Dixit and Londregan (1998). The dynamics of political conflict among many narrow interests, however, is likely to be quite different from political conflict among a few, large social groups defined by non-economic criteria.

David Austen-Smith and Michael Wallerstein

lower human capital on average. Individuals are otherwise assumed both color-blind and identical with respect to their fundamental (self-interested) preferences. The policy space consists of two policies. The first is a standard redistributive fiscal policy with a proportional tax that is used to finance a uniform benefit to workers in low-wage jobs. The second policy is an affirmative action target that requires employers to fill a given share of their higher paying jobs with minority workers.

The affirmative action policy is motivated by the historical discrimination resulting in the different current distributions of human capital between whites and blacks. In equilibrium this difference implies that, despite color-blind hiring by employers, the share of better jobs going to blacks falls short of the share of blacks in the population. Individuals' preferences over the policy space, therefore, are derived through equilibrium behavior in the economy and both race and income affect these induced policy preferences. The economy is modeled as a simple labor market in which the distribution of job opportunities is endogenous and workers are randomly matched with firms. Policy decisions are the outcomes of a legislative bargaining process.

Before going on, it is worth emphasizing that we do not deny the potential importance of racial or ethnic differences in preferences for determining redistribution policies. Our purpose in assuming that individuals behave in a color-blind fashion to maximize their post-tax and transfer income is to highlight the pure effect of introducing the possibility of redistribution by race, as well as by income, on the type and extent of redistribution that occurs in equilibrium. A different approach is adopted in the articles most closely related, as far as we know, to this paper. In Roemer (1998) and Roemer and Lee (2004), racial or religious differences are built into voters' preferences. Roemer (1998) assumes that voters care about their (post-tax and transfer) income and about government policy along a non-economic dimension such as race or religion.[2] In the case of two-party competition, Roemer shows that the existence of a second, non-economic policy dimension may reduce the equilibrium level of redistribution via a "policy-bundling effect." For example, the election may pit a party that favors redistribution and non-economic support for minorities against a party opposed to both. A low-income, white voter who think that minorities

---

[2] Roemer and Lee (2004) add an assumption that voters also altruistically care about aggregate inequality, with racially conservative voters attaching less weight to equality than racially liberal voters.

get more than they deserve may prefer a party that opposes redistribution but matches the voters' racial views, depending on the relative weights of the two dimensions in the voter's preferences.

Our approach differs from Roemer's in several ways. First, as mentioned above, we assume that voters have identical, self-interested preferences. Second, we focus on a different mechanism linking racial cleavages and redistributive politics. The political side of our model consists of a model of legislative politics rather than electoral competition. In our framework, the policy-bundling effect that drives Roemer's results is absent since all distinct combinations of derived preferences over redistributive taxation and affirmative action may be represented in the legislature. And a substantive argument for the legislative bargaining model is that, as we consider in more detail later (Section 5), it captures the political strategies that established affirmative action at the Federal level during the first two years of the Nixon administration. Affirmative action had a number of advantages for the Nixon administration, the most important of which, according to insider accounts, was that the plan drove a wedge between two parts of the Democratic electoral coalition, blacks and the (almost exclusively white) unions.[3] And although there were only thirteen black representatives in the House in 1969, Congressional support for African-American interests was more widespread. Thus our focus is on the trade-off between redistribution by income and by race that occurs through a process of legislative bargaining in which both white and black representatives are critical players.

The importance of developing a model such as the one we outline below is to gain the ability to address theoretically a variety of questions concerning redistributive politics in a racially or ethnically divided society that cannot be addressed with existing models. Does the presence of policies that redistribute according to ascriptive characteristics reduce support for redistribution according to income even with race-blind preferences? Who benefits and who loses when the policy space is expanded to include policies that redistribute by ascriptive traits? What are the net redistributive implications of using both racial and fiscal, rather than only fiscal, policies? How do the policies selected in equilibrium change as the distributions of income within the majority and minority social groups become more similar?

---

[3] See Skrentny (1996) or Anderson (2004).

In addition to a making a claim about how redistribution by race can reduce redistribution by income, we believe that our model captures the essence of the politics of affirmative action at the federal level with regard to the employment of minorities in jobs in the middle of the wage scale, a policy that reached its peak during the Nixon administration and has never been abandoned (Anderson, 2004). Affirmative action with respect to higher education, which concerns access to jobs at the top of the wage scale, has a different set of potential beneficiaries and losers and hence a different political dynamic; the model below is not well-suited to address this aspect of contemporary affirmative action policy.[4] We discuss briefly the federal policy of affirmative action after developing our model of the economy and the political equilibrium.

2. The Economy

In the standard competitive model of the labor market with complete contracts, affirmative action is pointless. If each worker receives a wage that is just equal to his or her best alternative, there is nothing to be gained from special treatment in hiring. For affirmative action to be of interest, some jobs must yield rents to those holding those jobs. There are a variety of reasons why some jobs might offer a premium above the competitive wage level, from the ability of unions to obtain higher wages via collective bargaining to employers' willingness to pay higher wages to reduce shirking. In this paper, we employ a model of the labor market in which the source of inefficiency is the holdup problem, whereby the workers obtain a share of the return on employers' investments via wage bargaining that occurs after the investment costs are sunk. We emphasize that we do not intend this paper to be a contribution to the large literature on the holdup problem and how it might be overcome.[5] The holdup model simply provides a convenient economic framework in which affirmative action policies can play a role. Other models that generate employment rents in the labor market, such as efficiency wage models, would yield similar results concerning the political equilibrium.

---

[4] See Chan and Eyster (2002) for a model of political conflict over affirmative action with regard to higher education.

[5] Grout (1984) was the first to discuss the hold-up problem in the context of the labor market, as far as we know. For more recent studies of the hold-up problem applied to the labor market, see MacLeod and Malcomson (1993), Agell and Lommerud (1997), Acemoglu and Shimer (1999) and Acemoglu (2001) among others.

2.1. Demographics and the Labor Market

We consider a large static economy with a continuum of individuals, each of whom belongs to one of two ascriptively distinct groups, whites (W) and blacks (B); let $p < 1/2$ denote the share of blacks in the population, the minority group. Individuals have one of two levels of human capital, hereafter called 'skill', $H \in \{0, h\}$, where $H = h > 0$ denotes a skilled individual, or worker, and $H = 0$ denotes an unskilled worker. Let θ_i be the share of skilled workers in group $i = W, B$ and let θ be the share of such workers in the population as a whole, $\theta = [p\theta_B + (1-p)\theta_W]$. A key assumption is that blacks are disadvantaged in the labor market through a historical racial difference in average human capital due to past discrimination; thus, $\theta_B < \theta_W$.

There is a finite number of competitive firms, each producing a homogenous consumption good and employing a continuum of workers, with firms and workers being randomly matched. We focus throughout on a representative match between a firm and a member of each of the four possible types (by group and skill) of individual.

Firms offer two types of job j, good jobs and bad jobs. All workers are equally productive in bad jobs, regardless of their skill. A worker's productivity in a good job at a given firm, however, depends both on the worker's skill and on the realization of an idiosyncratic, match-specific random variable, $x \in R$. Thus different workers with a common skill level may exhibit varying productivities at any given firm. Specifically, let $y(H, j, x)$ be the marginal product of a representative worker with skill H in job j at a given firm with realized match-specific variable x; then

$$y(H, j, x) = \begin{cases} 0 & \text{if } j = \text{bad} \\ H + x & \text{if } j = \text{good}, \end{cases}$$

where the zero marginal productivity in a bad job is a normalization. On average, skilled workers are more productive in good jobs than unskilled workers, but the most productive unskilled worker may be more productive in a good job than the least productive skilled worker. Assume x is distributed according to a differentiable and strictly increasing cdf $F(x)$ having full support on R and continuous density $f(x)$. Assume further that F exhibits a strictly increasing hazard rate:

$$\frac{f(x)}{1 - F(x)} \text{ is strictly increasing in } x, \text{ all } x \in R.$$

In effect, the assumption means that the probability density of any individual being more productive at any alternative firm, conditional on realizing a match x, is falling with x.

Bad jobs are costless to create and the labor market for such jobs is presumed competitive: firms make zero profit from workers in bad jobs and these workers earn their marginal product (zero). The same is not true, however, of workers in good jobs. We assume that a firm can create a good job only at cost $q > 0$ and the worker's wage is determined through bargaining with the firm. Furthermore, we suppose the firm's decision on whether to invest in a good job for a particular worker is made after observing the worker's productivity at the firm, but before bargaining over the worker's wage begins. Assume the outcome of such bargaining is defined by the generalized Nash bargaining solution.

Identifying the bargaining solution requires identifying the value of the worker's outside option. Assume the consequence of failing to agree in wage negotiations is that the worker obtains a bad job and the good job remains vacant. Let $b \geq 0$ denote the value of a bad job (that b might be strictly positive is justified below). Then, conditional on the firm having invested in creating a good job, the worker's gain from reaching agreement on wage w is $[w - b]$ and the firm's gain from the agreement is $[y - w]$. Hence, writing $w(y, b)$ for the wage of a worker in a good job with realized productivity y and outside option value b, we have

$$w(y, b) = \mathrm{argmax}(y - w)^{1-\beta}(w - b)^{\beta}$$
$$= \beta y + (1 - \beta)b \qquad (1)$$

where $\beta \in (0, 1)$ is the worker's bargaining power, assumed constant across all workers with an option on a good job, irrespective of their particular productivities. The corresponding profit for the firm from hiring a worker in a type j job, therefore, is given by

$$\pi_j(y, b) = \begin{cases} 0 & \text{if } j = \text{bad} \\ -q & \text{if } j = \text{good and the job remains vacant.} \\ y - w(y, b) - q & \text{if } j = \text{good and the worker is hired} \end{cases}$$

Substituting for $w(y, b)$ gives

$$\pi(y, b) = (1 - \beta)(y - b) - q \qquad (2)$$

as the profit earned from the creation of a good job if the worker is hired (and we suppress the subscript j on $\pi(y, b)$).

In the absence of any affirmative action policy, firms treat white and black workers identically, creating a good job for a worker with productivity $y = H + x$ if and only if it is profitable to do so; that is, if and only if $\pi(y, b) \geq 0$ or, equivalently,

$$H + x \geq \bar{y}(b) \equiv \frac{q}{1 - \beta} + b. \tag{3}$$

The fraction of group $i = W, B$ with good jobs when there exists no formal affirmative action policy, denoted $\sigma_i(\phi, b)$, is given by

$$\sigma_i(\phi, b) = [1 - G_i(\bar{y}(b))]$$

where $G_i(y) \equiv \theta_i F(y - b) + (1 - \theta_i)F(y)$ is the fraction of group i with productivity less than y. Hence, the share of good jobs held by minority workers in the absence of affirmative action, $\alpha_\phi(b)$, is

$$\alpha_\phi(b) = \frac{p\sigma_B(\phi, b)}{p\sigma_B(\phi, b) + (1 - p)\sigma_W(\phi, b)}.$$

By assumption, $\theta_B < \theta_W$ so $G_B(\bar{y}(b)) > G_W(\bar{y}(b))$ and, consequently, $\sigma_B(\phi, b) < \sigma_W(\phi, b)$. Therefore, lower average skill for the minority group implies the share of good jobs held by minority workers is less than the share of minority workers in the work force, $\alpha_\phi(b) < p$.

Because the cost of creating a good job is a sunk cost to the employer, there are match-specific rents over which employers and the prospective employees bargain. And since workers capture a share of the rents (that is, $\beta > 0$), the number of good jobs created is less than the number that maximizes the joint income of employers and workers.[6] The additional output obtained from a marginal increase in the number of good jobs exceeds the cost of job creation: $\beta > 0$ implies $\bar{y}(b) > q$. Moreover, workers with $y = \bar{y}(b)$ obtain a discrete jump in pay of $w(\bar{y}(b), b) - b = [q\beta/(1 - \beta)]$ in moving from a bad job to a good job, even though employers are indifferent between creating a good job or not when $y = \bar{y}(b)$. Thus, workers with

---

[6] In the context of our model, it is reasonable to ask why employers don't insist on negotiating the wage before investing in the creation of a good job, thereby avoiding the holdup problem. The assumption that wage bargaining takes place after the employer's investment is sunk can be seen as a reduced form version of a model where investments last for two or more periods. When investments last for more than one period, it is easy to show that workers receive rents and the number of good jobs is inefficiently low unless either (i) the initial wage contract covers the lifespan of the investment or (ii) employers can turn workers into co-investors by charging workers an upfront fee before investing in a good job.

David Austen-Smith and Michael Wallerstein

productivity slightly below $\bar{y}(b)$ would gain from a policy that forces firms to create good jobs for them.

2.2. Affirmative Action and Insurance

There are two types of policy in the society: social insurance and affirmative action. The social insurance policy provides a uniform transfer payment, $b \geq 0$ to all workers with bad jobs, financed by a budget-balancing flat tax $t \in [0, 1]$ on wages and welfare benefits (the assumption that benefits are taxed is purely for convenience; no result to follow depends upon it). Since workers with bad jobs receive zero wages, this benefit b defines the value of holding such a job. Affirmative action is modeled as a mandatory lower bound, $\alpha \in [0, p]$, on the proportion of good jobs filled by minority workers in any firm. If $\alpha \in [0, \alpha_\phi(b)]$ for any b, then the affirmative action policy is not binding; at the other extreme, if $\alpha = p$ the affirmative action policy requires firms to equalize the fraction of workers with good jobs in the two social groups.[7]

Typically, we expect $\alpha > \alpha_\phi(b)$ for any social insurance benefit b. In this case, affirmative action is binding and firms cannot use the same productivity threshold for both black and white workers when deciding whether or not to create a good job. Recall that each employer is large, in the sense of being randomly matched with a continuum of workers. Then a firm's optimal strategy with affirmative action policy α and benefit level b is to choose thresholds y_B and y_W to maximize expected profits

$$\max_{y_B, y_W} E[\pi \mid \alpha, b] = p \int_{y_B}^{\infty} \pi(y, b) \mathrm{d}G_B(y) + (1 - p) \int_{y_W}^{\infty} \pi(y, b) \mathrm{d}G_W(y)$$

subject to the constraint that

$$\frac{p\sigma_B(\alpha, b)}{p\sigma_B(\alpha, b) + (1 - p)\sigma_W(\alpha, b)} \geq \alpha \tag{4}$$

[7] Holzer and Neumark (2000) observe that the enforcement of equal opportunity legislation has lead to affirmative action targets in practice, $\alpha > \alpha_\phi$. Since the underrepresentation of minorities in broad occupational categories is considered to constitute evidence of discrimination if it falls below numerical yardsticks set by the Equal Employment Opportunity Commission, firms that want to avoid discrimination claims would treat the EEOC yardsticks as constraints. With respect to the upper-bound, $\alpha \leq p$, US courts have struck down affirmative action programs when the minority share of good jobs exceeded the minority share of the population at large: *Economist*, 10/4/03–10/10/03, p. 30.

328

Redistribution and Affirmative Action

where $\sigma_i(\alpha, b)$ denotes the share of group i workers with good jobs in the presence of an affirmative action policy α. Let $y_B(\alpha, b)$ and $y_W(\alpha, b)$ solve this problem; then all group i workers with $y \geq y_i(\alpha, b)$ are offered good jobs.

When the constraint (4) is binding, the first-order condition for a maximum can be written as two equations. The first equation replaces Eq. (3):

$$\alpha y_B(\alpha, b) + (1 - \alpha)y_W(\alpha, b) = \overline{y}(b) \tag{5}$$

The second equation is simply the constraint, Eq. (4), written as an equality. When the constraint is not binding, that is, when $\alpha \leq \alpha_\phi(b)$ for any benefit level $b \geq 0$, Eq. (5) reduces to expression (3) with $y_B(\alpha, b) = y_W(\alpha, b) = \overline{y}(b)$ and the share of good jobs allocated to blacks being the *laissez faire* level, $\alpha_\phi(b)$. Hereafter, where there is no ambiguity, the arguments of $y_i(\alpha, b)$ and $\sigma_i(\alpha, b)$ are suppressed and we simply write y_i, σ_i, etc.

Finally, it is useful to write the balanced budget constraint for financing the social insurance policy explicitly as

$$(1 - \sigma)(1 - t)b = tE[w \mid \alpha, b], \tag{6}$$

where $\sigma \equiv p\sigma_B + (1 - p)\sigma_W$ is the share of the population with a good job (so receiving no benefit) and, from Eq. (1),

$$E[w \mid \alpha, b] = \beta \left[p \int_{y_B} y \, dG_B(y) + (1 - p) \int_{y_W} y \, dG_W(y) \right] + (1 - \beta)\sigma b \tag{7}$$

is the average wage at (α, b).

The policies (α, b) are fixed at the opening of the labor market. In the next section we identify equilibrium in the labor market conditional on these policies, with the description of exactly how the two policies are chosen deferred to a later section.

2.3. Labor Market Equilibrium

Conditional on policy (α, b) and on wages in good jobs being defined by Eq. (1), an equilibrium in the labor market is a triple (y_B, y_W, t) that solves the system of three equations, Eqs. (4) (written as an equality), (5), and

(6).[8] Existence of a unique labor market equilibrium for any policy (α, b), ensuring that individuals' induced preferences over policies are well defined, and two salient facts regarding the equilibrium, are established in Lemma 1. Proofs for all lemmas and propositions are collected in an Appendix.

Lemma 1.

(1) There exists a unique labor market equilibrium associated with every policy (α, b).

(2) If $\alpha > \alpha_\phi(b)$ then $y_W(\alpha, b) > \bar{y}(b) > y_B(\alpha, b)$.

(3) In equilibrium, $\alpha_\phi(b)$ is strictly decreasing in b.

Lemma 1 is fairly self-explanatory. If the affirmative constraint binds, then profit-maximizing firms adjust their hiring policy by setting distinct thresholds for creating good jobs for blacks and for whites; the threshold for blacks being necessarily lower than that for whites, with the weighted average of the two being exactly the laissez faire threshold, $\bar{y}(b)$. And the laissez faire share of good jobs allocated to blacks, $\alpha_\phi(b)$, is decreasing in b because higher benefit levels reduce the incentive of employers to create jobs, thus raising the threshold $\bar{y}(b)$, which affects blacks proportionately more than whites because of the differential distributions of human capital across the two groups. In other words, if affirmative action were not an available policy instrument, successful demands for higher levels of benefit to address income inequality result in a reduction in the share of higher paying jobs allocated to the minority group.

The next result, Lemma 2, describes some useful comparative static properties of policy change.

Lemma 2.

(1) $\partial y_W(\alpha, b)/\partial \alpha > 0$ and, for all $b \geq 0$, $\lim_{\alpha \downarrow \alpha_\phi(b)} \partial y_B(\alpha, b)/\partial \alpha < 0$;

(2) $\partial y_W(\alpha, b)/\partial b > 0$; $\partial y_B(\alpha, b)/\partial b > 0$;

(3) $\partial t(\alpha, b)/\partial b > 0$;

(4) $\lim_{\alpha \downarrow \alpha_\phi(b)} \partial E[w + \pi \mid \alpha, b]/\partial \alpha > 0$;

(5) $\lim_{\alpha \downarrow \alpha_\phi(b)} \partial t(\alpha, b)/\partial \alpha \leq 0$ with strict inequality if and only if $b > 0$.

The first three claims of Lemma 2 are intuitive. Lemma 2(1) says that affirmative action always induces firms to raise the threshold for hiring white

---

[8] As we show below, there is a monotonic relationship between b and t. Therefore, it makes no difference whether voters vote over t (the conventional approach) or over b. In our model, the mathematics is simplified by letting b be the policy instrument.

workers and, at least for binding policies α close to the laissez faire level $\alpha_\phi(b)$, to lower the threshold for hiring minority workers.[9] For sufficiently onerous affirmative action mandates relative to the laissez faire level, and depending on details of the distribution function F, marginal increases in α may result in increases in the thresholds for both whites and blacks as firms reduce the overall level of good jobs in the economy. On the other hand, Lemma 2(2) states that both of these thresholds are strictly increasing functions of the benefit for any affirmative action policy α: an increase in benefits b raises the opportunity cost of a good job and thus the threat point for wage bargaining. As a result, profits fall and, as reported in Lemma 1, employers compensate by creating good jobs only for more productive workers which induces a fall in the laissez faire share of good jobs held by blacks. And Lemma 2(3) confirms that the tax rate is a strictly increasing function of the benefit that must be financed.

An increase in the benefit increases redistribution in three ways. First, the tax and benefit redistributes ex post from workers in good jobs, who pay taxes but don't receive the benefit, to workers in bad jobs. Second, the tax and benefit redistributes ex ante from skilled workers who are likely to obtain good jobs to unskilled workers who are less likely to obtain good jobs. Third, fiscal policy redistributes income from employers to employees. Consequently, while benefit increases may raise the aggregate income received by workers provided the benefit is not too large, they surely reduce aggregate output. On the other hand, under the assumption that the distribution of match-specific productivities F exhibits a strictly increasing hazard rate, affirmative action policies in the neighborhood of the laissez faire level enhance aggregate output (Lemma 2(4)) and permit a lower tax-rate for any positive level of benefits (Lemma 2(5)). In view of Lemma 2(1), when $\alpha \approx \alpha_\phi(b)$ the increase in the number of good jobs filled by black workers exceeds the decline in the number of good jobs filled by white workers and, since white workers are being replaced by black workers with similar levels of productivity at $\alpha \approx \alpha_\phi(b)$, aggregate output increases. Aggregate outcome may be reduced, however, with a sufficiently high affirmative action target as the acceptance thresholds y_W and y_B move further apart.

We now turn to consider the political choice of the two policy instruments.

[9] Holzer and Neumark (2000) report lower employment of white males (by 10–15%) and the employment of minorities with lower qualifications (as defined by test scores or education) in establishments with affirmative action hiring policies.

3. Induced Policy Preferences

A policy is a pair $(\alpha, b) \in \mathbf{P} \equiv [0, p] \times [0, \infty)$. The policy is chosen prior to a workers' knowledge of x or of whether he or she will be offered a good job. In evaluating policy, however, individuals are assumed to anticipate correctly the consequences of their choice. Individual preferences over policy are induced by an understanding of the resultant labor market equilibrium: a policy (α, b) is preferred by some individuals to an alternative policy (α', b') if and only if the individual's expected equilibrium consumption level under (α, b) is greater than that under (α', b'). Formally, let $c_{Hi}(\alpha, b)$ denote the expected consumption of an individual with skill $H \in \{0, h\}$ in group $i \in \{B, W\}$ at policy (α, b):

$$c_{Hi}(\alpha, b) = (1 - t)\left\{ F(y_i - H)b + \int_{y_i - H}^{\infty} w(H + x, b)\mathrm{d}F(x) \right\}, \qquad (8)$$

where y_i and t are defined by the labor market equilibrium at (α, b). The first term between the braces is the individual's income conditional on a bad job, and the second term is her expected income conditional on receiving a good job.

Although individuals' preferences are linear in consumption, Lemma 2 makes clear that consumption is nonlinear in policy. This greatly complicates explicit analysis. However, as $c_{Hi}(\alpha, b)$ is continuous on $\mathbf{P}$ and there is no loss of generality in assuming the maximal admissible benefit level is finite, there exists a global maximum for each individual type (H, i). And if this maximum is not a boundary point then it is generically unique; if the maximum is a point (α^*, b^*) with $\alpha^* \leq \alpha_\phi(b^*)$, however, definition of $\alpha_\phi(b^*)$ as the laissez faire share of good jobs going to blacks at the benefit level b implies that the individual's expected consumption is constant for all policies (α, b^*) such that $\alpha \leq \alpha_\phi(b^*)$. In this case, we simply report the most preferred policy as $(\alpha_\phi(b^*), b^*)$.

For each (H, i), let $(\alpha_{Hi}^*, b_{Hi}^*) \in \mathbf{P}$ denote the (H, i) type's most preferred policy pair. We are interested in identifying the relative locations of the ideal points across skill level and race. Because of the nonlinearities inherent in expected payoffs, additional restrictions on the parameters of the model are required to make some of the relevant comparisons. Essentially, these restrictions ensure that fiscal policy is politically salient across low and high types of worker, and that affirmative action policy is politically salient across blacks and whites. If the relative expected return from a good rather than a bad job is too small (q or β too low) or if there is insufficient distinction between high and low skill types (b too small), then there is too little variation in policy preferences for policy to matter differentially across types. The restrictions, therefore, are to guarantee that good jobs are sufficiently attractive to induce variation in ex ante policy preferences and so ensure that the policy choice problem is not trivial.

Lemma 3. *There exists a finite skill level $\overline{b} > 0$ and cost of good job creation $\overline{q} > 0$ such that $b \geq \overline{b}$ and $q \geq \overline{q}$ imply:*

(1) $[\alpha_{bB}^* > \alpha_\phi(0), b_{bB}^* = 0]; [\alpha_{0B}^* > \alpha_\phi(b_{0B}^*), b_{0B}^* > 0]$.
(2) $[\alpha_{bw}^* = \alpha_\phi(0), b_{bw}^* = 0]; [\alpha_{0W}^* = \alpha_\phi(b_{0W}^*), b_{0W}^* > 0]$.

Furthermore, firms' profits are maximal at $(\alpha_\phi(0), 0)$.

In sum, Lemma 3 says that blacks prefer higher levels of affirmative action to whites, and low skill types prefer more fiscal redistribution than high skill types. And it is worth noting here that, while blacks always prefer some affirmative action policy to the laissez faire level at any benefit level, in general whites might prefer no affirmative action or some modicum thereof. Unlike blacks, whites face a tradeoff: at any laissez faire level $\alpha_\phi(b)$ with $b > 0$, whites benefit from the efficiency gains induced by small levels of affirmative action (Lemma 2(5)) but are hurt by the distributional losses that such action implies for the majority group (Lemma 2(1)). So it is possible that, at least for some strictly positive benefit levels and a sufficiently small difference between high and low skill levels, the efficiency gains dominate the distributional losses. However, for sufficiently high skill level b and cost of job creation q, the distributional costs dominate the efficiency gains. Hereafter, we assume $b \geq \overline{b}$ and $q \geq \overline{q}$ as required for Lemma 3.

4. Legislative Policy Choice

We assume that legislators, when selecting between two alternatives, cast their ballot for the party that promises to implement the policy that generates the higher expected post-tax, post-transfer income for their constituents.

David Austen-Smith and Michael Wallerstein

A complete model of the political process would include (at least) two stages. The first stage involves voters' choice of representatives while the second stage consists of representatives' choice of policy. In this paper we focus exclusively on the legislative policy decision stage. With regard to voters' choice, we simply assume the existence of blocs of representatives or parties, each of whom represents a distinct constituency. While a variety of divisions of the legislature might be considered, here we restrict our analysis to the case in which the legislature is divided into three groups: legislators who represent high skill white workers ($\mathcal{H}$), legislators who represent low skill white workers ($\mathcal{L}$), and legislators who represent black workers ($\mathcal{B}$).

Two comments on this choice of partition are worth making explicit. First, firms are not directly represented which fits with the secondary role of employers in the political conflict over affirmative action at the Federal level, as we discuss in Section 5 below. Second, unlike white workers, we presume all black workers are represented by the same bloc of legislators, $\mathcal{B}$. In part this assumption is one of convenience; but more importantly it also reflects the empirical reality that while majority group parties have a history of development, with core constituents that are often separated by economic interests, the explicit representation of minority groups is a relatively recent phenomenon and as such, is better approximated as a single bloc.

For purposes of exposition, we refer to the three representative blocs of legislators as "parties", although we emphasize that a critical feature of such parties for the model is as coherent voting blocs. Each party is assumed to act in a unified manner to maximize the welfare of its constituents. Because the policy is chosen before workers know what job they will be offered, all white workers of a given skill are identical ex ante. Therefore, the objective functions for $\mathcal{H}$ and $\mathcal{L}$, respectively, are $u_\mathcal{H} = c_{hW}(.)$ and $u_\mathcal{L} = c_{0W}(.)$. Minority voters, however, include both high and low skill workers. In this case, we assume the legislative group maximizes a weighted average of the consumption of its two types of constituents: $u_B = \lambda c_{hB}(\cdot) + (1 - \lambda)c_{0B}(.)$ for some $\lambda \in [0, 1]$. The weight λ is a measure of the extent to which the minority party is concerned with high or low skilled minority workers and we presume throughout that λ is not so high that low skill blacks have no incentive to remain in a party with high skill blacks (we pursue this issue a little further in the comparative statics section below). Let $I_\mathcal{H} = (\alpha_H^*, b_H^*) \equiv I_{bW}$ and $I_\mathcal{L} = (\alpha_\mathcal{L}^*, b_\mathcal{L}^*) \equiv I_{0W}$ be the most preferred policy points for $\mathcal{H}$ and $\mathcal{L}$,

334

respectively, and let $I_B = (\alpha_B^*, b_B^*) \equiv \operatorname{argmax} u_B$ be the most preferred policy point for party B.

4.1. Bargaining Equilibrium

To avoid a trivial solution to policy conflict, we assume that no single group has a majority of seats in the legislature. If, for instance, the size or weight of each legislative bloc reflects the relative size of each bloc's constituents, then the weights of parties B, $\mathcal{H}$ and $\mathcal{L}$ respectively are $p < 1/2$, $(1 - p)\theta_W < 1/2$ and $(1 - p)(1 - \theta_W) < 1/2$. Thus any two of the three parties constitutes a majority. It is not hard to check that, as is usually the case with multidimensional policy spaces, the majority core is (generically) empty. By Lemma 3, if b_{0i}^* each i, the set of Pareto efficient policies in $\mathbf{P}$ for the three parties is (generically) two-dimensional and there is no majority core in $\mathbf{P}$ (Schofield, 1984). If there is a core, it is at the low whites' ideal point, but as this is a knife-edge possibility at best, we ignore it hereafter.

Because there is generally no core policy, we model the policy process as a legislative bargaining game. Specifically, we apply the generalized version of the Baron and Ferejohn (1989) legislative bargaining model due to Banks and Duggan (2006). In its simplest form, each party or bloc is associated with a probability of being selected to make a policy proposal (α, b) to the legislature in any period. If one (or both) of the non-proposing blocs accepts the proposal in some period then the proposed policy is implemented and bargaining ends; otherwise the process moves to the next decision period, a new proposer is randomly selected and the sequence repeats until some proposal is accepted.

The solution concept is a stationary subgame perfect Nash equilibrium with no-delay (hereafter, simply *equilibrium*). An equilibrium consists of a (possibly degenerate) probability distribution ζ_j over a (possibly infinite) set of policies $P_j \subseteq \mathbf{P}$ that party j proposes whenever j is recognized to make a proposal, and an acceptance set, $A_j \subseteq \mathbf{P}$ that specifies the set of proposals by others that party j supports; along the equilibrium path, the first party to be recognized offers its best proposal from among the set of proposals that will be accepted and the game ends. Let v_j be j's expected payoff at the beginning of the game. By stationarity, v_j is also j's continuation value or its expected payoff after a proposal has been rejected. Finally, let $\rho_j \in (0, 1)$ be party j's probability of being recognized to make a proposal. Then an equilibrium consists of a set of policy proposals and acceptance set for each

David Austen-Smith and Michael Wallerstein

$j = \mathcal{H}, \mathcal{L}, \mathcal{B}$ that satisfy the following conditions:

$$
P_j \subseteq \begin{cases} \operatorname{argmax}\{u_j(\alpha, b \mid (\alpha, b) \in (A_k \cup A_t)\} \text{ if } \sup[u_j(\alpha, b) \; : \\ \qquad\qquad\qquad\qquad\qquad\qquad\qquad (\alpha, b) \in (A_k \cup A_t)] \geq v_j, \\ \mathbf{P} \backslash (A_k \cup A_l) \text{ otherwise} \end{cases}
$$

$$
A_j = \{(\alpha, b) \mid u_j(\alpha, b) \geq v_j\}
$$

$$
v_j = \sum_{k=\mathcal{H}, \mathcal{L}, \mathcal{B}} \rho_k \left[\int_{p_k} u_j(\alpha, b) \mathrm{d}\zeta_k \right]
$$

The first condition states that any policy a party j proposes must yield at least its constituents' continuation value v_j from having the policy rejected: either there is such a policy within the acceptance set of some party $k \neq j$ that weakly improve on v_j (in which case the second condition implies that such a proposal must be acceptable to j itself), or exactly the value v_j is achieved by proposing a policy that is sure to be rejected. The second condition states that each party accepts any proposal that provides a higher or equal payoff than the party's continuation value. The third condition states that in equilibrium the continuation value equals the expected value of the game.

The most general (no-delay) equilibrium existence result for this game (at least, as far as we know) is due to Banks and Duggan (2006, Theorem 1). However, their theorem assumes utilities are concave on the policy space. Unfortunately, concavity is not a general property of induced preferences here.[10] The difficulty introduced by nonconcave utilities is essentially technical: the exclusive role of concavity for ensuring equilibrium existence is to ensure the existence of nonempty acceptance sets A_j. So, rather than attempt to finesse complications with equilibrium existence due to nonconvexities in parties' induced preferences, we simply assume in what follows that an equilibrium exists. And to show that the equilibrium concept is not vacuous in this regard, we later present a nonpathological example in which

[10] The absence of concavity is not an artifact of the model per se. A high benefit reduces the importance of affirmative action, since the difference in consumption between workers in good and bad jobs declines as the benefit (and the tax rate) increases. Conversely, the lower the benefit, the greater the impact of affirmative action policies on workers' expected after-tax and transfer income. Consequently, the marginal rate of substitution between affirmative action and welfare benefit can be increasing and preferences over policies nonconcave over some regions of the policy space.

336

all parties' induced preferences are strictly concave on **P** and calculate the legislative bargaining equilibrium.

Taking the existence of equilibrium (along with the sufficient conditions used for Lemma 3) as given, the impact of a second dimension of conflict over affirmative action on the legislative support for fiscal redistribution is summarized in our first proposition regarding equilibrium outcomes.

Proposition 1. *The expected level of fiscal redistribution when affirmative action is a policy variable is less than that most preferred by a majority of individuals when affirmative action is not a policy variable.*

The addition of a racial or ethnic dimension of redistribution reduces the amount of redistribution according to income, even when (i) the racial minority is poorer than the majority on average and (ii) the legislators who represent the minority group exclusively advance the interests of the less educated members of the minority group as in our example below. Although the low-type black might prefer an even greater b than low-type whites in the absence of affirmative action, blacks and high whites now have the potential to lower the tax rate and raise affirmative action targets in a way that makes both better off. The possibility of splitting the coalition between low-type whites and blacks is sufficient to reduce the average transfer payment and to increase the average affirmative action target in equilibrium.[11]

To see the intuition for Proposition 1, suppose first that affirmative action is not an available policy instrument. Then it is easy to check that all low skill workers share the same ideal benefit level, defined by the low skill white's most preferred benefit level, b^*_{0W}. Furthermore, b^*_{0W} is strictly greater than the high skill workers' most preferred level and low skill workers constitute a strict majority of the population. Therefore b^*_{0W} is a majority core allocation and this uniquely defines the equilibrium decision on social insurance policy.[12] Given the assumption of only two skill levels in the economy, the proposition is then immediate if, when affirmative action is an available policy instrument, the most preferred benefit level for the black party, b^*_B, is no greater than that for low skill whites, i.e. if $b^*_B \leq b^*_{0W} = b^*_L$. Now suppose that the most preferred benefits level for the black party when affirmative

---

[11] See Levy (2004) for a model that captures the same phenomenon of the rich reducing their tax bill by playing off divisions among poor voters with regard to paying for school.

[12] Strictly speaking, if parties are impatient and increasingly discount payoffs with the time taken to reach a legislative decision, the final outcome can be slightly less than b^*_{0W} depending on which party makes the first proposal.

action is an available policy is strictly greater than that for low skill whites, i.e. if $b_B^* > b_L^*$. Then it is a priori possible for the equilibrium benefit level to rise relative to the level when affirmative action is unavailable. But any proposal for such an outcome can be surely blocked by the high white party $\mathcal{H}$ proposing the low white party's ideal point, (α_L^*, b_L^*). It follows that no equilibrium policy pair can have a benefit level (and thus a tax rate) higher than $b_L^* = b_{0W}^*$.

A limitation of the result is that the argument uses the assumption of only two skill levels in the economy. If there were a middle skill level such that, conditional on affirmative action being unavailable, individuals with this level of human capital prefer a benefits level between those most preferred by the high and the low skill workers, then the proposition is not so transparent. When the affirmative action policy is not available, the ideal level of fiscal redistribution for the middle skilled workers is the core allocation and the unique bargaining outcome. As in the two-skills model, making affirmative action policy available admits a richer set of legislative coalitions and, in principle, there is scope for a coalition between low skill white workers and the black party to implement higher benefits in exchange for high levels of affirmative action. Whether or not such an outcome is sustainable in equilibrium, however, depends more subtly on the possible counter-coalitions in the legislature, as well as on details of the various individuals' induced preferences over the policy space. Nevertheless, the logic of the proposition, that being able to redistribute income through affecting job prospects induces a legislative substitution away from a reliance on redistribution through social insurance, seems compelling.

The second proposition summarizes the impact of adding a second dimension of redistributive conflict on the expected post-tax, post-transfer equilibrium income of each group of voters.

Proposition 2. *The possibility of redistribution through affirmative action (1) raises the expected income of both high whites and of blacks as a group (where the incomes of high- and low-type blacks are aggregated with weights $\lambda \geq 0$ and $(1 - \lambda)$ respectively), and (2) lowers the expected income of low whites.*

In expected value, the high-type whites gain more from a low tax and benefit level than they lose from a higher affirmative action target while blacks, in aggregate, gain more from the affirmative action target than they

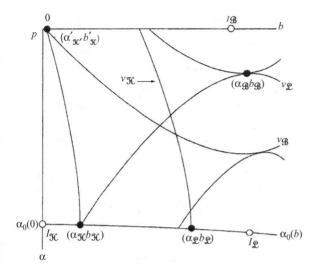

Figure 1 Legislative bargaining equilibrium.

lose from a lower benefit. The big losers, in comparison to the political equilibrium in the absence of affirmative action, are the low-type whites who are made worse off by both affirmative action and lower benefits.

Propositions 1 and 2 can be illustrated with the following example, that also serves to show the existence of bargaining equilibria here. It is worth observing that the example is similar to the equilibria generated by other parameterizations. Existence is not a knife-edge property of the model. In the case of a uniform distribution, the concavity property sufficient for equilibrium existence is satisfied for parameter values that cover most (but not all) of the feasible parameter space. While it is difficult to provide general conditions for the strict concavity of legislators' induced preferences, the central features of the equilibrium illustrated in the example are general characteristics of all equilibria of the legislative bargaining model.

Example 1. Assume x is uniformly distributed over the interval $[0, 1]$, $q = b = 1/4, \beta = 1/2, p = 1/3, \theta_B = 1/5$ and $\theta_W = 1/2$. These parameter values imply that 80% of minority workers and half of the majority workers are low skill and that the three groups are equal in size. We assume initially that the black party represents the 80% of minority voters with low skills, or $\lambda = 0$. Fig. 1 illustrates the preferences of the three parties over welfare benefits and affirmative action and the equilibrium of the legislative bargaining

David Austen-Smith and Michael Wallerstein

game. The western and northern borders of the Pareto set are given by
$b = 0$ and $\alpha = p$ respectively. The southern border is given by the function $\alpha_\phi(b)$ which represents the share of good jobs that the minority would
receive without affirmative action. Note that $\alpha_\phi(b)$ declines as b increases
(see Lemma 1). The ideal points of the three groups, $\mathcal{H}$, $\mathcal{L}$, $\mathcal{B}$ are denoted
$I_\mathcal{H}$, $I_\mathcal{L}$ and $I_\mathcal{B}$ respectively. The figure illustrates the unique equilibrium for
the case in which each group is recognized with equal probability: $\rho_j = 1/3$,
all j. If recognized, the high-type whites propose $(\alpha_\mathcal{H}, b_\mathcal{H})$ with probability (0.61) and receive the support of the low-type whites. With probability
(0.39), the high-type whites propose $(\alpha'_\mathcal{H}, b'_\mathcal{L})$ and receive the support of the
black legislators. The low-type whites, if recognized, propose $(\alpha_\mathcal{L}, b_\mathcal{L})$ with
probability one and win the support of the black legislators. Finally, black
legislators propose $(\alpha_\mathcal{B}, b_\mathcal{B})$ with probability one if recognized and win the
support of high-type whites.

Table 1 records some numerical details of the equilibrium in this example.
For comparative purposes, Table 1 also shows the expected value of the
benefit, the expected tax rate, and the expected share of good jobs held
by minorities associated with the legislative equilibrium. When there is
no racial divide, political conflict occurs over the single dimension of the
tax rate. Since, in the example, $(1 - \theta_B)p + (1 - \theta_W)(1 - p) = 3/5$ of the
population share the ideal point of poorly educated whites, the ideal point
of the poorly educated majority is a core point. Finally, we report the share
of goods jobs held by minorities for the laissez faire policy of $\alpha = \alpha_\phi(0)$ and
$b = 0$.

Using the equilibrium proposals reported in Table 1, the expected net
percentage gain in consumption from the equilibrium outcome when affirmative action is a policy variable relative to when it is not can be calculated.
Doing this yields, as predicted by Proposition 2, that the expected consumption (1) of high whites *increases* by 2.8%; (2) of low whites *decreases* by 2.8%;
(3) of high blacks *increases* by 5.1%; and (4) of low blacks *increases* by 1.0%.
Thus, the largest winners from the presence of redistributive policies along
racial lines are high skill workers, especially high skill minority workers.
High skill minority workers gain both from affirmative action and the tax
reduction, while high skill majority workers benefit from the tax reduction.
Even though black legislators were assumed to be representatives *exclusively*
of black workers with the low skills ($\lambda = 0$), such workers gain much less,
with the gains from affirmative action partly offset by the loss from the
lower benefit. The losers are members of the low skill majority who lose

340

Redistribution and Affirmative Action

Table 1. *Equilibrium for Example 1*

	Prob.	Affirmative Action Target	Benefit	Tax Rate	Minority Share of Good Jobs	Gini
Equilibrium with affirmative action						
$\mathcal{H}$'s proposal	0.61	None	0.04	0.07	0.301	0.448
	0.39	0.333	0.01	0.02	0.333	0.470
$\mathcal{L}$'s proposal	1	None	0.09	0.16	0.300	0.364
$\mathcal{B}$'s proposal	1	0.332	0.12	0.20	0.330	0.351
Expected value with affirmative action			0.08	0.14	0.314	0.392
Equilibrium without affirmative action			0.12	0.21	0.298	0.347
Laissez faire			0	0	0.306	0.482

from affirmative action and lose again from the reduction in the average amount of redistribution along income lines.

Proposition 2 and the numerical illustration raise a question about the effect of affirmative action on the inequality of post-tax, post-transfer income. In the setting in which the only policy dimension is fiscal redistribution, then the distribution of post-tax and transfer income is unequivocally more equal than the laissez faire distribution. To get some idea of the impact of choosing affirmative action along with fiscal redistribution on income inequality, we computed the Gini coefficient for the economy described in Example 1. Under laissez faire, the Gini is 0.482; in the case that only fiscal policy is available and there is no affirmative action constraint, the low white workers' most preferred tax-policy prevails and the resulting Gini falls to 0.347. Introducing affirmative action attenuates the extent to which income is redistributed: the expected (equilibrium) Gini from the legislative bargaining process is 0.392, with the high white party's proposal to the black party involving the least equalization and the black party's proposal to the low white party involving the greatest equalization. Nevertheless, although there is less equalization when affirmative action is subject to policy choice than when only fiscal redistribution is feasible, black workers benefit more as a group (at the expense of low white workers) when affirmative action is a policy issue than when it is not.

341

David Austen-Smith and Michael Wallerstein

4.2. Comparative Statics

In addition to existence, Banks and Duggan (2006, Theorem 3) prove that if the equilibrium is unique, as in our example, then it is a continuous function of the recognition probabilities and parameters of the legislators' utility functions, so justifying comparative static exercises.[13] And note that if the only political issue is fiscal policy (so the share of blacks with good jobs is invariably defined by the laissez faire level), then under our assumptions, there is surely a core allocation at the low white's most preferred benefit level conditional on no affirmative action policy.

4.2.1. Social Variation One motivation for affirmative action in divided societies derives from an intuition that increases in the accessibility of good jobs and in the numbers of minority individuals holding such jobs, provide both indirect (through role models) and direct (through expected economic returns) incentives for increased investment in human capital formation among minorities (e.g. Foster and Vohra, 1992; Coate and Loury, 1993; Chung, 2000). For this and for many other reasons, the educational gap between majority and minority groups is not static. The question of how the equilibrium changes with the distribution of human capital, therefore, is of interest. Proposition 3 states affirmative action and direct fiscal redistribution vary with the share of high blacks in the population (θ_B).

Proposition 3. *The political equilibrium approaches the majority core of the policy space where fiscal redistribution is the only dimension as $\theta_B \to \theta_W$.*

As the average level of human capital between white and blacks approaches equality, affirmative action drops out as a separate policy dimension, given the constraint that affirmative action target cannot exceed the share of minorities in the population. With both white and black workers receiving good jobs in the same proportion or as $\alpha_\phi(b) \to p$ for all b, redistribution politics is exclusively concerned with taxes and benefits.

We cannot prove that the convergence to the one-dimensional majority core is monotonic, but monotonic convergence seems to be the typical case.

---

[13] Although their argument assumes concavity of the utility functions, such concavity is used only to ensure equilibrium existence. Given existence, the continuity (strictly speaking, upper hemicontinuity) property depends only on the continuity of preferences and compactness of the set of equilibrium proposals.

Table 2. *Comparative Static on* θ_B

θ_B	Minority Share of Good Jobs	Average Benefit	Average Tax
0.2	0.314	0.08	0.14
0.25	0.318	0.09	0.15
0.3	0.321	0.09	0.15
0.35	0.325	0.10	0.16
0.4	0.328	0.11	0.18
0.45	0.331	0.12	0.19
0.495	0.333	0.14	0.22

Table 2 continues with the basic parameterization of Example 1 (in which x is uniformly distributed over the interval $[0, 1]$, $q = b = 1/4$, $\beta = 1/2$, $p = 1/3$, and $\theta_W = 1/2$), but varies θ_B between $1/5$ and $1/2$. Choosing $\lambda = 0$ implies the increases in the proportion of high blacks have no effect on their influence in the legislative bargaining process. As the proportion of high-type blacks among the black population rises, so too does the share of good jobs going to minorities and the expected equilibrium benefit and tax rates. Not surprisingly, given that an increasing share of good jobs are allocated to minorities independently of affirmative action (because highly educated blacks constitute an increasing proportion of the labor force and firms are color-blind), there is less pressure on affirmative action targets. Moreover, because $\lambda = 0$ and high blacks have no influence on the legislative bargaining process, the black party becomes increasingly allied with the low white party in the legislature as the importance of affirmative action diminishes.

4.2.2. Economic Variation Another comparative static concerns the degree of economic efficiency (q) (Table 3). So far we have assumed q sufficiently large to induce politically salient variations' in workers' preferences over policy.[14] As q falls the market inefficiency due to employers' investment costs being borne prior to any wage bargaining becomes less important and the corresponding wage-premium for securing a good job declines. Intuitively, then, the rationale and demand for affirmative action policy weaken with reductions in q. Exactly this intuition is contained in Proposition 4.

[14] It is worth noting that increases in the technical cost parameter q have a qualitatively identical impact on equilibrium outcomes as increases in the relative bargaining strength of workers, β.

343

Table 3. *Comparative Static on q*

q	Minority Share of Good Jobs	Average Benefit	Average Tax
0.25	0.314	0.08	0.14
0.22	0.314	0.12	0.17
0.19	0.315	0.15	0.19
0.16	0.316	0.19	0.21
0.13	0.317	0.23	0.22

Proposition 4. *The political equilibrium approaches the majority core of the policy space where fiscal redistribution is the only dimension as $q \to 0$.*

As q goes to zero, the difference between good jobs and bad jobs is reduced and affirmative action loses its importance. Again, the political equilibrium approaches to majority core when fiscal redistribution is the only dimension.

Table 4 continued the same parameterization as Example 1 (with $\lambda = 0$), letting q go from $q = 1/4$ to $q = 0$. The interesting feature to note in Table 4 is that, as q falls, the share of good jobs held by minorities goes up somewhat, reflecting a willingness of employers to create more good jobs in total, but the equilibrium benefit (and tax) rate goes up considerably. With a falling marginal return to obtaining a good job, increasing weight is placed by the black party on fiscal redistribution relative to affirmative action.

4.2.3. Political Variation From the political perspective, an important issue involves the impact of how interests are represented in the legislature on policy outcomes. And of particular concern here are the consequences of

Table 4. *Comparative Static on λ*

λ	Minority Share Good Jobs	Average Benefit	Average Tax	Percentage		Net Gain		Average Gini
				HW	LW	HB	LB	
0	0.314	0.08	0.14	2.8	−2.8	5.1	1.0	0.392
0.1	0.316	0.06	0.11	4.2	−3.2	6.8	0.8	0.410
0.2	0.317	0.05	0.09	5.1	−3.7	7.8	0.4	0.422
0.3	0.317	0.04	0.07	5.8	−4.2	8.5	0	0.433

shifting the balance of influence (λ) between high and low types within the black party. We are unable to obtain analytical results which respect changes in λ, but the numerical results are intuitive. Given the parameterization of Example 1 with x is uniformly distributed over the interval $[0, 1]$, $q = b = 1/4$, $\beta = 1/2$, $p = 1/3$, $\theta_W = 1/2$, and $\theta_B = 1/5$, Table 4 describes the unique legislative bargaining equilibrium as the weight given to high-type blacks in the black party, λ, is increased from zero (as in Table 1) to the share of high-types within the black population as a whole, $\lambda = \theta_B = 1/5$, and beyond to $\theta_B = 1/3$. The last four columns of the table report the expected percentage gain or loss of high-type whites (HW), low-type whites (LW), high-type blacks (HB) and low-type blacks (LB) of the expected equilibrium policy outcome with affirmative action relative to the equilibrium without affirmative action.

It is apparent from the table that an increase in the weight of highly educated blacks in the black party B increases the average affirmative action target (minority share of good jobs) and reduces the average level of fiscal redistribution. Intuitively, the shift of intra-party weight to high-types within B enables high-type blacks and high-type whites to reach more profitable compromises than they otherwise could when low-type blacks exerted more control over party bargaining. This in turn improves $\mathcal{H}$'s bargaining power relative to $\mathcal{L}$. Consequently, all high-types benefit from an increase in λ and all low-types do worse. In particular, once the relative influence of high blacks increases sufficiently beyond their share of the black population at large, low-type blacks are left strictly worse off with affirmative action than if taxes and transfers were the only redistributive policy, that is, where the market alone determines the allocation of good jobs.

Proposition 2 states that affirmative action can be expected to improve the lot of black workers *as a group* relative to when only fiscal policy is at issue when black incomes are aggregated using the weights λ and $1 - \lambda$ for high and low types respectively. On the other hand, Table 4 makes clear that the distribution of such gains between high and low-type black workers, however, need not leave low-type blacks better off as a subgroup. If enough weight is given to the high blacks (λ high) to leave the low blacks with strictly less in equilibrium than they would receive at the low white party's ideal point, $I_{\mathcal{L}} = (\alpha_\phi(0.12), 0.12)$, then representatives of low blacks prefer to defect from B and vote with $\mathcal{L}$ to ensure $I_{\mathcal{L}}$ as the legislative decision. In other words, for the parameterization of Table 4, $\lambda = 0.3$ provides an upper-bound on the politically sustainable representation of high blacks within the black party. It is worth noting that no such lower bound is apparent: high blacks benefit disproportionately even in the case $\lambda = 0$.

5. Discussion

In this paper, we explore the consequences of ethnic or racial divisions for redistributive policy choice in a world devoid of prejudice. There is no suggestion here that racial prejudice is in fact irrelevant, only that it seems sensible to identify what happens in the absence of racial prejudice. Results derived in a prejudice-free setting provide a clear illustration of the impact of the introduction of additional dimensions of potential redistribution on the amount of redistribution that occurs in equilibrium.

The motivation for redistribution along racial lines in the model is an inefficiency in the labor market creating rents for those holding good jobs, coupled with an exogenously (historically) given difference in the distributions of human capital across races. When racial divisions lead to demands for redistributive policies along racial lines via affirmative action, we show that legislative policy bargaining implies that the amount of redistribution along income lines is less on average than would exist were racial divisions absent. When affirmative action is on the agenda, redistribution along racial lines partly replaces redistribution along income lines and total redistribution, as measured by the change of the Gini coefficient, declines. We also show that the expansion of the dimensions of redistribution benefits both highly educated members of the majority (who gain from lower taxation) as well as members of the minority (who gain from the affirmative action policies). The losers are the low skilled majority (white) workers.

An advantage of the legislative bargaining model is that it captures the political strategies that lead to the adoption of affirmative action at the Federal level during the first two years of the Nixon administration.[15] The term "affirmative action" applied to race was first used in the Kennedy administration, but the meaning was to ensure that minority employees were treated "without regard to race, creed, color and national origin" by the federal government or by government contractors. Title VII of the 1964 Civil Rights Act makes it unlawful for any employer with more than 25 employees to discriminate according to race, religion, sex and national

---

[15] The story is told in two books: Skrentny (1996) and Anderson (2004). Our account follows Anderson closely. Holzer and Neumark (2000) also present a brief history and a discussion of how affirmative action worked in practice.

origin and gave the courts the power to enforce the act. When, in 1968, the Labor Department issued a regulation that federal construction contractors were required to have affirmative actions programs that had "specific goals and timetable", the goals were voluntary. After the US Comptroller General (who works for Congress) declared "goals and timetable" to be in violation of the intent of Title VII that all employees be treated in a race-blind manner, the attempt to encourage federal contractors to hire more minorities came to a halt until Nixon came to office.

Affirmative action was advocated by the Nixon administration with far more vigor than displayed by the previous Democratic administrations. Soon after Nixon's inauguration, Labor Secretary George Schultz presented a plan of affirmative action whereby the Office of Federal Contract Compliance would establish a target range for bidders on Federal construction projects that was related to the share of minority workers within a given area, plus timetables for progress toward the target. Affirmative action had a number of advantages for the Nixon administration. It was "consistent with the spirit of self-reliance," in Schultz' words (Anderson, 2004, 116). Unlike fiscal redistribution, affirmative action required no government money. But what was most important, according to insider accounts, is that the plan drove a wedge between two parts of the Democratic coalition, black and the unions. In the words of John Ehrlichmen, Nixon's aide, "The NAACP wanted a tougher requirement; the unions hated the whole thing. Before long, the AFL-CIO and the NAACP were locked in combat over one of the passionate issues of the day and the Nixon administration was located in the sweet and the reasonable middle" (Anderson, 2004, 120).

In 1969, the Comptroller General again declared affirmative action to be in violation of Title VII of the 1964 Civil Rights Acts. In the Senate, Democratic Senator Sam Ervin introduced a rider to an appropriations bill stating that Comptroller General, not the executive branch, should determine who could receive federal contracts and a second rider asserting that Title VII was the nation's only law regarding employment. In the House, where the key legislative vote was held, opposition to the riders and support for affirmative action was led by the Republican minority leader, Gerald Ford. In December 1969, the riders were defeated, first in the House and then in the Senate. In the House, affirmative action was supported by Republicans by 3–1, while a majority of Democratic representatives voted in opposition. In early 1970, Labor Secretary Schutz expanded affirmative action to include all businesses, not just construction companies, that obtained federal contracts of more the $50,000 and who employed more than 50 employees to submit minority hiring plans with goals, targets and timetables.

Nixon's strategy introduced a new policy dimension that split black workers and white union-members, establishing a Federal program of race-based hiring that has never been revoked. While the Office of Contact Compliance policed the hiring practices of federal contractors, the Equal Employment Opportunity Commission and, ultimately, the Department of Justice policed the rest of the labor market. Large firms, in particular, found that the best defense against the possibility of a costly lawsuit was to implement affirmative action targets based on the share of minorities in the local population. Affirmative action was effective in raising the employment of minorities. Holzer and Neumark (2000) estimate that affirmative action plans lowered the hiring of white men by 10–15% in favor of minority men and women.

It is worth noting that firms did not appear to play an active role in lobbying either for or against affirmative action. We came across no instances in which firms used affirmative action to lower their wage costs by replacing white workers with cheaper black workers, although that doesn't mean it never happened. Initially, most firms defended their hiring practices and their existing work force against the demands of minorities for increased employment. But once affirmative action was in place, firms found it easy to live with. Employers realized the advantages of having one federal law to comply with rather than a multiplicity of state regulations. Most importantly, employers found affirmative action to have small effects on profits. As Holzer and Neumark (2000) summarize the economic literature on the effects of affirmative action programs on efficiency, there is evidence that affirmative action resulted in the hiring of minorities with lower educational credentials than their white coworkers, but much less evidence that minorities recruited in affirmative action programs were less productive. In sum, our neglect of employers as a political actor does not appear to be an important lack in the politics of affirmative action.

There are several fairly obvious ways it would be desirable to extend the framework suggested here, short of explicitly including racial preferences. Among these, three seem especially salient. First, as observed in the text, it is important to explore the implications of allowing more than two skill levels for workers. Second, a natural extension is to expand the set of policies considered to include education. Education, however, is inherently a dynamic problem. At any moment, the distribution of human capital is relatively fixed. Over time, as new generations receive schooling, the distribution of human capital reflects investments in education as well as the distribution of human capital in previous periods. This in turn gives rise to dynamics in the politics of redistribution as earlier policies affect the distribution of resources and political interests in later periods.[16] And third, it is a commonplace in the contemporary political economy literature that details of legislative and party structures are important for understanding policy outcomes. Legislative bargaining is likely to differ in a parliamentary system with proportional representation where the government typically consists of a coalition of parties and party discipline is high. A general theory of the impact of introducing a second dimension of redistribution by race, religion or language to redistribution by income requires considering of the full range of political institutions that shape political conflict.

Acknowledgments

This paper is a revised version of an earlier working paper, "Redistribution in a Divided Society". We are grateful to the editor and two anonymous referees for very constructive comments and, among others, to seminar participants at CEACS of the Juan March Foundation, Madrid, at UCLA, and at the PIEP Political Economy workshop, Harvard University. We are also grateful to the NSF (SES-0212049) and the MacArthur Foundation for financial support. All responsibility for the content of the paper resides with the authors.

Michael Wallerstein died from brain cancer in January 2006. I am truly grateful for his friendship over many years and for all that I learned from him during that time.

Appendix

For convenience, recall from Eq. (3) in the text that

$$\bar{y}(b) = \left[\frac{q}{1 - \beta} + b \right]$$

---

[16] See Roemer (2004) for an analysis of a model of the political choice of taxes, transfers and investment in education in a dynamic setting where the current distribution of human capital reflects past investment in education and the past distribution of human capital.

is the laissez faire productivity threshold for a firm to create a good job. Also, for each $i = B, W$,

$$\sigma_i(\alpha, b) = 1 - G_i(y_i(\alpha, b))$$
$$= 1 - [(1 - \theta_i)F(y_i(\alpha, b)) + \theta_i F(y_i(\alpha, b) - b)]$$

is the share of group i workers with good jobs; let $g_i(y) = (1 - \theta_i)f(y) + \theta_i f(y - b)$ be the density $dG_i(y)$. Recall that $\sigma(\alpha, b) = p\sigma_B(\alpha, b) + (1 - p)\sigma_W(\alpha, b)$ is the share of the population with good jobs and, from Eq. (7)

$$E[w \mid \alpha, b] = \beta \left[p \int_{y_B(\alpha,b)} y \, dG_B(y) + (1 - p) \int_{y_W(\alpha,b)} y \, dG_W(y) \right]$$
$$+ (1 - \beta)\sigma(\alpha, b)b$$

is the average wage at (α, b). From the budget constraint (6),

$$t(\alpha, b) = \frac{(1 - \sigma(\alpha, b))b}{(1 - \sigma(\alpha, b))b + E[w \mid \alpha, b]} \tag{9}$$

is the budget-balancing tax rate. The laissez faire share of good jobs held by blacks at any benefit level b is

$$\alpha_\phi(b) = \frac{p\sigma_B(\phi, b)}{\sigma(\phi, b)} < p.$$

Because F has full support on R, b finite implies $\alpha_\phi(b) > 0$. Hereafter, where there is no ambiguity we take the dependency of y_i, σ_i, etc. on (α, b) as understood. Similarly, we occasionally write $E(w) \equiv E[w \mid \alpha, b]$ and $E(\pi) \equiv E[\pi \mid \alpha, b]$.

The following fact is used repeatedly in the arguments to follow. For any $x \in R$, define the difference

$$Z(x) = \left[\frac{g_B(x)}{[1 - G_B(x)]} - \frac{g_W(x)}{[1 - G_W(x)]} \right];$$

then we have

Lemma 0.   *For any $x \in R$ and any $b > 0$, $Z(x) > 0$ iff F has a strictly increasing hazard rate at x.*

Proof. Write

$$Z(x) = \frac{g_B(x)}{[1 - G_B(x)]} - \frac{g_W(x)}{[1 - G_W(x)]}$$

$$= \frac{g_B(x)[1 - G_W(x)] - g_W(x)[1 - G_B(x)]}{[1 - G_B(x)][1 - G_W(x)]}.$$

Since the denominator is positive, the sign of $Z(x)$ is the same as the sign of the numerator. Expanding the numerator we obtain

$$g_B(x)[1 - G_W(x)] - g_W(x)[1 - G_B(x)]$$
$$= [\theta_B f(x - b) + (1 - \theta_B) f(x)][1 - \theta_W F(x - b) - (1 - \theta_W) F(x)]$$
$$- [\theta_W f(x - b) + (1 - \theta_W) f(x)][1 - \theta_B F(x - b) - (1 - \theta_B) F(x)]$$
$$= (\theta_W - \theta_B)[f(x)(1 - F(x - b)) - f(x - b)(1 - F(x))].$$

Since $(\theta_W - \theta_B) > 0$ we have

$$Z(x) > 0 \Leftrightarrow \frac{f(x)}{1 - f(x)} > \frac{f(x - b)}{1 - F(x - b)},$$

which proves the lemma. □

Proof of Lemma 1. (1) To show the existence and uniqueness of the labor market equilibrium.

It is immediate from a firm's profit-maximizing problem that, for any $b \geq 0$ and any $\alpha < \alpha_\phi(b)$, the solution involves setting $y_i(\alpha, b) = \bar{y}(b)$, $i = B, W$, with the share of good jobs allocated to blacks being $\alpha_\phi(b)$. Moreover, $\bar{y}(b)$ is finite for any finite level of benefit. Hence, if the affirmative action constraint is not binding, that is, if $\alpha \leq \alpha_\phi(b)$, then the labor market equilibrium clearly exists and is uniquely defined by $y_i, (\alpha, b) = \bar{y}(b), i = B, W$, and Eq. (9). So assume $\alpha > \alpha_\phi(b)$ and, without loss of generality, suppose b is finite.

Fix $(\alpha, b) \in \mathbf{P}$, $\alpha > \alpha_\phi(b)$ and b finite. Equilibrium in the labor market is characterized by a system of two equations that jointly determine y_B and y_W and a balanced budget constraint (9) that determines t. Given the affirmative action constraint binds, Eqs. (5) and (4) in the text can be written, respectively, as

$$\left. \begin{array}{l} \alpha y_B + (1 - \alpha) y_W - \bar{y}(b) = 0 \\ p(1 - \alpha)\sigma_B - \alpha(1 - p)\sigma_W = 0 \end{array} \right\} . \tag{10}$$

David Austen-Smith and Michael Wallerstein

Writing $Y(y_W) \equiv \frac{1}{\alpha}[\bar{y}(b) - (1-\alpha)y_W]$ and solving for y_B from the first equation of (10) yields $y_B = Y(y_W)$. Substituting for y_B into the second equation and collecting terms yields

$$\frac{p(1-\alpha)}{(1-p)\alpha} = \frac{1 - (1-\theta_w)F(y_W) - \theta_W F(y_W - b)}{1 - (1-\theta_B)F(Y(y_W)) - \theta_B F(Y(y_W) - b)} = \frac{\sigma_W(y_W)}{\sigma(Y(y_W))}.$$

Since the affirmative action constraint is binding, $\alpha > \alpha_\phi(b)$. By assumption, $\frac{1}{2} > p \geq \alpha$ and so $\alpha > \alpha_\phi(b) > 0$ implies

$$\frac{p(1-\alpha)}{(1-p)\alpha} \in \left[1, \frac{p(1-\alpha_\phi(b))}{(1-p)\alpha_\phi(b)}\right].$$

On the other hand, we have that for any $b \in [0, \infty)$,

$$\lim_{y_W\uparrow+\infty} \frac{\sigma_W(y_W)}{\sigma_B(Y(y_W))} = 0 < \lim_{y_W\uparrow+\infty} \frac{\sigma_W(y_W)}{\sigma_B(Y(y_W))} = \infty.$$

Moreover, since F is continuous and strictly increasing, $\sigma_W(y_W)/\sigma_B(Y(y_W))$ is a strictly decreasing function of y_W. Hence, there exists a unique y_W and $y_B = Y(y_W)$ solving Eq. (10). And given b, y_W and y_B, the tax rate is uniquely defined by Eq. (9). This proves the existence and uniqueness of a labor market equilibrium.

(2) To show $y_B(\alpha, b) < \bar{y}(b) < y_W(\alpha, b)$. Suppose $\alpha \in (\alpha_\phi(b), p]$. If $y_B(\alpha, b) \geq y_W(\alpha, b)$ then the first equation of (10) implies that $y_W(\alpha, b) \leq \bar{y}(b) \leq y_B(\alpha, b)$ and so

$$\sigma_B(\alpha, b) = 1 - (1-\theta_B)F(y_B(\alpha, b)) - \theta_B F(y_B(\alpha, b) - b)$$
$$\leq 1 - (1-\theta_B)F(\bar{y}(b)) - \theta_B F(\bar{y}(b) - b)$$

and

$$\sigma_W(\alpha, b) = 1 - (1-\theta_W)F(y_W(\alpha, b)) - \theta_W F(y_W(\alpha, b) - b)$$
$$\geq 1 - (1-\theta_W)F(\bar{y}(b)) - \theta_W F(\bar{y}(b) - b).$$

Therefore

$$\frac{p\sigma_B(\alpha, b)}{\sigma(\alpha, b)} \leq \frac{p\sigma_B(\phi, b)}{\sigma(\phi, b)} = \alpha_\phi(b)$$

which contradicts $\alpha > \alpha_\phi(b)$. Hence $\alpha \in (0, 1)$ and Eq. (10) imply $y_B(\alpha, b) < \bar{y}(b) < y_W(\alpha, b)$.

352

(3) To show $\alpha_\phi(b)$ is strictly decreasing in b. Because $\sigma_B(\phi, b) > 0$, we can write

$$\alpha_\phi(b) = \frac{p\sigma_B(\phi, b)}{\sigma(\phi, b)} = \frac{p}{p + (1 - p)\left(\dfrac{\sigma_W(\phi, b)}{\sigma_B(\phi, b)}\right)}.$$

And

$$\text{sign} \frac{d}{db}\left(\frac{\sigma_W(\phi, b)}{\sigma_B(\phi, b)}\right)$$

$$= \text{sign}\left[\frac{1}{\sigma_W(\phi, b)}\frac{d\sigma_W(\phi, b)}{db} - \frac{1}{\sigma_B(\phi, b)}\frac{d\sigma_B(\phi, b)}{db}\right]$$

$$= \text{sign}\left[\frac{g_B(\overline{y}(b))}{1 - G_B(\overline{y}(b))} - \frac{g_W(\overline{y}(b))}{1 - G_W(\overline{y}(b))}\right]\frac{d\overline{y}(b)}{db}.$$

By assumption, F exhibits a strictly increasing hazard rate everywhere so Lemma 0 implies the term in square brackets is strictly positive. And since $d\overline{y}(b)/db = 1$, $\frac{d}{db}(\frac{\sigma_W(\phi, b)}{\sigma_W(\phi, b)}) > 0$. Hence, $\alpha_\phi(b)$ is strictly decreasing in b as required. □

Write the system of Eq. (10) as

$$\begin{pmatrix} \psi_1(y_B, y_W) \\ \psi_2(y_B, y_W) \end{pmatrix} = 0$$

and define Ψ as

$$\Psi \equiv \begin{vmatrix} \partial\psi_1/\partial y_B & \partial\psi_1/\partial y_W \\ \partial\psi_2/\partial y_B & \partial\psi_2/\partial y_W \end{vmatrix}$$

$$= \alpha^2(1 - p)g_W(y_W) + (1 - \alpha)^2 pg_B(y_B) > 0.$$

Proof of Lemma 2. (1) Write $\Delta \equiv (y_W - y_B)$; by Lemma 1, $\Delta \geq 0$. Differentiate Eq. (10) with respect to α to obtain

$$\frac{\partial y_B(\alpha, b)}{\partial \alpha} = \frac{\alpha(1 - p)g_W(y_W)\Delta - (1 - \alpha)\sigma}{\Psi}; \tag{11}$$

$$\frac{\partial y_W(\alpha, b)}{\partial \alpha} = \frac{p(1 - \alpha)g_B(y_B)\Delta + \alpha\sigma}{\Psi}. \tag{12}$$

Since $\Delta \to 0$ as $\alpha \to \alpha_\phi(b)$; it is clear that for all $b \geq 0$,

$$\lim_{\alpha \to \alpha_\phi(b)} \frac{\partial y_B(\alpha, b)}{\partial \alpha} = -\frac{(1 - \alpha)\sigma}{\Psi} < 0$$

and, for all $\alpha \in [\alpha_\phi(b), p]$,

$$\frac{\partial y_W(\alpha, b)}{\partial \alpha} > 0.$$

(2) Differentiating Eq. (10) with respect to b, one obtains

$$\frac{\partial y_B(\alpha, b)}{\partial b} = \frac{\alpha(1-p)g_W(y_W)}{\Psi} > 0 \qquad (13)$$

$$\frac{\partial y_W(\alpha, b)}{\partial b} = \frac{(1-\alpha)pg_B(y_B)}{\Psi} > 0. \qquad (14)$$

(3) Differentiating Eq. (9) with respect to $b \geq 0$ yields

$$\begin{aligned}
\frac{\partial t}{\partial b} &= \frac{1}{(1-\sigma)b + E(w)}\left[\frac{\partial((1-\sigma)b)}{\partial b} - t\frac{\partial(1-\sigma)b + E(w))}{\partial b}\right] \\
&= \frac{1}{(1-\sigma)b + E(w)}\left[(1-t)\frac{\partial((1-\sigma)b)}{\partial b} - t\frac{\partial(E(w))}{\partial b}\right] \\
&= \frac{1}{(1-\sigma)b + E(w)}\{[(1-t)(1-\sigma) - t(1-\beta)\sigma] + A_1\}, \qquad (15)
\end{aligned}$$

where

$$\begin{aligned}
A_1 &\equiv [(1-t)b + tw(y_B)]pg_B(y_B)\frac{\partial y_B}{\partial b} \\
&\quad + [(1-t)b + t_W(y_W)](1-p)g_W(y_W)\frac{\partial y_W}{\partial b}
\end{aligned}$$

and $w(y_i) = \beta y_i + (1-\beta)b$ is the wage of the marginal individual from group $i \in \{B, W\}$ with a good job. By Eq. (2) above, $A_1 \geq 0$ with equality if and only if $b = 0$. Subtracting $t(1-\beta)\sigma b$ from both sides of the balanced budget constraint (6) in the text, we obtain

$$[(1-t)(1-\sigma) - t(1-\beta)\sigma]b = [E(w) - (1-\beta)\sigma b]t$$

Since $E(w) - (1-\beta)\sigma b > 0$ the left-hand side of the equality must be positive for $b > 0$ and zero otherwise. Hence, $\partial t/\partial b > 0$ for $b > 0$. If $b = 0$, $\partial t/\partial b = (1-\sigma)/E(w) > 0$. Thus, $\partial t/\partial b > 0$ for $b \geq 0$ as required.

(4) In equilibrium, Eqs. (1) and (2) imply

$$E[w + \pi \mid \alpha, b] = p\int_{y_B}(y-q)dG_B(y) + (1-p)\int_{y_W}(y-q)dG_W(y).$$

Redistribution and Affirmative Action

Taking the derivative with respect to α yields

$$\frac{\partial E[w + \pi \mid \alpha, b]}{\partial \alpha}$$

$$= -\left\{ p(y_B - q)g_B(y_B)\frac{\partial y_B}{\partial \alpha} + (1 - p)(y_W - q)g_W(y_W)\frac{\partial y_W}{\partial \alpha} \right\}.$$

Taking limits then gives

$$\lim_{\alpha \downarrow \alpha_\phi(b)} \frac{\partial E[w + \pi \mid \alpha, b]}{\partial \alpha}$$

$$= -(\bar{y} - q)\left[pg_B(\bar{y})\frac{\partial y_B}{\partial \alpha} + (1 - p)g_W(\bar{y})\frac{\partial y_W}{\partial \alpha} \right]_{\alpha=\alpha_\phi(b)}$$

$$= (\bar{y} - q)\frac{\partial \sigma(\alpha_\phi(b), b)}{\partial \alpha}. \tag{16}$$

Since $\bar{y} > q$, expected income is increasing at $\alpha_\phi(b)$ if and only if the share of good jobs in the economy as a whole is increasing at $\alpha_\phi(b)$. So consider the effect of α on σ at $\alpha_\phi(b)$:

$$\frac{\partial \sigma(\alpha, b)}{\partial \alpha} = -\left[pg_B(y_B)\frac{\partial u_B(\alpha, b)}{\partial \alpha} + (1 - p)g_W(y_W)\frac{\partial y_W(\alpha, b)}{\partial \alpha} \right]. \tag{17}$$

Substituting for $\partial y_i/\partial \alpha$, $i = B, W$, and taking limits gives

$$\lim_{\alpha \downarrow \alpha_\phi(b)} \frac{\partial \sigma(\alpha_\phi(b), b)}{\partial \alpha} = [p(1 - \alpha_\phi(b))g_B(\bar{y}) - (1 - p)\alpha_\phi(b)g_W(\bar{y})]\frac{\sigma}{\Psi}$$

$$= [(1 - G_W(\bar{y}))g_B(\bar{y}) - (1 - G_B(\bar{y}))g_W(\bar{y})]\frac{p(1 - p)}{\Psi}$$

$$= \frac{p(1 - p)(1 - G_W(\bar{y}))(1 - G_B(\bar{y}))}{\Psi}Z(\bar{y}) > 0, \tag{18}$$

where the second equality follows on substituting for $\alpha_\phi(b) = p\sigma_B(\phi, b)/\sigma(\phi, b)$ and collecting terms; and the inequality follows from Lemma 0 and the assumption that F has a strictly increasing hazard rate. Thus, $\lim_{\alpha \downarrow \alpha_\phi(b)} \partial E[w + \pi \mid \alpha, b]/\partial \alpha > 0$ as claimed.

(5) Using Eq. (9), we have for all $b \geq 0$,

$$\frac{\partial t}{\partial \alpha} = -\frac{b}{[(1 - \sigma)b + E(w)]^2}\left[E(w)\frac{\partial \sigma}{\partial \alpha} + (1 - \sigma)\frac{\partial E(w)}{\partial \alpha} \right]. \tag{19}$$

By definition of $\alpha_\phi(b)$, $\partial E[\pi \mid \alpha_\phi(b), b]/\partial \alpha = 0$. Hence,

$$\frac{\partial E[\mid w \mid \alpha, b]}{\partial \alpha}\bigg|_{\alpha=\alpha_\phi(b)} = \frac{\partial E[w + \pi \mid \alpha, b]}{\partial \alpha}\bigg|_{\alpha=\alpha_\phi(b)}.$$

355

Taking limits, substituting from Eq. (16) and collecting terms yields,

$$\lim_{\alpha \downarrow \alpha_\phi(b)} \frac{\partial t}{\partial \alpha} = \frac{-[(1-\sigma)(\bar{y}-q) + E(w)]b}{[(1-\sigma)b + E(w)]^2} \frac{\partial \sigma(\alpha_\phi(b), b)}{\partial \alpha}. \tag{20}$$

Therefore, by Eq. (18), $\lim_{\alpha \downarrow \alpha_\phi(b)} \partial t / \partial \alpha \leq 0$ with inequality strict for all $b > 0$. $\square$

The expected consumption of an individual with human capital $H \in \{0, b\}$ in group $i \in \{B, W\}$ is given by Eq. (8) in the text; substituting for w, this expression can be rewritten:

$$c_{Hi}(\alpha, b) = (1-t)\left\{[1 - \beta(1 - F(y_i - H))]b + \beta \int_{y_i - H}^{\infty} (x + H)\mathrm{d}F(x)\right\} \tag{21}$$

Proof of Lemma 3. Differentiating Eq. (21) with respect to α and b yields,

$$\frac{\partial c_{Hi}(\alpha, b)}{\partial \alpha} = -\left(\frac{c_{Hi}}{1-t}\right) \frac{\partial t}{\partial \alpha} - (1-t)\beta(y_i - b)f(y_i - H)\frac{\partial y_i}{\partial \alpha}. \tag{22}$$

$$\frac{\partial c_{Hi}}{\partial b} = -\left(\frac{c_{Hi}}{1-t}\right) \frac{\partial t}{\partial b} + (1-t)[1 - \beta(1 - F(y_i - H))]$$

$$- (1-t)\beta(y_i - b)f(y_i - H)\frac{\partial y_i}{\partial b}. \tag{23}$$

The first two claims of the lemma follow from steps (1) through (5) below.

(1) To show $\alpha_{HB}^* > \alpha_\phi(b_{HB}^*)$, $H \in \{0, b\}$. Set $i = B$ in Eq. (22) and fix $b \geq 0$. By Lemma 2(1), $\lim_{\alpha \downarrow \alpha_\phi(b)} \partial y_B / \partial \alpha < 0$ and, by Lemma 2(5), $\lim_{\alpha \downarrow \alpha_\phi(b)} \partial t / \partial \alpha \leq 0$. Further, $\lim_{\alpha \downarrow \alpha_\phi(b)} (y_B - b) = (\bar{y} - b) > 0$. Hence, for all $b \geq 0$, $\lim_{\alpha \downarrow \alpha_\phi(b)} \partial c_{HB}(\alpha, b)/\partial \alpha > 0$ which suffices to show $\alpha_{HB}^* > \alpha_\phi(b_{HB}^*)$, $H \in \{0, b\}$.

(2) To show there exists finite $\bar{b}_{1i}$ and $\bar{q}_1$ such that $b \geq \bar{b}_{1i}$ and $q \geq \bar{q}_1$ implies $b_{bi}^* = 0$, $i \in \{B, W\}$. To prove $b_{bi}^* = 0$, note that Eq. (15) implies,

$$\lim_{b \to 0} \frac{1}{1 - t(\alpha_\phi(b), b)} \frac{\partial t(\alpha_\phi(b), b)}{\partial b} = \left. \frac{1-\sigma}{E(w)}\right|_{\alpha_\phi(0,0)} \tag{24}$$

in which case

$$\lim_{b \to 0} \frac{\partial c_{bi}(\alpha_\phi(b), b)}{\partial b}$$

$$= -\left[c_{bi}\frac{1-\sigma}{E(w)} - [1 - \beta(1 - F(\bar{y} - b))] + \beta\bar{y}f(\bar{y} - b)\frac{\partial y_i}{\partial b}\right]_{(\alpha_\phi(0,0))}.$$

By Lemma 2(2), the last term inside square brackets is nonnegative for all b. So, fixing the policy $(\alpha_\phi(0), 0)$, define

$$\Phi(b) = -c_{bi}\frac{1-\sigma}{E(w)} + 1 - \beta(1 - F(\bar{y} - b))$$

$$= -\frac{[\theta F(\bar{y} - b) + (1 - \theta)F(\bar{y})]\displaystyle\int_{\bar{y}-b}^{\infty} (x + b)\mathrm{d}F(x)}{\theta \displaystyle\int_{\bar{y}-b}^{\infty} (x + b)\mathrm{d}F(x) + (1 - \theta)\int_{\bar{y}}^{\infty} x\,\mathrm{d}F(x)}$$

$$+ 1 - \beta(1 - F(\bar{y} - b))$$

which is independent of i. Since (given $b = 0$) $\bar{y} = q/(1 - \beta)$ is constant and $\lim_{b\to\infty}(\bar{y} - b) = 0$,

$$\lim_{b\to\infty}\left(c_{bi}\frac{1-\sigma}{E(w)}\right)$$

$$= \lim_{b\to\infty} \frac{(1 - \theta)F(\bar{y})\left[\displaystyle\int_{\bar{y}-b}^{\infty} xf(x)\mathrm{d}x + b\int_{\bar{y}-b}^{\infty} f(x)\mathrm{d}x\right]}{(1 - \theta)\displaystyle\int_{\bar{y}}^{\infty} x\mathrm{d}F(x) + \theta\left[\displaystyle\int_{\bar{y}-b}^{\infty} xf(x)\mathrm{d}x + b\int_{\bar{y}-b}^{\infty} f(x)\mathrm{d}x\right]}$$

$$= \frac{(1 - \theta)F(\bar{y})}{\theta}$$

Hence

$$\lim_{b\to\infty} \Phi(b) = [1 - \beta] - \frac{(1 - \theta)F(\bar{y})}{\theta} < 0 \Leftrightarrow F(\bar{y}) > \frac{\theta}{1 - \theta}(1 - \beta).$$

Therefore, because $\lim_{q\to\infty} F(\bar{y}) = 1$ and $\theta < 1/2$, there exists $\bar{b}_{1i} > 0$ and $\bar{q}_1$ such that $b \geq b_{1i}$ and $q \geq \bar{q}$, implies $\lim_{b\to0} \partial c_{bi}(\alpha_\phi(b), b)/\partial b \leq 0$, $i = B, W$, in which case $b_{bi}^* = 0, i = B, W$.

(3) To show there exists finite $\bar{b}_{2i}$ and $\bar{q}_{2i}$ such that $b \geq \bar{b}_{2i}$ and $q \geq \bar{q}_{2i}$ implies $b_{0i}^* > 0$, $i \in \{B, W\}$. Evaluating Eq. (23) for $i = W$ at $(\alpha_\phi(0), 0)$ yields

$$\lim_{b\to\infty} \frac{\partial c_{0W}(\alpha_\phi(0), 0)}{\partial b}$$

$$= \lim_{b\to\infty}\left[-c_{0W}\frac{1-\sigma}{E(w)} + [1 - \beta(1 - F(\bar{y}))] - \beta\bar{y}f(\bar{y})\frac{\partial y_W(\alpha_\phi(0), 0)}{\partial b}\right]$$

$$= \lim_{b\to\infty}\left[\frac{-K(b) + [1 - \beta(1 - F(\bar{y}))] - \beta\bar{y}f(\bar{y})}{p(1 - \alpha_\phi(0))g_W(\bar{y})\Psi}\right],$$

where

$$K(b) \equiv \frac{[\theta F(\bar{y} - b) + (1 - \theta)F(\bar{y})] \int_{\bar{y}}^{\infty} x f(x)dx}{(1 - \theta) \int_{\bar{y}} x dF(x) + \theta \left[\int_{\bar{y}}^{\infty} x f(x)dx + b \int_{\bar{y}-b}^{\infty} f(x)dx \right]},$$

and we have substituted for $\partial y_W / \partial b$ from Eq. (14) and for $(\partial t / \partial b)/(1 - t)$ from Eq. (24). Therefore

$$\lim_{b \to \infty} \frac{\partial c_{0W}(\alpha_\phi(0), 0)}{\partial b}$$

$$= [1 - \beta(1 - F(\bar{y}))] - \beta \bar{y} f(\bar{y}) \frac{p(1 - \alpha_\phi(0))(1 - \theta_W)f(\bar{y})}{\Psi}$$

Hence

$$\lim_{b \to \infty} \frac{\partial c_{0W}(\alpha_\phi(0), 0)}{\partial b} > 0$$

$$\Leftrightarrow F(\bar{y}) > \frac{1}{\beta \Psi} [\beta \bar{y} f \bar{y}^2 p(1 - \alpha_\phi)(1 - \theta_W) - (1 - \beta)\Psi]$$

Now $\lim_{q \to \infty} F(\bar{y}) = 1$ and, by L'Hôpital's Rule and the assumption that F has a strictly increasing hazard rate, $\lim_{q \to \infty} \bar{y} f(\bar{y})^2 = 0$.[17] Hence the right-hand side of the last inequality is negative for q sufficiently large.

---

[17] To see this, write

$$\bar{y} f(\bar{y})^2 = \frac{\bar{y}}{1/f(\bar{y})^2}.$$

Both numerator and denominator go to infinity with q or, equivalently, with $\bar{y}$ and L'Hôpital's Rule implies

$$\lim_{\bar{y} \to \infty} \bar{y} f(\bar{y})^2 = \lim_{\bar{y} \to \infty} -\frac{f(\bar{y})^2}{2f'(\bar{y})}$$

if this latter limit exists. Since F has a strictly increasing hazard rate, at every $x > 0$ we have

$$\frac{d}{dx} \frac{f(x)}{1 - F(x)} = \frac{(1 - F(x))f'(x) + f(x)^2}{[1 - F(x)]^2} > 0$$

so that, for all $x > 0$,

$$1 - F(x) > -\frac{f(x^2)}{f'(x)}.$$

And since $\lim_{x \to \infty} [1 - F(x)] = 0$ and $f'(x) \leq 0$ for sufficiently large x,

$$\lim_{x \to \infty} -\frac{f(x)^2}{f'(x)} = 0.$$

Therefore, $\lim_{q \to \infty} F(\bar{y}) = 1$ implies there exists $\bar{b}_{2W} > 0$ and $\bar{q}_{2W}$ such that $b \geq \bar{b}_{2W}$ and $q \geq \bar{q}_{2W}$ implies $\lim_{b \to 0} \partial c_{0W}(\alpha_\phi(b), b)/\partial b > 0$. The same argument for $i = B$ likewise yields that there exists $\bar{b}_{2B} > 0$ and $\bar{q}_{2B}$ such that $b \geq \bar{b}_{2B}$ and $q \geq \bar{q}_{2_B}$ implies $\lim_{b \to 0} \partial c_{0B}(\alpha_\phi(b), b)/\partial b > 0$. In each case, therefore, we obtain $b_{0i}^* > 0$, $i \in \{B, W\}$.

(4) To show $\alpha_{bW}^* = \alpha_\phi(b_{bW}^*)$. By step (2), $b_{bW}^* = 0$ and, by Lemma 2(5), we have $\lim_{b \to 0} \partial t(\alpha_\phi(b), b)/\partial \alpha = 0$. Finally, by Lemma 2(1), $\partial y_W/\partial \alpha > 0$. Hence, Eq. (22) implies $\lim_{b \to 0} \partial c_{bW}(\alpha_\phi(b), b)/\partial \alpha > 0$, proving $\alpha_{bW}^* = \alpha_\phi(0)$ as required.

(5) To show there exists finite $\bar{b}_3$ and $\bar{q}_3$ such that $b \geq \bar{b}_3$ and $q \geq \bar{q}_3$ implies $\alpha_{0W}^* = \alpha_\phi(b_{0W}^*)$. Using Eq. (22), we have that for any $b \geq 0$,

$$\frac{\partial c_{0W}(\alpha, b)}{\partial \alpha} = -\left(\frac{c_{0W}}{1-t}\right)\frac{\partial t(\alpha, b)}{\partial \alpha} - (1-t)\beta(\bar{y} - b)f(\bar{y})\frac{\partial y_W(\alpha, b)}{\partial \alpha}$$

When evaluated at $\alpha = \alpha_\phi(b)$, we get

$$\lim_{\alpha \downarrow \alpha_\phi(b)} \frac{\partial c_{0W}(\alpha, b)}{\partial \alpha}$$

$$= -\left(\frac{c_{0W}}{1-t}\right)\frac{\partial t(\alpha_\phi(b), b)}{\partial \alpha} - (1-t)\left(\frac{\beta q}{1-\beta}\right)f(\bar{y})\frac{p[1 - G_B(\bar{y})]}{\Psi}$$

$$= \left\{\frac{c_{0W}}{(1-t)}\left[\frac{t[(\beta q/(1-\beta)) + b] + (1-t)b}{[(1-\sigma)b + E(w)]}\right]\frac{\partial \sigma(\alpha_\phi(b), b)}{\partial \alpha}\right.$$

$$\left. -(1-t)\left(\frac{\beta q}{1-\beta}\right)[1 - G_B(\bar{y})]f(\bar{y})\frac{p}{\Psi}\right\}$$

$$= \left\{\frac{c_{0W}}{(1-t)}\frac{[(t\beta q/(1-\beta)) + b](1-p)}{[(1-\sigma)b + E(w)]}\left[(1 - G_W(\bar{y}))\right.\right.$$

$$\times \left(\theta_B\frac{f(\bar{y} - b)}{f(\bar{y})} + (1-\theta_B)\right) - (1 - G_B(\bar{y}))$$

$$\left.\times \left(\theta_W\frac{f(\bar{y} - b)}{f(\bar{y})} + (1-\theta_W)\right)\right]$$

$$\left. - (1-t)\left(\frac{\beta q}{1-\beta}\right)[1 - G_B(\bar{y})]\right\}\frac{p}{\Psi}f(\bar{y})$$

$$= \left\{\frac{c_{0W}}{1-t}\frac{[(t\beta/(1-\beta)) + (b/q)](1-p)}{[(1-\sigma)b + E(w)]}\left[\left(\frac{1 - G_W(\bar{y})}{1 - G_B(\bar{y})}\right)\right.\right.$$

$$\times \left(\theta_B\frac{f(\bar{y} - b)}{f(\bar{y})} + (1-\theta_B)\right) - \left(\theta_W\frac{f(\bar{y} - b)}{f(\bar{y})} + (1-\theta_W)\right)\right]$$

$$\left. - (1-t)\left(\frac{\beta}{1-\beta}\right)\right\}\frac{p(1 - G_B(\bar{y}))}{\Psi}qf(\bar{y})$$

where we have substituted for $\partial y_W(\alpha, b)/\partial\alpha$, $\partial t(\alpha_\phi(b), b)/\partial\alpha$, and $\partial\sigma(\alpha_\phi(b), b)/\partial\alpha$ from Eqs. (12), (20), and (18), respectively, and collected terms. All of the terms outside the curly brackets are positive. Therefore,

$$\text{sign}\frac{\partial c_{0W}(\alpha_\phi(b), (b)}{\partial\alpha} = \text{sign}\left[\frac{K_1 f(\bar{y} - b)}{f(\bar{y})} + K_2\right],$$

where

$$K_1 = \frac{c_{0W}}{1 - t}\frac{[(t\beta/(1 - \beta)) + (b/q)](1 - p)}{[(1 - \sigma)b + E(w)]}\left[\left(\frac{1 - G_W(\bar{y})}{1 - G_B(\bar{y})}\right)\theta_B - \theta_W\right]$$

$$K_2 = \frac{c_{0W}}{1 - t}\frac{[(t\beta/(1 - \beta)) + (b/q)](1 - p)}{[(1 - \sigma)b + E(w)]}(\theta_w - \theta_B) - (1 - t)\left(\frac{\beta}{1 - \beta}\right)$$

Consider the term

$$\left[\left(\frac{1 - G_W(\bar{y})}{1 - G_B(\bar{y})}\right)\theta_B - \theta_W\right]$$

$$= \frac{\theta_B(1 - G_W(\bar{y})) - \theta_W(1 - G_B(\bar{y}))}{(1 - G_B(\bar{y}))}$$

$$= [\theta_B[1 - \theta_W F(\bar{y} - b) - (1 - \theta_W)F(\bar{y})]$$

$$- \theta_W[1 - \theta_B F(\bar{y} - b) - (1 - \theta_B)F(\bar{y})]]\frac{1}{(1 - G_B(\bar{y}))}$$

$$= \frac{(\theta_B - \theta_W) - (\theta_B - \theta_W)f(\bar{y})}{(1 - G_B(\bar{y}))}$$

$$= \frac{(\theta_B - \theta_W)(1 - F(\bar{y}))}{(1 - G_B(\bar{y}))} < 0$$

Therefore $K_1 < 0$:

Fixing b and letting $q \to \infty$ (so $\bar{y} \to \infty$) and $h \to \infty$ in such a way to ensure $\bar{y} - b$ is constant, we obtain

$$\text{sign}\lim_{\substack{q, b \to \infty \\ \bar{y} - b \text{ constant}}}\frac{\partial c_{0W}(\alpha_\phi(b), b)}{\partial\alpha} = \text{sign}\lim_{\substack{q, b \to \infty \\ \bar{y} - b \text{ constant}}}\left[K_1\frac{(\bar{y} - b)}{f(\bar{y})} + K_2\right]$$

$$= \text{sign}\left[\frac{(1 - p)tb}{[(1 - \sigma)b + E(w)]}\frac{(1 - F(\bar{y}))}{f(\bar{y})}\frac{f(\bar{y} - b)}{(1 - F(\bar{y} - b))}\frac{\theta_B - \theta_W}{\theta_B}\right.$$

$$\left. + \frac{(1 - p)tb}{[(1 - \sigma)b + E(w)]}(\theta_W - \theta_B) - (1 - t)\right]\frac{\beta}{1 - \beta}$$

where we observe $\lim_{q \to \infty} c_{0W} = (1 - t)b$ and, given $\bar{y} - b$ constant, $\lim_{q \to \infty}(1 - G_B(\bar{y})) = \theta_B(1 - F(\bar{y} - b))$.

By the argument above for $K_1 < 0$, the assumption that F has a strictly increasing hazard rate and $\overline{y} - b$ constant, $\lim K_1 \leq 0$. Hence the first term in square brackets is nonpositive, in which case

$$\lim_{\substack{q,b \to \infty \\ \overline{y}-b \text{ constant}}} \frac{\partial c_{0W}(\alpha_\phi(b), b)}{\partial \alpha} < 0$$

if

$$\left[\frac{(1-p)tb}{(1-\sigma)b + E(w)}(\theta_W - \theta_B) - (1-t) \right] < 0.$$

Using Eq. (6), this inequality can be written

$$\left[\frac{(1-p)(1-\sigma)b^2}{(1-\sigma)b + E(w)}(\theta_W - \theta_B) - E(w) \right] < 0$$

$$\Leftrightarrow (1-p)(1-\sigma)b^2(\theta_W - \theta_b) < E(w)[(1-\sigma)b + E(w)]$$

$$\Leftrightarrow (1-p)(\theta_W - \theta_B) < \frac{E(w)}{b} \frac{[(1-\sigma)b + E(w)]}{(1-\sigma)b}.$$

The left-hand side of the last inequality must be less than $1/2$ since $(1-p)\theta_W < 1/2$ and $\theta_B \geq 0$; and the right-hand side of this inequality must be greater that one since $b \leq E(w)$, benefits must be paid out of wages, and $b = b_{0W}^* > 0$. Therefore, there is some $\overline{q}_3 < \infty$ and some $\overline{b}_3 < \infty$ such that $q > \overline{q}_3$ and $b > \overline{b}_3$ implies

$$\frac{\partial c_{0W}(\alpha_\phi(b_{0W}^*), b_{0W}^*)}{\partial \alpha} < 0.$$

The claim follows.

To complete the argument for the first two claims of the lemma, let $\overline{b} = \max\{\overline{b}_{1i}, \overline{b}_{2i}, \overline{b}_{3i}\}_{i\in\{B,w\}}$ and $\overline{q} = \max\{\overline{q}_{1i}, \overline{q}_{2i}, \overline{q}_3\}_{i\in\{B,W\}}$.

(6) To show profits are maximal at $(\alpha_\phi(0), 0)$. Immediate from Eq. (2) and definition of $\alpha_\phi(0)$ as the outcome of profit-maximizing choice of the threshold $\overline{y}(0)$. $\square$

The argument for Proposition 1 uses the following claim. Let $\alpha_{Hi}^*(b)$ denote (H, i)'s most preferred level of affirmative action conditional on b.

Lemma 4. *There exists finite $\overline{b}_4$ and $\overline{q}_4$ such that $b \geq \overline{b}_4$ and $q \geq \overline{q}_4$ implies* $\alpha_{bW}^*(b_{0W}^*) = \alpha_\phi(b_{0W}^*)$.

David Austen-Smith and Michael Wallerstein

Proof. Consider the high-type whites' choice of α^*_{bW} at the point $\alpha_\phi(b^*_{0W})$:

$$\frac{\partial c_{bW}(\alpha_\phi(b^*_{0W}), b^*_{0W})}{\partial \alpha}$$

$$= -\left(\frac{c_{bW}}{1-t}\right)\frac{\partial t(\alpha_\phi(b^*_{0W}), b^*_{0W})}{\partial \alpha} - (1-t)\beta(\bar{y} - b^*_{0W})(\bar{y} - b)\frac{\partial y_W}{\partial \alpha}$$

Evaluating $\partial t(\alpha_\phi(b^*_{0W}), b^*_{0W})/\partial \alpha$ yields

$$\frac{\partial t(\alpha_\phi(b^*_{0W}), b^*_{0W})}{\partial \alpha} = \frac{[(1-\sigma)(\bar{y}-q) + E(w)]b^*_{0W}}{[(1-\sigma)b^*_{0W} + E(w)]^2}\frac{\partial \sigma(\alpha_\phi(b^*_{0W}), b^*_{0W})}{\partial \alpha}$$

Finally, evaluating $\partial \sigma(\alpha_\phi(b^*_{0W}), b^*_{0W})/\partial \alpha$ when $q \to \infty$ and $b \to \infty$ to ensure $(\bar{y} - b))$ is constant, yields

$$\lim_{q\to\infty} \frac{\partial \sigma(\alpha_\phi(b^*_{0W}), b^*_{0W})}{\partial \alpha}$$

$$= \frac{p(1-p)}{\psi}[(1 - G_W(\bar{y}))g_B(\bar{y}) - (1 - G_B(\bar{y}))g_W(\bar{y})]$$

$$= \frac{p(1-p)\theta_W\theta_B}{\psi}[(1 - F(\bar{y} - b))f(\bar{y} - b)$$

$$-(1 - F(\bar{y} - b)]f(\bar{y} - b)] = 0.$$

Since, by L'Hôpital's rule,

$$\lim_{\bar{y}\to\infty} \bar{y}\frac{\partial \sigma}{\partial \alpha} = \lim_{y\to\infty}\frac{\partial \sigma}{\partial \alpha} = 0$$

we have

$$\lim_{q\to\infty}\frac{\partial t(\alpha_\phi(b^*_{0W}), b^*_{0W})}{\partial \alpha} = 0$$

And therefore $\partial y_W/\partial \alpha > 0$ implies

$$\lim_{q\to\infty}\frac{\partial c_{bW}(\alpha_\phi(b^*_{0W}), b^*_{0W})}{\partial \alpha} < 0.$$

Hence, $\partial c_{bW}(\alpha_\phi(b^*_{0W}), b^*_{0W}/\partial \alpha < 0$ for $q > \bar{q}_4$ and $b > \bar{b}_4$. $\square$

Without loss of generality, assume $\bar{b} \geq b_4$ and $\bar{q} \geq q_4$.

Proof of Proposition 1. If affirmative action is not a political decision variable, the share of good jobs held by blacks in the economy is identically $\alpha_\phi(b)$ for all $b \geq 0$. In this case, the thresholds y_i satisfy $y_i \equiv y(b)$, $i = B, W$, and all low human capital types have identical preferences over fiscal policy. So, because the coalition of all low-types is a strict majority, $(1 - \theta) > 1/2$, the majority most preferred fiscal policy when affirmative action is not a decision variable, say b_0^*, solves

$$\left. \frac{\partial c_{0_i}(\alpha_\phi(b_0^*), b_0^*)}{\partial b} \right|_{\alpha = \alpha_\phi(b), \forall b \geq 0} = 0, i \in \{B, W\}.$$

By similar reasoning to that for Lemma 3,[18] $b_0^* > 0$; and that b_0^* is finite with $t(\alpha_\phi(b_0^*), b_0^*) < 1$ follows directly from Eq. (23) and $\partial t/\partial b > 0$ all $b \geq 0$. By Lemma 3 and the maintained assumptions, $\alpha_\mathcal{L}^* = \alpha_\phi(b_\mathcal{L}^*)$ for $b_\mathcal{L}^* = b_{0W}^* > 0$, in which case $b_0^* = b_\mathcal{L}^*$. Hence the core outcome when affirmative action is not a policy variable coincides with the low white party's ideal point when affirmative action is a policy choice. Now let affirmative action be a decision variable.

By Lemmas 3 and 4, for sufficiently high q and h, $b_{hi}^* = 0, i = B, W$, and

$$\alpha_\mathcal{H}^*(b_{0W}^*) = \alpha_\iota^*(b_{0W}^*) = \alpha_\phi(b_{0W}^*) < \alpha_\mathcal{B}^*(b_{0W}^*),$$

where α_j^* (b) is party j's most preferred level of affirmative action conditional on b. Therefore, if $b_{0W}^* \geq b_\mathcal{B}^*$ then surely $Eb_j < b_\mathcal{B}^* = b_0^*$, where $(\alpha j, bj)$ is the policy proposed by $j = \mathcal{H}, \mathcal{L}, \mathcal{B}$ in equilibrium and the expectation is with respect to the party first selected to propose a policy. Suppose $b_{0W}^* < b_\mathcal{B}^*$. Because $\nabla c_\mathcal{H}(\alpha_\phi(b), b) < 0$ for all $b \leq b_\mathcal{L}^*, \alpha_\mathcal{L}^* < \alpha_\mathcal{B}^*(b_\mathcal{L}^*)$ and $0 < b_\mathcal{L}^* < b_\mathcal{B}^*$ imply $c_\mathcal{H}(\alpha_\mathcal{L}^*, b_\mathcal{L}^*) > c_\mathcal{H}(\alpha_\mathcal{B}^*, b_\mathcal{B}^*)$. Moreover, high whites can obtain $c_{hW}(\alpha_\mathcal{L}^*, b_\mathcal{L}^*)$ with certainty by proposing $(\alpha_\mathcal{L}^*, b_\mathcal{L}^*)$ if selected to be the proposer (a proposal low whites would certainly accept) and accepting all proposals such that $c_{hW}(\alpha, b) \geq c_{hW}(\alpha_\mathcal{L}^*, b_\mathcal{L}^*)$ (a proposal low whites would certainly make). If blacks proposed a policy that entailed lower utility for both the high and the low white party than the low whites, ideal point, $I_\mathcal{L} = (\alpha_\mathcal{L}^*, b_\mathcal{L}^*)$, both white parties would reject the black party's proposal and wait until $I_\mathcal{L} = (\alpha_\mathcal{L}^*, b_\mathcal{L}^*)$ or better was proposed. Hence, the high white party's equilibrium continuation value in the bargaining game, $v_\mathcal{H}$, must be at least $c_\mathcal{H}(\alpha_\mathcal{L}^*, b_\mathcal{L}^*)$, in which case there is some $b' \leq b_\mathcal{L}^*$ such that $v_\mathcal{H} = c_\mathcal{H}(\alpha_\phi(b'), b') \geq c_\mathcal{H}(\alpha_\mathcal{L}^*, b_\mathcal{L}^*)$. Therefore, if $c_\mathcal{H}(\alpha, b) = c_\mathcal{H}(\alpha_\phi(b'), b')$, then $\nabla c_\mathcal{H}(\alpha_\phi(b), b) < 0$ for all $b < b_\mathcal{L}^*$ implies $\alpha > \alpha_\phi$ (b); if $b = b_\mathcal{L}^*$, then we have $\alpha = \alpha_\phi(b)$; and, finally, the party's indifference curve $c_\mathcal{H}(\alpha, b) = v_\mathcal{H}$ is downward sloping in (b, α)-space. Consequently, because $v_\mathcal{H}$ is the high whites' expected equilibrium payoff, it must be that $Eb_j < b_\mathcal{L}^*$ as required. $\square$

---

[18] Specifically, step (3) of the proof above.

David Austen-Smith and Michael Wallerstein

Proof of Proposition 2. Suppose part (1) was false. Then either high whites or blacks could do better by proposing the low white's ideal point, which would certainly be accepted. But then an equilibrium could not exist by the same reasoning as in the proof of Proposition 1. Part (2) is an immediate corollary of Proposition 1. Since the equilibrium with affirmative action results, on average, in a tax rate that is less than what low whites prefer and a binding affirmative action target, low whites are worse off. □

Proof of Proposition 3 and 4. Both of these results follow from the continuity result on the equilibrium correspondence proved in Banks and Duggan (in press, Theorem 3) and the convergence of interests between low-type whites and blacks, who jointly constitute a majority of the population. □

References

Acemoglu, D., 2001. Good jobs versus bad jobs. Journal of Labor Economics 19, 1–21.

Acemoglu, D., Shimer, R., 1999. Holdups and efficiency with search frictions. International Economic Review 40, 827–849.

Agell, J., Lommerud, K. E., 1997. Minimum wages and the incentives for skill formation. Journal of Public Economics 64, 25–40.

Alesina, A., Glaeser, E., 2004. Fighting Poverty in the US and Europe. Oxford University Press, Oxford.

Alesina, A., La Ferrara, 2000. Participation in heterogeneous communities. Quarterly Journal of Economics 115 (3), 847–904.

Alesina, A., Baqir, Easterly, 1999. Public goods and ethnic divisions. Quarterly Journal of Economics 114 (4), 1243–1284.

Anderson, T., 2004. The Pursuit of Fairness: A History of Affirmative Actions. Oxford University Press, Oxford.

Banks, J. S., Duggan, J., 2006. A general bargaining model of legislative policy-making. Quarterly Journal of Political Science 1 (1), 49–85.

Baron, D., Ferejohn, J., 1989. Bargaining in legislatures. American Political Science Review 83, 1181–1206.

Chan, J., Eyster, E., 2002. Admission impossible: self-interest and affirmative action Working Paper. The Johns Hopkins University.

Chung, K.-S., 2000. Role models and arguments for affirmative action. American Economic Review 99, 640–648.

Coate, S., Loury, G., 1993. Will affirmative action policies eliminate negative stereotypes? American Economic Review 83, 1220–1240.

Dixit, A., Londregan, J., 1998. Ideology, tactics and efficiency in redistributive politics. Quarterly Journal of Economics 113, 497–529.

Foster, D., Vohra, R., 1992. An economic argument for affirmative action. Rationality and Society 4 (2), 176–188.

Gilens, M., 1999. Why Americans Hate Welfare. University of Chicago Press, Chicago.

Grossman, G., Helpman, E., 2001. Special Interest Politics. MIT Press, Cambridge.

Grout, P., 1984. Investment and wages in the absence of binding contracts: a Nash bargaining approach. Econometrica 52, 449–460.

Holzer, H., Neumark, D., 2000. Assessing affirmative action. Journal of Economic Literature 38, 483–568.

Kinder, D., Sanders, L., 1996. Divided by Color: Racial Politics and Democratic Ideals. University of Chicago Press, Chicago.

Levy, G., 2004. Public education for the minority, private education for the majority Working Paper. London School of Economics.

Lipset, S. M., Bendix, R., 1959. Social Mobility in Industrial Society. University of California Press, Berkeley.

Lundberg, S. J., 1991. The enforcement of equal opportunity laws under imperfect information: affirmative action and alternatives. Quarterly Journal of Economics 106 (1), 309–326.

Luttmer, E., 2001. Group loyalty and the taste for redistribution. Journal of Political Economy 89 (5), 500–528.

MacLeod, W. B., Malcomson, J., 1993. Investments, holdups, and the form of market contracts. American Economic Review 83, 811–837.

Meltzer, A. H., Richard, S. F., 1981. A rational theory of the size of government. Journal of Political Economy 89 (5), 914–927.

Myrdal, G., 1960. Beyond the Welfare State. Yale University Press, New Haven.

Quadagno, J., 1994. The Color of Welfare. Oxford University Press, Oxford.

Roemer, J. E., 1998. Why the poor don't expropriate the rich. Journal of Public Economics 70 (3), 399–424.

Roemer, J. E., 2004. The democratic dynamics of educational investment and income distribution. In: Mansfield, E. J., Sisson, R. (Eds.), The Evolution of Political Knowledge: Democracy, Autonomy, and Conflict in Comparative and International Politics. University of Ohio Press, Columbus.

Roemer, J. E., Lee, W., 2004. Racialism and redistribution in the United States: a solution to the problem of American exceptionalism. Working Paper. Yale University.

Romer, T., 1975. Individual welfare, majority voting, and the properties of a linear income tax. Journal of Public Economics 14, 163–185.

Schofield, N., 1984. Classification Theorem for Smooth Social Choice on a Manifold. Social Choice and Welfare 1 (3), 187–210.

Skrentny, J. D., 1996. The Ironies of Affirmative Action. Chicago University Press, Chicago.

PART IV

Labor and the Nordic Model
of Social Democracy

15

Introduction

Karl Ove Moene

Michael Wallerstein had a long-term research interest in social democracy in the Nordic countries, a theme that we worked on together for many years. Our first paper on the topic praised the Nordic achievements, but claimed that social democracy was in retreat. As we saw it, "both the egalitarian distribution of income and the security of income that distinguished social democratic societies from other capitalist democracies are declining" (Moene and Wallerstein 1993a: 231–232). As time went on and we continued our work, we became less certain that the era of social democracy was actually over, and more certain that whatever the future of the social democracy in Europe, the Nordic lessons were highly relevant for social reformers in other parts of the world, including developing countries.

The societal model of northern Europe goes under many names. While the Swedes call the system the "Swedish model," the Danes and Norwegians insist on the "Scandinavian model." More recently, representatives of the European Union have started to use "Nordic model," which now seems to be the most popular term. Outside Europe the model is best known simply as "social democracy," a term that most Europeans associate with specific political parties and ideologies rather than with an economic and political system.

Social democracy in the Nordic countries is strong evidence for the achievements of unions as opposed to workers' ownership. The success of unions may seem obvious today, but to many early leaders of the labor movement in the nineteenth century, worker cooperatives were as relevant a goal as extensive union membership – and just as distant. But while unions grew to become important actors in the labor markets of northern Europe and elsewhere, worker cooperatives remained on the margins.

One of the first joint papers that Michael Wallerstein and I wrote explored why worker cooperatives are so strikingly absent where unions are particularly strong. We emphasized that without unions able to enforce a floor on wages throughout the economy, competition and free entry would drive the returns to labor down to their competitive level whether firms are owned by the employees or the shareholders. Thus, unions provide a smaller share of a bigger pie, and union leaders consider workers' cooperatives as a threat to union solidarity (Moene and Wallerstein 1993b).

A comprehensive union movement is indeed an important characteristic of the Nordic model of social democracy. Yet one should not underestimate the importance of strong employer associations to the system. Together the two parts of the labor market tend to take wages out of competition by way of centralized wage negotiations. The role of employers is often forgotten by the critics of the system. If the employers so desired, they could easily dissolve the system by withdrawing from central wage negotiations.

In addition, the Nordic model is distinguished by a large welfare state and a system of routine consultation among government and representatives of interest organizations. Its policies include wage leveling through "solidaristic bargaining," the provision of basic goods for all citizens as a right of citizenship, and a government commitment to full employment.

Wallerstein and I wanted first of all to explain how the Nordic countries achieved the most egalitarian wage distribution and the most generous welfare states in the world without obvious macroeconomic costs. We focused on the key institutions and policies that have dominated northern Europe since the Second World War. We wanted to emphasize the general lessons and to resolve the many puzzles that are associated with the Nordic model of social democracy.

The lessons for mainstream economics may be particularly harsh. The Nordic countries of Denmark, Finland, Norway, and Sweden seem to violate what the economics profession has long viewed as necessary requirements for an economy to prosper. Their wage differentials are too small, their taxes are too high, their public sectors are too large, their welfare states are too generous, and their unions are too strong. Despite these violations, the Nordic countries have for decades done extremely well. What most economists see as a recipe for serious economic trouble seems, in the Nordic countries, to be consistent with high growth, low unemployment, low inequality, and a fairly efficient allocation of resources.

So, has economics got it wrong? Or are the Nordic countries just a special case? Clearly, economics cannot have gotten it universally right, and the

Nordic experience may be a good example of why and how. But the Nordic lessons should be interpreted with caution. The lesson is not that there is a universal positive relationship between equality and economic performance. The lesson is that under some institutional arrangements, equality and prosperity go together and reinforce each other. Under other institutional arrangements this is not the case. A narrow economic approach, however, that neglects institutional complementarities and social spillovers does not capture such mechanisms and may easily misinterpret the Nordic experience.

Several complementarities between institutions and policies make Nordic social democracy a broader societal model. On the one hand, it would be difficult to maintain full employment in the Nordic countries without a comprehensive union movement that provides wage moderation in central wage negotiations even when unemployment is low. Full employment, on the other hand, is important for central union leaders to obtain wage moderation without too much resistance among their members. All this can be viewed as a mutual gift exchange (Moene and Wallerstein 1993a).

A comprehensive union movement would also lobby for generous welfare state arrangements. Yet the greatest influence of unions on welfare spending comes via their wage policies. The Nordic countries' unions have a much stronger influence on the distribution of wages among workers than on the functional distribution of income between labor and capital (Wallerstein 1999; Moene and Wallerstein 1995). And in turn, the distribution of wages among workers has a strong influence on welfare spending. The small wage differentials that centralized wage setting creates provide support for universal welfare state arrangements (Moene and Wallerstein 2001, 2003a). The generosity of the welfare state, on the other hand, supports weak groups in the labor market, which compresses the wage distribution even further. Together the two sides can generate an equality multiplier (Barth and Moene 2006).

The Nordic model is also characterized by high female labor force participation. Again, there are mutual dependences between the labor market and the welfare state. As women joined their husbands in the labor force, households naturally demanded more public care for children and the elderly. The gradual expansion of the welfare state made it easier for even more women to enter the workforce, which in turn led to higher support for welfare spending and to stronger economic growth.

These are all examples of how policies, institutions, and behaviors fit together and strengthen one another. One can argue, as we did, that they constitute a form of institutional equilibrium. Still, one may wonder whether such an institutional equilibrium supports lasting social and economic achievements.

Skeptics have long doubted the long-run feasibility of reformed capitalism. In 1899, Rosa Luxemburg (1970: 43) characterized social reforms under capitalism as "a sort of a labor of Sisyphus" in which partial victories would continually be eroded by market forces. More recently, conservative critics, such as Erik Lundberg (1985), have made the reverse argument that market forces are steadily eroded by social reform with negative consequences for economic performance.

Neither view has been proven correct. Social equality and worker security have persisted in the Nordic countries, and economic growth has been on par with the US. In the US, rising inequality has gone hand in hand with social cleavages and lower welfare for at least one-third of the population. In contrast, most of Europe has experienced only a modest rise in inequality, but a sharp increase in unemployment. The Nordic countries, however, have combined social equality with good macroeconomic performance and full employment.

One reason why so many scholars nevertheless have remained skeptical may simply be that they misunderstand what the Nordic model entails. In popular debates one can distinguish between different views.

Capital against labor. This is the most conventional view, derived from the classic conflict between labor and capital. It assumes that the Nordic model is built on a basic compromise between the interests of employers and employees, in which a strong labor movement has pressed employers to give political and economic concessions – historically to stop ideological contagion from the Soviet Union. The logic of capital against labor implies that a stronger labor movement stabilizes the system and its achievements, while stronger capital owners undermine the system.

Nordic exceptionalism. This view insists that the Nordic model is an exception that is only feasible in small, homogeneous societies with an extraordinary commitment to equality. It emphasizes that the Nordic countries historically were homogeneous with respect to religion, language, and ethnicity. In addition, the countries had a rather egalitarian distribution of land. Social homogeneity and the small differences in initial wealth lead to more egalitarian preferences in the population than elsewhere. The logic of Nordic exceptionalism implies that the stability of the system and its achievements depend on the viability of the egalitarian preferences in the population, while more self-interest and less solidarity would undermine the system.

Capitalism without entrepreneurs. This view is often held by representatives of the political right, who claim that the Nordic model is based on too much equality, too much worker security, and too much regulation for the good of the economy. The model lacks the dynamics of entrepreneurial creativity – the essence of capitalism. The logic of capitalism without entrepreneurs implies that the stability of the system and its achievements require regulated markets. On the other hand, more markets, more globalization, and less regulation will undermine the model.

Unwarranted class collaboration. This view is often held by representatives on the political left, who claim that the labor unions misrepresent the interests of their rank and file by accepting wage moderation in central wage negotiations and by imposing restrictions on industrial actions in local wage negotiations. The logic of unwarranted class collaboration implies that the stability of pro-labor outcomes requires class struggle and not cooperation between labor and capital. More class collaboration will undermine the best features of the Nordic model.

Although there may be some truth in all of these views, none of them captures the essence of the Nordic model as Michael Wallerstein and I saw it. While Nordic exceptionalism underestimates the conflicts inherent in the system, labor against capital gets them wrong. The arguments behind both capitalism without entrepreneurs and unwarranted class collaboration fail to see that the social arrangement of the Nordic countries may well benefit both labor and capital.

In fact, implicit worker-employer coalitions have led to both wage compression and improved performance over the last 50 years, especially in Norway and Sweden. Initially the main concern of the two parties was not equality, but rather macroeconomic efficiency by way of encouraging structural change through investment in good modern jobs. "Equal pay for equal work" achieved exactly that. This was the first step towards the solidaristic wage bargaining that became institutionalized in the 1950s.

This policy is the most dramatic instance of union-sponsored wage equalization in the world. "In both Norway and Sweden, an ambitiously egalitarian wage policy was adopted by the central blue-collar confederation in the early 1950s and pursued steadily for three decades. Solidaristic bargaining, as the policy was named, called for the equalization of workers' pretax income by eliminating or reducing the wage differentials that existed between plants within the same industry, between industries, between regions and ultimately between occupations" (Moene and Wallerstein 1995, 1997).

While solidaristic bargaining was part of a wider social democratic package that included substantial increases in the generosity of welfare programs, the most important support for solidaristic bargaining came from those who benefited directly. In principle the same egalitarian goals could have been achieved with steeply progressive taxes and targeted transfer payments instead of wage equalization. In practice, however, political support for an analogous and equivalent redistribution through taxes and transfers would have been more difficult to obtain.

The significance of solidaristic bargaining extends beyond the labor markets of the Nordic countries. The main beneficiaries from solidaristic bargaining are to be found in the tails of the income distribution, among low-paid workers and capitalist employers; the losers are high-skilled middle-class workers. Solidaristic bargaining was initially supported by important actors opposed to redistribution. The efficient and innovative enterprises gained from wage setting with small wage differentials. A compressed earnings distribution was supported by a coalition between numerous workers *and* influential capital owners. Such concurrent interests, typically categorized as *alliances of ends against the middle*, may explain the viability of the Nordic model and why it is associated with high economic growth (Moene and Wallerstein 1995, 1997, 2003b).

Despite the claims made by supporters of the capitalism-without-entrepreneurs view, wage compression does in fact stimulate innovation, as firms with advanced new technologies do not have to pay excessive wage premiums. While wage inequality operates as though high-productivity firms were taxed and low-productivity firms were subsidized as wages adjust to local conditions, wage compression works in the opposite way: it is as though high-productivity firms were subsidized and low-productivity firms were taxed. As a result, wage equality implies that inefficient firms close down earlier as newer and more productive firms enter – contributing to the process of structural change that Schumpeter (1942) called "creative destruction."

The Nordic experience reminds us of the importance of implementation and procedures for policy outcomes. In the Nordic countries, and maybe

374

more generally, interests may play out very differently in the labor market than in parliamentary politics. This is important, as coalition structures and economic interests in the economic base obviously affect policies chosen in its superstructure. What made the Nordic countries distinct is precisely the strength of the coalitions of ends against the middle in the labor market, which compressed the distribution of wages among workers. The wages of high-skilled middle-class workers were held back in the name of solidarity, raising profits and investments, which in turn made it possible to increase the wages of the low-paid workers without creating unemployment.

The small wage differentials that emerged led again to a change in the pattern of political competition in the electoral arena. As economic differences within the electorate became smaller, there were fewer divergent interests in the determination of welfare spending. Moreover, wage compression for a given total income implied that the majority of workers received higher pay and thus demanded higher social insurance, simply because insurance against income losses is a normal good the demand for which rises with income (Moene and Wallerstein 2001, 2003a).

Recently, the Nordic model has been in the headlines in the globalization debate. Some observers have foretold the death of Nordic egalitarianism as trade becomes freer, capital mobility higher, and migration flows stronger. Michael Wallerstein and I (together with Erling Barth) took up these challenges in a small book, *Equality under Pressure*, that we wrote in Norwegian (Barth, Moene, and Wallerstein 2003).

We insisted that freer trade is not a threat to the Nordic model, since the small open economies of Scandinavia have long been used to the discipline of international competition (Finland has quite a different trade history). In all Nordic countries freer trade has in fact helped sustain institutions necessary for wage coordination. In addition, freer trade has tended to raise, not reduce, support for welfare spending to protect voters against fluctuations in the world economy.

Higher capital mobility is also no basic threat. Great mobility of capital implies that capital owners must at least earn international returns on their investments to remain in the country. It does not imply that wages have to be distributed more unequally, or that we have to dismantle the welfare state. As long as profits are high enough, capital mobility provides employers with no credible threats.

It is true that greater labor mobility might be a threat to the Nordic model if workers became sufficiently mobile. If workers were hypermobile, egalitarian countries would attract many more low-skilled workers and lose many more high-skilled workers. In the European Union, however, there have been no formal restrictions on labor migration since 1993, and yet the level of migration has been low in spite of large wage differentials. Despite the absence of any formal restrictions on migration, an unskilled worker in Portugal would earn four times his wage if he moved to Denmark.

External threats to Nordic equality are much more widely discussed than internal threats to equality. Yet, there remains a question whether the Nordic model can withstand the growth in the middle class that an egalitarian educational policy implies. More generally, we might ask whether the social and economic results of the Nordic model will really reproduce the conditions for its continuation. Michael Wallerstein and I have argued repeatedly that the Nordic model is likely to become a victim of its own success.

If in fact the Nordic model is robust in the face of globalization, but not in the face of the internal social changes it generates, the model should not be considered an end state. Maybe the best way to look at the Nordic model of social democracy is as a productive development strategy for poor countries – as we discuss further in the final essay in this part.

It is encouraging to observe that the Nordic model is in fashion again as a source of inspiration to a number of countries. In China, the government has ambitions of building a "harmonious society" with an emphasis on redistribution, welfare, and social security. Leaders in Latin America and in South Africa refer explicitly to Scandinavia as a role model for equitable growth. It has recently been reported (Fuller and Ekman, 2005) that "European leaders want to know how Sweden and its Nordic neighbors, so heavily laden with cradle-to-grave welfare systems, float high above the struggling economies of much of the rest of the Continent." Michael Wallerstein would have liked that.

References

Barth, E., and K. Moene. 2006. "The Equality Multiplier." Unpublished manuscript, University of Oslo.

Barth, E., K. Moene, and M. Wallerstein. 2003. *Equality under Pressure. Challenges for the Scandinavian Model of Distribution.* (In Norwegian.) Oslo: Gyldendal Norsk Forlag.

Fuller, T., and I. Ekman. 2005. "The Envy of Europe: Success of Nordic Economies Is Turning Heads." *International Herald Tribune*, September 17, 2005.

Introduction

Lundberg, E. 1985. "The Rise and Fall of the Swedish Model." *Journal of Economic Literature 23*: 1–36.

Luxemburg, R. 1970. *Reform and Revolution*. New York: Pathfinder Press.

Moene, K., and M. Wallerstein. 1993a. "What is Wrong with Social Democracy." In P. Bardhan and J. Roemer (eds.), *Market Socialism. The Present Debate*. Cambridge University Press.

Moene, K., and M. Wallerstein. 1993b. "Collective Bargaining versus Worker Ownership." *Journal of Comparative Economics 17*:, 628–645.

Moene, K., and M. Wallerstein. 1995. "Solidaristic Wage Bargaining." *Nordic Journal of Political Economy 22*: 79–94.

Moene, K., and M. Wallerstein. 1997. "Pay Inequality." *Journal of Labor Economics 15*: 403–430.

Moene, K., and M. Wallerstein. 2001. "Inequality, Social Insurance and Redistribution." *American Political Science Review 95* (4): 859–874.

Moene, K., and M. Wallerstein. 2003a. "Earnings Inequality and Welfare Spending: A Disaggregated Analysis." *World Politics 55* (4): 485–516.

Moene, K., and M. Wallerstein. 2003b. "Does the Logic of Collective Action Explain the Logic of Corporativism?" *Journal of Theoretical Politics 15* (3): 271–297.

Schumpeter, J. 1942. *Capitalism, Socialism and Democracy*. New York: Harper and Row.

Wallerstein, M. 1999. "Wage Setting Institutions and Pay Inequality in Advanced Industrial Societies." *American Journal of Political Science 43* (3): 649–680.

16

How Social Democracy Worked: Labor-Market Institutions

Karl Ove Moene and Michael Wallerstein

I. Introduction

Social democracy is, in essence, a series of political and economic compromises.[1] Early social democrats were forced to compromise between their Marxist program and their commitment to abide by the rules of electoral competition that rendered the implementation of the Marxist program politically infeasible. Later, social democrats were forced to compromise between promoting the interests of their core constituency of manual workers in manufacturing, transportation, construction, and mining and the need to obtain support from much broader groups if they were to obtain a majority. Finally, social democracy represents a compromise between egalitarian goals and the need to promote economic growth and employment in a market economy driven by private investment.

Compromises are frequently unpopular. At the crest of left-wing mobilization in Europe and North America during the late 1960s and early 1970s, social democratic parties were denounced for having joined forces with their supposed class enemies in opposition to growing rank-and-file militancy.[2] Defenders of social democracy on the Left responded by arguing that the apparent loss of social democracy's revolutionary aspirations was

[1] The best book-length description of social democracy as a series of political and economic compromises is Adam Przeworski and John Sprague, *Paper Stones: A History of Electoral Socialism* (Chicago: University of Chicago Press, 1986).

[2] Leo Panitch, "Recent Theorizations of Corporatism: Reflections on a Growth Industry," *British Journal of Sociology* 31, no. 1 (1980): 159–87, and "Trade Unions and the Capitalist State," *New Left Review* no. 125 (1981): 21–43.

We thank Gøsta Esping-Andersen, Peter Swenson, and Erik Olin Wright for helpful suggestions and comments.

temporary. In the long run, a number of scholars argued, social democracy will be credited with creating the conditions that make the final transition from capitalism to socialism possible.[3]

Today, the pendulum has swung the other way, and predictions of a radicalization of social democracy appear to be little more than wishful thinking. In the current climate, social democracy is charged with being already too radical for the good of the economy. Social democracy, according to its contemporary critics, introduced too much equality, too much security, and too much employment.[4] In the words of Michael Novak, "Social democracy is based on the same errors as socialism, but in a form that takes a little longer to effect self-destruction."[5] According to recent views, a labor market dominated by powerful unions with strong egalitarian commitments that are protected by pro-labor governments is bound to function badly.[6]

In this article, we offer a dissenting, more positive view of the economic effects of social democratic policies and institutions in the labor market. In our view, social democracy is neither a way station on the road to socialism nor a deviation from sound economic management of a capitalist economy. Social democracy is a distinctive set of institutions and policies that fit together and worked relatively efficiently to reduce both the insecurity and the inequality of income without large sacrifices in terms of economic growth or macroeconomic instability.

Social democracy can be characterized in terms of political relations, institutions, or policies. In political terms, what is exceptional about social democracy is the influence of organized workers as represented by unions. This is not to say that the unions could achieve whatever they wanted. Employers are better organized than workers in North and Central Europe, and neither could dominate the other. In a comparative perspective,

---

[3] John Stephens, *The Transition from Capitalism to Socialism* (Atlantic Highlands, NJ: Humanities Press, 1979); Walter Korpi Korpi, *The Democratic Class Struggle* (London: Routledge and Kegan Paul, 1983); and Gøsta Esping-Andersen, *Politics Against Markets: The Social Democratic Road to Power* (Princeton: Princeton University Press, 1985).

[4] Erik Lundberg, "The Rise and Fall of the Swedish Model," *Journal of Economic Literature* 23, no. 1 (1985): 1–36.

[5] Michael Novak, "The Urgent Need for Virtuous Capitalism," *Los Angeles Times*, 13 March 1994, M5.

[6] Lars Calmfors and Henrik Horn, "Employment Policies and Centralized Wage-Setting," *Economica* 53, no. 1 (1986): 281–302; Assar Lindbeck and Dennis J. Snower, *The Insider-Outsider Theory of Employment and Unemployment* (Cambridge: MIT Press, 1988); and Lars Calmfors, "Lessons from the Macroeconomic Experience of Sweden," *European Journal of Political Economy* 9, no. 1 (1993): 25–72.

however, the political influence of the unions in Scandinavia and in Austria is exceptional. Union influence is not restricted to direct negotiations with employers over wages and working conditions. A distinctive feature of social democracy is the influence of the unions within the social democratic parties, and the centrality of the social democratic parties in parliament.

Institutionally, Scandinavian social democracy is distinguished by a large, universalistic welfare state, active labor-market policies that provide retraining and subsidized work for workers who are unemployed, encompassing trade unions, a centralized system of wage determination, and a system of routinized consultation and cooperation between government, union, and employer representatives. In terms of policy, social democracy in Northern Europe is characterized by a commitment to wage leveling through solidaristic bargaining, the provision of basic goods and services to all as a right of citizenship, and full employment as the primary objective of macroeconomic policy.

Applied strictly, this definition would only include Norway from 1945–65 and Sweden from 1945–76.[7] If we relax our definition to include periods in which the social democratic party lost its parliamentary dominance in the sense that social democratic governments alternated with bourgeois governments, the social democratic period in Norway and Sweden could be extended further. Other countries share some, but not all, of the features we have identified. Denmark and Finland share most, although wage setting was never as centralized as in Norway or Sweden, nor was the social democratic party able to dominate parliament in the same way. Austria shares social democratic dominance after 1970 and many of the institutional features, such as a highly centralized union organization and an extensive system of tripartite consultation and negotiation. But central social democratic policies in Scandinavia, such as solidaristic bargaining, were never attempted by the Austrian social democrats.[8] Germany also shares many social democratic characteristics, excluding solidaristic bargaining, especially during the sixteen years of social democratic participation in

---

[7] The starting point is arbitrarily chosen to be the end of the Second World War. In fact, the social democratic parties first came to power in Sweden in 1932 and in Norway in 1935. But many of the distinctive social democratic policies and institutions were not implemented until after the end of World War II.

[8] Bob Rowthorn, "Corporatism and Labour Market Performance," in *Social Corporatism: A Superior Economic System?* ed. Jukka Pekkarinen, Matti Pohjola, and Bob Rowthorn (Oxford: Clarendon, 1992), 82–131.

government (1966–82). If we take individual parts of our definition, counterparts can be found in almost all Western European countries.

Today, social democracy is clearly in decline. To measure the end in terms of loss of solid social democratic government is too stringent, since subsequent bourgeois governments in Norway and Sweden largely continued the policies of their predecessors. It is better to measure the decline of social democracy by the retreat from social democratic policies and institutions that has occurred, regardless of the party in power. In the 1980s, deregulation of housing and financial markets was promoted by socialist as well as bourgeois governments. In Sweden, twenty-seven consecutive years of centralized bargaining came to an end in 1983 when a separate agreement was signed in the metalworking sector. Although centralized bargaining has been restored in Sweden in most years since 1983, subsequent negotiations at the industry or plant level are subject to fewer constraints than before.[9] Wage inequality has increased in all of the Nordic countries since the mid-1980s, even in the absence of formal changes in the rules of collective bargaining.[10] Most dramatic, however, is the rise of unemployment. Throughout the 1970s and most of the 1980s, unemployment in the Nordic countries, with the exception of Denmark, remained low even as unemployment increased rapidly in most other countries in Western Europe. Since 1988 in Norway and 1990 in Sweden and Finland, however, unemployment rates have risen sharply. In Sweden and Finland, the decline of production and employment in the early 1990s is worse than the decline that occurred during the 1930s.[11]

The primary focus in this article is how social democratic labor-market institutions worked when they worked. In particular, we focus on three features. In the next section, we discuss corporatism, trade dependence, and the origins of centralized wage bargaining. In the third section, we examine

[9] For a detailed comparison of changes in the bargaining institutions of Norway, Sweden, Denmark, and Finland since 1950, see Miriam Golden, Peter Lange, and Michael Wallerstein, "Trade Union Organization and Industrial Relations in the Postwar Era in 16 Nations" (paper presented at the 1995 annual meetings of the Midwest Political Science Association, Chicago, 6–8 April 1995).

[10] For time series data on wage compression in Sweden, see Douglas A. Hibbs, Jr., and Håkan Locking, "Wage Compression, Wage Drift, and Wage Inflation in Sweden," working paper no. 87, Trade Union Institute for Economic Research (FIEF), Stockholm, 1991.

[11] See Asbjørn Rødseth, "Vegen til Høg Arbeidsløyse," in *SNF Årbok 1994: Perspektiv på Arbeidsledigheten*, ed. Agnar Sandmo (Bergen: Fagbokforlaget, 1994). Because of active labor-market policies and unemployment insurance, the economic hardship caused by the rise of unemployment in the 1990s is much less than in the 1930s.

the politics and economics of the reduction of wage differentials through solidaristic bargaining. In the fourth section, we offer a partial explanation for the maintenance of full employment in a period when unemployment rose rapidly elsewhere in Europe and North America. Reasons why social democratic policies and institutions have been widely abandoned in Northern Europe, in spite of (what we argue to be) their past success, are discussed in the concluding section.

The major prominent social democratic labor-market institution that we do not discuss is the set of mobility grants, retraining programs, and relief work that comprise the active labor policy pioneered in Sweden in the 1950s and copied in Norway in the 1970s. Active labor-market policies command general admiration among academics.[12] There is an ongoing debate in Sweden and Norway regarding the appropriate size and design of active labor-market programs. Recent econometric studies suggest that active labor-market policies have been increased to such an extent that the marginal cost exceeds the marginal benefit.[13] The proposition that active labor-market policies are preferable to the alternative of providing long-term passive unemployment benefits, however, is widely accepted.

II. Corporatism and Competition

Industrial relations in the Nordic countries are often given the label of "corporatist." But corporatism is a particularly bad choice of word to describe the Nordic system of centralized wage setting, since corporatism has connotations of anticompetitive practices and trade protection, not to mention fascism. The connection between corporatist wage setting and economic autarky is not merely an accident of history. According to the standard understanding of trade unions in economics, union power and protection from competition in the goods market are closely linked.

Even pro-union books like Richard Freeman and James Medoff's *What Do Unions Do?* presume that the exercise of monopoly power is one of the

---

[12] Richard Layard, Stephen Nickell, and Richard Jackman, *Unemployment, Macroeconomic Performance and the Labour Market* (Oxford: Oxford University Press, 1991).
[13] Calmfors, "Lessons from the Macroeconomic Experience of Sweden," and "Active Labour Market Policy and Unemployment – A Framework for the Analysis of Crucial Design Features," seminar paper no. 563, Institute for International Economic Studies, University of Stockholm, 1994. For a study using Norwegian data, see O. Raaum, H. Torp, and H. Goldstein, "Employment Effects of Labor Market Training in Norway," unpublished paper, ISF/SNF, Oslo, 1994.

main functions of unions.[14] Most economists think that in the long run, the rents that exist in the absence of monopoly power, the cost advantage particular firms might have due to their possession of an input that is in fixed supply, are relatively small. Unions can only raise wages significantly if the firm has some monopoly power, or if the union is able to "take wages out of the competition" and push the industry up its demand curve. Since international unions do not exist (except between the United States and Canada), raising wage costs throughout the industry is only possible if an industry is shielded from international competition, either naturally, as in the non-traded-goods sector, or as the result of government policy. Thus it is natural for economists to think that strong unions and trade protection go hand in hand.

In fact, the Nordic variety of corporatism was associated, not with protectionism and monopolistic pricing, but with free trade and the subsequent need to remain competitive in export markets. In Norway, Sweden, and Denmark, the leading proponents of centralized bargaining were not the unions at all, but employers. This is not to say that the unions were irrelevant. The centralization of bargaining remained limited in Denmark because the single largest union, the union of unskilled and semiskilled workers, remained adamantly opposed.[15] The establishment of centralized bargaining required support from both sides.

In both Norway and Sweden, the initial step toward centralization took the form of a conflict between the national organization of employers and the national confederation of unions, on the one side, and construction workers on the other.[16] In Norway, the LO intervened to end an illegal strike of construction workers in 1928, a strike that threatened the unity of

[14] Richard B. Freeman and James L. Medoff, *What Do Unions Do?* (New York: Basic Books, 1984). *What Do Unions Do?* is pro-union because Freeman and Medoff argue that the exercise of monopoly power is not the only thing unions do. In particular, Freeman and Medoff argue that unions also allow workers to express their preferences in the labor market in a manner that is superior, in some instances, to the way that preferences are revealed in workers' choice of jobs.

[15] Walter Galenson, *The Danish System of Labor Relations* (Cambridge: Harvard University Press, 1952).

[16] The best accounts of the centralization of bargaining in Sweden and Denmark are Peter Swenson, *Fair Shares: Unions, Pay and Politics in Sweden and West Germany* (Ithaca, NY: Cornell University Press, 1989), and "Bringing Capital Back In, or Social Democracy Reconsidered," *World Politics* 43, no. 4 (1991): 513–44. A detailed description of the Norwegian case, which parallels the Swedish case, can only be found in Norwegian, for example in Jorunn Bjørgum, "LO og NAF 1899–1940," *Tidsskrift for Arbeiderbevegelsens Historie* no. 2 (1985): 85–114.

the national employers' association. In Sweden, the first step toward centralization occurred with the intervention of the LO in a strike of construction workers in 1933. In both countries, there were political considerations in the background. The Norwegian LO was afraid that the strike would provoke the bourgeois majority in parliament to pass antiunion legislation. The Swedish LO feared that the new social democratic government would intervene to end the strike if they did not do so themselves. In Sweden, the LO was also fearful that employers would respond with a general lockout.

In addition to the political considerations, however, there was a powerful economic rationale for intervention by the LO. The centralization of bargaining in Sweden and Norway (and, much earlier, in Denmark) represented, in essence, an attempt by employers and workers in the metalworking sector to control wages throughout the economy in line with prices in the traded-goods sector.[17] Construction workers were the target in both Sweden and Norway because they were highly paid, militant, and sheltered from foreign competition. When foreign demand collapsed in the 1930s, metalworkers accepted large wage reductions in order to stem the decline of employment. Construction workers came under no such pressure, in large part because of government policy. In both Norway and Sweden, social democratic governments responded to the crisis by increasing government spending on housing. Since construction workers were employed in the export sector as well as in home construction, higher construction wages raised labor costs in the export sector. The more construction workers were paid, the more metalworkers had to reduce their wages in order to maintain employment (and the more metalworkers had to pay for housing). In addition, to the extent that higher government spending for nontraded goods led to higher wages instead of greater employment, the ability of the social democratic governments to reduce unemployment was undermined.

With decentralized bargaining, the cost of declining foreign demand would be concentrated, at least initially, on employers and workers in the export industries. In gaining control over the wage demands of workers in the non-traded-goods sector, metalworkers and their employers were able to force all workers to share the burden of lowering wage costs in the export sector. Indeed, the impact of centralized bargaining on the relative wages of construction workers was dramatic. As we discuss in the next section, solidaristic bargaining reduced the wage differentials received by skilled

---

[17] This argument was first made with reference to Sweden and Denmark by Swenson in "Bringing Capital Back In."

workers in both countries to exceptionally low levels. What is relevant here is that centralized bargaining was created as a mechanism for allowing those workers who were directly subject to international competition to set the pace of wage increases for the entire economy.

Rather than being associated with protection, the centralization of bargaining was associated with liberal trade policies and an export orientation. In the 1930s, the common response of unions and employers in the traded-goods sector in larger, less trade dependent countries when foreign demand fell was to seek trade protection. In small economies that are specialized in production for export markets, the option of protecting domestic industry was limited by the smallness of the domestic market. The only way to recover from falling prices in export markets, from the point of view of industries in countries with high levels of specialization in nonagricultural exports, was to lower costs. Centralized bargaining provided workers in the export sector a means for sharing the burden of cost reductions by controlling wage increases throughout the rest of the economy. Far from being the product of a closed economy, centralized bargaining at the national level was a product of an exceptionally high degree of trade openness and trade dependence. Like Marx, social democrats have always advocated free-trade policies.[18]

III. The Efficiency of Wage Equality

Unions probably had little influence in Scandinavia on the distribution of income between wages and profits. The need to maintain adequate profitability of private investment and employment ensured that the share of profit in national income was not dramatically reduced. This does not mean, however, that unions were without significant influence on the distribution of income. The unions had a large impact on the distribution of wage income among wage earners. In Norway, Sweden, and Denmark, the national union confederations pursued an ambitiously egalitarian wage policy. Solidaristic bargaining, as the policy was named, called for the equalization of workers' pretax income by eliminating or reducing wage differentials between plants in the same industry, between industries, between regions,

---

[18] The major exception was agricultural policy where social democratic governments adopted an extensive system of price supports and trade restrictions. Subsidies and protection for agriculture were the prices social democrats had to pay to form a parliamentary coalition with the farmers' party.

and ultimately, between occupations. "Equal pay for equal work" is a common demand of unions, easily explained by unions' desire to reduce managerial discretion and competition from low-wage employers. The Nordic unions are unique, however, in extending the principal of "equal pay for equal work" from one industry to the entire economy, and then moving beyond the demand for "equal pay for equal work" toward the goal of "equal pay for all work."[19]

The egalitarian wage policy was remarkably effective. In Sweden between 1970, when comprehensive wage data on individuals began to be collected, and 1983, when the system of centralized bargaining collapsed, the variance of the log of hourly wages among private-sector blue-collar workers declined by over 50 percent.[20] That dramatic decrease does not include the equally prominent reduction of the wage differential between blue-collar and white-collar workers. Douglas Hibbs estimates that a similar decline occurred during the 1960s as well, implying that the variance of log hourly wages in 1983 was only one-quarter of what it was in 1960.[21] Similar longitudinal data are not available for Norway, but the pattern appears the same. According to survey data reported by Arne Kalleberg and Tom Colbjørnsen, wage inequality in 1980 as measured by the coefficient of variation (standard deviation divided by the mean) of log earnings was even lower in Norway than in Sweden.[22] Industry-level wage data reported by Freeman indicate that Norway, Denmark, and Sweden have lower interindustry wage differentials than other OECD countries.[23]

The most common view today is that such wage equality creates severe problems with the allocation of labor and workers' productivity.[24] Too

[19] See Jonas Pontusson and Peter Swenson, "Markets, Production, Institutions, and Politics: Why Swedish Employers Have Abandoned the Swedish Model" (paper presented at the Eighth International Conference of Europeanists, Chicago, 27–29 March 1992) for a description of changes in the goals of solidaristic bargaining over the postwar period.
[20] Hibbs and Locking, "Wage Compression, Wage Drift and Wage Inflation in Sweden."
[21] Douglas A. Hibbs, Jr., "Wage Compression Under Solidarity Bargaining in Sweden," working paper no. 30, Trade Union Institute for Economic Research (FIEF), Stockholm, 1990, and "Wage Dispersion and Trade Union Action," in *Generating Equality in the Welfare State – The Swedish Experience*, ed. Inga Persson (Oslo: Norwegian University Press, 1990).
[22] Arne L. Kalleberg and Tom Colbjørnsen, "Unions and the Structure of Earnings Inequality: Cross-National Patterns," *Social Science Research* 19 (1990): 348–71.
[23] Richard B. Freeman, "Labour Market Institutions and Economic Performance," *Economic Policy* 3 (1988): 64–80.
[24] See, for example, Assar Lindbeck, "Comment on Moene, Wallerstein and Hoel," in *Trade Union Behavior, Pay Bargaining and Economic Performance*, ed. Robert Flanagan, Karl Ove Moene, and Michael Wallerstein (Oxford: Oxford University Press: 1993).

much solidaristic bargaining and too little connection between work performed and wages received became a prominent and persistent complaint of Swedish employers during the 1970s and 1980s.[25] The reduced sensitivity of wages either to the performance of the firm or to local conditions in the labor market that result from imposing a common wage at the industry or sectoral level is often blamed for the persistence of European unemployment. Comparisons are frequently made between the impressive growth of private-sector employment in the United States during the 1980s and the stagnation of private-sector employment in Europe. By preventing the decline of wages at the bottom of the wage distribution, the restriction of wage differentials is viewed as blocking American-style employment growth.

Not all forms of wage leveling result in efficiency losses, however. Local wage setting, with or without collective bargaining, generally results in unequal pay for equal work. Even without unions, the cost of filling vacancies or training new workers endows many workers with some degree of bargaining power.[26] Empirical work on relative wages in the United States reveals large interfirm and interindustry wage differentials that cannot be explained by union membership or any other observable characteristics of the job or the workers.[27] The explanation that best fits such empirical findings as the negative correlation between wage premiums and quit rates, the positive correlation between wages and profits, and the high correlation of wage premiums among different occupations in the same firm or industry is that rent-sharing is widespread with decentralized wage setting, even in the absence of unions.[28] Perfectly competitive equilibria are natural benchmarks to use in economic analyses, but one should not be too quick to identify the model of perfect competition with the reality of decentralized labor markets. In fact, the principal of equal pay for equal work that initially

---

[25] Hans-Göran Myrdal, "The Hard Way for a Centralized to a Decentralized Industrial Relations System: The Case of Sweden and SAF," in *Employers' Associations in Europe: Policy and Organization*, ed. Otto Jakobi and Dieter Sadowski (Baden-Baden: Nomos Verlag, 1991).

[26] See the model of A. Shaked and John Sutton, "Involuntary Unemployment as a Perfect Equilibrium in a Bargaining Model," *Econometrica* 52 (1984): 1351–64.

[27] Alan B. Krueger and Lawrence H. Summers, "Efficiency Wages and the Inter-Industry Wage Structure," *Econometrica* 56 (1988): 259–93; Erica L. Groshen, "Sources of Intra-Industry Wage Dispersion: How Much Do Employers Matter?" *Quarterly Journal of Economics* 106 (1991): 869–84.

[28] Robert Gibbons and Lawrence Katz, "Does Unmeasured Ability Explain Inter-Industry Wage Differentials?" *Review of Economic Studies* 59 (1992): 515–35.

guided solidaristic wage bargaining may have created a labor market that more closely approximated the competitive model than the wage differentials that result from decentralized wage setting.

It is usually assumed that the Scandinavian unions fought for reduced wage differentials out of an ideological commitment to equality, while employers resisted giving up their ability to use wage differentials as an incentive and recruitment device. In fact, the original arguments made on behalf of solidaristic bargaining when the policy was first proposed in 1951 by two Swedish union economists, Rehn and Rudolf Meidner, concerned macroeconomic stability and efficiency, not equality.[29] Even more surprising, Peter Swenson's historical investigations reveal that the goal of equalizing wages among firms and among industries had the strong support of the Swedish Employers' Association as well as the national union confederation.[30]

Both Rehn and Meidner's argument for the efficiency of solidaristic bargaining and the initial support of employers for such a policy can be explained in a growth model with embodied (exogenous) technical change. To take the simplest case, consider the difference between local and industry-level bargaining in the traded-goods sector with firms that are price-takers in world markets.[31] New plants are assumed to be more productive than old plants, but older plants are assumed not to become more productive over time. In other words, all productivity growth is embodied in new plant and equipment in the model. Over time, the industry becomes more productive as new plants are built and older plants are closed. For simplicity, we assume that employment is fixed at the plant level.[32] Employment varies at the industry level with the number of plants in operation. We restrict our attention to equilibrium paths along which the price of output

[29] LO (*Landsorganisationen i Sverige*), *Trade Unions and Full Employment* (Stockholm: LO, 1953).

[30] Peter Swenson, "Managing the Managers: The Swedish Employers' Confederation, Labor Scarcity, and the Suppression of Labor Market Segmentation," *Scandinavian Journal of History* 16 (1992): 335–56.

[31] In this section we summarize the results of Karl Ove Moene and Michael Wallerstein, "Egalitarian Wage Policies," unpublished paper, University of Oslo and Northwestern University. The assumption of an exogenous price is not critical for our argument. We adopt the fixed price assumption here solely because it facilitates the presentation of the argument through pictures rather than equations.

[32] The assumption of a fixed labor requirement per plant can also be relaxed without altering the conclusions.

is constant while the productivity of new plants, workers' average wage, and the cost of building new plants all rise exponentially at the same constant rate.

With both prices and employment per plant fixed, firms face only two decisions: when to build new plants and when to shut down existing plants. Investment costs are sunk when the plant is built. It follows that firms will keep existing plants in operation as long as revenues exceed or equal wage costs (since wages are the only variable costs in the model). Firms build new plants in each period as long as the expected present value of profits generated over the plant's lifetime exceeds or equals its building costs. The number of new plants built every period and the age of the oldest plants that remain in operation determine total output and employment in the industry.

In systems with decentralized wage setting, workers in each plant bargain separately. Even when local wage bargaining takes place within a frame agreement negotiated at a higher level, the outcome is equivalent to purely local bargaining if local bargainers are free to call strikes or lockouts when pressing their demands.[33] Since we have assumed that employment does not vary at the plant level, union members will want the highest wage possible subject to the constraint that the plant is not closed. In the event of a strike or lockout, we assume that workers receive zero income. This implies (a) that workers remain unemployed during labor disputes and (b) that striking workers do not receive strike support from nonstriking workers. In other words, workers who receive strike benefits are assumed to be drawing on their own collective savings.

Formally, the payoffs for workers at time s in a plant of vintage t with decentralized bargaining are given by

$$u(s,t) = \begin{cases} w(s,t) & \text{if there is an agreement,} \\ 0 & \text{if there is a strike or lockout} \end{cases}$$

where $w(s,t)$ is the wage. (Since employment is assumed to be fixed at the plant level, we choose units so that each plant employs one worker.)

---

[33] See Karl Ove Moene, Michael Wallerstein, and Michael Hoel, "Bargaining Structure and Economic Performance," in *Trade Union Behavior, Pay Bargaining and Economic Performance*, ed. Robert Flanagan, Karl Ove Moene, and Michael Wallerstein (Oxford: Oxford University Press, 1993), 100–3, for a discussion of the conditions under which two-tiered bargaining is equivalent to purely local bargaining.

Karl Ove Moene and Michael Wallerstein

Similarly, the income received by employers is assumed to fall to zero during a conflict. Therefore, the payoffs to the owners of the plant are given by

$$\pi(s, t) = \begin{cases} pb(t) - w(s, t) & \text{if there is an agreement,} \\ 0 & \text{if there is strike or lockout} \end{cases}$$

where p is the price of output and $b(t)$ is the productivity of a plant of vintage t.

Applying standard bargaining theory, the outcome of local negotiations is a wage that is a fraction of the plant's revenues per worker, provided the fraction of the plant's revenues exceeds workers' outside option. Let $\alpha \in [0, 1]$ be the share of the plant's revenues received as wages when workers are paid above their outside option, $r(s)$. Then we can write the wage that results from local bargaining as

$$w(s, t) = \max(\alpha p b(t), r(s)). \tag{1}$$

Workers' outside option acts as a constraint on the bargaining outcome in that employers cannot offer less than $r(s)$ and still attract workers. Otherwise, $r(s)$ has no impact on the outcome.[34] In Ariel Rubinstein's bargaining model, workers' share, α, is determined by the relative impatience of the two sides to settle during a conflict.[35]

The time path of wages in a single plant with local bargaining is illustrated in Figure 1. The horizontal line, pb_0, represents the revenues earned by a plant of vintage 0. Workers' outside option is given by the exponentially rising curve. As long as the wage exceeds workers' outside option, the wage in each plant is constant over time since the negotiated wage depends on the price, which is constant by assumption, and productivity, which is determined by the date the plant was built. As the plant grows older and the outside option rises, the gap between the union wage and workers' outside option falls. Eventually, at $s = \sigma$ in Figure 1, r reaches $\alpha p b_0$ and the constraint that $w \geq r$ becomes binding. At $s = \theta^L$ (the superscript L is for local bargaining), the plant ceases to be profitable and closes.

[34] See John Sutton, "Non-Cooperative Bargaining Theory: An Introduction," *Review of Economic Studies* 53 (1986): 709–24, for a discussion of the impact of the outside option on the bargaining outcome.
[35] Ariel Rubinstein, "Perfect Equilibrium in a Bargaining Model," *Econometrica* 50 (1982): 97–109.

390

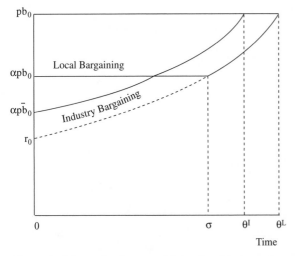

Figure 1   The path of wages with local and industry bargaining.

We model industry-level bargaining as setting a uniform wage for all plants in the industry. In all countries with industry-level bargaining, such an assumption exaggerates the leveling impact of industry-level bargaining since union locals were regularly able to obtain wage increases above the centrally negotiated wage through supplementary bargaining at the plant level.[36] In most countries with industry-level bargaining, however, unions and firms are forbidden to engage in strikes or lockouts once the central agreement is signed. These restrictions on permissible forms of industrial conflict limit the extent to which local bargainers can raise wages above the central agreement.

For ease of comparison, we maintain our prior assumption that the union seeks to maximize the wage received by its members, subject to the constraint that the wage is uniform throughout the industry, although in the case of industry-level bargaining, this assumes an extreme insensitivity to layoffs on the part of the union. On the employers' side, we assume that the industry association seeks to maximize the sum of the profits earned in

---

[36] In some countries, like Germany and Austria, workers' local organization is nominally independent of the union and legally prohibited from bargaining over wages. Even in such countries, informal local bargaining occurs on a regular basis. See Kathleen Thelen, *Union of Parts: Labor Politics in Postwar Germany* (Ithaca, NY: Cornell University Press, 1991) for a description of the relationship between works councils and unions in Germany.

existing plants. As before, both sides receive zero income during an industrial dispute. Thus the payoffs for the two sides can be written

$$u(s) = \begin{cases} w(s) & \text{if there is an agreement,} \\ 0 & \text{if there is a strike or lockout} \end{cases}$$

for the union and

$$\int_{s-\theta^I}^{s} n(t)\tau(s,t)dt$$

$$= \begin{cases} \int_{s-\theta^I}^{s} n(t)(pb(t) - w(s))dt & \text{if there is an agreement,} \\ 0 & \text{if there is a strike or lockout} \end{cases}$$

for employers, where θ^I denotes the age of the oldest plant in operation with industry-level bargaining and $n(t)$ denotes the number of new plants built of vintage t.

Again applying standard bargaining theory, the outcome of the labor negotiations with industry-level bargaining is a wage of

$$w(s) = \max(\alpha p \bar{b}(s), r(s)) \text{ with } \bar{b}(s) = \int_{s-\theta^I}^{s} n(t)b(t)dt / \theta^I \int_{s-\theta^I}^{s} n(t)dt.$$

(2)

The term $\bar{b}(s)$ is the average productivity of the industry at time s. With industry-level bargaining, the wage is equal to the share α of the average revenue per worker in the industry as a whole, $p\bar{b}(s)$, rather than the revenues earned in the plant where the worker is employed. The time path of the wage with industry-level bargaining is also illustrated in Figure 1. Since the average productivity of the industry increases continually over time, as new plants are opened and old ones are closed, so does the wage with industry-level bargaining.

In our model, local bargaining produces a wage in each plant that is constant over time (until the plant becomes so old that workers receive the outside option), while wages in different plants vary according to the plant's age. With industry-level bargaining, wages are constant across plants but rising over time at the same rate as productivity growth. Figure 2 illustrates the difference in wage inequality implied by the two bargaining systems. Plants are arrayed along the horizontal axis from newest to oldest. The declining exponential curve that begins at pb^0 is the revenue produced by a plant of each vintage. With decentralized bargaining, wages vary in proportion to the productivity of the plant, until wages hit the lower bound of r.

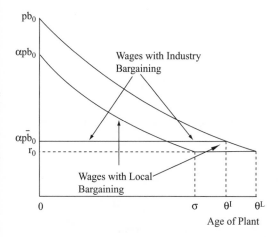

Figure 2 The distribution of wages across plants with local and industry bargaining.

In contrast, industry-level bargaining implies that all plants pay the same wage.

The two bargaining systems differ in terms of the average productivity of the industry, aggregate employment (and output), aggregate profits, and average wages. Decentralized wage setting allows wages in the oldest plants to fall to workers' reservation wage. With industry-level bargaining, wages everywhere may be held above the reservation wage, forcing marginal plants out of operation. As long as $\alpha p \bar{b}(s) > r(s)$, industry-level bargaining reduces the average age of plants ($\theta^I < \theta^L$) and raises average productivity.

An increase in productivity that merely reflects a decline in employment and output is not an improvement, however. Whether or not industry-level bargaining increases efficiency depends on how industry-level bargaining affects the entry of new plants. In our model, industry-level bargaining has two counteracting effects on entry. On the one hand, entry is encouraged since industry-level bargaining holds wages down in the newest, most productive plants. On the other hand, entry is discouraged by the anticipation that wages will rise independently of the plant's (stagnant) productivity, and will eventually exceed what they would be with decentralized bargaining. Which of these two effects dominates depends on the value of α, as illustrated in Figure 3.

Figure 3 illustrates the present value of a new plant as a function of α. For low levels of α, i.e., $\alpha \leq r_0/pb_0$, α does not affect the wage or the value of new plants with either bargaining system. For $r_0/pb_0 < \alpha \leq r_0/p\bar{b}_0$ only

393

Karl Ove Moene and Michael Wallerstein

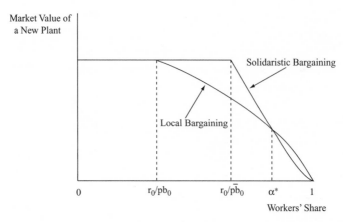

Figure 3 Market value of a new plant with local and solidaristic bargaining.

decentralized bargaining raises the wage in newer plants, since α times the productivity of the most efficient plants exceeds the reservation wage while α times average productivity does not. For $\alpha > r_0/p\bar{b}_0$, the wage in newer plants exceeds workers' outside option (and the value of new plants is lowered) in both bargaining systems. But as long as $\alpha < \alpha^*$ in Figure 3, the market value of new plants is higher with equal pay in all plants. The higher the market value of new plants, the more new plants are constructed. In fact, it can be shown that if α is sufficiently close to $r_0/p\bar{b}_0$, industry-level bargaining results in greater employment in the industry, higher profits, and lower average wages than local wage setting.[37]

Thus the answer to the question of whether industry-level bargaining is more efficient than decentralized bargaining, in the sense of raising productivity, employment, and output simultaneously, depends on the value of α. There are not many studies of the union wage differential in Western Europe, partly because in many industries almost all workers are covered by union contracts. Nevertheless, the studies that exist suggest that union wage differentials are smaller in Britain than in the United States, and even smaller in West Germany and Austria.[38] Given the low unemployment that

[37] See Moene and Wallerstein, "Egalitarian Wage Policies" for a proof.
[38] For example, David G. Blanchflower and Richard B. Freeman, "Unionism in the United States and Other Advanced OECD Countries," *Industrial Relations* 31 (1992): 56–79, see especially 64, use survey data to estimate that the union-nonunion differential is 18–22 percent in the United States, 10 percent in the United Kingdom, 6–8 percent in West Germany, and 5–7 percent in Austria.

existed in Norway, Sweden, Finland, and Austria until very recently, the difference between the wages set in the central or industry-level agreement cannot have been significantly higher than the level that would have existed without unions. Therefore, α close to $r_0/p\bar{b}_0$ appears to be the relevant case in North and Central Europe. Rehn and Meidner's belief in the efficiency of a union wage policy that reduced wage differences among plants is supported by our model, provided union wage demands are sufficiently moderate.

So far we have only discussed the difference between local and centralized bargaining at the industry level. The same reasoning on the elimination of wage differences among plants within an industry, however, can be applied to the elimination of wage differentials between industries. With industry-level bargaining, wages will differ by industry in accordance with industry-level differences in productivity or profitability. Solidaristic bargaining, applied over the national economy, limits the ability of the most efficient industries to pay a wage premium and prevents the least efficient industries from staying in business by lowering wages. In fact, the elimination of wage differentials between industries can be understood as a subsidy for new industries and a tax on older ones.[39] The result of nationwide solidaristic bargaining is to force older industries to shut down while encouraging the growth of new industries. The consequence is a national economy composed of more modern industries than would be the case with less centralized bargaining.

Local bargaining is sensitive to local conditions. That, in fact, is among the chief virtues claimed by its supporters. Sensitivity to local conditions means that fewer less efficient plants are driven out of business compared to centralized wage negotiations. The other side of the coin is that wages in decentralized bargaining systems are sensitive upwards in the most efficient plants or industries. This implies that building new plants may be less profitable with local bargaining than with centralized bargaining. Centralized bargaining forces less efficient plants to shut down and less efficient industries to shrink, but local wage bargaining may reduce the building of more efficient plants and the growth of more efficient industries. In this way, the elimination of interfirm and interindustry wage differentials through solidaristic bargaining aided rather than hindered economic performance in our view. The elimination of interplant and interindustry wage

---

[39] See Jonas Agell and Kjell Erik Lommerud, "Egalitarianism and Growth," *Scandinavian Journal of Economics* 95 (1993): 559–79.

differentials also increased aggregate profits, according to our model, which helps explain the employers' confederations' support for centralized bargaining. The effects of reducing interoccupational wage differentials, the third and most controversial effect of solidaristic bargaining, may have been quite different, as we discuss in the conclusion.

IV. The Maintenance of Full Employment

In addition to wage equality, the primary objective of social democratic governments and unions in the postwar period was the maintenance of full employment. Like the Democratic party in the United States, the social democratic parties in Northern Europe came to power near the peak of unemployment during the Great Depression and established a long-lasting parliamentary majority by presiding over an economic recovery and the achievement of full employment. Throughout the postwar period, social democrats successfully appealed for votes on the basis of their record as guardians of full employment.

The basis for the identification of social democracy with full employment can be seen in Table 1. In the 1960s, full employment was achieved throughout Western Europe. In most of Western Europe, however, the era of full employment ended abruptly in the mid-1970s. By the 1980s, the average rate of unemployment in the eight members of the European Community since 1973 exceeded 10 percent. In contrast, the average unemployment rate in the five continental members of the European Free Trade Association (EFTA) – Austria, Finland, Norway, Sweden, and Switzerland – remained below 3 percent. In the 1982–88 period, every EC country had an unemployment above the highest level of unemployment found in an EFTA country.

Today, the difference between the Nordic social democracies and the rest of Europe in terms of unemployment has disappeared. In Norway, unemployment rose from below 2 percent in 1987 to over 6 percent by 1993. In Sweden, the rise in unemployment came later but faster. In 1990, unemployment in Sweden was still below 2 percent. By 1992, Swedish unemployment had risen above 5 percent. In 1993, the Swedish unemployment rate reached 8.5 percent. Unemployment in Finland rose from 3.5 percent in 1990 to 15 percent by the end of 1992. Moreover, standard unemployment figures do not include the participants in active labor-market policies. Including workers enrolled in active labor-market programs would increase

Table 1. *Unemployment in EC and EFTA Countries: 1975–92*

	Average Rate of Unemployment		
	1975–81	1982–88	1989–92
EC countries			
Belgium	7.8	11.4	7.5
Denmark	6.7	9.1	10.1
France	5.4	9.6	9.5
Germany	3.5	6.7	4.9
Ireland	8.2	15.4	14.8
Italy	7.1	9.8	10.4
Netherlands	5.9	10.6	7.4
United Kingdom	6.1	11.0	8.1
EC average	**6.3**	**10.4**	**9.1**
EFTA countries			
Austria	1.7	3.5	3.4
Finland	4.9	5.1	6.8
Norway	1.8	2.7	5.4
Sweden	2.0	2.7	2.6
Switzerland	0.3	0.7	1.3
EFTA average	**2.1**	**2.9**	**3.9**

Source: OECD, *OECD Economic Outlook* 52 (December 1992): 218–9.

Note: The unemployment rates are the standardized rates except in Denmark, Austria, Switzerland, and Ireland before 1983 for whom standardized rates are unavailable. German unemployment figures exclude East Germany.

the 1993 rate of unemployment to 8 percent in Norway and 12 percent in Sweden.[40]

Two factors are generally credited for the superior performance of the social democracies of North and Central Europe in terms of unemployment and job creation until the late 1980s and early 1990s. The first factor is the centralized system of wage bargaining that characterized Norway, Sweden, Finland, and Austria. For a variety of reasons, national-level wage setters are likely to be more sensitive to unemployment than industry-level

[40] Organization for Economic Cooperation and Development, *Economic Surveys – Sweden* (Paris: OECD, 1994).

wage setters.[41] The second factor is the collection of active labor-market policies that directly reduce unemployment by enrolling the unemployed in training programs (thus removing them from the unemployment rolls) and indirectly reduce unemployment by upgrading the skills of the labor force.

It is now recognized that the effect of the active labor-market policies on unemployment is ambiguous.[42] In the long run, increasing the skills of the workforce may yield significant benefits. In the short run, the active labor-market policies reduce the extent to which unemployed workers compete in the labor market with employed workers. The restraining effect of layoffs on wage increases is diminished.

Therefore, the low level of unemployment compatible with nonacceler-ating inflation that characterized the EFTA countries until very recently is particularly remarkable. Although centralized wage setting at the national level has contributed to the restraint of wage increases under conditions of full employment, the experience of Switzerland and Japan, both with equally low levels of unemployment and far less centralized bargaining systems, suggests that centralized bargaining is not the whole story.

A significant part of the social democratic success in maintaining low levels of unemployment may be due to the effects of past success. Conditions of general labor scarcity induce adaptations on the part of employers that help maintain low levels of unemployment. In particular, when filling vacancies and keeping workers is difficult, employers adapt by hoarding labor. Even if current conditions would warrant a reduction in the workforce, employers may keep their entire workforce employed if demand is expected to increase in the future and if workers are sufficiently difficult to replace. It is widely recognized that raising the cost of laying off workers inhibits firms from hiring. Less appreciated is the reverse point: The greater the cost of filling vacancies, the fewer workers firms will lay off.

Let us define two types of employment policies.[43] A "flexible employment policy" is the policy of hiring when production is profitable and laying

---

[41] Reasons why union negotiators might be more sensitive to unemployment when bargaining is centralized are summarized in Moene, Wallerstein, and Hoel, "Bargaining Structure and Economic Performance," and Lars Calmfors, "Centralization of Wage Bargaining and Macroeconomic Performance Survey," seminar paper no. 536, Institute for International Economic Studies, Stockholm University, 1993.

[42] Calmfors, "Active Labor Market Policy and Unemployment."

[43] See Karl Ove Moene and Michael Wallerstein, "Full Employment as a Worker Discipline Device," in *Property Rights, Incentives and Welfare*, ed. John Roemer. London: Macmillan, 1997, for full details of the economic model that underlies the argument of this section.

off when production is unprofitable. By following a flexible employment policy, firms avoid losses when the price of output is below variable costs. But firms may pay a price in terms of forgone profits during the time it takes to fill positions once the price of output rises sufficiently to make production profitable again. The alternative employment policy could be called a "fixed employment policy." This is the policy of hoarding labor when demand is low in order to have a full workforce available immediately when demand rises again.

Which employment policy is better in terms of the present value of the firms' current and future profits depends on the properties of the stochastic process that describes future prices and on the wage. The shorter the likely period of time before the price increases enough so that production is profitable, and the higher the profits that are expected once the price increases, the more likely firms are to hoard labor when the price is low. Which employment policy is better from employers' point of view also depends on the ease with which vacancies can be filled. Clearly, if vacancies could be filled immediately at no cost, a flexible employment policy would dominate. But if the cost of filling vacancies or the time it takes to fill a vacancy is sufficiently high, firms may increase their long-term profits by hoarding labor during temporary downturns.

This can be illustrated in a simple model if we relax our steady-state assumption of the previous section and allow the price of output to be a random variable. Consider the case in which the output price follows a continuous time Markov process with two states – a high price, p_H, and a low price, p_L – and stationary transition parameters – λ_d and λ_I. When the price is high, there is a probability of $\lambda_D dt$ that the price will fall within the small time period dt. Similarly, $\lambda_I dt$ is the probability that the price will increase within dt when it is low. If the wage was higher than $p_H b$, where b represents the productivity of labor, all firms would close. If the wage was lower than $p_L b$, no firm would ever lay off. The interesting case, therefore, is when $p_H b > w > p_L b$.

Figure 4 illustrates the present value of future profits with both flexible employment and fixed employment strategies when the price is low as functions of the cost of filling vacancies. The variable μ, on the horizontal axis, is the transition parameter that governs the speed with which firms can fill vacancies. The probability that vacancies will be filled within dt is μdt. Alternatively, $1/\mu$ is the average length of time it takes a firm to fill a vacancy. Firms that follow a fixed employment policy do not lay off, so their long-run profits are independent of μ. The market value of firms that

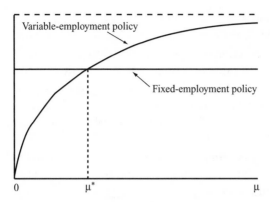

Figure 4 The value of a position when the price is low as a function of the ease of filling future vacancies.

follow a flexible employment policy rises with μ, however, since the more quickly vacancies are filled, the more quickly flexible employment firms can start production when the price rises.

If $\mu = 0$, vacancies remain unfilled forever. In this case, the fixed employment strategy is superior provided the wage is low enough relative to the prices and transition parameters such that production is profitable in the long run. If μ is sufficiently large, however, the flexible employment strategy is superior from the firm's point of view since, as $\mu \rightarrow \infty$, the variable employment policy approaches the best of all possible worlds for employers where they can lay off workers whenever the price is low and immediately fill vacancies when the price rises again. In general, the fixed employment strategy is superior from employers' point of view whenever μ is less than a critical value, μ^*, which depends on the prices, wage, and transition parameters.

From a single firm's point of view, the likelihood of finding a suitable worker within a given time period is exogenous, at least if the firm's wage offers are constrained by an industry-level wage agreement. But, in aggregate, the likelihood of filling a vacancy depends on the number of unemployed workers who are searching for work and the number of other firms that have vacancies to fill, which in turn depends on firms' choices of employment policy. The simultaneity of firms' choice of employment policies and the probability of filling positions can produce two stable equilibria: one where unemployment is high and firms follow a flexible employment strategy (since vacancies are easily filled) and the other where unemployment is low and firms follow a fixed employment strategy (since workers are hard to replace).

Unemployment rises with the number of firms that follow flexible employment policies. If the probability of filling a vacancy rises with the number of unemployed, as all models of the matching process presume, then μ rises with the number of firms that follow flexible employment policies.[44] The more firms follow flexible employment policies, the higher the long-run profits of firms following flexible employment policies. If, instead, most firms follow fixed employment policies, the number of unemployed is lower and the time it takes to fill a vacancy is longer. This, in turn, lowers the long-run profits in firms following flexible employment policies.

To see the possibility of multiple equilibria, consider a distribution of positions associated with differing productivity. Let $F(b)$ denote the cumulative density function of the productivity of different positions. For example, the growth model of Section III implies that the distribution of plants is uniform in the log of productivity, or $F(b) = (1/\gamma\theta)[\ln b - \ln b_{max} + \gamma\theta]$, γ is the rate of growth of productivity, θ is the age of the oldest plant in operation, and b_{max} is the productivity of the newest, most productive plant. For each level of μ, there will be a critical level of productivity, b^*, such that firms will follow a fixed employment policy labor if $b \geq b^*$ and a flexible employment policy if $b < b^*$. Firms will hoard labor in the most productive positions but hire and fire as demand fluctuates in less productive positions. Let $\beta = F(b^*)$ represent the share of firms that follow a flexible employment policy. Observe that b^* is an increasing function of μ since the easier it is to fill vacancies, the higher the level of productivity that is required to make labor-hoarding profitable. In addition, μ is a positive function of β, the share of firms that follow a flexible employment policy. Thus in equilibrium, we have the relationship

$$\beta = F[b^*(\mu(\beta))]. \tag{3}$$

Possible solutions to Equation 3 are illustrated in Figure 5. The LHS of Equation 3 is drawn as the 45-degree line from the origin. The RHS of Equation 3 is drawn as the cumulative density function of a log uniform distribution. As drawn, there are three equilibria at 0, B, and β^{**}. The equilibria at 0 and β^{**} are both stable in the sense that small perturbations

---

[44] In Moene and Wallerstein, "Full Employment as a Worker Discipline Device," we show that the number of unemployed workers rises relative to the number of vacancies as the number of firms using flexible employment policies increases.

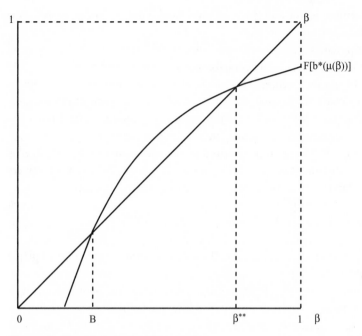

Figure 5 Equilibria in the labor market.

lead to reactions that return to the initial equilibrium. It is also possible that only one equilibrium will exist. A sufficiently large shift in the $\beta = F(\bullet)$ curve, either up or down, can reduce the number of equilibria to one. An increase in the wage, for example, shifts the $\beta = F(\bullet)$ curve upward while increases in λ_I, p_H, or p_L shift the $\beta = F(\bullet)$ curve downward.

In an environment of labor scarcity, firms that offer workers long-term employment contracts may earn higher profits than firms that use layoffs to reduce costs when the price falls. Thus labor scarcity may lead firms to adopt a no-layoff policy. In contrast, in an environment with a large pool of unemployed workers, companies that act quickly to reduce costs through layoffs may earn higher profits than firms that offer long-term employment guarantees. In both high and low unemployment equilibria, firms do worse if they deviate from the employment policies followed by other firms.

The difficulty of filling vacancies because other firms are hoarding labor is a friction in the labor market, a friction that was prominent in Norway and Sweden until recently. But the effects of such friction are not unambiguously harmful. On the one hand, there may be productivity losses from a lower turnover of labor. In a world in which some price declines are permanent, labor hoarding may slow the necessary transfer of capital and labor to other sectors. On the other hand, there may be productivity gains since workers who are protected from layoffs have greater incentives to acquire and develop firm-specific skills and knowledge.

Moreover, full employment that is supported by fixed employment policies may enable employers to motivate workers relatively cheaply. Recent models of wage setting emphasize employers' need to pay wages at a level that induces workers not to shirk. According to the literature on effort-inducing wages, workers only work diligently if the cost of being fired for shirking (multiplied by the probability that shirkers are detected) exceeds the cost of working hard.[45] For two reasons, the effort-inducing wage premium may be lower when most firms follow a fixed employment policy, even though unemployment is also lower.[46] The first is that the prospect of being fired for shirking is less of a threat when there is a chance that the worker will be laid off anyway, regardless of effort, should the price decline. The shorter the expected length of employment of workers who perform well, the higher the wage premium that must be paid to induce workers not to shirk. Secondly, layoffs are a clearer signal of workers' past performance when few workers are laid off for reasons that are unrelated to their work effort. When most layoffs consist of workers who have been caught shirking, the stigma attached to being laid off is amplified.

V. Social Democratic Decline

Social democratic labor-market institutions, in sum, worked reasonably well for a long period of time. To a significant extent, the socialist goals of equality and security of income were attained without disrupting the functioning of capitalist economies. Moreover, core social democratic policies benefited and received support from employers as well as organized workers. Nevertheless, it is not much of an exaggeration to say that the social democratic period appears to be over. While the extent of the retreat differs from country to country and from policy to policy, the movement

---

[45] See, for example, Carl Shapiro and Joseph Stiglitz, "Equilibrium Unemployment as a Worker Discipline Device," *American Economic Review* 74 (1984): 433–44; and Samuel Bowles, "The Production Process in a Competitive Economy: Walrasian, Neo-Hobbesian and Marxian Models," *American Economic Review* 75 (1985): 16–36.

[46] See Moene and Wallerstein "Full Employment as a Worker Discipline Device," for a formal demonstration.

today is toward less centralized bargaining, growing wage differentials, and higher equilibrium unemployment throughout North and Central Europe.

Although the primary emphasis in this article is on how social democratic labor-market institutions worked, our discussion of centralization and economic openness, solidaristic bargaining, and multiple equilibria in the labor market can be applied to the question of the causes of social democratic decline. The immediate cause of the rise in unemployment in the Nordic countries in the 1990s can be explained in standard macroeconomic terms.[47] In all three countries, the deregulation of credit markets and strong foreign demand resulted in a boom in employment, investment, and asset prices during the 1980s. Rapidly rising housing prices and easy credit encouraged a dramatic increase in private-sector borrowing. By the end of the 1980s, the boom in asset prices ended in a bust and an increase in private-sector saving as households struggled to reduce their accumulated debt. The result was a sharp decline in private domestic consumption that coincided with a decline in foreign markets as all of Western Europe entered into a recession. The consequent decline in aggregate demand resulted in one of the worst downturns of this century.

There is less agreement concerning the causes of the persistence of high unemployment, even after the governments eventually responded to the rise in unemployment with more expansionary macroeconomic policies. Our model of flexible and variable employment strategies may provide at least part of the explanation. With multiple equilibria in the labor market, as illustrated in Figure 5, the effect of a change in demand on unemployment may be discontinuous. If the labor market is initially at the low unemployment equilibrium, a small shift downward in the price distribution will not increase unemployment. But a larger decline in prices may shift the $\beta = F(\bullet)$ curve up sufficiently far that the low unemployment equilibrium ceases to exist. In this case, the labor market would move quickly to the equilibrium at β^{**}. Moreover, a subsequent recovery in which the price distribution returned to its original position would not, by itself, move the labor market back to the low unemployment equilibrium. The equilibrium would remain at β^{**}, and unemployment would remain high.

Thus the recent rise in unemployment in Norway, Sweden, and Finland could be said to represent, at least in part, a case of macroeconomic policy

[47] Our discussion of the recent rise in unemployment in Norway, Sweden, and Finland closely follows Rødseth, "Vegen til Høg Arbeidsløyse."

failure, as suggested by Asbjørn Rødseth and John Stephens.[48] The governments of all three countries can be faulted for failing to restrain the expansion of credit that led to an unsustainable boom in the mid-1980s and, perhaps, for persisting in a hard currency policy until late in the recession. There may be deeper reasons, however, why social democratic governments were unable or unwilling to do more to prevent the decline in aggregate demand that occurred in the late 1980s and early 1990s having to do with changes in the system of wage bargaining. The case is clearest in Sweden. In the early 1980s, the Swedish social democrats maintained a high level of employment with large devaluations in cooperation with the unions, who agreed not to seek compensatory wage increases. By the end of the 1980s, with Swedish labor costs rising significantly faster than in the rest of Europe, most economists thought another devaluation would just trigger faster wage increases. The capacity or the willingness of the unions to restrain wage increases under conditions of full employment had diminished to the point that the social democratic government saw no alternative to allowing unemployment to rise.

In all of the Nordic countries, central control over wage formation has weakened.[49] Since 1982, Sweden has moved from a system in which strikes or lockouts over disputes at the industry or firm level were prohibited once a central agreement was signed, as in Norway, to a system where the central agreement allows industrial conflict over industry-level disputes, as in Finland. In Denmark, the statutory system of wage indexation for inflation, an important source of the compression of wage differentials in the 1970s, was abolished in 1982. In all four countries, national or industry-level wage agreements are allowing greater scope for both interplant and intraplant wage differentials. Relative wages are less determined by the central agreement and more determined by the individual circumstances of the job and the worker.

The decline in support for centralized bargaining is, in large part, a consequence of the change in the implementation of solidaristic bargaining over time. Two changes were particularly important. The first was the treatment of wage drift or local wage increases above the centrally negotiated

---

[48] Rødseth, "Vegen til Høg Arbeidsløyse," and John Stephens, "The Scandinavian Welfare States: Development and Crisis" (paper presented at the World Conference of Sociology, Bielefeld, Germany, 13–18 July 1994).

[49] See Golden, Lange, and Wallerstein, "Trade Union Organization and Industrial Relations in the Postwar Era in 16 Nations."

wage. It is inevitable, when wages are set in a centralized fashion, that the wage is too high for some types of labor and too low for others. Where wages are too high, workers lose their jobs and, under conditions of full employment, rapidly find others. Where wages are too low, firms cannot fill vacancies. The solution was to add local raises on top of the centrally negotiated wage increase. The existence of local wage increases did not render the central agreement ineffective, since average drift could be predicted by the central negotiators and subtracted from their target aggregate wage increase when determining how much the centrally negotiated wage should rise.[50] But allowing drift limited the extent to which wages in different plants and industries could be equalized. Beginning in the mid-1960s, wage agreements began to include compensation clauses for workers who had not received drift. As the use of such compensation clauses spread, however, firms that faced labor shortages were less able to raise relative wages through wage drift. While employers benefited from low average wages, many wanted to raise the wages of their own workers.

The second significant change in the implementation of solidaristic bargaining concerned the treatment of interoccupational wage differentials. In the initial period, solidaristic bargaining meant reducing wage differentials between firms and between industries, but not within the firm between different occupations. Over time, however, wage policy became increasingly egalitarian. From equal pay for equal work, the goal became more equal pay for all work.[51] The increasingly ambitious implementation of solidaristic bargaining created both political and economic problems.

In the 1950s and 1960s, the goal of greater wage equality was supported by a general increase in the demand for low-skilled workers that reduced occupational differentials in many advanced industrial societies. Since the mid-1970s, however, technological change, international trade, and solidaristic bargaining have been pushing in opposite directions. In recent years, the attempt to raise the wage of low-paid workers has been undermined by a general reduction in the demand for low-skilled and semiskilled labor that has occurred in all advanced industrial societies as a result of

[50] See, for example, Steinar Holden, "Wage Drift and Bargaining: Evidence from Norway," *Economica* 56 (1989): 419–32; and Hibbs and Locking, "Wage Compression, Wage Drift, and Wage Inflation in Sweden."

[51] Pontusson and Swenson, "Markets, Production, Institutions, and Politics: Why Swedish Employers Have Abandoned the Swedish Model." An important reason why social democracy has been more stable in Austria than in Scandinavia may be that the Austrians never attempted to reduce wage inequalities through solidaristic bargaining.

a combination of technological change and increased competition from manufacturers in East Asia.[52] Keeping wages low enough to maintain full employment in the context of declining demand for unskilled labor while raising the relative wage of low-wage workers required increasingly severe wage restraint on the part of workers at higher pay levels.

Eventually, high-wage workers revolted. The goal of reducing interoccupational wage differentials split the union movement. As solidaristic bargaining reduced wage differentials between different occupations, high-wage workers joined militant unions dedicated to restoring traditional wage differentials. Union membership increased in the 1970s and 1980s, but union solidarity declined as nonsocialist unions of white-collar and professional workers grew relative to the socialist, blue-collar confederations. Resistance to the reduction of interoccupational wage differentials also increased among skilled, private-sector, blue-collar workers, most notably in metal working.[53]

Inside the blue-collar confederations, the increased support for egalitarian wage goals corresponded to the increased influence of public-sector unions whose membership included a large number of low-paid workers. For such unions, solidaristic bargaining represented the promise to raise the wages of their members faster than others. Moreover, such workers are not subject to the constraint of international competition. Appearances to the contrary, the long-run trend in Western Europe is toward reduced trade dependence of the labor force. While the Nordic countries are more dependent than ever on exports, productivity gains in manufacturing have meant a continual decline in the share of the workforce employed in the traded-goods sector. As late as 1970, the largest single union in both Norway and Sweden was the metalworkers. By 1990, the largest union in both countries was the union of local government employees.

Throughout Northern Europe, private-sector employment in manufacturing has declined while employment in the sheltered public sector has increased. As the outcome of central negotiations became increasingly influenced by union demands in sheltered sectors, many employers no longer

---

[52] See Adrian Wood, *North-South Trade, Employment and Inequality: Changing Fortunes in a Skill-Driven World* (Oxford: Oxford University Press, 1994) for an attempt to estimate the impact of increased manufacturing export from developing countries on the demand for unskilled labor in developed countries.

[53] See Scott Lash, "The End of Neo-corporatism?: The Breakdown of Centralized Bargaining in Sweden," *British Journal of Industrial Relation* 23 (1985): 215–39, for a description of conflicts over wage compression in the metalworking sector.

view centralized bargaining as a good instrument for the control of wage costs. Social democracy was a product of a time when the labor movement was dominated by blue-collar workers in export industries. Today, the number of blue-collar workers in traded-goods sectors has declined too much, in relative terms, for their unions to set the pace for wage increases throughout the economy without resistance.

There is probably no going back to the past, if the past is characterized as highly centralized wage setting that imposes a highly egalitarian wage distribution. The unions have grown too heterogeneous and competitive with each other to agree to a common goal of increased wage equality. Employers have hardened in their insistence on the relaxation of constraints on the payment of wage differentials. To the extent that central wage setting continues, it will entail less wage equality and fewer constraints on wage increases at the plant level. Nevertheless, wage setting may remain sufficiently centralized to provide a floor that protects the income, but not the employment, of workers at the bottom of the labor market. In spite of the recent retreat, the legacy of social democracy in terms of a relatively egalitarian income distribution may be long lasting, at least in comparison to other societies.

17

Earnings Inequality and Welfare Spending

A DISAGGREGATED ANALYSIS

Karl Ove Moene and Michael Wallerstein

I. Introduction

Governments collect and spend on average around 45 percent of GDP in advanced industrial societies, and about half of government spending goes to fund the various expenditures on transfer payments and services that constitute what is commonly called the welfare state. Perhaps the most common view of welfare spending is that these policies are the outcome of a long political struggle in which workers and their allies used the power of the ballot box to obtain some redress for the inequalities generated by the market. In the words of Huber and Stephens: "The struggle of welfare states is a struggle of distribution, and thus the organizational power of those standing to benefit from redistribution, the working and lower middle classes, is crucial."[1] Other scholars have emphasized the political influence of the beneficiaries of welfare spending who are outside the labor market, such as the elderly.[2] But whether the key groups are defined by

---

[1] Evelyne Huber and John D. Stephens, *Political Choice in Global Markets: Development and Crisis in Advanced Welfare States* (Chicago: University of Chicago Press, 2001), 17. For other recent books that emphasize the centrality of either the political mobilization or the economic organization of workers for explaining cross-national differences in the size of the welfare state, see Alexander Hicks, *Social Democracy and Welfare Capitalism: A Century of Income Security Politics* (Ithaca, N.Y.: Cornell University Press, 1999); Harold Wilensky, *Rich Democracies* (Berkeley: University of California Press, 2002); and Duane Swank, *Global Capital, Political Institutions, and Policy Change in Developed Welfare States* (Cambridge: Cambridge University Press, 2002).

[2] Fred C. Pampel and John B. Williamson, "Welfare Spending in Advanced Industrial Democracies 1950–1980," *American Journal of Sociology* 93 (May 1988).

We thank Nolan McCarty and three anonymous referees for helpful comments. We thank the MacArthur Foundation and the Norwegian Research Council for financial support.

class position, income, or age, most scholars have viewed welfare policies in redistributive terms.

The redistributive view of welfare policy, as formalized in a series of papers by Romer, Roberts, and Meltzer and Richard, implies that higher inequality of market incomes generates higher levels of political support for redistributive policies.[3] The basic intuition is that low-income earners have more to gain and less to lose than do persons with high incomes from expansions of welfare spending. Thus, the poorer the majority of voters relative to the average income, the greater the expected support for welfare expenditures. In the one-dimensional model of voting over welfare spending where the voter with median income is decisive, the key statistic is the ratio of the median income to the mean income. The more skewed the distribution of income or, more precisely, the lower the ratio of the median to the mean income, the higher the level of welfare expenditures desired by a majority of voters. Welfare policy is expected to "lean against the wind" in the sense that the greater the inequality of pre–tax and transfer income, the greater the electoral support for government policies that redistribute from rich to poor.

An alternative view of the welfare state is that social-insurance policies provide insurance rather than redistribution. As Baldwin observed in a study of the origins of the welfare state in five European countries, "Protection against risk has been sought more universally than a redistribution of resources."[4] Of course, all insurance policies are redistributive in the

[3] Thomas Romer, "Individual Welfare, Majority Voting, and the Properties of a Linear Income Tax," *Journal of Public Economics* 14 (February 1975); Kevin W. S. Roberts, "Voting over Income Tax Schedules," *Journal of Public Economics* 8 (December 1977); Allan H. Meltzer and Scott F. Richard, "A Rational Theory of the Size of Government," *Journal of Political Economy* 89 (October 1981).

[4] Peter Baldwin, *The Politics of Social Solidarity: The Class Bases of the European Welfare State* (Cambridge: Cambridge University Press, 1990), 18. For a survey of the economic arguments in favor of public provision of insurance, see Nicholas Barr, "Economic Theory and the Welfare State: A Survey and Interpretation," *Journal of Economic Literature* 30 (June 1992). Iversen and Cusack interpret the welfare state as insurance against the risk of income loss occasioned by the shift of jobs from manufacturing to the service sector, while Rodrik and Garrett interpret the welfare state as insurance against the risks entailed by increased international economic integration; see Torben Iversen and Thomas R. Cusack, "The Causes of Welfare State Expansion: Deindustrialization or Globalization?" *World Politics*, 52 (April 2000); Dani Rodrik, "Why Do More Open Economies Have Larger Governments?" *Journal of Political Economy* 106 (October 1998); and Geoffrey Garrett, *Partisan Politics in the Global Economy* (Cambridge: Cambridge University Press, 1998). The redistributive insurance framework used in this paper was first presented in Karl O. Moene and Michael Wallerstein "Inequality, Social Insurance and Redistribution," *American Political Science Review* 95 (December 2001).

sense that fire insurance redistributes resources from those lucky enough to never experience a fire in their house to those who have the misfortune of experiencing such. Nevertheless, fire insurance is not redistributive ex ante. We do not expect fire insurance to be more popular among the poor than among the rich.[5]

The typical social-insurance program, however, is neither pure redistribution nor pure protection against risk but rather a mixture of the two. Social-insurance policies in advanced industrial societies generally provide insurance against common risks on terms that are more favorable for low-income individuals than for high-income individuals. In this article, we suggest that neither redistribution nor insurance alone can explain how income inequality affects the demand for social insurance. We argue, instead, that it is the mixture of the two motives – a mixture that differs from one social-insurance policy to another – that determines the relationship between the distribution of income and support for welfare expenditures.

We begin by showing that extending the framework of Romer and Meltzer and Richard to include the provision of insurance on redistributive terms generates predictions concerning the impact of inequality on support for social-insurance expenditures that depend on the mixture of redistribution and insurance in the policies' design. We then conduct an empirical examination of the impact of earnings inequality on welfare spending disaggregated into spending on pensions, health care, insurance against unanticipated income loss, family benefits, housing subsidies, and poverty alleviation. We find little or no relationship between earnings inequality and expenditures as a share of GDP for pensions, health care, family benefits, and means-tested policies. In contrast, we find significantly *lower* spending in countries with higher earnings inequality for welfare policies that provide insurance for workers who have lost their income because of layoffs, ill health, or accidents, policies that constitute about 30 percent of total social-insurance spending. Instead of "leaning against the wind," a substantial share of welfare spending is better characterized as "bending in the wind," that is, declining as inequality increases.

---

[5] The strong correlation that exists between social-insurance spending as a share of GDP and GDP per capita in data sets that include both high-income and low-income countries suggests that richer voters prefer to spend a larger share of income on social insurance; the correlation is documented in Harold Wilensky, *The Welfare State and Equality* (Berkeley: University of California Press, 1975). An alternative explanation is that the capacity of governments to collect revenues without imposing large deadweight costs rises with economic development.

A simple model of voting over redistributive insurance predicts exactly this pattern.

Our study is not the first to present evidence that the relationship between income inequality and social-insurance expenditures in advanced industrial societies is not consistent with a purely redistributive model. Looking at OECD countries, Rodriguez and Moene and Wallerstein found higher income inequality to be associated with lower social-insurance spending as a share of GDP.[6] In the United States, Rodriguez found no relationship between welfare spending and inequality at the state level, while Moffitt, Ribar, and Wilhelm found spending on Aid for Dependent Children (AFDC) to be lower in states where the distribution of income was most unequal.[7] Using a broader sample of fifty rich and poor countries, Perotti found no significant relationship between inequality and social-insurance spending.[8] In contrast to these studies, Milanovic finds that more unequal countries redistribute more in a sample that includes advanced industrial societies and the newly industrializing countries of East Asia, where redistribution is measured by the difference between the pre–tax and transfer Gini coefficient and the post–tax and transfer Gini coefficient.[9] Since social-insurance programs are not the only policies that redistribute income, studies of redistribution in general and studies of social-insurance expenditures in particular may arrive at different conclusions.

In this article we study the relationship between earnings inequality and the major components of social-insurance expenditures. Our contribution is to highlight the differences among the main categories of social insurance in the relationship between income inequality and expenditures, differences that are obscured in studies of aggregate welfare spending, let alone in studies of redistribution in general. In the next section we describe a simple model of voting over redistributive insurance and the different comparative static results concerning income inequality and support for expenditures for different categories of social-insurance policies. In Section III we analyze

---

[6] Francisco Rafael Rodriguez Caballero, "Essays on the Political Economy of Inequality, Redistribution and Growth" (Ph.D. diss., Harvard University, 1998); Moene and Wallerstein (fn. 4).

[7] Rodriguez (fn. 6); Robert Moffitt, David Ribar, and Mark Wilhelm, "The Decline of Welfare Benefits in the U.S.: The Role of Wage Inequality," *Journal of Public Economics* 68 (June 1998).

[8] Roberto Perotti, "Growth, Income Distribution and Democracy: What the Data Say," *Journal of Economic Growth* 1, no. 1 (1996).

[9] Branko Milanovic, "The Median-Voter Hypothesis, Income Inequality, and Income Redistribution: An Empirical Test with the Required Data," *European Journal of Political Economy* 16, no. 2 (2000).

disaggregated data on social-insurance expenditures in OECD countries and show that the relationship between inequality and social-insurance spending varies among social-insurance policies in a manner that matches the model of Section II. In the final section we summarize our findings and discuss other possible explanations of the differences we observe among social-insurance programs in the relationship between inequality and expenditures. The proofs of the claims made in Section II are presented in Appendix 1.

II. *Theoretical Framework*

The argument of this article rests on a simple model of politics: voters are assumed to have well-defined, strictly single-peaked preferences over the level of funding for each of the various social-insurance policies that depend on each voter's income relative to average income. With strictly single-peaked preferences that depend on voters' income, the voters with the median income are pivotal in the sense that their preference between any two alternatives is always shared by a majority of the electorate. In such an environment, it is natural to identify the ideal policy of the median voters as the political equilibrium. Electoral competition between two parties or two blocs of parties, as in Scandinavian-style multiparty systems where the parties organize into socialist and bourgeois blocs, forces both the right and the left to compete for the support of voters around the median of the income distribution. Regardless of which party wins the election, the policy that is adopted is close to the policy preferred by the median group of voters.

This highly stylized model of the politics of social insurance can be criticized on many grounds. Voters, it is claimed, are generally ill informed about policy choices.[10] Instead, many have argued, welfare policy is determined by the political influence of the labor movement,[11] the policy innovations of bureaucrats,[12] or even the preferences of employers.[13] In the formal literature the two-party, one-dimensional model of redistributive politics has

---

[10] Donald Kinder, "Diversity and Complexity in American Public Opinion," in Ada Finifter, ed., *Political Science: The State of the Discipline* (Washington, D.C.: APSA, 1983).

[11] Walter Korpi, *The Working Class in Welfare Capitalism* (London: Routledge and Kegan Paul, 1978); Hicks (fn. 1); Huber and Stephens (fn. 1); Wilensky (fn. 1).

[12] Hugh Heclo, *Modern Social Policies in Britain and Sweden* (New Haven: Yale University Press, 1974).

[13] Peter Swenson, *Capitalists against Markets* (Oxford: Oxford University Press, 2002).

been extended to include more than two parties[14] and more than one policy dimension.[15]

Nevertheless, in this article we rely on the one-dimensional, two-party model of redistributive politics developed by Romer and Meltzer and Richard, extended to cover social insurance. While unions, bureaucrats, and employers have all played important roles in negotiating the details of social-insurance policies, in the end social-insurance policies are adopted or not by parties or coalitions of parties that manage to win a majority of votes. Voters may know little or nothing about the details of the policy choices facing legislators, but if voters vote retrospectively, rewarding the incumbent government if their welfare has increased and punishing the incumbent otherwise, the parties in government have a strong electoral incentive to adopt policies that raise the welfare of a majority of voters.[16] For these reasons, we believe that the policy preferred by a majority of voters to all alternatives, when such a policy exists, is an important (albeit not necessarily the only) determinant of the policies that are adopted. But before the framework developed by Romer and Meltzer and Richard can be expected to explain the politics of social insurance, the model must be modified to include risk.

Consider an electorate composed of self-interested, risk-averse voters who differ in their income when employed but face a common risk of losing their employment in the next period. In particular, we will rely on the following assumptions:

1. The wage distribution is lognormal. Let σ^2 denote the variance of the log of wages. Since we will consider changes in inequality (that is, in σ^2), holding the average wage constant, there is no loss of generality in assuming the average wage equals one.

2. All voters receive a known wage with probability π. There is, however, a nonzero probability, $(1 - \pi)$, that each voter will lose his or her income because of unemployment, injury, or illness. To keep the

[14] David Austen-Smith, "Redistributing Income under Proportional Representation," *Journal of Political Economy* 108 (December 2000).

[15] John Roemer, "Why the Poor Do Not Expropriate the Rich," *Journal of Public Economics* 70 (December 1998); idem, *Political Competition* (Cambridge: Harvard University Press, 2001); David Austen-Smith and Michael Wallerstein, "Redistribution in a Divided Society" CMS-EMS Discussion Paper 1362 (Evanston, Ill.: Northwestern University, 2003).

[16] Christopher Achen and Larry Bartels, "Ignorance and Bliss in Democratic Politics: Party Competition with Uninformed Voters" (Paper presented at the annual meetings of the Midwest Political Science Association, Chicago, April 25–28, 2002).

model as simple as possible, the probability of being employed, π, is assumed to be the same for all voters.[17]

3. Voters are assumed to be identical in terms of their aversion to risk. As our measure of voters' willingness to accept a lower average income in exchange for less uncertain income, we use the coefficient of relative risk aversion, $\mu \equiv -c\,u''(c)/u'(c)$ where $u(c)$ represents voters' preferences over consumption, c. The higher μ is, the more voters are willing to pay for insurance against the loss of a given fraction of their income. We assume that μ is the same for all voters and that $\mu > 1$, which implies that the demand for insurance rises as income increases.[18]

4. Social-insurance expenditures are financed by a flat tax on wages, denoted by t, that can take any value between zero and some $t_{\max}$.[19] Taxation is assumed to impose a deadweight cost which we model implicitly by assuming that total tax revenues per capita, T, are given by a twice differentiable function of the tax rate, $\tau(t)$, multiplied by average earnings, π (since the fraction π are working and the average wage is one), or $T(t) = \pi\,\tau(t)$. The function $\tau(t)$ is assumed to satisfy the following properties: (1) $\tau(0) = 0$ (no taxes are collected when the tax rate is zero); (2) $\tau'(0) = 1$ (there is no deadweight loss at $t = 0$); (3) $\tau''(t) < 0$ (the dead-weight cost of taxation rises as the tax rate

[17] We discuss relaxing this assumption below.

[18] The assumption that μ is constant is made to simplify the mathematical expressions, but it is not necessary. The assumption that $\mu > 1$ is critical for our results. Both assumptions regarding μ are supported by studies of the allocation of household savings. See Irwin Friend and Marshall E. Blume, "The Demand for Risky Assets," *American Economic Review* 65 (December 1975).

[19] We have made the modeling choice to represent differences in social-insurance policies in terms of differences in the distribution of benefits, rather than in terms of differences in the tax that finances the benefits. A more general approach would be to define post–tax and transfer income as a function of pre–tax and transfer income, as in John Roemer, "Does Democracy Engender Equality," in Edward Mansfield and Richard Sisson, eds., *Political Knowledge and Public Interest* (Columbus: University of Ohio Press, 2003). For the purposes of this paper, however, the assumption of a flat tax is a reasonable approximation. In most of the countries we study, much of the welfare budget is financed by a payroll tax that is usually flat. (Denmark is an outlier in relying almost exclusively on income and value-added taxes.) Moreover, a recent study of the progressiveness of the personal income tax in twelve OECD countries by Wagstaff et al., found "no link between pre-tax inequality and the degree of redistribution brought about by the personal income tax"; see Adam Wagstaff et al., "Redistributive Effect, Progressivity and Differential Tax Treatment: Personal Income Taxes in Twelve OECD Countries," *Journal of Public Economics* 72 (April 1999), 83. Thus, in neglecting cross-national differences in the redistributive impact of the income tax, we do not appear to be neglecting a factor that is systematically related to pretax income inequality.

increases); and (4) $\tau'(t_{max}) = 0$ for some $t_{max} < 1$ (there is some tax rate $t_{max} < 1$ beyond which further increases in the tax rate do not increase tax revenues).

5. Social-insurance policies are represented by two functions, $b_E(w, t) \geq 0$ and $b_N(w, t) \geq 0$, where $b_E(w, t)$ represents the transfer payment received by an employed worker who earns a wage of w and $b_N(w, t)$ represents the transfer payment received by a worker without employment when the tax rate is t. Note that the benefit may be a function of the worker's wage or, in the case of a worker without current employment, the worker's past wage.

Voters' preferences regarding social-insurance expenditures are derived from their expected utility

$$Eu = \pi u(c_E) + (1 - \pi)u(c_N) \tag{1}$$

where c_E is the voter's post–tax and transfer income when employed and c_N is the voter's income when not employed. Post-tax, post-transfer income when employed is equal to the post-tax wage $(1 - t)w$ plus the welfare benefit, or $c_E = (1 - t)w + b_E(w, t)$. Voters who are not working receive $c_N(w) = b_N(w, t)$.

A voter's ideal policy is the tax rate or spending level that maximizes (1) subject to the budget constraint that

$$\int_0^\infty [\pi b_E(w, t) + (1 - \pi)b_N(w, t)] f(w)dw = \pi \tau(t) \tag{2}$$

where $f(w)$ is the probability density function of the wage distribution. Equation 2 states that the average of benefits received by those employed and those not employed at each wage level must equal tax revenues per capita.

Different social-insurance policies can be represented by different specifications of the functions $b_E(w, t)$ and $b_N(w, t)$. Since voters have strictly single-peaked preferences with all of the specifications of $b_E(w, t)$ and $b_N(w, t)$ that we examine, the tax rate or benefit level preferred by the voter who receives the median wage is preferred by a majority to any other alternative. Therefore, we identify the preferred policy of the voter with median income as the political equilibrium.

Consider, as a benchmark, the simple case in which all benefits are paid as equal payments to employed workers, or $b_E(w, t) = b(t)$ and $b_N(w, t) = 0$. The budget constraint implies that $b(t) = \tau(t)$. This is a purely redistributive policy that provides no insurance against job loss. In this case, an increase in wage inequality increases the equilibrium level of spending, as stated in the first claim:

Claim 1. When $b_E(w, t) = b(t)$ and $b_N(w, t) = 0$, the equilibrium tax rate and benefit level rises as the inequality of the wage distribution increases.

The proof of this and all other claims are presented in Appendix 1. This claim simply reproduces the main result of the Romer and Meltzer and Richard model of voting over redistributive spending. An increase in the variance of a lognormal distribution, holding the mean constant, implies a decline in the median income. From the point of view of the median voter, a given benefit can now be obtained at a lower price since the median voter's share of the tax burden declines as the median voter's income falls. Hence, the median voter prefers a higher level of expenditures.

Social-insurance policies, however, do not pay benefits to currently employed workers only. Social-insurance policies either target benefits to those who are not currently employed (such as unemployment insurance) or provide benefits to everyone (such as health care). Consider, first, the family of policies that provides income replacement for those who have lost their earnings due to unforeseen circumstances such as layoffs, sickness, or accidents. The benefits from income-replacement policies are received only by workers without current employment, implying $b_E(w, t) = 0$. In addition, benefits are typically tied to past earnings according to a redistributive formula that we write as $b_N(w, t) = [\xi + (1 - \xi)w] b(t)$ where $0 < \xi \leq 1$.[20] In other words, income-replacement policies are assumed to provide an income floor of $\xi b(t)$ plus the fraction $(1 - \xi)b(t)$ of past earnings. The term $b(t)$ is the average benefit received by those who receive benefits. Since

---

[20] The assumption that income-replacement policies are redistributive, or that $\xi > 0$, is consistent with the way most social-insurance programs are designed. For example, the average replacement ratio for unemployment insurance, $b_N(w, t)/w$ in the notation of the paper, is 18 percent higher for a worker who receives two-thirds of the median wage than for a worker who receives the median wage in the countries in our data set; Organization for Economic Cooperation and Development, *Dataset on Benefit Replacement Rates* (Paris: OECD, no date). Of course, it would be preferable if $\xi > 0$ was a conclusion rather than an assumption. However, the one-dimensional model of politics no longer applies when both ξ and b are chosen simultaneously. For a model where ξ is chosen at a "constitutional" stage to maximize a social welfare function while $b(t)$ is chosen by self-interested voters in a second "electoral" stage, see Georges Casamatta, Helmuth Cremer, and Pierre Pestieau, "Political Sustainability and the Design of Social Insurance," *Journal of Public Economics* 75 (March 2000).

taxes are collected from the fraction π of the population while benefits are paid to the fraction $(1 - \pi)$, the budget constraint implies that: $b(t) = [\pi / (1 - \pi)]\tau(t)$.

In contrast to the case where the benefit is paid to those who are employed, an increase in inequality reduces the demand for welfare spending when the benefit is received by those without employment, as stated in the second claim.

Claim 2. When $b_E(w, t) = 0$ and $b_N(w, t) = [\xi + (1 - \xi)w]b(t)$ where $0 < \xi \leq 1$, the equilibrium tax rate and benefit level declines as the inequality of the wage distribution increases.

In this case a reduction in the income of the median voter has two effects that work in opposite directions. As in the previous case, the price of a given level of benefits for the median voter declines, thereby increasing the median voter's demand for expenditures. But now there is an income effect that pushes in the opposite direction. A decline in the income of the median voter reduces the amount of insurance the median voter wishes to purchase. We demonstrate in Appendix 1 that the income effect dominates the price (or substitution) effect in this case, which implies that support for benefits for those without employment declines as inequality increases.

Neither pure insurance nor pure redistribution can explain why rising earnings inequality lowers the political support for income-replacement policies among voters with below-average earnings. The key is the mixture of insurance and redistribution. When income-replacement policies are redistributive (that is, when $\xi > 0$), a change in an individual's earnings, holding average earnings constant, induces a less than proportional change in the social-insurance benefit that would be received in the event of unemployment, illness, or accident. Workers whose earnings have risen relative to the social-insurance benefit prefer to increase the benefit a little, even at the cost of a higher tax. Conversely, workers whose earnings have fallen relative to the social-insurance benefit prefer to reduce the benefit a little in order to restore some of their posttax income when working. Thus, a mean-preserving decline in inequality that raises the wage of the majority of workers who earn less than the average also raises the level of social-insurance spending that the majority prefers.

In contrast to social insurance against unforeseen income loss, social-insurance programs like health care are universalistic in the sense that the benefit is the same at all income levels and is received regardless of whether or not the beneficiary is currently employed. A reasonable characterization of programs like health care is simply $b_N(w, t) = b_E(w, t) = b(t)$.[21] Pensions are like health care and unlike unemployment insurance in the sense that public pension systems provide income upon reaching retirement age to all workers. Unlike health care, however, pensions depend upon earnings, typically with a redistributive formula for calculating benefits.[22] Pensions, therefore, might be represented by $b_N(w, t) = b_E(w, t) = [\xi + (1 - \xi)w] \, b(t)$, with $0 < \xi < 1$. The third claim covers both programs such as health care, where $\xi = 1$, and pensions, where $\xi < 1$.

Claim 3. When $b_E(w, t) = b_N(w, t) = [\xi + (1 - \xi)w]b(t)$ where $0 < \xi \leq 1$, the equilibrium tax rate and benefit level may either rise or decline as the inequality of the wage distribution increases. In particular, the equilibrium tax and benefit increase as inequality increases if the coefficient of relative risk aversion, μ, is sufficiently close to one, while the equilibrium tax and benefit declines as inequality increases if μ is sufficiently large.

Whether benefits are the same for all ($\xi = 1$) or depend on earnings ($\xi < 1$), the equilibrium level of benefits is an increasing function of inequality when $\mu \to 1$ and a decreasing function of inequality when $\mu \to \infty$. For moderate levels of risk aversion, the effect of inequality on spending can go either way. The median voter's preference for greater redistribution and less insurance as the median income falls relative to the mean roughly balance each other.

Finally, there are policies that explicitly target poverty alleviation. Means-tested policies, which constitute a minor part of the welfare budget but an important part of the budgets of very poor households in advanced industrial societies, cannot be examined in a model of self-interested voting. The probability of receiving payments targeted for poverty alleviation are virtually zero for a majority of voters. Support for such policies must be based on factors such as altruism or fear of criminal acts by the desperately poor.

---

[21] The U.S. is exceptional in devoting roughly 25 percent of public health expenditures to a family of means-tested programs known as Medicaid; United States Bureau of the Census, *Statistical Abstract of the United States 2001* (Washington, D.C.: U.S. Government Printing Office, 2001).

[22] Walter Korpi and Joachim Palme. "The Paradox of Redistribution and Strategies of Equality: Welfare State Institutions, Inequality and Poverty in the Western Countries," *American Sociological Review* 63 (October 1998).

To summarize the results that can be derived from an extension of the Romer and Meltzer and Richard framework to include the risk of job loss, the relationship between pretax income inequality and equilibrium level of expenditures on social-insurance policies depends on the policy's design. A compression of the wage distribution that increases the income of workers with below-average earnings relative to the mean has two effects when insurance is provided on redistributive terms. The demand for insurance rises while the demand for redistribution falls among the majority of workers whose income has increased. In the case of income-replacement policies, the greater demand for insurance dominates the reduced demand for redistribution and support for social-insurance expenditures increases. In the case of policies that provide benefits for the employed as well as for those without employment, the enhanced demand for insurance and the reduced demand for redistribution roughly cancel each other out. Therefore, spending on redistributive social-insurance policies targeted to those who have lost their income unexpectedly because of layoffs, sickness, or accidents is predicted to be higher in countries with more egalitarian distributions of pre–tax and transfer income. By contrast, spending on social-insurance benefits that are received by all workers is not predicted to have a strong relationship with inequality one way or the other.

Our assumption that the risk of job loss is uncorrelated with earnings is not critical. None of the results are altered by allowing the risk of job loss to depend on a worker's position in the income distribution provided the worker with the median ideal point with regard to social-insurance expenditures has below-average income. It is important to note that the redistributive-insurance framework does not imply that high-wage workers desire higher spending on income-replacement policies than do low-wage workers. The demand for insurance depends on risk as well as on income. Low-wage workers may express greater support for unemployment insurance than high-wage workers, for example, since the probability of being laid off is higher for low-wage workers. What the redistributive-insurance framework implies is that a worker's demand for unemployment insurance would increase if the ratio of the worker's income to average income increased, holding constant the risk of job loss. In a comparison of two countries with the same distribution of the risk of income loss but different distributions of income, the more skewed the distribution of income, the lower the level of insurance against income loss desired by a majority of voters.

III. Empirical Analysis

In this section we describe the empirical relationship between the main categories of social-insurance spending and earnings inequality in eighteen OECD countries from 1980 to 1995. We show that the relationship between spending levels and earnings inequality varies across social-insurance programs in the way that is predicted by the extended framework of Romer and Meltzer and Richards. We begin with a discussion of the data used in the statistical analysis and of the methodological issues that we confronted. We then present our empirical results. Details regarding data sources can be found in Appendix 2.

Description of the Data

According to OECD statistics, social-insurance expenditures averaged 23 percent of GDP and 51 percent of total government spending in advanced industrial societies between 1980 and 1995.[23] The welfare budget can be divided into three large categories and three smaller categories. Pensions (old-age cash benefits) make up 30 percent of the welfare budget on average. Public spending on health consumes an average of 26 percent of welfare spending. Policies that provide income support in a wide variety of circumstances (unemployment, disability, sickness, occupational injury, death of a spouse) constitute 31 percent of social-insurance expenditures on average. The remaining 13 percent of the welfare budget is spent on benefits and services for families with children (9 percent of welfare expenditures), benefits targeted to low-income individuals, refugees, and indigenous groups (3 percent of welfare expenditures), and housing subsidies (1 percent of welfare expenditures). Note the smallness of the share of spending on policies explicitly dedicated to poverty alleviation. Government spending for what is known as "welfare" in the U.S., that is, programs in which eligibility for benefits is based primarily on low income, averages only 0.6 percent of GDP in advanced industrial societies. Table 1 presents summary statistics, while Table 6 in Appendix 2 presents country means for each of the main categories of social-insurance spending.

In the one-dimensional model of voting over welfare, support for welfare expenditures depends on the ratio of the income of the median voter to

---

[23] Organization for Economic Cooperation and Development, *Social Expenditure Database 1980–1996* (CD-ROM) (Paris: OECD, 1999).

Table 1. *Summary Statistics*[a]

Variable	Mean	S.D.	Minimum	Maximum
Total welfare spending/GDP	23.0	6.2	11.3	33.4
Pensions/GDP	6.9	2.2	3.0	11.0
Public health spending/GDP	6.0	0.9	4.3	8.1
Income replacement/GDP	7.1	3.4	1.6	13.2
Unemployment support/GDP	2.4	1.5	0.3	6.6
Other insurance/GDP	4.7	2.3	1.2	9.6
Family benefits/GDP	2.0	1.2	0.4	4.7
Antipoverty programs/GDP	0.6	0.6	0	3.1
Housing subsidies/GDP	0.3	0.4	0	1.9
Inequality (90/10)	1.06	0.25	0.68	1.70
Inequality (90/50)	0.55	0.12	0.38	0.88
Inequality (50/10)	0.51	0.16	0.27	0.89
Right government	41.5	36.7	0	100
Turnout	78.5	13.2	40.0	95.6
Percentage elderly	13.5	2.1	9.5	17.7
Unemployment rate	7.2	3.1	1.7	17.2

[a] See Appendix 2 for data sources.

the mean income. Unfortunately, there are only limited data on the ratio of the median to the mean income. However, the OECD has published data on the ratio of earnings at different percentiles of the earnings distribution covering most OECD countries from 1980 through 1995.[24] The data refer to the annual income from wages and salaries received by full-time employees, both men and women. We can use the fact that the distribution of wages and salaries is well approximated by the lognormal distribution to write the ratio of the median to the mean as

$$\frac{\text{median}}{\text{mean}} = \exp(-\sigma^2/2) \tag{3}$$

where σ^2 is the variance of the log of wages and salaries.[25] The variance of the log of wages, in turn, can be derived from the ratio of the wage at any two percentiles of the earnings distribution according to the formula

$$\sigma = k_{ij} \ln(w_i/w_j) \tag{4}$$

---

[24] Organization for Economic Cooperation and Development, *Employment Outlook* (July 1993); idem, *Employment Outlook* (July 1996).

[25] For a discussion of the properties of the lognormal distribution and its use as an approximation of the distribution of income, see J. Aitchison and J. A. C. Brown, *The Lognormal Distribution* (Cambridge: Cambridge University Press, 1957).

where w_i is the wage or salary received by a worker at the ith percentile of the earnings distribution, w_j is the wage or salary received by a worker at the jth percentile of the earnings distribution with $j < i$, and k_{ij} is a positive constant that depends on i and j. Equations (3) and (4) imply that $\ln(w_i/w_j)$ is a reasonable proxy for the ratio of the median income to the mean.[26]

The OECD provides data on the 90/10, 90/50, and 50/10 wage ratios. As equations 3 and 4 indicate, the statistical results should not depend on the wage ratio that is used. In practice, the lognormal distribution is a good approximation but not a perfect characterization of the actual distribution of wages and all variables are measured with error. Therefore, we used all three available wage ratios in our analysis. To save space, we only report the results using the 90/10 wage ratio, but our findings do not differ significantly when the 90/10 wage ratio is replaced by either the 90/50 or the 50/10 wage ratio.

Because wage and salary inequality data are not available on an annual basis for many countries and because we do not think that small annual changes in distribution of income have an immediate political impact, we used the average value of the 90/10 wage ratio for each five-year period. That is, to explain social-insurance expenditures in, say, 1985, we use the average of all measures of the 90/10 wage ratio that are available for the time period 1980–84. Thus, our data set consists of data on spending in various social-insurance programs as a share of GDP in the eighteen countries in the years 1985, 1990, and 1995, with measures of wage inequality (and most other control variables) averaged over the time periods 1980–84, 1985–89, and 1990–94. We have fifty observations after subtracting the four cases in which there is no measure of wage inequality within the five-year time period.[27]

On average, a worker at the 90th percentile received three times the earnings of a worker at the 10th percentile. The most egalitarian earnings distribution in the data set is Norway in 1990–94, where the ratio of earnings at the 90th percentile to earnings at the 10th percentile was less than two to one. The least egalitarian earnings distribution was achieved by the U.S.

[26] Both our model and the data we use to measure income inequality refer to wage and salary earners who are either working full time or are temporarily without employment. Of course, not all voters fit into these categories. Some work part time. Others are permanently outside the dependent labor force. To take all categories of attachment to the labor market into account would greatly complicate the analysis, both theoretically and empirically.

[27] The countries and years in the data set are listed in Appendix 2.

in 1985–89, when workers at the 90th percentile received a wage or salary that was 5.5 times the earnings received by workers at the 10th percentile.

As control variables, we include the dependent variable lagged one period (five years), the rate of unemployment, the share of elderly in the population, voter turnout, and a measure of conservative party participation in government. We discuss each briefly in turn.

Lagged Dependent Variable

Budgeting is incremental. The best single predictor of the next period's welfare budget is the current welfare budget. Indeed, the simple regression of current total social-insurance spending on past total social-insurance spending (plus a constant) yields an R^2 of 87.7 percent.[28] Therefore, we include the lagged dependent variable in the set of regressors.

Unemployment Rate

Once the parameters of unemployment insurance are fixed, expenditures on unemployment benefits vary directly with the rate of unemployment. Expenditures on active labor-market policies and even disability insurance may also be sensitive to the unemployment rate. Thus, we include the rate of unemployment in the same year as the data on expenditures when analyzing categories of spending that might be sensitive to the unemployment rate.[29]

Share of Elderly in the Population

Government spending on pensions and health care may be affected by the share of elderly in the population, both because the larger the share of elderly, the greater the need for spending to maintain the elderly in reasonable comfort and because the larger the share of elderly, the larger the share of the electorate with a keen interest in spending on pensions. We use the average share of elderly in the population in the previous five years (as is appropriate if the share of elderly primarily measures the political strength

---

[28] The regression equation is

$$y_t = 3.03 + .938y_{t-1}$$

with $R^2 = 87.7$ and $n = 50$, where y_t is total welfare expenditures as a share of GDP in period t, and the standard error of the coefficient on the lagged dependent variable is .050.

[29] The possible endogeneity of unemployment is discussed below.

424

of the elderly) rather than in the same year (as would be appropriate if the share of elderly primarily measures need) because the five-year average fits the data better than the same-year figure, although the difference in fit is small.

Turnout

Since the electorate is not a representative sample of the adult population as a whole, the level of turnout may affect support for welfare expenditures, as argued by Lijphart and Franzese.[30] Therefore, we include the average turnout in elections to the lower house of parliament (except in the U.S., where we use turnout in presidential elections) in each five-year period.

Partisan Composition of Government

The simple spatial model of electoral competition between two parties competing on a single policy dimension predicts that the two parties offer identical policies in equilibrium in the absence of uncertainty. In the presence of uncertainty about the precise electoral consequences of offering one policy rather than another, however, parties that care about policy outcomes (and not just about winning) would propose divergent policies in equilibrium.[31] With uncertainty, the positions of parties that care about policy choices represent a compromise between the platform that maximizes the probability of winning (that is the policy preferred by the median voter) and the platform the party would most like to implement. Therefore, we include the party in power as a control. Like many others, we find the greatest partisan difference with respect to welfare expenditures is that which separates conservative parties from both center and left parties.[32]

---

[30] Arend Lijphart, "Unequal Participation: Democracy's Unresolved Dilemma," *American Political Science Review* 91 (May 1997); Robert J. Franzese, *Macroeconomic Policies of Developed Democracies* (Cambridge: Cambridge University Press, 2002).

[31] Roemer (fn. 15, 2001).

[32] Francis G. Castles, "The Impact of Parties on Public Expenditure" in Castles, ed., *The Impact of Parties: Politics and Policies in Democratic Capitalist States* (London: Sage Publications, 1982); Gösta Esping-Andersen, *The Three Worlds of Welfare Capitalism* (Princeton: Princeton University Press, 1990). The tripartite division of parties into left, center, and right follows Francis Castles and Peter Mair, "Left-Right Political Scales: Some 'Expert' Judgements," *European Journal of Political Research* 12 (March 1984). Socialist, social democratic, and labor parties (with the exception of the Italian Social Democratic Party) comprise the group of left parties, Center parties, farmers parties, liberal parties in countries with a

Accordingly, we use the average share of cabinet seats held by conservative parties in each period as our measure of the partisan composition of government. Summary statistics for our dependent and independent variables are listed in Table 1.

Finally, it is worth discussing common controls that we do not include. We do not include measures of union density, union concentration, or the centralization of bargaining, since previous studies have identified these variables as being the primary determinants of the inequality of wages and salaries.[33] Our assumption is that the effect of union organization and wage-setting institutions on welfare expenditures is indirect. Unions and wage-setting institutions affect the distribution of income, which, in turn, affects the political support for social insurance. The relationship between organization of the labor market and wage inequality is so close that it is impossible to separate the effect of union strength per se from the effect of a more egalitarian wage distribution.

We also experimented with controls for per capita GDP, trade openness (imports plus exports as a share of GDP), a dummy variable for federal systems of government as suggested by Huber, Ragin, and Stephens,[34] a dummy variable for systems of proportional representation and a measure of union participation in government policy formation and implementation with respect to nonwage issues developed by Traxler, Blaschke, and Kittel.[35]

---

conservative party on the right, Christian democratic parties in countries with a liberal party on the right, and the Democratic Party in the U.S. constitute the group of center parties. Conservative parties, liberal parties in countries where the liberal party is the main party on the right, and Christian democratic parties in countries where the Christian democratic party is the main party on the right, plus all small parties further right comprise the group of conservative parties.

[33] The impact of these three variables on the distribution of wages and salaries is analyzed in Michael Wallerstein, "Wage-Setting Institutions and Pay Inequality in Advanced Industrial Societies," *American Journal of Political Science* 43 (July 1999). For related studies, see Richard B. Freeman, "Labour Market Institutions and Economic Performance." *Economic Policy* 3 (April 1988); Francine D. Blau and Lawrence M. Kahn, "International Differences in Male Wage Inequality: Institutions versus Market Forces," *Journal of Political Economy* 106 (August 1996); and David Rueda and Jonas Pontusson, "Wage Inequality and Varieties of Capitalism," *World Politics* 52 (April 2000).

[34] Evelyne Huber, Charles Ragin, and John D. Stephens, "Social Democracy, Christian Democracy, Constitutional Structure and the Welfare State," *American Journal of Sociology* 99 (November 1993).

[35] Franz Traxler, Sabine Blaschke, and Bernhard Kittel, *National Labour Relations in Internationalized Markets* (Oxford: Oxford University Press, 2001). The measure of union participation in policy-making with respect to nonwage issues is described by Traxler, Blaschke,

None of these variables altered our results concerning inequality and all proved to be statistically insignificant in most of the specifications that we tried.

Methodological Issues

The model we estimate is

$$y_{i,t} = \alpha + \beta y_{i,t-5} + \gamma \cdot \text{Inequality}_{i,t} + \delta' x_{i,t} + u_{i,t} \qquad (5)$$

where $y_{i,t}$ is spending as a share of GDP in country i in year t ($t = 1985$, 1990, 1995), Inequality$_{i,t} \equiv \ln(w_{90}/w_{10})$ using the average value of w_{90}/w_{10} in country i from $t - 5$ to $t - 1$ and $x_{i,t}$ is the vector of control variables. Two methodological issues arise. The first is the question of the exogeneity of our right-hand-side variables. The second concerns likely deviations from the standard assumptions regarding the variances and covariances of the error terms.

Two right-hand-side variables, in particular, might be suspected of being endogenous. Few economists would accept the assumption that the rate of unemployment is exogenous with respect to spending on unemployment benefits. Since we are not concerned in this article with accurately measuring the impact of the unemployment rate on welfare spending, the endogeneity of unemployment only matters to the extent that it alters our inferences regarding γ in equation 5. Removing the unemployment rate from the set of controls results in only minor changes in the point estimates of γ and the associated standard errors. Therefore, the potential endogeneity of the unemployment rate does not affect our conclusions regarding inequality and welfare spending.

The other variable that might be endogenous is our central variable, the inequality of wages and salaries. While the w_{90}/w_{10} ratio is calculated on the basis of pretax wages and salaries, the welfare system may affect the pretax wage and salary distribution. Here we rely on the results of

and Kittel as "associational (union) participation in state regulation (non-wage issues)" (p. 68). The data are available by decade. We assigned the 1980–90 figure to 1985 in our data set, and the 1991–96 figure to 1995 in our data set. For 1990, we used the average of the 1980–90 and 1991–95 figures. We rechecked our results with 1990 removed from our data. In neither case did the inclusion of the index of union participation alter our findings with respect to inequality.

Wallerstein, who found that government spending had little effect on the w_{90}/w_{10} ratio after controlling for union density, the concentration of the union movement, the centralization of bargaining, and the level of wage inequality in the previous period.[36] Therefore, we maintain the assumption that the w_{90}/w_{10} ratio is determined by a country's labor market institutions and is exogenous with respect to spending on welfare policies.

The second problem concerns the implausibility of the assumption that the error terms associated with different countries in the same year are uncorrelated. The Norwegian government may not consider the U.S. a suitable model for its social policy, but the Norwegians pay close attention to the policy choices made in Sweden and vice versa. Instead of the usual assumption that $E(uu') = \sigma^2 I$, a more plausible assumption is to allow for heteroskedasticity and cross-sectional correlation of errors. The current conventional approach in comparative politics is to use OLS to obtain point estimates, since the OLS estimates remain unbiased but correct the estimated standard errors for heteroskedasticity and cross-sectional correlation.[37] However, the small sample properties of the correction for heteroskedasticity and cross-sectional correlation are unclear and our data has only three time periods.

To decide whether or not to use panel-corrected standard errors, we turned to simulations. The simulations revealed that the uncorrected estimates of the standard errors perform well, even in the presence of heteroskedasticity and cross-sectional correlations, while the panel-corrected estimates of the standard errors perform poorly with so few time periods.[38] Therefore, we report uncorrected standard errors in the regressions that follow.

---

[36] Wallerstein (fn. 33).

[37] Neal Beck and Jonathan Katz, "What To Do (and Not to Do) with Time-Series Cross-Sectional Data in Comparative Politics," *American Political Science Review* 89 (September 1995); William H. Greene, *Econometric Analysis*, 3rd ed. (Upper Saddle River, N.J.: Prentice Hall, 1997).

[38] We generated 400 data sets, each with 45 observations (15 countries, 3 time periods) and 3 regressors (a constant plus the first 2 regressors in column 1 of Table 2). The error terms were normally distributed with randomly selected, country-specific variances and randomly selected, cross-national correlations. In the simulations the 90 percent confidence intervals contained the true values of the coefficients roughly 90 percent of the time when calculated using OLS standard errors. When calculated on the basis of panel-corrected standard errors, by contrast, the 90 percent confidence intervals contained the true value of the coefficients only 77 percent of the time. See Karl O. Moene and Michael Wallerstein, "Income Inequality and Welfare Spending: Simulations" (http://faculty-web.at.nwu.edu/polisci/wallerstein/papers.html).

ble 2. *The Impact of Inequality on Major Categories of Welfare Spending as a Share of GDP in OECD Countries (1980–95)[a]*

ependent riable	1 All Welfare Spending	2 Pensions	3 Health	4 Income Replacement	5 Unemp. Insurance	6 Other Insurance
gged dep. var.	.749***	.965***	.777***	.728***	.582***	.759***
	(.063)	(.056)	(.103)	(.065)	(.077)	(.064)
equality (90/10)	−4.50***	−0.31	0.17	−3.32***	−2.12***	−1.37**
	(1.50)	(0.56)	(0.51)	(0.94)	(0.48)	(0.63)
ght govt.	−.0190***	−.0051**	−.0047**	−.0115***	−.0030	−.0070**
	(.0073)	(.0028)	(.0025)	(.0044)	(.0026)	(.0031)
rnout	−.0730***	−.0177**	−.0165**	−.0343**	−.0141*	−.0182**
	(.0250)	(.0097)	(.0085)	(.0150)	(.0086)	(.0101)
rcentage elderly	.326**	.065	−.020	.116		.116**
	(.170)	(.062)	(.052)	(.090)		(.063)
nemp. rate	.256***			.122***	.163***	−.016
	(.082)			(.050)	(.031)	(.032)
. R^2	92.3	90.7	61.2	90.4	82.5	90.7

)LS estimation; standard errors in parenthesis; $n = 50$. All regressions include a constant.
*$p \leq .01$; **$p \leq .05$; *$p \leq .10$

Results

We begin with total welfare spending as a share of GDP. As column 1 in Table 2 reveals, total welfare spending is significantly and negatively related to the inequality of wages and salaries. Spending levels are lower in countries that are more unequal. Total welfare spending is also reduced by conservative parties in government and high levels of voter turnout. The estimated negative effect of turnout on social-insurance spending may surprise readers. However, the electorate is both richer and older than the adult population as a whole, and the correlation between electoral participation and income is generally weaker than the correlation between electoral participation and age.[39] Thus, lower turnout may imply an older electorate on average. Both the share of the population who are elderly and the rate of unemployment are positively associated with welfare expenditures as a share of GDP.

Aggregating all welfare programs together, however, obscures where and how inequality matters. In columns 2, 3, and 4 we consider the three main pillars of the welfare state separately. Each pillar consumes roughly

---

[39] Mark N. Franklin, "Electoral Competition," in Lawrence LeDuc, Richard Niemi, and Pippa Norris, eds., *Comparing Democracies: Elections and Voting in Global Perspective* (Thousand Oaks, Calif.: Sage Publications, 1996).

30 percent of the total welfare spending or 7 percent of GDP. In column 2 the dependent variable is spending on pensions (old-age cash benefits) as a share of GDP. In column 3 the dependent variable is government spending on health care as a share of GDP. Since there is little reason to think that the rate of unemployment matters for spending on pensions or health care, and the estimated coefficient on unemployment is not statistically significant if unemployment is included in either regression, we removed the unemployment rate from the set of controls. It is apparent from columns 2 and 3 that inequality has little impact on spending for either pensions or health care. In both cases, the estimated coefficient on inequality is not significantly different from zero.[40]

By contrast, the inequality of wages and salaries has a significant, negative effect on spending on the set of policies that provide income replacement or insurance against the loss of income as a result of unemployment, sickness, disability, occupational illness or accident, and the death of a spouse (column 4 of Table 1).[41] The estimated impact of a permanent increase of wage and salary inequality of one standard deviation (.25) is to change spending on income-replacement programs by $-3.32 \cdot .25 \approx -0.8$ of a percent of GDP in the short run (five years) and by $-3.32 \cdot .25/(1 - .728) \approx -3.1$ percent of GDP in the long run. Since average spending on income replacement is 7.1 percent of GDP in the sample, this is a large change. To illustrate with an example, the difference between the average value of $\ln(w_{90}/w_{10})$ in the United Kingdom and Sweden in the early 1990s was .45. That difference in wage inequality is estimated to be associated with a difference of spending on income replacement of $3.32 \cdot .45/(1 - .728) \approx 5.5$ percent of GDP in the long run. The actual difference between spending on

---

[40] In the case of health expenditures, the estimated coefficient on inequality is even closer to zero if one subtracts means-tested health expenditures (Medicaid) from the U.S. figures. Excluding U.S. Medicaid expenditures (roughly 25 percent of total government expenditures on health in the U.S.), column 3 of Table 2 becomes

$$y_i = 2.92 + .801 y_{t-s} + .020 \, \text{Inequality} - .0046 \, \text{Right} - .0123 \, \text{Turnout} - .030 \, \text{Elderly}$$

where standard errors of the coefficients (excluding the constant) are (.103, .526, .0025, .0088, .052) and adjusted $R^2 = 65.8$. Only the coefficient on the lagged dependent variable and on Right government are significant at the .05 level.

[41] The category of income replacement in Table 2 is a subset of the policies included in insurance against loss of income in Moene and Wallerstein (fn. 4). The difference between the two is that the measure of insurance against income loss in Moene and Wallerstein (fn. 4) includes a share of expenditures on health while all health expenditures are excluded from spending on income replacement in Table 2.

income replacement as a share of GDP in Sweden and in the U.K. was 7.7 percentage points in 1995 (13.2 percent of GDP in Sweden as opposed to 5.9 percent of GDP in the U.K.). Thus, the difference in earnings inequality between the United Kingdom and Sweden explains about 75 percent of the actual difference in spending on income replacement as a share of GDP in the two countries.

The category of income-replacement programs can be subdivided into policies that provide insurance against the risk of unemployment, that is, the sum of spending on unemployment benefits and on active labor-market policies (2.4 percent of GDP on average) and policies that provide insurance against the risks of loss of income because of disability, sickness, occupational illness and injury, and death of a spouse (4.7 percent of GDP on average). Results for each of these two subcategories of income replacement are presented in columns 5 and 6 of Table 2. Inequality is most strongly related to spending on unemployment insurance and active labor-market policies, as column 5 shows, but the relationship is significant and negative for both categories of expenditures.[42] It is also worth noting that, in spite of the charge that employers, unions, and governments encourage workers to apply for disability payments under conditions of high unemployment, the unemployment rate does not have a significant effect on expenditures on disability insurance as a share of GDP. In addition, the partisan composition of the government makes less difference for spending on unemployment insurance and active labor-market policies than for spending in any other category of social insurance.

Readers may question the specification of the models displayed in Table 2. Perhaps unemployment should be dropped from column 6, since the estimated coefficient has the "wrong," that is, unexpected, sign. Perhaps the unemployment rate should be added to column 3, since unemployment may be damaging to health. Perhaps conservative government should be removed from the set of controls on the a priori grounds that electoral

---

[42] An alternative way to measure the generosity of unemployment benefits is the replacement ratio, which is available from OECD (fn. 20). Using the average replacement ratio for a worker at the median wage and at two-thirds of the median wage in the first year of unemployment as the dependent variable yields

$$y_t = 3.81 + .864y_{t-s} + .136 \text{ Inequality} - .0006 \text{ Right} - .0017 \text{ Turnout}$$

where standard errors of the coefficients (excluding the constant) are (.048, .054, .0003, .0010) and adjusted $R^2 = 90.5$. All coefficients are significant at the .05 level. Neither the share of elderly in the population nor the rate of unemployment are significantly different from zero when the replacement ratio is the dependent variable.

competition forces all parties to implement the same policies, as in the Downsian model. Rather than consider each possible objection, we investigated the robustness of the results in Table 2 by regressing each of the dependent variables on the lagged dependent variable, Inequality (90/10), and every subset of the "questionable" control variables, where the questionable control variables are Right Government, Turnout, Percent Elderly, and Unemployment Rate.[43]

The results are presented in the first two columns of Table 3, where we display both the minimum and the maximum value of the estimated coefficient on Inequality over all combinations of the questionable controls for each dependent variable. Table 3 shows that the qualitative results in Table 2 with regard to the three large components of the welfare budget are robust with respect to specification uncertainty. While the effect of uncertainty regarding the correct specification is larger than sampling uncertainty for any given specification, every specification implies that inequality is negatively associated at the .05 significance level with spending on income replacement as a share of GDP. In contrast, inequality is not significantly associated with spending on pensions as a share of GDP in any specification. In the case of government spending on health care, inequality is not significantly associated with spending as a share of GDP in most specifications.

To check whether our results could be upset by removing one of the countries from our data set, we redid the regressions of Table 2 for each subset of seventeen countries. The minimum and the maximum value of the estimated coefficient on Inequality (90/10) are presented in the third and fourth columns of Table 3. Again, the estimated coefficient on Inequality (90/10) is significant at the .05 level in every subset of seventeen countries when the dependent variable is total social-insurance spending (line 1), spending on income replacement (line 4), and spending on unemployment benefits (line 5) and is significant at the .05 level in all but one subset of seventeen countries when the dependent variable is spending on income replacement other than unemployment benefits (line 6).[44] In contrast, the

---

[43] This procedure is advocated and given a Bayesian justification in Edward E. Leamer, *Specification Searches: Ad Hoc Inferences with Nonexperimental Data* (New York: John Wiley and Sons, 1978). We did not consider the unemployment rate to be "questionable" when the dependent variable included unemployment benefits.

[44] In lines 1, 4, 5, and 6, the minimum estimate is obtained by excluding Austria and the maximum estimate is obtained by excluding Finland. In line 2, the minimum is obtained by excluding Norway and the maximum is obtained by excluding the U.S. In line 3, the

Table 3. *The Effect of Inequality on Expenditures: Robustness Tests[a]*

Dependent Variable	Extreme Bounds Analysis		Jackknife	
	Minimum	Maximum	Minimum	Maximum
1. All welfare	−5.52	−2.16	−6.90	−3.49
spending	(1.50)	(1.37)	(1.93)	(1.61)
2. Pensions	−0.75	0.32	−0.63	0.20
	(0.50)	(0.46)	(0.59)	(0.58)
3. Health	0.10	0.72	−0.01	0.50
	(0.52)	(0.44)	(0.55)	(0.63)
4. Income	−3.46	−1.93	−4.72	−2.54
replacement	(0.99)	(0.85)	(1.19)	(0.96)
5. Unemployment	−1.83	−1.28	−2.50	−1.83
support	(0.68)	(0.57)	(0.53)	(0.51)
6. Other	−1.71	−0.72	−1.79	−0.97
insurance	(0.61)	(0.52)	(0.86)	(0.66)
n	50	50	47	47

[a] Only the estimated coefficient for Inequality 90/10 is shown with standard errors in parentheses. Extreme Bounds Analysis summarizes the results of 2^q regression equations including all possible subsets of the q questionable controls. Jackknife summarizes the results of eighteen regression equations excluding each country one at a time. The Jackknife estimates include the same controls as Table 2.

estimated coefficient on Inequality (90/10) is not significantly different from zero in any subset of seventeen countries at the .10 level when the dependent variable is spending on pensions (line 2) or health care (line 3).

Kristov, Lindert, and McClelland distinguish between the political impact of inequality in the top half of the wage schedule and inequality in the bottom half of the wage schedule.[45] They argue that the closer the median is to the poor, that is, the smaller the w_{50}/w_{10} wage ratio, the greater the willingness of voters in the middle to support welfare expenditures. In contrast, the closer the median is to the rich, that is, the smaller the w_{90}/w_{50} ratio, the lower the willingness of voters in the middle to support welfare expenditures. In Table 4 we test the proposition that the 90/50 ratio and

minimum is obtained by excluding Finland while the maximum is obtained by excluding Austria.

[45] Lorenzo Kristov, Peter Lindert, and Robert McClelland, "Pressure Groups and Redistribution," *Journal of Public Economics* 48 (July 1992).

Table 4. *The Impact of the 90/50 Ratio and the 50/10 Ratio on Welfare Expenditures as a Share of GDP[a]*

Dependent Variable	1 All Welfare Spending	2 Income Replacement	3 Unemployment Support	4 Other Insurance
Inequality 90/50	−4.91 (3.37)	−3.60 (2.02)	−1.47 (1.17)	−2.11 (1.36)
Inequality 50/10	−4.19 (2.28)	−3.13 (1.44)	−2.48 (0.77)	−0.91 (0.95)
$F(1, n-k)$	0.20	0.16	0.27	0.29

[a] The regression equations include all of the controls included in Table 1 for each of the dependent variables; $n = 50$; $k = 8$ for columns 1, 2, and 4; $k = 7$ for column 3. The F statistic tests the null hypothesis that the coefficients on Inequality 90/50 and Inequality 50/10 are identical.

the 50/10 ratio have different political effects. The equations that are estimated are identical to the corresponding equation in Table 2, with the log of w_{90}/w_{10} replaced by the log of w_{90}/w_{50} and the log of w_{50}/w_{10}. Only the coefficients on Inequality (90/50) and Inequality (50/10) are displayed. The estimated coefficients on inequality always have the same sign. Moreover, the null hypothesis that the coefficient on $\ln(w_{90}/w_{50})$ and the coefficient on $\ln(w_{50}/w_{10})$ are the same is never rejected. Therefore, our use of $\ln(w_{90}/w_{10}) = \ln(w_{90}/w_{50}) + \ln(w_{50}/w_{10})$ as the measure of inequality in Table 2 is justified.

Pensions, health spending, and income replacement constitute most, but not all, of the welfare budget. In Table 5 we present an analysis of the remaining part, divided into family benefits and services (2 percent of GDP on average) and programs targeted to low-income individuals, refugees, and indigenous groups plus housing subsidies (1 percent of GDP on average). Column 1 reveals that none of the independent variables are good predictors of spending on family benefits, with the exception of the lagged dependent variable. The second column of Table 5 indicates that conservative parties in government are associated with more spending on housing subsidies and antipoverty programs, which probably reflects the preference of conservative parties for narrowly targeted programs over broadly targeted programs. In addition, countries with high rates of unemployment spend more on benefits targeted at those with low income. In neither category, however, is spending significantly associated with the inequality of wages and salaries.

Table 5. *The Impact of Inequality on Smaller Categories of Welfare Spending as a Share of GDP (1980–95)*

Dependent Variable	1 Family Benefits	2 Antipoverty Programs and Housing Subsidies
Lagged dependent variable	.521***	.986***
	(.102)	(.075)
Inequality (90/10)	−0.45	−0.24
	(0.63)	(0.26)
Right government	−.0025	.0028**
	(.0029)	(.0013)
Turnout	.0150*	−.0036
	(.0101)	(.0044)
Percentage elderly	.068	.024
	(.061)	(.025)
Unemployment rate	.035	.048***
	(.032)	(.014)
adj. R^2	63.8	82.7

[a] OLS estimation; standard errors in parenthesis; $n = 50$. All regressions include a constant.
***$p \leq .01$; **$p \leq .05$; *$p \leq .10$

IV. Conclusion

The empirical relationship between inequality and social-insurance spending as a share of GDP in advanced industrial societies differs across policies. For many policies – pensions, health care, family benefits, poverty alleviation – spending is largely uncorrelated with the inequality of wages and salaries. But for a significant set of policies that constitute roughly 30 percent of the welfare benefit – unemployment insurance, active labor-market policies, sickness pay, disability insurance, and occupational illness and injury – spending is significantly more generous in countries with a relatively egalitarian pretax distribution of wages and salaries.

These differences in the relationship between income inequality and social-insurance spending across policy areas can be explained by extending the Romer and Meltzer and Richard model to incorporate the fact that welfare policies provide insurance as well as redistribution. The demand for redistribution increases when income falls, but the demand for redistributive insurance increases when income rises. Thus an increase in inequality that lowers the income of the median voter relative to the mean generates two counteracting effects. With two counteracting effects, the impact of

435

Karl Ove Moene and Michael Wallerstein

inequality on support for welfare spending depends on the particular policy under consideration. Inequality lowers support for spending in policies
that provide insurance against unexpected loss of income. In welfare policies where the benefits are received by all regardless of current employment
status, the two effects roughly balance each other such that there is little or
no relationship between income inequality and spending levels. The fact
that we failed to find any category of welfare spending where inequality
clearly raises welfare spending can be explained by the absence of social-
insurance policies designed purely to provide redistributive benefits among
active participants in the labor market.

Our data analysis shows that the differences in the empirical relationship
between earnings inequality and expenditures in different social-insurance
policies match the predictions of the extended Romer and Meltzer and
Richards framework. But there are other possible explanations of the empirical pattern we found. Iversen and Soskice suggest a variant of the insurance
argument that emphasizes the relative importance of firm-specific skills
versus general skills.[46] According to Iversen and Soskice, the demand for
insurance against job loss is greater in countries where firm-specific skills
predominate, since firm-specific skills are lost by definition when workers leave their firm. In countries where general skills predominate, the
demand for insurance against job loss is less, since the cost of job loss is less.
In fact, there is a close empirical relationship between earnings equality
and the measures of firm-specific skills used by Iversen and Soskice.[47] An
egalitarian wage schedule that compresses the wage differential between
workers at different skill levels increases employers' incentive to invest in
firm-specific training and reduces workers' incentive to invest in general
training.[48] Thus, the effect of the wage distribution on the relative importance of firm-specific versus general skills is another route by which greater
wage equality may increase the demand for social insurance against job
loss.

A different approach is to emphasize the effect of wage inequality on the
disincentive effects of income-replacement policies, as suggested by Moffitt,

[46] Torben Iversen and David Soskice, "An Asset Theory of Social Policy Preferences," *American Political Science Review* 95 (December 2001).
[47] Iversen and Soskice (fn. 46), for example, report a correlation coefficient of .73 between
their measure of the extent of vocational training and the w_{40}/w_{90} ratio (p. 889).
[48] Daron Acemoglu and Jörn-Steffen Pischke, "The Structure of Wages and Investment in
General Training," *Journal of Political Economy* 107 (June 1999).

436

Ribar, and Wilhelm.[49] They argue that if wages at the bottom of the income scale are low, then the income floor provided by social-insurance benefits must not be so high that unskilled workers find living on the dole preferable to working. The higher are wages at the bottom, the higher the income floor provided by social insurance can be without creating severe disincentive effects. Such disincentive effects are less important for publicly provided health insurance or pensions. While there is some discussion of ways to keep the elderly in the workforce, voters are much more concerned about working-age adults choosing to live on social-insurance benefits instead of seeking employment than they are about the labor-force participation of retirees.

In our view, the political influence of unions, frequently cited as one of the most important determinants of cross-national differences in social-insurance spending, cannot easily account for the differences that exist in the relationship between earnings inequality and social-insurance spending across different categories of social insurance. We are not aware of any evidence suggesting that unions care less about pensions and health care than about income-replacement programs. After all, retirees make up a significant fraction of union members in Europe today.[50] Unions increase workers' ability to obtain the policies that workers want, but unions also change workers' preferences over policies. It is the indirect effect of unions in changing workers' preferences over social-insurance policies by changing the distribution of income that helps explain the differential impact of inequality on spending across policy categories that we have found in the data.

In conclusion, there is more than one reason why spending on social insurance against income loss from layoffs, sickness, or accidents might be greater in countries with lower levels of income inequality. We have emphasized the direct impact of wage equality on the political support for redistributive insurance policies against income loss. Iversen and Soskice focus on the relative importance of firm-specific skills versus general skills. Moffitt, Ribar, and Wilhelm argue in terms of the disincentive effects of income-replacement policies when wage inequality is high. The negative impact of income inequality on support for spending on important categories of social insurance, in turn, helps explain the strong association

---

[49] Moffitt, Ribar, and Wilhelm (fn. 7).
[50] Bernhard Ebbinghaus and Jelle Visser, *Trade Unions in Western Europe since 1945* (New York: Grove's Dictionaries, 2000).

of pre–tax and transfer income inequality and the proportion of households whose post–tax and transfer income falls below the poverty line.[51] Inequality matters for poverty, not because (or not only because) employed workers are paid so little, but because income inequality reduces political support for important categories of social-insurance spending.

Appendix 1: Proofs of the Claims in the Text

The ideal point of a voter with income w is given by the solution to the following problem

$$\max_{t} E(u) = \pi u(c_E) + (1 - \pi)u(c_N), \text{ where}$$
$$c_E = (1 - t)w + b_E(w, t)$$
$$c_N = b_N(w, t)$$

subject to the budget constraint

$$\int_0^\infty [\pi b_E(w, t) + (1 - \pi)b_N(w, t)] \, dF(w) = \pi \tau(t).$$

The first-order condition for the voters' maximization problem can be written as

$$H(w, t^*) = \lambda \tau'(t^*) - u'(c_E)w = 0 \tag{6}$$

where t^* is the optimal tax rate and λ (the Lagrangian multiplier) is the utility gain from a marginal increase in the per capita welfare budget $T(t)$. Equation 6 states that the gain in expected utility from a marginal increase in the tax rate, $\lambda T'(t) = \lambda \pi \tau'(t)$, just equals the expected utility cost of the tax increase, $\pi u'(c_E)w$. Equation 6 is not sufficient to characterize the solution, since λ depends on the definitions of the benefit functions $b_E(w, t)$ and $b_N(w, t)$ that describe different social-insurance programs.

---

[51] Kenworthy calculates the share of individuals in advanced industrial societies who would be classified as living in poverty in the U.S., that is, living in households with incomes less than 40 percent of the median household income in the U.S. after converting their household income to U.S. dollars according to purchasing power parity and adjusting for family size; see Lane Kenworthy, "Do Social Welfare Policies Reduce Poverty? A Cross-National Assessment," *Social Forces* 77 (March 1999). The partial correlation coefficient between share living in poverty and the log of the 90/10 wage ratio is .69, controlling for GDP per capita for the fourteen countries where Kenworthy's sample overlaps with the sample of this paper.

The wage of the median wage earner is $w_M = \exp(-\sigma^2/2)$ when the mean wage equals one with a lognormal distribution. We can derive the impact of inequality on the political equilibrium by calculating

$$\frac{dt^*}{d\sigma^2} = -\sigma w_M \left(\frac{dt^*}{dw_M}\right) = \sigma w_M \left[\frac{\partial H(w_M, t^*)/\partial w_M}{\partial H(w_M, t^*)/\partial t^*}\right].$$

The second-order condition $\partial H(w_M, t^*)/\partial t^* < 0$ is satisfied in all of the cases considered in the paper. It follows that:

$$\text{sgn} = \left(\frac{dt^*}{d\sigma^2}\right) = \text{sgn}\left[\frac{\partial H(w_M, t^*)}{\partial w_M}\right].$$

Therefore, we prove the claims in the papers by calculating the sign of $-\partial H(w_M, t^*)/\partial w_M$.

Proof of claim 1. When $b_N(w, t) = 0$ and $b_E(w,t) = b(t) = \tau(t)$, equation 6 simplifies to

$$H(w_M, t^*) = \tau'(t^*) - w_M = 0 \tag{7}$$

where w_M is the ratio of the median income to the mean (since the mean wage is assumed to equal one). Note that $\lambda = u'(c_E)$ in (7), since the benefit is received when employed. From (7), it follows immediately that $-\partial H(w_M, t^*)/\partial w_M = 1 > 0$.

Proof of claim 2. When $b_E(w,t) = 0$ and $b_N(w, t) = [\xi + (1 - \xi)w]b(t)$, equation 6 becomes

$$H(w_M, t^*) = u'(c_N)[\xi + (1 - \xi)w_M]\tau'(t^*) - u'(c_E)w_M = 0. \tag{8}$$

In (8), $\lambda = u'(c_N)[\xi + (1 - \xi)w_M]$ since the benefit is received when not employed and the median worker receives the multiple $[\xi + (1 - \xi)w_M]$ of $b(t)$. Differentiating (8) and simplifying yields

$$\frac{\partial H(w_M, t^*)}{\partial w_M} = \left(\frac{\xi}{\xi + (1 - \xi)w_M}\right) u'(c_E)(1 - \mu) < 0$$

since $\mu > 1$ and $0 < \xi \leq 1$.

Proof of claim 3. When $b_E(w, t) = b_N(w, t) = [\xi + (1 - \xi)w_1b(t)$, and equation 6 becomes

$$H(w_M, t^*) = [\pi u'(c_E) + (1 - \pi)u'(c_N)]$$
$$\times [\xi + (1 - \xi)w_M]\tau'(t^*) - u'(c_E)w_M = 0. \tag{9}$$

In (9), $\lambda = [\pi u'(c_E) + (1 - \pi)u'(c_N)][\xi + (1 - \xi)w_M]$ since the benefit is received whether or not the worker is employed. Differentiating (9) and simplifying yields

$$-\frac{\partial H(w_M, t^*)}{\partial w_M} \qquad (10)$$

$$= u'(c_E) \left\{ \frac{\pi u'(c_E)(1 - \eta_N) + (1 - \pi)u'(c_N)[1 - \mu\eta_E - (1 - \mu)\eta_N]}{\pi u'(c_E) + (1 - \pi)u'(c_N)} \right\}$$

where

$$\eta_E \equiv \frac{\partial c_E}{\partial w}\frac{w}{c_E} = \frac{(1 - \xi)wb + (1 - t)w}{[\xi + (1 - \xi)w]b + (1 - t)w}$$

is the elasticity of c_E with respect to w and

$$\eta_N \equiv \frac{\partial c_N}{\partial w}\frac{w}{c_N} = \frac{(1 - \xi)w}{\xi + (1 - \xi)w}$$

is the elasticity of c_N with respect to w. Observe that $1 > \eta_E > \eta_N \geq 0$ for $0 < \xi \leq 1$.

At $\mu = 1$, equation 10 simplifies to

$$-\frac{\partial H(w_M, t^*)}{\partial w_M} = u'(c_E)\left[\frac{\pi u'(c_E)(1 - \eta_N) + (1 - \pi)u'(c_N)(1 - \eta_E)}{\pi u'(c_E) + (1 - \pi)u'(c_N)}\right] > 0$$

since $1 > \eta_N$ and $1 > \eta_E$. By continuity, $-\partial H(w_M, t^*)/\partial w_M > 0$ for μ sufficiently close to 1.

As $\mu \to \infty$, equation (10) implies that

$$-\frac{\partial H(w_M, t^*)}{\partial w} \to \left[\frac{(1 - \pi)u'(c_N)u'(c_E)}{\pi u'(c_E) + (1 - \pi)u'(c_N)}\right](\eta_N - \eta_E)\mu < 0$$

since $\eta_E > \eta_N$. Therefore, $-\partial H(w_M, t^*)/\partial w_M < 0$ for μ sufficiently large.

Appendix 2: Data Sources

Unemployment support refers to unemployment insurance and active labor-market policies. Other insurance refers to disability insurance, sickness pay, occupational illness and accidents, and survivor's insurance. Income replacement refers to unemployment support and other insurance. Family benefits refers to both cash benefits and spending on family services. Antipoverty programs refers to spending on programs for refugees, indigenous groups, and the poor. Data are for 1985, 1990, and 1995 in the case of social-insurance benefits and the rate of unemployment. All of the other

Table 6. *Country Means for the Main Categories of Social Insurance Spending as Percent of GDP (1985–95)*[a]

Country	Total	P	H	IR	US	OI	F	AP&H
Australia	14.7	3.1	5.6	3.8	1.8	2.0	1.8	0.5
Austria	25.9	9.8	5.4	7.7	1.4	6.2	2.6	0.4
Belgium	27.7	7.9	6.8	10.0	4.0	6.0	2.3	0.5
Canada	17.4	3.9	6.5	3.7	2.3	1.4	0.7	2.6
Denmark	29.0	6.7	5.3	11.8	5.8	6.0	3.4	1.7
Finland	26.9	7.0	6.0	9.8	3.0	4.8	3.4	0.7
France	27.9	9.5	7.0	7.7	3.0	6.4	2.6	1.1
Germany	26.9	10.0	7.3	7.0	2.7	4.3	1.9	0.7
Italy	22.8	9.9	5.7	6.5	1.8	4.7	0.7	0.0
Japan	12.3	4.9	5.0	1.8	0.4	1.4	0.4	0.2
Netherlands	28.8	7.1	6.2	12.6	4.0	8.6	1.8	1.2
N.Z.	19.5	6.8	5.2	4.7	2.0	2.7	2.4	0.5
Norway	25.2	5.5	6.3	9.6	1.9	7.7	2.8	1.0
Portugal	16.6	5.3	4.6	5.6	1.4	4.2	1.0	0.1
Sweden	32.2	7.7	7.3	11.3	3.5	7.8	4.3	1.6
Switzerland	25.2	10.1	6.6	6.1	1.6	4.5	1.1	1.3
U.K.	21.2	6.3	5.2	5.6	1.7	3.9	2.2	1.9
U.S.	14.6	5.2	5.4	3.0	0.6	2.4	0.6	0.5
mean	23.0	6.9	6.0	7.1	2.4	4.7	2.0	0.9

[a] P refers to pensions; H refers to health; IR refers to income replacement, which equals US + OI; US refers to unemployment support (unemployment insurance plus active labor-market policies); OI refers to other insurance (disability, sickness pay, occupational injury, and other similar programs); F refers to family benefits and services; AP&H refers to antipoverty programs and housing. See text for further details.

variables represent the average value for the periods 1980–84, 1985–89 and 1990–94. The countries included in the data set are Australia, Austria, Belgium, Canada, Denmark, Finland, France, Germany, Italy, Japan, Netherlands, New Zealand, Norway, Portugal, Sweden, Switzerland, the United Kingdom, and the United States. The missing data points are Belgium 1980–84, Portugal 1980–84, and Switzerland 1980–89. Country means are presented in Table 6.

The source for spending on social insurance, health care, and pensions is the OECD.[52] Data on Medicaid expenditures in the United States is from the U.S. Bureau of the Census.[53] Inequality (i/j) is $\ln(w_i/w_j)$, where w_k

[52] OECD (fn. 23).
[53] United States Bureau of the Census, *Statistical Abstract of the United States 1990* (Washington, D.C.: U.S. Government Printing Office, 1990); idem (fn. 21).

55555

Karl Ove Moene and Michael Wallerstein

represents the wage or salary of a full-time employee at the *k*th percentile of the wage and salary distribution. The data on wage inequality are from the OECD.[54] Conservative government is from the Swank data set, updated using recent issues of *Keesings Contemporary Archive*.[55] The classification of parties in terms of right versus center and left is based on Castles and Mair, updated with Huber and Inglehart.[56] Turnout refers to turnout in elections in the lower house of parliament or for president in the United States. The source for turnout is Blais and Dobrzynska.[57] The share of elderly in the population and the rate of unemployment is from the OECD.[58] The data set is available upon request.

[54] OECD (fn. 24, 1996); OECD (fn. 24, 1993) in the case of the U.S.
[55] Swank (fn. 1).
[56] Castles and Mair (fn. 32); John Huber and Ronald Inglehart, "Expert Interpretations of Party Space and Party Locations in Forty-two Societies," *Party Politics* 1 (January 1995).
[57] Andre Blais and Agnieszka Dobrzynska, "Turnout in Electoral Democracies," *European Journal of Political Research* 33 (March 1998).
[58] Organization for Economic Cooperation and Development, *Statistical Compendium 1997/2* (CD-ROM) (Paris: OECD, 1997).

18

Social Democracy as a Development Strategy

Karl Ove Moene and Michael Wallerstein

"It is but equity, besides, that they who feed, cloath and lodge the whole body of the people, should have such a share of the produce of their own labour as to be themselves tolerably well fed, cloathed and lodged."

– Adam Smith 1776

"One has to understand that the ongoing crisis is not a crisis of real poverty, but an organizational crisis. The world is like a ship loaded with the goods of life, where the crew starves because it cannot figure out how the goods should be distributed."

– Ragnar Frisch 1931

Social democracy, it is often said, is nice but pricey. Whatever its merits in the rich countries of Western Europe, social democracy is frequently dismissed as an infeasible model for developing countries. Based on generosity towards the poor and protection against market competition, the argument goes, social democracy is only possible in consensual, homogeneous, and affluent societies with an extraordinary commitment to equality. In Third World countries that are conflict-ridden, heterogeneous, and poor, does the social democratic model have any relevance?

In this article we offer an agnostic view of the feasibility of the social democratic model of development in the Third World. First, we argue that consensus, homogeneity, and affluence are products of the social democratic model, not prerequisites. Second, we claim that the central social democratic policy in terms of economic development is the policy of wage compression attained through highly centralized wage-setting institutions.

An earlier version of this chapter was presented at the Conference on Globalization and Egalitarian Redistribution, Santa Fe Institute, May 2002. We thank Pranab Bardhan, Sanjay Reddy, Asbjørn Rødseth, John Stephens and the participants at the conference for comments.

Third, we argue that the economic benefits of wage compression would be as significant in South Africa, Brazil, or India today as they were in the Nordic countries between 1935 and 1970. The political feasibility of a policy of wage compression, however, is open to doubt, hence our agnosticism regarding whether or not the social democratic road to affluence can be repeated.

In this chapter, we consider social democracy as a model of development rather than an end state. In particular, we will not enter into the debate regarding the future prospects of social democracy in Western Europe in the context of European economic integration, a common currency, an aging population, and the ever-increasing cost of providing the best health care that money can buy. The achievements of social democracy as a development strategy in terms of combining the socialist virtues of equality and security with the capitalist virtues of economic efficiency and technological dynamism are not seriously in dispute. What are disputed are the answers to the following questions: First, what was the contribution of specifically social democratic policies to the high level of affluence and equality in Northern Europe today? Second, would the policies that successfully promoted development in Northern Europe be equally effective and feasible in the Third World in the context of an increasingly integrated global economy?

Nordic Exceptionalism

Social democracy in the Nordic countries can be characterized in multiple ways. In political terms, social democracy represented the mobilization of industrial workers such that workers' organizations exercised significant power in both the labor market and in government. Unions negotiated the terms of employment for most of the labor force and exerted a strong influence in politics through close connections to a social democratic party. The Social Democratic party was (and still is) the largest party in parliament and a frequent participant in government. In Norway and Sweden, in particular, the Social Democratic party enjoyed a long period of uninterrupted government (1933–76 in Sweden, and 1935–65 in Norway, not counting the five years of German occupation).[1] Institutionally, social democracy was distinguished by the growth of a large welfare state, the organization

---

[1] The Norwegian government flew to London in April 1940 and operated as a government in exile during the years of occupation 1940–45.

444

of encompassing and centralized trade unions, and the establishment of a system of routine consultation and cooperation among government, union, and employer representatives that has been given the label "corporatism" in political science.

In terms of social policy, social democracy in the Nordic countries was characterized by a wage policy of "solidaristic bargaining," that is, a commitment to the reduction of wage inequality, and by a welfare policy of providing basic goods and services to all as a right of citizenship. In trade policy, social democratic governments embraced free trade.[2] Protection was viewed as an ill-conceived subsidy to inefficient employers who did not deserve public support. Financial markets, however, were not open to international competition. In Norway, social democratic governments maintained extensive controls on the allocation of credit after the war. Swedish governments were more concerned with guiding the timing of investment rather than the allocation of credit among prospective borrowers. In neither country were financial markets deregulated until the 1980s. In sum, the Social Democrats, once in power, adopted the economics of Keynes and Frisch rather than of Marx. Quietly discarding the part of their political program that called for elimination of private concentrations of wealth, Social Democrats sought to construct a system of incentives that would lead private businesses to act in socially desirable ways without altering property rights.

In this paper, we focus on the policy of solidaristic bargaining, that is, the policy of reducing wage inequality through centralized collective bargaining and, in Norway and Denmark, occasional government involvement. This is not because other social democratic policies, such as social insurance programs and free trade, are unimportant. Rather the policy of solidaristic bargaining was the most innovative and most distinctive policy associated with social democracy.[3] A commitment to free trade was shared with liberal

---

[2] Like many others, the Scandinavian countries introduced trade restrictions in the early 1930s. The trade restrictions were less heavy than in most other European countries, however, and they were introduced before the Social Democrats came to power. For several years after the war Norway maintained import restrictions, but more as an instrument of economic planning than of protection. For example, the import of private cars was prohibited, not to protect domestic car producers (Norway has none), but because private cars were not considered to be an essential commodity by the government.

[3] Another policy innovation associated with social democracy that is much discussed is the development of active labor market policies, that is, policies that offer retraining to the unemployed in place of unemployment benefits. We emphasize solidaristic bargaining because we think it had far more important effects on both equality and growth.

parties, while a commitment to social insurance was shared with all parties other than the liberal parties (Hicks 1999; Huber and Stephens 2001; Wilensky 2002). The nonsocialist governments in France intervened in. credit markets as much or more than the social democratic governments in Northern Europe in the early postwar period. Only the Social Democrats, however, explicitly promoted the reduction of inequality among wage earners as a development strategy. Moreover, the commitment to greater wage equality was not merely rhetorical. Solidaristic bargaining was highly effective in compressing the wage distribution. By all measures, Scandinavia had the most egalitarian wage structure of any advanced industrial society by the 1970s (Freeman 1988, Wallerstein 1999).

How should the social democratic success in reducing inequality be explained? The most common explanations emphasize the importance of social homogeneity (Alesina, Glaeser and Sacerdote 2001), a socialist (or Nordic) commitment to equality (Therborn 1986), a consensual model of decision-making (Wilensky 2002) and affluence. But conditions in Norway and Sweden in the period preceding the social democratic ascent to power were anything but consensual, egalitarian and affluent.

In the 1920s and early 1930s, Norway and Sweden experienced the highest levels of industrial conflict in the world. In Norway the number of working days lost in strikes and lockouts in one year – 1931 – was three times larger than the total number of working days lost in industrial conflict over the twenty-five-year period 1945–70. In one of the first studies of comparative industrial conflict, Ingham (1974) contrasted the extraordinary militancy of Nordic workers with the relative docility of English workers during the interwar years. Moreover, employers were equally militant in defending their interests. More working days were lost in lockouts than in strikes. The consensus between employers and unions that characterized social democracy after the war was nowhere to be seen when the social democrats entered government in the 1930s.[4]

While the Nordic countries were relatively homogeneous in terms of religion and language, the working population was far from homogenous in terms of living conditions. In particular, the social and economic gap

---

[4] One exception might be the Norwegian Labor Pact (Hovedavtalen) of 1935, an agreement between the employer association NAF and the unions in LO that stipulated negotiation procedures including rules for industrial conflicts. The Labor Pact, however, was highly controversial. A similar proposal was voted down by the LO members in 1934, and the leaders of LO who favored the pact were replaced. A similar pact was signed in Sweden in 1938, after the Swedish Social Democrats came to power.

between rural and urban residents was huge. In Norway in 1934, average income per capita in rural municipalities was one third of the per capita incomes of urban municipalities. Referring to the difference in the average, however, understates the extent of regional inequality. Measured by income per capita, the gap between the poorest and richest rural municipality was 1 to 15, the gap between the poorest and richest city was 1 to 10, and the gap between the richest city and poorest rural municipality was 60 to 1 (Falch and Tovmo 2003). As in most poor countries today, the numbers exaggerate the real inequality because home production in subsistence farming and fishing is underreported. Nevertheless, Scandinavian Social Democrats came to power in societies no less economically divided than many poor countries of today.

As in developing countries today, there was significant underutilization of labor in Norway and Sweden in the interwar years. Surplus labor in the form of open unemployment was most evident. The rates of unemployed union members, the only official statistics available, was, in 1921, as high as 18 percent in Norway and 27 percent in Sweden. The rate fluctuated during the interwar period, but never dropped below 9 to 10 percent. The peak of unemployment was reached in 1933 with 33 percent unemployed in Norway and 23 percent in Sweden. How representative these numbers are for the total rate of unemployment is debated.[5] Moreover, an unknown fraction of union members, upon losing their employment returned to the countryside to work on family farms or on farms owned by relatives. While the exact numbers are in dispute, it is clear there was a large surplus of workers relative to the number of jobs even before the sharp decline of employment in the 1930s.

In addition, disguised unemployment in the countryside may have been as significant as open unemployment in the cities. Around half of the population in Norway lived in sparsely populated areas where most made a living from farming and fishing. Many of these workers lacked a job that offered steady income. The common practice of sharing work and income among family members in rural areas meant that remaining family members would work more if some members left for the cities. A withdrawal of part of the work force could, therefore, leave production unchanged. Thus, according to the production test of employment (Sen 1975), there was widespread disguised rural unemployment throughout the interwar years.

---

[5] See Hodne and Grytten (1992) for a discussion.

Table 18.1. *Real per capita GDP (1996 USD)*

Norway 1935	4081
Sweden 1933	4535
Norway 1950	6598
Sweden 1951	7731
Brazil 1998	7103
South Africa 1998	7481

Sources: Center for International Comparisons (2002),
Penn World Tables 6.0; Maddison (1964).

Finally, the economies that the Social Democrats inherited in the 1930s were far from affluent. As Table 18.1 illustrates, the real per capita GDP of Sweden and Norway when the Social Democrats entered government (1933 in the case of Sweden, 1935 in the case of Norway) was far below the current real per capita GDP of middle-income countries like Brazil or South Africa. Northern Europe became rich under social democratic government, not before. In fact, the per capita GDP of Brazil and South Africa today is comparable to the per capita GDP of Norway and Sweden in the 1950s. If Norway and Sweden could afford an ambitious, egalitarian wage policies in the 1950s, so can Brazil and South Africa today.

Other economic and social indicators tell similar stories. Norway was less urbanized in the 1930s than Brazil or South Africa today. The share of GDP generated by agriculture and fishing was greater in Norway in 1930 or in 1960 than in Brazil or South Africa today, as illustrated in Table 18.2. One potentially important difference is educational attainment.[6] Compulsory primary schooling was introduced in 1842 in Sweden and in 1860 in Norway (Olsson 1987, Bergsgård 1964). By 1960, virtually the entire adult population had at least a primary education in both Norway and Sweden, as compared with roughly a quarter of the adult population of South Africa and Brazil who had no schooling in 1990 (Table 18.3). As Table 18.3 reveals, however, the percentage of the adult population twenty-five years or older who had some secondary education was roughly the same in Norway in 1960 as in South Africa or Brazil today. In Norway in 1930, the share of the relevant age group who completed secondary school was only 2 percent for women and 4 percent for men (Statistics Norway 1995). The expansion

[6] We thank John Stephens for insisting on the importance of universal primary education in Scandinavia.

Table 18.2. *Share of GDP by Sector*

	Agriculture and Fishing	Manufacturing, Mining, and Construction	Services
Norway 1930	16.7	30.4	52.9
Norway 1960	9.0	32.4	58.6
Brazil 2000	7.0	29.0	64.0
South Africa 2000	3.0	31.0	66.0

Sources: Statistics Norway (1995), World Bank (2002).

of comprehensive primary and secondary education in Norway came after, not before, the social democrats came to power.

Social democratic governments that were formed in Sweden and Norway in the midst of the Great Depression were committed to reducing unemployment and alleviating poverty. The main slogan of the Social Democrats in the thirties was employment for everybody, which was a popular demand under the circumstances. Both governments increased government spending on policies such as unemployment benefits, public housing, and agricultural price supports. Most economic historians, however, think that the contribution of the relatively cautious Keynesian policies implemented by the social democratic governments to the subsequent recovery in Norway and Sweden was negligible (Hodne and Grytten 1992). The improvement of export markets due to the revival of the German economy was far more important in ending the depression in Scandinavia than any policy adopted by the social democratic governments. As Table 18.4 shows, spending on social security, welfare, health, and education in Norway and Sweden in 1950, fifteen or more years after the Social Democrats came to power, was lower as a share of GDP than in Brazil today.

Table 18.3. *Educational Attainment of the Adult Population*

	Percent of Adults 25 and Older with No Schooling	Percent of Adults 25 and Older with Primary Education Only or Less
South Africa 1990	25.9	73.1
Brazil 1990	22.4	88.2
Norway 1960	2.0	83.9
Sweden 1960	0.1	58.6

Source: Barro and Lee (1996).

Table 18.4. *Spending on Social Security, Welfare, Health, and Education as a Share of GDP*

Norway 1950	9.2
Sweden 1950	11.3
Brazil 1997	13.9

Sources: Huber and Stephens (2003), Olsson (1987), Kuhnle (1987).

In retrospect, the key social democratic innovation in the 1930s was not the moderate increase in welfare spending but the institutional response to the problem that threatened the recovery program: What would keep the increased government spending from raising the wages of insiders in the labor market, rather than increasing employment? The problem came to a head in both countries in the construction industry.[7] Construction workers in Sweden and Norway were highly paid (although their work is seasonal), militant, and sheltered from foreign competition. When foreign demand collapsed in the 1930s, workers in the export sectors, such as metal workers, accepted large wage-reductions to stem the decline of employment. Construction workers came under no such pressure, in large part because of increased government spending on housing. Since construction workers were employed in the export sector as well as in home construction, higher construction wages raised labor costs in the export sector, threatening the jobs of metal workers. When construction unions called a strike in support of higher wages, the national confederation of unions intervened to force the strike to an early and, from the construction workers' point of view, unsuccessful conclusion.

The intervention of the national union confederation to end the strikes in construction was the initial step in a process of centralization of authority within the union movement in both Norway and Sweden, a process that was encouraged and supported by employers. "Basic agreements" between the national associations of unions and employers establishing rules for collective bargaining at the industry level were reached in 1935 in Norway and 1938 in Sweden. In the 1950s (1956 in Sweden, 1958 in Norway), bargaining at the industry level was replaced by direct negotiations over pay by the national associations of unions and employers. As white-collar

---

[7] Swenson (1989, 1991) describes the events in Sweden. Bjørgum (1985) describes the events in Norway. The events leading to centralization are very similar in the two countries.

and professional union confederations joined the centralized negotiations, the coverage of the central agreements expanded to include most of the working population in the private sector.[8]

The central agreements were necessarily general. The details of how the agreements were to be implemented was decided by subsequent bargaining at the industry and local level. The central agreements included an industrial peace obligation, however, that prohibited work stoppages once the central agreement was signed. After an agreement was reached at the central level, wage increases at the local level were limited to what could be obtained without the threat of a strike.

The centralized system of wage setting, which reached its zenith in the 1970s, had three important consequences. The first was the virtual elimination of industrial conflict. From the countries with the highest levels of strikes and lockouts in the world during the interwar year, Norway and Sweden became countries with some of the lowest levels of industrial conflict in the postwar period. The second consequence was to allow conditions in the export industries to determine aggregate wage growth. The centralized system of wage bargaining tied wage growth throughout the economy to the growth of wages in the export sector, since the unions in the export sector, the metal workers in particular, were the largest and most influential unions within the national confederations.

The third consequence of centralized wage setting was a gradual process of wage compression that, over time, generated the most egalitarian distribution of wages and salaries in the capitalist world. In the 1950s, wage compression was adopted as an explicit goal of the unions in both Norway and Sweden under the title of "solidaristic bargaining." But wage compression is closely associated with the centralization of wage-setting in all advanced industrial societies, whether the centralization is achieved by centralized collective bargaining or by government intervention in the form of income policies and whether or not wage compression is adopted as an explicit goal.[9]

While wage compression fit easily with the socialist heritage of the unions, the goals of solidaristic bargaining were defended more in terms of

[8] See Pontusson and Swenson (1996), Iversen (1996), and Wallerstein and Golden (1997) for contrasting studies of the rise and decline of centralized bargaining in Denmark, Norway, Sweden and Finland.
[9] For studies of the impact of centralized bargaining on the wage distribution, see Freeman (1988), Blau and Kahn (1996), Wallerstein (1999), Hibbs and Locking (2000), and Rueda and Pontusson (2000).

efficiency than in terms of equality. In the 1950s, two Swedish trade union economists, Gösta Rehn and Rudolf Meidner (Rehn 1952), argued that equalizing wages for workers with similar skills across Swedish firms and industries would promote economic development by raising wages in low-productivity firms or industries and restraining wages in high-productivity firms or industries. In a decentralized bargaining system, wages vary according to the productivity of the firm and the industry. In a centralized system, in contrast, wages are relatively insensitive to the profitability of the enterprise. On the one hand, centralized wage-setting implied that industries with low levels of productivity were prevented from paying low wages and were forced to reduce employment instead. On the other hand, workers in industries with high levels of productivity were prevented from sharing the profits generated by high levels of productivity in the form of higher wages. By reducing profits in low-productivity firms and increasing profits in high-productivity firms, labor and capital would be induced (or coerced) to move from low productive to highly productive activities, increasing aggregate efficiency as well as improving equality (Agell and Lommerud 1993; Moene and Wallerstein 1997).

Whatever the benefits of solidaristic bargaining in terms of efficiency – a study of productivity growth in Sweden by Hibbs and Locking (2000) finds evidence that the gain in efficiency was substantial – the cumulative impact on the distribution of wages and salaries was large. "Equal pay for equal work" is a common demand of unions, easily explained by unions' desire to reduce managerial discretion. Solidaristic bargaining extended the principle of "equal pay for equal work" from one industry to the entire economy, and then moved beyond the demand for "equal pay for equal work" toward the goal of "equal pay for all work." In Sweden between 1970, when comprehensive wage data on individuals began to be collected, and 1983, when the system of centralized bargaining collapsed, the variance of the log of hourly wages among private sector blue-collar workers declined by over 50 percent (Hibbs and Locking 2000). That dramatic decrease does not include the equally prominent reduction of the wage differential between blue-collar and white-collar workers. Hibbs and Locking (2000) estimate that a similar decline occurred during the 1960s as well, implying that the variance of log hourly wages in 1983 was only one quarter of what it was in 1960. In 1992, the ratio of the wage for a worker at the 90th percentile of the wage distribution to the wage for a worker at the 10th percentile was about 2 to 1 in Sweden, Norway and Denmark, the lowest ratios of any country in the OECD (OECD 1996). In contrast, the 90 to 10 ratio was 5.4 to 1 in the United States in 1992.

Many other features of the Nordic model of social democracy follow from the policy of wage compression. Wage compression directly encouraged the movement of capital from less productive to more productive activities, but the effect on the incentives for workers to change occupations was mixed. While wage compression would increase job loss in industries with low productivity and job creation in industries with high productivity, employers in highly productive firms lost the ability to attract workers with offers of higher pay. The government, unions and employers responded to the problem with an array of active labor market policies that subsidized the movement of workers from one industry to another with training programs and grants to cover moving expenses. To keep highly productive employers from undermining the policy of wage restraint by offering workers generous benefits (which were harder than wages to monitor at the central level), the Swedish employers' confederation lobbied the government to nationalize the provision of health care and pensions (Swenson 2002). Greater wage equality increased voters' willingness to support insurance-replacement policies such as social insurance against the loss of income due to unemployment, disability, sickness, and occupational injury.[10] The compression of wage differentials, in sum, had far-reaching economic and political consequences, one of which, we argue in the next section, was to increase the pace of economic development.

A Simple Model of Development

To see the potential importance of wage compression for economic development, we present a simple model of a developing economy. The central aspect of development that the model incorporates is that the growth of a modern sector at the expense of traditional production depends on the size of the market for modern goods.[11] The model distinguishes between modern and traditional sectors depending on the technology they apply. While

---

[10] On the relationship between wage inequality and spending on social insurance policies, see Iversen and Soskice (2001) and Moene and Wallerstein (2001, 2003a).

[11] The modern sector should not be equated with the industrial sector. Much of contemporary modern sector employment is in the service sector. For an empirical study that presents evidence in support of our assumption that growth is driven by the size of the internal market and exports demand, see Aides and Glaeser (1999).

old technologies are assumed to have decreasing returns to scale, new technologies are assumed to have increasing returns. Increasing returns to scale imply that the profitability of modern plants depends on the size of the market. Foreign demand for the output of the modern sector, we assume, is exogenous. Domestic demand, in contrast, is assumed to be an increasing function of the size of the modern sector. The idea is that many consumers of modern sector goods are other modern sector firms or workers in the modern sector. The dependence of the growth of the modern sector on the size of the modern sector creates a feedback loop. The result may be a poverty trap, in which growth fails to occur, or sustained development in which initial growth of the modern sector encourages further modern sector growth until the traditional sector disappears. A central determinant of whether the economy develops or not that we emphasize in this model is the wage differential between modern and traditional sectors.

We start with the modern sector. Let x represent both the value of output and employment in a representative modern sector plant. We assume, in other words, that one unit of labor is required to produce one unit's worth of revenue for the enterprise. Labor is the only variable cost of production. In addition, we assume that there is a fixed cost of plant and equipment, c, associated with modern sector enterprises. Implicitly we have assumed that the minimum plant size is large enough to supply the domestic market. Note that we have assumed a form of increasing returns to scale in the modern sector, since the average cost of production decline as output increases. If workers in modern sector plants receive a wage of w, then profit per modern sector plant can be written as

$$\pi = (1 - w)x - c \tag{1}$$

Modern sector workers, we assume, are covered by collective agreements. If wage bargaining is decentralized, the wage agreement depends on the two sides' willingness to engage in industrial conflict. In the event of a work stoppage, we assume that modern sector workers receive an income roughly equivalent to what workers earn in the traditional sector, which we denote by q, while firms receive $-c$, since sunk costs are sunk. Applying the generalized Nash bargaining solution implies a modern sector wage of

$$w = q + \beta(1 - q), \tag{2}$$

where $\beta \in [0, 1]$ represents workers' share of the joint surplus in bargaining. Equation (3) implies that profits in the modern sector can be written as

$$\pi = (1 - \beta)(1 - q)x - c. \tag{3}$$

The demand for modern sector output depends on foreign demand and domestic demand. Domestic demand, in turn, depends on the size of the modern sector. In particular, we assume that a fixed proportion of modern sector income is spent on the output of domestic modern sector firms. It follows that the demand for modern sector output is an increasing, strictly convex function of the size of the modern sector, or $x = x(n)$ where n represents the share of modern commodities produced by domestic firms. (See the appendix for a full description of the mathematical details of the argument.) Implicit in our formulation is a view that development entails a process of import substitution as domestic modern sector firms replace foreign suppliers of modern commodities for the domestic market. In other words, we assume some degree of home market bias, such that domestic producers are preferred in the domestic market over imports. Imports may rise with development, however, as increasing income in the modern sector generates greater demand for the full range of modern sector commodities, including those that are not produced at home.

The fixed costs include normal returns on capital. Thus, negative profits imply disinvestment while positive profits imply an above average rate of return that attracts increased investment in modern sector plants. This is captured by assuming that the change in the size of the modern sector over time, or dn/dt, is given by the equation

$$dn/dt = k\pi(x(n)), \tag{4}$$

where k is a positive constant. For a given wage, equations (2) and (4) imply that there is a minimum size, n^*, such that modern sector growth is positive. Indeed, if $n > n^*$, then the growth of the modern sector is an increasing, convex function of the size of the modern sector if there is sufficient excess labor in the traditional sector such that q remains constant. Alternatively, for a given size of the modern sector, n, equations (3) and (4) imply that there is a maximum wage differential $w - q = \beta (1 - q)$ such that modern sector growth is positive. A wage differential that is too large is incompatible with sustained development.

The impact of the wage differential between the modern and traditional sector on the growth of the modern sector is illustrated in Figure 18.1.

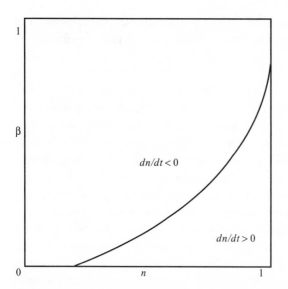

Figure 18.1 Workers' Share of the Surplus, the Size of the Modern Sector, and Growth.

The upward sloping curve represents the combinations of n and β such that profits are zero. If the initial pair (n, β) is below the curve, profits are positive and the modern sector grows. If the initial pair (n, β) is above the curve, however, profits are negative and the modern sector declines.

The assumption that unions would push the modern sector into extinction if they could seems extreme. A reasonable modification would be that unions limit their wage demands to the level that is compatible with constant modern sector employment. The wage would then be given by whichever is less, $w = \beta + (1 - \beta)q$ or $w = 1 - (c/x)$. In this case, the alternative to sustained development is stagnation, not decline. The conditions for sustained development, however, are unchanged. A sufficiently high wage differential between modern and traditional sector workers blocks development.

To complete the model, we need to include the determination of earnings in the traditional sector and unemployment. Earnings in the traditional sector are assumed to be a declining function of the number of workers seeking traditional sector employment, $q = q(l)$, with $q'(l) \leq 0$, where l is the number of workers employed in the traditional sector. Production in the modern sector is typically geographically concentrated. To be available for modern sector employment, workers may have to leave the countryside and their source of traditional sector employment. Let u be the ratio of unemployed workers to modern sector workers so that un is the number of workers who are unemployed, and let $f(u)$ be the probability of obtaining a modern sector job, where $f(0) = 1$ and $f'(u) < 0$. With these assumptions, migration takes place until expected earnings are identical in the two sectors, that is until[12]

$$f(u)w = q(l) \tag{5}$$

As long as modern sector workers have bargaining power that is derived from their ability to shut down production, wages don't fall to clear the urban labor market.[13] Unemployment is involuntary in the sense that the unemployed would prefer to work at the wage that is offered by modern sector firms. Finally, the share of workers who are employed in modern enterprises, of unemployed workers, and of employed in traditional activities must equal the total labor force, L, or $nx + unx + l = L$. Thus, the model posits three groups of workers: modern sector workers, traditional sector workers in the countryside, and informal sector workers who are unemployed (or underemployed) in the cities.

The allocation of labor and the distribution of earnings for a given n are illustrated in Figure 18.2, with employment on the horizontal axis and earnings on the vertical axis. Modern sector employment is represented by the distance from the left-hand vertical axis while employment in the traditional sector is represented by the distance from the right-hand vertical axis. Modern sector workers receive $w = \beta + (1 - \beta)q$, which does not depend on employment in the modern sector, while traditional sector workers receive q, which is a declining or constant function of employment in the traditional sector. The number of unemployed workers is determined by the intersection of the curve $f(u)w$ and $q(l)$ since migration is assumed to equalize expected earnings of traditional sector workers and the unemployed.

In Figure 18.2, the curve $q(l)$ is drawn as flat until the number of workers in the traditional sector becomes sufficiently small. A flat $q(l)$ curve represents the case of a labor surplus economy where expansion of the modern sector has little effect on earnings in traditional activities, as postulated

---

[12] This expression is just a variant of the Harris and Todaro (1970) mechanism for rural urban migration.

[13] The presence of unions is not the only reason why wages in the modern sector might fail to fall to clear the urban labor market. Even if unions were absent, employers may not reduce wages until unemployment is eliminated for fear of the effect of wage reductions on workers' effort and turnover. See Weiss (1990) for a review of the literature.

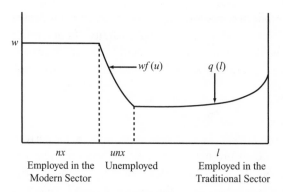

w

$wf(u)$ $q(l)$

nx   *unx*   *l*
Employed in the   Unemployed   Employed in the
Modern Sector   Traditional Sector

Figure 18.2 Wages and Employment with Surplus Labor.

by Lewis (1954). If wage differential between the modern and traditional sectors is sufficiently low, then the modern sector will grow and the traditional sector will decline. Eventually, the share of workers in the traditional sector will fall enough such that $q(l)$ and w will rise. But if the wage differential is too high, either the modern sector will stagnate or contract and development will not occur.

The model has Keynesian features in the sense that the level of demand determines modern sector output. A positive demand shock, such as an increase in exports, g, implies higher modern sector employment with a multiplier greater than one. Thus an increase in the demand for modern sector exports, such as occurred in the Nordic countries with the revival of the German economy in the 1930s, may create conditions of sustained development. Although we haven't included a government sector in the model, it is easy to show that increased government spending on modern sector output has the same impact as an increase in foreign demand.

The simple model we have described omits important considerations. In particular, the treatment of prices and foreign demand as exogenous forces us to ignore the effect of wage demands on the competitiveness of exports, an important part of the Norwegian and Swedish story. But the model is sufficient for the purpose of demonstrating the potential importance of large wage-differences between the modern and traditional sectors in blocking economic growth. Adding a channel whereby modern sector wage setting would effect foreign demand, in addition to domestic demand, is to add further reasons why growth might be increased by a policy of reducing the wages earned in the most productive enterprises. Reducing the share of surplus received by relatively privileged workers, we suggest, was the essence of the social democratic development strategy. Essentially, centralization took wage setting out of the hands of the unions representing relatively high-paid workers and put wage setting in the hands of leaders of the labor movement as a whole.

In the end, the social democratic model of development owed more to Adam Smith than to Karl Marx. Both Adam Smith and the social democrats were ardent defenders of the poorest groups in society. Both saw modernization and expansion of markets as the key to escaping poverty. Both saw the primary task as being one of removing the obstacles to rapid modernization. Adam Smith viewed the primary obstacles to modernization as restrictions on the free movement of labor and capital, such as guild privileges and monopolies, that limited the size of the market and the extent of specialization. The Social Democrats, in effect, saw the primary obstacle to modernization as strong local unions whose wage premiums restricted the expansion of the most productive sectors. What distinguished the Social Democrats from more conservative followers of Adam Smith like Margaret Thatcher was their solution to the problem of restricting the power of local unions. While Thatcher's solution was to weaken unions as institutions, the social democratic approach was to strengthen unions as institutions and to structure collective bargaining in a highly centralized manner that reduced the influence of highly paid workers in the wage setting process.

The Political Feasibility of Solidaristic Bargaining

Many economists, social democrats and non-social democrats alike, would accept the argument that development can be promoted by reducing the wage differential between modern sector and traditional sector workers. What makes the social democratic experience exceptional was that the policy of wage compression was voluntary, not coerced, and implemented by a union movement that included as members many of the high-wage workers whose wages would be restrained in the name of greater equality. Thus, the great challenge faced by those who would apply the lessons of social democracy in the Third World today is political. How can a democratic political movement with close ties to the unions implement a development strategy that centers on wage restraint?

It may be helpful to review the balance of political forces behind the implementation of solidaristic bargaining in the Nordic countries. Employers provided critical support for both centralized wage setting and solidaristic bargaining (Swenson 1989, 1991). While the Nordic countries are well known for the strength of unions, employers also achieved an extraordinary level of organization. Employers much preferred to bargain with the "sensible" leadership of the union confederations, rather than with the militant union leadership on the shop floor. Solidaristic bargaining can increase aggregate profits relative to the wage schedule associated with decentralized bargaining by eliminating the rents that workers would otherwise obtain in local bargaining (Moene and Wallerstein 1997). Solidaristic bargaining can even increase aggregate profits relative to the wage schedule associated with a non-union labor market by limiting competition among employers for the workers (Swenson 2002, Moene and Wallerstein 2003b).

Another group that supported the policy of wage compression was the leadership of unions of low-wage workers. Since the union movement was encompassing, both unions representing low-wage workers and unions representing high-wage workers had a voice in setting the union wage policy. While the policy of wage compression was controversial in unions of high-wage workers, it was enthusiastically supported by unions of low-wage workers. Thus, the political coalition that prevailed in the 1950s and established the pattern of centralized and solidaristic bargaining that was to last until the 1980s was comprised of the low-wage unions and employers. The unions with large numbers of low-wage members provided support for an egalitarian wage policy within the union confederations, while employers' preference for bargaining with the union confederation rather than with individual unions made it difficult for high-wage unions to bargain separately. It is unlikely that the low-wage unions and the leadership of the union confederation would have been able to force the high-wage unions to accept an egalitarian wage policy without the backing of employers and the threat of lockouts against recalcitrant unions.[14]

In addition, we believe that the policy found support in the widespread preference of Nordic workers for a more egalitarian wage scale. We do not believe that Nordic workers are inherently more egalitarian than workers in other countries. Rather, our belief is that a preference for greater equality is widespread. The preference for greater equality, however, can be acted upon only to the extent that wages are set centrally. When wages are set at the plant level, wage compression can occur only within the plant. When wages are set at the industry level, wage compression occurs within the industry.

---

[14] In Norway, but not in Sweden, compulsory mediation and compulsory arbitration have frequently been used to force high-wage unions to accept wage moderation.

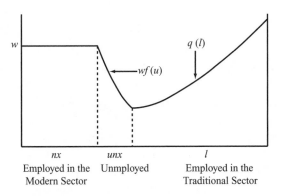

nx   unx   *l*
Employed in the   Unmployed   Employed in the
Modern Sector   Traditional Sector

Figure 18.3 Wages and Employment without Surplus Labor.

When wages are set at the national level, wage compression occurs at the national level.

Social heterogeneity does not eliminate the preference for more egalitarian pay. Unions compress wages within the scope of the bargaining agreement even in racially and ethnically divided societies like the United States (Freeman and Medoff 1984). European countries divided by religion, such as the Netherlands and Germany, or by language, such as Belgium, have relatively centralized wage-setting institutions and relatively egalitarian wage distributions (Wallerstein 1999). It is possible, however, that the centralization of wage setting is easier to achieve in countries that are not divided by religion, language or race. In addition, it is easier to centralize wage setting in countries with a small population.

The Nordic countries may have had another important advantage that countries in the Third World today do not. At the end of World War II, when solidaristic bargaining began to be implemented, the Nordic economies were operating at full employment. Full employment may seem like inauspicious circumstances to implement a policy of wage restraint, but it had an important advantage that is illustrated in figure 18.3. Figure 18.3 duplicates figure 18.2, except that the $q(l)$ curve is upward sloping throughout. Without surplus labor, any increase in modern sector employment will lead to an increase in the earnings of traditional sector workers. Since $w = \beta + (1 - \beta)q$, the rise in q generated by the reduction in β reduces the cost of solidaristic bargaining for modern sector workers. In addition, the increase in q implies that all traditional sector workers benefit from higher wages, not just those who move from traditional-sector to modern-sector jobs.

461

Conclusion

Is the social democratic model of development relevant in the contemporary world of economies increasingly integrated in global markets for goods and capital? The social democrats were committed to free trade but not the free flow of capital. We have de-emphasized, however, the importance of credit controls as an important part of the social democratic approach. The free flow of capital and of goods makes a policy of reducing wage differentials more, not less, effective as a strategy of development. Capital mobility implies that investment will be more responsive to policies, like solidaristic bargaining, that raise the return to capital. As the degree of international economic integration and capital mobility increases, so do the potential economic gains from reducing the wage differential between workers in the formal and in the traditional and informal sectors.

Is the social democratic model of development politically feasible in the Third World? This, it seems to us, is the critical question. The elements that appear to have been important in allowing wage differentials to be reduced through collective bargaining in Nordic countries were (a) well-organized employers, (b) encompassing trade unions that included the low-paid workers, and (c) immediate benefits of wage compression in terms of the earnings of those at the bottom. These conditions are not notably present in Africa, Asia and Latin America today.

The Nordic countries had important advantages that enhanced the feasibility of the social democratic strategy of development, including universal primary education which meant that traditional sector workers were literate; small size which promoted the growth of encompassing unions and employers' associations (Wallerstein 1989); and luck in the form of booming export markets.[15] But we still understand little of the political dynamics that made wage compression possible in an environment with strong unions and a government that considered industrial workers to be its core constituents. Thus, we are reluctant to conclude that the social democratic experience cannot be repeated.

---

[15] We do not include the absence of a politically powerful class of large landowners on our list. While the lack of a powerful landed elite may be an important part of the explanation for the political dominance of social democratic parties (Luebbert 1991), we do not think it had a direct bearing on the feasibility of the social democratic strategy of development. An egalitarian distribution of land can coexist with an inegalitarian distribution of wages and vice versa.

Social Democracy as a Development Strategy

Appendix

In this section, we present the details of the model underlying Figure 18.1 in the text. Let there be a continuum of measure one of modern commodities, all with prices fixed on the international market. Of these modern commodities, the fraction n is produced by local enterprises. For the sake of simplicity, we assume that each modern commodity is produced by one enterprise. As described in the text, output is linear in hours worked, with one unit of labor producing one unit of output. In addition, there are fixed costs of $c > 0$.

We assume that the fraction μ (with $\mu < 1$) of modern sector income $(x - c)n$ is spent on each of the modern commodities. Thus, the domestic demand for each modern sector enterprise is $\mu n (x - c)$. If we write foreign demand for each modern commodity produced locally as g, then output and employment in each modern sector enterprise is given by

$$x = \mu n(x - c) + g. \tag{6}$$

Equation (6) implies that production and employment in modern enterprises is an increasing, convex function of n

$$x(n) = \frac{g - \mu nc}{1 - \mu n},$$

provided $g > c$. If $g \leq c$, there is no wage low enough to make the first modern enterprise profitable. Note that the multiplier with respect to changes in the demand for export, that is, the partial derivative of $x(n)$ with respect to g, is greater than one. The assumption that the domestic demand for modern commodities is unaffected by the income earned in the traditional sector can easily be relaxed without altering the way the model works. The central assumption is that the growth of the modern sector increases the demand for modern sector output and higher output in the modern sector lowers the average costs of production.

Given a wage of $w = \beta + (1 - \beta)q$, the condition that profits are positive and the modern sector grows can be written in terms of the size of the modern sector:

$$\pi > 0 \Leftrightarrow n > \frac{c - (1 - \beta)(1 - q)g}{\mu c [1 - (1 - \beta)(1 - q)]} \equiv n^*.$$

Note that the minimum size compatible with sustained development, n^* is an increasing function of c, β, and q, and a decreasing function of μ and g.

Alternatively, we can write the condition that profits are positive in terms of the share of the joint surplus obtained by modern sector workers:

$$\pi > 0 \Leftrightarrow \beta < \left(\frac{1}{1-q}\right)\left[\frac{g-c}{g-\mu c n} - q\right] \equiv \beta^*$$

The maximum share of the surplus compatible with sustained development, β^*, is an increasing, strictly convex function of n. This is the function drawn in Figure 18.1 in the text.

References

Agell, Jonas, and Kjell Erik Lommerud. 1993. "Egalitarianism and Growth." *Scandinavian Journal of Economics*, 95: 559–579.

Aides, Alberto F., and Edward L. Glaeser. 1999. "Evidence on Growth, Increasing Returns and the Extent of the Market." *Quarterly Journal of Economics*, 114(3): 1025–1045.

Alesina, Alberto, Edward Glaeser and Bruce Sacerdote. 2001. "Why Doesn't the U.S. Have a European-Style Welfare State?" Paper presented at the Brookings Panel on Economic Activity, Sept. 7, 2001, Washington D.C.

Barro, Robert J., and Jong Wha Lee. 1996. "International Measures of Schooling Years and Schooling Quality." *American Economic Review*, 86(2): 218–228.

Bergsgård, Arne. 1964. *Norsk Historie, 1814–1880.* Oslo: Det Norsk Samlaget.

Bjørgum, Jorunn. 1985. "LO og NAF 1899–1940." *Tidsskrift for Arbeiderbevegelsens Historie*, 85–114.

Blau, Francine D., and Lawrence M. Kahn. 1996. "International Differences in Male Wage Inequality: Institutions versus Market Forces." *Journal of Political Economy*, 104: 791–837.

Center for International Comparisons. 2002. *Penn World Table 6.0.* University of Pennsylvania, Available at: www.pwt.econ.upenn.edu/.

Falch, Torben, and Per Tovmo. 2003. "Norwegian Local Public Finance in the 1930s and Beyond." *European Review of Economic History*, 7: 127–154.

Freeman, Richard B. 1988. "Labour Market Institutions and Economic Performance." *Economic Policy*, 3: 64–80.

Freeman, Richard B., and James L. Medoff. 1984. *What Do Unions Do?* New York: Basic Books.

Frisch, Ragnar. 1931. "Plan eller kaos." *Tidens Tegn*, November 5.

Harris, John R., and Michael P. Todaro. 1970. "Migration, Unemployment and Development: A Two-Sector Analysis." *American Economic Review*, 60: 126–142.

Hibbs, Douglas A. Jr., and Håkan Locking. 2000. "Wage Dispersion and Productive Efficiency: Evidence for Sweden." *Journal of Labor Economics*, 18(4): 755–782.

Hicks, Alexander. 1999. *Social Democracy and Welfare Capitalism: A Century of Income Security Politics.* Ithaca: Cornell University Press.

Hodne, Fritz, and Ola Honningdal Grytten. 1992. *Norsk Økonomi 1900–1990*. Oslo: Tano.

Huber, Evelyne, and John Stephens. 2001. *Development and Crisis of the Welfare State*. Chicago: University of Chicago Press.

Huber, Evelyne, and John Stephens. 2003. Globalization and Social Policy, Paper prepared for the conference on Globalization, the State and Society; School of Law, Washington University in St. Louis; November 13–14.

Ingham, Geoffrey. 1974. *Strikes and Industrial Conflict: Britain and Scandinavia*. London: MacMillan.

Iversen, Torben. 1996. "Power, Flexibility and the Breakdown of Centralized Wage Bargaining: The Cases of Denmark and Sweden in Comparative Perspective." *Comparative Politics*, 28: 399–436.

Iversen, Torben, and David Soskice. 2001. "An Asset Theory of Social Policy Preferences." *American Political Science Review*, 95: 875–893.

Kuhnle, Stein. 1987. Norway. In Peter Flora, ed., *Growth to Limits*, vol. 4 (Berlin: Walter de Gruyter).

Lewis, Arthur. 1954 "Economic Development with Unlimited Supplies of Labour." *The Manchester School*, 22, 139–191.

Luebbert, Gregory M. 1991. *Liberalism, Fascism or Social Democracy*. Oxford: Oxford University Press.

Maddison, Angus. 1964. *Economic Growth in the West*. New York: Norton.

Moene, Karl Ove, and Michael Wallerstein. 1997. "Pay Inequality." *Journal of Labor Economics*, 15: 403–430.

_____. 2001. "Inequality, Social Insurance and Redistribution." *American Political Science Review*, 95(4): 859–874.

_____. 2003a. "Earnings Inequality and Welfare Spending: A Disaggregated Analysis." *World Politics*, 55(4): 485–516.

_____. 2003b. "Does the Logic of Collective Action Explain the Logic of Corporatism? *Journal of Theoretical Politics*, 15: 271–297.

Olsson, Sven. 1987. "Sweden." In Peter Flora (ed.), *Growth to Limits*, vol. 4 (Berlin: Walter de Gruyter).

Organization for Economic Cooperation and Development (OECD). 1996. *Employment Outlook*, July. Paris: OECD.

Pontusson, Jonas, and Peter Swenson. 1996. "Labor Markets, Production Strategies, and Wage Bargaining Institutions: The Swedish Employer Offensive in Comparative Perspective." *Comparative Political Studies*, 29: 223–250.

Rehn, Gösta. 1952. The Problem of Stability: An Analysis of Some Policy Proposals. In Ralph Turvey, (ed.), *Wages Policy under Full Employment*. London: W. Hodge.

Rueda, David, and Jonas Pontusson. 2000. "Wage Inequality and Varieties of Capitalism." *World Politics*, 52: 350–383.

Sen, Amartya. 1975. *Employment, Technology and Development*. Oxford: Clarendon Press.

Smith, Adam. 1776. *An Inquiry into the Nature and Causes of the Wealth of Nations*. Reprint. Chicago: University of Chicago Press.

Statistics Norway. 1995. *Historical Statistics*. Oslo: Central Bureau of Statistics.

Swenson, Peter. 1989. *Fair Shares: Unions, Pay and Politics in Sweden and West Germany.* Ithaca: Cornell University Press.

———. 1991. "Bringing Capital Back In, or Social Democracy." *World Politics,* 43(4): 513–544.

———. 2002. *Capitalists against Markets.* Oxford: Oxford University Press.

Therborn, Göran. 1986. *Why Some Peoples Are More Unemployed Than Others.* London: Verso.

Wallerstein, Michael. 1989. "Union Organization in Advanced Industrial Democracies." *American Political Science Review,* 83: 481–501.

———. 1999. "Wage-Setting Institutions and Pay Inequality in Advanced Industrial Societies." *American Journal of Political Science,* 43: 649–680.

Wallerstein, Michael, and Miriam Golden. 1997. "The Fragmentation of the Bargaining Society: Wage-Setting in the Nordic Countries, 1950–1992." *Comparative Political Studies,* 30(6): 699–731.

Weiss, Andrew. 1990. *Efficiency Wages.* Princeton: Princeton University Press.

Wilensky, Harold. 2002. *Rich Democracies.* Berkeley: University of California Press.

World Bank. 2002. *World Development Indicators.* Washington D.C.: World Bank.